Fundamentals of Arts Management

Sixth Edition

Editors: **DEE BOYLE-CLAPP** and **MAREN BROWN**
with **MARYO GARD**

Arts Extension Service

College of Humanities and Fine Arts
University of Massachusetts Amherst

Fundamentals of Arts Management
Sixth Edition

Arts Extension Service, University of Massachusetts Amherst
(413) 545-2360; www.artsextensionservice.org

© 2016 Arts Extension Service

All rights reserved. Published 2016.
Second printing.

Permission to reproduce worksheets is granted for noncommercial purposes only. Please credit the book title, chapter author, and the Arts Extension Service. No other part of this publication, including any electronic versions, may be reproduced or transmitted in any form, or by any means, electronic or mechanical, including photography, recording, or any information storage and retrieval system without permission in writing from the Arts Extension Service.

Book design by Tekla McInerney and Jeff Potter

Library of Congress Cataloging-in-Publication Data
ISBN 978-0-945464-16-7

First published in 1987 as *Fundamentals of Local Arts Management*, this 6th Edition was supported by a grant from the National Endowment for the Arts (NEA). The Arts Extension Service is grateful to the NEA and for the ongoing support from the Massachusetts Cultural Council and the College of Humanities and Fine Arts at the University of Massachusetts Amherst.

Table of Contents

Preface vi
Acknowledgments ix
Introduction xi

PART ONE—ARTS AND CULTURE IN COMMUNITY

Chapter 1—Community Organizing: Building Community through the Arts 2
History and What It Tells Us
Isolation of the Arts
Headwaters Goals
Community Arts Stories
Ways that Arts Organizations Lead in Community Organizing
Endnotes

Chapter 2—Arts and the Economy: Fuel for the Creative Engine 14
The Arts and the Creative Economy
Definition of Terms
Where Culture, Economics, and Communities Meet
When Culture Goes to Work
Eight Culturally-Driven Strategies for Economic Development
Selected Resources
Appendix
Endnotes

Chapter 3—Creative Placemaking 50
Connecting People, Places, and Stories
The Making or Production of Space
Creative Placemaking and Traditional Community Planning and Development
Finding Assets in All the Right Places
Stories Our Communities Tell
Creative Process and Practice: The Medium is the Message
Sustainable Creative Economies
Outcomes and Measures
Sustainability and Unintended Consequences
Assessing Readiness and Getting Started
Endnotes

Chapter 4—Cultural Advocacy 70
What Is Politics?
Arts and Culture as a Public Issue
Four Levels of Government
Other Advocacy Audiences
Building a Foundation for Your Advocacy
Your Advocacy Goals
Planning and Executing the Campaign
Make Advocacy Part of Your Daily Mission
Appendix

Endnotes
Appendix

Chapter 5—Arts and Cultural Policy 94
What are Arts and Cultural Policies?
Culture in Cultural Policy
Agency and Organizational Policies
United States Arts Policy
Who Sets Policy?
How to Influence Public Policy
Conclusion
Endnotes

PART TWO—FUNDAMENTALS OF MANAGING ARTS ORGANIZATIONS

Chapter 6—Strategic Planning 114
PART I: PRINCIPLES OF PLANNING
Why Plan?
Four Key Concepts
Types of Plans
Planning Approaches
The Language of Planning
The Structure of a Strategic Plan
PART II: METHODS OF PLANNING
How to Plan: The AES Eight-Stage Planning Process
Stage 1: Organize
State 2: Envision
Stage 3: Assess
Stage 4: Make Decisions
Stage 5: Write the Plan
Stage 6: Approve and Commit
Stage 7: Implement
Stage 8: Evaluate and Adapt
The Learning Organization
Further Resources
Appendix
Endnotes

Chapter 7—Board Development 162
A Flexible Approach to Board Development
A Board's Governing Responsibilities
Are Expectations of Boards Reasonable?
Two Strategies for Board Development
Examples of Organizational Structures
Keys to Board Improvement
Resources
Endnotes
Appendix

Chapter 8—The Art of Fundraising 196
An Overview of Sources and Strategies

Fundraising is "Relationship Building"
The Five Elements of Successful Fundraising
Why People Give
Incorporate Long-Range Planning into Your Fundraising Plans
Start Fundraising from the Inside
Raise Money from the Top Down
Position Your Organization for Successful Fundraising
Determine Your Fundraising Capability
The Role of the Board and Staff in Fundraising
Raising Money from Individuals
Develop a "Friends of…" Program
Tax-Deductibility of Contributions
Methods of Individual Giving
Special Event Fundraising
Raising Money from Local and National Corporations
Raising Money from Foundations
Raising Money from Governments
How to Write a Proposal
Build Ongoing Relationships
Endnotes
Appendix

Chapter 9—Essentials of Proposal Writing 238
Proposal Summary
Introduction
Problem Statement or Assessment of Need
Goals and Objectives
Methods
Evaluation
Future and Other Necessary Funding
Budget
Appendix
Endnotes

Chapter 10—Online Fundraising 252
What Makes Online Giving Work?
Simple Steps to Online Fundraising
Online ASKS – How is this Different?
Protect Top Donors
People to People
Crowdfunding
Conclusion
Endnotes
Resources
Appendix

Chapter 11—Volunteers in the Arts 270
Age-Old Motivations, Changing Conditions
The Need for a Volunteer Program
Evaluating Who You Need and Where to Find Them

Recruitment
Selecting and Placing Volunteers
Getting a Good Start
Volunteer Management
Conclusion

Chapter 12—Financial Management 288
The Management Control Cycle
Board Responsibility
The Budget
Eight Steps to Budgeting
Tracking and Measuring Performance
Additional Resources
Endnotes

Chapter 13—Greening Your Arts Nonprofit Organization 316
Environmental Sustainability – What and Why?
Myths, Fears, and Inertia
Steps to Greening
Green Teams
Assessments
Plan Capital Changes
Public Program Considerations
Changes to Core Practices
Gift Shop, Supply Shop, Café
Financial Considerations and Fundraising
Boost Profile and Stand Out
Conclusion
Endnotes
Resources

PART THREE—PROGRAMMING AND PARTICIPATION

Chapter 14—Program Development 338
Program Philosophy
Program Planning
Program Design
Strategies to Connect Art and Audiences
Programming Considerations
Logistics
After the Program
Conclusion
Endnotes

Chapter 15—Marketing the Arts 372
Building on the "Four P's"
Understanding Your Products and Services

Understanding Your Audiences
Selecting the Best Marketing Channels
Evaluate the Effectiveness of your Marketing Strategies
Conclusion
Resources
Appendix: The Marketing Plan

Chapter 16—Cultural Access: Extend the Complete Invitation 402
Cultural Access is Social Justice
Knowing the Language of Cultural Access: Terms and Types
Building Inclusive Communities
The Process for Cultural Accessibility
Tools for Creating a Universal Environment for the Arts
Funding Accessibility
Conclusion
Endnotes

Chapter 17—Arts Education: Policy and Practice 430
Arts Education: Promise and Challenge
Arts Education Policy and Advocacy: Evolving from Frill to Focus
First Things First: Preparing to Take the Plunge
Planning and Implementing the Program
Conclusion
Endnotes
Appendix

Chapter 18—Program Evaluation: Looking For Results............................456
Understanding the Principles of Program Evaluation
Preparing for the Evaluation
Undertaking the Evaluation
Conclusion
Appendix
Resources
Endnotes

Contributors 484
About The Arts Extension Service...489
Index 491

Preface

Fundamentals of Arts Management has been a resource for countless arts managers, artists, students, instructors, and others who have used this book as it was intended, as a clear "how-to manual" and a reliable partner in getting work accomplished properly and effectively. First created in 1987 as *Fundamentals of Local Arts Management,* the topics covered, and consistently revised, have been prescient and are more important than ever. This book teaches arts leaders how to do their best work, and more, how to do their best with their community, staff, board, supporters, and audiences. In an era where ideas are shared in a very limited number of characters, topics such as inclusion, serving communities, advocacy, outreach, and the very latest on arts education policy are addressed in detail by experts in their particular arenas.

This edition is noticeably larger, not only because there are four new chapters, but because we made it possible for the most relevant items in the former Online Companion to fit here. We have also placed further resources lists and bibliographies at the end of each chapter to make it easier for the reader to follow and to conduct additional research. Focusing primarily on nonprofit arts organizations, the principles in the 6th Edition can also be applied to those organizations that operate under a fiscal sponsor or take place sporadically, like a pop-up gallery or once-a-year festival.

This book, like the 5th Edition, is divided into three sections.

Arts and Culture in Community

Part One provides the reader with an excellent overview, beginning with the launch of this field and concluding by emphasizing the impact that arts leaders can make on policy that can invigorate the arts now and decades into the future.

In Community Organizing: Building Community through the Arts, author Maryo Gard provides an important historical context for the work of local cultural organizations and arts organizing, work which remains timely and central to the field.

In Art and the Economy, Tom Borrup lays the foundation for how to build a community's Creative Economy, or financial base by tapping into the power of the arts as an economic driver. Tom's Creative Placemaking chapter informs the reader, in rich detail, of the history of this work and explains the opportunity, value, and positive impact that such work can provide. His argument that every community has something special means that creative placemaking is available to every community, regardless of its population, size of its arts community, or financial strength. Tom acknowledges the concerns of gentrification, uses case studies to illustrate points, and shares the progress some communities have made by using the arts as a means of building their economy and their community.

In Cultural Advocacy, Dan Hunter, with Stan Rosenberg (AES's founder and currently President of the Massachusetts State Senate), details how and why to advocate for the arts or for your own organization, citing when advocacy is acceptable and dispelling the myths that prevent too many arts organizations from exercising their right to reach out to their own government officials.

This section closes with a new chapter, Art and Public Policy, co-authored by former AES directors Bob Lynch and Craig Dreeszen. In this chapter, they explore what arts policy is, who makes it, how advocacy works hand in glove with those who write policy, and they underscore the influence that even a small number of activists and arts leaders can have on policy makers, and therefore, on those issues that will impact the field.

Fundamentals of Managing Arts Organizations

Part Two — Fundamentals of Managing Arts Organizations could have easily been named "the nuts and bolts of running an arts institution" as this section provides the tools needed to run an arts organization.

Craig Dreeszen's Strategic Planning chapter, the most-read according to our surveys, has been extensively revised, so much so that there two significant sections that could have been chapters in and of themselves. Craig defines the many types of strategic plans, then describes how to create the right plan to meet the organization's unique needs. Craig's Board Development chapter clearly details the important roles and duties of a board member, and should be "must" reading for anyone who is considering joining or who serves on a board, and for executive directors looking to train their board members to become effective leaders and visionaries.

The imperative of fundraising for nonprofit arts organizations sparked the need for three distinct chapters. The Art of Fundraising, by Alice and Halsey North, details the steps involved in raising money and the power of people giving to people. The Essentials of Proposal Writing, by the late Norton Kiritz, is so well written it deserved a place in this edition. Finally, the new Online Fundraising chapter, by Dee Boyle-Clapp, discusses the impact on fundraising created by the Internet and subsequent technology, and shares tips on how to enhance an organization's effectiveness online, with the caveat that all things will change, and likely rapidly!

Pam Korza's Volunteers in the Arts shows how to tap the energy and commitment of those who wish to give their time for the arts organization.

The Financial Management chapter, by Christine Burdett with Sally Zinno, clarifies how to read and use financial statements and apply basic accounting principles, while contributing editors Maren Brown and Carol Harper have updated the process for building budgets and planning for adequate capitalization.

The new Greening Your Arts Nonprofit Organization, by Sarah (Brophy) Sutton and Dee Boyle-Clapp, offers a step-by-step process for saving energy and resources, improving staff and visitor health, and inspiring others to reduce their water use and carbon footprint while saving money.

Programming and Participation

Part Three is the section that focuses on audience, inclusion, outreach and marketing, creation of exciting and effective programming and evaluation of the programs.

The Program Development chapter, written by Pam Korza with contributing editors Denise Boston-Moore and contributing editor Maren Brown, shares the latest information on developing effective programs for one's community while balancing community interests and addressing issues of inclusion.

Marketing the Arts, written by Barbara Schaffer Bacon plus Dorothy Chen-Courtin and Shirley Sneve, contributing editor Maren Brown has focused on the fundamentals and theory of marketing, including the marketing mix, the marketing cycle, connecting art and audiences, and how to pursue the organization's goals for outreach and understanding audience needs while acknowledging the importance of social media and the internet.

In Cultural Access: Extend the Complete Invitation, Gay Hanna and Lisa Kammel share the benefits of making arts organizations and their programs accessible to people with differing abilities. As was stated in the 5th Edition's preface, readers of this chapter will learn to "adapt existing facilities and programs that will bring the community into the organization and the organization into the community."

Marete Wester and Judy Conk, who co-taught the Arts Extension Service's Arts Education & Policy course, teamed up here to produce the Arts Education: Policy and Practice chapter, providing a substantive history lesson on arts education in America, then returned at the very last minute to insert the new ESSA rulings and explain the opportunity that this change in policy could produce.

Finally, we conclude the 6th Edition with one of the most important aspects that any arts organization could and should engage in: Program Evaluation. Craig Dreeszen details how to approach evaluation, and the steps involved to define hoped-for results, and he shows how to determine if the desired results were reached.

The *Fundamentals of Arts Management* 6th Edition has been years in the making, yet we hope it is worth the wait. Our goals were many:

- First, to provide the essential information that arts managers and others need to run their organizations to the highest possible standards and make this book a partner in that effort.
- Second, to provide the arts management student with an affordable and comprehensive resource that they can not only use in school, but from their first internship to the conclusion of a long career in the arts. As one graduate student shared, "I read the book for classes, but I didn't fully realize its importance until I used the book, and followed it to the letter, as I wrote my first grant proposal."
- Third, to provide the arts management instructor with a single textbook to save students from having to purchase more than one book, and by providing a straightforward means to teach both theory and practical information on how to run an organization, while leaving room for creative teaching.
- And finally, to the current generation of arts managers, who one day find that their job has expanded and they need a patient, informed tutor to walk them through their new work, be it marketing, finance, fundraising, programming, or finding ways to cut costs while increasing the audience experience: this 6th Edition of *Fundamentals of Arts Management* was written for you.

Acknowledgements

Fundamentals of Arts Management 6th Edition was only possible with help from many individuals who shared their unique skills to serve the arts and to support the Arts Extension Service (AES). I am grateful to all.

This good work, of course, is only possible thanks to the remarkable team of authors who have contributed chapters to this book. I am deeply indebted to each who wrote the initial chapters, and to those who contributed to subsequent editions.

In creating the 6th Edition I am particular grateful to the following authors:

- Craig Dreeszen, Ph.D., for all of his work on so many of these chapters and for his patient and kind guidance.
- The team of Bob Lynch and Craig Dreeszen for the new Art and Cultural Policy chapter, creating a rare opportunity to merge on-the-ground experience with scholarly rigor while uniting two former AES director's.
- Tom Borrup, for sharing his wonderful work on Creative Placemaking here, providing the latest research to readers from a practitioner who always seems to be in the right place at the right time.
- Marete Wester and Judy Conk, for their deep revision of the Arts Education: Policy and Practice chapter, and for ripping it apart at the very last minute to add in the new Every Student Succeeds Act (ESSA) rulings while saying a heartfelt goodbye to No Child Left Behind. Special thanks to Marete and friends at Americans for the Arts for allowing us to use their illustrations.
- Maren Brown for the substantive changes to the ever-evolving field of Arts Marketing, plus her good work on Volunteers and Arts Programming, and with Carol Harper, Financial Management, .
- Sarah Sutton (aka Brophy) for working with me on the Greening Your Arts Nonprofit Organization chapter, a topic we both care deeply about, and want to see every possible arts organization adopt.
- Dan Hunter and Stan Rosenberg for their important work in Cultural Advocacy teaching arts managers how to advocate for what they want and what the field needs.
- Alice and Halsey North for allowing us to reprint their Fundraising chapter, and Mrs. Norton Kiritz for granting permission to reprint Norton's evergreen Essentials of Proposal Writing.

Special thanks to the many others, editors, copyeditors, designers, and especially AES staff members, who made this book possible:

- Maryo Gard, thanks for stepping in and editing when we needed it most.
- Chris Rohmann, copyeditor for his good eye, endless patience and unquestionable allegience to the Style Guide.
- Jodi Devine for proofreading and excellent advice.
- Nic Canning for copyedits.
- Tekla McInerney for her design of the book, the cover, and wonderful eye.
- Jeff Potter for so deftly getting us over the finish line.
- Perry Huntoon for her excellent ideas and work on the Cover Contest.
- Emma Pampanin for her energy and enthusiasm.
- The team at the College of Humanities and Fine Arts business office for their professionalism and support, and making sure that the bills are paid and the authors kept happy.

- Terre Vandale for her excellent critique of, and assistance with, the Online Fundraising chapter.
- Priya Nadkarni for her rare mix of editing and graphic skills and willingness to learn as we go, and
- Todd Trebour for reading and supporting the Financial Management and Marketing chapters, and for being every bit an INFJ. Thanks to you and Priya for all you do each and every day.

Thanks to the scores of photographers and staff from arts organizations from three countries who submitted images for the Vote for the Cover Contest; to the editorial team for narrowing the field to 18 images; then the many hundreds of people who voted to place six images on the cover. Details about and links to these 18 institutions can be found on the Arts Extension Service's website at www.artsextensionservice.org. See the Introduction section on the next page for the list.

A sincere thank you to the National Endowment for the Arts and the Massachusetts Cultural Council for the support — and gift of time — which made this book possible.

Maren Brown, co-editor and long-time friend, for leading the way, then making room so I could walk in front. When your rule that *"family first"* was deeply tested, you passed with flying colors.

Finally, sincere thanks to the Dean of the College of Humanities and Fine Arts, Julie C. Hayes, for her support of the Arts Extension Service and for recognizing the importance of sharing the resources of the University with our national audience.

Dee Boyle-Clapp, *Director, Arts Extension Service, University of Massachusetts Amherst*

Introduction

The Arts Extension Service was founded in 1973 to support the work of Local Cultural Councils and extend the resources of the University to the community to support the arts. We firmly believe in the power of the arts. Beyond self-expression and a critique of our culture, the arts are an effective PTSD therapy at veteran's hospitals, giving soldiers an opportunity to dig deep and release their pain. In cities across the U.S, transportation, public art, and mural projects not only reclaim space and the dignity of residents, they become points of pride for locally engaged citizen-artists. The art works that promote awareness and change deeply impress us, ranging from Michael Rakowitz' Enemy Kitchen Food truck which creates art and opportunities for dialog when they offered Chicago resident's Iranian food (using recipes from his Jewish-Iranian mother), cooked and served by Iraq Veterans Against the War; to the First Generation Project, Springfield, MA, whose teens self-describe as "first generation" whether they are first U.S. citizen, first drug-free, first LGBTQ, or other important milestones, create theater.

It is therefore fitting that we clothe this *Fundamentals of Arts Management 6th Edition* in images that come from a wide range of local cultural councils and community arts organizations. Our Administrative Assistant Perry Huntoon ignited the idea for a Cover Contest, suggesting that we reach out to the community to pay tribute to their good work. A call went out via social media and the images came in. The editorial team sorted the work by categories including children's art, music, dance, theater, writing, public art, and more. Many of the images were truly stunning, but were too dark, the resolution was too low, they were horizontal and could not fit the book layout, or they would not translate well from color into black and white. We whittled the number down to 18 – one for each chapter. We then took a risk and offered the public the opportunity to vote. Would the images hold together to create a good cover? Would our favorites make the cut? Would they fit? We had reason to worry, as the designer had to place one image on the back cover, which in our opinion, makes the back cover special, too.

Perry sent out a weekly tally, showing some images neck and neck for first, but more importantly, tied for sixth place, and organizations called upon their members to vote! The result is in your hands, and we are grateful to all who participated.

Each of the eighteen organizations has their image inside the book as a chapter cover page, and each has a special page on our website with links to their sites. We encourage our readers to take a moment to learn the amazing history of these institution to not only expand appreciation for the images, but to learn more about the many diverse ways in which the arts truly serve the community. Find them all at www.artsextensionservice.org.

Cover Winners

1. Old Deerfield Productions, Truth, Deerfield, MA. (Photographer: Kristin Angel)
2. Sacramento Metropolitan Arts Commission, Leap by Lawrence Argent. Sacramento International Airport Public Art Project. Sacramento, CA. (Photographer: Jeremy Sykes.)
3. San Francisco Arts Commission, Noontime Dance at U.N. Plaza. San Francisco, CA. (Photographer: Mackenzie Grimmer.)

4. Community Art Center, Beneath the Surface, Community Painting Day, Cambridge, MA. (Photographer: Liz McEachern Hall.)
5. Casa Esperanza, Esperanza Community Mural Project, Roxbury, MA. (Photographer: Tova Speter.)
6. Anna Vigeland & Cassia Project, If Dusk Tangled with Dawn, Athens, Greece. (Photographer: Chris Petmazoglou.)

Interior Chapter Cover Winners

1. Art Garden: Design Your Own T-Shirt Workshop, Shelburne Falls, MA. (Photographer: Sienna Wildfield.)
2. Charleston Ballet: D. La Bayadere (The Temple Dancer), Charleston, WV. (Photographer: Jurgen Lorenzen.)
3. Easthampton Bearfest, Luminous Bear by Crystal Popko, Easthampton, MA (Photographer: Crystal Popko.)
4. Libby Elementary: Pure Joy, Carthage, TX. (Photographer: Dr. Kimberly Rose.)
5. National Steinbeck Center: In a Nutshell! by Tandy Beal, Salinas, CA. (Photographer: Laura Werde.)
6. New England Youth Theater: *Annie*, Brattleboro, VT. (Photographer: Laura Bliss.)
7. Northwest Choral Society: The Christmas Star, Chicago, IL. (Photographer: Tom Perles.)
8. Onion River Community Access Television (ORCA), ORCA Media Internship Program, Montpelier, VT. (Photographer: Peter Arthur Weyrauch.)
9. Orange Arts & Culture Council: Through the Garden Gate, Orange, CT. (Photographer: Lexi Crocco.)
10. San Francisco Arts Commission, Two Blocks of Art, San Francisco, CA. (Photographer: Glenn Halog.)
11. Vermont Arts Council: Poetry Out Loud, Montpelier, VT. (Photographer: Peter Arthur Weyrauch.)
12. Vision Maker Media: Growing Native, Tulalip, WA. (Photographer: Shirley K. Sneve.)

PART ONE

Arts and Culture in Community

Community Organizing: Building Community Through the Arts

MARYO GARD

Certain phrases crop up a lot in the mission statements of community arts organizations. One such phrase that is popular is community building. The arts have an important part to play in community building, but let's be clear about what it means.

Community has become one of those much used feel-good words. Political candidates running for office use it in speech after speech. Marketing firms trying to sell anything from cars to Internet access use it in ad after ad. It is clearly a word that people respond to powerfully. If people weren't hungry for "it," politicians and advertisers wouldn't use it so much. In fact, it is used so often it is starting to lose its meaning.

Community defined. For the purposes of this chapter, "community" refers to geography: a neighborhood, a town, a watershed. We are not referring to the "community of Jamaicans in Michigan," the "community of users of America Online," or the "community of gay people." These are groups of people who are demographically similar. Group power is a valid and important process in creating a sense of group identity, but is not within the scope of this chapter. Here, community refers to places where people who are different from one another live together and try to carve out a good life together. It is used in the sense that Lewis Thomas, the biologist, did when he said, "…[there are] no independent creatures. The life of any given individual, of any species, is dependent on other individuals, on other species. Moreover, the existence of a given species depends upon the genetic diversity of that species."

Community organizing defined. Within the arts world, the term community-building is frequently used as a synonym for audience development—creating groups of people who attend new music events or diversifying the demographics of an audience. Although audience development is covered in the Marketing the Arts chapter, this is not what is addressed here. What is under discussion is the process by which people in geographic communities make use of the arts to create, in Thomas' terms, an "effective interdependency leading to a better life for all." To do that, effective organizing skills are necessary. Accordingly, this chapter on community arts organizing is about building the capacity of the community and its key leaders to use the arts to create an effective interdependency among people in a geographic place. An effective interdependency refers to bettering the community, with better defined by the diversity of people who live there.

> Community arts organizing is about building the capacity of the community and its key leaders to use the arts to create an effective interdependency among people in a geographic place.

There are several points that are critical about this definition of community arts organizing:
- It refers to a geographic place.
- It recognizes the diversity of people who live in that place.

- It recognizes that though community members may be very different from one another, they are all interested in creating a good life for themselves and their families.
- It recognizes that a neighbor's idea of a "good life" is as important as your own.
- It recognizes that different people in a community need to work together on common goals and ways of addressing those goals.
- It recognizes that the arts are a key to doing this and so may be most important.
- It makes a "good community" the end, with arts of excellence as the means.

Our intention is community building. This last point is a very important one. For those people who use community building as a synonym for audience development, the arts are still the end goal. Our intention is to get more people, or different people, to arts events. Since increased artistic activity is a hallmark of a livable community, arts people often concentrate on producing more, and better, arts events. While we believe that is the job of many arts organizations, it too is outside the scope of this chapter. (See the chapter, Program Development for guidance on how to create better arts events.)

Here, our intention is a good community, as defined by the diversity of people who live there, not as defined by the art organization. Thus, the organization offers its knowledge and skills as a service to this concept of a built community, and works collaboratively with other community groups in order to do so.

Arts excellence matters. Let us put aside once and for all time the common idea that doing this kind of work somehow prostitutes the arts or minimizes their quality in the interest of social service. This is an old, tired argument. Community-building work is most effectively undertaken when artists or arts organizations with impeccable standards of excellence are involved. This is not "just social work"; rather, the melding of arts knowledge and skills with community ends is creating a new aesthetic, one which may, in time, be considered the cutting edge aesthetic of the early twenty-first century. This kind of work is forging new definitions and standards of what excellence means. Initiatives like Americans for the Arts' Animating Democracy program have begun to do just this in the critical writing experiment and resulting book titled *Critical Perspectives*.[1]

> Community-building work is most effectively undertaken when artists or arts organizations with impeccable standards of excellence are involved.

Community change takes time. Change takes time, and truly effecting deep change is the work of generations. You may make some short-term improvements, but larger-scale cultural change isn't going to be effected in your lifetime. We will address this in the part of this chapter on necessary skill sets, but this kind of work requires a person who thinks of him or herself as a player in a game that takes decades to "win," and is prepared not to see any deep results right away—maybe not in their lifetime.

Outcomes for This Chapter

By the end of this chapter, you should know something about your own history and the importance of keeping the "big picture" as your guiding star. Knowing your history will ground and connect you to a lineage of community arts ideas and people. We as community arts organizers need this kind of lineage as much as we need to know who our family forebears were.

> **The Music Man as Example of Community Building**
>
> Is this all getting a little too heavy? Take a break and rent the video of Meredith Wilson's The Music Man! with Robert Preston. Turn your Saturday night movie-watching experience into a learning experience (with humor, of course). Note that:
>
> - Early on, the people of River City explore what it means to live in Iowa.
> - Professor Hill spends a good deal of time considering, and rejecting, possible issues to organize around before he hits on the pool hall idea.
> - Professor Hill, the outside organizer, nonetheless collaborates with a local partner, Marian the librarian.
> - Marian moves into a position of community leadership, culminating in a very strong stand at the end of the film, and co-leading the final celebration.
> - The people (the Mayor) see no reason to change. What about his wife who sees "art" as only about the classics? What can we learn from them?
> - The people (the City Council) realize that, through the arts, they have more common ground than they were aware of.
> - Change for the youth at risk in the community (the kid with the speech disability; or Tommy, the potential juvenile delinquent) comes in the form of the arts.
> - The Think System of preparing for a concert is based on the art of keeping the "big picture" in mind, as well as an unwavering faith that it is the right thing to do.

History and What It Tells Us

Before we get into the mechanics of this kind of work, it is important to talk a bit about the past, for community arts is not a new idea. These stories will connect you to generations of other community arts organizers. First, your lineage is that of the community "griot," or cultural story-holder. In communities everywhere, the storyteller passes on knowledge to subsequent generations. These are not just good anecdotes; they are ways by which a culture shares its goals and its successes, what it knows, and how to evaluate its progress. Look, for example, at the work of the Roadside Theater in Kentucky (www.roadside.org). They are not just making plays based on stories, but works whose purpose is to articulate wisdom and evaluate cultural progress.

Village Improvement. Consider Anglo cultures in the United States, circa 1853. The Village Improvement movement, started in Massachusetts, addressed issues of ugly billboards and the need for community trees, paved roads, and recreational facilities. By 1900, there were about 3,000 such groups in the United States, trying to develop a sense of place through aesthetics.

City Beautiful. The Village Improvement movement led in turn to the City Beautiful movement, exemplified by the architectural ideas showcased at the Chicago World's Fair at the end of the nineteenth century. City Beautiful emphasized a return to grand, classical architecture for public buildings. The Museum of Science and Industry, the Shedd Aquarium, and the Midway were all World's Fair buildings.

Olmsted and Wright. At about this time, Frederick Law Olmsted was stressing the importance of parks in cities and a few public art commissions were created in urban areas. Two things slowed this civic aesthetics movement down, however. First, there was the idea that grandeur was classist, just another amenity for the wealthy. Second, efficiency and functionalism were replacing aesthetics as values in the United States. There were a few voices raised in opposition to this. A notable one was Frank Lloyd Wright, who believed that the middle class had the same right to aesthetics that the upper class did; he even designed a line of wallpaper, drapes, and so forth to be marketed through F. Schumaker & Company. In this story are the roots of contemporary public art and design. As we take action to ensure that artists serve on city engineering teams for the design of everything from manhole covers to bridges, as we design public art processes based on public input, as we consider icons at the edge of town to welcome us to the community, we are acting in the tradition begun in the United States 150 years ago.

Lyceum movement. Now return to the early 1800s and follow another thread. In this story, Josiah Holbrook of Massachusetts started inviting neighbors to his home for discussions of books. Gradually, he started inviting professors, and the discussions expanded to encompass new ideas. This led to the founding of the American Lyceum Association in 1831; by 1850 there were about 3,000 of these groups. However, the idea was introduced that discussion leaders should be paid honoraria and the discussions should become lectures. The next logical step was to put lecturers on "the circuit," and James Redpath started a management organization to do exactly that. He valued efficiency, so naturally favored lectures in communities that could afford the fee and that were on the railroad line. The grassroots movement, begun as discussions by ordinary folks in people's homes, began to wither as this more "professional" movement grew.

Chautauquas. Cut to Chautauqua, New York, where Reverend John Vincent was experimenting with the use of the arts to teach the Bible. This approach proved very popular, and pretty soon Reverend Vincent's study packages were being shipped to scores of local Chautauqua Circles. Back at the Redpath agency, now-manager Keith Vawter had a big idea; he had lecturers and the Chautauqua Circles were a network of potential presenters. So he brought the two together; if the lecturer was hot enough and the town was small enough, he even provided tents for the lecture. Do you see our presenting roots in these stories? Furthermore, they reveal the linking of the arts to the introduction of new ideas and new ways of thinking, as well as the notion of learning about a given topic through artistic methodology.

Now think about the growth of the arts themselves. There were theater companies in America in the eighteenth century, especially in the urban areas, though a performance by a so-called professional company was reported in rural Kentucky in 1797. There were performances on showboats and there were Mexican vaudeville companies traveling throughout the southwest. Artists like Edwin Booth and Sarah Bernhardt appeared in many small towns. It was even said that in the Rocky Mountain West, the first building built after the assayer's office and the saloon was the opera house, and in many places that was probably true.

Community concerts. Redpath's idea of traveling lecturers spawned groups like Columbia Artists Management, and suddenly there were community concert series growing throughout the country. Community-based arts were growing too, especially in small towns. Fargo, North Dakota, had an art league well-established by 1911. Quincy, Illinois, had an orchestra with a paid conductor by 1947.

Local arts agencies. In 1944, the Junior League of America took arts management one step further, offering consulting services to communities wanting to expand the number of arts activities and to coordinate existing arts activities. The woman behind this idea, Virginia Lee Comer, was insistent that when she visited a community, she should talk to all groups of people—not just arts groups—about creative activity in the community. She saw churches, union halls, and housing projects as obvious places for arts activity because people already gathered there. (Is this not the forerunner of the "community cultural planning" that our generation believes we invented in the 1980s?) Comer's manual on assessing, coordinating, and stimulating arts activities in small communities, and her work in Winston-Salem, North Carolina, in 1946–1947, probably led directly to the institution of local arts agencies.

Settlement House movement. At the turn of the twentieth century in urban areas, the Settlement House movement begins. Jane Addams founded Hull House in Chicago to provide entry, orientation points, and basic social services for new immigrants to the United States. She was adamant that neither poverty nor language barriers should mean disenfranchisement from one's culture. Her comprehensive social service program included meals and help to locate housing, but it also included a gym, men's and women's clubs, programs in native languages as well as English, a library, art classes, an art gallery, and a drama group.

University extension services. Meanwhile, in rural areas, the extension services of the land grant universities were doing similar work with rural people. They were producing opera in Iowa, encouraging folk arts in Kentucky, inserting the arts into community planning efforts in Ohio—linking arts and recreation, arts and homemaking, and arts and the meaningful use of leisure time. Some individuals stand out.

In upstate New York, Alexander Drummond was disgusted by the quality of so-called "rural plays" marketed by Samuel French, which portrayed rural people as hicks. So Drummond called for farmers who might want to write plays, and deployed his graduate students in theater as the dramaturgs to help them do so.

In North Carolina, Frederick Koch believed that because of the nature of the American ideal, America's culture could ONLY be recorded by ordinary Jo(e)s. So he required students in his theater program to start writing "folk plays"—plays about their background, about people in their communities. He insisted that his program be a mix of students rich and poor, sharecropper and landowner, black and white. Literally thousands of these "folk plays" were written in North Carolina during his time on the faculty and in other communities where he was asked to stimulate community playwriting.

Alfred Arvold, in North Dakota, was passionate that a community was an organic whole, and that the arts must not be broken off from the ongoing life of the community. To this end, he promulgated the notion of the community center where there would be a wonderful jumble of activity; it would be a recreation center, science center, arts center, and government center, where the boundaries between activities blurred. In 1917, he wrote:

> A community center is a place, a neighborhood laboratory, so to speak, where people meet in their own way to analyze whatever interests they have in common and participate in such forms of recreation as are healthful and enjoyable. The fundamental principle back of the community center is the democratization of all art so the common people can appreciate it, science so that they can use it, government so that they can take a part in it, and recreation so they can enjoy it. In other words, its highest aim is to make the common interests the great interests. To give a human expression in every locality to the significant meaning of these terms, "come let's reason and play together" is in reality the ultimate object of the community center.[2]

Robert Gard. In Wisconsin, Robert Gard's initial dream was to get every Wisconsinite writing; this ideal grew from the notion of populist government that prevailed in Wisconsin at the time. This "Wisconsin Idea" interrelated civic involvement, public education, access to the newest ideas, and fulfillment of creative potential for all of the citizens of the state. (Indeed, Gard's arts extension program at the University of Wisconsin inspired the founding of the Arts Extension Service at the University of Massachusetts, the publisher of this book!). In 1955, Gard wrote in *Grassroots Theater*[3] about the deep relationship between art and "sense of place." But Gard's dream kept expanding, and in 1967, in *The Arts in the Small Community*,[4] he urged arts groups to work with athletic groups like football teams, churches, ethnic organizations, senior citizens, and others, in the service of a healthy, whole community. These historical projects resonate with the notion of the role of the arts in whole communities, as well as our expressed commitment to empowering the individuals.

Baker Brownell. Another arts activist, working a little earlier than Gard, was Baker Brownell. He was a philosopher from Northwestern University, brought to Montana in the 1940s to help small towns think about their future, especially their economic future. He believed that this process started with a review of the community's economic, religious, creative, ethnic, and educational histories. The self-study process that he designed culminated in the production of a pageant that didn't just recite these histories, but used them as a way of addressing the future. Brownell believed that there are periods when specialists are needed in a society, giving way to periods when generalists are needed. It is tempting, and easier, to remain in a world of specialists, but he saw overspecialization as the path to the death of the soul and of society. Generalists, however, must stride forward and apply their knowledge to issues of the whole, integrated society. Brownell saw artists as people with this special knowledge. He juxtaposed the human community to the culture of specialism. In the human community, a place where the scale is shrunk so that people can know one another as whole persons, he saw the arts as a tool in community planning, but more importantly, as the way to reclaim a society's soul. He believed that art is a verb, that everyone is latently creative and thoughtful but that the art system too often reinforces passivity, and the way of passivity is the way of death. In 1950, Brownell wrote:

> Ours is a culture of displaced persons. It is tattered with escape and wandering, and as such is a culture founded on being lost… What the Germans did to millions in the concentration camps, and the Russians to tens of millions in the mass deportations, the western world in general does less dramatically but as effectively to hundreds of millions swarming homelessly to centers of vicarious and secondary culture. Their lives die out, love rots, and hope is replaced by avid stimulation. In all this, art may become merely one of the seducers to death. Or it may become the insight of life and survival itself.[5]

Brownell tied artists literally to the life of a society, and this, too, is something to which we are awakening today.

Rachel Davis-Dubois. An educator in New York working in the 1930s to 1950s, Rachel Davis Dubois[6] had a lifelong devotion to multicultural education. But even more than this, she articulated the notion of cultural democracy as the neglected third leg of the American stool, with the other two legs being political and economic democracy. She believed that the American dream could not be realized without equal emphasis on cultural democracy. In 1943, she said:

> The melting pot idea, or "come-let-us-do-something-for-you" attitude on the part of the old-stock American, was wrong. For half the melting pot to rejoice in being made better while the other half rejoiced in being better allowed for neither element to be its true self… The welfare of the group…

> means [articulating] a creative use of differences. Democracy is the only atmosphere in which this can happen, whether between individuals, within families, among groups in a country, or among countries. This kind of sharing we have [is] called cultural democracy. Political democracy—the right of all to vote—we have inherited. Economic democracy—the right of all to be free from want—we are beginning to envisage. But cultural democracy—a sharing of values among numbers of our various cultural groups—we have scarcely dreamed of. Much less have we devised social techniques for creating it.[7]

Much of her work was about enabling groups to study, understand, and value their own cultures, and to equally value and delight in the cultures of others. Here again, you surely see some of your roots.

Finally, in the first half of the nineteenth century, we see an articulation of the responsibility of the artist to building a stronger civic society. Percy MacKaye, from a long family of theater people, articulated the responsibility of the artist to think explicitly of him or herself as building civic infrastructure: "This potentiality of the drama could never be realized until the theatre…should be dedicated to public, not private, ends."[8]

Certainly, the artists later in the century, who were put back to work by the Works Progress Administration (WPA), wrote and produced plays and murals that challenged and raised questions while they also beautified and delighted. The film, *The Cradle Will Rock,* offers an important and provocative look at the WPA.[9]

Isolation of the Arts

Despite their positive approaches, something happened in each of these stories, and the arts were left isolated. Civic beautification often reaches a point where it is seen as optional, expensive, and something just for the wealthy (How many truly glorious public buildings are being constructed now?), and there is a constant debate about the appropriateness of public funding for artists and arts organizations. The Lyceum-Chautauqua story, which began as two grassroots, participatory endeavors, evolved into one-way presentations by artists to audiences; true engagement evolved into outreach. The Jane Addams and extension service stories have evolved so that now we separate "real" art from social work or recreation; indeed, the successors to Drummond, Koch, and Arvold were charged by their university with "professionalizing" the art in their departments. As schools struggle, arts education and multicultural education are left behind the "core" subjects of reading, science, and math.

Interestingly, each of these stories began with a deep-seated notion of personal wholeness and community interdependence and acknowledged the role of the arts in helping individuals and communities attain this wholeness and interdependence. Each of the stories ended with the arts being isolated—an amenity, an educational option, a one-way artist-audience relationship.

Let's consider our own organizations. We have done a good job in the past decades becoming institutionalized in the best sense. We do many high-quality shows, we're asked to a lot of community meetings, we've learned how to raise money, we are part of the concept of livable cities, we are becoming skilled in making the political process work for us. Yet as we have become institutionalized, the stakes have also risen. We need more money to keep the doors open. We need more political goodwill to build a facility. As we have struggled to secure more money and political support, it has often been at the expense of other groups in the community against whom we have had to compete for increasingly scarce resources of money, goodwill, and volunteers' time. We are, in fact, segregating ourselves from our communities even, ironically, as the idea of "more arts for all the people" is becomingly an increasingly accepted slogan.

Yet interestingly, in a RAND Corporation study, we learn that "institutions seeing the biggest gains [in diversity and engagement of audiences] are those that are making service to their communities as important as promoting artistic quality." [10]

Headwaters Goals

It is important to be aware of the philosophical origins of the stories we have just told. Yet we must also be aware that they can evolve into relatively simple projects with few philosophical "teeth," which are easily set aside when "times get tough." For example, endeavors whose goals were about relating civic aesthetics to democracy evolved into programs about beautification. The Lyceum, whose goal was to engage neighbors in discussion, evolved into a program about "audience development." As an analogy, consider the Colorado River; it begins as a profoundly important source of life, but it is diverted, used, and dammed so much that by the time it gets to the Gulf, it is but a dusty trickle. In community arts organizing, you must not start with goals analogous to that trickle; rather, start with goals that are analogous to the headwaters. For purposes of community arts organizing, a goal that is about "civic aesthetics and democracy" is a headwaters goal; a goal that is merely about "beautification" is a dusty trickle goal (without the passion to carry you when you are tired, impatient, and feeling as though it's just not worth it). Think about the philosophical "headwaters" of the historical stories recounted above, and see which, if any, relate to your situation.

- **A better physical community.** Beauty and invitations to gather are civic values—because in a democracy, public spaces and public buildings and thoroughfares ought to embody the highest aspirations of human beings. This is the story of the Village Improvement, City Beautiful, and Frank Lloyd Wright movements.
- **A more thoughtful community.** Here people engage in genuine dialogue—questioning, critiquing, leading to more informed personal and collective action—because every individual has a right to improve or change his or her life. This is the story of Josiah Holbrook and his discussion groups, and the Chautauqua clubs.
- **A multicultured community.** People prize the cultures of one another as they value their own—because coexistence is not enough. We cannot move to true globalism without deep understanding. This is the legacy of Frederick Koch and Rachel Davis-Dubois.
- **A community of empowered individuals.** Each person explores his or her own creativity—because each person has a birthright of dignity and a wealth of individual opinions and ideas. This is the story of Alex Drummond, Robert Gard, and extension services.
- **A human community.** People learn to know one another well—because moving forward meaningfully as a community cannot happen until groups move past being special interests and learn to relate as people. This is the story of Alfred Arvold and Baker Brownell.
- **A just community.** Here the norm is decency, dignity, and tolerance for all—because this is the meaning of being an American. This is the legacy of the Settlement House and the Civil Rights movements.

- **A civic community.** Here everyone sees him or herself as responsible to the community and its public processes—because without this individual commitment there can be no true democracy. This is the legacy of Percy MacKaye and the artists who participated in the arts programs of the New Deal.

Community Arts Stories

Let's look at a few examples where people are thinking about community arts programs with this kind of depth and considering the deep philosophical context that leads to community arts organizing.

Animating Democracy. In the late 1990s, the Ford Foundation and Americans for the Arts undertook a bold new venture called Animating Democracy. Its purpose is to "foster artistic activity that encourages civic dialogue on important contemporary issues." The Land Bridge Project, one of many such projects supported by Animating Democracy, shows how community arts organizing can be approached.

In collaboration with The Children's Theatre Company and the Perpich Center for Arts Education, the Land Bridge Project brought together rural and urban residents of Montevideo and Minneapolis, Minnesota, in dialogue around issues of the expanding farm crisis. The Minnesota farming community is deeply divided between farmers struggling to maintain family farms and those who contract with agribusiness. Related tensions exist between farmers and banks, legislators and rural activists, and between neighbors. The Children's Theatre Company aimed to use the creation of a new play to illuminate the complexity of the issue and to make those further along the food chain aware that this crisis of food, economy, land use, and social well-being is also their crisis.[11]

Pathway to Peace Neighborhood Gateway. A good example of community arts organizing at the local neighborhood level is the Pathway to Peace Gateway in the East Harriet Farmstead neighborhood in south Minneapolis. The Gateway Pathway began as an effort of the local neighborhood association and Lyndale Park, which includes a peace garden, a contemplative place secluded from the rest of the park. Peace garden activists wanted to create a stronger link between the neighborhood and the garden and solicited support from the City of Minneapolis Art in Public Places project for the creation of a gateway. Artists were commissioned to create a series of seven sculptural columns spanning the four-block area from the neighborhood to the garden. Each artwork contains text derived from community dialogues, where people shared their feelings and questions about peace in the community, across the world, and within themselves.

Engaged arts. During a 2001 Grantmakers in the Arts conference panel addressing the topic of meaningful community-building through the arts, Mark Valentine, of The David and Lucile Packard Foundation, said:

> It's about knitting… It's not about expansive kumbaya moments where everybody practices guitar around the campfire… It's about finding places where programs are active concurrently, but in a disaggregated context, and bringing them together. My own bias is that art and culture are a significant part of that conversation. They're woven into the very heart of that community. As you envision what the future might look like, I think it's essential that it be engaged.[12]

He cited projects reviewed by his foundation in which artists are paired with environmentalists to help their community really think about issues of climate change. Similarly, Peter Pennekamp, of the Humboldt Area Foundation, said, "Art outside the context of everyday life, art within a consumption model which is really almost all of what the professional arts world lives in, rather than a participation model, is what makes art not as important as I think all of us would like it to be." [13]

The point is that the arts can both become more important and serve an urgently needed role in our society now, if we shift our thinking back to the original ideas behind each of these historical tales. So whether you are an idealist ("this is the right thing to do") or a pragmatist ("we might not survive if we don't start thinking differently"), consider the idea of committing your arts organization to the community-building process.

Ways That Arts Organizations Lead In Community Organizing

Investigate the things we have in common. An example is the work of Roadside Theater. In Appalachia, its home, the dramatic material is drawn directly from community knowledge and stories there.

Investigate our differences. Another of Roadside Theater's artistic thrusts is to collaborate with theater companies from other cultures, exploring what their cultural stories do not have in common as well as what they share.

Further community conversation. Any of the activities in Americans for the Arts' Animating Democracy program fall into this category. Whether the issue is the health of a river on which a town is dependent, youth violence, blighted neighborhoods, or a debate over whose history should be told and how in the local historical museum, examples abound. Go to www.animatingdemocracy.org for case studies and publications.

Educate others about us. In Crested Butte, Colorado, which depends heavily on tourists for its economic life, the buses that transport skiers to the ski area are all painted with something important about the town—its history, current community members, even the dogs that everyone knows. It says, "We live here. Don't just spend money here. Respect our place and people. Get to know us."

Mobilize people. In Los Angeles, the Bus Riders Union collaborated with Cornerstone Theater Company to create a series of mini-plays which were performed on the buses. A small team of players boarded dressed in costume, did their playlet (which had to do with an issue faced by bus riders), distributed leaflets, and got off the bus several stops later.

Prevent issues from developing. In Calgary, Alberta, a neighborhood planner is thinking about a new kind of planning process involving the community theater. Act One might portray the status quo in the community, and groups of citizens would sketch scenarios for Act Two depending on which key decision is made about a particular issue. Visualizing alternatives and their consequences is difficult; this idea could lead to avoidance of poor choices.

Heal. Artists who had been in residence at Columbine High School in Littleton, Colorado, were among the first people that the school turned to after the shooting tragedy in which many students died. Within two days the artists were offering activities to students and teachers, the first of a series of activities that continued for two years. Artists served a similar healing function following the September 11 World Trade Center attacks in 2001 and the devastation wrought upon the Gulf Coast in 2005 by Hurricanes Katrina and Rita.

What is essential in all of these ideas is that the arts organization is not isolated. It must work with a wide variety of nonarts groups in the community—teachers, therapists, "ordinary citizens," planners, union organizers, businesses, farmers. Each group must be equal in bringing what they know, and how they know it, to the table. Together, they devise a new approach to furthering the health of the community that they, as interdependent people, have in common.

Endnotes

1. Atlas, C., & Korza, P., (Eds.). (2005). *Critical Perspectives: Writings on Art and Civic Dialogue.* Washington, DC: Americans for the Arts.

2. Arvold, A. (1917, May-June). *The Community Center Movement. College and State,* 1(3). North Dakota Agricultural College.

3. Gard, R.(1999). *Grassroots Theater: A Search for Regional Arts in America.* Madison, WI: University of Wisconsin Press.

4. Gard, R., Kohloff, R., & Warlum, M. (1995). *The Arts in the Small Community.* Washington, DC: Americans for the Arts.

5. Brownell, B. (1950). *The Human Community.* New York: Harper & Brothers.

6. Rachel Davis-Dubois was no relation to W.E.B. Dubois, though she did work with him.

7. Davis-Dubois, R. (1943). *Get Together Americans: Friendly Approaches to Racial and Cultural Conflicts Through the Neighborhood-Home Festival.* New York: Harper & Brothers.

8. MacKave, P. M. (1909). *The Playhouse and the Play.* New York: MacMillan.

9. Robbins, T. (Producer/Writer/Director). (1999). *The Cradle Will Rock* [Motion picture]. United States: Touchstone Home Video.

10. RAND Corporation. *Examining Why People Participate in the Arts.* Retrieved from www.rand.org/publications/RB/researchprofile/.

11. Americans for the Arts. *Children's Theatre Company.* Retrieved from www.americansforthearts.org/animating-democracy/labs/lab_065.asp.

12. Pennekamp, P., McPhee, P., Valentine, M., & Zollar, J. W. J. (2001, November 5). *Beyond "Art": A Community Perspective.* Presented at the Grantmakers for the Arts 2001 Conference. Retrieved from www.giarts.org/usr_doc/BeyondArt.pdf.

13. Ibid.

Arts and the Economy: Fuel for the Creative Engine

TOM BORRUP

The Arts and the Creative Economy

> You can go to any city in America and find an arts organization creating vitality in every neighborhood. And leaders still don't get it. Arts and culture is the genesis of the revitalization of communities. — former Pittsburgh Mayor Tom Murphy[1]

Increasingly, civic leaders are "getting it," but ironically, artists and nonprofit arts groups are sometimes the last to fully appreciate what they can do to be potent forces in shaping their local communities. By recognizing and understanding this capacity— and responsibility —cultural leaders acting with purpose can be larger contributors to the well-being of their communities. In turn, as communities acknowledge the value of the arts and culture, they, too, will thrive.

In this chapter, we'll look at the role culture and the arts play in the economic health of their communities, and how artists and arts organizations fit into economic-development strategies. We'll examine the idea of the creative economy and look at eight arts-centered economic-development strategies typically used by cultural organizations to impact economic development through culture and the arts. We'll also review language and tools that help cultural leaders and managers better understand their community's economy and their role in it.

In the APPENDIX to this chapter, you'll also find the following processes for implementing community-development strategies:

- How to map and leverage a community's creative assets for economic development;
- How to identify and form strategic partnerships; and
- The important role of the "intermediary" in arts and economic-development work.

Definition of Terms

WHAT IS THE CREATIVE ECONOMY?

The term creative economy came into popular use in the 1990s as creative-sector industries have grown in the post-industrial era. Generally part of the for-profit arena, these industries include advertising, media, entertainment, and the design professions, including product, fashion, and packaging, as well as handmade products from wood, ceramics, metal, and glass. In the nonprofit sector, they include arts producing, presenting, and preservation organizations, big and small, and individual artists, who make up a large number of creative sector workers. In fact, artists, who are often self-employed, each represent a small-business enterprise. Not only have creative industries grown in size at a faster rate than others since the 1990s, but their importance in shaping and propelling other economic sectors has become clearer.

> A culture persists in time only to the degree it is inventing, creating, and dynamically evolving in a way that promotes the production of ideas across all social classes and groups.
>
> — Shalini Venturelli, "From the Information Economy to the Creative Economy"

Since 2000, creative communities, creative workforces, and other dimensions of the creative economy have also come into sharper focus. That year, the New England Council, an association representing major business concerns in that region, issued a report, "The Creative Economy Initiative", examining the nature of this emerging sector and charting its relative size and remarkable growth. The report acknowledged the considerable contribution made by the arts industry to "nurturing innovation, developing a skilled workforce, and helping businesses remain competitive."

A 2012 report by the National Governors Association cites some of the ways arts, culture, and design can assist states with economic growth. These growing and productive sectors, the report notes, can assist states with economic growth because they can:

1. provide a fast-growth, dynamic industry cluster
2. help mature industries become more competitive
3. provide the critical ingredients for innovative places
4. catalyze community revitalization
5. deliver a better-prepared workforce

According to a report prepared for the National Governors Association in 2012, "Globalization and the changing economy have affected individual states differently, but all are searching for ways to support high-growth industries, accelerate innovation, foster entrepreneurial activity, address unemployment, build human capital, and revive distressed areas. Using the five roles as a framework, state leaders— governors, economic-development officials, and state arts agencies —have a way to intentionally and strategically make arts, culture, and design an important part of an economic growth agenda. States have already undertaken initiatives that are highly relevant to that agenda."[2]

This productive ground is shared by cultural leaders, economic-development practitioners, and policymakers alike. It is essential for arts managers to understand their part in it. That is the goal of this chapter.

THE USE OF THE WORD COMMUNITY

In this chapter, we will use the term community to refer to the people and the natural and built environments within a geographically-defined area, together with their social, economic, and civic institutions. Not to deny or diminish other definitions of community, such as communities of interest or virtual communities, we will talk only about place-based communities. In this sense, community includes not only the physical connections but the social, civic, and economic bonds between people who reside, work, or otherwise consider themselves part of a geographic place. Whether it is a rural, suburban, small-town, or densely populated urban community, 100 square miles or 10 city blocks, what's important is that it has identity as a place, and those in it have reason to coalesce around common interests.

HOW THE WORD CULTURE IS USED

What makes a community function, in every respect, is its culture. Culture can be defined as the "values, attitudes, beliefs, orientations, and underlying assumptions" that exist between people.[3] This contrasts with narrower definitions that have been associated with the practice of highly skilled artists, often within the context of institutions that adjudicate and possess artifacts of culture. Culture comes in forms that include food, language, religion, music, home life, holiday observances, rituals, dance, poetry, visual art, crafts, behaviors, and creative endeavors. They are influenced by the systems of values and aesthetics that evolve and are practiced over a long period of time among people in a particular place. They are dynamic and constantly evolving.

Background

WHERE CULTURE, ECONOMICS, AND COMMUNITIES MEET

While intuitively part of the community-building process for centuries, cultural activities have only recently come under serious study as part of economic and human development. Two of the more influential authors in the fields of economics and social development since the late 1990s are economist Richard Florida and social scientist Robert Putnam. While these thinkers disagree on what constitutes a "successful" community, they are on the same page with regards to the often overlooked role of culture and art. See the Creative Placemaking chapter for further discussion on Richard Florida.

In *The Rise of the Creative Class*, Florida proposes a definition of a city's *creative class* — workers in creative, communications, managerial, financial, legal, or any occupation in which information is the central tool or product — and postulates that a critical mass of workers who fit this definition fuels the city's economic engine. He cites characteristics of tolerance, cultural activity, and social climate as key to attracting and retaining these workers. In turn, he argues, their presence results in industries becoming and remaining competitive. Putnam, for his part, argues in *Bowling Alone: The Collapse and Revival of American Community* that the well-being of a city or region pivots on the ability of people to act constructively together around mutual interests. He measures this through a community's level of "social capital." This term describes the social connectedness of people across cultures, ages, and other divides (what he labels bridging social capital), as well as within groups who are more alike and who organize to advance their well-being (bonding social capital).

Florida finds that an active and participatory cultural scene is essential to a strong, creative economy, especially in places that are "bohemian" in character and offer diverse and edgy arts, music, film, food, and entertainment. Larger, more passive forms of cultural consumption or entertainment, he says, are of less interest to residents of these places. Putnam makes a similar case for an active cultural environment that includes activities to help people better share their cultures and stories, and to learn, cooperate, and build social and civic connections.[4]

Other scholars are finding that the practical and symbolic significance of creative people, bohemian neighborhoods, and iconic institutions have additional impacts. Economist Ann Markusen and David King[5] draw different connections between the presence and influences of thriving artist communities and successful industries. She argues that standard economic impact studies underestimate the full contribution of an artistic community to a regional economy; that is, they fail to trace the many ways in which creative talent contributes to regional productivity.

Markusen counters the parochial view of the arts as a consequence of, or even a parasite on, a successful business community. She makes the case that productivity in a regional economy rises in correlation to the number of artists within its boundaries, producing an *artistic dividend.* In other words, in a healthy economy, an abundance of artists may be more cause than effect. While Florida's *creative class* is more broadly defined, he and Markusen come to similar conclusions about the importance to economic growth of creative thinkers — and the environments that attract and stimulate them.

Florida's theories have been characterized as promoting "talent attraction," provoking cities to cater to a more mobile and upscale group of professionals to the detriment of existing populations, including manufacturing and service workers. Markusen and others advocate the development of local assets, the people and unique qualities of each place versus the dedication of resources to induce competition among cities to draw talent and resources away from each other. This *asset-based* approach to community building and economic development developed by John McKnight and John Kretzmann is the underlying concept driving this chapter and the projects highlighted here.[6]

ECONOMIC ENGINES DON'T MOVE WITHOUT WHEELS

While this chapter is focused on the economic dimensions of communities, there is a larger system at work that must be recognized. For an economic engine to move a community forward, the rest of the vehicle has to be in working order. Natural and built environments, as well as social, political, and cultural infrastructures, are integrally related. If they are not working together, the community is not advancing and is not healthy. Cultural leaders are key players in the overall well-being of their communities and bear responsibility for appreciating their key role in a holistic system. Some planners have begun to cite four key elements — cultural, economic, environmental, and social impacts — as equally essential to community health and sustainability.[7]

> What draws people to the arts is not the hope that the experience will make them smarter or more self-disciplined. Instead, it is the expectation that encountering a work of art can be a rewarding experience, one that offers them pleasure and emotional stimulation and meaning.

A 2004 report from the RAND Corporation surveyed recent literature and research on the social, economic, and human-development impacts of the arts, as well as on the more difficult to quantify "intrinsic" values. The findings bring together for the first time the multiple ways arts activities change lives and communities. Importantly, however, they point out that "what draws people to the arts is not the hope that the experience will make them smarter or more self-disciplined. Instead, it is the expectation that encountering a work of art can be a rewarding experience, one that offers them pleasure and emotional stimulation and meaning." The RAND researchers concluded that instrumental benefits of the arts are "grounded in compelling arts experiences."[8]

It is the instrumental impacts and intrinsic power of the arts *together* that make them profoundly effective catalysts for personal and community transformation. While the arts' capacity to invigorate an economy cannot be denied, it is impossible to divorce them from their multiple meanings, applications, and effects.

CULTURE AND THE CREATION OF HEALTHY PLACES

We shape our cities and then our cities shape us.

—Andres Duany et al., Suburban Nation[9]

Like the arts, the design professions have a bigger impact on communities than we often attribute to them. In his groundbreaking work *The Social Life of Small Urban Places,* William H. Whyte observed and documented human behaviors in urban settings and how design and policies regulating public spaces, buildings, and cities affect social behaviors. Whyte asserted that crowded, pedestrian-friendly, active spaces are safer, more economically productive, and more conducive to healthy civic communities. "What attracts people most in an urban place is other people," he wrote.[10]

Promoting constructive interaction among people in public spaces is a nearly forgotten art. Planners, architects, and public administrators have been focused more on creating physical structures and providing for the unimpeded movement and storage of automobiles than on creating good urban spaces that serve people.[11] More recently, public officials have been concerned with security and maximizing their ability to observe and control people in public spaces.

Active public space provides opportunities for people to meet and be exposed to the variety and multiple dimensions of their neighbors. These meetings often take place by chance, but also can come through active organizing. Public spaces include streets, sidewalks, parks, waterfronts, and civic buildings. Other important spaces include marketplaces, coffee shops, and restaurants.

"*Place* is something people do together, it's not just a container," said sociologist David Brain.[12] Place refers to a destination or iconic location within a community that has achieved deep and widespread meaning and value to locals and visitors alike. Taking mere space and turning it into *place*—what some call *placemaking*—means creating something collectively valued and used. (See Creative Placemaking chapter for more information. ▌)This is an area to which cultural programmers are uniquely well equipped to contribute—especially when they work together with, or complement the work of, planners, designers, and public officials. Culture contributes to the creation of healthy spaces and meaningful places. Desirable public space, in turn, can translate into economic benefits.

ARTS ACTIVITIES AND COMMUNITY DEVELOPMENT

A study led by professor of social welfare and history Mark J. Stern and urban planner Susan Seifert for the University of Pennsylvania's Social Impact of the Arts Project (SIAP) found that as the presence of small arts groups in neighborhoods increased, there were multiple positive effects. In areas with higher levels of cultural activity — both poor and middle-class neighborhoods — there was positive impact on school truancy, youth delinquency, civic engagement, teen pregnancy, and a host of other factors. The researchers also cited positive relationships between arts participation, population stability, and real estate values. They asserted that small cultural groups are typically more important to communities and to revitalization of neighborhoods than major institutions.

Stern and Seifert found that cultural activities stimulate community revitalization less through their direct economic impact than by building the social connections between people that in turn stimulate the formation and success of new enterprises. They motivate neighbors and give them increased capacity to see possibility and make changes in their community. They increase connections between neighborhoods of different ethnic and economic groups. Community arts organizations are associated with broader civic engagement and residents' sense of collective efficacy, or capacity to act together.[13]

A 2003 Chicago-based study by Diane Grams and Michael Warr[14] also looked beyond the art "product" and examined the social and economic activity that goes on in and around cultural organizations. It found that small community-based arts organizations leveraged a variety of relationships, capacities, and activities in unusually effective ways. The study cited three overarching results of arts groups' presence in a community; they:

- build social relationships;
- enable problem solving; and
- provide access to resources.

CULTURE IN COMMUNITY DEVELOPMENT

The economic, social, and physical dimensions of community building are not only interrelated but inseparable. Over the past 40 years the newly established field of community development has focused its efforts on construction and management of low- and mixed-income housing, job training or workforce development, commercial real estate development, and small business start-up and incubation. It sometimes operates youth development, health, recreation, family counseling, human services, and— in rare instances— cultural programs.

The field of community development includes planners, trainers, housing, real estate, and economic-development specialists, community organizers, and advocates. They typically function through entities known as community development corporations (CDCs), which are supported locally and nationally by a widespread network of intermediaries such as the Local Initiatives Support Corporation (LISC), the Enterprise Foundation, and Living Cities: The National Community Development Initiative. These intermediaries depend largely on government, philanthropic, and corporate support and provide operating dollars, training, loans, and loan guarantees, as well as guidance in commonly accepted standards of community-development practice. Local CDCs that become successful in housing and commercial real estate gradually build their own base of revenues from leasing, rental, sales, and development fees. Over the long term they accrue significant portfolios of real estate assets and become expert at property and small business development.

A 2002 report by New York's Center for an Urban Future saw great potential for synergy between CDCs and cultural organizations. It called for integrating cultural and business development and found that while the two had the greatest impact side by side, coordination was rare. The report states, "In our survey of over 150 [New York City—based] economic and community-development organizations, only six were involved in efforts that directly linked the arts with business."[15] Not only are many arts groups in need of some of the expertise housed within CDCs, but neighborhood development strategies have been found to be more successful and equitable when cultural, economic, social, and environmental assets and advocates act in concert.

Over the next decade, a growing number of CDCs have increasingly found new ways to revitalize communities by working with the arts. In 2014, LISC, the nation's largest network of CDCs, took a major step towards leveraging partnerships with the arts. A $3.5 million grant from the Kresge Foundation helped LISC launch "a national effort to drive millions of dollars into arts-related businesses and cultural activities that will help transform some of America's most distressed neighborhoods into safe, vibrant places of economic opportunity."[16]

> Neighborhood development strategies have been found to be more successful and equitable when cultural, economic, social, and environmental assets and advocates are acting in concert.

The Ford Foundation, together with a team of leaders in the culture and community-development fields, looked at innovative community-building strategies during 2002 and 2003 and reported similar findings. They observed that as art and cultural organizations support community involvement and participation, they help increase the potential for people to understand themselves and change how they see the world. This, in turn, bolsters community pride and identity, which bolsters the local economy. The study group also saw that the arts improve derelict buildings; preserve cultural heritage; transmit values and history; bridge cultural, ethnic, and racial boundaries; and stimulate economic development.[17]

The study group found a few cases where community-development practitioners in distressed communities successfully partnered with arts and cultural organizations in their community-development strategies. However, they observed that community-development and arts organizations were typically disparate and isolated from one another: an important synergistic relationship exists but is rarely acknowledged or exploited.

In 2010, the Ford Foundation joined forces with 12 other regional and national foundations, six federal government agencies, and six major financial institutions to form ArtPlace America, a 10-year funding initiative to "to position art and culture as a core sector of comprehensive community planning and development in order to help strengthen the social, physical, and economic fabric of communities."[18] ArtPlace makes grants to arts and culture organizations that are leading efforts to revitalize their communities. During its 10-year lifespan, ArtPlace expects to award as much as $150 million to communities nationwide.

When Culture Goes to Work

As partners in the larger process of building healthy and economically prosperous communities, arts organizations must ask what they can do for their community rather than what can their community do for them. To do so, they must first take a good look at themselves to identify what assets and core competencies they bring to the table and what unique qualities exist in their surroundings.

The ultimate success story is a sustainable and competitive local economy based on a community's distinct assets, particularly cultural assets that enhance the area's identity and character. Who wouldn't want to attract or nurture enterprises that emanate from and reflect local cultural values, that create jobs, are environmentally friendly, provide satisfying work, and give back to their community's civic and social life?

"Big box" solutions to local economic or social problems— imported from outside the community or costing the community enormous sums —tend to become long-term problems. Their impacts are inequitable, unbalanced, and unsustainable, whether the business is a single manufacturing plant, giant retail outlet, sports or convention center, or giant performing arts complex. Big box developments import and depend on outside capital, labor, goods, culture, and consumers. Typically, they take profits elsewhere, damage the environment, overshadow the unique identity of place, and diminish the integrity and value of the people and cultures of that community.[19] Just as a more diverse and balanced natural environment is a healthier one, a more diversified economy— rooted in a community's assets and in tune with the identity of that place —provides a more stable base and returns more to the local economy.

Locally owned small businesses, including individual artists and small arts organizations, engage in their immediate community and have a unique product that attracts and supplies customers from outside the community. A large number and diverse mix of such enterprises, in an environment that supports their start-up and growth, is ideal. Likewise, a cultural "ecology" that includes a mix of ethnic groups and a balance of cultural producers (artists), cultural presenters, and cultural preservationists— a balance that is reflective of the community and draws from both within and outside its boundaries —is eminently more stable, healthy, and productive.

Eight Culturally Driven Strategies for Economic Development

In this section we'll look at eight different, although often overlapping, approaches to economic development through arts and culture that readers can examine in relation to their own work. Observation and research has found the following successful strategies in use by arts centers, community-development corporations, business organizations, cities, and other civic agencies or nonprofits. These have been written about in greater length and with additional examples in *Creative Community Builder's Handbook*[20] by this author.

Typically, such efforts are successful when carried out in partnerships that straddle different sectors and include individual artists and/or arts organizations. It must also be noted that these eight approaches rarely function in isolation. Many of them are interdependent or build upon one another. They are singled out for purposes of understanding their impact, but rarely is any project so singular in focus or result.

Creative Community Building Strategies:

1. Create jobs by nurturing artists and small cultural organizations as businesses to increase employment;
2. Shape and enhance identity by developing civic pride, stewardship and brand identity through good placemaking and community-centered practices;
3. Stimulate trade by creating the right conditions for cultural tourism and economic exchange to bring new resources to the community;
4. Attract investment by support artists and artists' live/work spaces as anchors around which to build local economies;
5. Diversify the economy by clustering arts organizations as anchors and promoting entrepreneurship to attract activity and create new enterprises;
6. Enhance value by employing the artists' touch to increase property values;
7. Build trust, social capital, and community capacity by creating and strengthening bonds between people of different backgrounds and enabling enterprises to grow;
8. Retain wealth by keeping dollars recirculating in communities through buying locally.

STRATEGY 1: CREATE JOBS

> For too long, creative enterprises have been overlooked by economic developers and public services that have consistently cast their nets for the big fish, rather than the more abundant — and ultimately more self-sustaining — schools of small fish.
>
> — Stuart Rosenfeld, "Crafting a New Rural Development Strategy"[21]

The arts and culture sector has not generally been considered a major contributor to the U.S. economy. However, individual artists and nonprofit cultural organizations account for significant economic activity while bringing other benefits. Nurturing artists and small cultural organizations as businesses can increase employment and boost the local economy. A 2011 study by Americans for the Arts[22] estimated that the country's nonprofit arts industry generates $135.2 billion in annual economic activity. This places nonprofit arts in the top ranks of national industries, drawing more audience participation and expenditures than professional sports, among other industries that are often aggressively courted by states and cities. The arts and culture sector itself employs 5.7 million full-time-equivalent positions.

Significantly, this study covers only formal nonprofit organizations, not individual artists or any of the "informal arts," traditional arts, or craft practices that take place outside institutional settings. Individual artists and nonprofit cultural organizations are small businesses that provide significant employment within communities. Small businesses in general employ more than half of the private sector employees and are more innovative than many larger firms. Small businesses are also faster growing than larger firms, creating 66 percent of all net new jobs since the 1970s.[23] In 1970, the Bureau of Labor Statistics estimated 730,000 artists in the United States and by 2013 estimated that number to be just over two million.[24] As many working artists operate "under the radar," and many more supplement their primary income through arts and craft activities, these figures are likely even higher.

Arts entrepreneurs work in all corners of the country creating unique products and services that have value well beyond the raw materials they use. When recognized and nurtured as small business enterprises, artists and small organizations can contribute even more. There are many examples across the United States where entrepreneurial artists have been essential to the revitalization of neighborhoods, towns, and cities.

The legendary urbanist Jane Jacobs said, "New ideas must use old buildings."[25] And old buildings are something many post-industrial communities have in abundance. Creative entrepreneurs are in no short supply either. Matching the two, and creating a nurturing environment for creative sector and arts-based enterprises, is often the key in transitioning to the knowledge or creative economy.

> **Example: Greenpoint Manufacturing and Design Center (GMDC), New York City**
> Greenpoint and other areas of Brooklyn contain buildings that once housed "smokestack" industries. With older, noisy, and often polluting industries now relocated away from population centers, these buildings and neighborhoods were ready for a new life. GMDC started in the late 1980s to reclaim derelict factories and sustain newer industries and manufacturing in New York City. Their location ensures the stability of manufacturing businesses within mixed-use environments by protecting them from displacement and the increasingly volatile real estate market. As a nonprofit industrial developer, GMDC provides space for occupancy by small manufacturing enterprises, artisans, and artists. It owns and manages five properties which represent more than half a million square feet of space. Over 500 people are employed and more than 100 businesses reside within these properties.

STRATEGY 2: SHAPE AND ENHANCE IDENTITY

> *"Space" is more abstract than "place." What begins as undifferentiated space becomes place as we get to know it better and endow it with value.* —Yi-Fu Tuan, Space and Place

Developing civic pride and stewardship through good placemaking and cooperative practices can help to create or enhance a community's identity, engage local residents, and welcome others in. This strategy builds on the idea that every community has its own unique identity that is sometimes hidden and just needs to be uncovered or refreshed.

When the people of a community come together to find its identity, they learn the importance of their own customs and traditions. These include the inherited traditions of long-term residents as well as those of recent immigrants and newcomers. This heritage comes from the stories, music, and customs passed down through generations, as well as the culinary traditions of the community and other celebrations of life, coming of age, and death.

Building or reviving a community's identity based on its history and people assures that it is authentic, which in turn can add value to the products created there, as well as developing a sense of "ownership" or stewardship of place. These assets can then be leveraged to attract new residents and visitors and to support businesses. Connecting local businesses and cultural groups also helps to build clusters of activities, which can lead to historic districts, arts districts, and Main Street neighborhoods.[26] All of these clusters can then be used to promote the neighborhood or town as a destination for all. See the Creative Placemaking chapter for a case study on Roxbury RTC.

STRATEGY 3: STIMULATE TRADE

> Traditional arts can support economic development by strengthening communities, stimulating demand for local products, and supporting the economic activities of other local businesses.
>
> —Chris Walker et al., *Culture and Commerce*

This strategy focuses on creating favorable conditions for and engaging in cultural tourism to bring new resources to the community. However, the side benefits of a tourism campaign can be just as important: building a unified identity and increasing cross-sector, cross-business partnerships to attract new spending and new business. This section reviews some of the trends in the growing industry of cultural tourism.

Leisure travel and tourism in the United States contributed $927.9 billion in 2014 and directly funded 8 million jobs,[27] making it one of the largest industries in the U.S., with one out of every nine jobs depending on the travel industry. According to one study, over 70 percent of all U.S. leisure travelers participate in cultural or heritage activities while traveling. Arts and culture have proven to be a magnet for travelers and their money. When choosing a destination for leisure travel, 16 percent of Americans find that a place with interesting culture is "extremely important" to them. According to a study by the National Assembly of State Arts Agencies, "In 2009, 68% of the Adult Population were leisure travelers with 78% of these classified as cultural heritage travelers.[28] In the 2009 State of the American Traveler survey, American adults were asked where they had traveled in the last 12 months:

- Visit an historical place or attraction 42.3%
- Visit small towns/villages 41.2%
- Sightseeing in rural areas 39.1%
- Visit a state or local park 27.8%
- Drive a designated scenic byway 24.9%

Well-managed cultural tourism also improves an area's quality of life and builds community pride. *Cultural heritage tourism,* "based on the mosaic of places, traditions, art forms, celebrations and experiences that portray this nation and its people,"[29] is generally focused on a local theme or landmark and binds multiple small-scale enterprises that complement one another to create a ripple effect within the regional economy. Sometimes a community's greatest assets are in plain sight yet invisible to locals. Appreciating and mobilizing local assets requires taking a new look at one's own community and working together across sectors.

Good examples are found in every type of location, from inner-city immigrant neighborhoods to small towns in rural regions. They are very much alike, in that their activities are rooted in the history and values of the people in the community and the communities invest heavily in themselves. Cultural tourism requires ongoing and cross-sector planning. Success comes from cooperation across government, business, and nonprofit sectors, and often leads to even greater collaboration and enhanced capacity for problem-solving on all levels.

> **Example: Lanesboro, Minnesota**
> Visitors to remote Lanesboro (population 754 in 2010) enjoy biking, canoeing, horseback riding, golf, tennis, and walking. They also enjoy theater, art, music, fine cuisine, and cozy accommodations. Lanesboro's leaders— key among them the Lanesboro Art Council, Commonweal Theatre Company, and Cornucopia Art Center —understand the "brand identity" of their community —the aesthetics of the natural environment, their penchant for hospitality, and a panoply of cultural activities as ingredients for a successful tourism economy. The town's frozen-in-time 19th-century main street, the scenic bluffs of the Root River, and the energy of local artists came together to build a remarkable success story in a small out-of-the-way place.

STRATEGY 4: ATTRACT INVESTMENT

> These arts facilities have distinguished themselves as extremely stable and highly desirable additions to the urban landscape,… generating an immediate and significant positive impact on the surrounding neighborhoods, providing the momentum necessary to further revitalize distressed urban areas. —John Villani, "A Call to Art"

Older urban and rural areas have a great deal in common when it comes to suffering dis-investment, poisoned industrial sites, and population loss. Regenerating a more viable, sustainable, and flexible economy can begin with existing assets and result in a place that attracts investment. Some communities have enlisted creative entrepreneurs, chief among them artists, and made use of vacant real estate— such as warehouses, mills, and factory buildings —to jump start their economic-development efforts.

In his 1999 "Call to Art," John Villani advocated developing artist "live/work" spaces as anchors around which to build local economies. "Being able to foster a local arts scene, provide low- and moderate-income housing, preserve historic buildings, and promote downtown and neighborhood economic revitalization— all at the same time —makes these types of projects rewarding far beyond their bottom line," Villani concluded.[30] Typically, artist live/work spaces are conceived in tandem with the reuse of historic, commercial, or industrial structures. It's the artists themselves, living and working in the community, who stimulate development of more active street-level environments while they create products of interest to wider markets.

Artists' lofts and artistic communities bring a new and different kind of excitement to buildings and their surroundings. "The thing about artists is they're around 24 hours a day," says economist Ann Markusen. "They have unusual hours; they're around coming and going. They have families. These kinds of patterns are really great for reducing crime and stabilizing a community. Galleries, cafes, and other arts-related developments tend to follow, and the revenue from those businesses stays in the community."[31]

A 2011 study of two live/work projects concluded that such spaces "generate clear benefits for arts tenants and the surrounding neighborhood and region."[32]

> **Example: Paducah Artist Relocation Program/Paducah Renaissance Alliance, Kentucky**
> At the junction of the Ohio and Tennessee rivers, Paducah, Kentucky, may seem an unlikely spot for an artist relocation program. Prior to this project, most outsiders had come to town on riverboat cruises that brought around 11,000 visitors to the declining area each year. Thanks to Paducah's highly successful Artist Relocation Program, LowerTown, an older, deteriorated neighborhood of once-grand homes adjacent to downtown, is now a proud Arts District of renovated Victorian homes and storefronts. Many artists relocated here from other cities and established studios, galleries, and small businesses. Artists are the major economic-development leaders making investments and attracting investments to enrich the historic areas of the downtown. With coordination from the Paducah Renaissance Alliance, a National Main Street program, artists continually breathe new life into the local scene. While different from an artist live/work loft building, LowerTown is now a neighborhood with as many as 100 artists who have moved there since 2000. The community has gained national awards and media attention. Abandoned properties have once again become part of the community and $1.2 million in city funds have been committed to infrastructure upgrades. Residents take pride and reinvest in their community, bringing vibrancy, economic activity, and a high quality of life.

STRATEGY 5: DIVERSIFY ECONOMY

The arts, increased tourism and community participation, and regional economic redevelopment are mutually reinforcing and inextricably linked.… The arts create and bestow community identity. Identity rallies hope, productivity and pride, and economic vibrancy.[33]

The more legs an economy has to stand on, the more resistant it is to a downturn in any one sector. Creative economies continually generate new enterprises and reinvent themselves, building new legs and repositioning old ones. Many creative community builders have revived both urban and rural economies by tapping existing assets and applying creative strategies to support a variety of businesses and activities, clustering arts organizations as community anchors and promoting entrepreneurship to create new enterprises. Building connections between sectors— the community's "legs" —may be their most creative act.

Cultural organizations and activities are able to attract people and investment, encouraging entertainment venues, retail, restaurant, residential, and office development. They tend to increase rental rates, decrease vacancy rates, and increase tax revenues, jobs, and incomes.[34] A critical mass of cultural activities in one district generates enormous interest and a base for building other consumer-driven enterprises. But they cannot stand alone. Large arts complexes or cultural districts planned or created in isolation are not a winning strategy.

Urban redevelopment and historic preservation writer Roberta Brandes Gratz warns against the "big fix" or the "grand plan." She cites successful projects where the key was "thinking small in a big way."[35] Not only did these projects have more equitably distributed economic benefits, but they retained and built upon threads of existing social fabric. Their purpose was to build stronger communities, not entice larger institutions, richer investors, or bigger corporate chains.

Communities that bring together the cultural, business, and civic sectors to create interdependent economic networks do so by combining the unique assets of their residents, natural environment, proximity to other resources, and cultural strengths. The cultures and creative abilities of residents, together with the entrepreneurial drive of small business owners, have served as effective catalysts for the revival of downtrodden and decayed towns and neighborhoods. Culture is the best way to assert or reassert the unique identity of the place, to organize stakeholders, and to attract outside attention and resources.

> **Example: Massachusetts Museum of Contemporary Art, North Adams, Massachusetts**
>
> The Massachusetts Museum of Contemporary Arts (MassMoCA) has had multiple impacts on the remote western Massachusetts town of North Adams. The museum, which opened in 1999 in an abandoned 700,000-square-foot 19th-century mill complex, now attracts over 100,000 visitors annually. It has been both a magnet and an incubator for artists and dozens of creative industries. According to research by Benjamin, Oehler, & Sheppard, (2006)[36], the museum is responsible for diversifying the North Adams economy through creative use of space, creating 230 new jobs, generating $9.4 million in local growth in 2002 dollars, and stimulating more than $14 million in new annual business spending. Creating new markets, good jobs, and the long-term enrichment of the region are instrumental to the museum's mission. MASSMoCA develops and leases space to a wide range of businesses, including not only a restaurant but a publishing house, a law firm, a photography studio, and a computer-generated special effects company. It also collaborates with partners across the county to strengthen tourism, improve infrastructure for small business development, and attract and retain residents. Most importantly, says founder and director Joe Thompson, "Local youth see these buildings as symbols of opening the imagination rather than hulking post-industrial remnants of exploitation."[37]

STRATEGY 6: ENHANCE VALUE

> Human cleverness, desires, motivations, imagination, and creativity are replacing location, natural resources, and market access as urban resources. The creativity of those who live in and run cities will determine future success.[38]

Cities and small towns across the United States are looking for ways to revitalize neglected areas and bolster real estate values and tax rolls. Increasingly, some are courting creative industries and creative class workers, but few see artists as investors and hands-on workers who will enhance property values. Employing "the artists' touch"—putting artists to work to improve real estate—can enhance property values as well as return financial benefit to the artists and help them build artistic careers.

In taking raw materials and creatively enhancing them or adapting them to other uses, artists enhance value and change meaning. When applying themselves to home construction or rehabilitation, artists create new or increased value. New and historic homes with unique features and handmade amenities retain value and embody local history and craftsmanship. They are places with greater meaning that, in turn, move their inhabitants to make greater investment in the place they call home.

In some cities artists or arts groups have been blamed for bringing about gentrification—the rapid escalation of real estate prices, rents, property taxes, or condominium conversion that results in dislocation of poor and working class residents. Sometimes artists are also among the victims of gentrification. Both changing economics and the influx of new people of a different socio-economic class can prompt dislocation. Jamie Peck[39] and Graeme Evans[40] are among numerous scholars who point to the growing spread between rich and poor and heightened ethnic tensions that have resulted in the promotion of strategies to bring about economic growth through growth of the creative sector. In many cities artists and small arts organizations have ventured into economically depressed areas and sometimes attracted followers with higher incomes and social means. This can result in new investment and in the formation of a new sense of identity of the area. Sharon Zukin and Laura Braslow[41] (2011) call this "symbolic capital" where city leaders "establish new place-identities for problematic industrial areas, rebranding them as 'creative' and increasing their economic value." Change happens in every place, the questions are how quickly? And, do there have to be winners and losers?

> **Example: The Northeast (Minneapolis) Arts District**
>
> An industrial working class area of Minneapolis, Northeast was populated by waves of eastern and southern European immigrants from the mid-1800s. They worked in factories and began small retail and service businesses. Social networks grew, reinforced by churches, social clubs, bars, and neighborhood associations. By the 1980s, the closure of most of the older industries opened low-cost working space for artists and some bought into the mostly small single-family housing stock. By 1995 artists launched an annual open studio event to draw visitors, attract attention, and sell work. The increasingly successful, weekend-long "Art-a-Whirl" led to formalization of an arts district in 2003. Over 500 artists, tens of thousands of visitors, monthly gallery openings, and other events earned Northeast *USA Today's* top pick among its "10 Best" arts districts in the country in 2015.[42] Commercial areas and housing stock had seen decades of disinvestment but by the early 2010s saw significant repair. Long-shuttered corner stores became artist studios. Modest homes saw new roofs, porches, windows, and landscaping. Changes reflect individuals reinvesting in their homes and neighborhood — far from what would be considered gentrification. An older Northeast population remains stalwarts of the neighborhood and welcome the generational change. One neighborhood association leader reflected, "Artists are on boards and committees, some belong to the chamber, they buy houses and have great yards. They're just part of the neighborhood."

STRATEGY 7: BUILD TRUST, SOCIAL CAPITAL, AND COMMUNITY CAPACITY.

> Culture is the "glue," the shared values and meanings that bind us together, that shape our lives and, indeed, shape our attitudes about development and stewardship. Yet it is this intangible dimension of culture that is frequently ignored in public policy discussion, where culture is too often seen as a "soft" topic or an impediment to progress.[43]

Imagine a community in which a diversity of people regularly mingle, where they build bonds across differences towards a better community and openly and creatively tackle tough and complex issues. Both social capital as described by Robert Putnam, and economic capital are central to the well-being of people and their communities, requiring people of different backgrounds to work together toward common goals.

As Francis Fukuyama observes, "The most useful kind of social capital is often not the ability to work under the authority of a traditional community or group, but the capacity to form new associations and to cooperate within the terms of references they establish."[44] Economic success, he finds, depends on the kinds of trust nurtured within different cultures, a capacity he calls spontaneous sociability. That process can begin with neighbors shopping side by side or exchanging goods in the marketplace. It can grow through volunteering to produce community theater, participate in a holiday parade, or visit an event at a neighborhood art center, church, or school.

The fabric or social capital that holds communities together and allows them to function is based on relationships that transcend family structures, race, class, religion, ethnicity, etc. Whatever it's called, we know that without social capital, trust, or collective efficacy,[45] communities' business and civic enterprises would grind to a halt. What is less well known is how these phenomena are produced or where they come from. Many believe that arts and cultural practices both nurture and build on spontaneous sociability, social capital, and the rest. As such, the public practice of the arts, and participation in arts enterprises, are a major factors in a community's capacity to generate and support the success of new business and social networks.

When people from many different social and ethnic groups come together, there is always an opportunity for mutual growth as well as a greater likelihood of innovation. Engaging various demographics in a collective project focused on their shared environment can build social networks that had never before been conceived. This collaborative experience can help people understand how important everyone's story is in their community's unique identity, giving all residents a sense of ownership of and pride in the community as well as more civic responsibility. Together, they can arrive at ideas and create activities and goods not imagined before.

> **Example: Midtown Global Market, Minneapolis, Minnesota**
>
> Vendors who fill the 40,000-square-foot Midtown Global Market (MGM) include refugees from Somalia, immigrants from many parts of Mexico, the Middle East, Sweden, and Greece, and entrepreneurs of Korean, Cambodian, Vietnamese, and Italian descent, among others. Foods are authentic and creative. Arts and crafts are locally made and imported. Developed by a consortium of nonprofits led by the Neighborhood Development Center, MGM is the heart of a much larger urban redevelopment project that opened in May of 2006. Once a vast Sears store, warehouse, and catalogue distribution center, it includes 1.2 million square feet of mixed-use residential, office, service, and retail space. The bustling market provides a welcoming gathering place for the wider neighborhood where the cultures of the world mix and build relationships. Market tenants work together to promote events and activities highlighting cultural celebration, food competitions, and programs for kids. Partnerships and joint ventures are sparked and new food innovations sprout up. Condominium residents on the floors above and doctors from an adjacent hospital have become investors in new enterprises. This multi-cultural marketplace serves as an incubator to connect people, ideas, and resources.

STRATEGY 8: RETAIN WEALTH

> Local leaders can increase employment in their rural economies by providing better consumption opportunities locally that will then alter the consumption patterns of residents and result in a form of import substitution. —Ann Markusen

"Buy Local" has become a catchphrase over the past few years in many communities, promoting a practice that has proven to be one of the quickest and most effective ways to contribute to community revitalization. There are many reasons for engaging in a buy-local campaign. Encouraging residents and tourists to buy locally grown or made products not only reduces the economic and environmental costs of long-distance transportation but allows a community to keep dollars recirculating in the local economy, keeping revenues local and constantly refreshing their economy.

Economist Ann Markusen has found that by buying locally produced products, residents not only support local business owners over imported businesses, they circle a larger amount of revenue back into the community through wages and services.[46] When extended to the arts, buying local has other benefits. The growth of a distinctive local culture and arts scene is fostered. Developing appreciation of local creativity encourages artists, teachers, youth, and others to participate in growing their creativity. And, as Markusen and Anne Gadwa have observed, "Creative places nurture entrepreneurs."[47]

Many cities across the country have embraced buy-local campaigns. In some cities this is a grassroots strategy and in others it is a political strategy, with the municipal government setting up and structuring programs to nurture a buy-local environment. Benefits include:

- Keeping money within your local economy.
- Embracing the unique assets in your community.
- Fostering job creation by creating more local jobs for residents.
- Building more face-to-face relationships and local trust.
- Local businesses are more connected with the natural environment in which they work. They are usually a walkable distance from other local businesses, creating a vibrant downtown core.
- Studies have shown that local businesses contribute twice as much of their revenue to the community and promote a sense of community pride in all they do.
- Small businesses conserve tax dollars by needing less public infrastructure and making more efficient use of city services.
- Local businesses offer diverse products that are closely connected to the community and not to national sales plans.
- The staff and managers of small businesses are often more passionate and excited about their products and have a greater interest in building personal relationships with clients.
- Entrepreneurs are the power behind local businesses. They offer innovation and growth in an economy that nurtures a community spirit of entrepreneurialism.

Example: Boyne City, Michigan

Boyne City sits at the eastern tip of Lake Charlevoix, a beautiful 20-mile-long lake extending inland from Lake Michigan in the northwest part of the state. Known for its culinary offerings and historic downtown, Boyne City leaders take pride in their wide array of food-related businesses, festivals, and entrepreneurial wherewithal. Restaurants featuring wild and homegrown prepared and packaged foods, the National Morel Mushroom Festival, and widely regarded Farmer's Market are part of the community and its economic fabric. The region around Boyne City is also full of farmers and specialty regional food producers as well as all-season outdoor recreation amenities. An effort organized by the Chamber of Commerce and Main Street Program focuses on making Boyne City the go-to destination in Michigan where food, the outdoors, and the arts can all be enjoyed together and where farmers, food producers, restaurants, markets and festivals work together, buy from one another, and build on their local brand. The combination of culinary, creative, and recreational assets strengthens local identity and gives Boyne City a unique place in the region. Working together and buying local helps build networks and the synergy that both attracts and retains wealth, enhancing Boyne City's economy and quality of life.

ECONOMIC DEVELOPMENT BASED ON CULTURAL ASSETS

Looking across these eight culturally driven strategies for economic development, several best practices can be seen to emerge—practices that put cultural assets to work at building community and sparking economic development:

- **Project an authentic and unified identity** that focuses on cultural and natural amenities and taps artists and entrepreneurs who reflect and contribute to that identity.
- **Build mutually beneficial relationships** or "horizontal" networks across sectors and between artists, trades, developers, local business, arts groups, and policymakers from tourism and economic-development agencies.
- **Engage diverse populations,** including youth, in the design and realization of cultural activities, learning experiences, projects, and neighborhood and city planning, to both reflect the identity of the community and build a base of ownership and participation.
- **Utilize accessible and familiar public spaces** and provide opportunities for social interaction between diverse neighbors, artists, other community partners, and visitors.
- **Foster multicultural leadership** with intermediaries who understand the arts, economic development, and cultural diversity, and who can "translate" skills from one sector or culture to others.
- **Help artists and entrepreneurs establish ownership** of underutilized spaces that have the capacity for mixed-used development, so they can become active community contributors.
- **Advocate cultural planning** as a central dimension of town and city planning, cross-cultural understanding, creative economy development, and cultural events for their long-term impacts and benefits

The projects described above, and many others that have had similar impacts on their communities, result from the efforts of civic entrepreneurs, artists, philanthropists, visionary mayors, or other leaders. They often grow out of initiatives already at work or are hybrids of successful programs people saw work elsewhere.

See the APPENDIX for this author's outline of a general process that can be adapted in your community to mobilize the human, physical, creative, and economic assets unique to your place to realize your community- and economic-development goals through the arts.

Selected Resources

These national organizations have incorporated arts, design, and/or heritage among their interests in community and economic development.

Americans for the Arts
1000 Vermont Avenue, NW, 6th Floor
Washington, DC 20005
202.371.2830
www.AmericansForTheArts.org
Research, advocacy, and networking among arts agencies

Artspace Projects Inc.
250 Third Avenue North, Suite 500
Minneapolis, MN 55401
612-333-9012
www.artspaceprojects.org
Development and management of artist housing and arts organization space

The Center for Rural Strategies
46 East Main Street
Whitesburgh, KY 41858
606-632-3244
www.ruralstrategies.org
Rural economic, environmental, and cultural development and policy

Mayor's Institute for City Design
1620 Eye Street NW, 3rd Floor
Washington, DC 20006
202-463-1390
www.archfoundation.org/micd
Integrated design policy for economic revitalization

National Trust Main Street Center
National Trust for Historic Preservation
1785 Massachusetts Avenue NW
Washington, DC 20036
202-588-6219
www.mainst.org
Commercial district revitalization

Partners for Livable Communities
1429 21st Street NW
Washington, DC 20036
202-887-5990
www.livable.com
Integrated cultural, economic, and placemaking strategies

Project for Public Spaces
700 Broadway, 4th Floor
New York, NY 10003
212-620-5660
www.pps.org
Public markets and public space design

Appendix

HOW TO PUT THESE IDEAS TO WORK IN YOUR COMMUNITY

Now that we've looked at the ideas behind the creative economy and at practical strategies that have been working, we'll look at how you can put them to work in your community. The six creative community building strategies (shown below and described in the book) and the steps outlined below can be taken on by cultural organizations of any kind and any size in collaboration with others in the community.

> **Creative Community Building Strategies**
> 1. **Create Jobs.** Nurture artists and small cultural organizations as businesses to increase employment.
> 2. **Stimulate Trade.** Create the right conditions for cultural tourism to bring new resources to the community.
> 3. **Attract Investment.** Support artists and artist live/work spaces as anchors around which to build local economies.
> 4. **Diversify Economy.** Cluster arts organizations as retail anchors and activity generators to attract and support other enterprises.
> 5. **Enhance Value.** Employ the artists' touch to increase property values.
> 6. **Build Trust.** Create and strengthen the bonds between people of different backgrounds to enable enterprises to grow.

There is no one best way for this to happen. It depends on the characteristics of your community and the leadership and resources available. Projects described in the Arts and Economy book chapter, and many others that have had similar impacts on their communities, are the results of the efforts of civic entrepreneurs, artists, philanthropists, visionary mayors, other leaders, or some combination of these. They often grow out of initiatives already at work or are hybrids of things people saw work elsewhere. The processes outlined below provide a generalized path. It's one you can follow as you adapt to the ways things get done in your community and mobilize the human, physical, creative, and economic assets unique to your place.

First, you have to ask yourself whether this is the right road for you. Are you committed to building and expanding relationships you and your organization have with your community? Are you prepared to step into a leadership role? Wilder Research Center surveyed effective community building and recommends that you ask yourself a number of questions before embarking on such a journey.[1]

- Do you understand how decisions are made in the community?
- Do you understand the history of the community?
- Do you understand the demographic makeup of different groups in the community and how they relate to one another?
- Are you committed to the community's long-term well-being?
- Do you have a positive reputation among key community members and leaders? Will you be perceived as acting to serve the interests of the community at-large or to benefit an internal or external group?
- Do you have the ability to work with and motivate a wide range of people?
- Can you plan group activities that will be productive?

Understanding the Assets in People and Place

Understanding your own organization's and your community's special characteristics and assets provides an important context for creating successful strategies for economic growth and related social and physical development.

The key to building a stronger community is the ability to see and understand the things that make it special along with being able to make the connections between people and ideas that put these assets to work. Seeing possibility in raw materials, and understanding how those materials can create something of unique value and meaning, has long been the domain of the artist. These abilities are also necessary to the successful developer.

There are many factors that make your special piece of the planet unique, whether it is a city neighborhood, a small town, or a suburb. Your community's assets are lodged in the history, geography, traditions, people, and place. The most important assets to engage and maximize are the people—their cultures and creativity.

In mapping your community's assets, research and assess several aspects of your community, such as:

- history;
- demographic profile and trends;
- past and current economic base and trends; and
- contributions to community identity.

With all this information, you might affirm or challenge a particular strategy that is at hand, such as converting vacant industrial space to artist live/work space. Or you can assess which of various cultural strategies holds the greatest potential for economic and cultural development. Through this learning and planning process, you'll be able to pull a seat up to the table of community economic development. You'll be a central participant—even a driver—in a revitalization that taps the energies, cultures, and imaginations of the people. Done well, you'll put in motion a more equitable and sustainable economic engine that benefits the entire community.

Map the History

Interpreting the history of a place in relation to circumstances of the present—or an anticipated future—can be a creative and rewarding process. It will help you discover or deepen the identity of place.

To do this work, hook up with a partner such as a historical society or at least the unofficial town or neighborhood historian. It's important that you pull together a history that accounts for multiple points of view and considers environmental, cultural, economic, and social histories. If you can't find a single historian who meets these criteria, look to multiple sources. Form a team or put in motion an inclusive process to which others can contribute, such as a high school or community college class. More important than the quality or depth of research is that different perspectives are brought to bear, and that out-of-the-ordinary players or events come to the surface. This is where new ideas will emerge. Ask questions, such as those shown below.

- Does the geological history hold interest or value?

- How and why is there human settlement in this place, and who are the people who were here before? If they came and left, why?
- Who were key figures in recorded history? Significant events?
- Why does it have the name it does, and what significance has that identity had through time?
- Are there mythologies or popular stories that can amplify a sense of place? Artistic, literary, or technological creations or inventions?

Most likely, some segments of this story have been collected, but enlist more hands in contributing to and interpreting it.

Evaluate Census Data

Part of the overall mapping you'll undertake is to know more about the people who inhabit your community. You especially want to track changes that have taken place during the past few decades. Those changes are usually a good indication of what to expect in the future. If you're not familiar with this process, find someone in city planning or a local college who can assist you. Perhaps there's a newspaper reporter who can find an interesting story in census data who will work up a profile.

Even if you do get assistance from others, be sure to glean your own story from the census information because this data can tell many stories. Go to www.census.gov and learn to navigate the website. It's not difficult, but requires some focused time and analytical thinking. Census tracts provide the most precise comparison, but rarely correspond to more commonly known boundaries. The data is also available by zip code, which may be more meaningful. Pay particular attention to changes in age and ethnic groups and household sizes. Compare these facts with two, three, or more decades of the past. Make this information central to the narrative in your community's story.

Overview of Planning Process
Outlined below are key elements of a potentially larger and more formal community process. This process is described in full in The Creative Community Builder's Handbook.[2]

STEP 1: ASSESS YOUR SITUATION AND GOALS

1. Define the boundaries of the community you want to impact.
2. Identify your strengths and leadership capacity.
3. Conduct your own inventory of community assets.
4. Clarify your values and vision.
5. Write a concept paper.
6. Review readiness.

STEP 2: IDENTIFY AND RECRUIT EFFECTIVE PARTNERS

1. Identify potential partners.
2. Define expectations for potential partners.
3. Recruit partners.

STEP 3: MAP VALUES, STRENGTHS, ASSETS, AND HISTORY
1. Meet and establish group commitment.
2. Build group cohesion and identify community values.
3. Identify assets as a group.
4. Create a map of community assets.
5. Invite contributions from the larger community.

STEP 4: FOCUS ON KEY ASSET, VISION, CORE STRATEGIES, AND IDENTITY
1. Review data and narrow list of top community assets.
2. Choose your key community asset.
3. Envision the future.
4. Choose core strategies for cultural asset-based economic development.
5. Attach a clever name to your identity.

STEP 5: CRAFT A PLAN TO IMPLEMENT STRATEGIES
1. Create outcomes.
2. Attach measures to outcomes.
3. Set goals.
4. Generate a list of activities and needed resources.
5. Organize the plan with action steps.
6. Celebrate!

Understand What Makes the Economy Tick

Understanding the origins and trajectory of your community's economic base is essential to projecting and envisioning its future. Historically, your community's economy may have been based on resource extraction, food or raw material processing, shipping and trade, manufacturing, county or state government, education, or one (or more) of many such industries.

Twenty-first century success stories come from communities that have diversified or become centers of creative industries, whose raw material is human ingenuity. In some cases, it is the historic or cultural assets that define a particular identity and constitute the major industry, as in cultural and heritage tourism. Success lies in creatively building upon the assets and identity of the place, even if these assets include abandoned buildings or an idle workforce!

The Census website contains a wealth of information to help you tell this story. Use the search field on the home page to find County Business Patterns, where you can sort by zip code. This will allow you to build a profile of all the types of businesses in your community and their employment patterns. For instance, this might tell you that you have a concentration of auto repair shops, furniture retailers, or small manufacturers. This data can often be at least two years old, but you can paint a historic picture by tracking changes with past years. You can embellish the story with more current anecdotes from your own knowledge, such as the new housing development or industrial space conversion now under construction or the new Asian food businesses that opened during the past year.

Examining general trends in employment can also help paint that picture. Again, when online at America's Career InfoNet (www.acinet.org/acinet), you can see broader patterns in job types that are expected to grow or shrink. This is especially useful if any kind of job training or professional development services might be on your radar.

Community development leader and author Mike Temali lays out a detailed process to assess your neighborhood's economic conditions in T*he Community Economic Development Handbook*.[3] He also recommends drawing a map of your primary commercial corridor or district, labeling all the known businesses. It should include vacant properties. Often, this visualization can help you see clusters or combinations you otherwise hadn't noticed.

Through such research you can better understand what makes the local or regional economy tick. Ultimately, what you're looking for are ways that artist entrepreneurs, or the cultural bonds people share, can generate new industries or activities that stimulate the creative economy. You're also looking for ways in which your cultural organization can play a pivotal role in nurturing enterprises or in leveraging development or investment that lands new businesses or transforms existing community assets. These assets might range from vacant buildings to the community's image, both of which have been transformed by arts groups in many places.

Survey the Assets

Use the Community Asset Inventory (see the Forms section at the end of this document) to survey the assets of the place you call your community. The secret is not in the form, but in your powers of observation and analysis—how creatively you can see assets. Use this tool to list things that might be obvious (and not so obvious), and then go back over it and consider in what ways they might be of value in leveraging change, building on a larger initiative, or serving in concert with others as raw material for an entrepreneurial venture.

Articulate the Identity of Your Place

The distinctive qualities that shape the identity of your community can be considered assets in economic and cultural development efforts. By looking at the history and diversity of the community, and the other assets of your place, you've begun to uncover the ingredients that can go into its new or refreshed identity and that will "put it on the map." This identity can motivate and rally people and resources.

Finding and reinterpreting the identity of your place often poses a creative challenge. It can be difficult for someone within a community to see its identity anew. Maybe you feel your urban neighborhood is known for poverty, crime, and hopelessness—or that your rural town, widely considered a once important source of a special agricultural product, is now a nondescript truck stop on an interstate highway. This can be a key place to engage a consultant or to invite outsiders to weigh in on what makes it a meaningful place to live and makes it stand out. Identity cannot be forced on a place, and it may take time to emerge. You may need to travel to observe the identities of other places and talk with visitors about their impressions of your place in order to gain perspective.

ASSESS CULTURE'S PLACE IN THE ECOLOGY

Looking more expansively at what cultural organizations bring to their communities is a crucial step in repositioning them as vital contributors to economic and overall community well-being. It's not about changing what they do, but rather seeing what they do in a different light, and then building strategies and alliances that match their special capacities with broader community goals. A small theater company—in addition to presenting moving and enlightening plays—may generate active street life and restaurant patronage in a heretofore neglected neighborhood. Small nonprofit arts groups nurture new community leadership and prepare people for creative problem solving. They also help shape and reshape individuals' and communities' sense of identity.

The Massachusetts Museum of Contemporary Arts (MassMoCA) has had multiple impacts on its remote western Massachusetts town of North Adams. The museum opened in 1999 in an abandoned 700,000 square foot nineteenth century mill complex. It has been both a magnet and an incubator for dozens of creative industries. Research studies[4] have documented its impact on surrounding property values, residential stability, and the success of new and old businesses.

"Local youth see these buildings as symbols of opening the imagination rather than hulking postindustrial remnants of exploitation," said Joe Thompson, founder and director.[5] The importance of this change in the community's image of itself and its identity regionally and nationally shouldn't be underestimated. Hundreds of new jobs and millions of dollars in investment can be directly attributed to the museum and have turned around the economy of this small city. At least as importantly, it has begun to restore a sense of self-worth and hope to residents long buffeted by the economics and politics of disinvestment and labor exploitation. And it has done so while staying focused on presenting and commissioning the highest quality contemporary visual, performing, and media arts.

Develop Strategies Centered in Mutual Goals

Are you clear on your organization's or group's mission and goals as they relate to larger community challenges? Do they give you latitude to take a leading role in community building or suggest that you take a partnering role with some other entity in the lead? Do you have—or can you easily gain—the support of your board, members, funders, and staff to think bigger and step on to a larger stage? This is not about your organization getting bigger; it's about engaging in a larger, more holistic effort to build a more vibrant, sustainable community. It will probably return benefit to your organization, but only to the degree it benefits the whole community. When you begin to invite others to join you, you'll need to articulate your goals and why they're important to the wider community.

The City of Minneapolis, Minnesota, commissioned a plan in 2004[6] that looked specifically at ways in which its existing arts and cultural assets could be applied towards addressing its established goals. Positioning the arts as contributors to the economic, social, civic, and physical infrastructure of a city is a way to find synergy with other services and to multiply the return on investment.

Assess Community Goals

Look at each of the eight goals established by the City of Minneapolis, and the ways in which cultural assets are related to particular goals. As an exercise think of ways that your cultural organization or other culturally based activities might contribute to similar goals set by your city, town, or region.

> **Intersecting or Related Goals of My Organization**
>
> **CITY GOAL 1: BUILD COMMUNITIES WHERE ALL PEOPLE FEEL SAFE AND TRUST THE CITY'S PUBLIC SAFETY PROFESSIONALS AND SYSTEMS.**
>
> Arts and cultural activities are recognized as important tools for community development and neighborhood revitalization. Often, cultural activities like free concerts in neighborhood parks and cultural facilities are a forum through which neighbors meet neighbors, a critical step in what public safety professionals testify is a basis for crime prevention.
>
> **CITY GOAL 2: MAINTAIN THE PHYSICAL INFRASTRUCTURE TO ENSURE A HEALTHY, VITAL, AND SAFE CITY.**
>
> The city's physical infrastructure includes its public art works, historic theaters, and many cultural spaces for which the city has provided capital support and/or financing. It also includes many streetscape and other built environment elements that integrate cultural elements. Cultural spaces and the economic and social activity they stimulate contribute to neighborhood and commercial corridor revitalization as well as to the safety of residents and visitors.
>
> **CITY GOAL 3: DELIVER CONSISTENTLY HIGH QUALITY CITY SERVICES AT A GOOD VALUE TO OUR TAXPAYERS.**
>
> **CITY GOAL 4: CREATE AN ENVIRONMENT THAT MAXIMIZES ECONOMIC DEVELOPMENT OPPORTUNITIES WITHIN MINNEAPOLIS.**
>
> The city has several neighborhood-based culture nodes in addition to a downtown theater district and a concentration of arts facilities on the edge of the University campus. These can do more to stabilize and promote surrounding business and residential areas. Tourism and convention business can highlight these assets. A thriving corporate sector relies on both the creativity of its workers and a stimulating urban environment that helps attract new talent.
>
> **CITY GOAL 5: FOSTER THE DEVELOPMENT AND PRESERVATION OF A MIX OF QUALITY HOUSING TYPES.**
>
> Artist loft conversion has stimulated the renewal of a former warehouse district, attracting the development of new mixed income housing while making the area a highly desirable place to live and seek stimulation through cultural activities. Artists have also helped to rejuvenate older neighborhoods of single-family homes as they looked for low-cost housing in areas with traditional neighborhood amenities, such as corner bars and former social clubs.
>
> **CITY GOAL 6: PRESERVE AND ENHANCE OUR NATURAL AND HISTORIC ENVIRONMENT AND PROMOTE A CLEAN, SUSTAINABLE MINNEAPOLIS.**
>
> **CITY GOAL 7: PROMOTE PUBLIC, COMMUNITY, AND PRIVATE PARTNERSHIPS TO ADDRESS DISPARITIES, AND TO SUPPORT STRONG, HEALTHY FAMILIES AND COMMUNITIES**
>
> **CITY GOAL 8: STRENGTHEN CITY GOVERNMENT MANAGEMENT AND ENHANCE COMMUNITY ENGAGEMENT.**

Get to Know and Appreciate Your Own and Your Partners' Unique Assets

Asserting yourself and your cultural organization as a leader or key partner in community economic development can be a tough move because of how others tend to see you. Arts organizations are typically considered entertainment providers or as attractions to draw a crowd to listen to an important message provided by another, more "serious" organization.

As you think about assets you envision putting to work and partners who can help move that work along, you first want to be clear what you bring to the table. Conduct an inventory of strengths and capacities for yourself as a leader and for your organization. See the Organizational and Partner Assessment Form (in the Forms section at the end of this Online Companion), and list your greatest strengths in areas such as visioning, planning, management, marketing, fund development, advocacy, organizing, etc. Personal strengths you should assess include group leadership skills and knowledge of various sectors and professions within your community. Also important is your familiarity with political, philanthropic, nonprofit, and business leadership, as well as readiness to learn and venture into new territory! Be honest about your strengths and the areas in which you need to find partners who complement what you bring.

You've looked at your core competencies and analyzed your community's assets and identity. You have at least a raw vision for putting your organization and creativity to work for larger community interests. You may be the upstart and you may stumble with the right words to describe how you hope to leverage assets to propel your community into a serious role in the creative economy. The important thing is that you're coming to the table with things to offer, not with a hand out for more support. You still may face an uphill battle in convincing others that you have valuable assets to share, or you may just find you're welcomed to the table.

The same assessment form can also be used to assess what each prospective partner brings to the endeavor.

Collaboration Across Sectors is Necessary

Building a creative economy is about getting people to work together across sectors and across differences, traits at which many arts groups excel. To devise and put to work a set of strategies requires reaching across business, government, nonprofit, and voluntary organizations. It requires tapping the expertise, creativity, and resources embedded in each of these organizations. A larger goal must connect them, a concern for the future of the community and the people in it.

A healthy community embraces a culture of collaboration—a concurrent respect for both mutual and individual interests—and an ongoing willingness to work together and learn from each other. The process of building working partnerships that cross professions, sectors, and cultures presents special challenges. Getting busy people around the same table and learning to "speak the same language" while keeping them on task is hard.

Parties need to learn to think in the language and practices of other professions or industries. They will ultimately find that these other ways of thinking foster innovation within their own. When love of place and devotion to common values govern, collaborators can better overcome issues around the mechanics of terminology, resources, and turf. Artists seasoned in community building can offer creative processes to help build trust, think outside the box, and even communicate nonverbally to help a set of collaborators warm up to each other more easily.

The Role of "Intermediary"

The Urban Institute's study, Commerce and Culture[7] found that when artists and economic developers joined forces, the best results came when a key player had well-developed intermediation skills. By this it means a person or entity that can "translate" between the languages and practices of each sector. Successful projects cited earlier included leaders or key partners who possessed these skills.

Entrepreneurial small cultural groups, art gallery managers, and individual artists who crisscross art and business and who build economically viable small businesses are among the more well equipped to serve this role. It's equally important to have a holistic view of the role of culture in communities and good working relationships in the arts, local government, and business.

Consultants and visiting leaders from other communities can teach these skills or can draw out and identify others in your community who may have them. If you are not a good intermediary, you can team up with someone to serve in this role. If you represent a cultural organization and bring these skills and a holistic vision, it would be good to join forces with at least one colleague so it doesn't appear that your efforts are self-serving. It needs to be clear that this is not an effort to advance the arts groups by rallying the community around them. It's an effort to raise the tide and lifts all boats.

Identify Partners

You learned a lot about the community you hope to impact. You clarified your own values and strengths, took inventory of the unique assets your community possess, and evaluated preliminary strategies. Now you're going to seek others to join in. It's time to identify the key players you believe are needed to tackle the job, to talk with them one–on–one, to bring them together and determine the right working relationships to fit what you see as your community's character, capabilities, and vision.

Build Effective Partnerships

When you've made your list of prospective partners, use the Organization and Partner Assessment Form to evaluate their respective strengths based on the skills and resources that will complement yours and bring into play the community assets you've identified as important. Some potential partners will float to the top.

Meet one-on-one with prospective partners. Start with those you know best and believe to be the strongest candidates to develop your thinking and to build momentum. Branch out quickly and try your ideas on someone who will ask you tough questions. You likely need partners who function in areas with which you're less familiar. Talk about your ideas by asking questions. Allow your vision to evolve as a result of lively, open conversations and your expanding knowledge. You want their ideas, not their approval. This give and take is important, so don't get ahead of yourself. If you're successful, the idea no longer belongs to you. You become the steward of a community vision.

Paying for this Work

In moving forward with community economic development work, and in teaming up with partners from other fields and sectors, you are opening up a vast new landscape of funding opportunities. Community economic development work is supported by an infrastructure and a field of dedicated public and private funders, just like the arts. The partners with whom you build relationships will guide you in that world. At the appropriate time in the formation of those partnerships, the topic of funding must be addressed; you must bring to the table your resources in that area and expect the partner to do the same.

Each city, county, and state has different resources and uses different names to describe them. Contributors to your work can come in all forms and sizes. Sometimes a $500 investment by a key group or individual has symbolic value and can get the ball rolling. Also, think about the contributions of volunteers, staff time, space, food, publicity, transportation, or other items to get and keep positive momentum. Like a snowball, if a project keeps moving, it will pick up more of what it needs along the way.

Below is a list of places to look for financial support. Some may be more suited to planning, some to implementation, some to both. Getting someone invested in planning creates a greater likelihood of their larger investment later. For further information about fundraising, also see the chapters, The Art of Fundraising and The Essentials of Proposal Writing.

Private Sources
- Banks—charitable contributions and Community Reinvestment Act funds
- Business associations, chambers of commerce, and individual local businesses
- Church programs
- Corporate public affairs departments and foundations
- Larger nonprofits—start-up investments or planning support
- Local Initiatives Support Corporation (LISC) or Enterprise Foundation—predevelopment, training, and planning funds

Public Sector Sources
- CDBG (Community Development Block Grant) funds—community and economic development agencies
- Citizen or civic participation programs
- Community or neighborhood planning departments
- Empowerment zone funds
- Local, regional, state, and federal arts agencies
- Mayor or council member office budgets
- Municipal and state bonding
- Small Business Administration
- Special city and legislative appropriations
- Tax increment financing (TIF) or other special taxing districts for historic, low-income housing, new markets, and other new business
- University partnership programs and urban planning and architecture applied research projects

Philanthropic Sources
- Community foundations—discretionary and designated use trusts
- Private and family foundations, all program areas
- Program-related investments (PRIs)—real estate acquisition and development
- United Way—seed funds, research funds, and special project funds
- Wealthy individuals, especially those with business or real estate interests in your community, or who have family roots there

SAMPLE COMMUNITY ASSET INVENTORY

Quality Geographic area and demographics	
History/Industries Native American/Precolonial Significant events/people Products manufactured/grown Cultural/technological innovations Key economic drivers/employment base Other	
Geography Natural/geological features Climate Recreational amenities	
People Level of tolerance Age range/balance Ethnic mix Economic status Education levels Other	
Reputation Receptivity to visitors Location/accessibility Navigability Safety Aesthetic experience Other	
Proximity Natural amenities Widely known attraction(s)/features Urban center/district	
Major or Unique Service(s) Well known institution(s) Special places Other	
Infrastructure Transportation Education/culture Architecture/built environment Power/water/sewer adequacy/capacity Underutilized structures/real estate Health care Other	

SAMPLE ORGANIZATIONAL AND PARTNER ASSESSMENT FORM

Capacity to invest time	
History of collaboration	
Public profile or image	
Staff/board stability	
Financial stability	
Depth of constituency	
Breadth of constituency	
Broad concern for community	
Bring key skill set	
Openly share information	
Represent a strategic constituency	
Special leadership position or quality	
Gut instinct	

READINESS CHECKLIST

If you can check off the items of this list, you're in a position to launch an entrepreneurial venture or initiative to contribute to your community's economic engine.

- You have clear, value-driven, but not rigid, community building goals.
- You can describe and tell the story of your community, its history, and its current identity.
- You are aware of, and have connection to, your community's populations.
- You can articulate your key leadership strengths.
- You know many key leaders in your community and how things get done.
- You understand asset-based organizing and development and can articulate what you consider key assets of your community.
- You understand and can articulate what cultural assets and culturally-based development strategies are and why they're important.
- You have the support of your board, staff, and/or constituency to take a leadership role in a project of this type or size.
- You know what resources you already have that can be leveraged to plan and launch an innovative, visionary project.

Endnotes

1. P. Mattessich and B. Monsey, *Community Building: What Makes It Work*. St. Paul, MN: Wilder Publishing, 1997.

2. M. Temali, *The Community Economic Development Handbook*, St. Paul, MN: Wilder Publishing, 2002.

3. Ibid.

4. Stephen Sheppard, Ph.D., an economist with Williams College, launched with Mass MoCA the Center for Creative Community Development, a research center to examine the economic and social impacts of arts organizations.

5. J. Thompson, *"Post Voodoo Cultural Economics."* Speech given at the Berkshire Conference, Sterling and Francine Clark Art Institute. Williamstown, MA: February 12, 2005.

6. A. Greenberg and B. Bulick, *City of Minneapolis Plan for Arts and Culture*, St. Louis, MO: AMS Planning and Research, 2004.

7. C. Walker, M. Jackson, and C. Rosenstein, *Culture and Commerce: Traditional Arts in Economic Development*, Washington, DC: The Urban Institute and The Fund for Folk Culture, 2003.

Endnotes

1. Speech given at the 2004 National Performing Arts Convention, Pittsburgh, June 20, 2004. *Cincinnati Enquirer*.

2. Erin Sparks and Mary Jo Waits, *New Engines of Growth: Five Roles for Arts, Culture and Design,* National Governors Association Center for Best Practices, 2012, p. 5.

3. Lawrence E. Harrison and Samuel P. Huntington, eds., *Culture Matters: How Values Shape Human Progress* (2001), p. xv.

4. Robert D. Putnam and Lewis Feldstein, *Better Together: Restoring the American Community,* 2003.

5. Ann Markusen, with David King, *The Artistic Dividend: The Arts' Hidden Contributions to Regional Development,* Humphrey Institute of Public Affairs, University of Minnesota, 2003.

6. John P. Kretzmann and John L. McKnight, *Building Communities from the Inside Out: A Path Toward Finding and Mobilizing a Community's Assets,* 1993.

7. See, e.g., Jon Hawkes, *The Fourth Pillar of Sustainability: Culture's Essential Role in Public Planning,* 2001.

8. Kevin F. McCarthy et al., *Gifts of the Muse: Reframing the Debate about the Benefits of the Arts,* RAND Corporation, 2005, p. 37.

9. Andres Duany et al., *Suburban Nation: The Rise of Sprawl and the Decline of the American Dream,* 2000, new ed. 2010, p. 83.

10. William H. Whyte, *The Essential William H. Whyte,* Albert LaFarge, editor. Fordham University Press, 2000, p. 229.

11. Fred Kent and Kathy Madden, *How to Turn a Place Around: A Handbook for Creating Successful Public Places,* Project for Public Spaces, 2000.

12. David Brain, "Placemaking and Community Building," speech at the University of Miami School of Architecture, March 2004.

13. Mark J. Stern and Susan C. Siefert, Cultural Clusters: The Implications of Cultural Assets Agglomeration for Neighborhood Revitalization, *Journal of Planning Education and Research,* 29, No 3 (2010) p. 262—279.

14. Diane Grams and Michael Warr, *Leveraging Assets: How Small Budget Arts Activities Benefit Neighborhoods,* Richard H. Driehaus Foundation, 2003.

15. Neil Scott Kleiman, *The Creative Engine: How Arts & Culture is Fueling Economic Growth in New York City Neighborhoods,* Center for an Urban Future, 2002, p. 3.

16. "New national initiative will fuel arts and cultural investments in low-income communities." PRNewswire, November 13, 2014.

17. One project supported by the Ford Foundation's Asset Building and Community Development Program was a motion picture by Nancy Kelly, Downside Up, which looked at the arts-based revival of a dying postindustrial town, North Adams, Massachusetts.

18. www.artplaceamerica.org.

19. Mark Peterson and Jeffrey E. McGee, "Survivors of 'W-day': An Assessment of the Impact of Wal-Mart's Invasion of Small Town Retailing Communities." *International Journal of Retail & Distribution Management,* 28, nos. 4/5 (2000), 170—80; and Stephan J. Goetz and Anil Rupasingha, "Wal-Mart and Social Capital," *American Journal of Agricultural Economics,* 88 no. 5 (2006), 1304—10.

20. Tom Borrup, *Creative Community Builder's Handbook: How to Transform Communities Using Local Assets, Arts, and Culture,* 2006.

21. *Economic Development America* (Summer 2004): 11-13. A publication of the Economic Development Information Coalition, U.S. Department of Commerce Economic Development Administration.

22. Americans for the Arts, *Economic Prosperity IV: The Economic Impact of Nonprofit Arts Organizations and Their Audiences,* 2011, www.artsusa.org.

23. U.S. Small Business Administration, *Small Business Trends,* www.sba.gov.

24. http://arts.gov/news/2013/national-endowment-arts-releases-new-research-tool-working-artists.

25. Jane Jacobs, T*he Death and Life of Great American Cities,* 1961, p. 188.

26. See the National Trust for Historic Preservation's Main Street Program, www.preservationnation.org/main-street.

27. U.S. Travel Association, 2014. https://www.ustravel.org/sites/default/files/page/2009/09/Economic Impact of Travel and Tourism_2014.pdf

28. National Assembly of State Arts Agencies, *The Cultural and Heritage Traveler,* Mandal Research, 2013.

29. National Assembly of State Arts Agencies, Cultural Visitor Profile, cited in *Cultural Heritage Tourism,* Partners for Livable Communities, 2014. livable.org.

30. John Villani, "A Call to Art." *Urban Land* 58, no. 7 (July 1999): 56—59.

31. Quoted in the *Minneapolis Star Tribune,* May 8, 2005, D4.

32. Anne Gadwa & Anna Muessig, *How Art Spaces Matter II,* Metris Arts Consulting, 2011, p. 6.

33. Massachusetts Museum of Contemporary Art website, www.MassMoCA.org.

34. Hudnutt, *The Economic Impact of Arts Centers.*

35. Gratz has observed community redevelopment strategies for several decades, first in the United States and more recently in Eastern European countries. In *The Living City* (1994) and *Cities Back from the Edge* (2000), she advocates building from within, employing grassroots and bottom-up strategies.

36. Benjamin, B., Oehler, K, & Sheppard, S.C. (2006). *Culture and revitalization: The economic effects of MASS MoCA on its community.* North Adams: Center for Creative Community Development

37. "Post Voodoo Cultural Economics," speech given at the Berkshire Conference, Sterling and Francine Clark Art Institute, Williamstown, MA, February 12, 2005.

38. Charles Landry, *The Creative City,* 2000, p. xiii.

39. Jamie Peck, Struggling with the creative class. *International Journal of Urban and Regional Research,* 29(4) 2005, 740-770.

40. Graeme Evans, "Creative cities, creative spaces and urban policy." *Urban Studies,* 46(5-6) 2009, 1003-1040.

41. Sharon Zukin & Laura Braslow, (2011), The lifecycle of New York's creative districts: reflections on the unanticipated consequences of unplanned cultural zones, *City, Culture and Society,* 2(3) 2011, p. 131.

42. USA Today Best Art District: As chosen by readers of USA TODAY and 10 Best, http://www.10best.com/awards/travel/best-art-district/

43. Caroline Marshall, *Envisioning Convergence: Cultural Conservation, Environmental Stewardship and Sustainable Livelihoods,* The Fund for Folk Culture, 2004.

44. Fukuyama, Trust, 27.

45. Robert Sampson, "The Neighborhood Context of Well-Being," *Perspectives in Biology and Medicine,* 46(3), 2003, p. S53-S64. A research team from the Harvard School of Public Health conducted a 15-year study in Chicago neighborhoods and found the single most important factor differentiating levels of health from one person to the next was what they called collective efficacy. It wasn't economic status, access to health care, crime, or some more tangible factor that topped the list. This more elusive ingredient — the capacity of people to act together on matters of common interest — was the greatest variable in the health and well-being of individuals and neighborhoods.

46. Ann Markusen, *A Consumption Base Theory of Development: An Application to the Rural Cultural Economy.* Presentation at the conference on Opportunities and Challenges Facing the Rural Creative Economy, Northeastern Agricultural and Resource Economics Association, Mystic, CT, June 13-14, 2006.

47. Markusen and Anne Gadwa. *Creative Placemaking.* A white paper for the Mayors' Institute on City Design, National Endowment for the Arts, 2010.

3

Creative Placemaking: Arts and Culture as a Partner in Community Revitalization

TOM BORRUP

Introduction: Connecting People, Places, and Stories

> To share the same place is perhaps the most primitive of social bonds, and to be within view of one's neighbors is the simplest form of association.
>
> — Lewis Mumford[1]

This chapter examines the contemporary practice known as creative placemaking, including some key principles and best practices for artists, arts organizations, and communities engaging in creative placemaking, as well as some of the challenges they may face. Creative placemaking brings people and organizations together to create better lives for those sharing a geographically defined community. The term was coined by economist Ann Markusen and arts consultant Anne Gadwa in a 2010 white paper for the National Endowment for the Arts. As they explained it:

In creative placemaking, partners from public, private, non-profit, and community sectors strategically shape the physical and social character of a neighborhood, town, city, or region around arts and cultural activities. Creative placemaking animates public and private spaces, rejuvenates structures and streetscapes, improves local business viability and public safety, and brings diverse people together to celebrate, inspire, and be inspired.[2]

Creative placemaking builds on local human, physical, and cultural assets to enhance the social and civic fabric. It builds on distinctive local character and story. It is a long-term, partnership-based strategy that results from a commitment to social equity and a meaningful life for its residents as well as an interesting experience for visitors and a stronger economic base for the area.

A key thread through the creative placemaking process is building on the identity and historical trajectory of the place — with all the gifts and baggage that history carries. Ultimately, creative placemaking attempts to strengthen relationships between and among people, and between people and place, building a community where stewardship of one another and of place is central.

In creative placemaking, art and culture work as partner and catalyst, not as the center of attention. In their 2010 white paper, Markusen and Gadwa gave useful definition to this growing field. However, their suggestion that communities are shaped "around" arts and culture was incorrectly interpreted by some to mean that arts and culture should be "at the center" of creative placemaking. Equitable community building cannot place any one sector at the center; it requires what Kresge Foundation CEO Rip Rapson called "the willingness and capacity of arts and cultural organizations to take an outward orientation," or as Debra Webb said, referring to the "silo mentality" that blocks institutional and cross-sector communication and interaction, "to get out of their silos and into their neighborhoods."[3]

Others in community building — city planners and economic and community developers — must also try new approaches. Urban planner Leonardo Vazquez has noted that "to accept creative people as full partners, communities and leaders must be open to new ways of seeing their environments."[4]

Rapson cited four principles of creative placemaking:

- It is grounded in the particulars of place;
- it employs authentic and ongoing community engagement;
- it embraces existing community development systems; and
- it assumes the willingness and capacity of arts and cultural organizations to take an outward orientation. In the process, artists at community-building tables can realize a new catalytic role in their community.

Creative placemaking is an ongoing process with key outcomes that serve to ensure the vitality of the process. These include:

- Enhancement of the unique qualities and identity of place.
- Connections between and among people, and between people and place.
- Processes that include planning; animation of spaces and actions to secure permanent places for living, working, creating, socializing, recreating; and exchanging goods and ideas.
- Capacity building for local civic sector and organizations to maintain engagement of the community and to exercise local stewardship and governance.
- Including examples from communities across the United States, this chapter explores benefits that can accrue when creative and civic sectors, together with planning and development sectors, expand their tool boxes and enter new kinds of partnerships.

1. Overview: The Making or Production of Space

> Objects alone do not make a place. It is how people feel about and respond to the elements in their environment, as well as other people who share their space, that help determine what a place is.
>
> — Leonardo Vazquez[5]

Creative placemaking sits within a broader and longstanding discourse that goes by many names, including urban renewal or regeneration, revitalization, community building, culture-led regeneration, city-making, placemaking, and more. French social philosopher Henri Lefebvre proposed a construct he described as "production of space" that included:

- the perceived, or physical (land use, design, and physical structures);
- the conceived (the legal, economic, and the political systems applicable to or within the physical area); and
- everyday lived experience (the social, cultural, and other activities of daily life).[6]

Most practitioners who typically drive the process of building and rebuilding of cities and towns focus first on the uses of land and basic infrastructure such as water, sanitation, and transportation as well as physical structures. They also generally include the social and economic systems and civic infrastructures. However, most fail to account for the everyday lived experiences, including the cultures and stories of place — the ways people make space their own and create a sense of belonging and ultimately a sense of stewardship. When they are in balance, the three forces described by Lefebvre also generate social cohesion or social capital without which communities face disintegration with every challenge or obstacle.[7]

If creative placemaking is to fulfill its promises, practitioners must grapple with a wide range of age-old issues facing towns, cities, and neighborhoods — and this presents challenges. Good creative placemaking, however, must commit to building holistic and sustainable places that are of, by, and for people — all people.

Cultural administrator and thought leader Roberto Bedoya asserted that the same people often excluded from the dominant processes of city building also find no place for themselves in creative placemaking. The social dynamics of creating urban spaces, he wrote, should enable "identity and activities that allow personal memories, cultural histories, imagination, and feelings to enliven the sense of 'belonging' through human and spatial relationships."[8] Effective creative placemaking must generate, among other things, this sense of belonging. Particular artistic visions, cultural assumptions, or aesthetic sensibilities incorporated in design choices that speak to one group of people over others exclude some people.

PLACEMAKING AND CREATIVE PLACEMAKING: A HISTORY

> The practice of placemaking is about "everything," and it is always about different things. There is often no easy way to bound the sphere of intervention or the starting or stopping of it.
>
> — Lynda Schneekloth and Robert Shibley, Placemaking[9]

The term "placemaking" became popular in the 1960s and '70s in the planning and urban design fields. It supported a growing practice of community participation towards development of distinctive and livable places at the neighborhood and block level. In their 1995 book on placemaking, scholar-practitioners Lynda Schneekloth and Robert Shibley found the practices they developed were "not in the mainstream of academic theory, nor were they necessarily consistent with the dictates of any singular discipline or professional practice." Placemaking, they wrote, "is not just about the relationship of people to the places; it also creates relationships among people in places." Finding people disconnected from stewardship of their cultural and physical surroundings, they advocated the role of professionals as "enabling and facilitating others in the various acts of placemaking. ... The allocation of such work to a small body of professionals," they wrote, "ultimately disempowers others because it denies the potential for people to take control over events and circumstances that take place in their lives."[10]

The fields of arts and culture have not been immune from this phenomenon. In his book Arts, Inc., Bill Ivey, former chair of the National Endowment for the Arts, similarly lamented the professionalization of 20th-century artistic practices that removed what he called expressive forms from daily life. Music

> **A key principle to keep in mind**
> Community building is ongoing work and has its difficult times and issues. It can easily lose its joy. Keep building on the social and civic fabric and relationships in the community. In doing so, be sure to find ways to make community building fun: share food, stories, and cultural and personal celebrations; this is the core of the process and the work of creative placemakers.

education, for example, shifted from teaching young people to make music to "music appreciation." A variety of social and economic changes, Ivey pointed out, "steadily drained from society some of the most obvious incentives to becoming a citizen-artist" as growing institutions and corporate media "ushered in the age of cultural consumption."[11]

In the making of places, just as in the making of art, people turned into consumers rather than active participants. A central focus for the placemaking professional, Schneekloth and Shibley argued, is to restore a sense of empowerment and active engagement in the process of making places and sharing space. These early practitioners of placemaking defined a more inclusive process akin to the contemporary practice of creative placemaking. However, few of those in planning, design, community development, and other professions related to city building followed their lead. In the ongoing process of making cities and neighborhoods, leaders, planners, and community developers deferred to their specific area of professional training. Charles Landry, an early leader in culture-led regeneration, and community vitality wrote:

Planners find it easier to think in terms of expenditure on highways, car parks and physical redevelopment schemes rather than on soft infrastructure such as training initiatives for skills enhancement, the encouragement of a lively night-time economy, grants to voluntary organizations to develop social networks or social innovations and the decentralization of powers to build up local capacity and encourage people to have a stake in the running of their neighborhoods.[12]

While city planners are often expected to draw together the disparate parts of the process of making cities into a cohesive whole, Landry, as well as Canadian researcher Neil Bradford[13] and others have argued that the skills required for a holistic approach are typically outside the purview or training of the planning and community development professions. Bringing different skills, sets of knowledge, professional fields, and approaches together into a synthesized whole is what placemaking (as defined by Schneekloth and Shibley) aspired to do, just as creative placemaking now aspires to.

Silo-based structures and professional practices result in what social scientists who explore contemporary urban communities call a "crisis of social cohesion."[14] Practitioners and advocates of creative placemaking have staked out the challenging—if not impossible—task of breaking through or bridging an entire cluster of silos.

Harvard sociologist Robert Putnam's research on social capital had a profound impact on the community development profession. In his widely influential work Bowling Alone: The Collapse and Revival of American Community, he argued that communities large and small have become increasingly fragmented, resulting in a dramatic decline in social capital over the second half of the 20th century. Maintaining social cohesion and building new social capital, Putnam argued, is further complicated by globalization and growing ethnic and cultural diversity within neighborhoods. Concepts related to trust, social capital, social cohesion, and the capacity for collective action of people in place-based communities are central to forming sustainable and equitable cities and neighborhoods. These can be especially elusive in ethnically or racially diverse communities.

The holistic practice of placemaking, supplemented with participatory art-making and a commitment to building social capital, among other ingredients, has added up to the contemporary construct of creative placemaking. As an emerging field, creative placemaking must find ways to employ cultural awareness and cultural differences as assets in the process of building vibrant, distinctive, diverse, and sustainable communities and economies. Culture and creativity can and must cross ethnic, economic, professional, and other boundaries to become a galvanizing force.

2. Creative Placemaking and Traditional Community Planning and Development

> It is not enough to inject a vacant lot with quirky art happenings, or develop an artist live/work collective in an old, dank warehouse district. Before we can envision placemaking, we must first acknowledge our legacy of place-taking and seek to establish places of connection, social equity and economic opportunity for everyone.
>
> — Debra Webb[15]

The foundations of modern urban planning are rooted in the allocation of real estate and the provision of infrastructure and municipal services to meet expanding or changing needs and populations. The primary function of "land use planning" remains the core concern of the profession.[16] In its earlier forms, planning required technical and engineering skills to coordinate the resources and materials to implement top-down design and development schemes. Primary tools employed in these practices include allocation of space uses through zoning and the leveraging of public and private capital to generate housing, jobs, retail shops, service businesses, green space, and institutional uses (schools, health care, etc.). But as democratic societies and cities evolved and requirements became more complex during the 20th century, planners and developers had to be more responsive on a local level.[17]

The emerging role of public or local citizen participation in planning stems from the middle of the 20th century. By the 1970s, organized pressure from neighborhood associations, local business groups, and others required planners and city leaders to open up to "local knowledge" and accommodate more local concerns through formal participation processes. Increased citizen participation in the planning process set the stage for the creative placemaking process.[18]

Case Study 1. Bringing Creative Placemaking and Community Development into a Cohesive Strategy: *Madison Park Development Corporation, Boston, Massachusetts*

Once the second-largest shopping district in Boston, the Lower Roxbury/Dudley Square area is home to over 40,000 people, numerous cultural organizations, artists, and the city's largest bus transfer hub. In its 1940s and '50s heyday as Boston's most vibrant African American neighborhood, it boasted ballrooms, theaters, jazz clubs, and an ice cream parlor as vital parts of community life. In the 1950s the area began to experience disinvestment, loss of local businesses, and an increase in crime and poverty.

Madison Park Development Corporation (www.madison-park.org) began in 1966 as the Lower Roxbury Community Corporation. One of the nation's first community development corporations, it grew from local opposition to highway construction through the heart of the neighborhood. The community lost wide swaths of housing, businesses, and jobs to demolition but mounted a campaign that stopped construction. In its first 30 years, Madison Park Development rebuilt housing for low and mixed-income residents and conducted job training programs. It then looked to new strategies for bringing back business and a sense of active community vitality.

In the late 1990s the city's Community Development Corporation formed Arts Culture Trade (ACT) Roxbury to build on cultural assets as a strategy to bring retail and service businesses and renewed energy to the Dudley Square Business District and Lower Roxbury community. Addressing the business development and marketing needs of artists was a key piece of that puzzle. ACT Roxbury's mission was to engage arts and culture to enrich and strengthen physical, economic, and social revitalization.

A cornerstone in the strategy to generate more positive street-level activity was to rehabilitate Hibernian Hall, a four-story former Irish social club built in 1913 and left vacant for decades. The building now houses the Roxbury Center for Arts that hosts year-round events and transforms the image of Roxbury from a community filled with violence and poverty to a community rich in creative talent and cultural heritage. Through multiple partnerships, ACT Roxbury (now Roxbury Center the Arts) built a variety of events and invested in support structures for artists. It helped launch and promote the Roxbury International Film Festival, the Roxbury Literary Annual and Roxbury Open Studios, and other programs to encourage cultural tourism for both locals and outsiders.

Combined with other efforts of Madison Park, a new identity and revitalized economy has formed in Roxbury, built on a proud identity as an African American cultural hub with a mixed economy that includes growing creative-sector businesses.

Creative placemaking finds connection to traditional urban planning and city development, and goes beyond. It grows from a philosophy of equity and broad participation in the planning process. In creative placemaking the basic commodity or raw material is the creative and celebratory interaction among the people who share a place, including residents, workers and visitors. Primary tools include civic, cultural, and social events, organizational capacity, and public spaces, employed to generate physical and aesthetic improvement, as well as new or revitalized economic enterprises.

One of the challenges in creative placemaking is getting traditional practitioners of planning and community development to join with arts and cultural development practices. Kresge Foundation CEO Rapson said, "We believe that rather than standing outside the community development fence-line and looking in, arts and culture can step inside it and join in a multi-textured fabric of land-use, housing, transportation, environment, health, and other systems necessary for strong, more equitable, and vibrant urban places." One obstacle pointed out by Vazquez is "cynicism among creative sector professionals about their ability to influence public debate." This self-limiting or silo-based thinking and pre-conceived ideas about capacities keep people apart—people with much to contribute to the whole when they work together.

Offering a different observation, Canadian scholar-practitioner Steven Dang wrote that "while the planning profession may be reluctant to engage in community cultural development work, community-based artists are hard at work in community planning."[19]

At its best, creative placemaking finds common ground, blends organizational goals and creates scenarios where the whole is greater than the sum of the parts. Creative placemaking focuses on the local, the neighborhood unit where face-to-face relationships are frequent and essential; in Robert Putnam's terms, it builds social capital. It brings new dimensions and new tools to localized planning, community development, and community animation in the century-long drive to think more holistically about the goals of making space.

Characteristics of Creative Placemakers[20]

The term creative placemakers includes everyone who is actively involved in creative placemaking, as defined above. Individual skills and talents are not always immediately evident and yet they are probably the most important assets to bring into the process. To achieve their mission, creative placemakers:

- **are collaborative.** Just as no single person can lead and manage all aspects of a society, creative placemaking by one person or one interest group is unsustainable. Collaboration should be shared among as many groups as possible within a community.

- **are creative and compassionate creators.** Creative people can see opportunities and connections that others might not. Creators generate ideas that lead to new ways of thinking and doing. Creative placemakers are not mere facilitators or technicians; they are actively involved in creating from the beginning of the initiative. But because they are also collaborative, creative placemakers use compassion to temper any desires to make their ideas rise above others.

- **are culturally competent.** Creative placemakers recognize that artists, developers, and elected officials, as well as distinct communities, can have very diverse hierarchies of values and tolerances of risk. Effective creative placemakers understand and respect these differences, and engage in strategies that meet the diverse interests of stakeholders to build consensus for action.

- **intend to guide, but not control, market activity.** No one can accurately predict the comprehensive array of transactions that is called "the market." But all human activity is guided by awareness, intent, action, reflection, and response. Through such activities as market analysis, thought leadership and place marketing, creative placemaking works to understand the values, interests and concerns of audiences, and to address them in ethical, sustainable ways.

- **recognize that shaping awareness and beliefs is as critical as shaping the built environment.** One of the reasons that the Municipal Art and City Beautiful movements of the late 19th and early 20th centuries could not achieve broad, sustainable results is that their members put too much emphasis on physical determinism—the theory that social behavior can be predicted and directed through changes in the built environment. A person's willingness to risk time, energy, money, and other resources depends on his or her values, beliefs, perceptions, tolerance of risk, and experiences. The physical environment is only one of several elements that impact a person's willingness to engage in a place.

- **value, and promote the value of, creative processes and creators.** Creative placemakers seek to produce sustainable and predictable outcomes through processes that have internal order and can be managed. Creativity is inherently disorderly and unpredictable. Creative placemakers strive to balance idea generation with idea resolution, and seek to build the capacity of others to get more comfortable with the yin and yang of creative placemaking.

3. Finding Assets in All The Right Places

Asset-based strategies have emerged in a variety of fields, from youth development to social services and from business entrepreneurship to community development. More recently the arts and culture community has begun to integrate asset-based thinking into its work in relation to communities and their cultural resources.

These strategies were articulated by Chicago-based practitioner-scholars John McKnight and John Kretzmann as an approach to more equitable place-based revitalization.[21] Their Asset-Based Community Development (ABCD) practice encouraged communities to become more aware of their own resources and power, have confidence in their own capacities, and take charge of solving their own problems. This process begins with engaging community members in the process of making an inventory of community assets. They look to all corners for strengths and capacities that neighborhoods, organizations, and individuals can put to work to address challenges. Creativity, individual talents, and constructive relationships are high in those asset categories. The practice endeavors to identify and marshal new forms of internal (endogenous) power and capacities while leveraging and maintaining local control of outside (exogenous) forces and resources.

Focusing attention on holistic connections and the capacity of people to weave together assets within their communities is not only energizing, but foundational to creative placemaking. The ABCD process emphasizes active broad-based participation in asset identification as a vehicle in itself to build relationships and networks within communities. British planning scholar Patsy Healey addressed similar ideas, suggesting that relationship building may not have immediate purpose but can serve to prepare people for unknown or future challenges. Lewis Mumford described neighbors connecting through "intermediate links of association" and wrote that "in times of crisis, a fire, a funeral, a festival, neighbors become vividly conscious of each other and capable of greater cooperation."[22] Links of association —social capital—remains the most important deposit in any community's bank of assets.

4. Stories Our Communities Tell

Culture is sometimes described as the DNA of a community; or, in computer terms, it is the operating system that enables the hardware and software to work together. A community, like an organization or computer, won't work if its culture — its DNA, its operating system — is dysfunctional. Creative placemakers try to understand how organizational cultures drive places, learn how to function with and within that culture — and sometimes learn how to change it. Every culture, as well as every place, is an accumulation of the layers that nature and earlier people left behind. Everyday lived experience — one of Henri Lefebvre's three ingredients for the production of space — becomes an essential starting point for community planning based on creative placemaking. These experiences take the form of stories that define places. These stories can move the community forward — or hold it back.

A core component of every creative placemaking effort is to listen and gather stories, to find the storytellers and to seek out shared narratives. One key to learning how not to repeat mistakes is to respect and appreciate the stories or histories of place. Providing ongoing places for those stories to be told and to be shared is both one of the first and one of the last jobs of the creative placemaker. A fitting job for the arts!

Schneekloth and Shibley emphasized that the first and "most important activity of professional placemakers" is making "an open space for dialogue about place and placemaking." Effective creative placemakers bring people together to share stories in a psychological space—if not an actual physical space—where "all knowledges are valued, shared, and used in the process of decision making." Steven Dang described artists as community storytellers: "They can provide a planner not only deep insight into a community, but ready-made and powerful means of communicating them." Debra Webb similarly observed, "Artists are storytellers, preservers of cultural identity, and critics to the injustices that stagnate humanity." [23]

Creative placemakers draw on local stories to set their sights on a vision for a future that is consistent with its past. To fail to connect with the historical trajectory that shaped the place is to move down a dark or empty path. In some places creative placemaking explicitly includes historic preservation or the reinvigoration of 19th- or early 20th-century cultural resources (a jazz scene, for instance). While not every place has an immediately evident trove of significant period architecture, music legends, momentous events, or even important crossroads, every place does have stories which illuminate the ways people have used or interacted with the place over centuries, or even millennia, and the dynamics and relationships between the people in that place as it evolved.

The story of place may include its geology, indigenous peoples, waves of immigrants, economies that have come and perhaps gone, and the skills people employed to make their livelihood working with wood, stone, leather, or metal. The story may include a product or service of special significance that explains why that place was used for gathering, resting, or healing. There is never just one story of place, nor one correct story. The biggest mistake for the creative placemaker is to not listen to as many stories as possible or to fail to give stories an ongoing place in the process of community building.

Schneekloth and Shibley observed that "to appreciate a place and people does not, however, imply an uncritical stance toward it." They pointed out that "to act responsibly in the historical moment requires knowledge of that time/place/cultural reality; wisdom to recognize that one never has sufficient information or insight on which to base a 'rational' decision; and courage to proceed anyway."[24]

The critical process of exploring and sharing stories as a visible and ongoing part of creative placemaking demonstrates a respect for place and for the people who are there, who have been there, and who will be there in the future.

Creative placemakers must remember to utilize approaches that recognize, honor, and contribute to their community's ways of getting things done:

- Plan, engage, and work with others in every step of the process.
- Make small changes that signal momentum—both symbolic and meaningful steps.
- Understand and employ the unique capacities the arts bring to the table.
- Build bridges across difference.
- Visualize possibilities.
- Create and manage spaces where people feel free to express new and different ideas.

5. Creative Process and Practice: The Medium Is The Message

When social theorist Marshall McLuhan famously introduced the phrase "the medium is the message,"[25] he furthered our understanding that means and ends, or process and product, are not distinct. As Leonardo Vazquez has stated, "The value of creative placemaking is as much in the doing as in what is done."[26] Unfortunately, this can be a most difficult message to convey to policy-makers, philanthropists, and business leaders who want results. There is often a tendency to short-cut the process to get to the product. If the desired product is a creative, inclusive, and highly engaged community but the process to get there is formulaic, closed, and/or top-down, then formulaic, closed, and top-down is the kind of place that will be made.

To build creative places that exemplify inclusion, equity, and open dialogue, creative methods that employ those same values are required. Artists maintain the flow of intellectual capital and refreshing ways of thinking, as Patsy Healey has argued, and according to senior Canadian cultural planner Greg

Baeker, artists are boundary-crossers who bring an array of tools to foster the exchange of ideas both within and across communities.[27]

Artists working in community settings during the past 40 or more years have developed an extensive array of techniques and practices that foster community building.[28] Scholars such as Louis Albrechts,[29] Steven Dang, and Leonie Sandercock, as well as Australian creative planning practitioners Wendy Sarkissian and Diane Hurford, have advocated ramping up the involvement of creative people in community planning and bringing artists into central roles. Writing about the process of cultural planning, Greg Baeker observed, "The tools of the artist become key to the participation of all."[30] Sarkissian and Hurford described the impact of these techniques as "bridging conflict, changing the flavor of community discussions, opening participants to new possibilities and forming lasting partnerships to transform our communities and our futures."[31]

Case Study 2. Creative CityMaking: Arts-Infused and Inclusive Community Planning, Minneapolis, Minnesota[32]

The cutting-edge Minneapolis art center Intermedia Arts (www.intermediaarts.org) built on its history of work with surrounding neighborhoods and with various municipal agencies to form the Creative CityMaking Program (CCM) in 2011. CCM operates as a partnership with the City of Minneapolis to foster fresh and innovative approaches for addressing long-term transportation, land use, economic, environmental, and social issues.

The program formed artist-planner teams involving local practicing artists and city planners. They initiated discussions with community members through a variety of planning projects with the goal of increasing participation of under-represented communities in determining the city's future. During 2013, CCM focused on a set of short-term goals and small community changes with the idea that small and strategic change that impacts individuals, ecosystems, economies, and/or social systems will lead to larger changes.

Artist-planner teams focused on small-area plans for distinct geographic areas of the city and on an evaluation of the city's survey efforts to inform historic preservation policy. Other teams focused on action plans around a Light Rail Transit Station Area. Artist-planner collaborations brought new people together and inspired innovation that bled into other city departments.

In assessing their early efforts, artists, planners and evaluators came to define the practice as arts-infused and inclusive community planning. By 2014 the project had resulted in many new tools and strategies that foster engagement in community planning among under-represented communities.

The arts also brought playful and more accessible qualities to the process of engaging communities in complex planning processes.

One artist reported: The project has allowed me to make artwork and to do things that I am really passionate about. It has given me faith that art can change people's lives and provide perspectives that were not there.

A city planner said: This project has affirmed how useful a partnership like this can be. It has made me think about the creative process and how it interfaces with what we do.

Community planners, development professionals, artists, local policy makers and cultural practitioners have a great deal to learn from one another. In fact, some artistic processes parallel planning processes and complement them. Steven Dang asserted that "as a means of conversation, the arts are often more accessible and inclusive than the standard town hall meeting or open house."[33] Artists often have skills to help individuals less skilled at verbal debate or at using the traditional vehicles of civic engagement to find their voice. They can help individuals, groups, and communities use forms of expression beyond words to address their fears, questions, emotions, dreams, and visions.

The dialogic space advocated by Schneekloth and Shibley can be seen to be working if, "as the work progresses to decisions about action, all voices can see themselves in the approach." This results in community members with "a higher level of commitment to the decisions, and often more willing to live with and care for the resultant conditions."[34] And according to Rip Rapson, "The centrality of arts and culture to social cohesion is one of the arts and culture community's secret sauces."

6. Sustainable Creative Economies

Much of the interest in creative placemaking stems from its promise to improve local economies, open new employment opportunities, bring prosperity to artists and arts organizations, and expand or reinvigorate municipal tax bases.

Standard economic development strategies are dominated by outside (exogenous) investors or corporate entities. They generate economic activity but typically return little value or equity to the local community. Development activities are generally composed of industry attraction strategies and major infrastructure investments such as shipping ports and power generation. Creative placemaking emphasizes local (endogenous), people-centered, productive livelihoods. This is often pursued through synergistic growth of the creative sector and small entrepreneurial businesses.

In his book on creative placemaking, Leonardo Vazquez wrote, "In economic development practice, attracting a big employer would have a bigger immediate impact than many arts initiatives." He went on to argue that big employers are more mobile and thus contribute less to local sustainability while creative enterprises, which that often require more time to grow, provide "the greatest returns on investment for the goals of both community and economic development."[35]

The grassroots economic development practices of creative placemaking are drawn from economic gardening, a practice that nurtures and grows start-ups generated by local entrepreneurs who tap local assets and resources. Economic gardening builds on existing endogenous assets and is considered more sustainable.[36]

Local economic development typically grows a diverse mix of locally owned, interdependent enterprises that produce goods or services with local raw materials or skills. They export goods and/or attract customers, clients or tourists who seek out their unique or highly distinctive qualities. They also produce local social networks that keep them connected to and invested in place.

In recent decades, city leaders witnessed the industrial era, characterized by large manufacturing plants and pools of nominally-educated labor, give way to an economic era based increasingly on knowledge production, innovation, global exchanges, and creativity.[37] Cities in many parts of the world moved into this realm of creativity and culture, sometimes in desperate attempts to regain their economic and socio-cultural footing. "'Be creative—or die' is the new urban imperative" wrote British sociologist Jamie Peck, and Italian economists Sacco and Segre argued that "creativity and innovation —or lack of it—make the difference, specially when cities face a period of transition."[38]

Increasingly, city leaders have come to believe that arts and cultural institutions can play a catalytic role in regeneration. Some have made significant investments in the arts in order to make their cities more appealing, boost their image, and attract people with wealth and/or sophistication. American planning scholar Amanda Johnson traced a history of arts-led urban regeneration projects through the 1950s and '60s in the United States. She found early efforts characterized by construction of large-scale performing arts centers and implementation of tourism strategies. "For sixty years policymakers have been experimenting with clustering different arts activities as a revitalization strategy and a way to demonstrate a city's cultural reputation" she said.[39]

The concept of creative industries surfaced in the United Kingdom in the mid-1980s. Creative industries are characterized by for-profit entrepreneurial activities to produce goods and services, such as the design and/or production of ceramics, film, fashion, furniture, jewelry, wines, etc., and enterprises based in intellectual property development, including advertising, architecture, software, and video games.[40] A broad definition of the creative sector used by some in the United States gathers both for-profit creative industries and the not-for-profit sector under the umbrella of the creative economy, creating a larger interdependent ecosystem.[41]

Case Study 3. Yellow Springs, Ohio

Nestled in the softly rolling landscape of Southwest Ohio, the village of Yellow Springs (population 3,500) bustles with creative activity. Small artisan shops, galleries, restaurants, and cafes — even a small independent cinema — sit at the heart of the village. The village center is walkable and active day and evening. Youth hang out in front of the grocery store and older people gather across the street at the Senior Center. About 20 miles from Dayton, 50 miles from Columbus, and 60 miles from Cincinnati, Yellow Springs' distinctive identity is still rooted in the healing properties of the mineral spring once frequented by Native Americans. It is home to Antioch College, founded in 1852, open to women and people of color from the start, led by its first President, the iconic American educator Horace Mann, and later by Tennessee Valley Authority architect Arthur Morgan.

Yellow Springs illustrated the creative economy long before the term was coined. Many well-established artists and intellectuals have been drawn to the liberal community and teach at some of the 25 colleges and universities within an hour's drive. Festivals, art fairs, and gallery/studio walks have been a feature of the community for decades. Theater, music, dance, poetry, cinema, and other organized cultural and arts events clog the calendar of the town's award-winning weekly newspaper. Many in Yellow Springs earn their living in the creative sector and the vibrant retail economy is dominated by creative enterprises, including fine food. The kind of "artistic dividend" Markusen and King described, in which creative energies fuel innovation and entrepreneurship across sectors, is evident in abundance.[42]

This synergy across disciplines and sectors can be seen in the multiple enterprises the community has spawned. In addition to one of the most concentrated, active small arts communities in the U.S., this small village has fostered businesses producing innovations in aluminum casting, seed hybridization, industrial design, and high-precision thermostats, as well as water-monitoring devices, industrial surface-plates, high-stress rubber bearings, and the first known EMT training program. In one of his many books, Industries for Small Communities, Arthur Morgan concluded that these enterprises sprouted from a quality of life that included interdisciplinary education in which both art and science were central, inclusive racial and labor relations, and a highly engaged civic community. Some of these old-line companies remain and continue to employ area residents, joined now by countless small start-ups springing from the community, including clothing, medical technology, software design, and sustainable animal and plant nutrients.

In his 2002 study, The Rise of the Creative Class, Richard Florida set off a global firestorm of debate with his assertion that what he termed the *creative class* serves as fuel to power the post-industrial economy. Many cities began chasing creative talent — highly educated designers, scientists, engineers, software developers, artists, marketers, and others — and abandoning older economic development and industry attraction strategies. Transformation of old factories into loft living spaces, coffee shops, and art galleries became the operative strategy. As Sacco and Segre put it, "Human cleverness, desires, motivations, imaginations and creativity [are] the driving forces; replacing location, natural resources and market access." Politicians and planners wanted their communities to appear innovative, exciting, creative, and safe places in which to live, visit, play, and consume. Festivals, spectacles and displays, cultural events, flagship arts institutions, and a robust arts scene were increasingly appropriated as symbols of a dynamic city.[43]

But is this creative placemaking, or simply a strategy for cities to compete with one another to attract talent, capital, and stature in global trade and tourism? Most scholars, including Florida, now acknowledge the talent attraction strategy has heightened economic inequity and set off waves of gentrification that have harmed many of the poor and elderly as well as many artists. Creative placemaking, instead, focuses on endogenous assets and economic gardening to generate and keep wealth within the community.

7. Outcomes and Measures

Assigning measures to assess the success or failure of creative placemaking has proven one of the more complex arenas for practitioners and scholars alike. Some of the difficulty may lie in the classic left-brain/right-brain conundrum. Can quantitative tools measure "a sense of belonging" or "cultural stewardship" along with "walkability scores" and "local tax generators"? While some believe they can, others have asked if such measures are as applicable in a Philadelphia neighborhood with half a century of disinvestment as they are in a fast-growing Seattle suburb looking for more active social spaces.

A set of "Vibrancy Indicators," designed to assess placemaking outcomes, was issued in late 2012 by ArtPlace America, a creative placemaking funding consortium of over a dozen major U.S. foundations. They were divided into three categories: people, activity, and value, and included specific indicators and data sources for the people and activity categories. When compared year to year, the indicators measure changes in communities where ArtPlace has made grants and are available for use by others interested in measuring community outcomes. Because "a recurring issue in creative placemaking is whether the process of neighborhood change leads to places becoming less economically and racially diverse," ArtPlace also developed two measures of economic and racial diversity in neighborhoods — the racial and ethnic diversity index and the mixed-income, middle income index.

Ann Markusen and other cultural leaders and scholars have challenged standard quantitative measures while expanding the dialogue on the purpose and practice of creative placemaking. "Efforts based on fuzzy concepts and indicators designed to rely on data external to the funded projects are bound to disappoint," she wrote in 2013. Markusen argued for development of a new framework for assessing creative placemaking that transcends economic growth and instead values social equity and belonging. Creative placemaking, she argued, should not automatically equate higher property values and more people walking with success.[44]

Around the same time, the National Endowment for the Arts issued livability indicators addressing four areas:[45]

- Positive effect on artists and arts community
- Residents' attachment to community
- Improvement of quality of life for residents
- Positive effect on local economic conditions

Like the ArtPlace indicators, certain publicly available data sources are used to track changes in each of these areas. For instance, government jobs data tracks numbers of people employed in arts-related occupations; housing values and the numbers of people buying homes might be indicators of attachment to place.

While neither of these indicator systems have been fully implemented as of this writing, proponents and critics alike point to the challenges inherent in what Markusen alternately called "indicator mania" and "one-size-fits-all indicators." Community change through creative placemaking requires many years, even decades. Major short-term changes in communities rarely benefit residents, artists, nonprofits, or even local businesses.

8. Sustainability and Unintended Consequences

Community-based work is not easy. It involves people, their cultures and identity, the places to which they have emotional attachment, and politics. As in any community-development process, there are too often winners and losers. When it comes to economic development, it is increasingly rare in the current era to see economic outcomes generated equitably across all members of a community.

Creative placemaking and culture-led regeneration have room for improvement. Most critics maintain that while creative placemaking holds great promise, it is sometimes not carried out with a holistic agenda and set of strategies, or with clarity of means and ends. "Public art, cultural districts and performing arts centers are not the outcomes of creative placemaking — they are strategies" wrote Vazquez. He warned of the "lack of awareness or concern about the negative effects arts-based economic development can have on disadvantaged communities."[46] A pair of Taiwan-based researchers found encouragement in arts-based strategies because "unique-cultural resources of place, civic society strength and place-identity [serve] as vehicles for local sustainability and urban social cohesion in the globalising context," but they also expressed concern that homogeneous places result from "formulaic models of urban regeneration [that] result in standardized landscapes in localities, displacing local symbolic content."[47]

Sharon Zukin and Laura Braslow argued in 2011 that "real estate developers and public officials often use the symbolic capital of the 'artistic mode of production' to establish new place-identities for problematic industrial areas, rebranding them as 'creative' and increasing their economic value."[48] They went on to describe how this economic value becomes a profit center for developers and a tax generator for cities. In its wake, it causes dislocation of artists, the poor, elderly, and others who find they no longer belong in their neighborhood.

Using the label and strategies of creative placemaking, some cities or neighborhoods seek to capture, retain, and brand creative "space"—artist districts or quarters, live-arts scenes, or an overall 'cool city' image. However, as singular achievements, these are not enough. Charles Landry called these failed regeneration strategies favored by many political leaders the "Starbucks and Stadiums" approach. Critics cite such limited approaches as largely image makeovers that tend to further the process of gentrification and dislocation of the less affluent.[49] A consequence of creative placemaking or culture-led regeneration—whether intended or not—is often income inequality, gentrification, and displacement, as well as cultural conflicts. These are well-known, predictable phenomena that creative placemakers have scarcely addressed.

According to Jamie Peck, the global creative cities competition "gives way to a form of creative trickle-down; elite-focused creativity strategies leave only supporting roles for the two-thirds of the population languishing in the working and service classes."[50]

The potential to blend together urban planning, economic development, and cultural policy with values related to equity and social justice has proven a difficult recipe for creative placemakers. Part of the reason for this, Ann Markusen and Anne Gadwa have argued, is that public, private, and nonprofit sectors and professional fields within urban planning, design, arts, and economic development find it hard to understand each other, let alone coordinate efforts.[51] Another part of the equation, according to Sharon Zukin and Laura Braslow, is that cities become beholden to aggressive global investors and top-shelf developers. City and political leaders do not always assert values that protect their populations from growing inequity and political disenfranchisement.[52]

Peck also cited abandonment of comprehensive planning in favor of the selective development of "urban fragments"—neighborhood nodes of upscale housing, coffee shops, and cultural and entertainment amenities designed to attract creative-class residents. Whether such efforts represent a fragmentation or a move towards localized democracy and empowerment is the subject of ongoing debate among scholars in planning and municipal management. He argued that notions of the creative class would not be sweeping cities around the globe if they fundamentally ran counter to established business and political interests. "For the average mayor, there are few downsides to making the city safe for the creative class—a creativity strategy can quite easily be bolted on to business-as-usual urban development policies."[53]

Case Study 4. Jacobs Center for Neighborhood Innovation and Market Creek Plaza, San Diego, California

Within a five-minute drive of downtown San Diego, an abandoned 20-acre factory sat in the center of a diamond-shaped business improvement district. The Diamond, as it came to be called, includes parts of 10 different neighborhoods and has a total of 88,000 residents. Latinos and African Americans make up about 75 percent of the population, along with a mix of immigrants from various parts of the globe speaking more than 15 languages. This part of the city suffered over 25 years of disinvestment and a 1998 study found that, as is true in many poor communities, residents of the Diamond were going outside their neighborhood and spending over $60 million annually for basic products and services not available locally.

Market Creek Plaza and the Village at Market Creek emerged through a partnership between a San Diego community and a family foundation to redevelop the abandoned factory site, but it became much more. In 1996 Joseph and Violet Jacobs and the Jacobs Family Foundation formed the Jacobs Center for Neighborhood Innovation (www.jacobscenter.org) to explore new ways of helping communities, and soon decided to focus on the Market Creek project. The project grew into a skill and asset-building opportunity of considerable scale. "Working and learning together" became its motto and central strategy.

Early public projects included construction of the Malcolm X Library and Performing Arts Center and the Tubman-Chavez Multicultural Center. Market Creek Plaza opened for business in 2001 on a ten-acre parcel adjacent to a San Diego light-rail and bus transfer station. The Village at Market Creek, a housing development, and additional enterprises came on line over the next decade. The development includes office space, a 500-seat amphitheater, cultural center, walkways along a restored creek, myriad public art works, over 800 units of mixed-income housing, and 60 new businesses. The Jacobs Foundation and the hard work and imagination of community residents set in motion developments designed to encompass over 45 acres.

At least as important is how the project works. The process began when the Jacobs Center hired seven residents to survey 700 neighbors. Hundreds of community meetings followed and planning teams were launched to work on areas such as art and design, business development, employment, youth, childcare, community ownership, and a community center. Community art projects brought participation into the thousands. The art and design team created a unique design aesthetic to blend styles, colors, and designs derived from the neighborhood's multiple cultures. The number of working/learning teams grew and involved hundreds of residents bringing out the residents' natural creativity, problem-solving abilities, and appetite for risk-taking.

Market Creek Plaza evolved into a holistic community building project with culture and creativity at the center. Its imperative was to tap the creativity of residents while bringing about a new multicultural identity and building the skills and assets of the neighborhood. Arts and culture became a key strategy to engage residents and build the sense of connection and stewardship. Another key to the project

> was resident ownership through an equity stake for residents in businesses and homes. The community has become a growing employment center, with residents literally building the neighborhood.
>
> Market Creek Plaza is about building community block-by-block in an inclusive, participatory, and focused way, and it's based on the theory that social, cultural, and economic goals are interdependent.
>
> In their critique of a creative-class initiative in Baltimore, Davide Ponzini and Ugo Rossi acknowledged that an inclusive approach to culture-led regeneration can renew the image of long-deprived cities and neighborhoods, provide a strengthened sense of belonging, and improve the liveliness and attractiveness of places. However, they found that the city and its cultural district promoters appeared "not to be concerned with the issues of social inclusion and life-chance provision that are most relevant in socially deprived areas."[54]
>
> The challenge for creative placemakers is to move beyond activation of public spaces and to do more than improve conditions for the creative class with the economic and intellectual benefits artistic involvement can bring. As part of a more holistic effort at people and place revitalization, they need to influence the values and outcomes of a larger set of collaborators with whom they aligned themselves in creative placemaking.

9. Assessing Readiness and Getting Started

> Celebrate and stabilize distinctiveness with modest-scale investments ... paying more attention to the animation of places with economic and cultural activity.[55]

Creative placemaking leaders and prospective leaders need to assess their own readiness and that of their community and of some key organizations, including local levels of government. A central question to ask is: Does the community have the requisite internal self-governance experience and capacity, as well as cross-sector partnerships that are functional and can be built upon?

Over a period of three decades in the U.S., the community-development movement and the designers and advocates of large-scale urban renewal programs, initially launched by federal and state agencies, have learned that the development of local capacity is essential to the success of local efforts. Top-down, large-scale, or imposed and formulaic solutions have not often been well received and are simply not successful.[56]

In building a bottom-up, people-centered placemaking effort, some questions creative leaders need to ask include:

- Is there adequate appreciation of the history, stories, and unique qualities of the community?
- Are the creative leaders personally invested in the community and do they know their neighbors?
- Are the creative leaders familiar with how things get done in the city and with major actors in neighborhood, political, social, and business arenas?
- Are the creative leaders familiar with existing planning strategies and documents: city comprehensive plans; district, downtown, cultural, and neighborhood plans; and proposals for development in and around the neighborhood?
- Do the creative leaders understand how the development of major infrastructure projects in the past — and any pending infrastructure development — has altered and defined the community?
- Are the creative leaders and organizations prepared to make this work an ongoing part of their missions?

- Do the creative leaders share a meaningful vision for the community with other members of the community? How flexible is the creative leaders' vision? (If the answer is "Not open to adapting, amending, or making significant changes to it" based on the ideas of others, then the creative placemaking project may need to be postponed as the key players may not be prepared for such an undertaking.)

The emerging and evolving field of creative placemaking builds on a variety of formal and informal practices that shape, animate, and govern place-based communities of all sizes. It is not a new invention but a re-casting, re-articulation, and fresh combination of existing ideas and practices. The field tackles a broad and inclusive agenda, addressing the many ingredients that make places tick — the three components of "the production of space" described by Lefebvre: the perceived, conceived, and everyday lived experiences.

Only by thinking holistically and by actively working to bridge existing silos of practice can creative placemakers achieve success. Those from the arts and culture sector who have stepped up and stepped out from their own silo are taking on important work, but work that comes with a constant need for learning and often unpredictable challenges and rewards.

12 Steps: Preparation and Ongoing Practice in Creative Placemaking

1. Start with knowing and valuing the history and its multiple origins and interpretations.
2. Design and implement a process to engage people in identifying the community's assets; keep that process open to fresh ideas.
3. Value, engage, and honor local knowledge.
4. Identify appropriate outside thinkers and learn from their ideas.
5. Put in place an ongoing program or vehicle to connect community leaders across sectors, interests, ethnicities, always working to build new bridges and maintain existing ones.
6. Connect with, listen to, and meaningfully engage the talents of youth.
7. Get people talking and keep them talking. Use multiple strategies, including local media.
8. Include artists, culture bearers, designers, and other creative people on every team or committee and keep them involved at all stages.
9. In all aspects of the process, use creative approaches and maintain a creative environment.
10. Walk—literally—with people, and listen, as an ongoing practice.
11. Try new technologies to engage people in creative thinking, to keep people talking, and to inform people—but don't rely on it completely.
12. Generate and leverage the public visibility you generate to engage more people, to promote events, and to build political capital.

Endnotes

1. Lewis Mumford, "The Neighborhood and the Neighborhood Unit," The Town Planning Review, 24 no. 4 (1954), pp. 256—70.

2. Ann Markusen and Anne Gadwa, Creative Placemaking, white paper for the Mayors' Institute on City Design, National Endowment for the Arts, 2010, p. 3. www.artsbuildcommunities.com.

3. Rip Rapson, "Creative Placemaking: Rethinking the Role of Arts and Culture in Strengthening Communities," speech at League of Historic American Theatres conference, Minneapolis, July 17, 2013 (kresge.org); Debra Webb, "Placemaking and Social Equity: Expanding the Framework of Creative Placemaking," Artivate: A Journal of Entrepreneurship in the Arts, 3 no. 1 (2013): 35—48.

4. Leonardo Vazquez, "Creative Placemaking: Integrating Community, Cultural and Economic development," white paper, 2012. www.artsbuildcommunities.com.

5. Ibid, p. 15.

6. Henri Lefebvre, The Production of Space, 1974, repr. 1991.

7. Ade Kearns and Ray Forrest, "Social Cohesion and Multilevel Urban Governance," Urban Studies, 37, nos. 5—6 (2000): 995—1017; Kerstin Hermes and Michael Poulsen, "Determining the Structure of Neighborhood Cohesion: Applying Synthetic Small Area Data in Sydney and Los Angeles," International Journal of Applied Geospatial Research, 3 no. 4 (2012): 20—42.

8. Roberto Bedoya, "Placemaking and the Politics of Belonging and Dis-Belonging," Grantmakers in the Arts READER, 24 no. 1 (2013): 21.

9. Lynda Schneekloth and Robert Shibley, Placemaking: The Art and Practice of Building Communities, 1995.

10. Ibid., pp. xii—5.

11. Bill Ivey, Arts, Inc.: How Greed and Neglect Have Destroyed Our Cultural Rights, 2008, p. 10.

12. Charles Landry, The Creative City: A Toolkit for Urban Innovators, 2000, p. 18.

13. Neil Bradford, Creative Cities Structured Policy Dialogue Backgrounder, background paper for Canadian Policy Research Networks, 2004. www.cprn.org.

14. Kearns and Forrest, ""Social Cohesion and Multilevel Urban Governance," p. 995.

15. Webb, "Placemaking and Social Equity," p. 38.

16. See Patsy Healey, Making Better Places: The Planning Project in the Twenty-First Century, 2010; William Peterman, "Advocacy vs. Collaboration: Comparing Inclusionary Community Planning Models," Community Development Journal, 39 no. 3 (2004): 266—76; Sharon Zukin and Laura Braslow, "The Lifecycle of New York's Creative Districts: Reflections on the Unanticipated Consequences of Unplanned Cultural Zones," City, Culture and Society, 2 no. 3 (2001): 131—40.

17. See Peterman; also William Rohe, "From Local to Global: One Hundred Years of Neighborhood Planning," Journal of the American Planning Association, 75 no. 2 (2009): 209—30.

18. See Healey, Making Better Places; Leonie Sandercock, "Towards a Planning Imagination for the 21st Century," Journal of the American Planning Association, 70 no. 2 (2004): 133—41; Rohe, "From Local to Global"; Paul Grogan and Tony Proscio, Comeback Cities: A Blueprint for Urban Neighborhood Revival, 2000.

19. Steven Dang, "A Starter Menu for Planner/Artist Collaborations," Planning Theory and Practice, 6 no. 1 (2005), p. 123.

20. From Leonardo Vazquez's Creative Placemaking.

21. John McKnight and John Kretzmann, Building Communities from the Inside Out: A Path Toward Finding and Mobilizing a Community's Assets, 1993. See also Alison Mathie and Gord Cunningham, "From Clients to Citizens: Asset-Based Community Development as a Strategy for Community-Driven Development," Development in Practice, 13 no. 5 (2003): 474—86.

22. Mumford, "The Neighborhood and the Neighborhood Unit," p. 258.

23. Schneekloth and Shibley, Placemaking, pp. 6, 14; Dang, "A Starter Menu," p. 124; Webb, "Placemaking and Social Equity," p. 46..

24. Schneekloth and Shibley, pp. 8, 10.

25. Marshall McLuhan, Understanding Media: The Extensions of Man, 1964.

26. Vazquez, "Creative Placemaking," p. 2.

27. Patsy Healey, "Building Institutional Capacity through Collaborative Approaches to Urban Planning," Environment and Planning A., 30, (1998): 1531—46; Greg Baeker, Beyond Garrets and Silos: Concepts, Trends and Developments in Cultural Planning, Municipal Cultural Planning Project, Canada, 2002.

28. See Tom Borrup, Creative Community Builders Handbook: How to Transform Communities Using Local Assets, Art, and Culture,. 2006; Bill Cleveland, Art in Other Places: Artists at Work in America's Community and Social Institutions, 2000; Arlene Goldbard, New Creative Community: The Art of Cultural Development, 2006.

29. Louis Albrechts, "Creativity in and for Planning," Planning Theory, 4 no. 3 (2005): 14—25.

30. Baeker, Beyond Garrets and Silos, p. 24.

31. Wendy Sarkissian and Diane Hurford, Creative Community Planning: Transformative Engagement Methods for Working at the Edge, 2010, p. 5.

32. Adapted from Kristin Johnstad and Patricia Seppanen, Creative CityMaking Evaluation Report, January 2014.

33. Dang, "A Starter Menu," p. 124.

34. Schneekloth and Shibley, Placemaking, p. 17.

35. Vazquez, "Creative Placemaking," p. 9.

36. See National Center for Economic Gardening, hosted by the Edward Lowe Foundation, edwardlowe.org.

37. Richard Florida, The Rise of the Creative Class, and How It's Transforming Work, Leisure, Community and Everyday Life, 2002; John Montgomery, "Beware 'The Creative Class': Creativity and Wealth Creation Revisited," Local Economy, 20 no. 4 (2005): 337—43; Allen Scott, "Creative Cities: Conceptual Issues and Policy Questions," Journal of Urban Affairs, 28 no. 1 (2006): 1—17.

38. Jamie Peck, "Struggling with the Creative Class," International Journal of Urban and Regional Research, 29 no. 4 (2005): 740—70; Pier Sacco and Giovanna Segre, "Creativity, Cultural Investment and Local Development: A New Theoretical Framework for Endogenous Growth," in Ugo Fratesi and Lanfranco Senn, eds., Growth and Innovation of Competitive Regions: The Role of Internal and External Connections, 2009, pp. 281—94.

39. Amanda Johnson, "Urban Arts Districts: The Evolution of Physical Arts Development," presentation at Urban History Association Conference, Las Vegas, October 20, 2010.

40. John Howkins, The Creative Economy: How People Make Money from Ideas, 2001; see also Scott, "Creative Cities."

41. Douglas DeNatale and Gregory Wassall, The Creative Economy: A New Definition, New England Foundation for the Arts, 2007; Ann Markusen, Nurturing California's Next Generation Arts and Cultural Leaders, report for Center for Cultural Innovation, 2011.

42. Ann Markusen and David King, The Artistic Dividend: The Arts' Hidden Contributions to Regional Development, 2003.

43. Mary Donegan and Nichola Lowe, "Inequality in the Creative City: Is There Still a Place for 'Old-Fashioned' Institutions?" Economic Development Quarterly, 22 no. 1 (2008): 46; see also Sacco and Segre, ""Creativity, Cultural Investment and Local Development"; Peck.

44. Ann Markusen, "Fuzzy Concepts, Proxy Data: Why Indicators Would Not Track Creative Placemaking Success," International Journal of Urban Sciences, 17 no. 3 (2013): 291-303.

45. National Endowment for the Arts, The Validating Arts & Livability Indicators (VALI) Study: Results and Recommendations, 2015. Available for download at nea.gov.

46. Vazquez, "Creative Placemaking," p. 3.

47. Cheng-Yi Lin and Woan-Chiau Hsing, "Culture-Led Urban Regeneration and Community Mobilisation: The Case of the Taipei Bao-an Temple Area, Taiwan," Urban Studies, 46 no. 7 (2009): 1318, 1321—22.

48. Zukin and Braslow, "The Lifecycle of New York's Creative Districts," p. 131.

49. See Susan Bagwell, "Creative Clusters and City Growth," Creative Industries Journal, 1 no. 1 (2008): 31—46; Eugene McCann, "Inequality and Politics in the Creative City-Region: Questions of Livability and State Strategy," International Journal of Urban and Regional Research, 31 no. 1 (2007): 188—196; also Landry; Montgomery; Peck; Zukin and Braslow.

50. Peck, "Struggling with the Creative Class," p. 766.

51. Ann Markusen and Anne Gadwa, "Arts and Culture in Urban or Regional Planning: A Review and Research Agenda," Journal of Planning Education and Research, 29 no. 3 (2010): 379—91.

52. Zukin and Braslow, "The Lifecycle of New York's Creative Districts."

53. Peck, "Struggling with the Creative Class," p. 760.

54. Davide Ponzini and Ugo Rossi, "Becoming a Creative City: The Entrepreneurial Mayor, Network Politics and the Promise of Urban Renaissance," Urban Studies 47 no. 5 (2010): 1039.

55. Markusen and Gadwa, Creative Placemaking.

56. See Grogan and Proscio, Comeback Cities.

4

Cultural Advocacy

DAN HUNTER *and* STAN ROSENBERG

> I have come to the conclusion that politics are too serious a matter to be left to the politicians.
> — Charles de Gaulle[1]

Understanding and engaging in the political process is essential for a successful cultural organization. This chapter discusses how to navigate local, state, and federal politics to find the opportunities and know the limitations for nonprofit cultural organizations.

What Is Politics?

In 1936, Harold Lasswell defined politics as simply "who gets what, when, and how?"[2] Politics is the process of allocating resources. It is how human beings resolve differences, assign authority, and establish rules at all levels.

The word "politics" has several meanings. It may refer to electoral politics. It may refer to the process of establishing priorities in a democracy. It can mean the art of governing. Or, it can be defined as conflict resolution—the negotiations, compromises, and reconciliations between nations, factions, and individuals. We engage in politics whenever we try to resolve differences. Politics is also the tool that we use to work with others to create and implement a shared vision for our future.

Effective arts leaders apply well-developed political skills in working with a board of directors, supervising employees, soliciting donations, or allocating resources within their organizations.

But when it's time to allocate resources as a society, too many arts leaders disengage from politics. They may mistakenly believe that they are legally prohibited from engaging in politics, or that politics is a "dirty" business of conflict and partisanship.

Politics, however, is a process, a tool that is neither good nor bad. Any tool can create or destroy, according to the intent of its user. The Czech playwright and politician Václav Havel wrote that "politics worthy of the name ... is simply a matter of serving those around us: serving the community and serving those who will come after us. Its deepest roots are moral because it is a responsibility expressed through action to and for the whole."[3]

Arts organizations work to serve society by the nature of their charters and missions. They help build stronger, healthier, and more vital communities, and they are integral to education and public learning. Because they contribute to and depend upon their communities, arts organizations cannot thrive if they are isolated from the public resource-allocation process happening around them. Therefore, arts leaders must engage in the politics of their municipalities, states, and nation. If arts organizations do not advocate for their priorities, their needs will be ignored in favor of other interests. To paraphrase Havel, the roots of politics are moral and citizens must take action in support of their values.

SOME DEFINITIONS

Arts organizations are usually incorporated as public charities or nonprofit corporations, classified by the Internal Revenue Service (IRS) as 501(c)3 organizations because of their educational mission. The 501(c)3 designation allows donors to the charity to deduct their contributions on their federal income tax returns. This deduction reduces the taxpayer's gross income, thereby reducing the tax paid to the government. For example, a taxpayer in the 28-percent tax bracket could see her taxes reduced by $28 on a $100 donation. The charity receives $100, while the net cost of the donation to the tax-paying donor is $72.

In other words, contributions to nonprofit arts organizations are subsidized by the federal government. Without the tax deduction, the $28 in the above example would have been paid in taxes to the government. The tax deduction essentially allows the taxpayer to redirect public money. The charity provides a service to the public that the government supports. However, to protect the public from unfair use of this subsidy, government requires transparency, disclosure, and some restrictions.

Most arts organizations understand the need for transparency and reporting. However, many arts leaders misunderstand the restrictions. For the following discussion of IRS rules and restrictions, it helps to understand these definitions:

- **Political campaign intervention.** Political campaign intervention is prohibited. A 501(c)3 cannot use its resources to support or oppose any candidate for elected office or any political party.
- **Partisan vs. non-partisan election activity.** Partisan election activity is prohibited. Partisan activity seeks to boost one political party or one candidate over another. Non-partisan election activity is permitted. Non-partisan activity promotes citizen participation in the political process. For example, partisan activity would be registering only Republicans to vote. Non-partisan activity would be registering any and all new voters regardless of party affiliation.
- **Lobbying and Advocacy.** Lobbying and advocacy are permitted within a limit. The IRS defines lobbying and advocacy as any effort to influence the outcome of specific legislation. Nonprofits are generally prohibited from lobbying, but they have every right to advocate for public policy that they support. Saying that the arts strengthen communities and should be supported by the government is not lobbying. However, when the policy becomes legislation—such as Senate Bill 2342 or "An Act to Protect Wildlife"—then the ability to advocate is slightly limited.

What are the IRS limits on nonprofit advocacy?

According to IRS rules:

> In general, no organization may qualify for section 501(c)3 status if a *substantial part* of its activities [emphasis added] is attempting to influence legislation (commonly known as *lobbying*). A 501(c)3 organization may engage in some lobbying, but too much lobbying activity risks loss of tax-exempt status.[4]

Note that this is not a blanket prohibition against any lobbying or advocacy activity. However, what constitutes "a substantial part" is open to interpretation. Still, assume for a moment that "substantial part" could be defined as a percentage of a nonprofit organization's budget: it is very unlikely that an arts organization with an annual budget of $3 million would spend $150,000 (5%) on lobbying. Recognizing that, Congress has supported the fair use of advocacy by nonprofits by creating the 501(h) election. 501(h) allows an eligible 501(c)3 organization to formally choose to limit its expenditures to influence legislation at 20 percent of its mission-related expenditures.

What is not subject to interpretation is the right of nonprofits to engage in advocacy and civic engagement, supporting the arts in general and seeking assistance in achieving their mission as part of their responsibility to serve their community.

See the Appendix for "How Much Advocacy Can a Nonprofit Do?"

Arts and Culture as a Public Issue

The arts provide a public benefit. They strengthen our communities and improve our schools. The arts educate and challenge our minds. Should government, then, support the arts to enhance those public benefits? This has been an issue since the earliest days of our republic.

John Adams, later the second president of the United States, drafted the Constitution of the Commonwealth of Massachusetts, the first state Constitution, adopted in 1780 and later a model for the federal Constitution. The Massachusetts Constitution assigned to government a responsibility to support arts and culture:

> … it shall be the duty of legislatures and magistrates, in all future periods of this commonwealth, to cherish the interests of literature and the sciences …. to encourage private societies and public institutions, for the promotion of agriculture, arts, sciences, commerce, trades, manufactures, and a natural history of the country.[5]

Adams establishes that the promotion of the arts, literature, and sciences is a shared responsibility between public and private institutions. That same year, in a letter to his wife, Abigail, Adams described his vision of how a maturing society would be reflected in his own family:

> I must study politics and war that my sons may have liberty to study mathematics and philosophy. My sons ought to study mathematics and philosophy, geography, natural history and naval architecture, navigation, commerce and agriculture, in order to give their children a right to study painting, poetry, music, architecture, statuary, tapestry, and porcelain.[6]

Adams positioned the arts as an ideal—the natural outgrowth of commerce and government. Nevertheless, the government's role in the promotion of the arts has been an evolving and controversial issue since 1780. The question is still debated in the United States: how should government promote the arts?

In the 17th and 18th centuries, the arts were considered instructive repositories of American values. Portraits of religious and political leaders displayed their virtues—piety, industry, frugality, seriousness—as an inspiration. In the early 19th century, the government commissioned artworks to provide similar inspiration in public buildings. Congress commissioned four historical paintings for the Capitol rotunda at a cost of $32,000. When they were hung in 1826, one Congressman said he wouldn't give 32 cents for them. Another said that if the "Fine Arts cannot thrive without government jobs … let them fail."[7]

In 1835, Alexis de Tocqueville observed the shortage of fine art in the United States, noting that in a democracy, citizens "will habitually prefer the useful to the beautiful."[8] Should government support the arts for its usefulness or for its intrinsic values? With little exception, in the 19th century, government supported the arts for its utility, its instrumental benefits. For example, Massachusetts became the first state to institute statewide arts education in the public schools through the Free Instruction in Drawing Act of 1870. Was Massachusetts addressing the "shortage of fine art?" In fact, arts education was established to serve the economic interests of the state's leading manufacturers, who had petitioned for drawing instruction because, as they complained, "We are becoming tired of sending so many millions to Europe for articles that we might produce cheaper at home if we had skillful designers."[9]

Aside from commissioned work, the government first provided funds directly to artists during the Great Depression, through the Works Progress Administration (W.P.A.) jobs program. Artists were among the unemployed, so the government put them to work—for a paycheck, not for the sake of the art itself. A precedent was established, though, and in the next 30 years artists and arts supporters advocated for an increased governmental role in the arts. The 1930s marked a significant change in American government. Many issues that were previously private concerns, such as health care, retirement, the environment, transportation, and housing, became public issues. As a society, we now recognize that government plays a role in individual health care and retirement.

Arts and culture have seen a similar, though more recent, transformation. In 1965, the National Endowments for the Arts (NEA) and Humanities (NEH) were established. To meet federal requirements for receiving NEA funds, the fifty states and six territories quickly established state arts agencies. By the end of the 1960s, every state had an arts agency and most major cities devoted public funds to support arts and culture using a wide variety of funding mechanisms.

In 2013, local, state, and federal governments invested $1.14 billion in the arts.[10]

- County and municipal governments: $727 million
- State and regional arts agencies: $279 million
- NEA: $139 million

Culture, then, is part of the public purse at all levels of government. The laws, regulations, and budget allocations—public policy developed through politics— that benefit arts and culture are also subject to the constant tug and pull of political debate. Public funding for the arts, sciences, and humanities typically rises gradually during times of economic growth, followed by steep reductions during lean times. State funding for arts and culture rises and falls with the economic tides. In the past decade, state arts budgets have been slashed and, in some cases, nearly eliminated. Political priorities shifted to stimulating state economies through job creation and budget balancing. State spending was scrutinized for "return on investment." In many states, cultural funding was an easy target, even though cultural spending was typically less than half of one percent (.5%) of a state's total budget.

The competition for public funding is intense. Arts advocates must demonstrate the public value earned for public investment.

FOUR LEVELS OF GOVERNMENT

The United States has four levels of government: federal, state, county, and municipal, each having jurisdiction over specific geographic areas. The lines of authority overlap on some issues like health care and education, but in general, each level of government affects cultural organizations in different areas of operation.

The federal government provides direct funding to cultural organizations through grants and earmarks, and provides indirect subsidy by granting tax-exempt status. Since the federal tax code's 501(c)3 designation allows donors to take a federal income tax deduction for gifts to nonprofit, tax-exempt organizations, tax-deductible contributions are an invaluable form of public support to nonprofits of all kinds. The *Chronicle of Philanthropy* used IRS data to determine that in 2012, taxpayers claimed $180 billion in charitable-giving deductions. How important is the tax incentive for private donations? The *Chronicle of Philanthropy*, using *Giving USA* data, estimates that $180 billion in deductions is approximately 80 percent of all charitable giving.[11]

Would donors give to 501(c)3 organizations regardless of the tax deduction? There is no clear answer, though the tax deduction is used or factored into $4 out of every $5 donated. Nor is it clear how much of the $180 billion deducted in 2012 went to cultural organizations. However, it is clear that the deduction for cultural organizations is fundamental: the federal government has allowed a cultural tax deduction since the establishment of the income tax in 1917. Often overlooked, this tax policy demonstrates that funding the arts is important to the country.

The federal government also provides funding for cultural organizations through the National Endowment for the Arts (NEA). Most state arts agencies were created after 1965, when the federal government required one for a state to be eligible for NEA funding. Under current law, the NEA must direct 40 percent of its funding to state arts agencies.

State governments are a major source of the public funding for cultural organizations, including NEA funding directed to state arts agencies and funding appropriated by state governments. There is a wide disparity in state funding for arts and culture. Some states provide generous support, while others don't. State governments must balance their budgets, so when state revenues fall during tough economic times, state spending falls. Consequently, state cultural funding has seen many peaks and valleys, with increases in prosperous times, followed by funding cuts during lean times, as shown in Figure 1.

States can also assist arts and culture through tourism promotion, percent-for-art-programs, and statewide arts education mandates, among others.

Local governments—counties, cities, and towns—provide the largest source of public funding for the arts, nearly 74 percent more than direct state and federal support combined in 2013. Local governments control the nuts and bolts of an organization's day-to-day operations, providing mundane but critical services such as police and fire protection, garbage removal, water, utilities, parking, and street repair.

Local governments are also critical to long-term planning through zoning regulations, building and fire codes, and infrastructure investment. For example, a museum's plan to expand its load-in facilities requires city permission for new construction. Or a performing hall might seek to expand its seating and ask the city to increase nearby parking facilities. Local governments can assist in promoting cultural organizations through directional street signs or streetlight banners.

In the last 15 years, many cities have invested in new or restored performing arts centers as an anchor for downtown economic development. The cities range from large to small throughout the country,

Figure 1. Federal, State and Local Government Arts Funding, 1992–2012

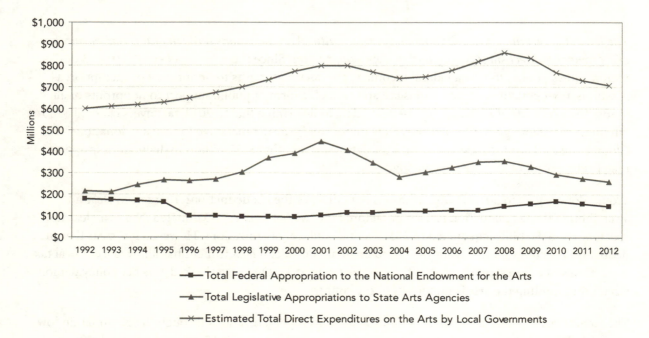

Graph courtesy of National Assembly of State Arts Agencies (NASAA). Constant dollar adjustments for inflation are calculated using Bureau of Labor Statistics Consumer Price Index (CPI) figures with a base year of 1992. Fiscal year 2013 forecasts for state arts agencies are available from www.nasaa-arts.org.

including Philadelphia, PA; Appleton, WI; Kansas City, MO; Salt Lake City, UT; Worcester, MA; and Charleston, SC.

OTHER ADVOCACY AUDIENCES

Advocacy is more than working to influence public policy. The maintenance and development of our cultural resources are, as John Adams wrote, a shared responsibility among individuals, the private sector, and the public sector. We must advocate, that is, effectively communicate the value of arts and culture, to multiple audiences. These include charitable foundations, large and small businesses, the media, and individuals.

Foundations are as many and varied as individuals in the world. But they are dedicated to promoting the public good through their giving. Since cultural organizations contribute to the public good and strengthen communities, through advocacy we can persuade more foundations to include arts and culture in their funding priorities. Many foundations support their communities through arts grants, yet, like many arts leaders, they may shy away from supporting arts advocacy, missing the opportunity to strengthen the cultural environment. Foundations can support advocacy with the same limitations as other nonprofits.

Businesses work to make a profit. However, they often recognize that a stronger community creates a better economic climate for business. Businesses can assist cultural organizations through sponsorships, program advertising, employee incentive programs, and direct contributions. Consider the many businesses that benefit from cultural organizations: neighborhood restaurants, vendors, and printers, to name a few. Far-sighted business leaders learned long ago that supporting their community enhances business in the long run.

Nonprofit cultural organizations are also businesses, concerned about costs, payroll, capital investment, and long-term planning like any other business. Both types of businesses are incorporated under IRS and state regulations. The difference between nonprofit and for-profit corporations is the mission. Traditional businesses earn profits to be distributed to their owners or shareholders. A nonprofit reinvests any income over expenses back into the mission of the organization.

Cultural leaders should participate in community and business forums. Local Chambers of Commerce and service clubs connect arts leaders with business leaders. These forums offer advocacy opportunities for describing the community value of your arts organization. Working effectively with business leaders also can also connect arts leaders with individual donors.

The media—newspapers, radio, television, magazines, and the Internet—distribute a daily barrage of news, stories, data, and images that shape how citizens see their society. Media create the context for political debate and monitor public perception, which is then interpreted by political leaders. Effective advocacy needs a media strategy. Cultural leaders should communicate with the press—formally and informally—and develop relationships with the local media. A long-term relationship with a reporter requires that one be honest, helpful, and prompt (they are always on deadline.) With the deluge of daily information, it can seem impossible to make your voice heard. But today's media need new stories every day. Create a narrative that truthfully serves your goals and share it freely.

On the Internet and social media, the cultural organization becomes its own reporter, creating, reporting, and publishing its own news. To be successful, your organization must provide accurate, entertaining information. Like a long-term plan, your organization must develop a social media strategy by identifying audiences and cultivating followers through compelling visual content, special promotions, and regular updates. Consistent blogging and linked social media platforms like Twitter and Facebook allow audiences to share, interact, and talk back. What niche does your organization fill? The goal is to determine what's distinctive about your organization and create an online community of supporters. For example, a craft museum may focus on regional crafts and local artisans. An art museum could carve out expertise in a period of art history or painting styles.

Every person you meet is a potential voter and we often overlook the vital one-to-one advocacy we can do. In fact, each individual represents more than one vote and more than one opinion. Everyone has a network of friends, family, and contacts. When you share your story with one person, you are also linking to an extended network. A wise campaigner once said, "Every election is won one vote at a time." That is equally true in advocacy campaigns.

Cultural organizations interact daily with government, ranging from the mundane (garbage removal) to the empowering (a federal grant for new programming). While each organization faces distinct challenges, all cultural organizations must engage in advocacy to achieve their missions. Advocacy plays a critical role in building public understanding of the value of arts and culture and the role of government. As you advocate in the political arena, you are also communicating to the general public. Likewise, advocating with foundations, businesses, individuals, and the media will build broader public support that will help convince elected officials.

See "The Advocacy Continuum" in the Appendix for an inventory of the many ways to advocate.

Building a Foundation for Your Advocacy

Some cultural leaders are reluctant to approach government. They may mistakenly believe that the tax-exempt status of their organization prevents them from engaging in advocacy. They may be unfamiliar with and even intimidated by the political world, or, as nonprofits functioning in a profit-driven society, they may feel that they lack the power to influence government.

But you are only powerless if you do nothing. You have sources of political power that you can cultivate. You can recruit allies who support your cause.

YOUR ADVOCACY NETWORK

The Advocacy Inventory

First, make a list of everyone you know, including family, co-workers, friends, and neighbors. This is the beginning of your advocacy network. Think of all the people connected with the organization—board members, donors, volunteers, vendors, and patrons. All of these people believe in the mission of the organization and can be recruited for an advocacy network. As each person has his or her own network, the list quickly grows. You have more power than you think. The goal is to harness and apply that power. That is effective advocacy.

The board of directors or trustees should be the leaders of an organization's advocacy. They have wealth, connections, and expertise. They help the organization connect with its community as eyes and ears and as spokespersons. Directors are effective advocates because they are not acting out of self-interest. They are volunteers dedicated to the mission and to improving the community. Political and public advocacy is a critical board responsibility.

The next step in the advocacy inventory is to chronicle how the broader community benefits from the organization.

Most important, the organization plays a cultural role in the community. But have you considered its economic, social, and educational contributions? Cultural organizations provide educational programs for school children, adults, and seniors. They anchor a neighborhood. And, like any other business, they create jobs, generating tax revenue through their payrolls. Here are some questions to answer for your advocacy inventory:

- What role does your organization play in the community?
- Who benefits from its services?
- How many full- and part-time employees are there?
- What is the total payroll?
- What are the organization's total expenditures in the community?
- Which local businesses are regular vendors?
- Which businesses indirectly benefit from your organization, such as nearby restaurants, hotels, coffee shops, and bookstores?
- Which schools and how many students benefit from the organization?

- How does your organization foster a spirit of community in the neighborhood and town?
- Which social service and civic agencies collaborate with or benefit from your organization?

Many of these questions address the local economic impact of your nonprofit organization, and answers can be found relatively quickly through various state arts agencies, as well as Americans for the Arts' Prosperity Index, WESTAF's Cultural Vitality Index, and the New England Foundation for the Arts. The mission of your cultural organization is vital to you, your colleagues, and your patrons. However, outside of the cultural world, not everyone shares this view of the importance of arts and culture. Economic impact studies are valuable because they offer another measure of community value, readily understood in business and political spheres. Though the organization is not a for-profit business, it is still a business with economic impact: making payroll, paying vendors, paying employment taxes, paying utilities, and filing tax reports.

Defining economic value is critical to successful advocacy, but it is not the only way to describe the value created by a cultural organization. The organization may educate young people; support tourism by drawing people to the region; help youth-at-risk; provide senior citizens with opportunities for creative activity and intellectual stimulation; be a catalyst for neighborhood revitalization; serve as a forum for cultural exchange to strengthen bonds between diverse communities.

While the value of your cultural organization grows out of its educational/cultural mission, it extends to other areas. Successful advocacy requires telling the full story of your organization, including its economic value.

Key Allies

Local, state, and national advocacy groups are part of your advocacy inventory. These groups have government contacts and strategic insights gained through experience with cultural issues and politics. Advocacy groups like Americans for the Arts and state arts advocacy groups have conducted valuable research to support and inform your advocacy. Americans for the Arts posts extensive information and current news on its website (www.americansforthearts.org) and links to advocacy software that allows arts supporters to send emails to elected officials quickly and efficiently.

Currently, almost all states have arts advocacy organizations. The average state advocacy group functions with a limited budget and one full-time employee. Many advocacy groups are run by volunteers. But all of these organizations provide expertise to answer your questions and networks to facilitate both state and local advocacy. Many cities and towns also have local arts agencies dedicated to supporting arts organizations and coordinating advocacy.

By working with established advocacy groups, you may find a network of arts organizations with similar goals. In our political system, there is strength in numbers. Advocacy groups connect diverse colleagues to establish broad goals and increase political effectiveness. Local, state, and national advocacy groups benefit from this support.

YOUR ADVOCACY GOALS

After careful assessment of the cultural, economic, and community value created by your organization, the next step is to determine your advocacy goals. The broadest goal is to increase public recognition of the value of the cultural organization and of the arts and humanities in general. It is also important to identify goals that can provide assistance to the organization's mission. It may be a general goal, such as increased operational support from the state arts agency, or it may be specific to the organization, such as a zoning variance from the municipal planning commission.

Advocacy goals must dovetail with your strategic plan. Too often, planners and cultural leaders neglect advocacy, effectively ruling out any assistance governments might provide.

Government actions affect cultural organizations in myriad ways beyond public funding. For example, municipal budget cuts could reduce subsidies for school bus transportation, forcing schools to cancel field trips to the cultural organization. Tax laws, too, have significant consequences for arts organizations. For example, one state tried to close a loophole in the income tax withholding laws and, as an unintended consequence, forced cultural organizations to withhold tax in advance on exempt international performers.

Achieving advocacy goals will take time. Government moves slowly and serves constituencies more than individual organizations. But advocacy does bring results. The NEA, established in 1965, would not have been created without advocacy that can be traced back to 1948 and, arguably, even earlier. Today, advocacy success can come much sooner because it builds on the continuing efforts of cultural advocates over many years. Making advocacy a part of your daily work will pay benefits down the road—for the organization, peer organizations across the nation, and the future of arts and culture.

Planning and Executing the Campaign

Advocacy takes time: plan for immediate, mid-term, and long-range goals.

SETTING THE AGENDA

Consider how many ways a cultural organization interacts with government at all levels. How do government policies help or impede the organization's mission? Prepare an advocacy assessment, and determine which issues are the most important. This assessment will range from the nuts and bolts of daily operations (garbage removal, street signs, utilities, and so on) to the visionary (substantial grants for capital improvements.) Here are some examples of typical government interaction for a cultural nonprofit:

- Food and beverage license
- Fire and building safety inspections
- Government-supported infrastructure such as access roads
- Police and public safety
- Federal and state filing requirements
- Payroll taxes
- Operating support grants
- School funding for student field trips
- Tourism signs on state highways and sign permits
- Publicity opportunity through convention and visitors bureaus
- Water and sewer capacity

- Federal grants from the NEA, the Institute of Museum and Library Services (IMLS), the Department of Transportation, and more
- Bonded loan pools for economic development
- Entertainment tax on tickets
- Changes in insurance regulations such as liability, unemployment, and health insurance for employees
- Tax incentives for charitable contributions
- Zoning variances

Cultural leaders may know how to apply for a grant from the state arts agency, but what about bonding, insurance regulations, or federal funds from unexpected sources? Probably not. You don't need to know the answers to every question; instead, know whom to ask. One of the best sources is an elected official, typically your state legislator.

With the completed list, rank priorities from two perspectives. First, what are the most beneficial and most urgent for the organization? The assessment of advocacy goals must be coordinated with the organization's long-term goals and strategic plan. Rank the goals in order of urgency, strategic importance, and timing. Is the first priority more parking? more operating support? better nighttime security? zoning permits for artist live-work space? a capital loan for new construction? It may be that the first goal is more parking, but does that fit with the goal of building an addition in three years' time?

The second perspective is a realistic assessment of what can be achieved. Which of these goals can be solved by a phone call or a meeting? Which goals require a longer time to achieve? What can be achieved in conjunction with the state advocacy group? What can you achieve with key allies? For example, if the priority is increased operating support from the state arts agency, then join forces with the state advocacy group.

Effective advocacy requires a balance between what is possible and what is ideal. Politics has been called the art of the possible, and no elected official, no matter how brilliant or powerful, can make all your dreams come true. Your organization's advocacy agenda will evolve through learning what is feasible by consulting board members, staff, leaders, and elected officials. The agenda is formed by blending what is best for the organization with what is politically possible.

MAKE A SPECIFIC REQUEST

Now that the agenda has been defined, state what you want in the clearest terms possible. You may have identified a broad issue like capital funding as your goal. However, in formal meetings with elected officials, be more specific. Examples of specific requests include:

- "We need a capital grant for $3.7 million, which will be matched two-to-one by private funding, to expand our educational wing."
- "Our audiences have grown, so we need the city to help us find 32 more parking spaces within a two-block radius of our theatre."
- "We would like you to reduce filing costs for small nonprofit cultural organizations by voting yes on the public charities bill, House bill #4234."
- "Vote yes for a 22% increase in funding for the state arts agency."

> **Do You Need A Lobbyist?**
>
> A lobbyist cannot solve all political problems, but there are times to hire a good one. There are also times to keep your checkbook in your pocket. The first step in making the decision is to define your political goals. What do you hope to achieve? An experienced lobbyist can assist with all aspects of advocacy. They can design your campaign, devise strategy, write and prepare lobbying material, provide training, assist in developing your advocacy network, set up constituent meetings, coordinate media relations, and, of course, do the traditional buttonholing of key legislators.
>
> However, a lobbyist is not a substitute for the work you must to do, such as setting goals, building an advocacy network, meeting personally with state legislators, and long-range planning. But the right lobbyist can be the most important ally you'll ever have. Look for someone who understands the legislature, who has a solid reputation for integrity, and who can help you fill the missing pieces of your advocacy inventory. Most of all, find a lobbyist who is a good personality fit and is someone you can work with easily.

Most legislators want to help, but they need to know what to do. Simply asking for support for arts and culture is too vague—it's easy for a legislator to say she supports the arts. Instead, make clear, detailed requests. Legislators will often say how much they love the arts, but the proof of their commitment is in their votes and actions on specific requests.

CREATING THE MESSAGE

With or without a lobbyist, you, as a cultural leader, will be directly engaged in cultural advocacy. Politics depends on personal relationships. Just as you would cultivate a relationship with a significant donor, you need to work with politicians and elected officials. Politicians don't want a relationship with an institution. Institutions don't vote. Politicians want a relationship with you.

The first step is to know what you are asking for. The second step is to answer why you are asking—not just why it is good for your organization, but more important, why it is good for the elected official's constituency. Your message serves not only as a rationale for your request, but also as a call to action. You need to explain why an expansion of your facility is good for the community. To receive public support, you must demonstrate public benefit. For example, in Massachusetts, a campaign for cultural facilities funding argued that upgrading the state's aging cultural facilities formed the infrastructure for tourism, the state's third-largest industry. The message linked investment in cultural facilities as a strategic investment in the broader economy.

Creating your campaign message means capturing the most significant public benefits in a concise, memorable way. Everyone—especially a politician—is inundated with messages clamoring for her attention. You don't need to outshine Madison Avenue. But, you need a compelling reason told with clarity: "This funding will allow us to create five full-time jobs and allow 125 low-income students to participate in our after-school programs."

The message and its accompanying justification will shift, depending on the audience. If your elected official is committed to economic development, you will emphasize the jobs created and the amount of local spending. If she is working on juvenile justice issues, you will talk about how you serve at-risk youths. In a campaign for facilities funding, you would emphasize different benefits based on each legislator's interests. Here are three messages designed for three different legislators:

> - "Facilities funding will provide much-needed capital support to help the concert hall in your district repair its roof."
> - "Facilities funding will create a lot of construction jobs, particularly for skilled, union workers in your district."
> - "The art museum in your district provides significant after-school education for school children. This money will allow that program to have its own facility."

There are two key elements in these messages. Notice that the phrase "in your district" is in all three messages. All politics is local. A legislator's job is to help her district; that's who "hired" her by electing her. You are more likely to win her support by demonstrating the benefits of your issue to the people of her district.

Second, each message answers the first questions everyone asks: "What's in it for me and why should I care?" You are passionate about your work. But never assume that the world shares your view of the inherent value of arts and culture. Many do, but often the ones who don't are sitting in the legislature or Congress. Always remember that public dollars must be invested for public benefit, and the more tangible the benefit, the easier it is for politicians to understand.

THE CAMPAIGN

Now, you design your campaign. The first question to ask is "Who decides?" Who has the power to enact your proposal or address your concern? Is it the zoning board, the legislature, a bureaucrat in the Department of Education, or the city council? Is it one person or a majority of the legislature?

Usually, you will be trying to persuade the majority of a deliberative body, like a legislature or county board of supervisors. There are a variety of strategies to build a majority (50%+1) for your side. You can try to persuade the leadership, such as the Speaker of the House or a powerful committee chair, to champion your cause. Legislators need favors from leadership and will often support an initiative because their leadership supports it.

Another tactic is to bring political pressure from outside the deliberative chamber demonstrating popular support among voters. This entails a grassroots campaign that could include personal letters, visits, emails, postcards, rallies, petitions, and letters to the editor. A grassroots campaign requires that you build and activate your advocacy network.

Every political situation is different. Your strategies and tactics—your campaign—will vary according to the situation and your resources. A campaign is a set of planned and coordinated activities to map out who will do what tasks and when will they be done. The following are activities that may be part of a campaign:

- Schedule meetings with your core activists
- Collect and interpret any necessary research, such as economic impact studies
- Identify your supporters and how you will communicate with them (for example, a phone tree or email network)
- Strategize ways to connect with decision makers
- Develop a newspaper strategy, including press releases, editorial endorsements, op-ed pieces, and letters to the editor

- Develop a media strategy to put your spokespersons on the air
- Write a one-page summary of your goals and their value, to distribute to decision makers
- Meet with decision makers
- Coordinate letter writing campaign to decision-makers
- Organize a rally at the capitol, such as an arts advocacy day
- Celebrate your victories
- Thank everyone involved, particularly decision-makers, both privately and publically

See the Appendix for the layout of a sample campaign in "Restoring Our Competitive Advantage."

KNOW YOUR ELECTED OFFICIALS AND LEGISLATORS

People enter public service and politics for honorable reasons—they want to help people—and they need to be recognized for their contributions. Along the way, they encounter endless demands on their time and energy, and they endure long hours and frustration. Merely becoming a candidate is enough to earn distrust and hostility from some people. Yet, at their core, every elected official entered politics to make a difference for his or her constituents. Most legislators want to help you.

However, politics is a two-way street. You will succeed when there is mutual benefit. You know what you hope to achieve, but what does your legislator need?

To do their jobs, elected officials need the voters to get to know their values and goals. This communication and recognition develops into the political capital necessary for the elected official to represent the voters. Recognition comes in many forms, but ultimately, political recognition depends on elections. In order to achieve her goals (and yours), your legislator must be elected (and re-elected). Therefore, her goals include satisfying 50%+1 of the voters in her district. Her job is not to work for the greater good of all—though she may want to. Her job is to represent the voters in the district that elected her. "All politics is local."

Therefore, you must establish a relationship with legislators just as you would with a major donor. Your first steps are to learn about your legislator—her background, the issues she focuses on, her ambitions, and her political record. The more you learn about her, the easier it will be to connect your issue to her concerns. For example, if she is concerned about the economy, your discussions with her will focus on the local economic impact of your cultural organization. If she is interested in education, you will emphasize the educational services your organization provides.

The consistent message to your legislator is how your organization benefits the people in her district. This includes the inherent value of your mission as well as how many local people are served, how many tourists are drawn to the area (boosting the local economy), how much is spent on local vendors, how many people work for the organization, how much tax revenue is generated, and so on.

You cannot develop a relationship in one 15-minute meeting during advocacy day at the capitol. It takes time and persistence. Invite your legislators to events; invite them to tour your facility. Always remember that legislators need recognition, so never pass up an opportunity to introduce and thank your legislators to the audience. Ask the legislator to speak at appropriate events. Any time that you can put a legislator in front of an audience and make her look good, you are assisting her in her job.

That job includes winning elections. As an individual, you can and should become involved in campaigns so that your friends and allies win elections—the political recognition that counts the most. Get involved in an election as a private citizen. By law, you cannot use the name, facilities, resources, or staff time of a 501(c)3 in support of a candidate for elected office. However, you do not give up your first amendment rights when you work for a nonprofit. Away from your job, you have every right to fully participate in elections. You, your staff, trustees, and directors, as private citizens, all have the right to engage in all aspects of elections.

There are three ways to get involved in campaigns:

- First and foremost, you must vote. Voting is your admission ticket to the political process.
- Second, Contribute money to your candidates' campaign. You don't need to give a lot of money—candidates welcome contribution because it represents a commitment to their candidacy. Consider hosting a fundraising event for your candidate, even if all your guests write small checks. This gives the candidate two important things: needed campaign funds and a chance to meet voters. Your fundraiser could be a neighborhood coffee, a cookout, or a cocktail party at someone's home. Remember, a 501(c)3 cannot take sides in a partisan election, so be sure to host your political events separate from your cultural organization in private homes or commercial establishments.
- Third, Volunteer to work in the campaign. Candidates may not immediately remember every contributor, but they never forget the volunteer who walked the streets with them. Offer to go door-knocking with your candidate or help organize an event. If you're not comfortable door-knocking, volunteer in the campaign office. There is always more work to be done in a political campaign. One of the most valuable tools in legislative campaigns is writing postcards to friends urging them to vote for your candidate. For the right candidate, you should activate your private advocacy network to rally voters.

MEETING IN PERSON

Ideally, you have met your legislators in the district. Now, they are in session at the capitol and you need to approach them on your issue. Or, you may have an urgent issue that occurs before you have met your legislator or elected official. What's the most effective way for you and your advocacy network to communicate? Legislators receive a barrage of communications, so they and their staff members quickly learn to prioritize. The most important communications come from constituents in the district.

The most effective communication is meeting with the legislator in her office. This allows for discussion and both sides can gauge the intensity of commitment. Prepare for your meeting by designating speakers, honing your talking points, and writing brief, yet informative materials on your issue. Do your homework, even if you've already met the legislator in the district: What committees does he serve on? What are her political interests? You should read about your legislator on websites and political almanacs, and follow his/her tweets or blog posts. Ask your state advocacy group, ask your board members and ask people in the district for their input. Knowing the legislator allows you to tailor your message and shape the conversation.

Begin with a specific request: "We are here to ask for your support on House Bill 4234." Keep your talking points precise. Allow time for the legislator to ask questions. If you don't know the answer to a question, say so and promise to provide the information as soon as possible.

Do not expect the legislator to make a commitment to your request right away. Legislators need to balance many conflicting interests and any worthy issue requires time for consideration. End the discussion by repeating your specific request and thanking the legislator for his time and consideration. Give the legislator your briefing material, which contains a succinct (one-page) summary of the pertinent information about your issue. You should be able to explain your request and its benefits in five minutes or less. Be informed, because you want your legislator to value you as a resource for information about the arts community.

Keep the meeting on track. You are there for one reason—asking for support for House Bill 4234. If the legislator wants to discuss baseball or an unrelated issue, politely return the conversation to your issue.

Legislative meetings should be short and concise. The demands on the legislator's time are intense. In a typical day, a legislator must bounce from meeting to meeting and from subject to subject. Follow up your meeting with a thank-you note, and then stay in touch. Put him on your mailing list. Give him a call when there is an opportunity to appear before the public or at a gathering with a significant number of voters.

Sometimes you will be asked to meet with the elected official's staff. Talking to staff members is as valuable as talking to the elected official. Because legislators deal with so many issues, they rely on staff to learn about an issue in depth. The information that the staff collects is vital to the legislator's decisions. Get to know the official's aides—they can be helpful.

COMMUNICATING IN WRITING

We live in an era of instant communication. But, e-mail and the Internet have not surpassed the effectiveness of direct human communication—face-to-face.

If you can't meet, though, write a letter that is thoughtful and respectful. The effort you make demonstrates the importance of the issue. Identify yourself as a constituent and include your address. Make your letter straight and to the point. Communication with legislators should always be clear and concise.

State why you care and your relationship to it. State how the issue impacts the legislator's district. Stating your views clearly is the first priority of your personal communication, but another goal is to begin a dialogue with the legislator. You can help ensure a response by making a request, such as asking for information, a copy of the bill, or for help. A personal request lifts your letter out of the pile of opinions to be counted and moves it to the correspondence file.

How many letters does it take to have an impact on a state legislator? Not as many as you may think. Depending on the size of the district, five to ten letters on the same subject will get the legislator's attention.

Form letters, postcards, and standardized emails are less effective. How committed are you to your cause if you can only spare a few seconds to communicate it? However, these communications are sometimes counted by staffers, particularly if many of them come from inside the district. Email and social media on the Internet allow you to expand your advocacy network, urging hundreds, even thousands of supporters to take action. However, emails can be effective only if they are not all the same. Like a thoughtful letter, each email should be customized by each advocate.

The least effective advocacy tool is the petition. Most people will sign anything when asked. A measure of the effectiveness of your communication is to ask how much energy you put into it: did you sign something at the grocery store, click on a website, or did you compose a thoughtful personal letter?

Hierarchy of contact, from most to least effective:

1. Meet with your legislator either face-to-face or by phone. You tell your own story in your own words about why this issue is important.

2. Write a letter telling your own story and concerns.

3. Participate in a postcard or email drive, but still include a personal message.

4. Simply sign a postcard or email.

5. Sign a petition.

Always treat legislators with respect. They have made a sacrifice of time and sometimes money to serve you. Legislators are not paid well, typically making much less in public office than they could in their chosen profession. So you have to find a balance between respect and persistence. Legislators have private lives and families. Respect that. There is a time and place for discussion of your issues. Say hello to your legislator in the grocery store, but pick another time for debate and discussion. Treating your legislators with respect also shows respect for the office and the institutions of our democracy—they are doing the people's work. Treating elected officials with respect is more than good manners—it's good politics. You never know when the tides will change and the legislator who opposed you on one issue becomes your new ally on another.

Make Advocacy Part of Your Daily Mission

An elected official makes decisions based on her perception of the public good and how it impacts the people in her district. Her perception of what the public wants grows from a variety of sources, such as the media, public opinion polls, lobbyists, and political advisors. But for most elected officials, the most important sources are the conversations, formal and informal, with voters in the district. To an elected official, everyone is a potential voter. That's why arts advocacy must go beyond elected officials. The average voter in a casual conversation helps a legislator understand what's best for the district.

Therefore, the more you spread the word about the public benefit of your issue, your organization, and the arts in general, the more likely elected officials will recognize the value of the arts. Advocacy works one voter at a time, so your likely supporter could be anyone you meet. Cultural leaders, whether volunteer trustees or paid staff, should make advocacy a part of their daily mission. The process of converting elected officials into active supporters begins with earning public support. Arts advocacy will be successful in the long run when the average voter understands the benefits of government support for the arts.

Public funding for arts and culture has an impact on the economy. It has an impact on education. It spurs economic development. It sparks revitalization of neighborhoods. It supports the cultural resources that attract tourists. To succeed in these broad and diverse missions, the cultural community needs support through public policy that provides adequate funding, infrastructure support, arts education in public schools, and a chance to participate in the debate on the future.

Arts and cultural organizations contribute far more to our communities than jobs and economic impact. They are integral to education, serving as classrooms during and after school. They provide programs that give at-risk youth and disadvantaged citizens the empowerment of self-expression. They are the distinctive institutions that build community pride. They challenge our assumptions, open our eyes, and nourish our society.

Simple statistics cannot measure the depth and breadth of the contributions of cultural organizations. Arts and cultural organizations are good for our schools, our communities, our economy, and our souls. We must engage in consistent advocacy, so that public investment in arts and culture benefits all the citizens for the common good.

Endnotes

1. Quoted by Clement Attlee in Francis Williams, *A Prime Minister Remembers*, 1961.
2. Harold Lasswell, Politics: *Who Gets What, When, How,* 1936.
3. Vaclav Havel, *Summer Meditations: Politics, Morality and Civility,* 1993.
4. See Charities-&-Non-Profits/Lobbying at www.irs.gov.
5. Constitution of the Commonwealth of Massachusetts, Chapter V, Section II. malegislature.gov/Laws/Constitution
6. Letter from John Adams to Abigail Adams, post 12 May 1780 [electronic edition], Adams Family Papers: An Electronic Archive, Massachusetts Historical Society, www.masshist.org.
7. Cited by David A. Smith in *Money for Art: The Tangled Web of Art and Politics in American Democracy*, 2008.
8. Alexis de Tocqueville, *Democracy in America*, vol. 1, chapter 1; 1835, reprint 2000.
9. Paul E. Bolin, "The Massachusetts Drawing Act of 1870: Industrial Mandate or Democratic Maneuver?" In Donald Soucy and Mary Ann Stankiewicz, *Framing the Past: Essays on Art Education, National Art Education Association,* 1990, www.noteaccess.com.
10. Public Funding for the Arts: 2013 Update, Grantmakers in the Arts, www.giarts.org.
11. Alex Daniels, "As Wealthy Give Smaller Share of Income to Charity, Middle Class Digs Deeper," *The Chronicle of Philanthropy,* Oct. 5, 2014, www.philanthropy.com.

Appendix

SEGMENT 1: HOW MUCH ADVOCACY CAN A NONPROFIT DO?

Nonprofit organizations have every right to engage in advocacy. You can (and should) talk to your elected officials about anything related to your work, including the necessity of government funding. Many nonprofit leaders misunderstand their advocacy rights, and mistakenly view the legal limitations as a prohibition.

Here's what a nonprofit **can** do:

- Advocate on behalf of its political and economic interests within a limit.
- Advocate for or against a ballot referendum:
- A nonprofit, 501(c)3 organization is legally allowed to take a public position on ballot referendums. A ballot referendum is considered legislation (as opposed to a partisan election) and voters are considered legislators.

Here's what a nonprofit cannot do:

- Take a position for or against any candidate for elected office.

What is the limit on nonprofit advocacy?

Section 501(c)3 states that a tax-exempt organization will lose its tax-exempt status and its qualification to receive tax-deductible contributions "if a *substantial part* of its activities is attempting to influence legislation (commonly known as *lobbying*)."

"Substantial part" is open to interpretation. However, assume for a moment that "substantial part" could be defined as a percentage of a nonprofit organization's budget: it is very unlikely that an arts organization with an annual budget of $3 million would spend $150,000 (5 percent) on lobbying.

What is not subject to interpretation is the right of nonprofits to engage in advocacy. While advocacy cannot be the primary focus of the organization's activities, nonprofit organizations have substantial latitude to engage in advocacy. They have a responsibility to serve their community—and that includes advocacy and civic engagement. Arts organizations can and should engage in advocacy, not only to promote the arts in general, but also to find assistance in achieving their missions.

According to IRS regulations and U.S. law, attempting to influence legislation is:

- Any attempt to influence legislation through an effort to affect the opinions of the general public or any segment thereof (grassroots lobbying), and
- Any attempt to influence any legislation through communication with any member or employee of a legislative body or with any government official or employee who may participate in the formulation of legislation (direct lobbying).
- Attempting to influence legislation does not include the following:
- Making available the results of nonpartisan analysis, study or research.
- Examining and discussing broad social, economic, and similar problems.

Providing technical advice or assistance (where the advice would otherwise constitute the influencing of legislation) to a governmental body or to a committee or other subdivision thereof in response to a written request by that body.

Appearing before, or communicating with, any legislative body about a possible decision of that body that might affect the existence of the organization, its powers and duties, its tax-exempt status, or the deductions of contributions to the organization.

Communicating with a government official employee other than communication with the purpose of influencing legislation.

An Escape Clause:

In the unlikely event that your organization has exceeded the "substantial part of its activities" guideline, the board of directors can elect to temporarily reclassify your organization. This is called a 501(h) election. Section 501(h) permits eligible 501(c)3 organizations to limit their expenditures to influence legislation to 20 percent of their mission-related expenditures. In a 501(h) election, you are limited to no more than 20 percent of your nonprofit organization's budget.

Under 501(h), donors will still be able to take a tax deduction for their contributions to your nonprofit and your nonprofit will also continue to be eligible for donations from other 501(c)3 funding organizations such as foundations.

A 501(h) election requires a vote by the board of directors. The board can make the election anytime in the fiscal year and it can be applied retroactively. For example, if a year-end audit shows that the organization has spent 20 percent on advocacy and lobbying, the board can make the 501(h) election as late as the last day of the organization's fiscal year. A 501(h) election can be rescinded at any time by the board.

You still have your Constitutional rights:

As a private citizen—separate from your nonprofit—you have all the rights provided by the Constitution to petition, advocate, and communicate with your government. And, you have the right to fully participate in elections. As a private citizen, you can contribute to campaigns and make public statements separate from your organization. Make contributions and volunteer your time to candidates who support arts and culture, and make it clear that your contribution is linked to their support for your issues. Business leaders seek support for their business issues by giving money as private citizens.

In your official capacity, you can be an effective advocate within the broad limits of the IRS's guidelines. As a private citizen you can fully participate in the political process. Speak up on cultural funding; support the issues that support your organization and your vision for the future.

SEGMENT 2: THE ADVOCACY CONTINUUM

The following chart outlines a range of activities defined by the level of your commitment. At the top are activities that are relatively easy, inexpensive, and straightforward. As you progress down the list, the activities require greater commitment of time, dedication, and resources. As you gain advocacy experience, you and your colleagues will become skilled at all the tasks outlined here. However, if you feel like a newcomer to advocacy, try the activities at the top of the chart. Dip your toe in here and you will soon be swimming with all the political fish (and the sharks as well).

Information	• Newsletters, online briefs, etc. • Telling your story to the public without links to an agenda
Workshops/Training	• Advocacy discussion and training • Enabling people through training
Speakers Programs/Forums	• Informing key audiences about your advocacy • Topics are not controversial
Research	• Conducting research to measure community value, including economic impact, etc. • Leads to positioning papers
Position Papers	• Using the research to guide policy positions outlined in position papers • Communicating the research to the public
Advocacy Days	• Establishing a community of advocates local and statewide • Developing shared agenda and common message
Agenda Setting/Public Policy	• Setting an advocacy agenda targeted to national, state or local government

Awards to Politicians, Business Leaders & Others	• Recognizing past support and effort • Developing champions for your cause
Accountability Organizing	• Getting candidates to state their opinions, commit to action or support • Publish the information about candidates/officials without offering support • Track official actions and votes taken after they are elected
Endorsing Candidates	• Publicly endorsing one candidate over another based on voting records or opinion surveys • (Cannot be done by a nonprofit organization) • Endorsing candidates is risky—your candidate may lose and your endorsement may antagonize other candidates and their supporters
Campaigning	• Contributing personal money to a candidate's campaign • Volunteering to work in the campaign. • (Cannot be done by a nonprofit organization)
Lobbying	• Hiring a lobbyist • Registering as a citizen lobbyist • Working at the statehouse to affect legislation/legislators
First Amendment Issues	• Arts and culture often sit on the fault lines of intense societal disagreements. Taking sides carries the risk of earning enmity. Not taking sides carries the risk of losing your self-respect • Responding to public attacks on the arts based on misinformation, bias or preference

SEGMENT 3: RESTORING OUR COMPETITIVE ADVANTAGE

A Statewide Campaign for Cultural and Heritage Facilities Funding:
SAMPLE STRATEGY AND TIMELINE

The cultural community has identified a growing crisis of inadequate cultural facilities due to age and deferred maintenance. The average age of the state's cultural facilities is 93 years. Cultural organizations need substantial financial support to address issues of building code compliance, fire safety, handicapped accessibility, energy efficiency, and improvements and expansions. This campaign plan is designed to achieve the filing of a bill in the state legislature to provide cultural facilities funding.

JANUARY

- Develop a legislative advocacy strategy based upon committee appointments in the state's House of Representatives and Senate. Identify a list of targeted legislators who chair key committees or occupy positions of leadership.
- Develop a fundraising strategy for private-sector matching requirement. Development of the Steering Committee works in tandem with this fundraising strategy.
- Take first steps to form an Advisory Committee of cultural leaders from organizations throughout the state. We will recruit board leaders from cultural organizations with a goal of two organizations per targeted legislator and two board members from each organization.
- Meet with Historic Preservation leadership.

JANUARY–MARCH

- Meetings with potential fundraisers.
- Identify key business leader to be co-chair of the campaign.
- Telephone survey of cultural organizations with facilities, to document needs and develop a database of maintenance issues for cultural institutions in the targeted legislative districts.

JANUARY–FEBRUARY

- Invite business leaders as potential Steering Committee members to February meeting.
- Develop research on public support for the preservation of cultural and historic buildings through public funding.
- Schedule series of speeches for Chambers of Commerce, January—September.
- Explore partnership with tourism and lodging industries.
- Recruit university or foundation to donate or commission a public opinion poll.

MARCH–APRIL

- Continue to grow the Steering Committee of business and cultural leaders. Continue to work on raising private-sector match.
- Collect documentary photos through site visits to cultural facilities as identified in the telephone survey. Photos will be used in collateral material and in the rally planned for the Statehouse.
- Obtain the support of key municipal leaders including the mayors of targeted municipalities.
- Identify mayors to participate in a Mayors' Forum to be held in September.
- Develop collateral material, including list of examples of cultural institutions in need of support. Possibly develop a Top 10 list of threatened organizations.
- Develop a database of potential supporters in each targeted legislative district, including Board members of each institution, major suppliers, volunteers, and employees. This can be done with the assistance of the Advisory Committee.
- Schedule meetings with industry leaders such as a high-tech council, biotech council, and industry associations.
- Private discussion with editorial writer for state's largest newspaper.

MAY

- Continue to recruit the Steering Committee of business and cultural leaders. Continue to work on private-sector match.
- University collects polling information.
- Schedule 40 legislative site visits in targeted districts.

JUNE–AUGUST

- Continue to grow the Steering Committee. Continue to work on private-sector match.
- Site visits with local representatives and state senators in the targeted legislative districts.
- Local press coverage for each visit.

SEPTEMBER

- Continue to grow the Steering Committee. Continue to work on private-sector match.
- Meet with newspaper editorial board.
- Mayors' Forum with press conference.
- Delivery of mayors' letter of support at press conference.
- Generate press coverage in media.

OCTOBER

- Meetings with editorial boards of newspapers serving in targeted legislative districts.
- State House event with coalition advocates, including large-size photos. Advocates meet with representatives and senators.
- Announcement of fundraising goal.
- Recognition of donors.
- Obtain sponsors and cosponsors of the legislation. Schedule meetings with targeted legislators with key cultural leaders from their districts to ask them to cosponsor the legislation.
- Filing of the bill.
- The following campaign steps will be coordinated with the legislative process:
- Organize key supporters to testify at House and Senate Committee hearings.
- Implement grassroots advocacy strategy as follows:
- Collect letters of support addressed to legislators from the trustees and directors of nonprofit cultural organizations. Letters should be on the business, professional, or personal stationery of the individual trustee. These letters will be collected at the campaign headquarters to be delivered by hand at the right political moment.
- Begin email campaign through advocacy group's website using advocacy software. Target: 1000 emails over two months.
- Coordinate a letters-to-the-editor campaign in support of the bill.
- Host a series of political fundraisers in private homes for the bill's legislative sponsors and leaders.
- Organize a series of meetings with business leaders, cultural supporters, and key legislators.
- Organize an advocacy rally at the State House.
- After the bill passes each chamber, send a thank-you note to all the legislators who supported the bill, especially those in leadership positions.
- Celebrate.

Arts and Cultural Policy

CRAIG DREESZEN *and* ROBERT L. LYNCH

What Are Arts and Cultural Policies?

Waiting for an appointment, a visitor scans an arts leader's office bookshelf. Yes, there is *Fundamentals of Arts Management,* along with several other management journals and texts. But where is the organization's policy manual? In fact, you are unlikely to find documents labeled "arts policy" or "cultural policy" on an elected official's or cultural leader's desk.[1] Arts and cultural policies are not highly visible, but as we shall see, cultural policies, both explicit and implied, help define and support much of arts, humanities, and creative industries work.

Even if cultural policies are not always apparent, most readers of this text will have encountered a grant application process. The agencies offering grants, their funding sources, eligibility requirements, deadlines, guidelines, funding criteria, application form, cash-match requirement, peer panel reviews, appeal process, accountability requirements, and more have all been determined through policy decisions. While a federal, state, or local funding agency may have no section on their website titled "policy," policies are embedded throughout: in the agency's legal status, funding sources, mission and strategic plan, funding priorities, and grant-making procedures.

While agencies may have a few explicit policies, especially as required by authorizers and the Internal Revenue Service (for example, conflict-of-interest and record-keeping policies), policies are more often expressed through planning, governance, and many years' accumulation of programmatic and administrative decisions, most of which are not routinely thought of as policies. Yet the existence of the National Endowment for the Arts is the result of federal legislation,[2] grants to nongovernment agencies were first established by the Rockefeller Foundation, and matching grants were inventions of early Ford Foundation directors.[3] We may now think of these as givens, but these precedents were at one time innovative policy decisions. Prior to these policy initiatives, nearly all philanthropy to U.S. cultural organizations was from individuals.

The aim of this chapter is to 1) define arts and cultural policy; 2) explore some of the ways such policies are manifested, primarily in the public sector in the United States; and 3) consider how policies are developed, by whom, and how small organizations and individuals may influence public policy.

Arts and Cultural Policy

Kevin Mulcahy defines cultural policy as "the sum of a government's activities with respect to the arts (including the for-profit cultural industries), the humanities, and heritage."[4] Cultural policy is what governments and some private agencies do—or do not do—that encourage or limit cultural activities, cultural organizations, public access, and creative workers.

Arts policy is more specific than cultural policy. Arts policy is the domain of the visual, performing, literary, media, and other arts, artists, arts audiences, arts education, arts funders, and arts service

> Behind almost every action there is some kind of guiding principle. The name given to it is "policy." Consider a teenager who wants keys to the car. Parents set out rules or policies, ranging from the broadest policy, "We will have a family car" to alternative teen-use policies, "You may never have the keys to the car" or "You may sometimes have the keys to the car if you get good grades in school." Requirements to return the car filled with gas and return the keys to a hook by the door may be among the family's car-borrowing rules or procedures. Asking for the keys is called advocacy.

organizations. It is likely that the bulk of cultural policy in the United States has been developed for the arts.

Cultural policy is a broader construct. Culture can mean many things, but discussion of cultural policy includes the arts, humanities, heritage, and sometimes interpretive sciences and for-profit creative industries. It may also include cultural practices such as ethnic traditions. However, this chapter does not consider the policy implications of culture, understood even more broadly as the way of life of a people. In this chapter, cultural policy draws upon examples from U.S. arts agencies. While arts and culture have specific separate meanings, writers often use the terms "arts" and "culture" interchangeably as the policy principles apply throughout the cultural sector. Scholars often consider arts policy in the larger context of cultural policy, so many of our references draw from cultural policy research.

"POLICY" DEFINED

A policy is a decision that establishes principles, guidelines, limitations, or requirements that guide future decisions. Policies can be explicit or implicit. They may be developed through inclusive planning, by executive order, or by precedent. Policies may be written and well understood or informal and ambiguous. Policies may be firm requirements of law or flexible guidelines. Formal policies are generally approved by governing boards of nonprofit organizations or senior officials of public agencies. Policies establish boundaries that guide future decisions. Policies may be formally approved documents that govern subsequent decisions or may be implied by actual programs and procedures. Policies may be implemented through plans, procedures, or regulations.

Almost every area of life and action has a related set of guidelines, often termed policies. We speak of our nation's environmental policy, health policy, monetary policy, or defense policy. The guidelines for how we as a nation deal with the rest of the world are collectively called our foreign policy. Plug in almost any aspect of national life and we, through government, have laid out guidelines and laws for how we expect our nation, leaders, and citizens to proceed in these areas. Similar sets of guiding principles exist at our state and local government levels. These three levels of government policy have to coexist and often compromise with one another. Debating which policy and whose authority will prevail keeps our U.S. courts busy.

PROCEDURES

A state's arts policy might say that its state arts agency may, in the interest of the public, fund the arts. This policy is established by the enabling legislation of the arts agency. How this policy is actually implemented depends upon annual appropriations from the legislature and federal grants. Administrative and legislative budget procedures determine how much funding is actually appropriated to fulfill that policy. Policies may require champions within agencies and constituent advocacy to help ensure they are followed.

In general, policies are broader than procedures. Policies are generally in effect for a long time and approved by a governing authority while procedures may be more often amended and may be developed and approved by staff. For example, an NEA policy—public funds should be awarded to advance excellence and access—guides staff members to develop grant guidelines, invite applications, and identify panelists to evaluate proposals and recommend funding. Routine procedures like deadlines and application-form questions may be fully the responsibility of staff, while procedures like funding criteria or eligibility requirements that have policy implications may be presented by staff for approval by their board or commission. It is prudent for any critical procedure or policy to be backed by board authority. Board approval helps staff defend policy-based decisions with constituents.

While cultural policy is primarily the domain of government agencies, the policies of nonprofit organizations, especially foundations and service organizations, have significant influence. In Hartford, Connecticut, the Hartford Foundation for Public Giving, a community foundation, requires grantees' governing boards to fairly represent their constituents' diversity. This private Governance Diversity Policy[5] has resulted in significantly greater representation of and service to diverse communities throughout greater Hartford.

Culture in Cultural Policy

One of the challenges of cultural policy is the unbounded nature of the word "culture" itself. One text devotes 435 pages to concepts and definitions.[6] The term culture has become so ubiquitous that editors of the *Merriam-Webster Dictionary* picked culture as the 2014 "word of the year," given the frequency of its use in headlines and analyses. Culture has often been used in an anthropological sense to describe the way of life of a people or subgroup. Culture is now used in so many contexts that it defies a simple definition. Merriam-Webster cites examples of broad definitions of culture: "culture of transparency," "consumer culture," "winning culture," and "celebrity culture." In the context of cultural policy, we include the arts as a central part of culture, along with the humanities, history, heritage, and the beliefs and customs of ethnic groups.

Cultural politics

Our country's debates over cultural issues have included race, diversity, equity, religion, gender, sexual orientation, and the arts. The so-called culture wars raging over the last century have debated all of these aspects of our society and many have changed dramatically. The arts as a mirror of society have often been in the middle of much of this national dialogue, whether reflecting the issues of the civil rights movement in song, theater and visual art, or the antiwar sentiments of the sixties in music, fashion, and lifestyle. And the arts have sometimes taken on the brunt of the attacks from opposing sides, when artists have expressed themselves in ways that others considered pornography, such as the work of James Joyce or Robert Mapplethorpe, or blasphemy, such as the work of Andres Serrano. When congressional lawmakers charged that the works of Mapplethorpe and Serrano were funded by public dollars, the resulting controversy contributed both to policy and law, that no individual artists could be funded directly by the federal government, and to the slashing by 40 percent of the NEA's budget.[7] The far-reaching Depression-era arts program of the Works Progress Administration (WPA), a highly successful job creation tool through the arts, came to an abrupt end, in part after being accused of Communist leanings.[8] In these instances, the arts were caught up in the broader cultural issues of our society at the time.

CHARACTERISTICS OF CULTURAL POLICY

Cultural policies are also the aggregate of many decisions by multiple agencies with varying levels of authority and enforceability. A map of one state's cultural policies found that "cultural policy at the state level has been the sum total of the more or less independent, uncoordinated activities of a variety of state agencies and allied organizations and institutions."

J. Mark Schuster developed four premises to understand state cultural policy (and much of this likely also applies to federal and local policies): [9]

1. "Many more agencies than those that are commonly understood to be 'cultural agencies' are involved in cultural policy." These may include departments of parks and recreation, natural resources, transportation, planning and economic development, etc.
2. "It is not common to think of the aggregate of these agencies, institutions, actions, and policies as constituting a conceptual whole." While all these disparate policies may have an overall impact, they are not coordinated or even considered a state's overall cultural policy.
3. "Much of state cultural policy is implicit rather than explicit, being the result of decisions taken without expressed policy intention." Policies are more often implied through executive and board decisions, strategic plans, grant guidelines, and procedures. Policies may be determined more often by precedent than intentional planning and policy making.
4. "Much state cultural policy is indirect rather than direct, being the result of a wide variety of interventions beyond direct operation or direct financial support." Although the IRS' 501(c)3 regulation exempting contributions to charitable nonprofit organizations from federal taxes was not intended as a cultural policy, it has had a profound impact on U.S. nonprofit arts organizations.

Grants policy. It may be helpful to deconstruct a typical grants-making policy. Grants programs consists of procedures or regulations that may have been determined by program or administrative staff (for example, application forms or documentation requirements), agency policies determined by executive staff (eligibility requirements or proactive outreach to underserved populations), funding priorities determined through constituent assessment and strategic planning (a commitment to excellence and access), and board policies approved by the governing board or commission (board approval of grants process or budget allocations to grant programs). The funding agency's status may have been determined by law, such as enabling legislation or federal tax-exempt status. At one end of the continuum, administrative procedures tend to be the most flexible and may not even be documented. Precedence is a powerful force in policy. A program officer may say, "That's the way we've always done it." Policies embedded in law have the most authority, may be the least flexible, and could be enforced in the courts. In between these extremes policies may be more or less explicit, formal, and enforced.

Nested policies. John Carver described organizational policies as sets of nested bowls.[10] A governing board would set the broadest policies (the largest bowls) that identify broadly the results or ends that should be achieved. "The most critical policy … concerns itself with what human needs are satisfied, for whom, and at what cost. The governing board's highest calling is to ensure that the organization produces economically justifiable, properly chosen, well-targeted results." The Ohio Arts Council's grants policy includes a good example: "Sustainability grants ensure that public support of the arts continues to play an integral role in celebrating the rich past and sustaining the vibrant future of Ohio's cultural legacy through flexible and reliable funding for annual arts programming." Staff would develop operational policies and procedures, and "all organizational applications must be submitted electronically."[11] As with nested bowls, subordinate policies must fit within or align with higher policies approved by the governing board. For example, a state arts agency policy to credit in-kind contributions for developmental programs is consistent with the funder's broader policy to require cash matches for state grants. This nesting concept can apply to any agency, not just funders. A theater company may have a policy to present contemporary theater. Its nested policy may be to present contemporary Irish theater.

Carver argues that policies should be explicit, current, literal, available, brief, and comprehensive. "After addressing the largest of value choices (the biggest bowl), the board can either address the next level (the second largest bowl) or be content with having clarified the first level." The CEO can then deal with all smaller-level policies within the larger value articulated by the board. It is also important that policies be consistent—or at least not in conflict. As plans, policies, guidelines, and procedures evolve over years, sometimes grant-seekers are puzzled by application guidelines that do not align with application form questions, grants panel scoring rubrics, or final report requirements. Periodic evaluations of grant programs can help to align these so there is a consistent through-line of intentions.

CULTURAL POLICIES IN THE LAW

Significant cultural policies in the United States set the stage for support of the arts. Policies established in law have the most authority and are most likely to be enforced. Laws are enacted by

Congress, state legislatures, and county and municipal councils. In some cases laws are implemented or supplemented with regulations, policies, or procedures established by executive officials or administrative staff.

- The U.S. Constitution promises to "promote the general welfare," which can be interpreted to include access to the arts and humanities. Article I, Section VIII authorizes Congress "to promote the progress of science and useful arts" with protections for intellectual property.
- IRS 501(c)3 regulations establish that contributions to charitable nonprofit organizations could be exempt from federal taxes. This may be the single most significant U.S. cultural policy.
- U.S. Copyright law protects the creative work of writers and artists and patent law protects the rights of inventors and designers.
- Enabling legislation for the National Endowment for the Arts, National Endowment for the Humanities, Corporation for Public Broadcasting, Institute of Museums and Library Services and state arts agencies establishes the legal basis of federal and state cultural funding.
- Enabling ordinances for local arts commissions and articles of incorporation for nonprofit local arts agencies create the organizing structures of local arts councils and authority for their funding, programs, and services.
- Laws may require open meetings for public agencies and accessible entrance to buildings and access to records.
- Percent for Art state laws and municipal public art ordinances establish the legal authority to fund and manage art in public places.
- State high school graduation requirements may include requirements for arts education credits or service-based learning.
- Teacher certification requirements may include provisions to qualify practicing artists.
- Local home-based creative business zoning ordinances provide legal standing for arts businesses in neighborhoods.

- Creative enterprise zones in some cities establish tax benefits for establishing creative businesses in typically under-developed districts.
- Local ordinances may permit or deny street performances, outdoor festivals, loud music, and more.
- Local building codes and regulations for housing, accessibility, and fire and safety may determine what creative uses or building redevelopment is possible.
- Some federal, state and local executive orders have nearly the effect of law when they establish entities like the President's Committee on the Arts and the Humanities, Governors' Arts Awards, and mayor's offices of cultural affairs and creative industry departments. Executive action may also reorganize local arts commissions into larger departments of tourism or economic development. Executive actions can be amended or reversed by subsequent administrations.

CULTURAL POLICIES EMBEDDED IN PLANS

It is likely that more organizations have general plans than have explicit policies. Policies are often embedded within plans. These may not be labeled as policies but have the same effect as policies, in that they serve as an effective guide for subsequent decisions over time. This is especially true of mission statements, long-range goals, and core principles or values. It may be difficult to discern if an intention documented in a plan is a policy as defined here or a plan of action. Since policies are long-term parameters that guide or limit subsequent decisions over time, they tend to be general, timeless, and not quantified (similar to long-range goals in strategic plans (see the Strategic Planning chapter). Other elements of plans, such as strategies, objectives, and tasks, are specific, time limited, and may be quantified; they do not have the broad, parameter-setting function of a policy. However, it is more important that plans and polices be clear than correctly labeled. In practice, the distinction between plans and policies are sometimes subtle.

Community cultural plans may establish cultural policies (for example, universal access to cultural opportunities and education) or call for action to establish public policies (graduation requirements for arts education or affordable artist housing and studios). In some cases these have the effect of policy, as when a sponsoring local arts agency implements the cultural plan with funds and programs. In other cases, the plans have a role in advocacy that may or may not result in actual policy changes.

Regional or municipal comprehensive plans increasingly include sections on arts and culture, for instance, when they promote creative industries or cultural tourism. Some municipal master plans incorporate goals of their community's cultural plans as policies that guide local public investments and development.

Strategic plans of state and local arts agencies establish priorities for programs and funding. State arts agencies are required to update their plans with public input to qualify for NEA partnership funding. Some public funders and foundations require their grantees to present recent strategic plans as a requirement for operational funding.

Agency and Organizational Policies

Some agencies' policies, especially grant-makers', have significant public cultural policy effects. The grants policies of federal and state funding agencies likely have the most direct impact on arts funding and also influence private funding through public endorsement and cash-match requirements.

Foundations' policies also have had profound effect through direct funding. Foundation policies have also influenced how arts programs are organized as nonprofits, and have initiated concepts of matching grants and seed funding. Foundations have led the way to requiring evaluation of outcomes and requiring diversity in nonprofit boards.[12]

Most cultural organizations have policies that influence internal programs and operations. (These are addressed in more detail in the Board Development chapter.) ▌ These may include administrative and governance policies for personnel, finance, record keeping, conflict of interest, and programmatic policies like artistic quality, accessibility, freedom of expression, and cultural diversity. Organizational by-laws specify governance requirements. As in public cultural policy, these policies help staff and board members make decisions based on agreed principles, so that every time a problem or challenging issue arises it need not require board deliberation. Staff make decisions (for instance, presenting a challenging art program) within the bounds of approved policy (as in, the artistic director's authority), confident they will be backed by their board.

Many policies, especially state and federal arts policies, relate to funding. Organizational policies may also relate to arts programs and audiences. An arts center's implied or de facto policy might be, "We will present programs that we can make available for the cheapest price to our public," and that policy will affect their choices of the programs they produce or present. Or the leaders may say, "We will bring in only the best programs—but they must, to a large extent, pay for themselves with earned revenue, and therefore our ticket prices will be expensive." Or the directors may decide, "We want both excellent and affordable programs, so we must raise a significant amount from contributions and sponsorships." These are three very different policies or strategic choices that might govern an arts center's programming, pricing, and fundraising decisions. The decisions may be explicit policy statements, strategies in plans, or the result of trial-and-error practice, precedent, or response to competition.

Local arts agencies (LAAs) look at their publics and develop policy, either formal policy in a mission statement or de facto policy apparent from their actions. A typical LAA policy may be to offer all the arts to all the people: "We are not just about the few things; we are about the many things. We are not just about the few people; we are about the many people."

STATED AND ACTUAL POLICIES

Like so many aspects of public life, stated policies may differ from what is actually implemented. Foundation or arts council guidelines, for example, may have a stated policy to fund five priorities, documented in grant guidelines or strategic plans. However, a review of actual funds granted may reveal that they have only funded three of the five priorities in recent years. This suggests two options for the grants-seeker: (1) Focus applications for funding on the actual priorities that are being funded; or (2) advocate for the other priorities to be funded. Applied policy is not always clear; it is something that you have to determine by looking at precedent.

A public funding source may have a policy that it funds "dance." But if you look at their practice, you may see that they fund ballet and some modern dance but they don't fund folk dance. An Irish step dance company would not get a grant from this source. They may get funding through a folk arts program but not through regular grant channels. The funder may not have initially intended this, but it has become an implicit policy over time, perhaps relating to precedent or the choice of who is invited to serve on grant panels.

Figure 1. U.S. Nonprofit Organizations' Funding Sources

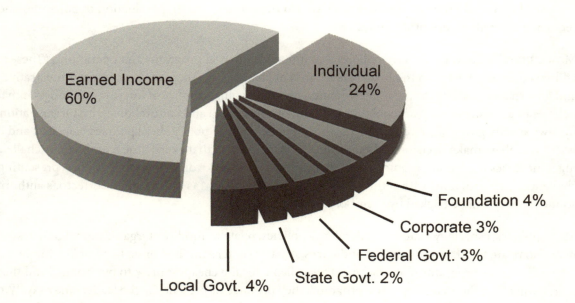

United States Arts Policy

In the arts, our work is guided by many policy principles; some, like funding policies, are easy to understand. Americans for the Arts' 2012 Arts and Economic Prosperity Study concluded that the collective budgets of all existing nonprofit arts organizations in the U.S. were $61 billion annually. That money, in the aggregate, came to the arts in the ways indicated in Figure 1.[13]

While the dollar amounts change every year, the chart in Figure 1 reflects the results of American policies for funding the arts in 2012. The chart indicates that the dominant arts-funding policy is to expect arts organizations to operate much like any small businesses, deriving the majority of their income from earned revenue such as ticket sales. Further, we as a country expect 31 percent of the income to be from donations—primarily private donations, led by individual giving—foundations, and the business sector. Finally, the chart indicates that U.S. arts policy is for government to have a modest role, 9 percent of the total, with just a tiny fraction from federal involvement, represented primarily by the NEA's investment of $146 million within the $61 billion total. Local government represents the largest public share, but still only 4 percent.

De facto U.S. arts policy. It is often said the U.S. has no national cultural policy. Policies tend to be dispersed through many agencies and tend to be more often implicit than explicit. As well, public funding agencies often make policy in reaction to input from constituents or pressure from legislators. In this way, U.S. cultural policies may be more reactive than proactive.

The U.S. arts policy is unlike that in most other parts of the developed world, where the national policy is to highly subsidize the arts with public funds. However, governments worldwide are looking at the U.S. government subsidy policy and much change is being contemplated. The argument is made by some that U.S. arts organizations are held back by this lack of government financial resources compared to other countries. Others argue that U.S. arts organizations are more abundant and more resilient and less likely to fail because they enjoy a highly diversified funding base.

While there may be no federally stated national arts policy in the United States, there is definitely a de facto policy or set of positions. The de facto U.S. federal arts policy is:

Financial self-determination for our nation's nonprofit arts organizations.
- High reliance on self-generated revenues.
- Reliance on a diversified portfolio of philanthropic giving that is primarily private incentivized by tax benefits to donors.
- Understanding of direct government money as a leverage investment rather than as subsidy.
- Division of the 3 percent of the $61 billion in total U.S. arts funding (in 2014) that comes from federal sources as $146 million toward helping the 95,000 non-profit arts organizations throughout the U.S. and some $1.7 billion in partial funding for a dozen or so national treasure organizations such as the Smithsonian, Kennedy Center, and the Corporation for Public Broadcasting

> The de facto U.S. arts policy is one of financial self-determination for the nation's nonprofit arts organizations, high reliance on self-generated revenues, and a reliance on a diversified portfolio of philanthropic giving that is primarily private, with a small amount of government money that serves more as a leverage investment than a subsidy.

The policy of our federal government is to have a national arts endowment that makes grants nationwide to arts organizations. It took many years of advocacy (feeding the cause and telling the story) and many years of lobbying (specifically to decision-makers, asking them for a "yes" vote on a late night in 1965) that led to President Johnson signing into law the National Foundation on the Arts and Humanities Act of 1965 on September 29, 1965. However, 50 years of practice has created many related and often unrelated policies that shape what the original policy means. For example, the act did not say how much money was to be given out, and so each year during the congressional appropriations process, advocates ask for a specific amount of money. Over those 50 years, that amounts has varied, but it is consistently small—about 35 cents per person in the U.S. in 2014. To put this in context, the

---

Arts Education Policy

Arts education is a policy issue with profound implications—implications that go well beyond basic arts instruction. Arts education helps students and schools thrive in the short term, but also ensure that there will be arts-educated mayors, legislators, bankers, and foundation heads in the long term. Americans for the Arts' ten-year report on the availability of arts education, released in 2012, confirmed that arts education is in trouble.[15] But, it found, while arts education wasn't in that much danger in the wealthier or even middle class communities, it was in deep trouble in poor communities. Thus, the unwritten, de facto policy was to feed the rich and starve the poor. This persuaded Secretary of Education Arne Duncan to say, "And unfortunately, the arts opportunity gap is widest for children in high-poverty schools. This is absolutely an equity issue and a civil rights issue."[16] See the Arts Education and Policy chapter for more information.

> **Some arts policies have influenced larger social policies.**
> The Winston-Salem arts council was one of the first places where the bathrooms were integrated. Some early rock and roll performers and agents also stipulated that they would only perform to an integrated audience. These arts policy changes fed into change in the larger community.[17]

NEA's budget has always been less than the Department of Defense's annual appropriations for military bands.[14]

So the unwritten U.S. arts policy is to keep the federal investment extremely small. This was not a single intentional policy decision, but the result of many years' aggregate of legislation, appropriations, and decisions by multiple agencies. The most recent decades of advocacy have taught us that the most persuasive argument for federal legislators is that the arts leverage the value that federal dollars bring to the table, attracting other public and private money. This ratio is 11:1, according to the NEA.

In addition to the NEA in the public sector, there are also 50 state and six territorial arts agencies that give out state government money and re-grant federal funds. There are approximately 3,000 LAAs that grant local government money and six federally funded regional organizations that create regional and national services.

As of this edition, the last full NEA reauthorization was in 1990.[18] This was while the NEA was under attack for allegedly funding work that was objectionable to some members of Congress.[19] Negotiations with Congress allowed the agency to survive, but with new policy restrictions on the NEA including a prohibition from directly funding artists (except writers and for special honors to folk and jazz artists). Congress also mandated that 40 percent of federal appropriations (previously 20 percent) to the NEA be distributed to the states and regions. And finally, as part of the 1990 agreement to keep the NEA alive, the budget was cut by 40 percent. This then led to decisions about the programs to keep and to eliminate. These seemingly financial decisions were in fact policy decisions. The NEA would no longer fund artists, no longer have artist or management fellows, no longer have NEA regional staff, would double the distribution to the states, and would include members of the U.S. Congress on the National Council for the Arts.

Policy is a long term business. At the time, some argued that these 1990 compromises were too high a price to pay just to keep the NEA alive. But it had taken a generation or longer to create the policy of having an NEA at all; and if eliminated, it could very well have taken another generation or more to get it back. Most would say that keeping an NEA was worth it. Since that compromise, the NEA has distributed $2 billion. Our nation had a policy of not funding the arts for 189 years and has had a

> **Policy Disappointments**
> Some policy initiatives have not worked as planned and have sometimes come and gone. These include some state cultural trusts, entertainment taxes, and entertainment district taxes. State-level trusts or endowments have sometimes been raided by legislators or have led to reduced annual appropriations. Entertainment taxes created a rift between the entertainment world, the for-profit world, and the nonprofit world.

> **Tax Potential**
> Hotel/motel taxes have been widely replicated policies that have led to massive investments for the arts.

policy of funding the arts for 50 years. We must distinguish between a short-term advocacy "victory" and a policy decision that will influence things for years to come.

Federal arts policies impact state policies. When the NEA was founded in 1965, it included a policy that any state with a state arts agency could get matching money from the NEA. In 1964 there were four state arts agencies. As a direct result of the federal policy, "by 1974, all the states—plus the District of Columbia and the territories—had created some form of arts agency."[20] The NEA has granted out about $5 billion since its founding.[21] According to the National Assembly of State Arts Agencies, those 56 state and territorial arts councils have received state government appropriations of over $10.1 billion during that time period.[22] Most of this amount, plus other funds from private sources, was granted out to support the arts. So the long-term leverage impact of one policy decision was profound, creating a national system of arts support agencies and leveraging public support for the arts for half a century.

Still, if we think about public sector policy purely in financial terms, local policy has had the greatest impact. As many as 5,000 local governments, local arts agencies and others have funded over $2 billion annually.[23] Compare this to state government policies that fund the arts at about $1 billion annually, and federal policy that provided $146 million in 2014 through the NEA.

Who Sets Policy?

Sometimes the term "public policy" is incorrectly used to refer to the output of think tanks and policy forums: ideas, research, and big new ideas. While these may provide context and lay the groundwork, policy is only made when a decision-making body accepts ideas or creates guidelines through law or actionable plans. Most often, policy is made evident in budgets. Federal plans, policies, and funding priorities influence corresponding grants, programs, and services of state arts agencies, which often shape local programs.

Federal arts policy. This most apparent in funding programs. The NEA supports state arts agencies with operating support grants through its State and Regional Partnership program. This in turn allows state arts agencies to make grants to support local arts programming. The NEA also funds state arts agencies with arts education and folklore grants. Accordingly, most state arts agencies have arts education and folklore staff and funding programs to support local arts education and folk programs. There are parallel state and local cultural policy systems influenced by federal policies of the Institute of Museums and Library Services, National Endowment for the Humanities, and Corporation for Public Broadcasting. Federal arts policy is developed primarily by the National Endowment for the Arts.

Many NEA policy initiatives (for example, Shakespeare on Tour and Our Town Creative Placemaking grants) are priorities of its Chair, who is nominated by the President and confirmed by the U.S. Senate. Other policies, such as those establishing state and regional arts agency partnerships and artist fellowships, are developed and refined over time by senior staff and approved by the Chair with advice from the National Council of the Arts. Planning and policy debates help decision-makers hear constituents' concerns and formulate or rebalance their policy positions. These may change over time as changes in the economy, political opinion, technology, demographics, or audience behavior suggest the need for adaptations.

State arts policy. It is the policy of the NEA to require state arts agencies (SAAs) to develop strategic plans to qualify for NEA funding through partnership agreements on a three-year cycle. The NEA requires SAA plans to be developed with inclusive participation by each state's constituents. State arts agencies then develop plans and policies based, at least in part, on constituent input. It is not unusual for a SAA to test a new policy with constituent assessment before implementing it (for instance, shifting from annual grants of operating support to two-year grants). State arts agency policies are generally recommended by staff and approved by their governing commissions (which may also be called boards or councils).

Local arts policy. Local arts agency (LAA) policy formulation varies according to the organizations' legal status and governance structure. Some public agencies report to a mayor or town council who may approve major policies. Subordinate policies may be approved by the agency director. A nonprofit local arts agency would set policy by approval of the governing board upon recommendation by staff as outlined in the Board Development chapter. ▌ Many city and county local arts agencies consult their constituents through community cultural planning. (See the Strategic Planning chapter). ▌ In Clearwater, Florida, a municipal percent-for-art ordinance was approved by the city council after being developed by city staff with community support, documented in its cultural plan. In Providence, Rhode Island, the cultural plan called for a public art policy, which the city's Department of Arts, Culture and Tourism subsequently developed.[24]

Roots of policy. Policies are often developed when policy-makers are confronted with a question or a problem. The question may be resolved with a one-time decision, or it may have long-term implications and benefit from establishing a general guideline or principle to help determine similar questions or problems in the future. A legislature may issue a mandate to support economic development; a constituent might ask a funder for an exception to a grant program requirement; or an editorial may question the judgment of an artistic director. The question might come from the mandate of the organization itself to try to figure out its mission and its vision to go forward. Related questions about audience, programs, and the systems to support them are nested within these broader policies.

Funding policy. In recent times, the lack of money has been a primary driver of policy change. Government only has its tax base to spend, and that money goes up and down in direct relation to economic cycles. Arts advocates use economic data in advocacy, but the larger issues are really about policy—advocacy is largely of the moment, but policy is long term. For example, suppose there is a downturn in the economy. An unsound policy response would be for government to eliminate the system of public funding for the arts altogether. Sound public policy would be to simply reduce the amount of funding for the arts and restore it when the economy improves. These are two very different policy approaches. Job-creation and economic-impact data help build the policy argument that government should keep the basic arts investment system in place, even in difficult times.

How to Influence Public Policy

If you are not an elected official, board member, or senior staff of a funding agency, it may seem difficult to influence public policy. As the Advocacy chapter ▌ of this book explains further, there are many ways to affect policy. One cannot do everything, but everyone can do something. The Advocacy chapter also makes a distinction between advocacy and lobbying. Advocacy is more general; it's the pleading of the cause. Lobbying is more specific; it's asking a legislator to make a particular decision. So creating policy may need both advocacy and lobbying, and continued advocacy helps ensure its implementation. For example, data may indicate some needed change in that policy. Those who care, advocate for that change.

The following list outlines the various ways individuals and organizations can help influence public policy:

- **State arts agency planning.** State arts agencies update their strategic plans every three or four years. They engage in constituent assessments through surveys, regional forums, focus groups, and interviews. Some also convene forums to test a funding policy change. It is simple to respond to a survey, attend a planning meeting, or send recommendations directly to the agency director. Even a few articulate suggestions can help shape state arts policy and plans.
- **Local cultural planning.** Whether a community does this once or periodically, cultural planning processes are important opportunities to test community opinion and shape plans and policies. As with state plans, constituents may respond to invitations to answer surveys or attend meetings. An individual might influence policy more directly by volunteering to serve on the steering committee or specific-issue task forces or planning committees.
- **Government planning.** States, municipalities, county governments, and regional planning authorities conduct plans that require citizen input. These include comprehensive land-use planning, capital improvement plans, neighborhood or downtown district planning, and plans for economic development, education, housing, tourism, zoning, and more. Savvy cultural advocates recognize these as opportunities to make arts and culture a part of the concerns and solutions for other sectors. Constituents can engage simply by responding to surveys or speaking up at a hearing, or they may become more deeply involved by volunteering for a planning committee or seeking an appointment to a policy board.
- **Legislative hearings.** State legislatures and Congress may convene hearings to reauthorize funding agencies, determine budget appropriations, or consider law. Constituents and their colleagues may be in a position to write a policy brief or offer expert testimony.
- **Candidate forums and transition teams.** State and local arts advocates often invite candidates to answer questions about their positions on arts policies or participate in candidates forums to discuss such issues. Individuals might help pose such questions. Sometimes an arts leader joins the transition team or is invited to help write a policy brief for a newly elected executive official.
- **Present to state and national associations.** Speaking to gatherings of opinion leaders like the American Planning Association or the U.S. Conference of Mayors can be effective in raising their awareness and influencing policy.
- **Press releases and conferences, news media interviews.** A nonprofit organization can take the initiative and issue news releases or convene press conferences to influence public policy. Over time an organization may become a trusted source of information and be called for media interviews or appearances on radio or television. It is important for an organization's spokespeople to be clear and consistent on matters of policy.

- **Letters to editors and guest editorials.** Local and state public policy can be influenced by individuals or organized campaigns on the opinion pages of newspapers.
- **Research.** Service organizations and academics conduct research that provides policy-makers with data to make informed plans and policies. Economic impact and cultural tourism data is often used to help support arts funding.
- **Position papers, blogs, social media postings.** Writing about a policy issue can be part of a larger awareness-building campaign to influence policy.
- **Advocacy actions.** Most states and some national service organizations maintain advocacy systems. They encourage artists and those who care about the arts to sign up for advocacy alerts and then ask them to send letters or emails or make appointments with elected officials, when requested, to influence funding or arts policy.

Policy development, much like creating a law or coming to almost any decision, goes through a cycle of steps such as those illustrated in the Policy Wheel developed by Robert Lynch, President and CEO of Americans for the Arts (see Figure 2). This wheel specifically illustrates the cycle of public policy development resulting in some kind of legislative decision.

1. **Ideas.** At some early point, ideas are floated and talked about and then, as facts are needed, research and opinions are put forward and debated. This is the same whether it's for a major national issue or for a teenager trying to get the keys to the car for the night.

Figure 2: The Policy Wheel

2. **Positions.** A specific position is put forward and this, too, will be debated and amended along the way. In order for a cultural policy idea to move forward, however, it needs help from individuals, supporters, alliances, partners.
3. **Leadership and Professional development.** Who is going to help move the policy forward and what do they need to know?
4. **Visibility.** This circle suggests that now information about the idea needs to be broadly distributed. Visibility and marketing will tell both the decision-maker and the public why a particular policy idea is a good idea. Telling the story is not necessarily specifically asking for anything, but is laying the groundwork for "the ask."
5. **Advocacy.** Visibility is general publicity; advocacy gets more specific. It is aimed at decision-makers, letting them know why a particular idea or cause is a good one. Advocates should expect ongoing dialogue with decision-makers who need to understand the value of the arts against the backdrop of all the other ideas they hear every day.
6. **Lobbying.** This is the most important step and often the step that is not taken. This step requires the advocate to be very clear about the decision that is wanted and to be very persuasive in making the case to the decision-makers. It is not the rally for support for the arts on the steps of a state capitol (that's advocacy), but rather the moment in the elected official's office where it is made clear that a "yes" vote is wanted on a specific bill that is being voted on a specific date. In the final step, a decision is made or not made in the way the advocate hopes, but nonetheless, policy is created. And finally, and most importantly for all policy and all law, the circle begins again immediately.

WRITING POLICY

When writing policy, be clear about why the policy is needed. Policies often have a brief opening statement explaining their purpose. The language should be concise and unambiguous, with simple wording. Section headings and bulleted or numbered lists work better than long narratives. The policy itself may be expressed in a sentence or two, supplemented with more detailed procedures.

Generally policies are broad enough to apply to a wide variety of situations and to allow for judgment within limits established by the policy. Remember John Carver's advice to "nest" policies. A broad policy to ensure artistic freedom may contain more detailed policies or procedures on the authority of the artistic director and artist selection processes. Policies should be consistent with each other and procedures should be consistent with their associated policies.

Policies sometimes accumulate amendments over time until they are a long aggregation of broad principles and specific rules that become unwieldy to the point of uselessness. An evaluator of a safety policy for a youth development program recommended converting a 24-page document of detailed random-order instructions into a one-sentence policy and a one-sentence summary of procedures, followed by details in logically sub-headed sections. The document was approved by the governing board, recorded and filed in a policy manual, posted on the organization's website, distributed to staff, and became part of volunteer teacher recruitment and orientation.

- **POLICY:** It is the policy of [our organization] to require staff and volunteers in our education program to comply with the Safety Policy and Procedures to ensure that children and youth in our education program may "…safely learn and grow." (quoting the mission statement)

> - **PROCEDURES:** Volunteer and professional staff sign an agreement to ensure commitment to abide by our Safety Procedures that are detailed in the following pages. Procedures may be revised by the Council.

Conclusion

Arts policy affects every aspect of how arts professionals operate. However, most of these policies are implicit, the result of many decisions made over time by disparate agencies and legislatures. Strategic arts advocates work to protect the overarching policies that have established funding and support for the arts.

First, it is imperative that arts lovers, artists, arts managers, and arts advocates protect the principles that public support for arts and culture is important; that institutions like the federal, state, and local arts and other cultural agencies are essential parts of our infrastructure; and that the arts and humanities should be funded. It took those in the arts in the United States nearly 200 years to achieve this policy. Even in economic downturns, this fundamental policy must be protected.

Second, it is equally important that those who care about the arts recognize the reality that the de facto cultural policy in the U.S. can be summed up as "the arts are not all that important and need little public support," and a result, arts advocates must keep working to affect subordinate, nested policies and funding decisions. We must advocate for long-term policy and for short-term annual financial appropriations.

Understanding that policies establish the principles that guide future decisions, effective cultural leaders must develop policies that are intentional, clear, and consistent with plans and with actual programs. Overarching policies establish broad boundaries that may be refined by incremental changes to subordinate or nested policies and implemented with plans, procedures, funding, and programs. Effective public policies are best created with input from constituents through inclusive assessment and planning, and by engaging with citizens who can influence cultural policy by participating in assessments, planning, and continued advocacy.

Endnotes

1. See J. Mark Schuster, ed., *Mapping State Cultural Policy: The State of Washington,* 2003.

2. Title 20 U.S. Code § 954 – National Endowment for the Arts, 1965.

3. John Kreidler, "Leverage Lost: The Nonprofit Arts in the Post-Ford Era," *Journal of Arts Management, Law, and Society* 26, no. 2 (1996) pp. 79–100, cited in Toby Miller and George Yudice, Cultural Policy, 2002, pp. 46–47.

4. Kevin V. Mulcahy, "Cultural Policy: Definitions and Theoretical Approaches," *Journal of Arts Management, Law and Society,* 35 no. 4, 2006.

5. hfpg.org/for-nonprofits/key-policies/

6. A.L. Kroeber and Clyde Kluckhohn, *Culture: A Critical Review of Concepts and Definitions,* 1963.

7. Miller and Yudice, "The United States, Cultural Policy, and the National Endowment for the Arts," in their Cultural Policy, 2002.

8. Don Adams and Arlene Goldbard, *New Deal Programs: Experiments in Cultural Democracy,* 1986, 1995. wwcd.org/policy/US/newdeal.html

9. Schuster, *Mapping State Cultural Policy,* p. 7.

10. John Carver, *Boards That Make a Difference: A New Design for Leadership in Nonprofit and Public Organization,* 2nd ed., 1997, p. 31.

11. Ohio Arts Council, *General Operating Support for Arts And Cultural Organizations: Sustainability.* oac.state.oh.us/grantsprogs/guidelines/Sustainability.asp

12. See John Kreidler, "Leverage Lost: The Nonprofit Arts in the Post-Ford Era," *Journal of Arts Management, Law, and Society* 26, no. 2 (1996) pp. 79–100, cited in Miller and Yudice, pp. 46–47; W.K. Kellogg Foundation Evaluation Handbook, 1998; United Way of America, *Measuring Program Outcomes: Training Kit,* 1996; Hartford Foundation for Public Giving, Governance Diversity Policy.

13. Americans for the Arts, *Arts & Economic Prosperity IV: Economic Impact of the Nonprofit Arts & Culture Industry,* 2012, figure used by permission. americansforthearts.org

14. Jane Alexander, *Comand Performance: An Actress in the Theater of Politics,* 2000.

15. Arne Duncan, prepared remarks on the NCES report, delivered at Miner Elementary School, Washington, DC, April 2, 2012.

16. Personal communication to Robert Lynch.

17. Basmat Parsad and Maura Spiegelman, *Arts Education in Public Elementary and Secondary Schools: 1999–2000 and 2009–10,* National Center for Education Statistics, Institute of Education Sciences, U.S. Dept. of Education, 2012.

18. Implementation of National Endowment for the Arts Reauthorization Act, GGD-91-102FS, Sept. 17, 1991.

19. Mark Bauerlein, with Ellen Grantham, eds., National Endowment for the Arts: A History, 1965–2008, NEA, 2009.

20. Kevin V. Mulcahy, *The State Arts Agency: An Overview of Cultural Federalism in the United States,* The Cultural Policy Center at the University of Chicago, 2001.

21. arts.gov/about-nea, accessed 1/7/2014.

22. National Assembly of Local Arts Agencies appropriations data. From 1983 to 2013—30 years—state arts agency grants totaled $7,085,089,459, or about $7.1 billion. NASAA does not have grant data from 1965 to 1983.

23. Americans for the Arts' Arts and Economic Prosperity Study IV.

24. Clearwater Cultural Plan, Clearwater, FL, 2002; *Creative Providence: A Cultural Plan for the Creative Sector,* Providence, RI, 2009; *Proposed Public Art Policy for the City of Providence,* 2014.

PART TWO

Fundamentals of Managing Arts Organizations

6

Strategic Planning

CRAIG DREESZEN

Successful organizations—whether community arts organizations or multinational corporations—have at least two things in common: a compelling vision and effective strategies. These organizations are guided by a clear sense of priorities and are able to adapt to changing circumstances without losing their way. They may be propelled by the inspiration of an individual who captures the imagination and commitment of others, or they may reflect the collective ideas of a group that has framed a common dream. You may also have encountered arts organizations that operate the way they always have, even as evidence mounts that things are no longer working, as they react to each new problem as a crisis with no idea how to respond, or change direction each time their leaders or funders change.

If the members of an organization, from the president to the newest volunteer, share an understanding of what that organization values and where it is headed, they may effectively realize shared intentions. An empowering vision expands personal dreams into ones that can unify, inspire, and mobilize people and resources. Translating that vision to clear strategies that yield results is what strategic planning is all about.

> When you are immersed in a vision, you know what must be done.... But you may not know how to do it. You experiment, err, try again, yet there is no ambiguity.
>
> —Ed Simon, president and CEO, Herman Miller Inc.[1]

So what is strategic planning? "Strategy" is a term so commonly used, and in so many contexts, that it is much misunderstood. Noted organizational theorist Henry Mintzberg offers the following definition of strategy in Strategy Bites Back: "Strategy is a plan—some sort of consciously intended course of action, a guideline (or set of guidelines) to deal with a situation." In Strategic Planning for Nonprofit Organizations: A Practical Guide and Workbook, Michael Allison and Jude Kaye define strategic planning as "a systemic process through which an organization agrees on—and builds commitment among—key stakeholders, priorities that are essential to its mission and are responsive to the environment. Strategic planning guides the acquisition and allocation of resources to achieve those priorities."

Strategic planning is a process through which an organization articulates what it may accomplish in the future, what opportunities and needs it hopes to meet, and how it plans to do so. Strategic planning answers questions like: What do we do best? Who do we serve and what do they want? What difference do we want to make? What are our priorities? Where should we invest our time and money for best results?

The intent of this chapter is to help you understand strategic planning well enough to organize this process for your nonprofit organization. We begin by discussing the principles of planning, then provide an outline of planning methods. We explore how strategy develops as part of a deliberate process that engages leaders and stakeholders in defining a plan to guide future decisions. We also briefly consider annual operating or work plans, budgets, business plans, program plans, and community cultural plans.

> A learning organization is a place where people are continually discovering they can create their reality.
>
> —Peter Senge, business strategy writer[2]

Part I: Principles of Planning

Why Plan?

A major economic downturn can shake nonprofit leaders' confidence in planning. Few strategic plans can anticipate the rapid and dramatic changes in funding and consumer behavior that follow a financial crisis. After the 2008–09 financial crisis, for example, public and private funders cut grants, businesses dropped sponsorships, and audiences shifted their ticket-buying habits, while other organizations downsized, merged, or failed. Little of this was planned in advance.

All this leads one to wonder, "Why bother planning when so little is predictable?" Consider, however, that when so much is changing, it is even more critical to be clear about what is most important, what values inform your choices, whom you serve, and what your organization ultimately intends to accomplish. Otherwise, your organization will be tossed about by economic, social, and technological forces, react impulsively to crises, and chase every grant or opportunity like a life saver thrown in a stormy sea.

Long-term stability may be a thing of the past, but this is not necessarily a bad thing. Nassim Nicholas Taleb argues in Antifragile: Things That Gain from Disorder that it may be a mistake to try to prevent instability. Volatility can actually improve organizations' resilience if their leaders continually learn from and adapt strategically to unforeseen turbulence.

Increasing unpredictability and the rapid pace of change means you cannot create a strategic plan every three or four years and operate with business as usual in between. In The Nonprofit Strategy Revolution, David La Piana calls for "real time strategic planning" as a proactive alternative to widely spaced strategic planning initiatives. He urges nonprofit leaders to "continuously monitor the organization's environment and respond immediately to Big Questions with appropriate strategies." When the answers to opportunities or threats to which the organization must respond—the Big Questions to which La Piana refers—suggest new strategies, the organization should be "quickly converting thought into action in real time to address opportunities and challenges in a rapid-response world."[3]

> You never want a serious crisis to go to waste.
>
> —Rahm Emanuel, former White House Chief of Staff

So why plan? Planning offers a number of benefits:

- Informing and exciting people about an organization's work, motivating staff, boards, and volunteers.
- Helping an organization communicate the potential impact of its work to funders, potential partners, and audiences. (See the Program Evaluation chapter to learn how to observe and report actual results achieved. ▌)
- Helping an organization allocate limited resources—people, funds, and facilities—to accomplish its goals.
- Defining the results an organization hopes to achieve and providing the basis for measuring how well it achieves them.
- Protecting an organization from potential artistic, financial, or political catastrophes.
- Providing a process that clarifies a group's intentions.
- Developing a product, the written plan, that summarizes these intentions.

Thinking about planning while attempting to keep up with daily tasks in the face of financial and personnel restrictions can be overwhelming. Certainly, if you are in the midst of a crisis, you may need to deal with the immediate emergency before undertaking broader-scope strategic planning. However, frequent crises indicate the need for strategic planning. If you are preoccupied with the mind-numbing details of daily operations, you may not notice opportunities or threats until it's too late. Planning can prepare you for some crises, mitigate others, and even prevent some catastrophes.

As former U.S. Treasury Secretary Tim Geithner was fond of saying, "Plan beats no plan."

KEEP PLANNING SIMPLE

Planning must be kept simple so that people will do it and the resulting plan won't be ignored. Most arts administrators intuitively use elements of the strategic planning process, such as when they organize a performing arts season, write a grant, or recruit volunteers. The process doesn't have to be perfect: what is important is that planning becomes a frequent and integral part of the life of the organization.

In short, a sound planning process mobilizes you to:

- gather together the people who care about your work;
- imagine what you could accomplish together, what the organization could become, and what difference it could make in the community;
- look around to identify what you do well or poorly, who your audience is and what they want or need, and your major threats and opportunities;
- determine what you will do and what you will not do;
- decide what steps will get you where you want to go, and what help and resources you will need;
- implement your plan; and
- evaluate, revise, and adapt your plan as you carry out programs and services.

Somehow, when we approach the task of systematically planning for an organization or community, all the discussion can make the task appear more complicated than it actually is. Planning is not as complicated as some would make it seem. It's a bit like riding a bike. While bike riding is easy enough for a five-year-old to master, describing how to do it is more difficult. Everyday planning is also easy and we all do it. Keep this in mind. Like bicycling, the real work of planning is intuitive, active, and forward moving.

Four Key Concepts

Before explaining the specific steps of planning, it may be helpful to consider four concepts that put practice into context. In the following section we consider: coping with the paradoxical nature of planning; the benefits of building plans on assets rather than problems; dealing with complex, adaptive changes; and managing seemingly contradictory either/or polarities.

THE PLANNING PARADOX

Planning's fundamental paradox is that the future is essentially unknowable. We plan to prepare for what cannot be known. In orderly times we forget this and plan with unquestioned assumptions about how we think the world will unfold. But if we think of planning as accurately predicting the future, we're defeated before we begin. When we think of planning as understanding community strengths, clarifying our organization's values, and articulating the kinds of differences we hope to make for our constituents and communities, we're on safer ground. These things are less volatile than the political, economic, and social environment in which we work. An organization's core values and mission don't often change, even as leaders continually adapt to changing circumstances with adaptive changes to strategies and short-term objectives.

However, it is still very useful to project actions and their intended results into the future. This is essential in the current era of accountability for outcomes. What we can't do is get too attached to our predictions or follow planned strategies without constant adjustment to changing conditions. We get in trouble when we use metaphors like "blueprint" and "road map," which reinforce the mistaken belief that planning is a reliably predictable, step-by-step guide to the future. The road changes—bridges wash out and new paths emerge. However, with a strong sense of direction we can navigate regardless of what changes we encounter in the terrain.

The planning paradox can be resolved by simply recognizing that you don't have to know the future to plan. In rapidly changing times, planning helps deepen our understanding of people's interests, centers the organization around shared values and vision, and describes the results we are trying to achieve.

PLAN TO BUILD ON ASSETS, NOT PROBLEMS

Many planners have been taught to assess needs and plan to resolve problems. A needs- or problem-based approach seems like common sense. Most managers are good problem solvers. As part of routine management, we identify problems and fix them. However, when we base strategic planning on needs and problems, we focus on weaknesses. We may also identify errors and seek to place blame. Our attention can be focused backwards. In evaluating results, we may focus too strongly on the question "What went wrong?"

Problem-centered planning is essentially reactive; asset-centered planning is creative. An assets-based approach asks "What do we do particularly well?" and "Where are we most successful?" These questions focus our attention on strengths and identify what works, making successes more common and less isolated by identifying what is working well and making this more the norm.

Of course, problems must be addressed in planning. They will arise in any planning conversation, no matter how affirmative the approach. The difference lies in the emphasis, looking backward with misgiving or forward with hope—and that makes all the difference.

> Problem-solving is about making what you don't want go away. Creating involves bringing something you care about into reality.
>
> —Peter Senge[4]

Appreciative Inquiry (AI) is a system for tapping the power of assets. It is used both in planning and in community and organizational development.[5] AI taps the collective intelligence of the group and helps build a sense of optimism and support for the resulting plan and actions. An Appreciative Inquiry approach starts with picking a topic to be thoughtfully studied within an organization or community (for instance, constituent services or board and staff development). Then leaders generate questions that explore this topic in an appreciative way (see sample AI questions below). In a small organization, such questions could be explored with interviews or in a planning retreat. In a large organization, an AI team trains volunteers to discuss the questions with people throughout the organization and in the community. The leaders then meet to synthesize what they learned and to dream of what might be, asking "What is the world calling us to do?"

Some appreciative inquiry questions:

- Can you recall a story that illustrates our organization really fulfilling its mission?
- What are our signature strengths?
- What do we do better than almost anyone else?
- What assets do we want to build upon?
- When do we really connect with our audiences?
- Can you remember an incident when we touched people in ways that you hoped we would?

> Human systems move in the direction of what they most frequently and persistently ask questions about. What you study, GROWS.
>
> —David L. Cooperrider and Diana Whitney,
> *Appreciative Inquiry: A Positive Revolution in Change*

ADAPTIVE CHALLENGES

Successful leaders scan the changing landscape while understanding what has worked well in the past. Not every program or practice that has helped an organization succeed will continue to work in the future. For example, subscription series that sustained regional theaters for decades are now much less predictably useful.

Adaptive Leadership. Not everything changes. The challenge is to discern what is essential and what must be let go. It still matters that we produce programs and services that people value and communicate this to our communities. Ronald Heifetz has described this as adaptive leadership. An effective leader and an effective plan help an organization adapt to changes. Even when so much is changing, Heifetz says, leaders must draw upon past successes to discover what will help the organization thrive into the future: "A challenge for adaptive leadership, then, is to engage people in distinguishing what is essential to preserve from their organization's heritage and what is expendable. Successful organizations are thus both conservative and progressive."[6]

Adaptive challenges are persistent. They may provoke conflicts and may require new learning and may require changes in organizational culture or structures. Adaptive challenges take time. If feelings are running high and you have no idea how to resolve the issue, or the same question comes up again and again, you are likely dealing with an adaptive challenge. Some adaptive challenges never go away. For example, you, your predecessor, and your successor will all be attempting to adapt to and serve changing audiences.

Many of the questions we consider in strategic planning are adaptive challenges:

- How do we diversify our audiences?
- What business model will work in the changing economy?
- What are the evolving roles and responsibilities of board and staff?
- How should our programs adapt to the changing demographics and consumer habits of our audience?

Adaptive Challenges vs. Technical Problems. It is important also to distinguish adaptive challenges from technical problems. A lot of planning considers routine questions that can be answered with some confidence: How shall we integrate social networking into our marketing? How shall we cultivate major donors to join the Gold Circle? Heifetz says these technical problems may be complex and critical, but "they can be resolved through the application of authoritative expertise and through the organization's current structures, procedures, and ways of doing things."[7]

In contrast, adaptive challenges are messy and defy easy solutions. Many nonprofit organizations are questioning whether the business models that have worked in the past (especially the mix of earned revenue, contributions, and grants) will continue to work in the future. The question "What business

Figure 1: Adaptive Challenges vs. Technical Problems

Technical Problems	Adaptive Challenges
Familiar terrain	"Wicked problems"
Clear definition possible	Persistent problem
Clear solution possible	May evoke conflict
Expertise exists	Clear definition difficult
Quick solution possible	Outside group's expertise
Authority may impose solution	Requires learning
	Requires change
	No clear solution
	Takes time and culture change
	Stakeholders must address challenge

model will sustain our work?" is not tidy. The question itself is not easily framed, leaders may not yet have the skill to respond, and answers may be ambiguous. These are adaptive challenges.

Heifetz suggests that "the most common cause of failure in leadership is produced by treating adaptive challenges as if they were technical problems." He suggests an experimental orientation, because leaders of adaptive change can never be sure what exactly will work and must improvise as they learn to adapt. This doesn't mean you should not plan, but it demands that you be continuously experimenting, monitoring results, and adapting strategies.

MANAGING POLARITIES

Barry Johnson, creator of the Polarity Management approach to problem-solving, believes that some adaptive challenges are essentially unsolvable. The good news, he says, is that you can learn to manage them even if they defy clear solutions.

For Johnson, much of what organizational leaders consider problems are instead "sets of opposites, which can't function well independently. Because the two sides of a polarity are interdependent, you cannot choose one as a 'solution' and neglect the other. The objective of the Polarity Management™ perspective is to get the best of both opposites while avoiding the limitations of each."[8]

Many planning questions are presented as dualistic, either-or choices: Should we present the best art of accomplished professional artists or show the promising work of emerging artists? Should we challenge our audiences with new and unusual work or play it safe with familiar artists we know will attract them? Shall we predict measurable outcomes in our plan or improvise to see what works?

Johnson suggests using a Polarity Matrix. Figure 2 explores this paradox of planning: to solve problems or to create anew. For each approach there is an upside and a downside, so we cannot entirely accept or reject either pole in the continuum.

Johnson suggests that successful leaders manage a dynamic balance between these apparent poles. The solution to any adaptive challenge that moves from one polarity to another will generally involve some

Figure 2: Problem-Solving and Creating Paradox

Problem-Solving—the upside	Creating—the upside
• Familiar approach • We are good at it • Necessary for technical problems	• Builds on success and strengths • Taps power of vision and core values • Driven by hope • Energizes • Future orientation
Problem-Solving—the downside	**Creating—the downside**
• Focus on what is wrong or who's at fault • Less effective with adaptive problems • Past orientation • Driven by fear • Saps energy	• A learned skill; there will be skeptics • Risk of ignoring problems

downside consequences. Responding to these problems invites a swing back to the opposite pole. An axiom of systems theory is that the solution to any problem sets the seeds for the next problem.

Consider the polarity of centralized vs. shared management. Central authority and dispersed responsibility are both valuable. However, when control is concentrated, the negative implications of central authority become apparent. When junior colleagues start to protest that their opinions are not considered, a manager may delegate more responsibility in response. As authority becomes more dispersed, uncoordinated efforts and other downsides of decentralized responsibilities appear, followed by a corresponding shift back to more central control.

Effective leaders move between the poles, seeking a harmony that takes the best of seeming opposites and avoiding the worst of each. When you are confronted with "either-or" choices, consider if "both-and" solutions can resolve the apparent conflict. The familiar images of a pendulum swing or the interconnected Ying Yang symbol may help envisage the concept.

Types of Plans

One of the complicating factors in thinking about planning is that there are many different kinds of plans, from the planning of routine operations, to program planning, to major organizational change. The leaders of a local arts agency may create a program plan for an annual concert series where the scheduling, budgeting, process of artist selection, and marketing are routine. These same leaders could also undertake strategic planning to reevaluate a role shift to service and advocacy in a community whose other dance, theater, and music presenters are beginning to fill programming needs for the community. This non-routine planning could dramatically transform the organization. This will be clearer after we define some types of plans. See Figure 3.

Strategic Plan

Strategic planning is the means by which an organization makes choices about its overall priorities, who its constituents are and how they will be served, what difference the organization hopes to make, and how it will achieve intended results. This is the most common type of organizational planning. Strategic plans recognize that organizations and the environments in which they operate are dynamic and unpredictable, requiring flexibility. After three years (or sooner in a volatile environment), the organization formally reviews and revises its strategic plan.

Annual Work or Operating Plan

Many nonprofits and public agencies write strategic plans that include goals and the major objectives built on their goals, and then develop annual work, or operating, plans with more specific objectives and tasks. The work plan is updated each year. A work plan contains specific operational objectives for the year, identifying related tasks, persons responsible, deadlines, costs, and other details too specific for a strategic plan. Work plans might be developed for a single staff person, a program, or an entire organization.

Figure 3: Common Types of Plans

Strategic Plan	Organization plan that documents an agreed mission, overall strategies, long-range goals, and short-term objectives for the next three to five years, stressing results and how they may be achieved.
Annual Work or Operating Plan	A detailed 12-month work plan that specifies short-term outcomes, tasks, responsibilities, deadlines, and costs. These are often organized by staff or program.
Contingency Plan	Emergency preparedness plan that specifies actions in the event of data loss, power interruption, severe weather, loss of key staff, or other significant business interruption. Also referred to as a business continuity plan.
Business Plan	Strategic plan that includes revenue and expense projections for the duration of the plan and may include marketing strategies and an analysis of competitive position.
Transition Plan	Short-term plan to help an organization navigate a significant transition like the departure of a long-time leader or a merger. Also referred to as a succession plan.
Program Plan	Plan for a specific program, project (like a performance series), or component of an organization's operations for example, marketing or fundraising).
Collaborative Plan	Plan for a joint venture or collaborative project among two or more independent organizations.
Budget	Financial statement that specifies anticipated revenues and expenses consistent with a strategic plan, for a specified period, usually one year. Budgets may also be done for a single program or funding proposal.
Creative Economic Plan	Plan to identify and strengthen a community's creative and cultural assets to spur economic development. May also be called cultural economic development planning.
Community Cultural Plan	Assessment and plan for arts and culture in a community, county, or region. It can be general or specific, as in a cultural economic development plan.

Contingency Plan

The catastrophic impacts of some emergencies can be mitigated by planning. Many leaders of museums and arts centers without contingency plans have unfortunately discovered that hurricanes, tornados, and floods move faster than they could prepare for in a crisis. Contingency, or business continuity, plans usually complement other plans and may include plans for fire, severe weather, sudden loss of key staff, or data loss and recovery. Visit South Arts' website, www.BeArtsReady.org, for online emergency preparedness tools, resources, and links.

Business Plan

As nonprofits are becoming more entrepreneurial, this shift is reflected in planning. When prospective donors ask to see an organization's "business plan," they may be asking for a strategic plan that includes three years of projected revenues and expenses, or a corporate plan that also includes an analysis of competition, market share, and market position.

Some nonprofits develop a strategic plan and then a separate three-year budget projection, which function together as a business plan. A marketing plan may also complement a strategic plan. When an organization has multiple plans and budgets, it must take care that these plans are consistent.

Budget

A budget is a kind of annual plan expressed in strictly financial terms. It should be influenced by, and reflect the priorities of, the annual operating plan. If the board has determined that arts education will be a greater priority next year, the budget should reflect increased organizational resources of staff time and money in that sphere. (For more information on budgeting, see the Financial Management chapter.)

> As a grant reviewer I expect the budget to reflect the values of the mission statement, and if I see no link, I'm concerned that the project is probably not an appropriate one. If the mission is about supporting artists but the budget shows artists' fees as in-kind contributions, I rarely read on.
>
> —Maryo Gard Ewell, arts organizer, former associate director, Colorado Council on the Arts

Program Plan

A program, or project, plan deals with a single aspect of an agency's operations, such as an arts education program, a marketing or fundraising project, or facility renovation. Such a plan can be assembled in a procedures manual, organized in a single binder, computer file, or web page. A procedures manual for an ongoing program is a good example of a plan that emerges from experience. Rather than just projecting how a project might be done, the plan documents what is being done and what needs improvement. For a volunteer-run organization, this can be a breakthrough. Each lead volunteer amends the procedures manual before he or she passes it on to the next volunteer. This makes it easier to recruit volunteers and ensure well-managed programs.

The Program Development and Marketing the Arts chapters contain more examples of program planning. ▌ See the Appendix for elements that might be included in a procedures manual.

THE CYCLE OF PLANNING

Strategic plans often follow a three-to-five-year planning cycle. In the first and second years of a comprehensive strategic plan, organization leaders may monitor progress, adapt the plan as necessary, and perhaps plan for specific initiatives. In the third or fourth year, the plan is thoroughly revised in anticipation of the next planning cycle. Leaders of a strategic planning process may write an overall agency plan with differing levels of specificity. Some aspects—such as arts programming, fundraising, and marketing—may warrant considerable specificity, while other areas—perhaps staffing or facility improvement—might need more assessment and planning than can be completed during the organization's strategic planning process.

David La Piana argues for real-time strategic planning with "ongoing consideration of strategy, as it is needed, not on a pre-determined three-year cycle." He reminds us that organization leaders cannot limit strategic thinking to occasional planning retreats; the world changes too fast to expect a plan to work for years without adaptation.[9] Still, an intentional planning process is the best way to achieve consensus about the organization's priorities and central strategies. Then, leaders must be continually alert to adapt strategies and tactics. If conditions change or plans do not achieve intended results, plans must change. But in the absence of a strategic plan, leaders have no basis from which to improvise; they risk being reactive, rather than proactive.

Remember, the process of planning is more important than the resulting plan. The critical value of planning is for an organization's members to agree on priorities, intended results, and an overall strategy to achieve them. Writing the plan requires rigorous thinking that translates broad concepts into decisive intentions. Yet, it is a mistake to follow the plan blindly. As emphasized above, using metaphors like "blueprint" or "roadmap" can imply a misleading sense of certainty or predictability. A compass is a more useful metaphor, if you think of the device as a tool you use to find your way when you know where you're headed, guided by the organization's values and strategy.

> In preparing for battle, I have always found that plans are useless but planning is indispensable.
>
> —Dwight D. Eisenhower

> No plan survives contact with the enemy.
>
> —German Field Marshall Helmuth Karl Bernhard Graf[10]

ALTERNATIVE TYPES OF AGENCY PLANNING

Scenario Planning

Recognizing that the future is uncertain, some planners develop plans for two or more alternative scenarios. If you have ever had a "Plan B," you've done scenario planning. As Peter Schwartz explains in The Art of the Long View, "In a scenario process, managers invent and then consider … several varied stories of equally plausible futures.… Scenario planners do not try to predict the preferred or most likely future, but rather the point is to make strategic decisions that will be sound for all plausible futures. No matter what future takes place, you are much more likely to be ready for it."[11]

Corporations use scenario planning to anticipate how they will react to a given set of variables under a number of conditions. For example, an arts center may prepare for two scenarios: in one, the capital campaign is successful and the facility is expanded; in the other, the organization prepares for a less successful campaign and minor facility renovation.

> Vision plus information plus unforeseen events equals opportunity
>
> —Peter Senge, *The Fifth Discipline*

Emergent Planning

While most planners anticipate future actions and develop a plan that describes what they intend to do, there is another, more intuitive approach, which Henry Mintzberg called emergent planning.[12] In this method, program managers run programs, try new initiatives, observe and document what works and what does not, and make adjustments accordingly. Emergent planning is a deliberate process of discovering a plan from experience. This is a more sophisticated approach than what some planners call "muddling through," in that planners are quite intentional about creating new written plans based on emerging experience. Program plans often use this method.

Collaborative Planning

You may find yourself planning for a program or larger initiative in partnership with other organizations; for instance, to develop arts education programs with schools, to produce a statewide arts advocacy campaign or launch a regional cultural tourism initiative. While many of the same strategic planning principles apply, there are some significant differences.

The partners will seldom have a common mission, so the partnership lacks this central organizing principle. Power among the partners may be unequal. Implementation is not under the authority of a single organization, and partners must create systems to determine how decisions are implemented, progress monitored, and results evaluated. See "Ten Steps to Plan Collaboratively with Another Organization" in the Appendix.

Community Cultural Planning

Community cultural planning is a structured process engaging multiple cultural and civic partners to assess a community's cultural assets and needs, develop a comprehensive plan, and mobilize resources to respond. Community cultural plans are explicitly concerned with the broader cultural assets, needs, and opportunities of the entire community, transcending the interests of any one organization.

There are several types of community-wide planning. A community arts plan focuses specifically on planning to understand and encourage artists, arts organizations and their related funding, facilities, audiences, and educational and communications systems. A community cultural plan is aimed at the more broadly defined cultural interests of a community, including areas like history and heritage, libraries, public celebrations, and interpretive science centers. Many cultural plans extend to urban design, including the look of streets and neighborhoods and the preservation of historic buildings. More recently, communities are organizing creative economy and creative placemaking plans (see below).

It is not unusual to combine elements of these types of plans. A local arts agency may conduct a community-wide cultural assessment and then create a strategic plan that responds to the issues raised in the broader assessment that most closely relate to the agency's mission and capabilities.

CREATIVE ECONOMIC DEVELOPMENT PLANNING

Creative (or cultural) economic development planning (CED) applies the principles of community cultural planning to local or regional economic development. As jobs and economic growth have become critical concerns for municipalities and regions, these creative-sector plans have become more common. Creative economic development plans are concerned with professional artists, creative workers in all sectors, nonprofit cultural organizations, for-profit creative industries, and the funding, service, and educational systems. CED thus positions arts, culture, heritage, and creativity as the creative economic sector.

CED planning is driven by economic data. An early step is to define and measure the local creative sector. Definitions vary widely. The New England Foundation for the Arts[13] defined the sector with a specific set of standard industry codes that permit apples-to-apples comparison across regions. Western States Arts Foundation (WESTAF) developed a Creative Vitality Index (CVI™) that measures for-profit and non-profit creative industries and enterprises as an economic sector and a measure of vitality.[14] Americans for the Arts developed the National Arts Index, an annual measure of the health and vitality of arts in the United States.[15] (See the chapter on Arts and the Economy for more information on this topic.)

CED processes include cultural and creative sector asset mapping, analysis of the creative sector's economic impact, and planning to use creative assets to enhance jobs and growth. Plans often help position a community for cultural tourism and to attract and retain creative workers, businesses, and young people. See the Arts Extension Service's Creative Economy Planning Workbook.

> Creative economy in its most basic sense addresses how organizational and individual output of creative capital economically impacts communities.[16]

ALTERNATIVES TO PLANNING

To be fair, not every successful organization embraces intentional planning. Some charismatic or authoritarian leaders simply decide what is best, based on their own vision or perceptions. If their vision is clear and their instincts are good, this can work as long as they are in charge. Other leaders seem to thrive on the high drama of crisis management, reacting to each new force as it confronts the organization. Some long-established organizations seem to run on automatic pilot, operating on the principle "We've always done it that way."

Some arts leaders value intuition, experimentation, and improvisation and make it up as they go. Emergent planning builds upon this approach with intentional plans drawn from experience. There is also a trend to value strategic thinking as an alternative to strategic planning. However, experimentation and strategic thinking work best if strategic planning establishes common understandings among staff and board about values, long-range goals, and overall strategy. This creates a base from which leaders can improvise or adapt strategies to novel situations.

Organizations with a strong central authority or no planning tend to have difficult transitions or fail when the leader departs. Reactively or intuitively managed organizations can lose their way as they chase grants and opportunities or respond to threats without a clear sense of direction. Those running on automatic pilot may not spot critical changes in their environment in time to adapt. While an improvisational, approach can work in times of stability, when times are turbulent strategic planning can be critical to an organization's success.

Planning Approaches

There are as many different approaches to planning as there are types of plans. In practice, short-term, project-specific plans are crafted more precisely and with a higher expectation of predictability than longer-range and more comprehensive strategic or community planning. Leaders of start-up organizations may plan differently than those of established organizations. Planning for ongoing operations is approached more routinely than planning for organizational transformation. There is no one planning approach that will suit every organization or situation. Organization leaders should feel free to adapt the planning methods outlined here to fit their group's culture and conditions. Planning need not be complicated or follow an expert's instructions to be effective.

THE BENEFITS OF COLLABORATIVE PLANNING

Effective leaders are able to articulate a vision of what an organization can accomplish, possess the energy to work on behalf of that vision, and have the power to persuade others to support the effort. Why, then, shouldn't a leader just make plans and then convince the organization's board and staff to support them? There are several reasons.

Even if an individually generated plan were as good as one created by a group, the apparent efficiency of individual leader doing the planning may be undermined by the time and effort required to sell the finished plan to others. Involvement in planning leads to ownership and ownership can translate into commitment to do the work necessary to implement the plan. Even more important, plans that arise from vigorous discussions among board members, staff, and key stakeholders are simply better than solo work. Organizations and their environments are often too complicated for any one leader to fully understand. Strategic thinking must be shared.

It is, of course, possible to involve board and staff members in token participation in planning where the leaders have predetermined the results. This Machiavellian sort of planning is usually recognized for what it is and backfires in the form of grudging support from board members, volunteers, and staff. When the work encounters obstacles, it is easy to give up on someone else's idea.

The difference between token and genuine participation in planning has little to do with the amount of time spent. A general sense of a group's priorities and intentions can be gathered in a relatively brief planning retreat or series of planning meetings. In genuine participation, the leader must be authentically open to new ideas, even those that may challenge the leader's own preconceptions. In a truly participatory process, a good idea gets tempered and improved, and a flawed one gets challenged and rejected. (See the Board Development chapter for more information on how a board can contribute creatively in planning.)

What If Planning Provokes Disagreement?

If board and staff members are largely united in their intentions and agree upon organizational priorities, the planning process can confirm this and provide the basis for coherent decisions on programming, marketing, fundraising, and volunteer recruiting.

On the other hand, planning may reveal differing visions of an organization's mission and priorities and may even provoke conflict.

Board and staff members should debate priorities in a planning retreat or series of meetings. In the case of conflict, the task of the planning team is to clarify the implications of each choice in terms of its fit with the organization's mission, fulfillment of community needs, financial implications, and audience outreach. The planning team then returns to a larger meeting of board and staff with a clearer picture of what the organization might look like if it moved along either of the proposed paths. For example, there may be financial consequences for one choice that was not obvious when the alternative was first proposed, or audience statistics may reveal a surprisingly high (or low) level of community support for one or the other option.

> The task of the planning team in the case of conflict is to clarify the implications of each choice in terms of its fit with mission, fulfillment of community needs, financial implications, and audience outreach.

At times it is necessary to agree to disagree. Disagreements may be so profound that they prompt people to withdraw from the organization. While such conflicts are unpleasant, it is better to openly clarify what members of an organization believe in and are prepared to support than to allow unaddressed conflicts to bubble up later when attempting to implement programs. It is usually better to at least achieve consensus on general principles. Then it becomes more obvious which specific decisions must be made.

The Language of Planning

Planning terminology can be confusing. One person's "goal" is another's "objective" or "outcome." Many vigorous planning discussions have been derailed by debating terminology: "Is this a goal or an objective?" While it is a good idea to think about the structure of a plan early in the process (for example, the hierarchy of mission, goals, strategies, and objectives), it may not be helpful to worry about labels until the group leaders' intentions are being translated into written form. In fact, "intention" is a great placeholder to label any decision the planning committee or board and staff make while planning.

Some commonly used planning terms and their definitions are suggested below, but don't be overly concerned if people in your organization are more comfortable with others. What is more important is that people within an organization understand the language used in their plan and that a word like "objective" means the same thing each time it is used throughout a plan.

In general, planning terminology ranges from more general, inclusive terms to the more specific. In this chapter, we use the following terminology: Broad terms like vision, mission, and purpose describe an organization's ultimate intentions in the broadest sense. Goals describe desired long-term results. Strategies usually mean the organization's overall approach or methods that will realize goals and objectives. Objectives or outcomes describe more specific results to be achieved in the short term. The most detailed short-term actions may be called tasks or activities.

TERMS DESCRIBING BELIEFS

Values or principles. Values are core beliefs or assumptions about how the world works and what is important. In some plans, important values that define the organizational culture and inspire ethical action are stated as explicit values statements. For example, the Maryland State Arts Council defined four core values, the principles that guide all its policy, plans, programs, and administrative decisions:

- **Excellence** in artistic practice and expression
- **Access** to the arts and to the Arts Council for every citizen of our state
- **Inclusion** of diverse voices that reflect the people of Maryland
- **Integrity** in policy development and program implementation ensuring fairness and equity[17]

Assumptions. Some plans make explicit the organization's beliefs about the forces in the world that influence their plans. Plans may express assumptions about demographic, economic, political, social, or technological trends that organization leaders considered in planning. For example, "Our planning considered increasing capacity to communicate to our community's changing demographic profile, evolving audience attendance patterns, and rapidly changing communications technologies."

TERMS DESCRIBING INTENDED RESULTS

Vision. A vision is a statement of an ideal or hoped-for future and describes what it would look like. If you can imagine the essential difference your organization is trying to make in the world, you have a vision. Sometimes these are tightly crafted statements that complement the formal mission, or they may be lists of idealized future results. Visions need not be practical. While not all plans articulate a vision, they can help to set the organization's sights high and provide context for a formal mission statement. Here, for example, is the vision statement of the Hawai'i Community Foundation:

> We want to live in a Hawai'i where people care about each other, our natural resources, and diverse island cultures; a place where people's ideas, initiatives, and generosity support thriving, responsible communities.[18]

Mission. An organization's mission statement captures its purpose or the ultimate result it hopes to achieve. The mission answers fundamental questions: why an organization exists, whom it aims to serve, and what business it is in. Here are some examples:

- Fractured Atlas … empowers artists, arts organizations, and other cultural sector stakeholders by eliminating practical barriers to artistic expression, so as to foster a more agile and resilient cultural ecosystem.
- Young Audiences New York … instills in young people from pre-kindergarten through high school an appreciation, knowledge, and understanding of the performing, visual, and literary arts.
- Sierra Arts … is a regional arts organization dedicated to enhancing the quality of life and human experience by supporting an environment where arts and cultural diversity thrive.

Slogans or tag lines. Organizations often condense their mission or vision into a very short, compelling phrase used as a memorable slogan or tag line. This is as much a marketing strategy as a planning issue. Especially if you choose to write a long mission statement, it is useful to capture the essence in a phrase that you reproduce on your letterhead, business cards, publications, website, email signatures, program notes, and fundraising materials. For example:

- Arts Extension Service: Connecting Communities and the Arts since 1973.
- Vermont Arts Council: We don't make art, we make art work.

Long-Range goal. Goals are general, long-term, result-oriented statements consistent with the mission. They often describe the overall intended results of major program areas. Think of long-range goals as the infrastructure upon which the bulk of the plan is built. If all goals are achieved, the mission is fulfilled. It is a good idea for a plan to lead with public-benefit goals and conclude with internal, capacity-building goals.

South Dakota Arts Council's Goals
- 1. Expand accessibility to the arts.
- 2. Advance the arts as essential to learning.
- 3. Encourage, support and promote artists.
- 4. Strengthen arts organizations in South Dakota.
- 5. Enhance the development of quality cultural tourism.
- 6. Promote public awareness and support of the arts.

In common usage, the word "goal" can mean virtually any intention. You will hear people say, "Our goal for this meeting is to conclude by 9:00 p.m." This of course, is not a long-range goal. Some planners and writers confusingly use "goal" to mean a specific measurable result. Do not be surprised if you find plans that label detailed targets as goals or if funders ask you to measure goals. In this chapter, we use goals only to mean long-term results, not specific, short-term results that can be measured. In practice, however, you may have to adapt to many different usages.

Objective and outcome. While the terms objective and outcome are often used interchangeably, objective is used more often in planning, to describe an intended future result and outcome is used in evaluation, to document an actual achieved result. An objective is a specific, measurable, and achievable short-term result that, if fulfilled, would help advance a long-range goal. Objectives are similar to goals, in that objectives describe desired future results. Objectives, though, are much more specific than goals and predict results in a shorter time frame—often a year or two. Objectives also are anticipated outcomes. Increasingly, however, strategic planners are using the term outcomes instead of objectives to stress the importance of achieving results. Funding agencies that have embraced outcome-based evaluation may ask you to present your plans in terms of outcomes. The difference is largely one of perspective and how the intended results are labeled can be simply a matter of semantics.

Objectives should describe an intended observable result. A good test is to ask what specific changes in people or the world you expect to observe. It is quite common to see action steps erroneously described in plans as objectives: "Offer a series of three professional development workshops for artists each fall." It is better to re-frame this to include the intended result of those actions: "Artists will learn to better manage their creative businesses through a series of three professional development workshops each fall." In evaluating your eventual success, the first, action-oriented version of the objective could be satisfied by counting the artists sitting through lectures. The second, results-oriented version (an intended outcome) could only be satisfied by asking artists if they learned something useful to advance their careers. Learning is a better outcome than attending.

Given the ubiquitous expectation of accountability, your plan will be more compelling and evaluation much simpler if you convert draft objectives describing projects or actions into the result you expect to see achieved. Ask what will change in the world as a result of your project or actions. Present this as your objective or intended outcome. This also forces organization leaders to decide what they want to accomplish and helps all team members to understand what is intended. Framing objectives as outcomes or intended results helps prevent business-as-usual thinking that perpetuates programs only because "we have always done them." (See the Program Evaluation chapter for more information on the relation of planned objectives to observed outcomes.)

When evaluating programs, it is helpful to compare an objective (determined in planning as an intended outcome) with its actual outcome (measured as an achieved objective). In the perfect world, these would be identical—you would achieve your objectives. In the real world, of course, that doesn't always happen, and distinguishing between objectives and outcomes performs a valuable function. Evaluations that document the extent to which outcomes vary from objectives clearly demonstrate the extent to which your programs met, exceeded, or failed to meet expectations, providing the basis on which to revisit and revise your plan.

> To determine objectives, ask what specific changes in people or the world you expect to observe.

As you write objectives, think SMART.[19] The SMART mnemonic will help you remember that an effective objective should meet five conditions. An objective should be:

- Specific (describe specific changes in the world or in people that will be achieved)
- Measurable (the result should be observable by either quantitative or qualitative measures)
- Attainable (result should be realistic and feasibly achievable)
- Relevant (result should help further one or more long-range goals)
- Time-bound (note when the result should be achieved)

TERMS DESCRIBING METHODS

Strategy. Strategies are general approaches or methods an organization utilizes to fulfill its plan. They describe the overall means to accomplish goals and objectives. Military and corporate planning limits the use of strategy to describing the broadest ways of working, using tactics to define more specific actions. Nonprofit organizations and public agencies tend to be less strict in planning language, using strategies as the means to achieve any element of a plan: an overall approach for the whole plan, a long-range goal, or specific objective.

David La Piana defines a strategy as "an organized pattern of behavior towards an end."[20] In general, strategies answer the question, How will we fulfill our plan? For example:

> An arts agency will shift activities from presenting arts events to providing information and services for arts presenting and producing organizations.
>
> A theater will cultivate more individual local donors and rely less on public agency grants.

Tasks and actions. These are activities which contribute to the achievement of goals and objectives, expressed in terms of who does what by when. Tasks are specific jobs to accomplish objectives. For example:

> The artistic director will present his proposed budget for the upcoming season of concerts to the board of directors for their approval by the March 15th meeting.

Assessment. Assessment is the process of identifying organizational strengths and assets, constituent needs, organizational health, and environmental trends. In planning, assessment is thought of as information gathering in preparation for taking action. In practice, assessment, decision-making, and action may happen concurrently. The term "assessment" may also be used to describe the monitoring and evaluation of programs to see what works and what doesn't, and to evaluate results at the conclusion of programs.

The Structure of a Strategic Plan

The elements of a written strategic plan, outlined above, are typically organized in a hierarchical structure that emphasizes their relationships. Plans generally start with the broadest statements of belief (mission, vision, values) then express overarching strategies (how, in general, the plan will be fulfilled), then long-range results (goals), specific results (objectives or outcomes), then very specific and short-term tasks, and finally, the funding that will support the plan.

Mission (why organization exists)

    Vision (ideal, written picture of an ideal or hoped-for future)

        Core Values (ethical principles that guide policy and action)

            Strategies (overall approach to achieve priority outcomes)

                Long-Range Goals (long-term, hoped-for results that can guide policy but can't be measured)

                    Outcomes (short-term intended objectives or results – progress evaluated annually)

                      Tasks (who does what by when – staff work plans)

                        Budget (approved and monitored by board)

Part II: Methods of Planning

How to Plan: The AES Eight-Stage Planning Process

Almost any planning process is beneficial if it regularly brings together people who care enough about an organization to answer important questions: How are we doing? What do our constituents want? What do we believe in? If your organization already has an effective planning process in place, stick with it. However, organizations without one often want to begin with a tested process known to work. The Arts Extension Service (AES) uses an eight-stage planning process that is simple, flexible, and can be adapted for a quick or more comprehensive process.

The AES planning process relies upon the combination of a small planning team or committee to organize it, and one or more planning retreats to engage the board and professional staff. One or more members of the planning committee may actually write the plan. Assessment can be comprehensive or simplified. The planning retreat can be a one-day meeting (usually four to six hours) or a day-and-a-half overnight.

The eight-stage planning process should be undertaken to initiate an organization into a cycle of ongoing planning. The sequence of steps can vary. An organization that knows its constituency very well may organize a planning retreat instead of doing an external assessment, while one that wishes to engage with its community may want to gather constituent input through surveys, public forums, interviews, and/or focus groups before having its first planning retreat.

After planning becomes part of the organizational culture, assessing, monitoring, adapting, and planning become ongoing activities. With practice, planning is not a separate activity but a fundamental way of working. It becomes second nature and intuitive. If planning is seen as a way to systematically learn about and adapt to changes in the organization's environment, the planning organization becomes a learning organization—one in which learning is an internalized value.

WHO'S ON FIRST?

Each organization will determine who is most able to take responsibility for each stage of planning. The board usually starts and concludes the planning and is ordinarily the final, approving authority. In some public commissions, the commissioners are advisory and ought to participate in planning even if they are not called upon to approve the finished plan.

While the board is ultimately responsible for planning, the professional staff should have key leadership roles. In many organizations, the board and staff together focus on the larger issues of mission, goals, and overall strategy, while staff may be primarily responsible for objectives and annual work plans. In the best case, the board and staff are partners in planning. If planning must consider reducing programs or staff, the board may need to meet without the program staff. In all-volunteer organizations, committee chairs may provide the equivalent of a staff perspective.

The sequence of events involved in strategic planning and the roles of board and staff in carrying them out are outlined below:

1. Board and staff initiate the plan by organizing and appointing a planning committee.
2. Organizations needing outside help find and contract with a consultant.
3. Board and staff participate in an initial planning retreat to discuss vision, mission, values, and questions that should be resolved in planning.
4. The planning committee leads a community assessment if required.
5. Board and staff gather in a second planning retreat or series of planning meetings to make sense of assessment results and make decisions about priorities. A volunteer or professional consultant facilitates.
6. The planning committee (and/or planning consultant) writes the draft plan.
7. The board considers the draft, amends it if needed, and approves the plan. If necessary, the planning committee writes a second draft before final approval.

Stage 1: Organize

A planning effort requires organization. Typically one or more board or senior staff members decide that the organization would benefit from planning and initiate discussion with other board members and staff. They consider the scope and scale of the plan, candidates for the planning team, and the time and funds needed for the effort. They decide how to involve the full board and staff. At a subsequent board meeting, the idea is raised and support is sought. If there are professional staff, the project is introduced to them at a staff meeting.

FIRST THINGS FIRST

To prepare for planning, some initial topics need to be considered.

Time commitment. When should planning start and finish? What time period should the plan cover? A simple plan can be accomplished with a single planning retreat, a few days of writing, and a board meeting. A more comprehensive plan may take three to six months. Ask how comprehensive the plan should be and match the time commitment to the scope of planning. The stage that requires the most time is seeking constituent input in the external assessment.

Figure 4: The AES Planning Process

STAGE	WHAT	WHO	HOW
1. Organize	Recruit planning team, budget, determine scope, and collect background information.	Chief executive and board president	Organize meeting.
2. Envision	Discuss vision, values, and who you are and what you believe in (to be expressed in a set of governing ideas).	Board and staff	Hold planning retreat for stages 2-4.
3. Assess	Discover current internal and external conditions. Simple plans involve only board and staff; more team-comprehensive plans assess community members' needs directly.	Board and staff	Conduct retreat and/or planning interviews, focus groups, surveys, and public hearings. Review records.
4. Establish Goals	Explore alternatives and choose desired results and most likely ways to achieve them. These may be expressed through mission, goals, objectives, strategies, and budgets.	Board and staff or planning team	Hold planning retreat and subsequent series of planning meetings.
5. Write the Plan	Write first draft; revise, review (board and staff), check with constituents, and revise final draft.	Planning team	Write, revise, and rewrite.
6. Approve and Commit	Confirm board approval and organizational commitment to implement. Distribute plan widely.	Board, staff, and volunteers	Explain, promote, and go public.
7. Implement	Determine who does what, and at what cost. Then do it.	Staff and/or volunteers	Link plan to budgets and program decisions.
8. Evaluate and Adapt	Regularly ask how you are doing. Monitor progress on objectives. Make course corrections as conditions change. Recycle through the planning process.	Staff and board	Recruit champions for goals, schedule discussions, and monitor progress.

Process. What process should be used to gather the information needed for the plan? At what point should the assessment be made? Will it involve people outside the organization—through interviews, focus group meetings, public forums, or surveys—or can the board and staff assume they know the community, audiences, funders, and potential collaborators and competitors well enough to proceed?

Planning team. Who will lead the planning effort and who should be on the team? AES recommends using a small planning committee. (See "Should We Use a Consultant?" in the Appendix.) Recruit people for the planning committee who can write, as well as those who represent a balance among the interests and constituencies served by the organization. A small, balanced group is needed to finish the planning work started at a retreat or series of planning meetings. The planning committee will not develop the plan by itself; it will organize the rest of the organization to do so.

Budget. What funds are required and from what sources will they be drawn? If a professional consultant or retreat facilitator is used, this will be the major expense. Consultants are sometimes helpful but not always necessary. Other expenses may include refreshments for the retreat and any assessment meetings, flip charts, photocopying, and space rental (if not using space in the organization). State and local arts agencies and community foundations often offer funding for planning. If you plan to seek a grant to underwrite your planning effort, this step will have to be accomplished well in advance of the start of planning.

Planning retreat(s). Reserve the retreat date on people's calendars. Allow enough time to collect information, including audience research or community assessment if they are part of your planning process.

Retreat site. Select an attractive, easily accessible location where people will be comfortable and productive. Retreats may be held in corporate boardrooms (to encourage hard work), in private homes (to encourage informality and sociability), or at conference centers (to encourage productivity or make the retreat more of a special event).

Useful materials. You will need an easel and large flip chart, markers, and tape. In addition, have on hand copies of existing plans, budgets, mission statements, audience statistics, sample promotions, etc. Refreshments are essential. Where possible, email information in advance to retreat participants, and only provide essential documents at the meeting. (See the Appendix for a Planning Retreat Checklist as well as a Sample Planning Retreat Agenda.)

Stage 2: Envision

The next three stages—envisioning, assessing, and making decisions—may be covered in part or in their entirety at the planning retreat. However, if your board and staff do not adequately represent the community you serve or wish to serve, an external assessment step is probably necessary. In that case, this process works best if the assessment is conducted before the planning retreat. Assessment then becomes the second step and Envisioning becomes the third.

Envisioning may be the most important step in the planning process. It is here that members of the group ask the most fundamental questions: In what do we believe? Why does this organization exist? What difference, ultimately, do we wish to make in this community? What is our vision for the future? What will that envisioned future look like?

For an organization with a clearly established vision, this step becomes an opportunity to introduce new board and staff to that vision and to remind everyone of the important work of which they are all a part.

THE IMPORTANCE OF VISION

A sense of vision—one that is meaningful, clearly articulated, and widely shared by members of an organization—is a powerful force in planning. A vision, a clear sense of mission, and core values are more valuable in a rapidly changing environment than a detailed set of tasks that may become quickly outdated. A planning retreat which achieves a clear sense of a desired future is well worth the effort. But how do we find one?

> Stripped of all the jargon, planning is, in essence, a creative act. A planner, like an artist, imagines what might be and then goes about to make it so.

Recall your vision. Sometimes discussions among founding members or a review of early plans and promotions will reveal a powerful founding vision which may have been forgotten. Ask members to recall why it was that they joined the organization, to regain a sense of this founding vision.

Recognize the vision of a leader. Sometimes arts organizations are blessed with a visionary leader. This is frequently the case for arts-producing organizations formed to support the creative work of a choreographer, music director, or curator. This envisioning stage can encourage the visionary leader to communicate her or his artistic vision to the rest of the organization's members.

Create a new vision. For arts organizations sustained by community needs for artistic programs and services, this approach may be the most successful.

It may be difficult for people to express their visions. While a vision must ultimately be expressed in writing, it may need to emerge from a less literal process. Too much talking and writing may inhibit more imaginative thinking. A planning retreat should include envisioning exercises to assist people to tap their right-brain creativity. These may include the use of drawing, metaphors, storytelling, games, and guided visualization.

It's likely that at this point in the retreat (or in a succession of planning meetings), the vision exists as a series of key words and phrases, perhaps some drawings or charts. Try to condense them onto one or two flip charts—the essential parts of the visioning exercises. Post the mission statement on a flip chart alongside the written elements of the newly described vision.

Imagining a Theater

An actor in Maine attended an AES planning workshop to learn how to start a theater company in her rural community. She had worked in other theaters and knew how they operated. There were a number of people interested in participating, but she was having considerable trouble getting started. How does one create an institution? She was daunted.

After she described her dilemma, it occurred to the instructor to ask if she could act and organize the production of a play. Of course she could. He suggested that she assume the role of an artistic director, imagine a scenario of her theater company in business, and then cast players in the roles needed to get the theater established. "But the theater isn't real yet," she said. He asked her at what point it would be: would it be real after they had built a theater, after they had produced their first play, or after they had a year's productions behind them? Why not create it now?

He suggested that she announce that a community theater had been started and that she was its artistic director. She was to print some business cards, call a meeting of interested community members, and plan its first production. She was to assume the role and act the part. Soon after she announced on her new letterhead that it worked just as she had imagined. She had tapped the creativity of the art she knew so well.

> **Questions to inspire people to express a sense of vision and mission**
> - What most inspires you about our work?
> - Recall an incident when you observed this organization at its finest.
> - When have you seen us doing the best work we were meant to do?
> - What business are we in?
> - If we went out of business, what would be the ultimate cost to our community? What would be lost?
>
> **How you might ask questions**
> - During a retreat or planning meeting, a facilitator asks one of the above questions.
> - Ask each individual to briefly write down one or more answers.
> - After individuals have worked alone for a time, ask people to form groups of two or three and share their stories. Planners call these *purpose stories*.
> - Ask a representative from each group to summarize stories that are typical of their group's discussion.
> - A facilitator summarizes themes and patterns from the discussion by writing keywords and phrases on a large pad of paper.
> - Compare the elements of these visions to the current mission or purpose statement.
> - If the formal mission statement seems to fit these stories, group members now have a better understanding of what that dry language now means. If the mission seems out of synch with the values that group members most often described, this suggests that the planners may need to revise the mission.

Compare the emerging vision with the existing mission statement. If the mission remains consistent with the language emerging as a vision, planners can reconfirm the mission. Some of the words and phrases generated in the retreat can be used to interpret the mission in promotions, fundraising appeals, and communications with volunteers or staff.

The comparison of the mission and vision may prove the mission to be out of date. In that case, the group should discuss whether it needs to revise the mission. It should resist the temptation to write a new mission statement as part of the retreat. Rather, the planning committee should work later with the intentions of the retreat participants. The committee should return to the board and staff with one or more versions of a revised mission for their consideration.

An inspiring vision is crucial. But the vision must balance with a clear-eyed look at where the organization is and how it is doing.

Stage 3: Assess

An accurate assessment of your current situation—both internal and external to the organization—is the usual next step in planning. Alternatively, assessment may precede envisioning if there is to be a single planning retreat or, as noted above, if a preliminary community assessment is required.

While assessment is considered here as a discrete phase in planning, the leaders of any successful arts organization are constantly observing and assessing what is going on within the organization and its community and adapting operations as required. In addition to this ongoing assessment, a deliberate taking stock of current conditions is a key part of a strategic planning process.

The eight-stage model assumes two assessment possibilities. Either the board and staff represent the community or constituencies served by the organization and understand their needs; or they do not. The first case assumes that organization leaders are in close contact with the people served, understand their concerns, and are aware of community changes like shifting demographics. It may be possible to develop a good plan without extensive community assessment. However, planning and the organization are usually improved through the relationship building that happens when you go out into the community to ask about people's interests and needs and how your organization can help serve them.

> External assessments fulfill two important functions: to gather information and build relationships.

If the group's leadership does not itself reflect and understand important resources or constituencies, then external assessment is essential for the planning to be authentic. Beyond the obvious advantage of the planning information you will gather, there are other critical benefits. Plans inevitably change, but if you've built relationships in planning, you can adjust. There is also a political or public relations benefit from constituent assessment. Your organization becomes visibly concerned with understanding community interests. This may put you on the radar screens of people who may be in a position to help you implement your plans. Many arts leaders find they are able to reach funders, political leaders, school officials, and newspaper publishers to ask questions in assessment in a way they could never do if they were asking for help.

External assessments can be accomplished by sampling the opinions of representatives of key funders, audiences, and potential collaborators through interviews, focus group meetings, public forums, or surveys. Internal assessments can be done by reviewing financial reports and evaluation results, by asking questions of staff, volunteers, and board members, and by identifying assessment issues as part of a planning retreat. Both of these are looked at in more detail below.

INTERNAL ASSESSMENT

Records. Before going out to the community to gather more data, look at what information you already have. Some may originally have come from external sources and may be useful in your assessment.

Financial statements. The current year's budget compared with actual expenses to date provides valuable assessment data. Get an even better sense of financial trends by reviewing the three previous years of operating statements (statements of annual income and expenses). While much can be learned from a look at how specific line items change, summarized charts may be more useful for strategic planning—for example, a pie chart showing the sources of income and the major expenses or a simple line chart with total income and expenses over a three- or four-year period.

If the data show changes, ask why. If ticket sales rose and then fell, ask if there were changes in programming or promotion that could explain the variation. The point of the financial analysis is to help make strategic decisions in planning.

> An arts agency board debated the wisdom of partnerships with non-arts agencies. A table, showing the relative amount of money that partners invested in the arts agency and directly to artists through employment contracts, quickly settled the debate.

Evaluation reports. Consider the findings of program or service evaluations in planning.

Grant panelist comments. Comments and scores by the panelists who considered a grant proposal may provide good assessment data. Consider what they say about your organization, good and bad, during planning.

Attendance statistics. A summary of attendance at programs, events, and services can be useful. Organize visitor tracking data, inquiries for information, ticket sales, etc., into summary charts or tables and then ask what the information reveals.

Benchmarking. Organizations participating in DataArts (formerly the Cultural Data Project) or who are members of national service organizations like American Alliance of Museums or Dance USA can see how their results compare with similar organizations locally or nationally. While planning, it can help to know, for example, if a shift from subscriptions to single-ticket buying at your organization is a trend shared by your peer institutions. Such a finding might inspire a new business strategy rather than doubling down to market more subscriptions.

Self-assessment questionnaires. It can be quite productive to ask questions of board and staff to elicit a clearer sense of what is—and is not—working inside the organization. Or you can frame questions specific to the issues you know to be of concern. Consider using a self-assessment instrument. The scoring of anonymous responses can identify issues that people might otherwise be hesitant to raise. More important than scores is that the questions that provoke reflection. Circulate assessment questions a couple of weeks before your first retreat to stimulate critical thinking about the organization's strengths and weaknesses. (For information on framing open-ended questions or fixed-response questions, see the Program Evaluation chapter.) ▌

Internal interviews. Administer assessment questions in one-on-one interviews or small group discussions. In one large arts center, the director met with small groups of professional and support staff, regular volunteers, and teaching artists to discuss their concerns and suggestions for planning. Then he summarized these discussions during a planning retreat for senior staff and board members.

Strengths, Weaknesses, Opportunities, and Threats (SWOT). Invite board and staff members to brainstorm and consider internal organizational strengths and weaknesses and external threats and opportunities. Planners call this step a SWOT analysis.

A SWOT analysis is best done as part of a more thorough internal and external assessment. However, in an abbreviated planning process, a SWOT discussion could be done in a planning retreat. This will work as an external assessment only if the board and staff understand their community well enough. If they understand the general intentions of important funders, the interests of audiences, the concerns of neighbors, and the likely impact of competitors and partners, they might skip a more thorough external assessment.

There are two popular methods of conducting SWOT analyses: brainstorming and nominal group process.

Brainstorming. The objective of brainstorming is to get as many ideas as possible from group members in a short time. The facilitator invites the group to think about the organization's internal strengths and weaknesses and external threats and opportunities. While ideas are being expressed, judgment should be suspended. People should feel free to propose whatever comes to mind, even if it seems far-fetched, bouncing new ideas off earlier ones. The facilitator or an assistant jots down key words or phrases to keep track of each idea as it is introduced.

> It is easier to tone down a wild idea than to think up a new one.[21]
>
> —Alex Osborne, inventor of brainstorming

If the group gets stalled, suggest some categories of ideas within the broader headings. It may help to focus first on the internal strengths and weaknesses and then on the external threats and opportunities.

In most SWOT sessions, internal strengths and external opportunities get intermixed. Don't worry. Just mark an "S" next to each strength and an "O" next to each opportunity. A threat may also be seen as an opportunity and vice versa. If the issue is both a threat and an opportunity, mark it "T/O." Brainstorming concludes when many issues have been identified and the pace of new suggestions slows.

Sometimes a group falls into a pattern of just listing problems. A perceptive facilitator will prompt for some strengths and ask if some of the threats don't also suggest opportunities. Don't gloss over real problems, but the productivity of the retreat will be compromised if everyone is depressed by a litany of problems without relief.

A variation on brainstorming is to break into smaller groups of five or six people and have each group brainstorm its own list. After a period of perhaps 40 minutes, the full group reconvenes and each small group reports on its assessment.

Nominal group process. In this variation, members of the group are invited to individually write out a list of strengths, weaknesses, opportunities, and threats. After 15 or 20 minutes, the facilitator asks each person in turn to identify one issue. Like group brainstorming, each issue is summarized on a flip chart until all ideas have been expressed.

Nominal group process gets everyone to participate and is easier to facilitate. This approach, however, does not take advantage of group synergy. The people are only "nominally" a group. Brainstorming is good for generating ideas, as it builds on group enthusiasm. But brainstorming is more challenging to facilitate, with lots of ideas being tossed out at once.

EXTERNAL ASSESSMENT

Often, important community interests are underrepresented on an organization's board or staff. Direct community input may be needed to identify and understand needs or test potential support for new initiatives. In these situations, the planning process should be adapted to conduct community assessment prior to the retreat or envisioning stage.

Four standard external assessment tools are interviews, focus groups, surveys, and public forums. A staff and board may conduct interviews and focus groups, though the outside perspective and research skills of a consultant may prove useful. Any complicated surveys should be designed and administered with the advice or help of experienced survey researchers.

For further detail on conducting interviews, focus groups, and surveys, see the Program and Evaluation chapters ▌ and "How to Run a Focus Group" and "Steps of Survey Research" in the Appendix.

Community interviews. The people outside an organization most frequently sought out for assessment interviews are community leaders—people who can represent the interests of larger groups of people, such as religious leaders and community organizers. Spokespersons, however, may not always fully understand the interests of their constituency, so it is a good idea to interview multiple leaders, if possible, or include some constituent types as well.

A good interview requires some preparation. First, determine what information is needed, whom to ask, and how to formulate questions. Typically, external perceptions are sought regarding community needs and interests, opportunities and threats, and potential resources.

Focus groups. Interviewing a focus group—several carefully selected representatives of a constituency with common interests or affinities—is a simple way to determine what a larger number of people are likely to think about a given subject. With a group of eight to ten people discussing a few questions for 90 minutes, you can gain a general sense of preferences—What kind of entertainment does your family prefer?—or reactions to specific programs—How did you like the jazz concert?

Surveys. Surveys are commonly used to collect assessment information from large numbers of people. They can be simple cards distributed in program notes to audience members, online surveys, social media polling, or intercept polling (volunteers stopping people leaving an event and asking a few questions). Mailed paper surveys and telephone polling are increasingly rare.

For general population surveys of the type needed for a community cultural plan, it is highly recommended that you seek professional advice. An experienced consultant or graduate student in an arts management program, school of business public policy, or sociology department may design and/or conduct a survey.

Public forums. Public agencies like state and local arts councils need to be especially accountable to their constituents. A public meeting can provide a forum for anyone to offer opinions or advice to the planners. A meeting may be convened early in the planning process to collect assessment data and/or later in the planning to share emerging strategies for feedback. Circulating links to a draft plan via email blasts or social media may complement or replace a face-to-face public forum.

IDENTIFY CRITICAL ISSUES

Conclude your assessment by distilling the information you have gathered into a short list of critical issues to resolve in planning. If your assessment was limited to a brainstormed list of SWOT issues in a retreat, you can do this quite simply. Post all of the flip chart pages around the retreat room and invite participants to walk around, reflect, and make notes about what issues seem to be the most significant. Then determine group consensus through discussion. Another method is to hand out colored markers or adhesive dots and ask people, for example, to put a red dot next to issues they consider critical and a blue dot by important ones. The issues with the highest number of red dots are likely to be the most critical.

If your internal and external assessments are more thorough, it is best to go through the data and look for themes, patterns, problems, and opportunities to be raised in the planning. It is best if the assessment is presented as a written report that concisely summarizes critical issues for planning. (See the Program Evaluation chapter for information about how to organize and interpret assessment data.)

The assessment concludes with planning team consensus on a pared-down list of critical internal and external opportunities and issues that must be considered during the remainder of the planning process. A local arts agency might conclude its assessment with this summary: "We are sustained by an effective staff, a well-connected board, and a reputation for quality programs and services; and yet we are challenged by inadequate information about community artists and arts organizations, and our audiences do not sufficiently include the community's growing Latino and Asian-American populations."

Stage 2 (Envisioning) and much of Stage 3 (Assessment) may be completed in a single planning retreat. If the facilitator keeps an eye on the clock, the agenda, and people's energy, it is often possible to take further advantage of the organization's gathered leadership in a retreat. Before people disperse, it is helpful to move on to the next stage of the process: planning more specifically for the next two or three years.

Stage 4: Make Decisions

WRITE OR REVISIT THE MISSION

A mission statement becomes the fundamental principle or foundation of your strategic plan. If planning is leading to the creation of a new organizational mission, you will need to write one. If there is an existing mission, determine if it should be revised. You should consider mission as part of an envisioning exercise early in your planning retreat, but also revisit your mission as you approach the conclusion of your planning.

DEVELOP OR REFINE LONG-RANGE GOALS

The vision expresses what could be; the mission expresses why the organization exists; the assessment describes what is; and goals are ideal, long-term future conditions that, if met, help to realize the vision or resolve critical issues. Goals tend to describe long-range public-benefit programs and services. Many plans also include organizational capacity-building or administrative goals.

> The vision expresses what could be; the mission expresses why the organization exists; the assessment describes what is; and goals are ideal future conditions that, if met, help to realize the vision or resolve critical issues.

Long-range goals may not be clear at the end of a single retreat. It is possible, though, to elicit general agreement on what the organization wishes to accomplish in the future. Then the planning committee or consultant writes goals based on their notes and observations from the retreat. Alternatively, the leaders can be convened for a second retreat that focuses on long-range goals and short-term objectives.

It is a common mistake for planners to draft goals that describe symptomatic problems or superficial solutions. Here's an example of an interaction between an artist advocate and a planner in which a short-term scheme is reconceived in terms of a more fundamental and long-range goal.

Advocate: Our goal is to renovate the front room of the arts center to serve as a local artists' gallery.

Planner: If this goal were resolved, what would that get us?

Advocate: It would provide artists a place to exhibit.

Planner: A more fundamental goal might therefore be: Provide for local artists opportunities to exhibit their work. What would that get us?

Advocate: If they had opportunities to exhibit their work, more people would see their work, and the artists could make more sales.

Planner: A still more basic goal statement might be: Provide opportunities for local artists to connect with their audiences.

Many initiatives may help fulfill such a fundamental goal: renovate the gallery, publish a map of local artist studios, encourage the local artists' guild to hold open studios, work with the local newspaper to feature local artists, etc. By seizing on the first obvious project as a goal, the planners may limit their thinking and subsequent programming.

A group can make headway in articulating long-range goals by breaking into smaller task forces with each one working on a separate program or goal area. In each case, the planners prepare rough notes for the planning committee to refine. (See the Goals/Objectives Worksheet in the Appendix.) Good plans wisely limit to only three to five the number of long-range goals an organization commits to in its strategic plan.

SET PRIORITIES

The critical results of the assessment should present organization leaders with strategic choices, such as: How can we respond to the changing needs of our diversifying population? Should we discontinue a favorite program that is no longer funded?

There is a distinct shift in emphasis as the planning process moves from assessment and envisioning to decision-making. Assessment is expansive and questioning. Exercises to elicit vision and clarify mission are not constrained by limitations of resources. Now the planners must answer questions raised in the assessment, and determine priorities.

This stage can be the most challenging part of planning. It can also be the most rewarding, as organization leaders respond to opportunities, solve problems, and resolve ambiguous questions.

Decision-making will occur throughout the planning process. Many planners prefer to determine overall strategies first (for example, "Shift from arts programming to arts services"), then establish long-range goals ("Provide capacity-building information and services to the arts community"), and then define specific objectives ("Establish a central ticketing office by the start of next year"). With clear goals and defined objectives, planners can determine a work plan for the first year with detailed tasks, deadlines, responsibilities, and evaluation measures. Such planning moves deliberately from general principles to specific actions.

Other planners start at the detailed level of programs and services ("Create a central ticketing service"). They then consider what goals and strategies are implied by that and other operational decisions, as described by an emergent planning model. Planning often blends deliberate decision-making with emergent strategies as leaders plan ahead and also learn from what works and does not.

DEFINE CRITICAL QUESTIONS

Decision-making starts with a list of the decisions to be reached. What are the critical questions and issues that surfaced in the assessment and must be resolved in planning? What specific opportunities and problems do we face? If the assessment raised dozens of questions, prioritize the few most compelling questions that must be resolved. Resist the temptation to pursue every interesting problem or to delve into the details of specific programs or operations. These questions become the central agenda for planning meetings. Many opportunities to answer major questions are wasted on debates about details.

Talk It Through

The simplest method for group decision-making is to sit down and talk through the planning questions. There are several structured ways to engage a team in problem solving, but don't ignore the old-fashioned way of sitting around a table to talk about it. Conversation works best for technical or uncomplicated decisions. Start by defining the question and then explore several possible solutions before settling on the best decision.

There are risks, however, to decisions arrived at by unstructured conversation. Sometimes the first suggested option is accepted as "good enough" before better, more subtle options are even considered. The most articulate or outspoken people may dominate and ignore good advice from others. "Group think" may lead to poor decisions: if no one in a group takes the initiative to voice a reservation about a proposal, then others with doubts may also not speak, and the group makes a bad decision that most do not support.

Resolve SWOT-Defined Issues

If SWOT (Strengths, Weaknesses, Opportunities, Threats) analysis was used in the assessment stage, now determine which of the identified issues are critical and within your power to influence. Then plan how to maximize strengths, minimize critical weaknesses, respond to the best opportunities, and avoid the most dangerous threats. This often provides just enough structure to planning discussions that you can make decisions and choose priorities. There is a risk, however, that this simple analysis will ignore the interrelationship among these forces.

Strategic planner Kevin Kearns recommends using SWOT to look for relationships among strengths, weaknesses, opportunities, and threats.[22] Try to match strengths with opportunities. An organizational strength (for instance, a track record of successful arts programming for kids) combined with an opportunity (demographic projections of increasing numbers of children) suggests a strategic choice to invest in children's programming. An area of organizational weakness (no experience coordinating centralized services) and an opportunity (community need for centralized marketing) requires a decision: strengthen organizational capacity, collaborate with another organization, or ignore the opportunity. Kearns further suggests that areas of strength provide the means to mobilize to defend against external threats (a strong capacity to organize advocacy can defeat threatened public arts funding cuts). If the threats are in areas of weakness, the strategy may be to control the damage.

LIST PROS AND CONS

A time-honored way for a group to make decisions is to simply frame the question, brainstorm alternative solutions, shorten the list of options to the few most feasible solutions, and then list pros and cons for each alternative response or solution. This may quickly reveal your best choice.

COMPARE ALTERNATIVES TO AGREED CRITERIA

You can create a matrix or grid to compare options against criteria. (See, for an example, Figure 5.) This allows for more sophisticated analysis of alternative solutions. Determine what criteria you will use to judge the alternatives. Common criteria include:

- fit with the mission (always the first criterion);
- fit with overall strategy and/or goal;
- focus on documented unmet need;
- fiscal feasibility (capacity to earn more than it costs or be funded);
- staff capacity to implement; and
- facility capacity.

Depending on the issue, problem, or opportunity at hand, the various alternatives may be compared to other criteria, such as the potential to increase organizational visibility, increase organizational capacity, develop partnerships, increase earned revenue, grow sponsorships, etc.

To rate each alternative against each criterion, the simplest approach is to put yes, no, or question mark (need more information) in each cell of a chart. Or determine a numeric score for example, +3 for an option that excellently matches a criterion, +2 for very good match, and so forth, down to −3 for an option that seriously undermines a criterion. Criteria may also be weighted, so that "fit with mission" carries more relative weight than "increase organizational visibility." Then each column of numbers is totaled to get relative scores for each option. If criteria are weighted, then the result of each column is multiplied by the number representing that criterion's relative weight. Build this in a spreadsheet to simplify calculations.

COMPASSPOINT'S DUAL BOTTOM-LINE MATRIX

Allison and Kaye[23] describe a decision tool that helps planners evaluate decisions based on two bottom lines: the impact of the decision on the mission and on financial viability, expressed in a four-cell matrix. (See Figure 6.) A good decision would have high positive impact on the mission and high financial viability. An option that would have low impact on the mission and low financial viability would be a good candidate to close down or give to another agency. This tool may be particularly useful if your planning decision is a choice between starting a new program and keeping or discontinuing an existing program. Decide if the program has a high or low impact on mission and high or low financial viability and place it in the appropriate quadrant. Then make a decision guided by the matrix. Note that organizations may also consider a Triple-Bottom Line approach (People, Planet, Profit), which fits many nonprofits' mission of service rather well.

Be careful, however. These types of decision-making tools may suggest an illusory precision of results. Much depends upon your assumptions. When you evaluate the results of an exercise like this, use your judgment. Ask if it makes sense. Ask what the results suggest. Creative problem solving often defies the tools planners invent to bottle it.

DOCUMENT PRIORITIES AND DECISIONS

Document your decisions as each one is determined! Some planning committees run in circles rehashing the same questions because no one recognizes or writes down decisions. (For a discussion of group decision-making, see the Board Development chapter). ▌ If you have an existing plan, you may wish to annotate it as you go with revisions or additions: amend a goal, write a strategy, adopt a new objective, or note a task. Or you can simply write down each decision and later integrate any

Figure 5: Comparing Options Against Criteria

Question: What capacity-building programs and services should we offer?					
Criteria:	Fits mission (weighted 2x other criteria)	Staff can handle	Advances core strategy: shift to services	Fiscally feasible	Weighted score
Option 1: Create central marketing	3	–2	3	–2 (requires 2-year subsidy)	5
Option 2: Start nonprofit management training program	3	–1	3	0 (revenue neutral)	8
Option 3: Provide consulting services	2	–3	3	3 (earns $)	6
Option 4: Create website with links to other resources	3	3	3	2 (good cost/ benefits)	15

Figure 6: CompassPoint's Dual-Bottom Line Matrix

	High mission impact ♥ Low $ viability Business decision: Keep a "heart" program that is critical to mission, but contain costs.	High mission impact ☆ High $ viability Business decision: Invest in this "star" program for continuance and growth.
	Low mission impact ? Low $ viability Business decision: Discontinue this questionable program or give it away.	Low mission impact $ High $ viability Business decision: Enhance the money-making option to increase impact on mission.

Mission Impact: LOW → HIGH (vertical axis)
Financial Viability: LOW → HIGH (horizontal axis)

label the decision an "intention" or "priority" and later sort out how it fits into the hierarchy of the written plan. If you haven't yet made a decision, but have narrowed choices to two options, record them both with a note to decide later.

DEFINE OBJECTIVES AND OUTCOMES

While some planning decisions become expressed as goals or strategies, more often the answers to planning questions may be written in the plan as objectives or outcomes. Objectives state specific intended results for board, volunteers, and staff to reach. This may be the first time in the planning process that some bottom-line, results-oriented staff and board members get interested! The elusive stuff of vision gets translated into how many of what kinds of programs are offered when, and at what cost. As discussed in Part I, these specific, intended results may be expressed as objectives or outcomes.

This is the stage of planning when the board and staff make the tough decisions to set priorities, determine what programs the organization will start or discontinue, and allocate scarce resources among competing demands. This process can be untidy and uncomfortable as tough questions are raised. As you delve into details, planning questions may appear to be increasingly ambiguous. Trust in the process and accept that decisions will become clearer as you move through planning. Acknowledge when questions have been resolved and take note when the list of ambiguous questions is getting shorter.

Specific objectives anchor the plan to the real, immediate opportunities and needs of the organization and its constituency. This is where the expressions of high purpose answer the question "So what are we going to do about it now?" At this point, goals become linked to resources:

- Who will organize and lead the program?
- How much will it cost?
- Where will the funds come from?
- If we do this project, what demands will it make upon staff time, facilities, and supplies?
- Which objectives are important enough to merit scarce funds and time?
- When will this objective be achieved?

Here competing priorities are balanced. Some priorities move forward as immediate objectives for the organization and community. Others are postponed until more resources can be secured.

But specificity has its limits. Because conditions inevitably change, a plan that projects overly specific objectives too far into the future may soon be out of date. To balance short-term specificity with long-term flexibility, many strategic plans project detailed objectives for the upcoming year and more general ones for the period thereafter, and then update annual work plans each year by updating objectives.

When you write objectives, you are setting the conditions for evaluation. If your objectives are specific and observable, you can evaluate the extent to which each is achieved. This will make evaluation simpler. (See the Program Evaluation chapter for more on the relationship of planning to evaluation.) ▌

LINK THE PLAN TO THE BUDGET

A budget must be developed that translates the next year's objectives into anticipated revenues and expenses. A first-draft budget will likely reveal that all the objectives can't be realized as first hoped. The budget process provides a forum for debating the relative merits of competing objectives and programs.

It is helpful to organize the planning process so that it parallels the organization's budgeting process. The planning team can then focus upon programmatic objectives, which the financial staff or committee converts into a budget. (See the Financial Management chapter for more on budgeting.) ▌

Stage 5: Write the Plan

Writing the plan is a dynamic phase of the planning process. The rigor of crafting words to clarify emerging directions and to identify dilemmas serves to ground ideas. It is not necessary that the planning committee leave a retreat with clear consensus on the organization's intentions or instructions for every element of the plan. Often it isn't until the planning team begins reworking retreat notes into the draft plan that areas of consensus and disagreement become apparent.

WHO WRITES?

Writing can be done primarily by one writer (chief executive, planning committee member, or the consultant), with the rest of the planning committee serving as editors; or the planning committee can write jointly; or sections of the plan can be delegated to various committee members. How you proceed depends on the skills and working styles of the committee; however, you may find that the single writer/multiple editor approach produces a more coherent, readable plan.

> **Format Options for the Finished Plan—Examples**
>
> **NARRATIVE FORMAT**
>
> "Commit to a policy of inclusion in every program, with particular attention to the unique needs of rural artists and rural communities. In the first year, convene a meeting of the Rural Arts Panel to explore alternative programs for rural arts advancement if federal support is not available."
>
> **OUTLINE FORMAT**
>
> 1. Commit to a policy of inclusion.
>   1.1 Serve the unique needs of rural communities.
>   1.2 Explore alternatives to federal funding.
>
> **GRAPHIC FORMAT**
>
> | Goal 2: Remove barriers to access. | | | |
> |---|---|---|---|
> | Objective 2.1: Commit to a policy of inclusion in every program with particular attention to artists of color and rural artists. | | | |
> | | Year 20___ | Year 20___ | Year 20___ |
> | Tasks | Convene a panel of artists to assess needs and evaluate programs. Make changes as indicated. Hold four regional forums. | Evaluate impact of changes. Secure additional funds for a full accessibility plan. Hold a state conference. | Complete accessibility plan. Establish artist fellowships. |

THE DRAFTING AND REVIEW PROCESS

Write drafts of the plan soon after each planning retreat or meeting while ideas are still fresh and momentum is strong. Express points of agreement clearly. Convey beliefs the group feels strongly about. Earmark for additional deliberation issues on which there is disagreement. Outline the implications of various goals on courses of action that must still be decided. Keep it simple! Aim for brevity, clarity, accessibility, and a usable document.

The planning committee or consultant works up a first draft from the flip charts and from their own notes. (See sidebar, Format Options for the Finished Plan.) Distribute the first draft for consideration at a scheduled board meeting or a second planning retreat. At the meeting, confirm portions of the plan with broad support, allowing enough time for thorough discussion. Fully debate alternative goals or versions of goals. Here the objective is to focus and reach closure on unresolved issues. The board should try to reach consensus in principle and let the planning committee revise the draft plan.

The planning committee meets again and incorporates these changes into a second draft. The second draft, if approved by the board, becomes the strategic plan. If there is disagreement about the intentions of the group or need for further clarification, debate until there is consensus or an agreement to disagree. The plan is then revised and finalized, copied, and distributed.

A comprehensive version of the plan, either in narrative form or in outline plus narrative, is produced to guide the organization's policymakers and those responsible for day-to-day operations and decision-making. Goals, objectives, and strategies are explained in greater detail in this version. Objectives for the upcoming year are linked to the budget so that various commitments are backed by line items in the budget.

Stage 6: Approve and Commit

The governing board ordinarily approves the final draft of the plan. This may be a simple manuscript for internal distribution. Since board members have been a part of the planning process from the start, this process should be harmonious. It should be an opportunity to celebrate the organization's new or renewed commitment to a shared sense of purpose and the clarification of strategies which will be pursued to help fulfill that mission. This stage should also be the occasion to present the entire strategic plan in overview.

Some board and staff members will not have participated in every planning step and some may have only a partial understanding of the plan, appreciating primarily those portions with which they are most closely associated. The strategic plan is meaningless unless members of the organization understand it and commit to carrying it out. Accordingly, the leadership should work to assure that everyone understands the group's intentions as expressed in the plan. If the plan can succeed in realigning the efforts of individual members toward a commonly shared sense of purpose, significant energy is released that can accomplish that purpose.

If the plan is a community cultural plan, the approval and commitment process should include a well-orchestrated publicity campaign and a celebratory arts and public relations event that presents the plan.

DESIGN AND PRINT A PUBLIC VERSION

Many organizations share a summary version of their finished plan with the public, partners, and funders. If so, the final, board-approved plan should be attractively presented with good graphic design and images. Recruit a graphic designer to produce a professional-looking document. It need not be slick to respect aesthetic quality.

Create a summary outline or graphic version to communicate the key points of the plan. Adding images may improve the plan's readability and power to communicate. A summary version, laid out as a single printed page, web page, PowerPoint presentation, or brochure, is then produced in quantity and distributed widely. Every staff and board member, volunteer, and committee member gets a copy of the plan. An online version of your plan can create layers, starting with a short summary and images with links to details. Copies of this plan are included in funding requests and made available to audiences, municipal officials, and community partners.

Stage 7: Implement

The point of planning is to inform actions, yielding intended results. Considering implementation as a discrete final stage suggests that planning is separated from action. In fact, the process is more circular. Assessing, monitoring, adapting, and implementing may be concurrent processes.

Decisions to act—that is, to implement—may occur at any point in the eight-stage process. For example, ideas expressed at the planning retreat may make such obvious good sense that staff resolve to implement the idea immediately, not waiting for the finished plan. Still, as strategic planning is mostly devoted to describing how the organization will relate to the future, most implementation follows the conclusion of the strategic planning process.

AVOID THE FATE OF ABANDONED PLANS

Here are some tips to help ensure that the strategic plan doesn't collect dust on the shelf and instead becomes a dynamic tool which will inform and guide the organization's leaders and members.

Use an authentic, inclusive planning process which fosters investment in the plan's success.

Keep the planning process and product simple. Planning should produce a few core strategies and goals. Take advantage of enthusiasm for the project—start and conclude the planning process in a short time, with no more meetings than are necessary. In the assessment stage, remember that you can never know enough to plan as thoroughly as you might wish, so be content with information that is "good enough." It will change anyway. Few people will read long planning documents. Write the plan simply and succinctly. As Strunk and White put it, "Omit needless words."[24]

Think strategically and adapt. A plan does not substitute for judgment. No plan can predict the future. Think strategically and creatively, and adapt as conditions change. Don't be quick to abandon a good strategy every time you encounter a problem, but be willing to adapt plans as you observe what works and what does not.

Go public with your plans. By publicly committing to your strategic plan, you have put yourself under some pressure to implement it.

"Keep your eyes on the prize." Keep the objectives of your plan before you. People who find they never have time for the crucial tasks that will help realize important goals should heed Stephen Covey's advice, "Don't prioritize your schedule; schedule your priorities."[25] Post your one-page plan above your desk or somewhere you'll see it often. The most useful plan is the note-covered copy that you keep handy. Highlight priorities, cross off strategies that haven't worked, check off accomplished tasks, and make notes about potential new objectives.

Recruit champions. Identify people who care about the issues expressed in your plan and ask them to advocate for the implementation of specific elements. The board member who is a parent concerned about arts in education can become the advocate of your new arts-in-education goal. She or he would work with staff to ensure that education programs are developed and get into the budget.

Link fundraising and spending decisions to the strategic plan. A plan that is not related to the budget can scarcely be called a realistic plan. If you don't plan to raise money for and spend money on activities to achieve planned goals, they probably are not your real priorities.

Acquaint new people with the plan. As new board members, staff, and volunteers join your organization, make it a point to orient them to your priorities as expressed in your plan.

Stage 8: Evaluate and Adapt

How are we doing? and What difference did we make? are the questions at the heart of evaluation. The point of planning is to help make a difference by supporting improved programs and services for a positive impact on the community. The inevitable question then is, Did we?

Strategic planning is an ongoing, dynamic process of action, observation, and reflection. Evaluation and adaptation are presented here as the final phase of the process. In practice, however, evaluation commences at the assessment stage of planning, and adaptation is something leaders do every day to cope with new information and unforeseen developments.

> Planning and then not evaluating is like producing a play and then not asking how good it was, or playing a football game and not keeping score.

Schedule periodic reviews of the plan. Armed with evaluation information, review progress on important plan objectives. Ask the advocates of planned programs to provide progress reports and note suggested changes in the plan at regular staff and board meetings. Many groups schedule an annual retreat for reviewing and evaluating existing plans.

Use evaluation to adapt the plan. Ongoing informal evaluations and periodic formal reviews provide information essential to keeping organizations on course. Your strategic plan was your best guess about how the future would unfold. Evaluations show how it is in fact unfolding. Adjust strategies accordingly. Please study the Program Evaluation chapter to learn how to measure results. ▌

The Learning Organization

This chapter has offered instruction on how to organize a strategic planning process. Once such a process has become a way of doing business, planning becomes simply an increased capacity to learn—what Peter Senge described as a *learning organization*.

Planning adaptively means being tightly committed to your principles and your vision of what the organization can accomplish while being loosely committed to your specific plans to get there. This is what Thomas Peters and Robert Waterman call the *simultaneous loose/tight* principle.[26] Mindlessly sticking to specific strategies that no longer make sense gives planning a bad reputation. Regularly recreate or revise your strategies as you learn from experience, but don't regularly recreate your value system or your sense of ultimate purpose.

Know what you believe in and care about. Know what difference you want your organization to make in your community. Keep your eyes and ears open for evidence about how you are doing—financially and in terms of audience impact and quality of programming—and look for unforeseen problems and opportunities. Waterman, in The Renewal Factor,[27] says that opportunities knock often, but may show up disguised as problems. Staying attuned to your vision for the organization, plus regularly gathering information about how the organization is doing, positions you to take advantage of opportunities. Effective planning becomes second nature in a learning organization. Learn by planning and you'll be able to recognize fruitful opportunities.

Further Resources

Barry, B. W. (1997). *Strategic Planning Workbook for Nonprofit Organizations* (Rev. ed.). St. Paul, MN: Amherst Wilder Foundation.

Bridges, William. *Managing Transitions: Making the Most of Change,* 2nd Ed. (2003). Da Capo Press, Perseus Books Group, Cambridge, Massachusetts.

Bryson, J. M. (2004). *Strategic Planning for Public and Nonprofit Organizations* (3rd ed.). San Francisco and Oxford, England: Jossey Bass.

Bryson, J. M., & Alston, F. K. (2004). *Creating and Implementing Your Strategic Plan: A Workbook for Public and Nonprofit Organizations* (2nd ed.). Jossey-Bass Public Administration Series. San Francisco: Jossey Bass.

Dreeszen, C. (1998). *Community Cultural Planning Handbook: A guide to community leaders.* Washington, DC: Americans for the Arts.

Dreeszen, C. (1999). "Who's on First: Resolving Problems of Implementation in Public Sector Planning." In *Lessons Learned: A Planning Toolsite.* Washington, DC: National Endowment for the Arts: Retrieved from www.arts.endow.gov/

Dreeszen, C. (2001). *Learning Partnerships: Planning and Evaluation Workbooks and Online Help for Arts and Education Collaborations.* Amherst, MA: Arts Extension Service.

Dreeszen, C., Aprill, A., & Deasy, R. (1999). *Learning Partnerships: Improving learning in schools with arts partners in the community.* Washington, DC: The Arts Education Partnership.

Drucker, P. (1990). *Managing the Nonprofit Organization: Principles and Practices.* New York: HarperCollins Publishers.

Mintzberg, H. (1994). *The Rise and Fall of Strategic Planning.* New York: Free Press.

National Endowment for the Arts. (1985). *Surveying Your Arts Audience.*

National Endowment for the Arts. (n.d.). *Lessons Learned: A Planning Tool Site.* Retrieved from www.mtnonprofit.org/uploadedFiles/_Pages/Organizational_Dev /ConferencePresentations/Cooney%20PreCon%20Part%202.pdf

Peters, T. J., & Waterman, R. H., Jr. (2004). *In Search of Excellence: Lessons from America's Best-run Companies.* New York: HarperCollins Publishing.

Radwan, Sue & Denise McNerney (2012) *Strategic Planning Successful Practices in Non-profit Organizations* (501c3), March 2012 National Survey – Initial Findings

Reported May 1, 2012 - Association for Strategic Planning Annual Conference http://www.ibosswell.com/wp-content/uploads/2013/12/ASP_Article_NPO_National_Survey_Initial_Findings_March_2012.pdf

Schwartz, P. (1991). *The Art of the Long View: Planning for the Future in an Uncertain World.* New York: Doubleday.

Warshawski, M., Barsdate, K. J., & Katz, J. (2000). *A State Arts Agency Strategic Planning Tool Kit.* Washington, DC: National Assembly of State Arts Agencies.

Waterman, R. H., Jr. (1987). *The Renewal Factor: How the Best Get and Keep the Competitive Edge.* New York: Bantam.

Wolf, T. (1999). *Managing a Nonprofit Organization in the twenty-first century.* New York: Simon & Schuster Inc.

Appendix

PROCEDURES MANUAL ELEMENTS.

- Program objectives
- Planning and implementation schedule (often presented as a graphic timeline)
- Program tasks, including how-to guidelines
- Staff and volunteer job descriptions
- Funding sources

- Grant and contribution proposals
- Projected budget and statement of actual income and expenses
- Samples of press releases and clippings, promotions, letters, contracts, brochures, advertisements, etc.
- Evaluation forms and results (compared to program objectives)

TEN STEPS TO PLAN COLLABORATIVELY WITH ANOTHER ORGANIZATION

1. Prepare for partnership.
2. Explore a shared need.
3. Decide to act in collaboration.
4. Define goals.
5. Set objectives.
6. Describe activities.
7. Budget.
8. Plan fundraising.
9. Anticipate evaluation.
10. Summarize plan and timeline.

SHOULD WE USE A CONSULTANT?

Consultants can help to organize your planning effort, facilitate a planning retreat, collect information about your community in the assessment phase, or advise you as you write the plan. The advantage of using a consultant is that you can get right to planning issues without attending much to the process. You can enjoy a more effective and efficient retreat with professional facilitation, and the amount of volunteer and staff time devoted to the planning effort can be reduced. The biggest potential disadvantage is that the organization's leaders may not acquire the skills to plan on their own and will remain dependent upon consultants. To avoid this, insist on participating in the organizing stage with the consultant. Another potential disadvantage is that the consultant may deliberately or inadvertently divert the organization toward the consultant's own values and interests. Consultants, of course, charge for their professional fees and expenses.

The facilitation of the planning retreat is the hardest to duplicate without a consultant. The retreat requires a skillful facilitator. A member of the organization can fulfill that role, though an in-house retreat facilitator must defer her or his own interests in favor of the interests of the group. If you use or adapt the AES eight-stage planning process, you can employ a consultant just for retreat facilitation and save on expenses. A recommendation from your colleagues in other arts organizations is a good way to find a consultant. Check with your local or state arts agency or your national arts service organization. Some state and regional arts organizations have assembled rosters of consultants. If there is a Business Volunteers for the Arts organization near you, they can refer you to business volunteers.

HOW TO CHOOSE A CONSULTANT
- Interview the consultant in person or over the phone.
- Ask the consultant to describe her or his approach to planning.
- Notice how well the consultant listens to you.

- Notice what questions the consultant asks and if she or he proposes a planning process before learning about your organization.
- Meet with more than one consultant.
- Ask for references.
- Ask for the consultant's fees and anticipated expenses.
- Ask for a simple written proposal.
- Trust your feelings. It is more important to respect each other's values and work well and comfortably together than to use the specific planning methods planned by the consultant.

HOW TO RUN A FOCUS GROUP

1. Determine what information you seek and compose specific questions to elicit that information. Limit focus groups to one or two general topics and no more than four or five specific questions.
2. Determine which community segments you wish to hear from—your audience, nonattenders, artists, educators—and select a representative sample. A common error is to invite only those who care most about the arts and then to assume that the entire population feels the same way. People who do not see themselves as interested in the arts may need an incentive to participate.
3. Schedule focus group meetings. Always convene more than one meeting, as a single meeting may provide information relevant only to that group's dynamics. Focus groups usually consist of six to ten people. The minimum number is four, and 12 is the manageable maximum. Allow about one hour per meeting.
4. Invite participants. Send a letter and follow up with a phone call. You may need to invite 12 people to get eight participants. Be sure to clearly explain why you seek their advice. Market and political researchers pay their focus group participants. Nonprofit arts groups tend more often to give tickets or just a thank you. Do understand, though, that payment would attract noninterested citizens who would give a different perspective than those motivated to come to a meeting without compensation.
5. Enlist a moderator who introduces the topic, poses questions, and facilitates the conversation. The moderator can take a high profile and closely direct the conversations or stay in the background and only intervene when the discussion gets off track.
6. Create the meeting agenda, which might include the following: explain the reason for the meeting, introduce the general topic, introduce participants, and then pose the first specific question. After some discussion of the first question, move on to subsequent questions. Summarize key points at the conclusion of the meeting.
7. Gather information or feedback as specific as possible. If someone says she likes film, probe and find out what types. Ask questions that your group is capable of answering. Don't ask nonattenders what they think of your programs. To determine what people think of your programs, show a video segment and invite reactions to it.
8. Document the meeting. Professional focus group researchers record focus groups, transcribe the discussions, and closely analyze the results. At the very least, take detailed notes.
9. Ask the same questions of each focus group. Be sure not to let one group know what another said. The point of conducting multiple meetings is to determine whether perceptions are shared. If you ask leading questions—We've been hearing that our ticket prices are too low. What do you think?—you will get biased results.
10. Determine when you've done enough. If you have conducted two focus group meetings and can successfully predict what the third one will say, you have done enough. If you keep getting new or conflicting information, you should continue.

11. Analyze the results. At the conclusion of all the focus groups, review notes with an eye for patterns of perceptions, interests, and preferences that show up in more than one meeting. Test conclusions for validity by comparing them to other sources of assessment information such as ticket sales, competitors' trends, surveys, or first-hand observations.

STEPS OF SURVEY RESEARCH

1. Identify the problem to be solved or general questions to be answered. What are the characteristics of your audiences? How do people find out about you? What kinds of programming would appeal to nonattenders?
2. Identify your sample. Start by identifying the overall population (community, neighborhood, or existing audience) and then select the study sample (specific individuals to be surveyed). A simple approach is to consider names in the telephone book to be the population and every hundredth listing (or other interval) to be the sample. (Remember that such a sample omits unlisted numbers and people without telephones.) A mailed survey requires getting names and addresses on mailing labels.
3. Optionally, conduct interviews or focus groups to explore the issue in order to prepare relevant survey questions.
4. Design the survey questionnaire, composing questions to elicit the required information.

> **Open-ended Question:**
> What kind of music do you like?

> **Closed-ended Question:**
> Check the most appropriate box: I like country and western music
> ☐ I strongly agree ☐ I agree ☐ I disagree ☐ I strongly disagree

5. Pretest the questionnaire with a smaller sample to weed out confusing questions or other problems. Some common errors are two questions in one, overly complicated questions, leading questions, and jargon.
6. Distribute the questionnaires. For a mailed survey, a higher rate of response will result from use of first class mail (more likely to be opened, but more expensive than bulk mail), a signed letter (explaining clearly and persuasively the importance of the survey), a return, self-addressed, stamped envelope, and a follow-up request with a duplicate survey.
7. Monitor returns, making up to two follow-up requests. A 50 to 60 percent return is acceptable.
8. Edit the completed questionnaires, correcting obvious respondent errors or omissions.
9. Look for patterns in open-ended questions. Read through all the surveys, noting frequent responses. Then assign codes, for example, a "CM" in the margin for those who prefer classical music.
10. Tabulate the survey results. The best way to do this is to enter the answers to survey questions in a file of a statistical computer program. Some spreadsheet and database programs also have statistical capabilities. If you conduct manual counts of responses, you can extract some simple summary information, such as how many people like classical music. With a computer program you can cross-tabulate between questions and determine the music preferences of your African-American respondents or the media habits of country and western fans.

11. Analyze the results. With manual tabulations you can determine totals, averages, and media figures. You can also pull out narrative responses that seem typical. With a computer program you can easily generate graphic portrayals of the data, such as bar and pie charts.
12. Report the results to the planners and policy makers.

GOALS/OBJECTIVE WORKSHEET

Mission:

Goal #:

OBJECTIVES	STRATEGIES (HOW)	RESOURCES NEEDED (WHAT)	UNDERTAKEN BY (WHO)	COMPLETION DATE (WHEN)

Evaluation Criteria:

Endnotes

1. Cited in Peter M. Senge, *The Fifth Discipline: The Art and Practice of the Learning Organization*, 1990, p. 209.

2. Peter M. Senge, *The Fifth Discipline: The Art & Practice of The Learning Organization*. New York: Currency Doubleday, 1990.

3. David La Piana, *The Nonprofit Strategy Revolution: Real Time Strategic Planning in a Rapid-Response World*. 2008, p. 110.

4. Senge, Peter and Bryan Smith, Nina Kruscwitz, Joe Laur, and Sara Schley. (2008). *The Necessary Revolution: How individuals and organizations are working together to create a sustainable world.*

5. Appreciative Inquiry was first developed by David Cooperrider and Suresh Srivastva of Case Western University in "Appreciative Inquiry in Organizational Life," chapter in Woodman and Pasmore's *Research in Organizational Change and Development*, vol. 1 (1987), pp. 129-169.

6. Ronald A. Heifetz et al., *The Practice of Adaptive Leadership: Tools and Tactics for Changing Your Organization and the World*, 2009. https://books.google.com/books?id=n5u ZBAAAQBAJ&pg=PT181&lpg=PT181&dq=A+challenge+for+adaptive+leadership, p. 15.

7. Ibid, p. 8.

8. Barry Johnson, *Polarity Management: Identifying and Managing Unsolvable Problems*, 1996, p. xviii.

9. David La Piana, *The Nonprofit Strategy Revolution*, 2008.

10. Eisenhower quoted by Richard Nixon in *Six Crises*, 1962. Graf quoted by Helmuth von Moltke in Daniel Hughes, ed., *Moltke on the Art of War: Selected Writings*, 1993, pp. 45–47 (paraphrased translation).

11. Peter Schwartz, *The Art of the Long View: Planning for the Future in an Uncertain World*, 1991.

12. Henry Mintzberg, "Crafting Strategy," *The Harvard Business Review* (July/August 1987), pp. 66–75.

13. NEFA's The Creative Economy: A New Definition (2007) used NAICS (North American Industry Classification System) codes, "the standard used by Federal statistical agencies in classifying business establishments for the purpose of collecting, analyzing, and publishing statistical data related to the U.S. business economy." www.census.gov.

14. www.cvi.westaf.org

15. www.artsindexusa.org.

16. Craig Dreeszen, with Tom Borrup and Maren Brown, *Partners in Creative Economy Planning Workbook*, Arts Extension Service, 2007.

17. From *Imagine Maryland: A Renewed Strategic Plan for the Maryland State Arts Council*, 2014-2019.

18. www.hawaiicommunityfoundation.org.

19. George T. Doran, "There's a S.M.A.R.T. Way to Write Management's Goals and Objectives," Management Review, 70, no. 11 (AMA Forum) (Nov. 1981), pp. 35–36.

20. La Piana, The Nonprofit Strategy Revolution, 2008. p. 4

21. "Alex F. Osborn: Father of the Brainstorm," in "Thinkers" section at www.skymark.com.

22. Kevin P. Kearns, Private Sector Strategies for Social Sector Success: The Guide to Strategy and Planning for Public and Nonprofit Organizations, 2000, cited in Michael Allison and Jude Kaye, Strategic Planning for Nonprofit Organizations, 2nd ed., 2003.

23. Allison, M., & Kaye, J. (2005). Strategic Planning for Nonprofit Organizations (2nd edition). Hoboken, NJ: John Wiley and Sons.

24. William Strunk and E.B. White, The Elements of Style, 3rd ed., 1979, p. 23.

25. Stephen R. Covey, The 7 Habits of Highly Effective People, 2013.

26. Thomas J. Peters and Robert H. Waterman, In Search of Excellence: Lessons from America's Best-Run Companies, 2006.

27. Robert H. Waterman Jr., The Renewal Factor: How the Best Get and Keep the Competitive Edge, 1987.

Board Development

CRAIG DREESZEN

Boards of directors, composed as they are of a changing mix of people with all their hopes and failings, are challenging to analyze and improve. When you think you finally understand your board, new board members join and the complexion changes. Even experienced board development consultants and trainers are wise to recall the observation of Sandra Hughes of BoardSource: "When you've seen one board, you've seen one board."[1]

Members of boards can be called board members, trustees, steering committee members, or (in public agencies) councilors, or commissioners. Boards govern nonprofit organizations and govern or advise public agencies. They may work with professional or all-volunteer staff. The most common type of arts board is the governing board of a professionally staffed nonprofit organization. While some corporate boards are paid, nearly all nonprofit and public agency board members are volunteers.[2]

Board members provide leadership, funding, connections, and skills. They represent the interests of their community and exercise accountability. Some boards do not live up to this promise, or worse, get bogged down in tedium or conflict.

Effective organizations usually credit a strong board as a key to their success, while struggling agencies often cite problems with their boards. Arts service agencies report that the most frequent calls for help from arts organizations regard boards and money. The most frequently prescribed cure for both problems may be board development.

A Flexible Approach to Board Development

A board-development text such as this one confronts a basic paradox. Board service is not an innate skill; board members must learn what they are expected to do and how to do it. At the same time, each board is different. Each has evolved from a unique combination of artistic vision, community needs, organizational resources, and leadership personalities. In addition to the variation among boards, each board itself changes. Most tend to evolve over time, as they adapt to changing leadership and conditions. The best advice on board development is tailored to the current specific circumstances of each board.

It is impossible to successfully prescribe generic solutions that will work for each board at each stage of its development. This chapter instead provides a framework to help you examine what works and how your board might be improved. Boards are so individually distinctive that you should think twice before changing something that works just because this book or someone outside the organization advises another way of working.

Most of this chapter is devoted to improving board members' understanding of their roles and governing processes, stressing the board's role as the governing entity. You may be attempting to learn how to work with an existing board of directors, although the principles apply equally to a start-up board. More experienced readers, who are in a position to significantly influence their organizations, will want to attend particularly to the concluding section, which questions basic assumptions about organizational structures, and refer to the books suggested in the references.

A Board's Governing Responsibilities

Most nonprofits have ambiguous expectations of their boards. Often board members confuse their governing role with the many other important functions that board members fulfill as individuals and volunteer staff in their organization. This is particularly true for all-volunteer and understaffed organizations. Board members also bring differing expectations from their corporate, civic, and other nonprofit board experiences. While individuals in many volunteer and staff roles help with operations, only the board of directors governs.

THREE MODES OF GOVERNANCE

Board leaders may operate with differing mental maps or paradigms that define how they see their governance roles. Some boards assume one prevailing approach to leadership, other boards have a mix of leaders whose differing understandings of their role creates a balance of complementary or conflicting approaches, while still others shift their emphasis according to need. Richard Chait, William Ryan, and Barbara Taylor, in *Governance as Leadership*,[3] introduced the helpful idea that a nonprofit board may operate in three leadership modes: fiduciary, strategic, and generative.

Fiduciary mode. Boards are legally bound to fulfill their fiduciary responsibility to act faithfully in trust to ensure the well-being of the organization. They must ensure fiscal accountability, monitor tangible resources, make sure the law is followed, and watch for problems that would threaten the solvency of the organization. A board working in a fiduciary mode organizes committees around functional areas like finance, governance, and personnel.

Strategic mode. In this more visionary role, boards work closely as partners with staff to strategically shape the organization's future. In this mode, the board may organize temporary teams around strategic priorities. While many organizations engage in strategic planning, to govern strategically, the entire board must be fully engaged and not just authorize and approve a plan.

Generative mode. The concept of generative governance is less familiar. Boards that govern through generative leadership consider their organization's values and principles, ask fundamental questions about who is being served and how well, identify and frame problems and opportunities, and seek to discover sense and meaning in the organization's work. This is a way of thinking that can work in various board structures. According to Chait et al., "As long as governing means what people think it means—setting the goals and direction of an organization and holding management accountable for progress toward those goals—then generative thinking has to be essential to governing. Generative thinking is where goal-setting and direction-setting originate."

Chait et al. also argue that each mode or type of governance is associated with a different mindset. Fiduciary governance can be watchful and cautious, strategic governance can be open and analytical, and generative governance can be intuitive and creative. Each of these has its place, and an effective board must operate in all three modes, emphasizing each approach as needed. A board operates generatively and strategically while planning and adapting to changing circumstances and shifts to fiduciary mode when budgeting or managing a fiscal emergency.

Most board development writers, this one included, have urged a clarification of roles that stresses a division between governance and management. Boards govern organizations, while staffs manage operations. This clarity helps prevent board micromanagement of programs and operations and ensures accountability. The governance/management separation of authority works especially well in the fiduciary mode. However, in the strategic or generative type of governance, the roles of the board and staff are less distinct and more partner-like. If board members and staff often engage in collaborative problem solving and strategic thinking, then strategic and generative governance may not be distinctly different modes of governance. For more information, see Summary of Governance and Management Responsibilities, below.

FIDUCIARY RESPONSIBILITIES

Fulfill the Law

The one unavoidable fiduciary expectation of all incorporated nonprofit boards or public commissions is that they ensure fulfillment of appropriate legal requirements. In many cases, staff or individual board officers will actually perform the legally required tasks, but the board as a whole is legally responsible to see that each is done.

BoardSource (a good resource to nonprofit boards) inspired the following list of legal duties of board members:

- **Duty of care,** the care that an ordinarily prudent person would exercise in a like position and under similar circumstances. This means that a board member owes the duty to exercise reasonable care when he or she makes a decision as a steward of the organization.
- **Duty of loyalty,** a standard of faithfulness: a board member must give undivided allegiance when making decisions affecting the organization. This means that a board member can never use information obtained as a member for personal gain, but must act in the best interests of the organization.
- **Duty of obedience,** which requires board members to act in a way that is consistent with the mission and goals of the organization. A basis for this rule lies in the public's trust that the organization will manage donated funds to fulfill the organization's mission.

Collectively, board members must:

- govern the organization in keeping with the charitable purpose for which the organization was incorporated;
- ensure that annual reports are filed with the Secretary of State (or equivalent);
- ensure that federal income tax returns are filed and earnings of contracted workers are reported (consult current IRS 990 and 1099 regulations at www.irs.gov);
- pay payroll and social security taxes for employees; and
- ensure that contracts are fulfilled.

Because of the duty of care, individuals or corporations suffering financial loss or personal injury as a result of alleged negligence may sue board members. For this reason, we recommend that board members obtain directors' and officers insurance or personal liability insurance.

Be Accountable

The board is the central link in an organization's system of public accountability. Externally, the board is accountable to local, state, or federal governments on behalf of the public. Governments entrust the board of a tax-exempt nonprofit with public funds in the form of grants and with the privilege of collecting tax-exempt contributions. The board is accountable to funders to fulfill their requirements and to implement grant-funded projects as promised.

The board is also crucial to internal accountability. In an effective organization, board members and professional and volunteer staff are actively accountable to each other to fulfill their responsibilities in keeping with policies, plans, and budgets. Board members govern on behalf of the organization or community members who "own" the nonprofit. In a volunteer organization, committee members and volunteers may be accountable to an individual board member—typically a committee chair—who, in turn, is responsible to the full board. In staffed organizations, volunteers and support staff members are responsible to senior staff who, in turn, are responsible to the board. The organizational hierarchy may be steep, with strict up-and-down reporting, or flat, with a more collaborative approach. In either case, the board is ultimately accountable.

Ensure the Financial Well-Being of the Organization

We trust boards to be responsible for the short- and long-term fiscal health of the organization. Boards fulfill this responsibility by fundraising, budgeting, and overseeing the group's financial management. Board members must understand and approve budgets and financial reports and not leave this entirely to a treasurer or financial officer.

Fundraising. A nearly universal expectation is that board members will donate funds to the organization and seek other donors to help support program, operating, and capital expenses. A common recommendation is that all board members make what is for each a significant annual personal cash contribution. Board members should also participate in soliciting contributions from individuals and businesses, such as making fundraising calls, writing fundraising letters or hosting fundraising events. See The Art of Fundraising chapter for more information.

Budgeting. The board must approve the organization's annual operating budgets. It may be that staff or a finance committee will actually draft the budget, but the board must be sure that the budget both protects the organization's financial interests and furthers its mission. Board members should insist that budgets are clearly presented and explained. While budgeting may be seen as a primarily fiduciary responsibility, it is also strategic. Organizational plans and priorities should be clearly expressed in financial terms through annual operating and program budgets. A common mistake is to agree on a priority in planning (for example, "reach more underserved community members with subsidized tickets") and then fail to budget for the costs required to implement that priority. See the Financial Management chapter for more information on budgeting.

Overseeing financial management. Day-to-day financial transactions are ordinarily the responsibility of the treasurer or staff. The board is responsible for seeing that financial controls are established and applied. The board sets financial policies to determine how money is accounted for, how expenses are approved, and the limits within which staff may adjust budgeted expenses without seeking board approval. The board should regularly (monthly for most nonprofits) compare revenues and expenses to budget projections. If revenues drop or expenses rise above amounts budgeted, the board should take corrective steps—usually by reducing expenses. Those boards that have neglected their responsibilities, accumulated dangerous deficits, and waited too long to act, have been put at risk, both legally and in the eyes of their constituents.

LEADERSHIP RESPONSIBILITIES

Govern and Lead

Board members help shape an organization's vision, express that vision in plans, and represent and advocate for the interests of the organization throughout the community. The board, a step removed from the details of the day-to-day operations of staff or committees, can take the longer view: What are the core organizational values? What are the long-range goals? The board is primarily concerned with values and ends—where we are going—and staff and committees are more concerned with means—how we will get there. In some organizations, the chief executive is the primary leader. In others, it is the board. In the best case, the board and staff partner in leadership.

> In a staffed organization, the board is primarily responsible to govern and the staff is primarily responsible to manage.

In many all-volunteer organizations, however, the board may do everything. The same people who plan programs may also manage every detail of their operation. In such organizations, the challenge of leadership is to rise above the details to see the larger picture, to reserve time from managing to also govern. Otherwise, everyone may end up rowing with no one steering. The board's central role in planning is further explained in the Strategic Planning chapter.

Represent the Community

A board that reflects the diversity of its community can best serve the community's varied interests. For example, if the organization needs to work closely with the public school system, it is helpful to have an educator on the board. If funds are to be raised from corporations, the board should have access to corporate leaders. Be wary, though, of recruiting community members to the board to represent a constituency if they do not also care about the organization's mission. An organization can seldom recruit board members to represent every constituency served, so ideal candidates bring more than one needed attribute to the board.

Are Expectations of Boards Reasonable?

Board members are volunteers who are expected to lead, govern, raise funds, oversee finances, and ensure internal and external accountability. It is a common complaint that boards do not fulfill their roles. Before taking steps to improve the board, it seems appropriate to ask whether the expectations are reasonable.

Fundraising is a central board function and a tough responsibility. Many arts organizations attempt to sustain levels of programming and services that have been growing, sometimes over decades, even as resources diminish. There is an increasing gap between the quantity and quality of arts programs and services offered and the human and financial resources that a community can provide to sustain them.

Many nonprofit cultural organizations have struggled to adapt to changing economic circumstances. Old business models that rely on public grants and business sponsorships sometimes no longer work. As funding decreases and boards try to reduce the funding gap by raising even more individual contributions, some arts organizations may reduce staff, then ask board members to help manage those programs. Such a strategy risks board members becoming so consumed with their volunteer staff roles that they neglect their governing responsibilities or quit from fatigue.

Sometimes it is reasonable to expect increased fundraising and volunteer work from the board, especially to get through a short-term crisis. However, a more successful remedy may involve a combination of reduced programs and expenses along with additional help recruited for specific operational tasks. The Strategic Planning chapter will help you develop a process to determine priorities and make tough choices.

Two Strategies for Board Development

There are two fundamental strategies for improving a board: 1) improve the board's understanding of governing and its own governing processes, and/or 2) revise the organizational structure.

- **The first strategy** focuses on improved understanding and procedures. With this approach, the board clarifies its role, how board members relate to one another, and how they do their work. This strategy also considers leadership needs, recruitment, orientation of new board members, and skills training. Examples of procedural changes include developing a new statement of governing responsibilities or designing systems for identifying and recruiting board members.
- **The second strategy** involves restructuring the board itself. Examples range from a simple reduction of the number of board members to a more comprehensive overhaul of structure, as outlined at the end of this chapter.

Structural changes have the most potential for impact. Dramatic structural change can sometimes be just the jolt needed to bring the organization into alignment with its current environment, such as when there is an extended economic downturn. In other cases, too many changes at once can be so disruptive to board and staff members that they fail to provide the arts programs and services for which they were organized.

STRATEGY 1: IMPROVE GOVERNANCE UNDERSTANDING AND PROCESSES

This strategy involves two approaches:

- improve the effectiveness of current board members and their interaction with staff and volunteers, and
- recruit additional people.

The First Approach: Improve Effectiveness of the Current Team

Recruiting additional board members into a poorly functioning organization without also improving the way they work together is a recipe for failure. If board members don't understand what is expected of them, or if they don't get the information they need to do their jobs, recruiting more people may only worsen the situation. However, if the existing team has neither the skills nor the inclination to make the required changes, the fresh perspectives of new board or staff members may be required.

Another common error is to assume that the only way to recruit people with the requisite expertise is to elect them to the board or to hire them. Instead, it may be more effective to invite people to undertake specific tasks as committee members, task force team members, or volunteer consultants. Given the difficulty of recruiting good people to serve on a board, a growing trend is to engage people with special skills to handle specific short-term tasks in ad hoc task forces rather than recruiting them to the board or creating standing committees. People who work effectively in such roles and want to continue working with the organization may then be good candidates for board membership.

Clarify the board's governing responsibilities.

Perhaps the most perplexing and contentious issue in board development is understanding the board's governing responsibilities.

> Nonprofit governance is the work of articulating mission, planning strategy, setting policy, and ensuring the organization has adequate resources to fulfill its mission.

To understand the board's role, we must first understand governance. A board of directors governs their organization in trust for constituents, members, the public, and all those who support and benefit from their work. In recognition of this stewardship role, board members are sometimes called trustees.

To understand a board's role, we must distinguish *governance* from *management*. The board governs, while volunteer and professional staff manage programs and operations. Understanding governance and management in a staffed organization will also help clarify the board's essential governing role when there is no staff. Leaders of all-volunteer organizations may substitute the terms *volunteer staff* or *committees* for *staff* to better understand explanations below.

Summary of Governance and Management Responsibilities[4]

Governance (Board)	Management (Staff and Volunteers)
Oversee policy and planning	Advise on policy and planning
Advise on programs, operations	Manage programs, operations
Concerned with *ends*	Concerned with *means*
Accountable to the public, law, and bylaws	Accountable to the board
Plan mission, goals, objectives	Plan objectives, tasks, annual work plans
Hire and supervise chief executive	Hire and supervise staff and volunteers
Ensure fiscal stability (raise funds, oversee budgeting, monitor financial performance)	Manage finances (handle accounting and reports, write grants, support board fundraising)

Figure 1. Governance and Management

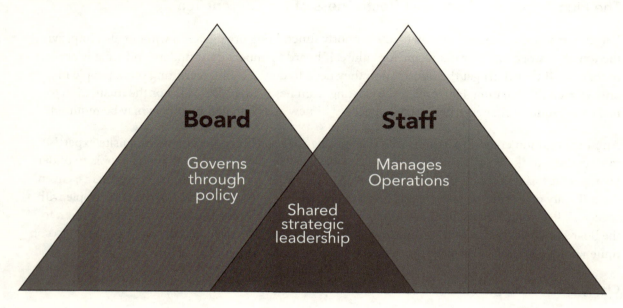

Governance   Programs & Operations

The simplest way to understand the differing board and staff roles is to make two lists: one for the board (governance) and one for staff (management). This approach stresses the separation of authority between board governance and staff management. Some writers, such as John Carver, argue this separation should be quite distinct.[5] In this view, the board makes plans and sets policy and staff implements it. Others, such as Dan Hotchkiss, argue that such distinctions are too rigid.[6] While it is helpful to see a stark separation of authority, it is important to understand that the reality is more nuanced. Staff often support or advise the board in governance and board members advise or help staff in management. For example, staff may develop a budget that the board considers and approves, while staff may plan a program with the advice of board members.

In *Governance and Ministry: Rethinking Board Leadership*,[7] Dan Hotchkiss developed a conceptual map that illustrates a system that both supports firm boundaries between governance and organizational management and allows for shared communication and accountability. (See Figure 1.) He asserts that the most productive relationship between board and staff is a partnership characterized by mutual support and respect for boundaries of authority.

The board is ultimately responsible for governance and the chief executive is responsible for operations. The boundaries are well defined at the top of their respective domains. Governance decisions are ultimately within the board's authority and management decisions lie within the staff's domain. The overlapping area illustrates that board and staff advise and assist each other as decisions move up the overlapping pyramids for resolution by either board or staff. Staff may exercise considerable leadership and the board may do many management tasks, assisting staff as volunteers. At the bottom of the pyramid—at the beginning of a plan or decision—the organization's leaders work collaboratively. Then, if a decision must be made on policy, the board decides. If the decision is administrative, the staff decides. As Hotchkiss observes, "Clear decision-making authority at the top actually makes it easier to share information, power, and influence throughout the organization."

Hotchkiss rejects the argument that boards should be solely concerned with ends while staff deals with means. A clear separation of the responsibilities of governance and management serves as the fiduciary function of check and balance. But when the board is operating in a generative or strategic mode, it is working in partnership with staff. Vision, leadership, insightful questions, and creative solutions transcend separate board and staff roles. The most productive relationship is a partnership characterized by mutual support and respect for boundaries of authority. An insistently strict division of duties may reduce the cooperative benefits of board and staff working together, each contributing his or her expertise in support of the central artistic vision.

Governing responsibilities in small and all-volunteer organizations. In small, understaffed, or all-volunteer organizations, board members often run the programs and manage operations, serving as volunteer staff. Some call these "working boards." Because directing a play or running a festival is time-consuming—and generally more interesting than writing policy— there is a real risk that board members will attend too much to programs and operations and too little to governance. A working board needs to be intentional about its governing responsibilities. One simple technique is to schedule regular governing or planning meetings where the agenda includes only strategic questions and policy issues: What are the pressing community needs that we can address through our programs and services? How well are our services fulfilling our mission? What external threats and opportunities should we address? These questions could be incorporated into a quarterly or annual planning retreat, or included at the start of every other board meeting. A change of meeting locations and even the playful wearing of "policy hats" can signal a governance discussion.

Helping Board Members Understand Their Roles

In order for board members to operate effectively within an organization, they must clearly understand their roles and responsibilities. These responsibilities should be shared with prospective board members as part of the recruitment and orientation process, and distributed to all board members in a board manual. Here are some of the ways in which boards can deepen understanding of their roles and responsibilities:

- **Arts conferences and board development workshops** offer opportunities to cultivate skills in board leadership, and expose board members to other arts leaders.
- **Board development readings and online resources** provide board members with insight into best practices.
- **Discussions of board responsibility,** organized by a board development or governance committee (or perhaps a single board member), enhance the board's understanding of how best to identify, cultivate, recruit, and orient new board members.
- **Participation in a structured exercise** can help boards clarify their roles and then discuss their responsibilities. (See sidebar, "Two Exercises to Clarify Board Responsibilities.") Their decisions should be documented in writing.

Board responsibilities change as the organization evolves and as external circumstances change. Reconsider board responsibilities annually.

Whenever a serious problem arises from an ambiguity about responsibilities (for instance, a missed opportunity or someone having overstepped their authority), rather than assigning blame, approach the problem as an opportunity to address the larger issue of distribution of responsibilities.

> **Two Exercises to Clarify Board Responsibilities**[8]
>
> **1. BOARD'S CRITICAL ROLE.**
>
> Imagine the board is meeting five years in the future and celebrating the achievement of a critical objective: [insert a priority objective from your strategic plan.] With that success in mind, complete the following sentence: "This result would not have been achieved if the board had not…"
>
> **2. SMALL-GROUP DISCUSSION.**
>
> - Present the following questions to the board in order to sort tasks into those that only the board may fulfill (governing) and those that volunteers or professional staff can fulfill (managing).
> - What are the essential governing responsibilities of our board of directors?
> - What specific responsibilities can individual board members undertake to contribute to good governance?
> - What expert help, advice, or volunteer work would be helpful for board members to offer that is not part of their official governing responsibilities?
> - What should board members avoid doing?
> - If you have an executive committee, what board responsibilities are delegated to the executive committee?
> - How should these executive committee decisions be communicated to the larger group?
>
> Convene small discussion groups of three to five people to elicit their responses. Then ask each group to present their recommendations for governing, managing, and volunteer tasks. Use uncertainty or disagreements as opportunities to clarify the essential roles of the board. It is much better to debate a list of duties now than fight over authority later. Seek consensus with a summarized list of the board's governing responsibilities. The list of activities that board members may do in their capacity as volunteer staff may be important, but competent volunteers may also do them. The board development committee should then draft a statement of board governing responsibilities for the full board to consider and adopt as policy.

Avoid the dilemma of the board president and chief executive competing for leadership authority. In most cases, the president looks *outward* toward the community, cultivating partners and support, while the executive looks *inward,* overseeing programs and operations. They will advise each other, but the wise board president will defer to the professional staff's judgment on organizational operations. If the executive is taking the organization off course, this is cause for collective board intervention. Remember, though, that the board as a body supervises the executive. This supervisory authority may be delegated to an executive or personnel committee, but an individual board member, even the president, cannot pull rank on staff.

For more on creating a constructive partnership between the board and chief executive, see Appendix for Constructive Partnership: Board and Chief Executive, excerpted from *The Source: Twelve Principles of Governance That Power Exceptional Boards.*

The board speaks as one body or not at all.

The board's role in a transition. A board that works well with an experienced president or chief executive must adjust when leadership changes. A founder's departure can be especially challenging. A board used to trusting the leadership of a seasoned executive will find itself much more actively involved in leadership during a transition to a new executive. In small organizations, the transition following the departure of a professional chief executive may require the board to temporarily adopt a more hands-on management style. As the new staff executive matures on the job, the board increasingly lets go of operations. A board may use a leadership transition to take stock and confirm the organization's mission and priorities, or to make a significant shift.

William Bridges' book *Managing Transitions: Making the Most of Change* (2003) is a good resource for navigating significant organizational change. As a generation of founding directors retires, many organizations are developing succession plans. Some boards hire a short-term interim director to help the organization manage a significant leadership transition.

Building a Sense of Team

Even an understanding of responsibilities does not ensure that individual board members will work together as a team. Members of any small working group such as a board require time to get to know each other, build trust, clarify roles, accept leadership, work out conflicting interests, and learn how to make decisions.

A group needs to have some history together before it becomes effective. One classic description of group process, first described by Bruce Tuckman,[9] predicts that a new group will spend time to *form*, then *storm* (encountering and resolving conflicts), then *norm* (working out effective procedures) before they can effectively *perform* as a group. Recognizing this process helps keep perspective when a group struggles at first.

Working groups, such as boards of directors, have two parallel group dynamics: accomplishing organizational tasks and navigating the members' personal and social needs. To accomplish tasks, board members identify problems, determine agendas, consider alternatives, and make decisions. A skillful chair or meeting facilitator can help the group advance through its tasks. At the same time, a social and emotional dynamic is being played out. Who is that new person? Should I volunteer? Who does he think he is, taking charge like that? These dynamics are as much a part of the board meeting as the tasks, yet they sometimes go unacknowledged.

If a board meets infrequently or only to conduct business, team building will proceed slowly. Team building can be accelerated if you create opportunities for less formal gatherings. If board members eat and laugh together, the chances are better that they can later debate the tough issues and still like and respect each other. Board members who care about each other work better together.

Consider team building activities:

- **Plan pre- or post-meeting gatherings** with snacks and drinks or a potluck supper so people can get better acquainted.
- **Hold a reception before or after an arts event.** This helps people get acquainted and connects them with the programs of the organization.
- **Conduct a board retreat.** A facilitated retreat can address issues of board responsibilities apart from or within the context of strategic planning, with the added benefit that board members get to know each other. Program the retreat loosely enough to encourage important informal conversations. See the Strategic Planning chapter for information on retreats.

- **Ask board members to write one-paragraph biographical sketches.** Provide these sketches to the entire board, along with a complete list of board members, their addresses and phone numbers, and the names of spouses or partners.
- **Periodically "check in" with people** to see what is happening in their lives as a preliminary to conducting business.
- **Identify one or more board members to concern themselves with the human, emotional side of board development.** Ask them to call a board member who missed several meetings to see what is going on, or speak with the person who doesn't participate in board discussions. This could be a task of the governance committee.
- **Celebrate successes.** People want to be a part of a winning team, and they need to be reminded when the organization is doing good work.

Managing Meetings

Meetings are occasions when both group tasks and social needs of the board can be accomplished. Most people have plenty of experience with agonizing meetings that waste people's time and fail to accomplish important work. Since meetings are so central to the board's work, learning how to make meetings productive and rewarding is important. The following are important elements of successful meetings.

Respect board members' time. Schedule meetings in consideration of busy volunteer schedules. Except for national boards that meet infrequently, meetings lasting more than two hours suggest that committees or staff should do more work between board meetings. A national trend suggests that boards are meeting less frequently than once was the case. BoardSource reports that on average, nonprofit boards meet six to nine times a year.[10] They should also meet annually in a retreat.

Select a skilled meeting leader. Any gathering of more than three people can benefit from a facilitator. Usually the president facilitates the meeting. If the president's skills do not include meeting management, consider appointing a meeting facilitator or rotating the task. The facilitator manages the agenda and time; guides discussions, reining in a longwinded speaker or drawing out a reticent one; clarifies issues; tests for consensus; and recognizes decisions. In some groups, the president or facilitator controls access to discussions by recognizing people who want to speak. In others, she or he intervenes only when someone can't get a word into a lively debate.

Figure 2. Sample Agenda Outline

Agenda Item	Presenter	Time Required	Tab in Binder	Outcome Wanted	Action Taken
				Discuss or vote…	

Work with an agenda. Board members appreciate receiving an agenda in advance of the meeting. In many organizations the president and/or executive committee, along with the chief executive, develop the agenda in advance of the board meeting. Start the meeting by confirming the agenda, and incorporate important and time-sensitive items brought forward by board members. Schedule important issues for consideration early in the meeting, and keep track of the time. In meetings where there is a large volume of material to consider, it is common to prepare a binder with tabs for each important agenda item.

Different types of agendas are appropriate for different meeting types or structures:

- **Traditional meetings** are used to approve minutes, give reports, revisit old business, conduct new business, etc. While this is the most familiar structure, it prioritizes past business and relegates new thinking to the end of the meeting, where it may be cut short if the rest goes overtime.
- **Operating meetings** are organized around major operations: finance, programs, or marketing. The meeting time is organized according to the areas of major work. This promotes better use of time than the traditional agenda, but runs the risk that the board oversees management instead of governing.
- **Planning meetings** are organized to discuss progress on each of the organization's goals. This is a fine way to ensure that the plan is active and not filed away. This approach is ordinarily blended with one of the other models to accommodate business unforeseen in the plan.
- **Functional.** The functional agenda starts with action items, then moves to matters that require discussion, and concludes with routine reports. This approach puts the important matters first.
- **Tabular.** A graphic presentation can be used for any of the agenda styles. (Figure 2 is an example.) In this format, the agenda itself can be used to note actions taken in the meeting minutes.
- **Timed.** A prediction of how much time should be allowed for each agenda item can be incorporated into any agenda style.
- **Consent agenda.** Organizations having a large number of routine matters to approve often save time by use of a *consent agenda,* also called a *consent calendar* or *unanimous consent agenda.* Consent agendas have long been used in government to streamline board meetings, yet the idea is relatively new to nonprofits. In this system, a portion of the printed agenda, listing matters that are expected to be noncontroversial and on which there are likely to be no questions, can therefore be voted on without discussion. Before taking the vote, the president allows time for the members to read the list to see if it includes anything on which they may have a question, or which they would like to discuss or oppose. Any member has the right to remove any item from the consent agenda, in which case it is transferred to the regular agenda to be considered and voted on separately. The remaining items are then unanimously approved in their entirety without discussion, saving the time that would be required for individual votes. Board members must take care, though, that they read the proposals on the consent agenda carefully in order to fulfill their governing responsibilities.[11]

Provide information in advance. In order to make decisions in a timely and concise manner, board members need to have important and relevant information prior to meetings. However, they will likely not read voluminous reports. Sandra Hughes of BoardSource recommends providing vital information in a one-page "dashboard report" that highlights critical information. (See Figure 3.) The concept is also known as Balanced Scorecard.[12]

Agree on how to make decisions. Parliamentary procedures, such as those detailed in *Robert's Rules of Order* and *The Standard Code of Parliamentary Procedure,* can be useful as a tool for running annual

Figure 3. Sample Arts Agency "Dashboard" Report: Quick assessment of critical indicators

Examples of Indicators (adapt to suit your specific needs)	April Base year	April Last year	April This year
New members			
Total members			
Number of grants written			
Grants receivable			
Grants received			
Earned revenues			
Administrative expenses			
Program expenses			
Other financial details			
Endowment balance			
Bank balance			
Audience numbers			
Other measures of interest			

membership meetings and meetings about crucial policy and financial decisions. Most board decisions, however, are more creative and are effectively managed by consensus. A formal, parliamentary motion for a specific action tends to fix the group on one alternative too early in a discussion. A bad idea gets proposed as a motion, amendments are offered and debated, and the only way to proceed to a good solution may be for the motion-maker to withdraw the motion or for the group to defeat it (and the person) by a vote. Consensus is a less formal process that is closer to the way people actually work together. A problem is clarified, alternatives are proposed in brainstorming fashion, and alternative solutions are discussed until the best options become clear. The president or another board member tests for consensus by a suggestion such as "I hear a lot of support for inviting key constituents to our fall board retreat. Have we reached a decision?" If people agree, the matter is decided. If not, there is need for more discussion.

Recognize when the group has made a decision. At the conclusion of a discussion, the president should acknowledge that a decision has been reached. Restate the decision. If the business item has financial or legal implications, or if people are more comfortable with formal rules of order, confirm the consensus decision with a motion and a vote. At the conclusion of a meeting, review the decisions that have been reached.

Document decisions. Decisions should be recorded in writing and promptly distributed as minutes. The trend is toward shorter minutes that do not include summaries of the discussions, but only decisions made and actions required, and need not be more than one page in length. Decisions that require action should acknowledge who does what by when and, if necessary, at what cost. If no one can be identified to take action, acknowledge that the group has not made a decision to act.

Monitor and follow through on agreed actions. A useful assumption is that even the best-intentioned board member needs encouragement or a reminder to complete board assignments. The minutes highlighting decisions and actions become a tool to provide that encouragement and to monitor implementation. Here are tips on monitoring:

Recruit a board member to monitor the fulfillment of important board or committee tasks. This is a good assignment for a vice president. The monitor should make timely calls to inquire on the status of tasks in process. This approach can be a huge improvement over the belated "What, you missed the deadline?"

Dispense with the routine reading of the minutes at the next meeting. Instead, determine the status of all of the action items.

Produce a timeline. A graphic summary of important actions and key dates is a useful task-monitoring tool. The timeline is consulted by staff and committee chairs and brought out at board meetings for a quick visual overview of work before the board. Seeing all projects and key tasks on one chart also helps to pinpoint bottlenecks and people being overburdened with work.

Conduct some business electronically. Boards are increasingly doing business electronically. Be sure that your bylaws accommodate virtual meetings. Agendas, minutes, and reports are often distributed by email, and actions requiring quick response are handled through email exchanges. National organizations sometimes conduct entire board meetings with conference calls, videoconferences, or email exchanges. Organizational websites sometimes have password-protected areas where board members can post communications and drafts of policies and plans. Do take care that no one is disenfranchised by lack of Internet access (this can still be a real consideration in rural areas). Consider also the limitations of electronic communications: avoid working through conflicts or distributing sensitive information by email. Consider developing email and social media protocols to avoid initiating or exacerbating conflicts. Virtual meetings work best when good personal relations are built and maintained through face-to-face contact.

Managing Conflicts

While it is beyond the scope of this chapter to teach conflict management, the issue must be addressed. Conflicts are virtually inevitable and are sometimes useful. They tend to be about policy, programs, or personalities.

Conflicts can identify important differences that need to be aired and resolved. A fundamental misgiving about the mission can manifest itself as a conflict over a detail. Rather than smoothing over the disagreement, leaders should use this opportunity to have a substantive discussion about the organization's purpose and its policies, programs, or procedures. Conflicts that are personality clashes also need attention.

In any conflict, two factors need to be balanced. One is a concern for the relationships of the people involved, and the other is a concern for the task or the principle at stake. If the cause of the disagreement (the color of the membership brochure) is less significant than the relationships, one party concedes or both agree to disagree. If the principle is vital (the policies and measures for genuine inclusion of people of color), it may be worth risking the angry resignation of a board member: a win/lose solution.

Sometimes the best solution is to simply ignore the minor conflict. More often the best course is to work toward a win/win solution that meets the interests of all parties. It is important to look beyond the specific positions taken by people to identify the interests they have in common and find a solution that satisfies the common interests rather than pitting one position against the other. (For further discussion, see the classic *Getting to Yes*.[13])

Policy Development

Policies reflect what is important to the organization as a whole. Written into formal statements approved by the governing board, they are used to guide individual and group action toward organizational goals and objectives. Policy development, therefore, is a primary board responsibility. A test of the need for a policy and of how clearly it is written is this: will the policy help staff make effective decisions related to this issue?

Policies allow for leadership continuity despite turnover. By setting policies to guide staff or volunteer action, the board is relieved from making day-to-day operational decisions. By setting limits, policies permit freedom of action within those limits. They simplify decision-making and provide for more consistent decisions.

The protection from political and personal pressures that policies provide to staff is also very important. For example:

- Mayor: "Why didn't my niece get accepted into your exhibition?"
- Gallery Director: "According to our exhibition policy, a jury of peers makes the selections. I am sorry, but the matter is out of my hands."

The Internal Revenue Service (IRS) monitors nonprofit accountability practices. Organizations required to file a 990 form (check current IRS regulations) must indicate each year if certain policies and procedures are in place. These include policies on whistleblowers; conflicts of interest; document retention; documentation of board and committee meetings; formal evaluation and compensation of the chief executive and key employees. The 990 form also asks how these policies and tax forms are made available for public inspection. As laws and regulations are subject to change, check with the IRS for current policies.

Board operating policies encompass how board members should function in relation to each other and to paid staff and volunteers. For example: "Board members are expected to attend all regularly scheduled meetings (four to six per year) and to serve on at least one committee." "Board decisions will be made by consensus and confirmed by formal vote."

Management policies concern planning and overall operation of the organization, as well as establishing accountability, responsibilities, budgets, and fiscal procedures. For example: "The operating budget for the upcoming fiscal year shall be approved by the board at least one month prior to the end of the current fiscal year." "Year-end statements will be reviewed by an independent auditor."

Personnel policies relate to recruitment, affirmative action, selection, placement, training and development, discipline, compensation, grievances, termination, and fringe benefits. For example: "Staff members should receive a formal performance appraisal each year."

Professional policies deal with the actions of staff members in relation to performance of their organizational duties, confidentiality, and ethical standards. For example: "It is the duty of board and staff members to act in the best interests of the gallery. Part of that duty is to exercise confidentiality on matters conveyed to the board."

Safety policies help protect staff, volunteers, and constituents from sexual harassment or threat of violence. Organizations working with young people need policies and procedures to protect children and youth from sexual misconduct. For example: "Every youth event will be overseen by at least two adult volunteers."

Artistic and program policies pertain to an organization's programs and the type and scope of artistic activity. For example: "The gallery is committed to representing the fine artists and craftspeople emerging from the four-county region whose work meets the artistic standards of the director." "In all programs, the agency has a policy affirming and supporting artistic freedom of expression."

Artistic policy in arts-producing organizations is a special case. A dance company, theater, or music ensemble is frequently founded by an individual artist or group of collaborators. The organization provides the support that allows the artist(s) to produce the work. A board is recruited to help institutionalize and sustain the organization, support the artistic vision, and fulfill the law. Such a board would not ordinarily develop an artistic policy on its own.

The board that attempts to set artistic policy may find itself in conflict with the founding artist or current artistic director. Some argue that arts programs should be solely the responsibility of the artistic director. The board of a producing organization would affect artistic policy only through the selection of an artistic director. Arts programs would also be subject only to the board's financial controls. A community arts board, however, often has dual obligations to its art and its community. The board may need to collaborate with its artistic personnel to balance artistic and community-development goals.

The Role of the President

The leadership provided by an effective board president is a key ingredient of a successful organization. In all-volunteer organizations, the president may act like a chief executive. In a staffed organization, the president complements the chief executive.

The president should have an overview of the organization's purpose and management process, and may be the public spokesperson. He or she is the one person, in addition to the chief executive, who is concerned with the organization as a whole and with its means of fulfilling its mission. To maintain an overview and to manage in the relatively little time available as a volunteer leader, the president must work by motivating others to act. To be effective, he or she must avoid getting bogged down with tasks that should be the responsibility of staff or volunteer workers.

The duties of the president may include:

- managing the board of directors;
- overseeing recruitment and orientation of board members (with the governance committee);
- calling and conducting board meetings;

- preparing board agendas (with the executive staff and/or chief executive);
- appointing ad hoc committees and committee chairs;
- representing the organization to the public; and
- serving as the liaison between board and staff.

The Second Approach: Improve Boards by Recruiting New Members

The previous section describes the first step in board development: ensuring that the existing team understands its role and the way it works together on behalf of the organization. However, community arts organizations often do not have enough depth of leadership on the board or staff to fulfill the necessary roles and tasks. When that is the case, the organization may need to recruit new members.

The Recruitment Process

Any strategy to improve the governing process will eventually involve identifying and recruiting new board members. Without conscientious attention to the recruitment process, boards tend to perpetuate themselves by recruiting people just like those who currently serve. This leaves the same gaps in skills, representation, contacts, and resources. A better approach is to identify the organization's governing needs and find people who can help meet those needs.

Create a board development or governance committee. Replace the short-term nominating committee with a year-round leadership development or governance committee that would oversee the profiling, recruitment, and orientation processes. This group could include a board member (someone in line to be president would be a good choice), a staff member, and someone with an outside perspective. In some organizations, the governance committee organizes board training, shares new resources or articles of interest, talks with nonperforming board members, and helps manage conflicts.

Profile governance needs. Produce a written profile of the skills, contacts, resources, and representation needs of the board. (See the Board Profile Grid in the Appendix.) Next, compare the existing board to this profile and summarize characteristics missing from the current board profile, or attributes that will be lost when members' terms expire. Prioritize the recruitment of new board members who meet these needs, and offer your recommendations to the board for discussion. Keep in mind, though, that some needs can be filled by recruiting people to serve as advisers, on committees or temporary task forces, or in other capacities. Only a few identified candidates would ordinarily be approached to join the governing board of directors.

In *Governance as Leadership,* Richard Chait and his colleagues remind us to, above all, seek board members who can lead and not to aim for a "Swiss army knife" board in which every conceivable skill is represented. Look for people who bring multiple attributes. It is dangerous to an artistic mission to recruit people who bring only financial expertise without some artistic sensibility. It is patronizing to invite a person of color for their contribution to diversity who does not also bring needed skills or provide access to resources.

Identify stakeholders. Do not limit recruitment to people personally known to board members. Work to broaden your reach by identifying community sectors or types of people who have a stake in the organization's success. (See the Sample Stakeholder Analysis in Figure 4.) Few people will make the commitment required of a board member unless they perceive they have a stake in your success.

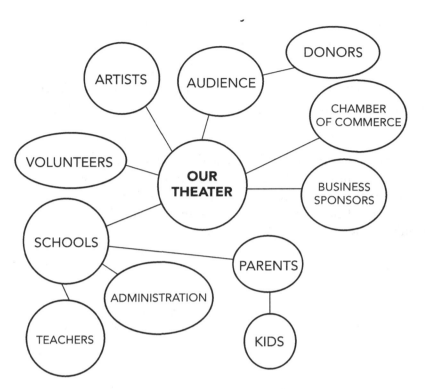

Figure 4. Sample Stakeholder Analysis by a New England children's theater

Sample Stakeholder Analysis. This stakeholder analysis was done by a New England children's theater. The theater operated in a barely adequate church basement. The board was wholly composed of theater professionals and parents who did not have access to potential contributors. Among the identified stakeholders were parents and the local publisher of a children's magazine. Looking at the clusters, a board member realized the obvious: a senior executive at the publisher had a child who participated in the theater. This individual provided the link to the corporate community. The president invited the executive to lunch, which led to the executive inviting a group of friends to another lunch, where it was agreed to form an advisory board which would plan corporate fundraising for the theater. Within two years, several corporate leaders joined the theater board and the advisory board was disbanded. The contacts provided by these new board members eventually helped yield contributions sufficient to buy and refurbish a performance facility.

Name potential candidates. With recruitment priorities in mind, look at the list of stakeholders and think of individuals who provide the priority attributes and who may see themselves as having a stake in your organization. People who fit into more than one category of stakeholder are more likely to appreciate the benefit of volunteer service.

Decide on individuals to approach. Make a shortlist of the most qualified candidates. Look first within your own constituencies: volunteers, committees, donors, audiences, etc. Some organizations require that a board candidate serve first in another volunteer capacity so they become familiar with the organization and vice versa. As in fundraising, board recruitment is best done by someone known and respected by the candidate. If no board or staff member knows the candidate well, determine who would be the most persuasive.

Assemble a fact pack that helps a candidate decide whether or not to accept your invitation. Such a kit might include a mission statement and plan, program descriptions, current year's budget and past year's financial statements, board and staff list, a statement of board responsibilities, a schedule of board meetings, and your "give or get" policy for board membership. (See the Fundraising chapter for more on this policy.)

Make a call to the candidate. Most people are flattered to be asked. If you have done your homework, this will lead to more conversation. The best way to do this is face-to-face; second best is an extended telephone conversation.

Meet to discuss the organization, explain why the candidate is being asked to help, and outline the benefits and responsibilities of board membership. This discussion is similar to a fundraising call, where you are trying to persuade the prospect of the value of your work, and to a job interview, where both parties can assess whether this is a mutually beneficial commitment. Determine the candidate's interests and how they may be served through your organization. This makes his or her involvement a two-way street, and is an important step in later assigning the board member responsibilities. If you want something specific from the candidate, this is the time to ask.

> One arts center, seeking someone to fundraise, recruited a woman who had just raised $5 million for the hospital. At her first board meeting she exclaimed to her dismayed colleagues how happy she was to be working with the arts and how tired of fundraising she had become.

Invite the candidate to join the board. If there is initial interest and the match between the candidate and the organization seems good, including personalities, skills, interests, experience from other boards, etc., extend the invitation. Your bylaws may specify that the invitation must be in the form of a nomination to be confirmed by a vote of the board or members. It may be that the candidate will need to think about your offer and consult family members or an employer before responding. In that case, leave the fact pack and get back in touch at a specific date.

Elect or appoint your new board members. Each organization's bylaws will specify how to formally approve new board members.

Board Orientation

New board members may not become productive team members without some deliberate orientation and team building.

Board manual. The materials in the recruitment fact pack referred to above form the core of a board manual or handbook. Create a digital version or assemble the materials in a three-ring binder with index tabs so that changes can be easily incorporated.

- Sample Contents of a Board Manual
- Mission statement and strategic plan
- Brief history of the organization
- Program descriptions
- Current year's budget and past year's financial statements
- Bylaws
- Major policies
- Standard operating procedures

- Statement of board responsibilities, including fundraising and personal donations
- Board member list
- Staff and committee chairs list
- Biographical sketches of board members
- List of major funders
- Calendar of upcoming events, including a schedule of board meetings.

Orientation meeting. The president and chief executive or the governance committee should meet with new board members to orient them to their responsibilities, the organization's ways of working, and current projects or issues being considered. This can be a separate meeting or can precede the first regularly scheduled board meeting.

Social gathering. A luncheon, dinner, or reception in honor of the new board members is a courteous gesture that may accelerate team building.

Board development and planning retreat. An annual planning retreat can serve both to advance the organization's planning and to build a team. Such an event takes time, energy, and perhaps money to do well, but can yield significant results. See the Strategic Planning chapter for more information on retreats.

Buddy system. Some groups find it helpful to assign an experienced board member to be a buddy to the new board member. Such a partner provides a direct and personal source of information, encouragement, and support in the first months of board service.

Specific assignments. People respond better to a request to "organize a team to raise $2,000 from downtown business" than to "do what you can to raise money." Assign one or more specific responsibilities.

Ongoing board development. Attention to board development does not end with the recruitment and orientation of new board members. This is one of the reasons why many organizations have board development or governance committees instead of nominating committees. Someone should be charged with providing ongoing attention as to how the board is functioning as a team. Personal attention to the human needs of board members goes a long way.

Keep Good Board Members

If board members misunderstand what is expected of them, or don't feel like an important part of the team, they may resign. In some boards, members feel uninvolved because the president or executive committee makes most of the important decisions.

It is also common for key board members to experience burnout. As one weary board president bluntly put it, "Our arts council recruits good people and sucks them dry."

Learn to delegate. Boards of all-volunteer organizations that spend too much time on programming and administration, and too little on policy and planning, may need to delegate detailed operational decisions and tasks. Set aside meetings or portions of meetings for policy discussions. In addition, if you delegate and involve more people periodically for shorter assignments over a longer period of time you can spread the workload and help prevent burnout. A good friend of the organization could serve on a cultural planning task force one year, coordinate a fundraiser the next, take a year off, join the board for two years, and then retire to be an occasional advisor.

Involve people in many different ways. Any organization needs multiple options to engage people in their work. Recruiting individuals to the board is only one way to attract expertise. Consider these options:

- A pool of volunteers under the direction of a volunteer coordinator. (See the Volunteers in the Arts chapter.)
- Short-term, task-specific volunteers referred by such agencies as Business Volunteers for the Arts, SCORE, or other local service organizations.
- Ad hoc committees, project teams, or short-term task forces organized for a specific task and then disbanded.
- Consultants or volunteers working in a consultant-like role to accomplish specific tasks. (Funds for paid consultants may be available from state and local arts agencies or foundations.)
- Peer advisers—local arts leaders trained to do short-term consulting and referred by a number of state arts agencies and statewide assemblies of local arts agencies. The Arts Extension Service offers these trainings.
- Here are additional measures you can take to retain good board members:
- Help them meet their needs. Try to understand why they are motivated to volunteer and match them to opportunities to fulfill those needs.
- Share successes. People like to win. Bring to the board positive news or feedback.
- Involve board members actively in decision-making. If you persist in bringing predetermined issues to the board, you'll lose members. Executive committees should be cautious of assuming too much authority and undermining the participation of other board members.
- Help them develop. Invite board members to professional conferences, management development workshops, and networking meetings.
- Recognize them. Acknowledge the interests and the work of board members at public functions or in your publications.
- Thank your board members. Never take them for granted.

STRATEGY 2: CHANGE THE GOVERNING STRUCTURE

The preceding section explored strategies to improve governing and managing processes. However, it may be that procedural changes or recruitment alone don't make enough difference to create an effective governing system. Structural changes may be required. Think of what an organizational chart would look like, showing all the players (board, committees, staff), their responsibilities, and how they relate to each other.

Structure should relate to the organization's mission. A major change in mission, long-range goals, or major programs may suggest a corresponding structural reorganization. Structural changes can be minor or dramatic. Simple changes could include the creation or elimination of some standing committees (for example, some organizations facing financial crisis have responded by abolishing their fundraising committee and making it the full board's priority), the creation of new officer positions, or a change in the number of board positions. More significant changes could include reducing the frequency of board meetings, eliminating the executive committee, or appointing the chief executive to the board as a voting member. A radical change might be reducing the board to the legally required number of members, who become charged solely with assuring the organization's fulfillment of legal requirements.

So much of the arts-support environment has changed that leaders of new arts organizations are questioning if they need to create a classic nonprofit organization, while existing organizations are questioning their basic business models. Board leaders may wish to consider alternative organization structures. As government and foundation grant funds have diminished or become more restrictive, new organizations may not find it necessary to incorporate and seek a 501(c)3 tax exemption. Some organize informally and use a fiscal agent when necessary for grants or tax-deductible contributions. Others have created low-profit limited liability companies (L3Cs) that aim to achieve public benefits with business structures.

Institutional Collaborations and Mergers. Nonprofit arts organizations often work in collaboration with complementary organizations to achieve greater impact or efficiencies. When funding gets tight, such collaborations may become a necessity to sustain organizations. While partnerships tend to be organized around discrete projects, collaborations are increasingly being sustained over time and may extend into closely-connected programs and operations.

There are many options for strategic restructuring in partnership with other organizations, ranging from shared projects to full mergers or acquisitions. Boards and their chief executives should be intentional about such realignments with careful planning. There are clear advantages as well as practical risks and legal considerations. Some funders and management service organizations offer technical assistance programs, funding, publications, and checklists to guide restructuring. MAP for Nonprofits has outlined eight restructuring options (see Restructuring Options+ in box on next page).

Rethink Old Assumptions

Many arts organization leaders have questioned long-held assumptions about nonprofit business models and how nonprofits are organized. Business models that worked in environments of relative abundance need rethinking in times of financial duress. That reconsideration may yield structural changes. Before considering specific structural changes, it may be helpful to question commonly held assumptions about nonprofit boards. Beyond what is required by law for incorporated nonprofit organizations, there is nothing carved in stone about the way boards, committees, and staff are organized.

Consider some common assumptions and some alternative thinking:

Assumption: Arts organizations must be federally tax-exempt, nonprofit corporations.
Alternatives: Some organizations remain ad hoc and informal. Some operate independent of grants or use a fiscal agent to process grants requiring tax exemption. Others organize as for-profit businesses while others are experimenting with L3C status.

Assumption: An organization should be steeply hierarchical, with information flowing up to a few leaders (board) and decisions flowing down to the staff.
Alternative: People in an organization can relate to one another as peers. Information is communicated throughout the organization at all levels. Decisions are, as much as possible, entrusted to the people who are closest to the action. While important policy decisions may be reserved for a governing board, everyone should have an opportunity to contribute to important decisions.

> **Restructuring Options+[14]**
>
> 1. Administrative consolidation: Restructuring that includes the sharing, exchanging, or contracting of administrative functions to increase the administrative efficiency of one or more of the organizations involved. Such functions may include accounting, human resources, information and technology systems, marketing and purchasing, among others.
>
> 2. Consolidation: Combining separate organizations into a single one. Consolidation differs from a merger in that a new entity is created in the consolidation.
>
> 3. Joint programming: Restructuring that includes the joint launching and managing of one or more programs to further the programmatic mission of the participating organizations.
>
> 4. Joint venture corporation: Joint ventures involve the creation of a new organization to further the specific administrative or programmatic ends of two or more organizations. Partner organizations share governance of the new organization.
>
> 5. Merger: The integration of all programmatic and administrative functions of two or more organizations, to increase the administrative efficiency and/or program quality of one or more of the partners. Organizations may also integrate to increase geographic reach or achieve synergy between programs. Mergers occur when one or more organizations dissolve and become part of another organization's structure. The surviving organization may keep or change its name. A merger also occurs when two or more organizations dissolve and establish a new structure that includes some or all of the resources and programs of the original organizations.
>
> 6. Parent-subsidiary: An integration that combines some of the partners' administrative functions and programmatic services. The goal is to increase the administrative efficiency and program quality of one or more organizations through the creation or designation of an existing organization ("parent") to oversee administrative functions and programmatic services of one or more other organizations ("subsidiary"). Although the visibility and identity of the original organizations often remain intact in a parent-subsidiary relationship, some organizations involved in such restructurings consolidate to the point where they look and function much like a merged organization.
>
> 7. Program transfer: One organization spins off or transfers administration of one or more of its programs to another organization.
>
> 8. 8. Strategic restructuring: Two or more independent organizations establish an ongoing relationship to increase administrative efficiency and/or further programmatic goals through shared, transferred, or combined services, resources, or programs. Strategic restructuring ranges from jointly managed programs and consolidated administrative functions to full-scale mergers.

Assumption: An organization needs standing committees and every board member should be assigned to one.

Alternatives:

—Create only those committees that are essential and convene meetings only when necessary. Eliminate conflicts or redundant efforts by removing committees that mirror staff functions. BoardSource promotes the idea of a zero-based committee structure. Like the parallel concept for budgeting, each committee should be justified each year or discontinued.

—Consider flexible committee structures. A committee can be a single board member who invites some friends to work on a fundraising event or who develops a proposal for a communications policy. A committee meeting can be a conference call or email exchange. A volunteer working in the role of a consultant can fulfill a governing task, such as designing a membership campaign. A temporary task force can be convened just for the life of a project. Ad hoc committees and task forces are becoming more common than standing committees. As a general rule, resist the temptation to set up a standing committee.

Characteristics of Nonprofit Boards

BoardSource conducts periodic surveys of nonprofit chief executives and board members from all types of organizations. Here are some highlights from its biannual Nonprofit Governance Index for 2012 (see www.boardsource.org for more and updated information).

BOARD STRUCTURE

- The average size of a nonprofit board is 16-17 members.
- Nearly three quarters (73%) of boards have term limits for board members and the most common structure is two three-year terms.
- Nonprofit boards commonly convene seven to twelve times per year for less than two hours or four to six times per year for two to five hours. Overall, the average is seven meetings per year.
- Committees: 79% of boards have an executive committee (21% of these meet more often than full board); 56% a fundraising committee; 46% combined finance/audit; 38% combined governance/nominating; 37% standalone finance; 29% standalone nominating; 27% program; 26% standalone audit; 23% marking/communications/PR; 23% planning.

FUNDRAISING

- Three quarters (75%) of board members make personal financial contributions.
- Six in ten (61%) board members identify donors.
- Six in ten (61%) board members attend fundraising events.
- Over four in ten (42%) board members solicit funds.

BOARD POLICIES

Nearly all boards:

- have a conflict-of-interest policy (96%);
- have a whistleblower policy (88%);
- have a document retention and destruction policy (88%);
- carry directors' and officers' liability insurance (95%).[15]

Assumption: More board members means more contributions.
Alternative: Recruiting someone to the board may help ensure her financial contribution, but it commits that board member to all the trappings of other board responsibilities. Consider instead cultivating a large number of contributors who have a stake in your organization's success and who commit themselves to giving, but not necessarily to joining the board.

Assumption: "But the bylaws say we can't."
Alternative: Bylaws have a clause that allows them to be amended. Use it.

Examples of Organizational Structures

A successful structure should evolve from an organization's unique history and community environment. The following models of organizational structures may stimulate constructive thinking about your own organization.

All-volunteer nonprofit organizations. The all-volunteer nonprofit can be structured in various ways. One variation is the board plus executive committee. The executive committee typically meets more frequently than the board and acts on behalf of the board. The full board is more concerned with policy and the executive committee with oversight of operations. Whereas in a staffed organization, the executive committee relates more directly with professional staff than the rest of the board does, in an all-volunteer organization the executive committee itself may serve as the volunteer staff.

Another variation is the governing board plus advisory board. An advisory board may be formed to connect your organization to community or national leaders who offer expertise, perspectives, and contacts not found on the board or needed for particular programs. They can be convened periodically for discussions, or called upon by staff or governing board members for advice on specific issues. Be sure to call upon advisors periodically to enhance organizational credibility and build your awareness of the needs of key stakeholders.

Staffed organizations. Within a staffed organization, a managing (or administrative) director administers the policies and programs of the board. The role of the managing director can range from a supportive, almost clerical role in support of board initiatives to one where the director assumes a leadership role.

As organizations grow, an artistic director is sometimes hired to manage artistic programs, and the managing director's responsibilities are limited to administration. Sometimes the two are peers who together report to the board. In other cases, either the managing or artistic director is the more senior staff member.

The title of chief executive or executive director connotes a staff person more generally responsible for the organization's well-being than either a managing or artistic director. In a large organization, the chief executive may have supporting management and artistic staff. In a smaller organization, the chief executive may possess overall programming and artistic responsibilities and may be assisted by board members and non-governing volunteers operating in the capacity of volunteer staff.

A trend in larger, well-established arts organizations is to promote the experienced chief executive to be the president and CEO. She or he assumes much of the policy-making responsibilities of the president, as well as the administrative responsibilities of the chief executive. The board president may be re-titled "chair" or "chairperson."

SOME ALTERNATIVE STRUCTURAL MODELS

Staff-driven with a nominal board. An organization that does not depend much upon individual or corporate contributions may reduce its board to the legally required minimum and ask that they simply ensure the fulfillment of the organization's legal responsibilities. They might assemble once a year for the legally required annual meeting, authorize the staff to sign contracts, note that tax reports have

> ### Special Cases: Public Commissions and Coalitions
>
> #### PUBLIC COMMISSIONS.
>
> A quarter of local arts agencies nationally are public commissions.[16] In some, the commissioners function like a nonprofit board of directors. They set policy, direct staff, and are ultimately responsible for the commission. In other local arts councils or commissions, the commissioners merely advise staff and elected officials without governing authority. The professional staff is accountable to the mayor, city manager, or city council. In these cases, the structure and governing procedures explicitly acknowledge the political role of a local arts agency. Problems arise when the commissioners don't understand their role. Especially problematic are commissioners who should be advising, but assume their role to be governance and supervision. In one city, the professional staff director of the arts commission had to seek a legal opinion from the city attorney to convince her commissioners that their role was to advise the staff and the mayor.
>
> #### COALITIONS AND NETWORKS.
>
> Another special case is local arts agencies that are organized as coalitions of arts organizations. Here the board of directors may comprise representatives of the member organizations. As such, these board members must learn to consider their collective interests and may encounter conflicting pulls on their time, energy, and loyalties. Avoiding conflicting interests while fundraising for the coalition and for the represented organization can be particularly difficult.
>
> In these two cases, the board and staff may have a limited role in recruiting new commissioners or board members. In a public commission, the mayor appoints new commissioners. In a coalition agency, the member organizations may select their representatives.

been submitted, and sign the annual report to the secretary of state. Otherwise they serve as advisers to the staff.

In a variation, the nominal governing board is supplemented by a larger advisory board, which may help provide the staff with specialized advice, representation, access to constituencies or resources, and fundraising assistance.

Ad hoc task forces. A traditionally structured board organizes committees as they are needed. These are often called task forces or ad hoc committees, to distinguish them from standing committees. When the project is completed, the team disbands.

Artistic and governing boards. Some producing organizations create both a governing board and an artistic one. The artistic board assumes the responsibilities that would be fulfilled by an artistic director in a larger organization.

Board composed of all members (member board). Alternate ROOTS, a coalition of artists and activists working with grassroots communities in the southern United States, is an example of an organization whose board is composed of every voting member of the organization.

Nonprofit board plus a profit-making subsidiary. Some nonprofits have organized profit-making companies. Typical of these are craft organizations, which, because of tax regulations, have been required to separate their retail marketing operations from their nonprofit educational programs. In some cases, the same professional staff supports two separate boards. In others, there is considerable—even complete—overlap between the memberships of the two boards. Over time some of these subsidiaries have grown so independent of the parent organization that they have split completely away and become wholly independent entities.

CAUTIONS REGARDING STRUCTURAL CHANGES

Experiment with incremental changes. See what works, and then expand upon what is successful and discard what fails. You may wish to live with a change for a while before entrenching it in your bylaws or articles of incorporation. Successful organizations are perhaps more effectively grown than built.

The Internal Revenue Service and funding agencies may prefer organizations with traditional boards of directors. Be prepared to do a lot of explaining if you innovate with other structures. It may be that you'll operate with an innovative board but describe it in a more standard format to funders.

Keys to Board Improvement

This chapter is likely to have raised as many questions as it has resolved about fundamental assumptions and long-accepted board models. Summarized here are the key suggestions for board improvement.

- Engage board members in creative problem solving and strategic thinking.
- Help board members get better acquainted with each other.
- Host a social gathering of board and staff members.
- Manage meetings more effectively.
- Document decisions and follow through on commitments.
- Help board and staff understand the governing responsibilities of the board.
- Create a board development or governance committee.
- Create a board manual.
- Review the committee list.
- Organize a board development/planning retreat annually.

Resources

BoardSource: Probably the best source of practical information, books, tools and best practices, training, webinars, and leadership development for board members of nonprofits. Much of it requires a paid membership. The website's Q & A section and Glossary offer good summaries of frequently asked questions. www.boardsource.org

Governance Matters: A New York–based service organization that engages and informs nonprofit leaders on governance issues and improves board governance. www.governancemattersusa.org

Independent Sector: A good source of nonprofit-sector trends. Independent Sector sponsors research and creates resources so staff, boards, and volunteers can improve their organizations and better serve their communities. www.independentsector.org

MAP for Nonprofits: A Minnesota-based service organization with good governance advice, especially on mergers and other legal matters affecting nonprofit organizations. www.mapfornonprofits.org

Nonprofit Finance Fund: Helps organization leaders analyze and strengthen their financial health. www.nonprofitfinancefund.org

Probono Partnership: Provides business and transactional legal services to nonprofits in New York, New Jersey, and Connecticut. Their website offers answers to frequently asked legal questions of interest to boards. www.probonopartnership.org

The Board Café: An electronic newsletter with short articles of ideas, information, opinion, news, and resources for board members of nonprofits. www.blueavocado.org/category/topic/board-cafe

Endnotes

1. Sandra Hughes, senior consultant with BoardSource (formerly National Center for Nonprofit Boards), quoted in Alice Cochran, Board Structure: Current Trends and Options, Charity Channel, 2007, www.charitychannel.com.

2. BoardSource reports just 3 percent of nonprofit organizations compensate board members. Nonprofit Governance Index, 2012.

3. Richard Chait, William Ryan, and Barbara Taylor, *Governance as Leadership: Reframing the Work of Nonprofit Boards*. BoardSource, 2005.

4. This chart of responsibilities is influenced by John Carver's concept of Policy Governance®, a prescriptive board system adopted by some state arts agencies and larger cultural institutions. Organizations adopting this model operate within explicitly defined roles for the board and chief executive. When done well, this system leaves little room for ambiguity. The board defines policies that carefully define parameters within which staff must operate. The board is responsible for defining ultimate ends, while staff is entirely responsible for the means to achieve those ends within the bounds of policy. Such a system may suit some large organizations with a professional chief executive and adequate staff so that the board can focus entirely on governing through policy. This system is less useful for under-resourced organizations, where board members also serve as volunteer staff, and is inappropriate for advisory boards. The Carver system stresses the board's fiduciary role to ensure accountability and may limit its potential to engage in generative leadership.

5. John Carver, *Boards That Make a Difference: A New Design for Leadership in Nonprofit and Public Organizations*, 2nd ed., 1997.

6. Dan Hotchkiss, *Governance and Ministry: Rethinking Board Leadership*, Alban Institute, 2009.

7. In *Governance and Ministry*, Hotchkiss translated lessons of nonprofit governance to religious congregations and clergy. It is helpful to translate them back to arts management. The "wall of separation" implied by a strict two-column model seems to Hotchkiss "a bit stiff and artificial." His insight is that while governance and ministry must have well-defined boundaries, their interests and contributions intersect with each other. According to Hotchkiss, "The three indispensable requirements of organizational effectiveness [are] a unified structure for making governance decisions; a unified structure for making ministry decisions; and a firm boundary, with active mutual communication and accountability between them."

8. Adapted by permission from Chait et al.

9. Bruce Tuckman, "Developmental Sequence in Small Groups." Psychological Bulletin 63 no. 6 (1965): 384–99.

10. BoardSource, Nonprofit Governance Index 2012, p. 13.

11. See American Institute of Parliamentarians, *New Standard Code of Parliamentary Procedure*, 2012.

12. Robert S. Kaplan and David P. Norton, *The Balanced Scorecard: Translating Strategy into Action*, 1996.

13. Roger Fisher, William Ury, and Bruce Patton, *Getting to Yes: Negotiating Agreement Without Giving In*, rev. ed., 2011.

14. Excerpted by permission from *MergeMinnesota: Nonprofit Merger as an Opportunity for Survival and Growth*, written by Ron Reed for MAP for Nonprofits, 2007.

15. Director and officer liability insurance data is from the BoardSource Nonprofit Governance Index 2010.

16. Mitch Menchaca and Ben Davidson, *Local Arts Agencies 2010*. Available from Americans for the Arts, www.americansforthearts.org.

Appendix

CONSTRUCTIVE PARTNERSHIP: BOARD AND CHIEF EXECUTIVE

Exceptional boards govern in constructive partnership with the chief executive, recognizing that the effectiveness of the board and chief executive are interdependent. Nonprofit boards have primary legal responsibility for governance—the exercise and assignment of power and authority—of their organizations. Boards reserve to themselves organizational oversight and policy setting and delegate to the chief executive responsibility for managing operations and resources.

While respecting this division of labor, exceptional boards become allies with the chief executive in pursuit of the mission. They understand that they and the chief executive bring essential, complementary ingredients to the governance partnership that, when combined, are greater than the sum of their parts. Exceptional boards forge a partnership with the chief executive characterized by mutual trust, forthrightness, and a common commitment to mission. They encourage a strong, honest chief executive to pose questions and offer answers, and to share bad news early and openly. In turn, chief executives provide boards with tools and information to govern exceptionally. They welcome differing points of view and strategic thinking at the board table. Members of exceptional boards communicate regularly with the chief executive, informally discussing concerns in and between board meetings.

Exceptional boards hold the chief executive accountable. They evaluate the chief executive's performance annually and formally and continually evaluate the organization's leadership needs as part of succession planning. As a sounding board and source of support, they encourage the chief executive to strengthen necessary skills.

They understand that fair and competitive executive compensation is important in attracting and retaining qualified staff. When it is in the best interests of the organization, exceptional boards undertake the difficult task of replacing current leadership and selecting the most qualified chief executive available.

BOARD RESPONSIBILITIES

The board of directors of the organization accepts the following collective responsibilities:

- Lead. The board commits to govern the organization, to further its mission, and to recruit and nurture new leadership.
- Connect with the community. The board represents the interests of the organization and its programs to the community, and relates the interests of our community to the organization.
- Plan. The board determines the organization's mission and long-range goals by means of a regularly updated strategic plan.
- Set policy. The board establishes policies for finance, fundraising, personnel, facilities, board operations, and artistic programs.
- Raise funds. The board sets and meets annual fundraising goals through active solicitation of gifts from individuals, small businesses, and corporations.

- Assure financial stability. The board approves an annual budget and oversees financial management through a monthly review of financial statements.
- Assure legal accountability. The board assures that all legally required records are maintained, reports filed, and fees and taxes paid. The board makes sure that all grant reports are properly submitted and that grant-funded projects are completed as agreed, or amended.
- Manage board development. The board oversees the recruitment and orientation of new board members and regular board development training; schedules board meetings, maintains board records and communications, and oversees its committee system.
- Oversee chief executive. The board hires, supervises, evaluates, and, if necessary, fires the chief executive. All support staff and program and operational volunteers report to the chief executive. (An all-volunteer organization might substitute committees and volunteers for chief executive.)

As an individual board member of the organization, I accept the following responsibilities:

- Fiscal. I understand that I am fiscally responsible to help assure the financial solvency of this organization. I accept the responsibility to participate in budgeting and to understand and help evaluate financial performance.
- Legal. I understand that I am legally responsible to see that the organization serves its mission and that legal responsibilities are fulfilled.
- Fundraising. I commit to participate in the ongoing cultivation of community support; to actively participate in fundraising; and to make an annual financial contribution that I determine to be a significant amount for me.
- Membership. I agree to maintain a current individual membership.
- Participation. I agree to attend and participate in board meetings. When I am unable to attend, I will notify the secretary in advance and then review the minutes to remain current. I agree to attend as many artistic programs as possible.
- Volunteer service. I may be asked to serve on a committee or to help as a volunteer with certain organizational tasks. When working as a program volunteer, I am accountable to the professional staff (or to the full board, depending upon organizational structure).

HOW TO PROFILE BOARD PERSONNEL NEEDS

In order to recruit new board members for an effective board, it is best to know just what you need. What skills, contacts, resources, and representation should the board ideally have to be truly effective? Which of these characteristics are met by the current board, and which ones are missing? Needs that are not now met become the priorities for recruitment. Determine which needs are best met by recruiting people as advisors or ad hoc committee members, and which call for board membership. Schedule an hour during a board meeting to profile the board's personnel needs. Invite staff to participate.

- Brainstorm. What sorts of people are needed on the board to provide the resources, contacts, cultural representation, and constituent perspectives to fulfill the organization's mission? What skills are needed?

- Record and prioritize the desired board characteristics. Record on newsprint the selected characteristics under the categories of arts knowledge, resources, skills, contacts, and constituencies.
- When the list seems thorough, take stock. The list may be impossibly comprehensive. At the same time, there also may be important omissions, such as the failure to notice that only the interests of the white, middle class are reflected. Look for such omissions and amend the list. Then rank in order those characteristics which are the highest priority.
- Chart board needs on a profile grid. The board development committee enters the desired characteristics as column headings across the top of a board profile grid. The names of existing board members are entered down the first column. Current board members are invited to check which desired attributes they are willing and able to provide. This step not only identifies what contacts, skills, resources, and constituencies are now represented on the board, it serves also to motivate board members to own those characteristics. (See the sample grid on the next page.)
- Observe the gaps. The committee examines the profile to see what important board characteristics are lacking. The profile grid may also identify a few board members upon whom the organization is heavily dependent.

Figure 5: Board Development Profile Grid.

	Year term ends	Donor	Major donor	Fundraising experience	Financial skills	Leadership skill	Passion for mission	Contributes to diversity	Education contacts	Business	Civic leadership	Artistic involvement	Other desired attributes
Existing Board Members													
Potential Candidates to the Board													

8

The Art of Fundraising

HALSEY M. NORTH *and* ALICE H. NORTH

This chapter is written to demystify the fundraising process. It describes the key elements—from basic fundraising events through sophisticated capital campaigns. Your organization may be ready to tackle a large campaign or your first request for gifts from members. Whatever the scale of your fundraising, you should be familiar with all of the alternatives.

A small, all-volunteer arts agency will find this chapter as instructive as the largest arts organization. The same principles apply to the approach of a corner grocer for an in-kind donation of refreshments for the opening reception and to the approach of a corporate CEO for the $20,000 sponsorship of a concert. The prospect is identified, contacted, and cultivated over time, presented with a well-considered idea, asked for the contribution, and thanked, and the relationship is sustained. The larger donor takes more research and cultivation and expects the idea to be presented as a tight case statement supported by financial reports. But the same clarity of purpose and decisiveness of approach is necessary for the smallest potential donor.

Those of you who work in arts commissions as part of a local government should read this chapter with the following four ideas in mind:

1. Making a case for the community impact and worthiness of your agency's work for public support is much like making a case for private contributions. The ongoing cultivation of private donors has its parallel in the public sector with the year-round preparation for the annual municipal budgeting process.
2. Cultivation of the public and their elected officials parallels the development of supportive relations with corporations, foundations, and individual donors.
3. Public commissions usually seek funds from outside local government sources. They write grants to state, regional, and national agencies and foundations. Some have arranged to seek contributions from businesses and individuals as well as by setting up a nonprofit organization or making arrangements for a dedicated municipal fund or community foundation to receive donations.
4. Arts commissions often advise their constituent arts organizations on fundraising and sometimes regrant funds themselves and should, therefore, know the principles of effective fundraising.

An Overview of Sources and Strategies

Earned revenue from sources such as admission tickets and participation fees, sales, and advertising provides the largest proportion of most arts organizations' income. A strong foundation of unrestricted earned income should be a central part of any organization's funding mix. However, it almost always costs more to produce arts programs and sustain organizations than can be earned through tickets, sales, and other earned revenue. Effective fundraising is therefore essential.

There are essentially four sources of contributed funds for the arts:

- Individuals and small businesses
- Corporations
- Governments
- Foundations

Individuals are widely documented as the largest source of contributed revenue. Understanding how to raise funds from individuals not only yields the most contributions, but also applies directly to raising funds from other sources. Consequently, this chapter will explain how to raise funds from individuals, and then will adapt the approach for corporations, foundations, and government grants.

Fundraising Is "Relationship Building"

Think of fundraising as an opportunity to share your passion about an arts organization with others you know. Successful fundraising is built on the infectious enthusiasm of a few dedicated volunteers who can show their acquaintances that a gift to the arts organization will not only benefit the community but also the donor.

Passion bends reality! The passionate support of volunteers can make the impossible possible for an arts group. Achieving that support takes time, organizational skills, and commitment. Fundraising is a continuous process. Asking for money is just one component. Fundraising is informing and educating prospective donors, keeping them interested and involved, and showing them how they can help.

People give money to people they know and trust. At its very core, all fundraising is built on the personal relationships and links between individual people. Individuals give money—whether they are representing themselves, corporations, foundations, or governments. People give money to people they know and trust. Many people equate fundraising with grant writing. Grant writing is only a small part of what is needed to be a successful fundraiser, and successful grants are often the end product of a personal relationship which has been established between the representative of a funding organization and an arts organization.

Never ask a stranger for money! Successful fundraising results when an organization develops relationships with potential donors before asking for money. The basic principle is never to ask a stranger for money.

Fundraising is nurturing a sense of ownership and trust over time. It is "friend raising," enabling people to feel such a part of your organization that they feel a sense of ownership. With ownership comes a sense of responsibility for the organization's financial well being.

Think of the needs of the donor. You develop a relationship with a potential donor by thinking about the donor's perceptions and needs, not the needs of the organization. The basic principle is: speak to the needs of the donor.

Your organization's needs are not a motivating force for a donor. Individuals, corporations, foundations, and governments all give to support their own needs or to fulfill their own agendas.

Find out what interests the donor has and think through how the donor will benefit by giving. A corporation, for example, may want visibility and an individual newly arrived in town may want opportunities to meet people.

The key is to define your organization's dreams in such a way that potential donors can buy into them. They need to know what they can do to help and how they will benefit.

Who Will Be Interested in Giving to Your Organization?

Donors are asked to give to many different causes and organizations. Those to which they contribute are ones in which they have developed a special intellectual or emotional interest or, even more importantly, one in which they have become involved or from which they have benefited.

In general, arts organizations that had established strong relationships with individual donors before the emotional turmoil of September 11, 2001, kept those donors because their donors had a sense of "ownership" and responsibility. Many of those donors were determined that the organizations they supported would thrive in spite of September 11. One donor to an arts center said to us, "It is my patriotic duty to make certain the arts center raises the money it needs." On the other hand, arts organizations that had passive mail-based relationships discovered their donors' loyalties had shifted to disaster relief and other human service causes.

Individuals give about 83 percent of the total dollars given in the United States to nonprofit organizations.[1] For you, these individuals can be those who attend your events and enjoy the art you produce as well as the friends, neighbors, and acquaintances of your volunteers. You, your board members, and other volunteers can help to strengthen your arts organization by exciting these individuals to join you in giving and asking others to give.

> Gifts from individuals are the key to successful fundraising; 68 percent of the gifts from individuals go to organizations to which the donor belongs.

When you study fundraising, you are learning how to develop a systematic approach for developing relationships with people. It is the human element of personal relationships that makes fundraising an "art" rather than a "science."

Whether your organization is volunteer-run, has a one-person staff, or is so huge that it has lots of staff, the same principle applies—fundraising is about relationships between individual human beings.

The Five Elements of Successful Fundraising

As you focus your organization's fundraising energy on developing relationships with donors, realize that there are five elements that are crucial for successful fundraising.

1. **Case.** A clear, compelling reason why your organization is raising money, what you are going to do with it, and who will benefit. Need is not a compelling factor. Most potential donors want to understand why their gifts will make a positive difference.

2. **Confidence.** Both in the organization and its board and staff, and that their gifts will be well used.
3. **Constituency.** A sufficient number of prospective donors who are capable and willing to give major gifts to the organization at a level that meets the organization's needs. Otherwise, the organization will operate at a level that the constituency is willing to provide.
4. **Leadership.** Access to effective volunteer leaders with clout in the community who are capable, available, and willing to commit the time and energy needed to make your fundraising successful. Leadership is often the most difficult fundraising component to put into place. Leaders will often give money but not time or, more usually, leaders will give time but do not have the clout or money your organization needs. The key is to find a balance of both. If you have to choose, go for the clout or money and support the leadership effort with additional staff or volunteer efforts.
5. **Organizational fundraising capacity.** Staff with enough time, knowledge, and organizational resources dedicated to the development of donor relationships, and key volunteers with the power, influence, and financial resources needed to raise funds successfully.

Why People Give

As of 2005, the number of 501(c)(3) organizations in the United States exceeded one million.[2] Most of them do good and important work. Individuals, businesses, foundations, and governments are besieged with requests. Why should they give to your arts organization and not something else?

Fundraising for the arts is different from other forms of fundraising. Individual donors to organizations such as the United Way, hospitals, American Cancer Society, American Red Cross, and Salvation Army generally hope they won't have to "benefit" from the services such organizations offer.

Arts and cultural organizations offer donors opportunities to support things not only where they will benefit directly, but also where being involved will be fun, exciting, and personally enriching. The arts can offer joy, hope, education, and improved quality of life. The arts can help people feel good about themselves. As arts organizations, we can ask people to invest in the quality of their own lives. Even better, we can ask them to invest in the quality of life for the next generation.

You can position your organization to foster active involvement and participation in ways which simply are not available to other nonprofits in the United States. This is an advantage you will want to utilize.

People will only give to your arts organization if you are doing demonstrably good work—but they will not give because you are doing good work (so does the Red Cross). People as individuals and in businesses, foundations, and the government will give to you because they:

- know the people asking for the gift and like, trust, and respect them; and
- perceive that they and/or the community will benefit from the work of an arts organization.

The best way to develop prospective donor confidence in the organization is to involve them in some way—through governing boards, advisory boards, committees, support groups, and special events, etc. Such involvement can bring them into the "family."

The Importance of Face-to-Face Visits

Personal visits and face-to-face discussions are also good ways to cultivate people's interest. By involving a person in the development and creation of ideas and solutions, a potential donor can become emotionally involved in the success of those ideas and solutions. People give more and are more likely to give when asked in person.

Personalize your solicitation! The more people give, the more personalized the approach must be. Personal calls raise more than phone calls. Phone calls raise more than letters. And personalized letters and handwritten notes raise more than form letters.

Incorporate Long-Range Planning Into Your Fundraising Plans

Potential donors will want to know what your organization is going to do with their money. You can't be vague with donors—you need to be able to tell them clearly what you are going to be able to accomplish with their support.

Planning defines your organization's future so funders can buy into it. It shows how the donors' money will be used and how the community will benefit. Planning also gives potential donors confidence because they will realize your organization has been thoughtful in determining what it would accomplish and how much would be needed to get the job done.

New philanthropists in the United States have grown up in an entrepreneurial era. They have a hands-on approach to their work and their philanthropy. One of the most effective ways to engage them in your organization is through the long-range planning process. When potential donors are involved in helping to determine what an organization is trying to accomplish and become emotionally involved in the success of the organization, they are much more likely to give at a level to ensure success.

Start Fundraising From the Inside

Raise money from the inside out! Start your fundraising with your organization's own board of directors. Each board member should be asked for and should give a gift which is, for him or her, an important gift. This is easier said than done. Board members often say, "I give time, I give my expertise, I give up hunks of my life working for this organization, and now you want me to give money?" Yes!!! It takes cash to run a nonprofit organization. If your board members are unwilling to give cash to your organization, why should others support it? Your board members should demonstrate a strong leadership commitment to your organization which is demonstrated to the rest of the community, in part, by their personal financial commitment.

> Each board member should give, what is for him or her, an important gift.

Reasons to start your fundraising with your own board members include:

- 100 percent board giving builds community confidence;
- a board member campaign teaches your board members how to ask and how it feels to give;
- a board member campaign helps your organization test its "case" for giving, refine its fundraising materials, and train staff on how to organize a fundraising effort; and
- your board members will become much more effective fundraisers once they have given and can say, "Won't you join me in supporting…"

Boards which, when they recruit new members, instill the "expectation" that all board members will give are more likely to be able to announce 100 percent board participation in the organization's fundraising.

Raise Money from the Top Down

Larger donors will set the pace. Once you have started raising money from your own board, then you can begin to approach your largest potential donors. Focus on the BIG gifts first. The larger donors will set the pace of giving for your campaign. Not all donors are equal in importance to a fund drive. Large, early gifts to a campaign help to build volunteer and staff confidence that the campaign will succeed. Go to these large donors before you go public and announce a goal because the size of the gifts from these early donors will, to a large extent, determine how much you can raise and the goal that can be set. These early, large gifts determine your fundraising fate because:

- 75 to 95 percent of all the money you raise will come from ten to 15 percent of your donors, usually 50 to 100 prospects; and
- these 50 to 100 prospects will usually be solicited by ten to 15 individuals.

In essence, effective fundraising consists of a few of the right people (leadership) asking people they know and can influence (constituents) to give.

Fundraising, by its very nature, may seem elitist. You will target your fundraising to those who have the most capacity to give. Only individuals, foundations, corporations, and governments with accumulated assets can contribute substantial amounts of money. Focus on their gifts first, and then broaden your base of support by going after smaller gifts.

Smaller gifts do matter. You can demonstrate your broad-based community support with larger numbers of contributors, even if individual gifts are modest. Your funding agencies will value the numbers of contributors in addition to the total amount of gifts. Note too that people who admire your work may be encouraged to increase their initial contributions in subsequent years.

Position Your Organization for Successful Fundraising

There are several key elements which need to be in place to enable you to raise money successfully.

MISSION

Why do you exist? First, you need a clear, concise mission statement specifying why the organization exists. A commonly agreed upon mission helps focus the energies of the board, staff, and volunteers. It ensures that the community is receiving a clear message about the purpose of the organization. Mixed messages about mission can confuse potential givers. Make certain your mission can be stated clearly during a fundraising call so that prospective donors will know to what purpose you will be using their money.

STRATEGIC PLAN

What are you going to do? Who will get it done, when, and at what cost? If your organization has established priorities in a strategic planning process as is recommended, these should be reflected in your fundraising goals.

The plan will also help you make a convincing case to funders who will have more confidence in your organization if they know you have thought through the options, established the priorities, and determined who will do what, when, and at what cost. Funders want to know how you will be spending their money, and a multiyear plan helps give them the answers they want.

Funders will also be reassured when they can see your fundraising history, how much you need to raise, and a reasonable projection estimating the sources of those funds. The details give an organizational plan credibility. Funders can see that you have a strategy to bring your vision from a dream to a possible future reality.

FINANCIAL INFORMATION

Show donors you will spend their gifts wisely. Clear financial information, in the form of Statement of Activities (operating statement) and Statement of Position (balance sheet), demonstrates an organization's ability to manage money. See the Financial Management chapter for more information about how to prepare these financial statements. ▌Figure 1 in the Appendix is a sample summary of historical and projected cash flow. It gives two years of financial history, the current budget, and six years of projections (two years is often sufficient). This sweep of information gives donors an understanding of your organization's operations, stability, and financial needs—current and projected.

You will notice that Figure 1 places expenses first and income second, reversing the format used by profit-making corporations. We recommend this format because it differentiates your organization as a not-for-profit enterprise and focuses a reader's attention first on the cost of the art, and then on how much money it takes to support those programs and services. This format enables you to put your request of a potential donor—and the level of that request—into the context of an overall plan.

Financial information can be presented as backup for a written request or taken along on a fundraising call as evidence of thoughtful planning. In either case, it will strengthen a potential donor's confidence that a gift will be well spent.

CASE FOR GIVING

Once you have developed a succinct mission, a clear multiyear plan, and businesslike financial projections, you will have the information you need to create a document known as *the case for giving, case statement,* or simply *the case.*

The case for giving outlines how your organization will serve the community, your qualifications to do so, how the donor will benefit, how much money you need to raise, and why. The case describes the programs and services your organization will provide and the funds needed to carry them out. It does not need to convince a prospective donor of the value of supporting the arts—that can be done, if needed, as part of the in-person call. Instead, the case focuses on how your organization will strengthen the community and the quality of life for the donor and the donor's children, family, employees, etc.

The case can be summarized in a single page or it can be printed in a multipage document which can contain, as appropriate:

- the community leadership and volunteers involved with your organization as board members and working on the fund drive (this list acts as a stamp of community endorsement);
- the mission of the organization, why you are raising money, and the amount of money being raised;
- the project's budget, how the community benefits, how donors will benefit and be recognized for their gifts; and
- your organization's goals, achievements, and financial health.

Make the case larger than the organization! From a fundraising standpoint, it is important to think about your organization in a larger community context. What is your organization's contribution to your community in terms of:

- Economic impact?
- Impact on downtown revitalization?
- Impact on the quality of life?
- Impact on the schools and education?
- Impact on corporate recruitment?
- Impact on tourism?

Package your organization's needs and dreams in such a way that donors can relate to you in terms of their own needs. Make the case larger than the organization. Give people a sense of how they can help your organization make a difference that benefits them.

ANNUAL REPORT

Show the donor you know what you are doing. An annual report is useful for showing what your organization can accomplish. It can list your volunteer leadership, professional staff, what you do for the community, and what it costs. It can state your mission and include clear and succinct financial information. It can outline next year's goals, discuss future plans, and list and thank donors. Annual reports demonstrate that you know what you are doing.

ORGANIZATIONAL ATTITUDE

Give fundraising the time it deserves, and incorporate fundraising into the everyday life of your organization. Every board member must be involved with fundraising at some level at appropriate times.

The act of giving money—like the act of participating in creating the long-range plan—enables people to feel that they are a part of the family, that they are important to the success of a worthwhile organization. Fundraising involves marketing, membership, and the cultivation of resources—leadership, constituencies, and money.

Fundraising takes time.

Fundraising is not effective when it is rushed or done at the last minute because the money has run out. Such a state of panic does not build confidence in volunteers or donors.

Fundraising cannot be "tacked on" to an organization's already full work load. It has to be given staff and board time and resources as well as the money to pay for supplies, receptions, meetings, computer software, printed materials, annual reports, etc. Fundraising is an ongoing process that needs advanced planning. Successful fundraising takes time and attention on a daily basis.

VOLUNTEER LEADERSHIP

To raise funds, you need time, money, power, and passion from your board and other volunteer leadership. To survive over the long run, your organization must have political and social access to the people who control public and private giving in your community, who can give as well as ask. This does not mean that every board member should have wealth and political clout. Your mission and commitment to the community may require that you also have artists and other community members of modest means. What you need is balance and a commitment from every board member and some key volunteers to cultivate potential contributors throughout the community, including those who have wealth and power.

Everyone enjoys being an expert. If you do not have "power people" involved with your arts agency, then you need to identify specific people who could help you develop an individualized cultivation strategy for each person you want to bring into the family. You can develop a series of small lunches, receptions, or special orientation meetings to ask for specific advice or help. Or you can ask them to work on projects, ad-hoc committees, an advisory board, etc.

Make volunteers feel important, and use their time wisely. The key is to use their time wisely. Recruit them using clear expectations (verbal or written). Enable them to feel helpful and important. Make certain they have fun, learn something, and enjoy the experience. Provide follow-up information by newsletters, notes, and phone calls.

To summarize, in addition to giving what is for them an important gift, campaign leaders should have:

- understanding of the case for giving;
- commitment to the organization;
- confidence the money will be used wisely;
- an opportunity to learn how to make a fundraising call;
- appropriate fundraising materials;
- clear tasks that are organized into doable bite-sized pieces; and
- the recognition and thanks they deserve.

Treasure your volunteer leadership! Good leaders are rare. Don't take them for granted once they are involved. Thank them often and in many different ways. Make them feel special and appreciated. Remember, you can't thank volunteers enough. And saying thank you leaves the door open to ask for their help again. See the Volunteers in the Arts chapter for more information about working with volunteers.

STAFF AND OFFICE RESOURCES

Fundraising requires professional or volunteer staff to provide the information and administrative support that board members and key volunteers need to raise funds.

For a larger organization, it is best to hire a part- or full-time staff member whose sole function is fundraising. When staff functions are combined, fundraising often comes up short. Someone responsible for both marketing and fundraising, for example, will spend more time on marketing: it is more fun to write a press release than a gift request which might be declined.

Many smaller arts organizations find that they can hire excellent part-time help from the pool of parents who want to work from 10 a.m. to 3 p.m. so they can be home with their school-age children. When hiring or recruiting volunteer fundraising staff, look for:

- fundraising experience;
- organizational ability and attention to detail;
- writing skills; and
- ability to work with and motivate volunteers.

Also make certain that you have the computer support you need, including software for record-keeping and word processing. There are a number of fundraising-specific software packages on the market, some of which, if you need, can interrelate to ticketing, accounting, and scheduling software. Even the smallest arts organization can find a board member or key volunteer with an adequate computer system to support fundraising.

CONSTITUENCY OF DONORS

Developing an ongoing process of cultivation to involve as many potential donors as possible is essential to effective fundraising. People usually do not give to strangers or causes with which they have no relationship. Your job is to bring potential donors into the family, develop their interest, and get them involved. Develop monthly newsletters, reminder postcards, annual reports, special receptions, preview parties, or post-performance gatherings. Develop guilds, friends groups, advisory boards, or volunteer committees. Try to involve as many community members as possible in your organization. If your arts organization is run with the input and involvement of only a few individuals, then those few people will be your only significant source of contributed income.

> People do not give to causes or good work.
> They give to people they know, trust, and respect.

The section, Raising Money from Individuals, discusses how you can identify, cultivate, and focus your search for specific prospects. Keep in mind that the best prospective donor is someone who already feels like they are part of the family. The next best prospect is someone who is beginning to feel part of the family. This is because fundraising is, in part, the process of giving people a sense of ownership in your organization.

LEGAL READINESS

Donors are not able to deduct their gifts to you unless you are designated as a 501(c)(3) tax-exempt organization by the IRS. To receive this status, you need to be incorporated as a not-for-profit tax-exempt organization by your state government. Corporations, foundations, the National Endowment for the Arts (NEA), and state arts agencies can, generally, only give to 501(c)(3) tax-exempt organizations. If you do not yet have your tax-exempt status from the IRS, it may be possible to find a 501(c)(3) organization willing to accept gifts and grants on your behalf as a fiscal agent.

Determine Your Fundraising Capability

Before you can establish how much you are going to raise, you have to determine not only how much you need but also how much your arts organization is capable of raising. As you evaluate your fundraising capacity, remember that fundraising is built on the relationships between individual human beings. So, in a real sense, what you are evaluating is your organization's capacity to initiate, strengthen, and maintain relationships with people who can give money.

> Is our board committed to fundraising? Do we have the key volunteer and staff support we need to make our efforts successful?

To determine your fundraising capability, begin by evaluating your organization's internal resources and its access to outside funding sources.

Does the organization have...
- board members/volunteers who have fundraising experience?
- board members/volunteers who have access to funding sources?
- board members/volunteers who are capable of providing leadership?
- advisors who can help provide information and assist with donor cultivation and solicitation?
- staff or dedicated volunteers who have the time and expertise to do the homework?
- computer capabilities or access to computers to do the record-keeping and reports?
- existing and prospective members/friends and donors who will give?
- the support of local businesses (including restaurants, stores, law firms, doctors' offices, real estate agencies, motels and hotels, grocery stores, etc.) in the area which know your work?
- the support of decision-makers in local and state governments whom you know and who will help you get funding?
- strong peer relationships with colleagues who will make grant decisions on local, state, and NEA panels?

THE SIX SOURCES FOR RAISING MONEY

There are six primary sources for raising money. Determine which should be your organization's focus in order to maximize the amount of money you can raise given the time and energy you can put into it. Remember that gifts from individuals are how most nonprofits get the most money. Public grants and national foundation contributions may be a part of your fundraising mix, but there is no substitute for cultivating local individual donors. The six sources, in priority order, are:

1. contributions from board members, former board members, and other key volunteers;
2. contributions from other individuals;
3. net contributed income from benefits and special events;
4. contributions from local businesses and foundations;
5. grants from local, state, and federal governments; and
6. contributions from national corporations and foundations.

Individuals

For most arts and cultural organizations, the best results are achieved when funds are first raised from board members who are then enlisted to solicit, face-to-face, other key, potentially significant donors. For those organizations limited by the number of individuals they can send out to ask for money, solicit other individuals by personalized letters followed up by personal phone calls. Why emphasize the "personal?" Because the basic component of successful fundraising is building and maintaining relationships.

Benefits

Fundraisers and special events are another source of funds for arts and cultural organizations. They can devour staff and volunteer time and take a lot of work. They require long-term planning to secure sponsorships, in-kind donations, and attendance that will generate maximum revenues and minimum expenses. They are most effective when they are run, from beginning to end, by a group of committed volunteers. The best benefits and special events can be a lot of fun and can help with donor cultivation and involvement.

Local Businesses and Foundations

Personally soliciting local businesses and foundations is very similar to asking local individuals for money. Success is based on cultivating a relationship with them. So, the key question to ask is: Do you have the manpower to develop and maintain good relationships with these folks? If you have been working with the chamber of commerce and its arts committee is willing to help you launch your first local business fund drive, one option is to develop a cultivation and solicitation strategy for the 50 to 75 most likely business prospects.

Governments

Many nonprofit cultural organizations receive grant support from their local and state governments, and this area is worth exploring. Contact your state arts agency and get to know the staff. Ask them to help you understand what grant programs they offer that might help your organization. Once you have established a relationship with your state arts agency, then you may want to ask them if there are any grant programs at the NEA to which your organization should apply.

Another strategy that is often overlooked is to enlist the assistance of state and local legislators in your fundraising efforts. Does your organization's staff or volunteers know any local or state politicians who can help you organize a lobbying effort for a major grant from your city, county, or state government? If no one knows any local or state politicians but there is strong feeling that the city, county, or state government should support the organization, then the strategy may be to develop a cultivation plan. Decision makers will then get to know and become involved in the organization so you can ask them for money in the coming year. See the Cultural Advocacy chapter for more detailed information about relationship building with your legislators as well as advocacy campaign strategies.

National Corporations and Foundations

Proposal writing to national corporations and foundations is generally the least effective form of fundraising for nonprofit arts and cultural organizations. Exxon, for example, won't give to you because there is a gas station on the corner. National corporations generally give only when they have a factory in your community and its officers have a relationship with your organization. National foundations generally give when an organization is doing something unique which can have national impact or which can become a model for other organizations.

CREATE A FUNDRAISING WORK PLAN

> Aim for success. Don't overreach. Fundraising success builds community, donor, and volunteer confidence so you can ask again.

Figure 2 in the Appendix is a chart you can use to get an overview of your organization's fundraising options and capabilities. The left-hand column lists fundraising options the organization might want to consider; the other axis evaluates internal and external resources. You do not have to, nor should you, attempt all options. Decide what strategies are best for your organization.

Once you have evaluated your organization's internal capacity to fundraise, you will need to make some choices. What fundraising options will realistically produce the most money from donors for the time, energy, and resources your organization invests? You do not have to attempt all options. Decide what options your organization can undertake effectively. If you have a board of directors, it is recommended that your board undertake the option of a personalized campaign to raise money from board members and other key volunteers. Then, option by option, develop a work plan to implement each fundraising option, as follows:

1. Select the fundraising options your organization will undertake.
2. For each option:
    - list the tasks that need to be done to raise the money;
    - negotiate with the staff, board, and other volunteers who will do what tasks;
    - establish a timetable (who is going to do what, when);
    - determine the costs (the direct costs in dollars) plus the staff/board/volunteer time needed (who, number of hours, tasks), and consultants, if any (who, number of hours, tasks, cost); and
    - determine the funds expected to be raised from each option.
3. Set the total dollar fundraising goal for your organization.
4. Step back, review the plan, and ask whether it is realistic and feasible. Can your organization—staff, board, and other volunteers—actually do the work you have outlined?
5. Revise the work plan as needed.

6. Distribute the work plan to those who will do the tasks and ensure buy-in from all involved. Revise the plan as needed.
7. Regularly update everyone on tasks accomplished and costs/funds raised compared to the work plan.

Figure 3 in the Appendix offers a sample fundraising work plan. Included are examples of a board giving campaign, a membership campaign, and a special event.

SET THE GOAL

Now you can compare the dollar goal established in the fundraising work plan (how much you think the organization can raise) with the numbers in the financial projections (how much it needs to raise). The two numbers usually differ. Arts organizations often find that their needs outstrip their fundraising capabilities. Groups get into trouble by increasing their estimates of how much they can raise to equal the amount needed. A goal set too high can demoralize volunteers and put the organization at financial risk because it arouses unrealistic expectations that cannot be met.

On the other hand, an organization which always reduces its staff or operations to reduce the demands on the organization's fundraising efforts will limit the organization's growth and ability to serve.

The goal should be a realistic stretch. The overall fundraising goal should be established by the board and staff as a compromise between the need and the fundraising capacity. The need should be lessened and the goal should be increased to slightly more than what the fundraising team feels is comfortable. The overall fundraising goal should at least balance the budget and be a realistic "stretch" for the fundraising team.

> The goal is a compromise between how much you need and how much your volunteers feel comfortable raising.

The Role of the Board and Staff in Fundraising

Simply stated, the primary role of the staff in fundraising is to do the homework, while the role of the board is to do the solicitation.

ROLE OF THE BOARD

The board of your arts organization has the legal and moral responsibility to make certain the organization has the financial resources it needs to operate. When the board approves the budget, they need to realize that they are setting their own fundraising goal. If they do not feel they can make the goal, they should adjust the budget.

Have the board help develop a fundraising work plan. To build confidence and a sense of ownership, have board members help to develop the fundraising work plan and present it to the rest of the board for approval. By participating in the development and approval process, board members are more likely to ensure that the fundraising work plan is implemented successfully.

Board members should ask each other. Board giving is essential. Many government, corporate, and foundation funders require 100 percent board giving before considering making a contribution to a nonprofit organization.

The amount a board member gives is also important. Board members should be recruited with the expectation that they will give, what is for them, an important gift. Set the expectation that board members give the organization an amount comparable to what they donate to the United Way, their place of worship, their college, or other nonprofits in which they are interested and involved. The actual dollar amount they give is not as important for setting the pace for giving as the perception that each and every board member is stretching to be as generous as possible. We are not suggesting that board members be required to give a specific minimum amount as a gift, but, rather, that each board member be challenged to maximize their personal giving commitment. So, the first step that board members take in fundraising is to give what is for them an important gift.

Personally, board members are more comfortable and effective as fundraisers when they have already given themselves and can say, "Join me!" Giving a cash donation strengthens board commitment to the organization and the fundraising process. Moreover, the giving enthusiasm of board members sets the pace of support for the organization.

Spend money to raise money.

In addition to setting the pace by giving, the board needs to accomplish these tasks:

- **Ensure fundraising staff and systems are in place.** It is a board's responsibility to make certain the organization is investing enough of its resources in fundraising. Staff time and fundraising information-gathering and record-keeping systems must be in place to help ensure success.
- **Identify and cultivate prospects.** Board members introduce their friends, business acquaintances, and associates to the organization and excite them about the organization's work. The board needs to make certain there is an ongoing, systematic approach to gathering and updating information about prospective donors from board members, and utilizing board members to cultivate prospects.
- **Advocate with local governments and businesses.** The board is the "good housekeeping seal of approval" for your organization. Board members' ability to talk about the organization knowledgeably and with enthusiasm will go a long way in convincing others to give. Board members are your best advocates to work with local government officials and businesses for support.
- **Be passionate.** How a community thinks about an organization is often determined by the hundreds of brief remarks and discussions people hear at meetings, social gatherings, and events. This gossip can set the tone for what community members think about your organization when they are approached for money. The board of an organization in small- and medium-sized communities can, to a very real extent, influence the tone of the community's perception by talking about the organization with enthusiasm and passion.

Board members should be passionate advocates.

- **Solicit gifts in a thoughtful manner.** Board members often want to ask others for gifts by phone or letter. It is easier and, on the surface, more efficient and less time-consuming. If board members want significant gifts from individuals, businesses, or foundations, however, they need to make the request in a considered and thoughtful manner. Taking the time to do it right will pay off in the long run. Expedient fundraising may create frustration, failing to produce the kinds of gifts the board needs to succeed.
- **Say thank you.** Board members can help keep donors interested by thanking them when they see them as part of their everyday work life. You can't thank a donor too often, and a thank you from a board member is much more powerful than a staff thank you. Board members can also help by writing personal notes or making phone calls to donors to thank them.

> Take the time to show prospects you care about them before you ask them to give.

ROLE OF THE STAFF

You need to cherish your volunteers and make certain you maximize their effectiveness and personal satisfaction by giving them the staff support they need. Good staff back-up is the key to good volunteer involvement. If you do not have adequate staff time dedicated to fundraising, then you need a few dedicated volunteers to fulfill the support role that staff would normally provide. Volunteers can help advocate for the organization, identify and cultivate prospective donors, and ask for money. Staff can support fundraising volunteers in these efforts with:

- background materials;
- data on potential donors;
- training materials;
- individualized solicitation letters;
- examples of thank-you letters;
- their presence on calls;
- confirmation calls for appointments;
- information on developments and funds raised to date;
- the calendar of meetings, appointments, and follow up;
- agendas for meetings; and
- meeting spaces, names tags, refreshments, and clean up.

Trust is an important part of fundraising. Volunteers need to know that they can rely on the fundraising staff. Donors need to trust in the people to whom they are giving. As a result, consistency in the fundraising staff is another element to consider when your organization is working to strengthen its fundraising efforts. The trust needed for successful fundraising is built upon hours and hours of staff time and dedication to building the relationships needed over time—with volunteers and donors.

Because relationship building takes so much time—as do day-to-day homework, information-gathering, and record-keeping—fundraising is not a project that can be dumped on top of everything else the staff is doing. To be successful, arts organizations must invest more and more money to hire and train fundraising staff. Each organization needs to make certain it has adequate staff or dedicated volunteer fundraising leaders in place to develop ongoing relationships with volunteers and donors; support volunteer fundraising efforts; organize the homework, making certain the record-keeping and accounting systems are up-to-date and accurate; and write grants and proposals.

If your organization is staffed by a single individual or if your organization has no staff, you must still find ways to provide the same fundraising support as is provided by a development director in a larger organization. Consider these alternatives.

- Recruit an exceptional volunteer to lead a time-limited fundraising campaign.
- Seek the loan of secretarial help from a local corporation or public agency.
- Seek the loan of database-design or data-entry personnel.
- Contract with an independent fundraiser to help staff your fundraising campaign.
- Seek the help of a fundraising consultant to advise how to manage your fundraising. Note: Be clear about whether you are seeking advice or supplemental staffing. Most fundraising consultants are in the advising business.
- Seek a donor to invest in fundraising staff.

Fundraising is 90 percent homework and ten percent solicitation. It is the staff's responsibility to give the board/key volunteers the support and information they need to do their jobs successfully. The staff collects, organizes, and produces information (the homework) and then develops the letters and materials needed for the board to implement the cultivation and solicitation process (the solicitation).

The reality is that the staff cajoles, prods, educates, and pushes board members and other volunteers to complete their fundraising tasks. The staff should do the following:

- Make certain that board members learn how to ask for money.
- Organize the fundraising tasks into doable, bite-sized pieces. When we ask board members to "fundraise," they often don't. The task is too open-ended. When we encourage them to "cultivate and solicit five people they know for gifts similar to their own," they usually respond positively.
- Organize the homework. Make certain a board member has all the information needed to make a successful call—that the right solicitor is asking the right prospect for the right amount for the right reason at the right time.
- Organize and develop the fundraising materials—solicitation letters, case statement, prospect information, pledge cards, receipts, brochures, newsletters, and calendars.
- Create giving opportunities with benefits. It is easier for board members to ask prospects to join them as a patron member or a sponsor of a special event.

Six "Rights" of Fundraising
- the right person asking
- the right prospect
- the right amount
- the right reason
- the right time
- the right way

- Say thank you for fundraising as well as for giving.

In summary, the staff is the glue that holds the fundraising effort together—setting up the meetings, gathering the information, educating the volunteers, and saying thank you. The board members and key volunteers are the community liaisons who say; "The work of this arts organization is important. Please join me in supporting it to enrich the lives of our children and the quality of life in our community!"

Raising Money from Individuals

As noted earlier, gifts from individuals account for more than 83 percent of U.S. philanthropic dollars.[3] Your organization's ability to keep potential individual donors happy and satisfied is fundamental to its future fundraising success. An organization has cultivated and involved a donor well when that donor believes the organization is an important part of his or her life.

Basically, what most donors want from a relationship with a nonprofit arts organization is to:

- be thanked in an appropriate and thoughtful manner;
- feel good about themselves and what they have done;
- be confident that their money will make a difference;
- feel special with access to select privileges, people, savings, or experiences not generally available to others; and
- have a sense of satisfaction, recognition, importance, appreciation, belonging, and being part of the family.

In general, individuals give money to people they know and trust for organizations in which they have a personal interest. The size of the gift will be influenced by:

- their capacity to give;
- their level of interest in the organization;
- who asks them for the gift; and
- the manner in which they are asked.

Your organization cannot influence an individual's capacity to give, but it can influence their level of interest, who asks, and the thoughtfulness of the ask. To develop an effective individual gifts campaign, you need a two-phased process.

- **Phase 1: Research, Planning, and Cultivation.** Identify the highest potential individual donors and find out their needs and interests. Determine the best way to position your organization potential donor by potential donor, develop a connection, and get them interested.
- **Phase 2: Solicitation.** Have people whom potential donors respect and trust ask them for a gift face-to-face in a thoughtful manner.

PHASE 1: RESEARCH, PLANNING, AND CULTIVATION

Step 1: Work Plan

Develop a work plan for the individual gifts campaign. Determine how much you need to raise, how many volunteers you need to recruit, how many prospects you need to identify, how you will cultivate the prospects, and the approaches you will use to ask them for money.

Step 2: Staff Support

Determine the staff support you need and have for the fundraising effort. Limited staff support will limit your fund drive efforts. Is your organization expecting too much from its current staff or do you need to commit additional staff time? Do you need to hire fundraising staff or do you need to free up more of the chief executive's time to devote to fundraising? Often, hiring fundraising staff (or staff to free up the chief executive's time) is a cash-flow issue rather than an expense issue. You should be able to expect competent fundraising personnel to more than pay for their salary and expenses after the first year because they should increase the organization's capacity to raise money.

Step 3: Job Descriptions

Develop job descriptions for staff, board, and volunteers so each person in the individual gifts campaign knows what their role will be and the timetable for getting work done. Deadlines are important in fundraising because they help give a sense of urgency so the work gets done in a timely manner.

Step 4: Prospect Lists

Begin to develop prospect lists for different elements of the campaign. Who are the prospects with the highest potential that require special personal attention? Who are the intermediate givers who will respond to some personal cultivation? Who are the others you should solicit by mail?

You have limited staff and volunteer time available to solicit gifts from individuals, so you want to develop a fundraising work plan to give you the greatest dollar return for the time invested. Prospects who have the capacity to give substantial gifts need a personalized, face-to-face approach which can be quite time-intensive.

The two primary sources of individuals whom you can solicit for your arts organization are:

- those who are involved or benefit from your services, such as audience members, constituents, board members, guild members, committee members, other volunteers, artists, students, alumni, parents of students, friends, group members, organizational members, etc.; and
- people known personally by your board members, other key volunteers, and staff.

To find those potential donors who can and are most likely to give, you first have to do some donor research and organize the information you have.

Step 5: Prospect Research

Do prospect research to gather as much information as possible about the prospective donors you have identified. Take all the lists of the names of people you serve—those who support you, encourage you, volunteer for you, get your newsletter, attend events, etc.—and gather them together with an annotation of where the name came from and their relationship to your arts organization. Then, using staff and key volunteers who know your community well, divide these lists into three categories:

- **high potential**—worth the time for personal cultivation and solicitation;
- **medium potential**—worth a personalized letter and telephone follow-up; and
- **little potential and don't know**—solicit by mass mail and telephone campaigns.

Once you have completed this broad-brush-stroke sort, you can begin to refine your placement of donors into appropriate solicitation categories.

> The more potential a donor has, the more time you want to spend getting to know and cultivating them.

First, review your high-potential list and make certain it is less than 200 names. Enter these names on a form similar to Figure 4 in the Appendix. (It takes about two hours for two to three volunteers to review 100 names on such a set of worksheets. If you have more names than that, you may want to have two sets of worksheets.)

Then ask a number of your staff members and key volunteers to review these worksheets and tell you (or your development staff or designated volunteer) as much as possible about the prospective donors. Do they actively participate in the arts? What is their occupation, interests, perceived worth, community involvement, and history of giving to other organizations? Is there anything else it would be helpful to know?

> Ask board members, other key volunteers, and staff who they know and can involve in your organization.

Another approach to developing a list of high-potential donors is to ask your board members and key volunteers who they know who has the capacity to give generously and who might be interested in your organization. Sit down with each board member and key volunteer and go through their contact list with them, noting names, addresses, and phone numbers on a worksheet such as is given in Figure 4. Ask them to tell you anything helpful to know about the donors. Also discuss lists of potential prospective donors that you have drawn up. Does the board member know any of the names on the lists? Then, using the upcoming year as a time frame, ask them to divide the resulting names into the three prospect categories.

Determine who is best to cultivate their interest in the organization, who is best to ask them for a gift, and what is the best strategy for cultivating and asking for the gift.

Step 6: Recruit Volunteers

Once you have done enough research to know the potential donors you want to cultivate and solicit face-to-face (and the best people to solicit them), you are ready to recruit the volunteers. The average fund drive volunteer can solicit between five and seven prospective donors. So, if you have 100 prospects that you want to cultivate and solicit face-to-face, you will need 15 to 18 dedicated volunteers.

Actually, you may need to recruit more volunteers: experience shows that volunteers are more effective, especially for major gifts prospects, when they work in teams of two people. These teams can consist of a volunteer and a staff person or any effective combination of board members, key volunteers, previous donors, and/or staff members.

> The average volunteer can solicit five to seven people face to face.

In a typical campaign, some wonderful volunteers may solicit 15 to 20 prospects and others may have to be hounded to follow through on only one or two prospect solicitations. So, determine how many volunteers you will need, recruit a chairperson or co-chairs, and work with the chairperson or co-chairs to identify and recruit the volunteers they believe will be effective and who they can motivate to do a good job. The volunteers can then review the list of prospective donors, tell you who they can help call upon, and give you additional information on the prospects.

Step 7: Case for Giving

Based on how much your organization needs to raise, and your capacity to raise these funds from your community, develop a compelling written case for giving—what will be accomplished with that money. If you need unrestricted annual operating support, look at your programs and services and package your need in a way that captures people's attention and calls out things in which prospective donors might be interested—such as subsidizing tickets for school children; enhancing the quality of productions; providing scholarship support; or strengthening the staff so you can take more artists into the schools.

As you write the case, include how your organization will benefit. For example, discuss the quality of education in the schools, the community's quality of life, economic development, downtown revitalization, corporate recruitment, and providing people with educational, enriching, and entertaining opportunities.

Step 8: Fund Drive Materials

Create the printed fund drive materials in such a way that they serve a two-fold purpose: (1) they inform potential contributors about the organization and help build confidence that contributions will be well utilized; and (2) they are tools designed to help the volunteers go on calls with confidence that they have in hand all the key information they need to complete a successful call. Fund drive materials can include:

- case statement;
- personalized letter requesting the gift;
- pledge form;
- volunteer information sheets;
- answers to most frequently asked questions;
- thank you letters;
- contribution acknowledgment and tax receipt forms;
- annual report; and
- record-keeping sheets for calls, gifts, and acknowledgments.

> Create fundraising tools to make the volunteer's job easier.

Step 9: Establish Information System

The person responsible for fundraising should oversee the creation and maintenance of a file—both electronic and hard copy/desk files—on each prospective high-potential donor. Establish a system to collect and enter information continuously into these files. Everyone having contact with these people on behalf of the organization needs to know how to feed information into the system so that the files are always up-to-date.

PHASE 2: SOLICITATION

Step 10: Solicit the Board First

Start the fund drive with a board campaign, that is, board members asking other board members (and former board members asking other former board members) for gifts.

> Board members can set the pace of giving.

Step 11: Solicit Fund Drive Volunteers

Concurrently with the board campaign, solicit the other volunteers who have agreed to work on the campaign. Arrange this effort so everyone has a chance to go on a call and experience being called upon before they start solicitations in the broader community. If your volunteers, and board members, have successful fundraising experiences with each other first, then they will have more confidence as they begin to approach prospects who are not as close to the organization.

Step 12: Solicit Major Gifts

Once the board and fund drive volunteers have been solicited, you can then move on to the select group of prospects who are capable of giving your organization larger gifts. The major gift prospects should be cultivated before they are asked for money. They should be personally invited to special events, receptions, private dinners, etc., where they can learn more about your organization before they are solicited. Remember the basic fundraising principal: never ask a stranger for money. Make certain the prospective donors know about your organization and how they personally and/or the community will benefit from your work.

Figure 5 in the Appendix lists steps and offers pointers for making a fundraising call to an individual. We recommend you use it, or something similar, as a basis for training board members and other volunteers.

Step 13: Announce the Campaign Goal

Once your organization has an understanding of how generous these advance donors will be, then you can project forward how much you will raise from a broader, public campaign. At this point, publicly announce a campaign goal that you have confidence in achieving. Remember that 75 to 95 percent of all the money raised will come from ten to 15 percent of your donors. The publicly-announced goal may be more or less than the actual need. It is often less than the organization had hoped to raise, but it is better to make a goal and even exceed a goal than to fail trying to raise too much.

Step 14: Launch the Broader Campaign

Once you have publicly-announced a goal and launched the campaign, then you can go after a broader range of gifts using personalized letters, telephone calls, mass mail, special events, and grant writing, etc.

Step 15: Acknowledge Donors

It is crucial that each donor be thanked properly, with major donors being acknowledged on multiple occasions. Proper thank-yous are personalized thank-yous. All donors should be thanked by the appropriate staff person who sends the formal acknowledgment for tax purposes. Major donors should also hear from the solicitor and the president. Hand-written notes—even if at the bottom of a personalized, computer-generated letter—are effective ways of making the donor feel special. At the beginning of the campaign, thank volunteers in advance for their hard work and, at the end of the campaign, thank them in writing and with some kind of celebratory event.

Develop a "Friends Of…" Program

People like to join or belong to groups. We are members of clubs and places of worship, and we live in neighborhoods. We belong to chambers of commerce, Rotary, and League of Women Voters. We are Republicans and Democrats. How do you position your arts organization so people will want to join and be identified as being a member?

By developing a "Friends of…" or membership program, you are giving people an opportunity to "join." You are also creating a structure of benefits which make people feel special and involved. It is important to build a structure where people receive more benefits the more they give—thus encouraging them to give generously. The package of benefits will be different for every organization.

> Focus on giving donors access, ease, fun, information, recognition, education, and special experiences.

Example Benefit Structure		
GIFT	CATEGORY	BENEFITS
$50	Donor	Member card + monthly newsletter + advance notice of events + volunteer opportunities
$100	Patron	All the above + recognition in the annual report + quarterly preview seminars and receptions
$250	Sponsor	All the above + advance ticket purchase capability + priority access to special trips + private receptions with artists
$500	Sustainer	All the above + access to house seats + private tours of exhibits with curators + recognition in monthly newsletters
$1000	Producer	All the above + special reserved parking privileges + annual dinner with the board
$1000+	Benefactor	All the above + use of the Green Room for a private party + curbside parking at all events

This kind of friends/membership structure helps formalize your organization's cultivation of donors. The newsletter, benefits, and special events will keep donors informed and make them feel special. The benefits can be important, too. You will attract some people you did not know to the higher levels of giving. For current friends/members, you will have mechanisms for involving them and encouraging them to give at higher levels. For potential donors, volunteer fundraisers will be able to say, "Join me as a sponsor. It will give us a good opportunity to see more of each other!", which is even easier to say than "Join me in giving $250 to a wonderful arts organization."

This kind of program is usually promoted through a mass-mail effort, but it can implemented more effectively through personalized letters, phone calls, and, at the higher levels, personal visits from volunteers.

> It is easier for a volunteer to offer benefits and to say "join me" than to ask for a specific amount of money.

Friends/membership programs take a lot of work. You have to write and send the newsletters, host the receptions, and provide the special tickets, dinners, and parking if you offer them. Start them out as volunteer-run programs. As they grow, hire staff, at least on a part-time basis, to provide the services you offer. The prompt, complete provision of these services and making people feel special is the best cultivation (fundraising) you can do.

> Make the benefits meaningful to the donor and of minimal cost to the organization.

Tax-Deductibility of Contributions

The IRS requires not-for-profit organizations to make clear, at the time contributions are solicited, exactly how much the donor can take as a tax deduction. The federal law is summarized in *IRS Publication 1771, Charitable Contributions—Substantiation and Disclosure Requirements*, which is available online at www.irs.gov. The law requires organizations that receive tax-deductible charitable contributions to:

- **Provide written acknowledgment to donors for any single contribution of $250 or more so the donor can claim a tax deduction.** Cancelled checks are no longer acceptable. Such acknowledgements must express the amount of a cash contribution and a description (but not the value) of a noncash contribution. The valuation of such donated noncash property is still the responsibility of the donor. Note: Even though the law only requires a written acknowledgement if a gift is $250 or more, consider doing it for all gifts. Donors will appreciate having the receipt, and you can take advantage of the opportunity to communicate, say thank you, and let donors know how much you value their support!

- **Provide written disclosure to donors with a description and good faith estimate of the value of goods or services received in exchange for a single contribution in excess of $75.** Written acknowledgments would state: "In exchange for your contribution, we gave you [description] with an estimated fair market value of [$__]" or "No goods or services were provided in exchange for your contribution."

The IRS allows full deductibility of a contribution and no written disclosure when:
- the goods or services given to a donor are considered insubstantial and meet either the "token exception" or "membership benefits exception" (see *IRS Publication 1771* for the current dollar amounts considered to be insubstantial); or
- there is no donative element involved in a particular transaction, such as a typical museum gift shop sale.

The benefits described on the previous page would be considered insubstantial. The written acknowledgement would state: "No goods or services were provided in exchange for your contribution."

If you have questions after reading *IRS Publication 1771*, seek advice from your organization's accountant or lawyer.

Methods of Individual Giving

Individuals may choose from a number of methods for making contributions. Larger gifts may require longer payment periods or more sophisticated methods of payment.

GIFTS THAT WOULD BENEFIT THE ORGANIZATION NOW

Cash gifts. These can be in the form of checks made payable to your organization or pledges paid over a period of time. The pledge form should state who the donor is, how much they are giving, and the date(s) when they will make the gift.

Matching gifts. Your donors or their spouses may work for or serve on the board of a company which will match their gift. Have your donor contact their company's matching gifts officer, if appropriate.

Gifts of appreciated securities. Larger gifts are frequently paid with long-term capital gains securities, which can provide donors with a more attractive income tax benefit. If your organization has the potential to attract gifts of securities, develop a relationship with a stock broker who will offer free or reduced-price services in facilitating the transfer and sale of the securities.

Gifts of tangible personal property. Gifts that are useful to your organization, including real estate, can provide donors with an immediate tax deduction and, if qualified as a long-term capital assets (held for a year and a day), offer avoidance of capital gains tax, removal of the assets from the donor's estate, and, if appropriate, elimination of maintenance costs of the property. Valuation for income tax purposes can require an independent appraisal. The deduction is limited to 30 percent of adjusted gross income. Excess beyond 30 percent can be carried forward for five additional years.

Charitable lead trusts. This planned giving method can enable a donor to reduce gift and estate taxes, leave property to heirs, and make a contribution to your organization. The donor contributes assets to a trust and sets an amount or fixed percentage that is paid to your organization for a specific period of time. At the end of the time period, the trust is dissolved and the property returned to the donor or the donor's designated beneficiaries, thereby removing the assets from the donor's estate. This and other planned giving transactions can be complex and offer the opportunity to involve professional advisors as volunteers with your organization.

Gifts of life insurance proceeds. A donor might decide to liquidate a life insurance policy no longer needed for family protection and give the proceeds to your organization. This would give the donor an immediate tax deduction (for the value of the gift) and would reduce the donor's estate and inheritance taxes by removing the asset from the donor's net worth.

GIFTS THAT WOULD BENEFIT THE ORGANIZATION IN THE FUTURE

Bequests/giving through a donor's will. A donor may make a bequest to your organization by preparing a new will or adding a codicil amending an existing one. A bequest is not subject to federal or state estate or inheritance taxes and is, in fact, deductible in calculating the taxable estate. There is no limit to the amount of that deduction. The following language is appropriate for making an unrestricted bequest: "I give ["the sum of _____ dollars" or "all or _____ percent of the residuary of my estate"], to [organization], for its general corporate purposes."

Charitable remainder trusts. These enable a donor to contribute to the future of your organization, retain lifetime annual payments, and generate significant tax benefits. The donor makes an irrevocable gift of cash or marketable securities and sets an amount or fixed percentage that is then paid to him or her, providing life income for the donor (and a survivor). For an annuity trust, the amount is set when the trust is created, either as a fixed percentage or a set dollar amount of the then fair market value of the trust assets. For a unitrust, the amount is a fixed percentage of the fair market value of the trust assets as determined annually.

Charitable gift annuity. A donor can make an irrevocable gift of cash or marketable securities for which your organization contractually guarantees to pay a specified annuity to the donor and/or another beneficiary for life. The donor receives a charitable deduction and other tax benefits (which depend on the type of gift) and, in return, secures a stream of income for life, often at the rate of return recommended by the American Council on Gift Annuities when the charitable gift annuity is set up. If the donor didn't need income now but wanted to secure income sources for retirement, a deferred gift annuity would allow for a gift and charitable deduction now with higher income payouts due to deferring the payments for a period of years.

Gifts of life insurance. A donor can name your organization as a beneficiary of all or part of the proceeds from a life insurance policy. Or the donor can give a paid-up policy, a new policy, or a policy on which you are still paying—naming the organization as sole owner and beneficiary—and take a deduction for the "present value" of the policy (approximately the cash surrender value or the cost basis, whichever is less). In these instances, the donor diminishes his or her estate and inheritance taxes by distributing part of his or her net worth during his or her lifetime. If the donor continues to pay the premiums to maintain the life insurance policy, he or she will also be able to deduct the premium payments as charitable contributions. A donor can also use life insurance as a replacement asset.

Gifts of real estate, reserving the right of occupancy as long as donor and spouse live. A gift of a remainder interest in a personal residence can entitle a donor to an income tax deduction of the asset's fair market value, an avoidance of capital gains tax, and the removal of the asset from his or her estate. To qualify, a donor must make the gift now rather than in a will. Through a "reserved life estate contract," a donor can reserve the right to occupy the property during his or her (and a survivor's) lifetime, while making an immediate and irrevocable transfer of title to the organization. Any real estate transaction is complex and should be reviewed with both the organization and a donor's financial advisors.

This outline is prepared as a guide to planning. Donors should be encouraged to consult their own legal, accounting, and other professional advisors as they consider the best possible ways to benefit their individual tax situation.

Special Event Fundraising

Special events can help your organization raise money creatively while attracting new members, developing new leadership, and providing opportunities for publicity. Special event fundraising can also be the fastest way to bankrupt your organization. Numerous arts organizations boldly decide to host a special event, spend lots of money on it, and then wake up to realize they did not focus enough energy on developing strategies for selling tickets.

Below are key points to consider with special events.

- Plan ahead. (Select your chairperson up to 14 months in advance, enabling him or her to help on the preceding year's event and to start planning early for a successful event.)
- Start small.
- Set the fundraising goal early and stick to it. Do not compromise later on.
- Evaluate the risk (expenses, break-even point, number of sales needed at what ticket price to reach your financial goal, potential for loss or net profit).
- Seek as many donations as possible of space, labor, food, beverages, entertainment, auctioned items, favors/gifts, and printing.

Pros and Cons to Special Event Fundraising

PROS	CONS
• They are fun.	• They are hard work.
• They cultivate prospects.	• They take staff time.
• They attract new friends.	• They take volunteer time.
• They get volunteers involved.	• They cost money.
• They raise money.	• They can lose money.

- Maximize volunteer involvement.
- Recognize and thank everyone involved.
- Keep the mailing list updated.

Special events have a life cycle of about seven years. Do not try to do something new every year. Build on the experience of past years until the event starts losing energy or no longer attracts the volunteer support it needs to succeed.

Always remember that the purpose of a fundraising special event is to raise money. Set the fundraising goal and do not compromise. If the volunteers want to fancy things up a bit, let them pay for it or seek donations. Do not spend any money you do not have to. Some examples of special events are silent auctions, dinner and dance events, walk-a-thons, private film screenings, and meet-the-artist receptions. Be creative and try to link the event to your organization's mission (i.e., if you are a music organization, build your event around music). Give yourselves plenty of advance time.

Raising Money from Local and National Corporations

Cultivation and solicitation of locally-owned businesses is similar in approach to raising money from individuals. You focus on the owners/decision-makers and do the same kind of homework, cultivation, record keeping, planning, and follow-through. Help them feel more like family and less like strangers.

The approach for national corporations with manufacturing plants or branches in your area will be different because the motivations for giving will be different. Often, plant/branch managers are from out-of-town and are emotionally uninvolved with the local community. They may look at your request and ask themselves, Does this make me look good in the community and/or the home office? Does it put me at risk? Does it meet our guidelines? Local managers have a limited contributions budget over which they have discretion. Normally, they can award grants of $1,500 to $2,500. Larger grants usually have to go to the home office but need the blessing of the local facility to have any chance of success.

> Corporate giving comes more easily when you first involve one or more executives in your work: they can help to position your request.

As you approach businesses for gifts, be aware that there are a number of ways in which businesses can support your efforts. There are four primary types of support.

- **Philanthropic gifts.** Tax-deductible as charitable deductions, these come out of the contributions budget and/or a separate corporation foundation. Corporations and foundations often have specific policies and guidelines for grant applications. Decision-making may take one to six months.
- **Sponsorships and ads.** These are often (but not always) considered marketing expenses and can come out of budgets other than for contributions. They are typically sought through the marketing, community, or public relations department. An ad sale might take a month; however, sponsorship solicitations and negotiations can take considerably longer. Allow a minimum of three months, six or more for larger corporations.
- **Employee matching gifts.** Some corporations offer programs to match the gifts their employees make to nonprofits like yours. Others have a matching gift program restricted to gifts to higher education. Such funds come out of the contributions budget.

- **In-kind contributions.** These are gifts of goods and services—paper, printing, newsletter mailings, office furniture and equipment, graphic design work, computer help, accounting services, space, office supplies, loaned secretarial services, loaned executives, food, lumber, hotel rooms, or rental cars for visiting artists. The expenses associated with such gifts are tax-deductible as part of the normal course of doing business, and this is often the easiest type of corporate support to attract. Often a frontline manager can make such a decision without getting elaborate upper management approval.

> In-kind gifts can lead to future cash gifts.

You will get more from a company if you first involve some of their key executives in your organization. They can guide you through the process of asking for various kinds of gifts from different departments within the company. We recommend the following strategy when asking national corporations for support.

- Do research.
- Prioritize and select the most likely prospects.
- Try to identify contacts of board and staff at the corporations.
- Cultivate the individuals identified on the local level.
- Ask for help positioning the gift request at national headquarters.
- Ask for the gift (make a formal proposal).
- Receive and acknowledge the gift.
- Maintain contact.
- Ask for help positioning the next gift.

Remember, the key to success is identifying, cultivating, and involving the key decision-makers so they will want to help you get money from the corporations for which they work. Enable them to help you determine the best strategy for approaching the corporation and deciding upon an appropriate request.

Raising Money from Foundations

Focus your efforts on raising money from local foundations which you know already have an interest in your community. You will raise more money per hour of time invested with local foundations than you will with national foundations.

Approach small family foundations without professional staff in the same manner as you would an individual. In these cases, the foundation is usually just a mechanism for giving which has certain personal tax advantages.

> The staff of foundations can often direct you to other potential donors if you ask.

For established foundations with professional staff, a more formal approach is required.

Do research through such places as:

- The Foundation Center, a nonprofit that provides extensive information on foundations, including which ones give to the arts and which ones give to the arts in your state. Its website and publications are excellent. Publications are found at most public libraries. It also has research centers across the country. www.fdncenter.org
- The Chronicle of Philanthropy. Published biweekly. www.philanthropy.com
- Websites of larger foundations and places such as GrantsStation. www.grantstation.com
- Colleagues with similar situations.

Develop a list of appropriate foundations, including those which fund organizations in your region/community, the type of work you are doing (arts, education, beautification, urban renewal, senior citizen projects), and the type of fundraising you are doing (annual operating support, project support, endowment campaigns, capital improvements, renovations).

Review the list and develop cultivation strategies. Meet with key volunteers to review the information gathered. Find out whether your volunteers know individuals on the staff or boards of the foundations. If no one knows anyone at the foundation, search within your organization's family of supporters for someone who does. Never ask a stranger for money! Once you make a personal contact, develop a cultivation strategy for each foundation to educate the foundation about your arts organization and how you serve the community. You will also need to learn about the foundation, what they fund, their guidelines, timelines, funding preferences, and criteria for funding decisions.

Review a draft proposal with the foundation. Based on this research, respond accordingly to the foundation's guidelines. Some will welcome an initial phone call. Others will require or encourage a letter of inquiry summarizing your request in order to determine whether a full proposal should be invited. Others may be willing to critique a draft proposal. In this case, you can ask how to strengthen or revise the request to best meet the foundation's needs. Then finalize the proposal and submit it to the foundation for review. If you take this step, build in at least six to eight weeks before any deadline to give the foundation time to review and to give you time to revise.

See the subsequent chapter, Essentials of Proposal Writing, reprinted with permission from The Grantsmanship Center, for information on how to develop a funding proposal.

Write a thank-you letter. Once the foundation makes a decision, say thank you in writing, even if the response is negative. Once you know the foundation representative, you can ask why your application was rejected. The answer may be simply that there were more good requests than could be funded. Reapply if you get any encouragement from the foundation.

Maintain contact. Maintain contact with foundation representatives. Make certain they get your newsletter, invitations to openings, etc. Keep them up-to-date on how your arts organization is serving the community.

Raising Money from Governments

Raising money from government agencies or other public funding sources is also a process of identifying the right people, cultivating them, and having them help you get funding. Each level of government requires a different approach.

> Local government fundraising equals politics and the art of persuasion through lobbying.

LOCAL GOVERNMENT FUNDING

City and county governments can be your best prospective funders if you organize those who believe in your work to help you lobby for government funds. Identify who has the power and makes the decisions on how local public funds are spent. Develop a cultivation strategy for each decision-maker. Make them understand how your organization serves the community and that you have a powerful constituency that supports your organization's work. Because many good organizations ask for money, make certain you are capable of making the politicians look good.

Local government funding can be delivered through:

- line item direct funding;
- local government departments such as libraries, school systems, and parks and recreation departments;
- community development funds;
- dedicated or special taxes such as ticket taxes, cable franchise fees, entertainment taxes, hotel/motel taxes, special tax districts, and voluntary tax check-offs;
- general county funds; and
- local access to federal community development funds (community development block grants), historic preservation, social service, and more. (Talk with municipal staff in various departments to see what sources you might tap through them.)

STATE GOVERNMENT FUNDING

State funding for the arts comes primarily through your state arts agency. Call your state arts agency and ask for guidelines and assistance to understand how and to what you should apply. The staff members are there to help you, and you will enjoy getting to know them. Typical state arts agency funding programs for arts organizations might include:

- project support;
- general operating support;
- artists-in-schools or in residence;
- technical assistance funds; and
- touring performance/exhibition funds.

In most states, peer panels recommend which grants should be funded. While it is ultimately the quality of your proposed project or use of funds that will reap a positive funding decision, it helps if peers in other arts organizations in the state know you, your organization, and the good work you are accomplishing.

Other avenues of state funding can include:

- line item direct funding;
- state government departments such as education, tourism, economic development, human services, humanities council, community development, rural development, rural health, and historic preservation;
- going through states to access federal funds; and
- state income tax check-offs.

See the Cultural Advocacy chapter to learn about advocacy principles and practices that can help secure local or state public funds.

FEDERAL GOVERNMENT FUNDING

The NEA is the most visible source of federal arts funding.

Local arts agencies can access some federal sources (some NEA funds are set aside for this purpose) through their state arts agencies or statewide assemblies of local arts agencies.

The NEA stresses quality, excellence, and professionalism in its funding considerations. You should have unique, special, or strong programs before you consider spending your limited fundraising time approaching the NEA. The NEA funds only specific, definable activities by professionally-staffed organizations. To learn about the NEA's current grantmaking areas, visit online at www.nea.gov. Talk to NEA staff before you apply.

As with state funding, NEA funding recommendations are made by peer review panels, so it can be helpful to be known nationally by your peers in the field. The best way to do this is by participating actively in national and regional conferences.

Other federal government sources. Listed below are some of the other federal departments and agencies that offer arts funding opportunities. Collaborations and partnerships with other organizations—often local government agencies—are essential for access to most of these federal grants.

- U.S. Department of Agriculture (USDA)
- U.S. Department of Commerce (DOC)
- U.S. Department of Defense (DOD)
- U.S. Department of Education (ED)
- U.S. Department of Energy (DOE)
- U.S. Department of Health and Human Services (HHS)
- U.S. Department of Housing and Urban Development (HUD)
- U.S. Department of Interior (DOI)
- U.S. Department of Justice (DOJ)
- U.S. Department of Labor (DOL)
- U.S. Department of State (DOS)
- U.S. Department of Transportation (DOT)
- Advisory Council on Historic Preservation (ACHP)
- Appalachian Regional Commission (ARC)
- Corporation for National and Community Service (CNS)
- Environmental Protection Agency (EPA)
- Federal Emergency Management Agency (FEMA)
- General Services Administration (GSA; surplus goods)
- Institute of Museum and Library Services (IMLS)
- National Endowment for the Humanities (NEH)
- National Science Foundation (NSF)
- Save America's Treasures
- Small Business Administration (SBA)

EXPAND YOUR OPTIONS THROUGH PARTNERSHIPS

Don't just consider arts sources. Be alert to opportunities in your own community to create innovative collaborations which can expand your resources, programming, and audiences. Local arts agencies around the country have partnered with such groups as school systems, universities/community colleges (good sources of interns, too), civic organizations and clubs, restaurants, radio/television stations, cable television systems, other businesses, chambers of commerce, schools of business, libraries, churches, festivals, rescue squads, volunteer fire departments, home extension service programs, outdoor recreation facilities and parks, tourist development authorities, planning departments, historic preservation agencies, community centers, transportation agencies, prisons, economic development organizations, elder care facilities, the United Way, health and social services agencies, and human services.

> Requests for funding are often strengthened by collaborating with other organizations.

How to Write a Proposal

Your state arts agency, the NEA, and some foundations and corporations have their own forms to fill out and/or guidelines to follow when you apply for funds. Follow the guidelines carefully. You do not want to give them an excuse not to fund you.

If you are writing a grant request to a foundation or other source without particular guidelines, keep your request short (two or three pages plus appendices).

For a more detailed explanation of how to develop an effective proposal, see the next chapter, Essentials of Proposal Development, reprinted by permission from Mrs. Norton Kiritz and The Grantsmanship Center. ▌

Build Ongoing Relationships

Once you have received a gift or a grant, you have the opportunity to create an ongoing relationship with the donor, which can produce major amounts of money in the years to come. Fundraising is built on trust and the development of ongoing personal relationships. Always be open and honest with your donors. Keep them informed about your successes, problems, and planning. Avoid surprises. Work to make certain they understand what is happening within your organization, and, if possible, involve them in ways they can feel helpful and supportive. Help your donors realize that a gift to your organization will enrich their lives.

> Maintain the relationship so that donors are never strangers again.

Endnotes

1. Draper, L. (2005, January/February). "Philanthropy in Action. Where the Money Is: Topping Overlooked Sources of Support for Nonprofits" [Electronic version]. *Foundation News & Commentary*, 46, 1.

2. Cohen, T. (2005, May 1). "Each 501(c)(3) Is Now." *The Nonprofit Times*.

3. Draper, L.

Appendix

Fiscal year ending June 30:	Actual		Budgeted	
	Year 1	Year 2	Year 3	Year 4
CASH DISBURSEMENTS				
Production	1,617,367	1,606,136	1,581,723	1,746,372
Administration	196,110	211,668	184,032	215,976
Other operating costs	209,772	213,872	166,781	216,417
Total Program+Operating Costs	2,023,249	2,031,676	1,932,536	2,178,765
Capital Needs:				
Construction costs+equipment purchases				
Architect+theatre consultant Development +marketing			28,179	159,342
Financing costs				
Endowment				
Total Capital Needs	0	0	28,179	159,342
Campaign Loan Retirement				
Total Cash Disbursements	**2,023,249**	**2,031,676**	**1,960,715**	**2,338,107**
CASH RECEIVED				
Earned Income:				
Ticket sales	1,123,467	1,028,915	1,057,710	1,353,280
Concessions	20,858	21,131	20,000	20,000
Advertising	69,017	71,309	60,000	65,000
Rentals+Miscellaneous	172,067	203,489	139,280	153,880
Foundation distribution		43,144	74,000	41,000
Total Earned Income	1,385,409	1,367,988	1,350,990	1,633,160
Contributed Income:				
To support operating needs	560,807	585,638	507,500	497,500
To support program needs	77,659	80,400	85,000	95,000
Proposed Capital Campaign			25,000	125,000
Total Contributed Income	638,466	666,038	617,500	717,500
Campaign Loan proceeds				
Total Cash Received	**2,023,875**	**2,034,026**	**1,968,490**	**2,350,660**
Cash in Excess of Disbursements	626	2,350	7,775	12,553

THE ART OF FUNDRAISING | 231

Figure 1: Capital and Endowment Campaign for the Well-Established Arts Center (Summary of Historical and Projected Cash Flows—Confidential/for Planning Purposes).

Year 5	Construction Year 6	Year 7	Year 8	Campaign Totals	
1,798,763	1,852,726	1,908,308	1,965,557		⎫
222,455	229,129	236,003	243,083		⎬ Cost of the art
222,910	229,597	236,485	243,579		⎪
2,244,128	2,311,452	2,380,795	2,452,219		⎭
548,320	596,230	935,142	693,230	2,772,922	⎫
	166,375	166,376		332,751	⎪
57,300	25,000			269,821	⎬ Campaign need:
15,274	98,821	60,582	17,736	192,413	⎪ $7,567,907
775,000	975,000	1,000,000	1,250,000	4,000,000	⎪
1,395,894	1,861,426	2,162,100	1,960,966	7,567,907	⎭
	347,000	600,000	275,907		
3,640,022	4,519,878	5,142,895	4,689,092	1,222,907	
1,393,878	1,435,695	1,478,766	1,523,129		
20,600	21,218	21,855	22,510		
66,950	68,959	71,027	73,158		
158,496	163,251	168,149	173,193		
1,639,925	1,689,123	1,739,796	1,791,990		
512,425	527,798	543,632	559,941		
97,850	100,786	103,809	106,923		
977,300	1,401,375	2,800,000	2,239,232	7,567,907	
1,587,575	2,029,958	3,447,441	2,906,096		
414,291	808,616			1,222,907	
3,641,791	4,527,697	5,187,237	4,698,086		
1,769	7,819	44,342	8,994		

The North Group, Inc.

Figure 2: Evaluating internal resources.

ORGANIZATION:

COMPLETED BY:

DATE:

Fundraising Options to Consider (in priority order)	Do we know how?	Do we have needed staff time?	Do we have needed volunteer time?
1. Board/key volunteer gifts			

2. Individual gifts
  a. Personal solicitation of major gifts
  b. Membership campaign
    1) Personal solicitations
    2) Personalized letters
    3) Telephone follow-up
    4) Mass mail campaigns			

3. Fundraisers/benefits/special events			

4. Personal solicitations
  a. Local businesses
  b. Local foundations			

5. Cultivation and grantwriting
  a. Local governments
  b. State government
  c. Federal government			

6. Cultivation and proposal writing
  a. National corporations
  b. National foundations			

Other			

	Do we have needed space/ equipment?	Do we have needed prospects?	How much can we raise?	How much will it cost?	Should we do it?

The North Group, Inc.

Figure 3: Fundraising Work Plan Example

Capital City Performing Arts Center Five-Year Plan

Goal: To increase annual contributed income by 250 percent from $77,100 to $1,927,500

1. BOARD SOLICITATION

- *Plan and rationale.* Our 18 board members have been pushed hard to give to their maximum over the last five years. They have given to the annual fund drive and capital campaign. There is little room for improved giving. Each board member is required to give to the best of his/her ability

- *Strategy.* Continue to have the board chair solicit the executive committee members and to have the executive committee members solicit other board members. All solicitations will be made in person.

- *Time commitment.*

     Chief executive . . . . five hours to help with "prospect research"
     Development director . . . . ten hours
     Board chair . . . . .six hours
     Executive Committee members . . . . four hours each

- *Timetable.* Board solicitation is to be completed within the month of September.

- *Direct cost.* Minimal

- *Projected Income.*

Year 1	Year 2	Year 3	Year 4	Year 5
$37,100	$40,000	$47,000	$58,000	$65,000

2. INDIVIDUAL GIFTS SOLICITATION

- *Plan.* Start small, build a strong base, and give our board and staff experience in raising money from individuals. By Year 5, achieve 400 high-level members, assuming we keep cultivating current members as we add more.

- *Enhance membership benefits.* New seven to eight member Individual Gifts Committee improves special privileges/benefits provided for those at $50 to $1,000 levels of membership.

- *Personal solicitation.* Given new benefits, board members submit information on 15 individuals/couples capable of memberships at $100+ a year. Staff compiles list and eliminates duplicates. Committee discusses list, prioritizes top 80 most-likely prospects, and determines who is best to cultivate/solicit each one. Those "best" personally invite prospects to attend a special show and private reception. That night, solicit prospects to become members at $100 to $1,000 a year. Repeat each year with new prospects.

- *Mail campaign.* Committee arranges for those next on the list to receive letters with hand-written notes from people they know, inviting them to become high-level members ("Please join me as a Patron-level member"). Committee organizes phone follow up by "best" person for mail prospects who did not respond. Start calls with "thank you" for past support and/or participation. The calls should be made within a month after mailing.

- *Time commitment.*

    Development director . . . . .30 days of coordinating, motivating, following up, record keeping, and list/letter preparation

    Individual gifts . . . . two meetings +

    Committee members . . . . five performances with guests + Ttwo evenings each for phoning

    Other board members . . . . .two performances each with guests + two evenings each for phoning

- *Direct cost.* Supplies and mailings, $3,800; receptions, $1,850; and 160 complimentary tickets
- *Projected income.*

	Year 1	Year 2	Year 3	Year 4	Year 5
Personal solicitation	$14,000	$25,000	$35,000	$48,000	$55,000
Mail + Follow-up	$6,000	$9,750	$13,500	$18,500	$20,000

3. SPECIAL FUNDRAISING EVENT

- *Plan and rationale:* Establish a gala cocktail party, sit-down dinner, and show as a special event to kick off the season. Involve up to 150 people and get donations in a way that is not extra work for our technical crew. We have already recruited to the board the head of food service at the Capital Hotel and his wife, former president of Junior League, specifically to establish this event as an important community occasion. They will recruit the Gala Team from prominent couples on the subscription list.
- *Strategy.* Secure a headline artist. Charge for dinner and tickets. Gala patrons can secure best seats in the house through the development director. Use this opportunity to get current and potential donors into the theater who don't have the time to come on a regular basis. Make the evening very special.
- *Time commitment.*

    Development director . . . . Several days for Gala Team back-up, invitations, ticket-related phone calls, ticket and dinner arrangements, and helping with marketing and publicity

    Co-chairs and Gala Team members . . . . One meeting + time to address envelopes and write personal notes to tuck in invitations + gala evening

- *Timetable.* Secure commitment of Capital Hotel, headline artist, and co-chairs up to 13 months ahead.
- *Direct cost.* Pay Capital Hotel for set-up, flowers, food, clean-up, etc.—an agreed upon $5,000 (rest of their cost is a contribution).
- *Projected net income*

Year 1	Year 2	Year 3	Year 4	Year 5
$20,000	$30,000	$35,000	$40,000	$52,750

Figure 4: Prospect Research Chart for intelligence gathering and cultivation. Complete the first two columns ahead of time.

ORGANIZATION:

COMPLETED BY:

DATE:

	Giving history	Capable of gift of	Likely gift	Best solicitor
1. Names Address Phone Email				
2. Names Address Phone Email				
3. Names Address Phone Email				
4. Names Address Phone Email				
5. Names Address Phone Email				

The North Group, Inc.

Figure 5: Steps for Making a Fundraising Call on an Individual.

ASK IN A FACE-TO-FACE MEETING.
- Solicit gifts in a thoughtful manner, not casually.
- Cultivate the prospect, and ask face-to-face if you are asking for a lot of money.

BE PREPARED AND BRIEF.
- Know as much about the prospect as possible.
- Be clear about the amount or range of money you are requesting.
- Have a personalized letter with you which asks for a specific amount or range (and includes the pledge form).
- Include attachments explaining the fund drive/organization which the prospect can review later.

BE CONFIDENT, POSITIVE, AND PASSIONATE.
- You are not begging; you are sharing an opportunity to enhance your organization and to satisfy the prospect's need.

FOCUS ON THE PROSPECT'S NEEDS.
- Successful fundraising speaks as much to the needs of the donor as it does to the needs of the arts organization.

ASK UP FRONT FOR A SPECIFIC AMOUNT OR RANGE OF MONEY.
- Mention a need or goal of the prospect which the gift will satisfy (based on your research). Lead with the strongest opportunity. (Mentioning more than one may give the prospect a chance to shoot down your request.)

DON'T FILL THE SILENCE AFTER YOU MAKE THE REQUEST.
- Give the prospect a chance to respond.
- Then continue based on the response.
- Involve the potential donor in the development of the idea/proposal so the donor is emotionally involved in its success.
- Remember that everyone wants to be a worthwhile member of a worthwhile organization.

MENTION THAT THE AMOUNT REQUESTED MAY BE HIGH OR LOW.
- It is only a suggestion.
- Only the prospect knows the appropriate gift level.

FOLLOW UP WITH A THANK-YOU LETTER.
- Follow up even if the prospect turns you down.
- In fact, thank donors every time you can.
- Saying thank you gives you the right to ask again.

"INVOLVE" THE DONOR AND FOLLOW THROUGH TO MAKE THE CONTRIBUTION AN ANNUAL GIFT.

9

Essentials of Proposal Writing

NORTON J. KIRITZ

The grant proposal package to a foundation or corporate funder will usually contain these three elements:

1. **Cover letter.** Signed by the chairperson of the board of a nonprofit agency or the top authority in a governmental agency, the cover letter describes the program and tells the grantmaker how important the grant would be to the community served by the applicant agency. The cover letter demonstrates the board's strong support of the proposed program, which is essential in gaining foundation grants.
2. **Grant proposal.** The body of the proposal may be as modest as one page (in the case of a foundation that limits requests to a page) or it may be quite voluminous. It may be in letter form or it may be more formally presented. The format described in the following article will help to assure that necessary items are included and that they are presented in a logical manner. It can serve as your proposal format where the funding source has not provided one—as is often the case with foundation proposals. But it should not be substituted for any format required by a foundation. If the funder asks you to follow a set format, do it!
3. **Additional materials.** These should be limited to the items required or requested by the funding source, supplemented by only the most important addenda. Reviewers don't grade proposals by the pound, so save your postage.

The proposal package to a government funding source will usually contain these three elements:

1. **Letter of transmittal.** A brief statement (two to three paragraphs) signed by the highest level person within your organization. It summarizes the request and the amount asked for, and it may indicate the significance and importance of the proposed project. It should indicate the support of your board of directors. It should also convey the approval of the request as reflected in the signature of the board chairperson (possibly along with that of the executive director/chief executive officer).
2. **Grant proposal.** A proposal going to a government funder is usually much lengthier than one going to a private foundation. The funder's guidelines will contain the sequence to be followed in writing the narrative portion. Quite often, government agency guidelines will also describe exactly how each section of your proposal will be weighed. This tells you what the reviewers look for and it helps you to organize your thoughts. Follow the guidelines meticulously because the reviewers will. Proposals are often disqualified simply because the applicant failed to follow specific instructions. Proposals for government grants may also contain unique forms, such as face-sheet forms where the entire project, names of key staff, budget, numbers of people impacted by the project, etc., are indicated, along with various assurance and compliance forms pertaining to is-

Copyright © 2005 by TGCI—The Grantsmanship Center. Reprinted by permission. This document may not be reproduced or redistributed without express permission of TGCI—The Grantsmanship Center.

sues such as handicapped accessibility and civil rights. It is important to understand which items must be submitted with your proposal and how they are to be completed, so read the instructions carefully.
3. **Additional materials.** These might include job descriptions, résumés, letters of support or commitment, your IRS tax exemption designation, an annual report, financial statement, or similar documents required or requested by the funder.

This section (or Appendix) can be extensive when a funding source requests a great deal of information. There are instances in which the funding source will request copies of certain agency policies and procedures, copies of negotiated indirect-cost rates, etc. Generally, this will happen only once, and for refunding packages to the same public agency, you will probably not need to resubmit the same documents.

We suggest the following basic format for planning all of your proposals. Thinking through the various sections should enable you to produce everything that either a private or government funding source will ask of you. It will also enable you to develop a logical approach to planning a program and writing the proposal for getting that program funded.

- Proposal Summary
- Introduction
- Problem Statement
- Program Goals and Objectives
- Methods
- Evaluation
- Future Funding
- Budget
- Appendix

Proposal Summary

The Summary is a critical element of any proposal—not just something to be written as an afterthought. There may be a box for a Summary on the first page of a federal grant application form. (It may also be called a "Proposal Abstract.") In writing to a foundation, the Summary should be the first paragraph of a letter-type proposal, or the first section of a more formal proposal. The Summary should succinctly describe who you are, the scope of your project, and the cost.

The Summary is probably the first thing that a funding source will read. In fact, it may be the only thing that some people in the review process will read—so make it clear, concise, and specific.

Introduction

In this part of the proposal you introduce your organization as an applicant for funds.

More often than not, proposals are funded on the basis of an applicant's reputation.

The Introduction is where you build your credibility and make the case that your organization deserves to be supported.

What gives an organization credibility in the eyes of a funding source? That may depend on the nature of the funding source. A traditional, conservative foundation might be more impressed by persons of prominence on your board of directors, how long it has been in existence, or how many other funding sources have been supporting it. A progressive funding source might be more interested in a board comprised of community representatives rather than corporate bigwigs, or in organizations that are new and promising rather than old and established.

Potential funding sources should be targeted because of their possible interest in your type of organization as well as their interest in the kind of program you are proposing. You can use your proposal's Introduction to reinforce the connection you perceive between your interests and those of the funding source.

Here are some of the things you can talk about in your Introduction:

- how you got started—your purpose and goals;
- how long you have been around, how you've grown, and the breadth of your financial support;
- unique aspects of your agency—the fact that it was the first organization of its kind in the nation, etc.;
- some of your most significant accomplishments as an organization or, if you are a new organization, some of the significant accomplishments of your board members or staff in their previous roles;
- your success with related projects; and
- the support you have received from other organizations and individuals (accompanied by a few letters of endorsement which can be attached in the Appendix).

Remember, in terms of getting funded, the credibility you establish in your Introduction may be more important than anything else. But here, as in all other parts of your proposal, be as brief and specific as you can be. Avoid jargon and keep it simple.

Problem Statement or Assessment of Need

From the Introduction, the reader should know your areas of interest—the field in which you are working. Now you will zero in on the specific problem or problems that you want to solve through your proposed program. If the Introduction is the most important part of your proposal in getting funded, the Problem Statement is the most important element in planning a good program.

> If the Introduction is the most important part of your proposal in getting funded, the Problem Statement is the most important element in planning a good program.

The Problem Statement or Needs Assessment describes the situation that prompted you to write this proposal. It should refer to situation(s) that are outside of your organization (i.e., situations in the life of your clients or community). It does not refer to the internal needs of your organization, unless you are asking someone to fund an activity to improve your own effectiveness. In particular, make sure you don't describe your lack of money as the problem. Everyone understands that you are asking for a grant. That's a given. The funder wants to know what external situation will be addressed if you are awarded the grant. That is what you should describe—and document—in the Problem Statement.

A Problem Statement is used to address such issues as homelessness, school dropouts, teen pregnancy, and the like. A Needs Statements deals with less tangible subjects.

It is especially useful for programs that are artistic, spiritual, or otherwise value oriented.

Don't assume that everyone knows the urgency or the dimensions of the problem you are describing. The funding source has no assurance that you will be able to deal with the problem if you fail to demonstrate your understanding of it. Use some appropriate statistics. Augment them with quotes from authorities, especially those in your own community. And make sure that you convey a knowledge of the problem in your area of service, not just on a national level. Charts and graphs will probably turn off the reader. If you use lots of statistics, include the key figures in your Problem Statement and save the rest for an Appendix.

In the Problem Statement you should present the following:

- **Make a logical connection** between your organization's background and the problem or needs you propose to address.
- **Clearly define the problems or needs** you intend to address. Make sure that what you want to do is feasible—that it can be done by your agency within a reasonable time and with a reasonable amount of money.
- **Demonstrate the existence of the problem or needs** by including credible evidence, such as statistics or statements from groups in your community who are knowledgeable about the problem, from prospective clients, from other organizations working in your community, and from professionals in the field.
- **Be realistic**—don't try and solve all the problems in the world in the next six months.

> Many grant applicants fail to understand the difference between problems and methods for solving problems.

Note: Many grant applicants fail to understand the difference between problems and methods for solving problems (or between needs and methods for satisfying needs). For example, an agency working with the elderly in an urban area said that what the community needed were vans to get the elderly to various agencies. They determined that this "need" existed because not enough seniors were able to get to the local Social Security office or access health services. What the organization had done was to immediately jump to a "method" by which seniors would now be able to receive services. But, of course, there are other methods for accomplishing the same end. For example, what about the possibility of working with institutions to decentralize services? Alternatively, volunteer advocates could work with seniors, acting on their behalf with some of these service providers. Ultimately, buying vans might be the best method, but it is clearly a method and not a problem or a client need. Be very cautious about this. If you find yourself using "lack of" statements in the Problem Statement, you are probably equating the problem with the lack of a method. This starts you on a circular reasoning track that will work havoc with your planning process.

Goals and Objectives

A good proposal flows logically from one section to another. Your Introduction can establish the context for your Problem Statement. Similarly, the Problem Statement will prepare the funding source for your Goals and Objectives. Editor's note: Please see the Strategic Planning chapter for more information about goals and objectives.

Goals are broad statements, such as:

- Develop additional resources to provide AIDS information to bilingual populations.
- Reduce underemployment rates among adults.
- Increase availability of resources to address the problems of adolescent pregnancies.
- Create an environment in which folk art is fully appreciated.
- Enhance self-images of senior adults.

These types of statements cannot be measured as they are stated. They suggest the general thrust of a program. They are not the same as Objectives.

Objectives are specific, measurable outcomes of your program. Objectives are your promised improvements in the situation you described in the Problem Statement. When you think of Objectives this way, it should be clear what your Objectives should look like. For example, if the problem is that certain children in your school read at least three grade levels below the norm for their age, then an objective would be that a certain number of those children would read significantly better when you have concluded your program. They would read better than their classmates who had also been reading poorly, but who did not have the benefit of your intervention. These outcome Objectives should state who is to change, what behaviors are to change, in what direction the changes will occur, how much change will occur, and by what time the change will occur.

Many, if not most, proposals state that the purpose of the program is to establish a program or provide a service. This results in Objectives that read like this: The objective of this project is to provide counseling and guidance services to delinquent youth between the ages of eight and fourteen.

The flaw in this sort of Objective is that it says nothing about outcome. It says nothing about the change in a situation that was described in the Problem. Objectives should be specific, estimating the amount of benefit to be expected from a program. If you are having difficulty in defining your Objectives, try projecting your program a year or two into the future. What differences would you hope to see between then and now? What specific changes would have occurred? Editor's note: Please see the Program Evaluation chapter for more information about outcomes-based measurement.

Outcome Objectives should not be confused with process objectives. You may be used to seeing statements like, "The objective of this training program is to offer classes in automotive repair three times each week, for a period of 36 weeks, to a group of 40 unemployed individuals," or "The objective of this program is to provide twice-weekly counseling sessions, for a period of 18 weeks, to no less than 50 parents who have been reported to Child and Protective Services for child abuse."

> If you are having difficulty in defining your Objectives,
> try projecting your program a year or two into the future.
> What differences would you hope to see between then and now?

Those are process objectives, and they belong in the Methods section of your proposal. They tell what you will do. They do not address the outcome or benefit of what you will do. If you do not distinguish between these two kinds of objectives, you will not be able to gauge the changes attributable to your program. Remember, you are proposing your program in order to make some change in the world, not to add one more service to a world already overcrowded with services and service providers.

Methods

Now you are ready to describe the Methods you will use to accomplish your Objectives. The Methods component of your proposal should describe, in some detail, the activities that will take place in order to achieve the desired results. The Methods section of the proposal is where the reader should be able to gain a picture in his/her mind of exactly how things work, what your facility looks like, how staff are deployed, how clients are dealt with, what the exhibits look like, how the community center recruits and assigns volunteers, or how a questionnaire is administered and the results interpreted.

There are two basic questions to be answered in the Methods section: (1) What combination of strategy and activities have you selected to bring about the desired results? (2) Why have you selected this particular approach of all the possible approaches you could have employed?

Justifying your approach requires that you know a good deal about other programs of a similar nature. Who is working on the problem in your community or elsewhere? What Methods have been tried in the past and are being tried now and with what results?

Considering alternatives is an important aspect of describing your methodology. Showing that you are familiar enough with your field to be aware of different program models and showing your reasons for selecting the model you have selected will add greatly to your credibility.

Your Methods section should describe who is doing what to whom, and why it is being done that way. Your approach should appear realistic to the reviewer, and not suggest that so much will be performed by so few that the program will be unworkable. Unrealistic programs do not win points for good intentions.

Evaluation

Evaluation of your program can serve two purposes. Outcome evaluation is used determine how effective the program is in reaching its stated Objectives. Process evaluation is used to make appropriate changes or adjustments in your program as it proceeds. Editor's note: Please see the Program Evaluation chapter for more information about evaluation methods. ▮

Measurable Objectives set the stage for effective outcome Evaluation. If you have difficulty in determining what criteria to use in evaluating your program, take another look at your Objectives. Chances are they weren't very specific.

> Showing that you are familiar enough with your field to be aware of different program models and showing your reasons for selecting the model you have selected will add greatly to your credibility.

Many Evaluation plans are subjective in nature. Subjective Evaluations tell you how people feel about a program, but they seldom deal with the concrete results of a program. For example, the Evaluation of an educational program that surveyed students, parents, teachers, and administrators of the program would be eliciting attitudes about the program. It would not speak to a statistical improvement in performance attributable to the program. Subjectivity also invites your own biases to enter into an Evaluation, especially if you feel that continued funding depends on producing what looks like good results.

One way to get a more objective Evaluation is to have an outside organization conduct the Evaluation for you. Sometimes it is possible to get an outside organization to develop an Evaluation design that can be submitted to a funding source as part of your proposal. This not only can suggest a more objective Evaluation, and if the evaluating institution has an impressive reputation, it can also enhance the credibility of your proposal.

It is essential that you build an Evaluation plan into your proposal and that you be prepared to implement it at the same time that you start your program. It is very difficult to start an Evaluation at or near the conclusion of the program. By then, you may not know the characteristics of your clients when they entered the program.

> No grantmaker wants to adopt you. Funding sources want to know how you will continue your program when their grant runs out.

Future and Other Necessary Funding

No grantmaker wants to adopt you. Funding sources want to know how you will continue your program when their grant runs out. If you are requesting funds to start a new program, or to expand an existing program, they want to know how you will maintain it after the grant funds have been spent.

A vague promise to continue looking for alternative sources of support is insufficient.

You need a real continuation plan that will assure the funding source, to the greatest extent possible, that you will be able to maintain this new program once the grant is over. Indeed, if you are having trouble keeping your current operations up and running, you will probably have even more trouble maintaining a level of operation that includes additional programs. The grantmaker may be doing you no favor by funding a new project and putting you in the position of having to raise even more money next year in order to keep it going.

At this point in your planning you may realize that there is little likelihood of any other sources of support one or two years hence. Should you even try to implement a new program at this time?

Where should you be looking for future funding? Could you get a local institution or governmental agency to help support the program, should it demonstrate the desired results? Can you get such a commitment in writing? Can you generate funds through the project itself—such as fees for services that will build up over a year or two, subscriptions to publications, etc.? Are there third parties available to provide reimbursement for services? Are you expanding your non-grant fundraising activities? The best plan for Future Funding is the plan that does not require continued grant support.

Other Necessary Funding refers to what are sometimes non-recurring grants—i.e., onetime-only requests. Examples would be a request for a vehicle to transport your clientele or the purchase of a piece of medical equipment for your hospital. While these are not program grants, the funds you request are not all you will need either to utilize the vehicle or to operate the medical device. For the vehicle to be used, you must cover the costs of a driver, insurance, gas, and maintenance. Similarly, the medical equipment must be operated by trained personnel. The funding source will want to know if you are aware of what you need beyond the purchase requested in your grant, and whether you have the funds needed to cover these costs. It makes no sense to find a bus that will sit in your garage for a year.

Budget

The requirements for Budgets vary widely. Foundations usually require much less detail than government funding sources require. Our recommended Budget contains three sections: the first covers personnel costs, the second covers non-personnel costs, and the third covers indirect costs.

Budgets should be built from the ground up—that is, they should be based upon your Goals and Objectives as well as your proposed Methods. It is important to go through this exercise in developing a Budget. Without it, there is a risk of developing unrealistic or impractical requests, where program and Budget are unrelated.

This is how we suggest you structure your Budget.

PERSONNEL

Salaries and Wages

In this section you can list all full- and part-time staff who will be working on the proposed program. Include the following information in columns running across the page.

- Number of persons per title
- Title
- Full monthly salary
- Percent of time employed during grant period
- Number of months during grant period
- Amount requested
- Amount donated or volunteered
- Total

If any of your staff are being paid out of another source of funds (for example, a staff person assigned to your project by a county agency), then you would total up their salary and put it in the "donated" column (also referred to as in-kind, local share, or applicant share).

The salary listed may represent the actual salary paid to a staff member, but not necessarily. If this is a new project, and if your organization has a multistep salary schedule for job classifications, you should request the mid-point unless you know in advance who will fill that position. That way, you have the flexibility to hire at any point along the range with the assumption that all staff salaries will average out toward the middle of the salary range. (This works if there are a number of positions in your project, not just one or two.)

How do you determine what the salary range ought to be? The federal government prefers that salaries be comparable to the prevailing practices in similar agencies in your community. To justify the salaries you build into your Budget you should obtain information from other local agencies regarding the salaries of persons with job descriptions, qualifications, and responsibilities similar to those of the jobs in your agency. You might go to the local city and/or county government, the school district, or United Way. By comparing the jobs in your agency with the jobs at other local agencies, you plan a salary for each position, and you keep the "comparability data" on hand, should you be asked by the funding source to justify your staff salaries.

Another item to be included in your Budget for most public agency applications is the matching support being contributed by your organization, or the donated services. They can either be personnel contributed by you (the applicant organization) or by a third party (another participating agency, a corporation giving you a loaned executive, students, etc.). In many cases this will involve the use of volunteers. You should place a value on the service being performed by that volunteer, e.g., plumber, attorney, carpenter, receptionist, etc. That value is based upon the function being performed by the volunteer, not on the professional background or education of the volunteer. A physician volunteering time at a community center where he/she helps out painting the facility is shown at the hourly wage paid painters, not physicians.[1]

Government grantmakers sometimes require financial participation on the part of an applicant, e.g., 25 percent match. You may be able to make this contribution in cash or in-kind. If you are going to pay the salary of a staff member, that qualifies as cash. If you are using volunteers, or receive an executive on loan from a local corporation, that is in-kind. If you promise volunteers in your program, you are required to deliver the promised services, just as if the funding source were actually paying their salary. You will be asked to document the work they perform and to keep records of their time. Records may be audited in the case of a government grant. Always be able to document five to ten percent more than the required percentage match just in case you are audited and some of your volunteer time is disallowed.

Why is it important to develop a match (applicant share) and show the total costs of a project when some of the money or services are not being provided by the funding source? First, the government funding source wants to know that there is a commitment on the part of your agency—a commitment beyond just conducting the program. It helps for them to know there is some likelihood that you have resources with which to continue the program after funding has ceased. It also provides some clarity as to the precise cost in delivering a service. If the program were to be replicated elsewhere, and donated services were not available, it tells the funding source what the total cost would be. Finally, when you have local resources (volunteers, cash, staff, equipment, etc.), it reduces the amount of money required of the grantor, thereby allowing additional projects to be funded in other locations.

Fringe Benefits

In this section you list the fringe benefits your employees will be receiving, and the dollar cost of these benefits. Some fringe benefits are mandatory, but those vary from state to state, so you will have to determine what they are for your agency in your state.

Mandatory fringe benefits may include state disability insurance, state unemployment insurance, FICA, etc. They are usually based on percentages of salaries.

Some fringe benefits, such as health insurance, are calculated on a flat amount per month per staff member, and not on a percentage basis. As with your salary schedule, your fringe benefits should be comparable to the benefits offered in similar agencies in your community. While you will need to calculate fringe benefits for your own information, in some grant applications you simply indicate the fringe benefit total as a percentage of salary.

Consultant and Contract Services

This is the third and final part of the Personnel section of your Budget. In this section you include paid consultants as well as unpaid consultants (i.e., volunteers). You can differentiate between the items that go here and those that go in Salaries and Wages according to the manner in which the individual or business normally operates. If a bookkeeping firm generally operates on a fee-for-service basis and is volunteering its services to your organization, that would fit best under Consultant and Contract Services. Essentially, be logical and if a Fed yells at you, change it. (Foundation persons never yell.)

Entries might look like these.

	Requested	Donated	Total
Bookkeeping Services@ $400/month x 12 months	$0	$4,800	$4,800
Contracted Fundraising Services @ $500/day x 10 days	$5,000	$0	$5,000
Trainer @ $450/day x 8 days	$3,600	$0	$3,600

NONPERSONNEL

Space

In this section you list all of the facilities you will be using, both those on which you pay rent and those which are being donated for your use. Rent you pay, or the valuation of donated facilities, should be comparable to prevailing rents in the geographic area in which you are located. In addition to actual rent, you should also include the cost of utilities, maintenance services and renovations, if they are absolutely essential to your program, insurance on the facility, telephones (number of instruments needed, installment cost, and monthly cost of instruments), and out-of-town facilities needed.

Include these items in line item fashion like this:

	Requested	Donated	Total
Office Space (900 sq. feet) @ $1.25 foot/month/ x 12 months	$13,500	$0	$13,500
Contracted Fundraising Services @ $600/year	$0	$600	$600

Rental, Lease, or Purchase of Equipment

Here you list all the equipment, donated or to be purchased, that will be used in the proposed program. This includes office equipment, desks, duplicating machines, computers, etc. Use discretion. Try to obtain as much donated equipment as you can. It not only lowers the funder's cost, but it shows the funder that other people are involved in trying to make the program happen. Read guidelines closely when working with government grant applications, especially as to their definition of "equipment" and the restrictions that apply. For example, equipment is often defined as something costing more than $500 per unit and/or having a lifetime of greater than one year. In addition, there may be prohibitions against purchasing equipment, and you may be encouraged to lease rather than purchase.

Supplies

This generally means "desktop" supplies, such as paper clips, pens, stationery, etc. If you have any unusual needs for supplies—perhaps you are running an art education program, a sheltered workshop, or some classroom activity requiring lots of educational materials—then have a separate line item for such supplies. This component can also include publications, subscriptions, and postage.

Travel

All transportation-related expenses are included here. Don't put in any big lump sums which will require interpretation or raise eyebrows. Include staff travel at per diem rates approved by your agency and/or the state or federal agency to which you are applying, ground transportation, taxi, reimbursement to staff for use of their automobiles, consultant travel costs, use of agency vans or automobiles (if this has not been included under equipment), etc. Be sure that you use per diem rates (covering hotel and meals) which are appropriate for the location. Attending a workshop in Iowa will be considerably less expensive than attending one in Manhattan.

Other Costs

This is generally a catch-all category which includes items not reasonable to include elsewhere. Examples:

> Bonding of employees
> Tuition for classes
> Professional association dues
> Printing (unless this was included under Consultant and Contract Services)

Indirect Costs

The federal government defines indirect costs as "those costs of an institution which are not readily identifiable with a particular project or activity, but nevertheless are necessary to the general operation of the institution and the conduct of the activities it performs. The cost of operating and maintaining buildings and equipment, depreciation, administrative salaries, general telephone expenses, general travel, and supplies expenses are types of expenses usually considered as indirect costs." While it is possible for all such costs to be charged directly—that is, to the line items listed above, this is often impractical, and you may group them into a common pool.

The federal government indicates that an Indirect Cost Rate is "simply a device for determining fairly and expeditiously…that proportion of an institution's general expenses each of its projects or activities should bear." An organization or institution can negotiate an Indirect Cost Rate (generally a percentage of Salaries and Wages or Total Direct Costs) with any federal agency from which it has received funds. This is an important issue, since many larger institutions find that every new project undertaken costs the institution money unless it is reimbursed for the indirect costs associated with operating the project.

For further clarification of Indirect Cost Rates, contact the federal office's regional comptroller or your program officer or contract officer to find out exactly how to go about negotiating Indirect Cost Rates. Once you have such a rate, there may still be instances in which the funding source refuses to pay indirect cost rates or places a cap (a maximum) on the percentage of total direct costs they will pay. Nevertheless, this is an area which should be thoroughly explored and understood.

Appendix

Addenda to a foundation or corporate proposal should be minimal. It is an imposition to make reviewers plod through pages and pages of "window-dressing" material. In the case of a government grant, however, the Appendix may well be longer than the body of the proposal. The Appendix should contain material which needs to be submitted to the funding source but which would detract from the continuity and flow of the proposal if it were included in the narrative. Ask yourself, "Do I really want the funding source to read/scan the census runs, flow chart, or job descriptions while reading the proposal?" If the answer is yes, then definitely include the item at that juncture. If the answer is no, then include the item in the Appendix and refer the reader to it.

Funding sources will usually stipulate the specific attachments they want you to include with your grant application. The following items are routinely requested.

- **Financial statements.** Funding sources generally require an audited financial statement. Many smaller organizations do not routinely have an audit conducted, so an unaudited financial statement is developed by the agency's accountant or bookkeeper. It is important that applicants know whether the funding source will accept an unaudited financial statement. Call the program officer or other contact person at the offices of the funding source for an answer.
- **IRS determination letter.** Your organization should have a letter from the Internal Revenue Service indicating its tax exempt status. It contains important information regarding the basis for your exemption and the requirements associated with maintaining it. In some cases, individual states also grant such exemptions, and copies of both letters may be appropriate for submission.
- **Indication of nonprofit corporation status.** A copy of the receipt of nonprofit corporation status by the state in which your organization was incorporated may be required. In most instances, the favorable determination of tax exemption (above) will be sufficient in that it lists the name of the incorporated nonprofit organization.
- **Board roster.** Funders are not simply interested in knowing the names of your board members, but who they represent. Are they ministers, doctors, bankers, social workers, building contractors? In the cases of retired individuals, indicate their former job or profession. In situations where organizations have board members who are welfare recipients, unemployed persons, students, etc., select an area of interest or specialty indicate that after their name. Don't just list a name without any affiliation.
- **Organization chart.** This should include the proposed staffing pattern for the project for which funds are being requested, and should also include the larger agency/department/section to whom the new project personnel report. With large organizations, it is not critical that each position be indicated, but units or departments should be shown. In many instances it is more important that the funding source understand how the major functions of the organization are carried out, and how boards, committees, and staff interrelate.

- **Organizational budget.** Some funding sources will require submission of an organizational Budget for the current or forthcoming program year. This organizational Budget differs from the Budget for the project itself, previously discussed. This allows the reviewer to put the grant request in a larger context.
- **Summary chart of key activities.** Most public grant applications will require that you submit some form of timeline for major milestones or activities. This can be done in a variety of formats—Gannt charts, PERT charts, flow charts, etc., and can be done by month, quarter, or time elapsed from the initiation of the project. Whatever format you use, it should be clear and easily understood by the funding source.
- **Negotiated indirect cost rate.** A copy of your agency's negotiated indirect cost rate should be included in the Appendix when you are citing a percentage amount for indirect costs. This is required when submitting public agency applications where such costs are being charged.
- **Letters of support or endorsement.** Letters from elected officials or from other interested parties may be required by a funding source. Or your organization may decide that such letters are good indicators of support and include them in the Appendix.
- In general, such letters should be addressed to your organization (executive director, board chairman, etc.) and sent along with the proposal. Letters should not be sent under separate cover to the funding source because they may not get there in time or they may not be filed appropriately with your proposal.
- **Résumés.** Résumés/curricula vitae of key staff should be updated periodically. They should also be written in the same format. With the exclusion of academic and medical personnel, they need be no longer than two to three pages.
- **Job descriptions.** While in some instances it is important to create a capsule résumé for inclusion in the body of the proposal, in most cases the description of positions should be an Appendix item.

Endnotes

1. Editor's note: Please see the Independent Sector website at www.independentsector.org/programs/research/volunteer_time.html for an estimated dollar value for volunteer time per hour.

The Grantsmanship Center (TGCI) was founded in 1972 to offer grantsmanship training and low-cost publications to nonprofit organizations and government agencies. TGCI conducts some 200 workshops annually in grantsmanship, enterprise development, and fundraising. More than 100 local agencies across the country host these workshops. TGCI alumni attend regular meetings in Los Angeles and other cities, receive continuing support from the TGCI organization, and benefit from technical assistance and other forms of support delivered through its website.

TGCI publishes *The Grantsmanship Center Magazine*. TGCI's "Winning Grant Proposals Online" collects the best of funded federal grant proposals annually and makes them available on CDROM. The TGCI proposal writing guide, *Program Planning and Proposal Writing* (PP&PW), is available in short and long versions (this chapter represents the short version) and is a widely utilized publication with more than a million copies in print.

Essentials of Program Planning and Proposal Writing

The Grantsmanship Center. All Rights Reserved.

P.O. Box 17220, Los Angeles, CA 90017; phone 213-482-9860; fax 213-482-9863; info@tgci.com

---

Editor's note: A special thank you to Mrs. Kiritz for granting reprint permission.

10

Online Fundraising

DEE BOYLE-CLAPP

Donating online, just like shopping and banking, has quickly become an accepted practice. For donors, giving online is about convenience and many appreciate the opportunity to do something good with minimal effort from their phone, tablet, laptop, or desktop. For arts nonprofits that create and maintain good email lists and learn to develop compelling messaging, online fundraising is one of the simplest means to increase income, reduce costs, easily and consistently connect with existing and new donors, and have the flexibility to reach out quickly if circumstances require it. Keep in mind that just as (most) banks have not moved 100 percent online, there will be donors who are either not comfortable with online giving, or their donations will be too large to simply put on a credit card. For this, and all the reasons covered in this chapter, online fundraising is one important part of a nonprofit organization's fundraising mix.

Online fundraising combines the arts nonprofit organization's website, social media, and email into an integrated host of opportunities to reach out to and receive support from donors who engage via some form of online device. This chapter will focus on the online fundraising process and tools, crowdfunding, and how to reconcile the notion of people giving to people in the online environment, which is well detailed in the Art of Fundraising chapter. See the Appendix for a few hints for applying for grants online. For those new to online fundraising, this chapter could be the start of an exciting host of possibilities, while the development staffer with more experience may find tips and suggestions that corroborate practices or suggest additional opportunities.

First, online giving is not only increasing, it is rapidly increasing while other forms of giving are only slowing increasing - or depending upon the study - decreasing. Charity Navigator's **Online Giving Statistics**[1] quick overview of three studies included the following observations:

Network for Good's Digital Giving Index:

- Online giving is the primary source of growth for nonprofits
- Overall giving rose 3% between 2013-2014

M+R Benchmark Study Comparing 2014-2015:

- Online giving increased 13%
- Monthly online giving grew 32%
- One-time online giving grew 9%

Clearly there is great potential online, in particular since other avenues are stagnant. The key is to be ready to take advantage of each and every opportunity while remembering to focus resources, both financial and staff time and energy, on those areas that will produce the best results; and utilize the full potential of putting out a consistent marketing and appeal message online and offline; and to continue to deepen relationships with new and existing donors.

What makes online giving work?

Simply put; ease. The donor is already online, so the time is convenient for them, and set up properly, online giving should entail just a few mouse clicks and the entering of credit card numbers. Compare that to a phone solicitation that takes the donor away from work or family time (or dinner), or having to reach out and grab a checkbook, then find an envelope and a stamp.

That said, the process of giving has to be simple and without glitches for a prospective donor to get all the way to the end and complete their donation. Test your site and be objective! What is the process? Is it cumbersome? Students in several of the Arts Extension Service's fundraising classes revealed that they lost interest in donating online when they had to move from page to page, when the copy on donation pages was too long, or if they had to hunt to find where to make their gift. Watch the complexity at the end as well; are there many options for membership or premiums? Streamline each step.

> One example of a website shared in a UMass Fundraising class required moving from the home page to the "support us" page which contained a lengthy description of each program. Deeply embedded in the copy about each program were links that then brought the weary (or very determined) donor to yet another page where the donor could either download a form to then mail in, or go to yet another page, select from a long list of "opportunities" and press donate. This is asking too much from donors.

Simple Steps to Online Fundraising

STEP 1: GET READY — TAKING STOCK

Starting, or growing an online fundraising program, like anything new, offers many opportunities and options. Starting out will require assessments of time, expertise, internet capacity (many arts nonprofits operate in areas where broadband is limited!), and at least some financial resources. Several of the following steps can be done concurrently, if there is ample staff or human power.

Personnel: Paid Staff and Volunteers

Arts organization staff members already have much to do. Make sure that they can add online fundraising work in addition to their other duties. If staff has the expertise or if the nonprofit arts organization is large enough to have online ticket sales or class registration capabilities linked from their website, creating online fundraising platforms will be straightforward. If not, then determine how much the organization can invest (money and hours) before adding online fundraising to the income mix.

Online donations are so important that this should be a priority for board and staff. If there is not adequate staff time, get help by hiring qualified temporary or permanent staff, or ask experienced board or committee members to devote the necessary number of hours for a very finite period of time. Know no one? Consider asking another nonprofit organization whose online donation system you admire to work with you or recommend someone, or bring in a computer consultant who has the skills you need. Regardless of who is brought in, check references, even if they volunteer. An art organization's online fundraising presence is not a training ground for an intern. A good intern can conduct research, but should not be tasked with creating an online fundraising program.

Begin with an inventory of existing practices and staff capacity. Be realistic and assess how much staff can undertake before launching anything new. While online giving should be relatively seamless, someone will still have to monitor and reconcile money in the bank, enter donor records and add these names to prospect research lists, craft the fundraising copy and the thank you templates, install everything, test, retest, and make sure the website, payment platform, email synced to the organization's database (more on this below), and automatic responses are working. It is imperative that this system be set up so a thank you is immediately sent when an online donation is received.

Ask staff who will be assigned this work to create a realistic outline of how much time they have available, or could make available, to invest in establishing or growing an online fundraising process. Is it possible to streamline other giving channels, for example the annual campaign or annual event, in order to free up staff time? Determine how much time staff will need per week, and over how many months to conduct research, implementation, testing, and then operation and maintenance of the new or expanded online fundraising program(s).

If staff members need to attend workshops or webinars, add that time and cost in. If staff members need time to explore software, meet with other nonprofit leaders, or even sales people, include this as well. Before anything is adopted, be prepared to answer the question: do we have the time? Next, determine the costs and potential for online fundraising. What are the implementation costs? Is there software to purchase or will the nonprofit use free programs? How much can be realistically raised, and how much saved, by switching most of the fundraising from paper mail to email? Will the work pay off later in more income and staff time saved? Once that is determined, the director and the fundraising committee should create a presentation and ask the board to prioritize resources to create an online fundraising program.

Website

Don't forget the potential to turn passive observing, such as when a visitor finds the website, or hears about the organization through another means (story on the radio or a shared item from a friend), into an opportunity to connect. The website has to be viewed as the organization's front door and must offer ways for the visitor to become a part of the organization. The visitor must easily find how to join the mailing list, sign up to receive the online newsletter, find links to other forms of social media so they can engage with the organization in the form they are most comfortable (Facebook, Twitter, Instagram among others) or if so inclined, to become a donor. Just as few who attend their first concert become members, first-time visitors to a website do not become an immediate donor, but their awareness of the arts organization has been heightened, and if the visitor has been moved to take an action, the potential is there to grow a relationship. Send an immediate (and automatic) thanks for joining the mailing list email, and if a physical address was requested, consider sending a thank you post card.

> The website must offer ways for the visitor to become a part of the organization.

Before you do anything, determine your short and long term website needs. If the website is outdated, it makes little sense to rework only the online donation section. Balance opportunities with effort, and remember that every website should be mobile ready, otherwise known as responsive design, in which the screen size instantly collapses to fit the smaller screen of a smart phone or tablet.[2] Having a responsive design is required by Google and other search engines to be easily found and be kept high in the ratings so when someone searches for the arts organization, it appears near the top of the listings.

Dream and explore, but make sure that the nonprofit arts organization's website is both donor friendly and well represents the good programmatic work being done. Ask a large handful or more staff, board members and key supporters to go online, look around, and then share the top two or three websites that inspire them to give. Don't get too many at once; you can always reach out a second time. Have them report the website address and describe in one or two paragraphs what it is about the website they find inspiring, and another one or two paragraphs describing their perception of the donation page or donation form. Ask what they found appealing, what was interesting, unique, or what could be easily applied to the arts organization's own website. Don't be surprised if these observers and dreamers are only drawn to one part of a website, such as the description of the symphony's longstanding mission, or the exciting, upbeat style of images and short bursts of text introducing the new makerspace or pop-up gallery. The sites can be arts organizations with a mission/program similar to yours or completely unrelated to the arts. What matters is that they are inspired by it. It will be up to the small task force group, outlined below, to decipher what's in that "secret sauce" of color, images, layout and information. Are their donation forms unique? Do they offer clear donation levels or premiums, an inclusive-sounding membership opportunity and more? See Figure 1 for suggested questions to ask, but feel free to create those more relevant to your needs.

Create a small task force to sort the Website Comparison Worksheets (found in Figure 2) and ask them to consider key themes, donation processes (such as using PayPal or another third party site) and to make recommendations knowing that it's a wish list that may be restrained by budget, and what is realistic for staff and the existing website and financial resources. It is also possible that staff may have questions or will need to conduct deeper research to move forward (see examples below).

Examples of possible task force recommendations and staff responses.

Task force recommendation:	Staff questions:
Install a *Donate Now* button	Where should it be located? Should it appear only on the home page, above the navigation bar, or on the side of every page? Will the donor be taken to a donation page where they can get more information, or be taken directly to a place to type in their credit card information? Will the donations be processed through the organization or through a secure, third party source like PayPal?
Create a unique donate page	Accessed from the navigation bar, will you create inner pages with details on why you give? Will premiums and giving societies be listed? Who will determine premiums?
Add a "join the mailing list" segment to capture visitors	Can this be automated so new names are automatically added to the mailing list?

Once the recommendations have been adopted, staff and/or a web designer can create some mock ups, and the task force can preview and test the changes before they go live. Build in time for feedback.

Images and testimonials on the importance or the impact of the programs and services offered may be more interesting and impactful to the reader than paragraphs of well-scripted text. Remember that more than ever, the donation form or page will be read on a mobile device, so edit to as few choice words as possible.

Remember that it will be important for staff to make regular updates of website donation options as technology evolves. This means that arts nonprofits must keep abreast of changes and adopt only what makes sense for their organizations. Wholesale upgrading of donor interfaces should be done only if it provides more opportunities to better serve supporters and donors, saves staff time and organizational

Figure 1: Website comparison worksheed.

Name of reviewer: _____

Relationship to org: _____

	Website 1	Website 2	Our Arts Nonprofit	Notes or comments
URL (website address) Name and type of org	www._____	www._____	our-arts.org Community arts	
Focusing on the entire site:				
Where did you learn about this organization?				
Overall, what was most inspiring? How was it shared?				
Overall, what was most visually appealing?				
Focusing on Fundraising:				
What was most appealing?				
Impression of donation process? Easy, complex, impossible!				
Test giving a gift: how long did it take? How many links or other pages were required to make a gift?				
Impressions of the donation form? Did it feel insecure? Well or poorly branded?				

resources, and increases donations because the new system is easy and attractive. Regardless of what one chooses, keep it simple. Donors are busy and you want to inspire and capitalize on their immediate instinct to give.

Monitor the Mobile Realm

The exponential rise of mobile device use has changed behaviors. In part because people read in short bursts, and certainly because small device size demanded it, copy length has changed. People can only see so much on a small screen, and they expect short, to-the-point information.

Keep up with voice activated technology. In addition to wanting a phone's persona (Siri for Apple, for example) telling donors how to get to your location, the voice activated portion of tablets must be able to read the organization's information. Logos and photos, for example, do not substitute for the name of the institution, nor should it substitute for a donate button.

Determine which individual, or what team of individuals is most excited about technology, and who can translate what they learn into plain language for the rest of the board and staff. Assign or ask the most tech savvy, or most interested mix of board and/or staff members, to keep abreast of this information and report it at staff or board meetings. It is imperative that the arts nonprofit not be taken by surprise, but to keep up, and plan for sequential improvements in technology so donors can be served, including those who find email a challenge as well as those who are already hungrily waiting for the arrival of the next new technological invention.

> The power of a mobile device was immediately apparent at the UMass Campus following the earthquake in Haiti. Students texted gifts (back then the only option was $10) and discussed their experience with peers. They quickly realized that their simple act of generosity could influence others, and together they could make a difference on a device that they were well familiar with and already held in their hand.

STEP 2: GET SET — SELECT THE RIGHT SOFTWARE AND SYSTEMS

CRM - Customer Relationship Management System

Determine where to store your data. Nonprofit arts organizations have many options for holding data and donor records; from excel spreadsheet lists to sophisticated and costly donor database systems. In between is a lot of room and opportunity.

The first decision to be made is to understand who uses this information, who maintains it, where it is stored (in the cloud, linked via a shared network, or on a single volunteer's laptop) and ensuring that it can be accessed by the organization's staff when needed. Always plan for ease of use, safety of data, and continually back it up. For example, every new contact should be saved immediately, a clear advantage that almost any CRM has over an excel spreadsheet. No nonprofit organization, regardless of budget, should ever keep their donor records on an aging laptop that could suddenly cease to work, be lost or stolen, or (cruelest of all) disappear with a volunteer who may leave the organization and not return the information. Unfortunately, some arts organizations operate this way. For these organizations, it is time to explore the amazing potential of free, open source, or low-cost online Customer Relationship Management software. While it may first appear to be larger than the organization needs, it offers scalability and the reassurance that the organization will not likely outgrow it.

A CRM offers the opportunity for field customization. Name, address, email address, etc., are fields. So are occupation, partner name, interests, donor giving history, etc. A CRM also offers integration with email systems, so email news (aka e-blasts) can be sent from this system, allowing nonprofits the opportunity to have one holder of information.

Which to adopt? It is important that the nonprofit arts organization staff or key volunteers take the time to explore a number of CRM programs. Like financial management software, one can download and test drive them for a period of time, and take the time needed to pick which is best for the organization. Test drive and decide which are easy to use, affordable and most compatible for your nonprofits' other systems. For arts organizations like pop-ups or annual festivals, there are tools that can be used perpetually or for one-time events.

Select a CRM integrated with an email service provider. The top four CRMs, according to crmsearch.com, are Salesforce (which integrates with the email service provider Vertical Response), Microsoft, Oracle and SAP. The largest segment of CRM market share belongs to "other"[3] platforms - a growing list of easy to use, low-cost or even free CRMs, including Insightly (which integrates with MailChimp).

> No nonprofit organization, regardless of budget, should ever keep their donor records on an aging laptop that could suddenly cease to work, be lost or stolen, or (cruelest of all) disappear with a volunteer who may leave the organization and not return the information.

API — Application Programming Interface

Once the website has been prepared for online fundraising, there has to be a place where the donor's credit card is processed. This is the role of an API, an application programming interface, which is an online tool that is integrated within the arts organization's website via a button or a page. When the donor is directed from the arts organization's website to a separate company's page to donate, the page should not only look and feel like the arts organization's website, but should be secure and be able to accept a variety of debit, credit cards and possibly e-checks. These API companies will take their fee out of donated funds and then deposit the balance into the arts organization's bank account.

Whatever API is selected should be scrutinized for fees. Are there set-up fees? Monthly fees? A holiday pop-up or summer festival will not want to commit to a monthly fee, but could agree to a reasonable cost per donation. Most readers want to be given recommendations, however API's are so critical for one's nonprofit that the following are just examples, and any under consideration must be thoroughly researched before signing on. Familiarize yourself with options such as PayPal, Authorize.net, Inuit, and search online articles for the newer and most trusted options available, and contact peer networks and ask what they use, what they like most, find the most cumbersome, and then look at their ratings by customer. An API that is slow to pay, has high fees, or has poor customer service should be avoided.

Other options to explore include: Donor Tools, which at this writing has no set up fee, and offers several packages that offer a variety of tools including Quickbooks export, that could save valuable staff time, and the nonprofit Tessitura system, created for arts and culture organizations that combines fundraising, CRM, ticket sales and memberships in one, and boasts no internet transaction fees. As these products change quickly, do your research, and be sure that what you select has a track record, and longevity so it will thrive as the arts organization does.

STEP 3: GO!

Email

Build your email list! Depending upon the size and scope, age, and resources of one's organization, this may be old hat, or dauntingly new. The organization may have a prospect or a donor list, but if you have not been capturing emails, you need to start now. Add a line for email address at every possible opportunity including sign-in sheets at events, art class registration forms, open house forms, and raffle tickets. Ask for addresses when selling performance tickets, following surveys or answering a phone call.

Teach staff to ask those who call for information if they would like to be added to the email list or obtain the newsletter (specify electronic or printed). Have them repeat name, address, phone, and spell back email address. If the organization puts out a printed newsletter, consider adding a section asking donors if they want the next one emailed to them to help save the organization resources. Inside every donation envelope request email address and add a preference section, asking if the donor would like to receive their donation requests via post or email. Track these requests and make no assumptions. The eldest donor may be tech savvy while the youngest board member may not be. You cannot build an online donation program without email addresses!

> Making people feel connected and involved is imperative. The Art Garden in Shelburne Falls, Massachusetts has a policy that a gift of ANY size, be it a donation of a stack of clean, recycled yogurt containers or a gift of $500, automatically makes the donor a "member."

Tie Social Media

Tie social media to fundraising. Brand the nonprofit and the fundraising online presence so they are seamless. Invest wisely not only in development staff and software, but in the full staff. Require those who write online content, tweet or post to Facebook, to clear anything related to fundraising or to events with the development staff. It is imperative that everyone is aware of the policies, needs, desires, campaigns, and progress of these campaigns so fundraising news is shared across appropriate platforms. Good development efforts are supported by all in the organization and there should be no contradictory information going out. This may mean sending memos to staff, holding weekly updates at staff meetings, sending intramail (internal to the nonprofit) updates, or requiring that staff clear their copy before posting during campaigns or special times of the year, such as the two weeks prior to Giving Tuesday (see below for details).

Run an Online Fundraising Campaign

An online fundraising campaign is conducted very much the same way as a traditional fund drive sent via mail. Donors are segmented, appeals are written and prepared for donor tiers (more on this below), mailing lists are created, edits are made and campaigns approved by staff and the development team member or volunteer, and the dates for mailing and reminders, are established. With online fundraising campaigns, there are additional advantages, including having the ability to schedule the campaign to go out via email and arrive at special times (for example, noon on the first Tuesday) or creating the campaign when staff has time (for example, between the close of the summer season and the start of the fall semester) and schedule them to go out in the final weeks in December. Setting up a campaign in advance allows staff time to do their work when it is more likely to be done well, under less pressure, and with the most creativity and care. One other clear advantage is that instead of relying upon one letter to reach one prospective donor, online fundraising campaigns include multiple opportunities to connect via an emailed request, posts on Facebook and Twitter, and other social media, a notice on the website that a fund drive is underway, and reminders and updates sent out over several days (or longer) until the goal is met. Any bit of news, such as meeting the half-way point, or reaching a new donor milestone (we have just surpassed our 1000th donation in four days, a record for our arts organization!)

> **A word about numbers.**
> Numbers and statistics used well can quickly illustrate a story. Put into context, they ARE the story. For example: the arts nonprofit organization wants to raise $200,000 and it is well on its way. In a follow-up email it can share that they are making headway, are half-way, or that they have raised $100,000. These are important distinctions, from vague to specific. Add information about the duration of time in which that amount was raised (Just over a week!) and the number of donors (30 donors or 5,000 donors) and now there is a full story.

should be, or could be, news to be shared and made a part of the campaign. If it gets staff excited, then it should get donors excited. Share it.

Online *Asks* — How Is This Different?

For a traditional fundraising campaign letters are crafted, printed and personalized (Dear Sue and Chris, or Dear Dr. and Mr. Jones), sorted by zip code and sent out via bulk mail. The arts nonprofit could create one, two or three different appeal letters according to donor level, and online appeals are written, and personalized through an email service provider from the organization's email list, and can and should be, segmented via queries. Queries are requests that allow the donor to be pulled out and assigned to receive a specific appeal letter by any number of factors, including donation history (size or frequency), special interest, etc. The template letter is prepared for select groups and sent to the segmented mailing list only.

The email subject lines must be carefully crafted so they are interesting to the donor and will be opened. Do not waste precious real estate; remember that subject lines do not have to include the name of the organization, as that is visible above. The subject line should be fun, and timely. Do not send out anything that appears to be "all about the organization" but instead appeal to the individual donor's interests and history with the organization.

Test subject lines for their open rate, and capitalize on those that work. If the organization's typical email appeal letter subject line has been as uninspiring as "It is time to give again" then it is time to think more creatively! How can the donor be made to feel included in an ask? Consider a problem and how the donor can solve it. If, for example, the organization's annual holiday performance sold out again, and most patrons who wanted to attend have been unable to obtain tickets, are they being asked

> **How to Test Subject Lines**
> First, craft two subject lines. Create a mailing query that captures 15-20% of the total email list (again, do not send email appeals to top donors or to those who may not want email asks.) Randomly divide this in half. For Group A, test the more fun, witty, timely, problem-solving, or more personal subject line. For Group B, send out a subject line typical of the organization's last few online appeals. For Group A, create and assign a unique URL and send this group to a new landing page so you can track this on Google or through other analytics. See the Marketing Chapter for more information on analytics. The landing page can be identical to the organization's donor landing page. Compare the email open rates, compare the gift size, and track the analytics and see what worked best. Send the balance of the email list the subject line that does best. Repeat this process periodically until the institution sees an uptick in online donations and finds "the voice" that appeals most to online donors.

> **Protect Top Donors**
>
> Every organization has people they consider top donors, those who can or do give a substantial gift or have the potential to do so. These individuals deserve personalized treatment and are not simply invited to give online, but instead may be sent more personalized, mailed or otherwise delivered appeals. These are the people that the staff and board must prioritize and invest time in. Ask if they want e-blasts for news and updates, but do not burn them out with many requests.
>
> Any donor who requested or indicated that an appeal be sent in writing should have their preference honored. Be sure that staff checks the box in the organization's donor database software so these people do not feel harassed by information and appeals they do not want. Never give a donor a reason to be annoyed with the organization.
>
> While the advantage of having a donate button on one's website makes donating to the organization an option for donors every day of the year, there are special moments when donors are more likely to give, and smart nonprofits are not only aware of, but plan to take advantage of them.

to donate now so there are more funds available to add another performance? Consider what the organization does, or has recently done and share the good news, and then ask for support of it. If there was a demand for late evening studio hours in the makerspace, consider: "You asked, we delivered! Find out how…" Be prepared to show that attendance went up, that the mission is being met, and now there are additional costs or scholarships to support. Test ideas and themes.

In the 2014 election, an attempt by one party to increase open rates and achieve donations lead to some very unusual subject lines. "*All is lost! We are Doomed!*" and similar subject lines were used. This is not recommended for the nonprofit arts organization. It should be the goal of every arts leader to instill confidence in the organization's ability to operate, not to manipulate donors.

END OF YEAR GIVING

According to the M+R study noted at the start of this chapter, 31 percent of annual giving occurred in the month of December and 12 percent of annual giving occurs on the last 3 days of the year. This is not new. People have always taken advantage of tax deduction opportunities, and others are spurred into action during the season of giving. What this underscores is that every arts organization should evaluate their end-of-calendar year donations, and plan to take advantage of this trend. It makes sense for the arts nonprofit to plan ahead and be present at the top of donor's minds by sending out e-news articles or well-timed e-blasts. Remind arts supporters that their support is needed and deserving all year, but in particular at the end of the calendar year.

SPECIAL GIVING DAYS

The international "Giving Tuesday" is an opportunity for the arts nonprofit organization to test or expand online fundraising by taking part in an orchestrated, marketed, and joint day of giving. According to the M+R study noted above, "donations made on 'Giving Tuesday' rose 148 percent from 2013 and 2014."[4]

Again, determine if staff or the board have the time or ability to devote new, or renewed, energy. If not, who can help? If this event was tried and failed in the past, revisit what happened. Was the email list insufficient? Did the staff and board make a concerted and planned effort and nothing happened? Did overwhelmed staff make a lukewarm attempt to spread the news?

It may be worth another try if the email list has grown, if the organization has a stronger marketing presence, and if there is ample staff and board interest and support.

Not only should organizations reach out to the appropriate names on the donor list, but this is the time to reach out and connect with social and other forms of media. Remember that many organizations will be doing the same, and instead of viewing this as competing, consider the possibility that so much attention to one special giving day is actually helping to remind donors to do their part.

Some communities create their own events, such as ValleyGives in the Pioneer Valley of Western Massachusetts, which celebrates a day of giving in early May. While many nonprofits promote this day for themselves, they and the other organizations listed on the ValleyGives site, collectively benefit from the extra marketing and the last minute reminders to donors. There may be other opportune dates which are, or could be, widely marketed as days of giving in one's area. Consider joining forces with other nonprofit organizations to cross-promote such mutually beneficial days. Ideas for such events include a date of historic significance, a celebration of a region's seasonal highlights or opportunities to make fun of regional uniqueness. For example, many communities celebrate foods grown (strawberry or asparagus events) and Vermont makes great fun out of its "mud season". Be creative and make connections for the arts. Work with the regional tourism council or chamber of commerce to create something special.

People to People

The Art of Fundraising chapter clearly details the importance of recognizing that **people give to people**. This Online Fundraising chapter does not contradict this concept, as in reality, people do give online all the time, but few people give a *significant* gift online without personal contact or without being solicited and carefully developed. While people may do research and consider an arts nonprofit for a legacy gift, rarely will they do so without speaking to another human being within the institution of choice.

Increasingly this **people give to people** "relationship" can begin, and can be grown, online. Personalities, be they an arts leader or a celebrity musician promoting a cause, can be "present" on one's own desktop, laptop, tablet or mobile phone at any time, and anywhere. This pervasiveness of possibility means that one can easily feel connected to their institution of choice, or closely follow a leader who shares more than a story, idea or commentary on occasion through a website or email. This connection can also continue multiple times a day via Facebook, Twitter, Snapchat, and other platforms. This online relationship, however one-sided, can prompt a first time gift or tie a donor to the organization deeply, and this can be shown not only by the number of donors, but the frequency by which they give.

Treat all new prospects equally. Do your research, learn as much as you can about them so you can target appeals, but more importantly, be sure to give them more of what they want from your organization, such as invitations to special events, opening receptions, or online news, so they feel a genuine connection to and feel that they are a part of the institution.

> One day the director of a small nonprofit opened the door after hours to greet a visitor who came to deliver a small, in-kind gift. The organization sent a thank you letter with a small handwritten comment (So nice to meet you!) added. A week later, a $1,000 check came in the mail from this same gentleman. After the second thank you letter, he called to ask to meet, stating that he and his wife wanted to "do more." Understaffed and under-resourced, staff did not have time (or the prioritization) to do any research about this donor with the first or second gifts. It turned out that this couple had owned, and recently sold, a magazine and were looking for a cause to support.
>
> Apply the same lessons to online giving, and do your homework! Online donors, even those who give small gifts, may turn out to be capable of giving something more!

Crowdfunding

Simply put, crowdfunding is another online fundraising opportunity in which the organization creates a campaign, teams of volunteers or board members send news out to their personal email contacts, and then all donors are asked to give on a specific crowdfunding site for a specific cause. Crowdfunding, unlike the annual fund drive, can create a sense of urgency as the campaign should be compelling and focused on a specific project or issue. Creating a buzz and a sense of excitement is imperative, as people must be compelled to give quickly to help the organization meet a goal. The buzz can compel those who give to invite their peers to do so as well, and this can bring the organization not only their much-needed income, but new supporters as well.

Crowdfunding has its drawbacks. First, it has become somewhat overused in recent years as organizations have seen grant and foundation support wane, and as individuals use crowdfunding for everything from launching items for commercial or social good to supporting school trips and paying for dire medical needs.

Second, crowdfunding comes with costs. Review the options carefully as the platforms vary widely in terms of fees charged to the nonprofit and/or the donor. At this writing, fees ranges from 2 to 9.5 percent plus some sites charge an addition fee of 30 cents per donation. Some sites, such as Kickstarter focus on creative projects while other crowdfunding platforms are open to any campaign. Another cost to consider is donor fatigue. Be certain not to detract from annual operations by holding an additional call for donations that will be designated funds for a specific project. Never let an important donor give $15 to one campaign in lieu of their annual gift of $150 to support operations. Instead, make certain that donors are well aware that this campaign, just like a capital campaign, is above and beyond annual support.

Most important, however, is understanding the ramifications of an all-or-nothing concept used by some crowdfunding sites. In this scenario if the goal is not met, funds are returned to the donor. Some swear by all-or-nothing, citing that it is the urgency itself that makes the campaign timely and compelling. Organizations must be continually draw attention to the campaign, share updates on progress, thank supporters, and urge them to bring others out to help. The all-or-nothing option also means that organizations will create a very strong budget and have the ability to state their needs succinctly for those who want just the key points, as well as have the details available for those donors who want to know more. This is important advice not only for a crowdfunding campaign but for every campaign, grant and budget. See the Financial Management chapter for building a budget. ▌ Other crowdfunding platforms give an organization the funds it raised minus fees, and allows for organizations to test how this concept works for their institution.

> **Support a Winner!**
> When asked about giving to crowdfunding sites, students in the University of Massachusetts Amherst arts management classes were primarily interested in supporting those sites that had already, or nearly reached their targets. Students reported the most excitement in giving to those that had surpassed their financial targets, and when pressed said that they wanted to support a winner. This phenomenon may prompt an interesting research study someday, but for now, such anecdotal evidence suggests that arts nonprofits should do as much behind-the-scenes work for their crowdfunding campaigns as possible, getting people ready and waiting to donate and create buzz on social media to immediately build momentum, and pull in those, like these students, who want to support a winner.

To ensure that the organization makes it goals, make certain that the pitch is perfect; no typos compelling content and excellent images. Use video! People expect it, and it works. With a decent smart phone or a good laptop, most anyone can record a video, but it is important that this be a quality video; short, with great images and sound. Be creative, it is what arts organizations do best. What is the money to be used for? Tell the story in as interesting, clear, lingo and jargon free terms as possible. Show examples of students taught, art works created, music performed, behind-the-scenes views of how something is created, and, include different voices if possible. If the Executive Director and the Artistic Director can make the pitch together, this could show a unified front. If any local celebrities are invested in the project, invite them to participate. If a professional is to be hired be sure to include that fee in the amount that needs to be raised.

If rewards (perks) are to be given, make them meaningful. Ask for input here, since it is too easy to think from the organization's perspective, not from the donor's. Not every reward has to cost money. A drawing or print made in the children's art class, or a back-stage tour with the lead in the next performance can be very meaningful. Lunch with the executive director and board chair plus the top five donors could become a fun way to meet new people, and if a local restaurant (or pizza delivery place) donates the meal, this becomes an opportunity to gain an additional gift, and share in the publicity.

PEER TO PEER FUNDRAISING

Peer to Peer Fundraising also plays an important role in crowdfunding. In this process, an organization's supporter creates his or her own campaign on a crowdfunding site, and then asks all of their personal friends to give on the organization's behalf. This can be done for general operations or specific needs like new easels for the paint studio, but not larger initiatives like rolling out plans for a new dance floor or wing or launching a new program. This is a lovely concept that not only deepens a relationship from one supporter to the organization but provides an opportunity for the organization to be connected to new networks of supporters, the friends, family and co-workers of the original supporter, with the potential that each of these individuals will learn about and then support the nonprofit arts organization as well. There is both the potential for a gift and free advertising to those who may otherwise never learn what the organization does.

Is this a good idea for an individual arts nonprofit organization? The drawback(s) could be that the organization has no control over the content of the message nor does it control who is contacted nor when. If there are content errors, this is out of the arts organization's hands. For this reason, the individual interested in creating the peer-to-peer campaign should ask the arts nonprofit for permission, and at minimum there should be an agreement made that all content sent out via email or posted on any form of social media, be approved in advance by the nonprofit. Timing should also be controlled. An independent peer-to-peer campaign should not coincide with or negate the organization's own campaign. It may behoove the arts nonprofit to state upfront that certain individuals (i.e. major donors) should not be asked, though this could be hard to control once the campaign is underway and shared beyond the initial peer-to-peer leader.

Conclusion

There are many exciting possibilities with online fundraising, from both the organization's or the individual's perspectives

Online donations start with the donor learning about, getting curious or excited about, and wanting to participate or, in some way, be a part of the nonprofit arts organization. The act of giving, and being thanked, makes the donor feel like an ally in the work, and good thank you letters (yes, they can be sent via email!) reinforce that belief.

The donor finds donating online easy and prefers the process to be straightforward and quick whether clicking a link posted on Facebook, responding to a call for action in an email, or finding the website donation page and filling in credit card information.

For the arts nonprofit, online fundraising has the potential to engage an entirely new audience of people who follow the organization on social media, but who rarely enter the facility and who have no interest in receiving mail. The organization can save money by not printing or mailing hard copy letters or newsletters, and may save time not folding letters or taking checks to the bank. Another plus with online fundraising is that staff can create the email requests weeks or even months in advance, and take advantage of light schedules or when this work is more convenient for them. The email can be scheduled to go out at a day and time that works for the organization.

Not all is rosy with online giving.

Online fundraising means that nonprofit arts organizations are opening the door very wide and can be passive recipients of gifts. Through the website, the organization is inviting random strangers who wander onto the website to become supporters. The majority of visitors may never give; some will give once, but will remain one-time donors no matter how much effort has been made to prompt a second gift. This is a reality for all nonprofit organizations, and one that can be perplexing as the arts organization may never learn why the first gift was made, and more importantly, why there is no ongoing interest.

Even when asked, the donor can feel minimal commitment. An email request for a gift is easy to ignore. The donor may feel that she or he did their part by giving once, and their loyalty has concluded. If the giving process is interrupted by a slow-loading photo, or the donation page looks insecure many donors give up. If the donor was not expecting to be moved to a PayPal page that looks nothing like the organization's website, they may simply stop the donation process and not give it a second thought. Some donors tire of what they feel are perpetual asks, and they can easily unsubscribe and be lost.

Staff may have to learn new processes, and troubleshoot problems. Email copy, no matter how carefully written, may be unappealing or donors may be busy and never open it. Email requests can be sent to spam folders and never be seen. Despite the effort, online fundraising generally reaps gifts on the smaller side of the arts nonprofit's gift range. Some people do not want to give a large gift and pay the credit card interest. Still, others want to take advantage of "cash back". Others give small, but consistent monthly gifts add up to make the online donor a valued friend.

Online fundraising is a part of the arts nonprofit's income stream mix. This is not, or should not, be the only channel by which the nonprofit arts organization receives income. The development team still has to engage in donor research, development, and find the time to reach out personally to donors. Good stewardship of the online donor requires immediately thanking the donor, regardless of the size of the gift. Remember, any first-time donor (whether they give a fifty dollar or five hundred dollar gift), will require research (though any first-time donation is an opportunity for research, organizations must prioritize staff time), and then staff must do everything possible to keep and engage the donor through genuine gratitude, ongoing news via email or other forms of social media.

Online fundraising is both passive and active, but in the end it is built on the same principal as traditional fundraising - people connecting with people, the donor has to be found, researched, asked, thanked, nurtured, and then thanked again.

Endnotes

1. https://www.charitynavigator.org/index.cfm?bay=content.view&cpid=1360

2. This is where nonprofit arts organizations need to keep abreast of change, as "the internet of things" (the internet on watches, eyeglasses and other devices) becomes a reality. Websites must adapt to whatever that technology is. Falling behind in online donations is not an option.

3. http://www.crmsearch.com/crm-market-share.php

4. Giving Tuesday is an international day of giving, traditionally held the Tuesday following Thanksgiving in the U.S. Their website makes this easy to remember: Black Friday, Cyber Monday, Giving Tuesday. See www.givingtuesday.org for more information.

Resources

https://www.charitynavigator.org/index.cfm?bay=content.view&cpid=1360

http://www.crmsearch.com/crm-market-share.php

http://www.giarts.org/article/public-funding-arts-2014-update

http://www.gsb.stanford.edu/alumni/volunteering/act/service-areas/earned-income-assessment

http://www.guidestar.org/rxa/news/articles/2014/top-10-major-donor-fundraising-trends-for-2014-2015

http://mashable.com/2011/03/14/social-good-fundraising-tools/#mPiXORsMkmqH

https:nonprofitquarterly.org/philanthropy/24406-study-retaining-donors-through-and-after-recession-most-difficult-for-small-nonprofits.html

http://www.nten.org/article/report-release-the-2014-nonprofit-benchmarks-study/

http://mcs.smu.edu/artsresearch2014/articles/blog/smu%E2%80%99s-national-center-arts-research-publishes-second-major-report-arts-industry-health

http://www.socialvelocity.net/2014/04/does-your-nonprofit-know-how-to-attract-big-donors/

Appendix

ONLINE GRANT HINTS

NEA and other online grant applications are complex and as THE ART OF FUNDRAISING chapter says, "the (NEA) grantmaking stresses quality, excellence, and professionalism." The arts organization should have unique, special, or strong programs before contemplating spending limited fundraising time applying to the NEA. The NEA funds only specific, definable activities by professionally-staffed organizations. Review their grants and do talk to NEA staff before applying so your questions are answered and you are prepared to upload documents.

All NEA grants are administered through the portal www.grants.gov which requires a DUNS (Data Universal Numbering System) number, SAM (System for Award Management) number, and a series of verification steps prior to grants submission. This is time consuming, and staff will need weeks - or months - in advance of the application deadline to accomplish this work. SAM passwords will need to be updated regularly (They send out reminders, so make sure that key staff update and then carefully save the new password, or for organizations without staff, recruit a very small circle of committed board members to get the reminders.) You want only one person changing the password, but it is a good idea to give more than one staff and board member access so there is redundancy.

This process is rife with pitfalls. In the hours following the Stimulus, when the NEA fought for and was given an extra $50 million to award, systems were overloaded, yet there were no options to circumvent the online portal. At least one applicant was saved from being turned down, by documenting the steps they tried, and then reporting them to NEA staff, but diligence and a sincere effort had to be demonstrated. One should not assume that this will be repeated, so document, create a check off list, put dates on the calendar when to check back, and follow up.

(Note: To both aid in evaluation and statistics gathering, several foundations and state arts agencies use a Common Application form that asks questions in a specific order, limits word counts, and calls for letters of reference or letters of agreement, stating that organizations are partnering on a grant. The Arts Extension Service offers a grantwriting course that covers the Common Application in depth.)

Volunteers in the Arts

PAM KORZA

Volunteers constitute a key resource for arts organizations. In a field where economic pressures make the flexible use of people and skills a must, volunteers can provide essential services at all levels from staff to board to one-time helper. They extend staff resources by assisting or even running ongoing programs and services, launching new projects, serving on committees, providing invaluable clerical or technical support, researching, and documenting. Volunteers may lend professional skills and advice—accounting, carpentry, graphic design—which can save arts organizations considerable money. And volunteers lend fresh and diverse perspectives and enthusiasm. In addition, volunteer involvement in your organization reflects the community's commitment to your organization, as well as your interest in having its input.

This chapter focuses on integrating volunteers into a cultural organization which can support both ongoing and special activities. The principles presented regarding motivating, managing, and rewarding volunteers are equally applicable to your arts education committee chairperson, a college student intern working on a social media campaign, or the helper who occasionally assists with bulk mailings. Considerations about recruiting, orienting, and managing board members as a specific type of volunteer are discussed in the Board Development chapter.

Age-Old Motivations, Changing Conditions

The enjoyment and artistic stimulation the arts provide has always attracted people to volunteer. In general, the things that motivate people to volunteer have remained much the same over time. They reflect an individual's values, needs, interests, and desire for self-fulfillment. Volunteer work offers opportunities to:

- help others and make a difference;
- learn new things and develop new skills;
- belong to a group or institution;
- be needed;
- have fun;
- grow personally and gain self-esteem;
- share skills, knowledge, or talents;
- gain meaningful acknowledgment;
- enhance one's public image;
- gain valuable career insights;
- make professional contacts;
- enjoy social contact with others; and
- support causes in which one believes.

Who is most likely to volunteer? According to the U.S. Bureau of Labor Statistics, over a quarter of the population volunteers their time to support nonprofit causes. These volunteers tend to be women (28.3% vs. 22% of men), between the ages of 35-44 (29.8% of all volunteers), married (30% of all volunteers), and employed part-time vs. full-time (31.7% vs. 26.5%).

Yet, while the desire to volunteer remains strong, the conditions which enable people to volunteer have changed dramatically over the years. According to the Bureau of Labor Statistics, working adults are the most often tapped pool of volunteers (volunteering at a rate of 27.5 percent). Because they have to juggle demanding jobs and family obligations, many are cautious about making long-term commitments they might be unable to fulfill. Today's volunteers want to serve responsibly within the limited amount of time they have to devote to volunteer activities.

For arts organizations to succeed at developing a volunteer base of support given such competing demands for volunteers' time, they must make volunteering as easy and accessible as possible. Best practices to overcome these obstacles include: structuring a volunteer program so that it involves short-term commitments and flexible hours, providing choices about the types of jobs that match an individual's skills and preferences, minimizing arduous paperwork that might discourage people from applying, and appealing to motivations unique to certain groups, such as those over 55 and people of color.

The Need For a Volunteer Program

To recruit discerning prospective volunteers, organizations must "sell" themselves. It is essential to plan ahead of time what you want and can offer. This means developing a serious, well-planned volunteer program.

GETTING THE ORGANIZATION READY

A first step in preparing your organization to fully incorporate volunteers is to assess staff attitudes and preconceived notions about volunteers.

Attitudes. The planned integration of volunteers into an organization may elicit from staff a variety of concerns and questions: Can we maintain our standards of quality with volunteers providing service? How much time will it take to effectively manage them? I've been burned before when I counted on volunteers who didn't come through; I'd rather do it myself. What about the safety of children in our care with volunteers? These concerns must be acknowledged and dealt with in order to agree upon the purpose of the volunteer program and to foster an environment in which volunteers are respected and nurtured, but also where policies and expectations are clear to volunteers.

Roles. Organization staff and board members should also clearly communicate their roles and degree of involvement in each volunteer's work. Who will coordinate the volunteer program—recruitment, placement, and tending to volunteer group needs? Assuming there is staff, what will be individual staff members' roles regarding interviewing, selecting, training, evaluating, and firing? Such planning also clarifies a volunteer's rights, for example, to have information that enables her to carry out her work, defining limits, responsibilities, and authority. This could include selecting artists for the arts agency's community gallery or negotiating advertising rates when selling ads for a program book.

Practical concerns. Also consider the following practical issues:

- **Work space.** Can you provide work stations, phones, office supplies, and computers to enable volunteers to be effective?
- **Accessibility.** Can you make volunteer opportunities accessible to people with disabilities or for whom transportation might be a problem (teens, seniors, low-income individuals)?
- **Policies.** What are your policies regarding reimbursement of expenses related to volunteering, benefits such as free or reduced tickets, or grounds for termination? Will you acquire volunteer liability insurance?
- **Risk management.** If you serve young people, how will you manage the risk of volunteers working with children? How will you control access to sensitive information on internal database systems? If your organization has valuable collections, how will you secure these collections? How will you address the risk of volunteers who are injured in the course of their work for you?

COMPONENTS OF A VOLUNTEER PROGRAM

A successful volunteer program has the following components:

- **Purpose statement.** This statement describes why the organization includes volunteers, and how volunteers can contribute meaningfully to the mission and vision of the organization.
- **Coordinator.** Someone, either paid or volunteer, should have primary responsibility for planning and implementing the volunteer program and monitoring volunteer needs.
- **Policies.** Policies can include reimbursements, insurance, free tickets to events and other perks, methods of communication, as well as disciplinary policies.
- **Recruitment.** Volunteer recruitment requires methods and tools to identify and enlist prospective volunteers; discover volunteer interests, abilities, and experiences; and determine potential positions.
- **Selection and placement.** For proper placement, one must first determine which persons are most qualified or have potential for particular volunteer positions, and what positions are most suitable for each individual.
- **Training.** All volunteers should engage in an orientation process that prepares and equips them with the necessary information, knowledge, and skills to do an effective job.
- **Support.** Volunteers need ongoing guidance, support, recognition, and gratitude for their work.
- **Evaluation.** Appropriate processes must be put in place to solicit volunteers' evaluations on their experiences. These evaluations should be used to make necessary changes to the volunteer program and keep it functioning effectively.

Evaluating Who You Need and Where to Find Them

In order to be clear with potential volunteers about what specifically they can do, it is first necessary for you to evaluate your own organizational needs.

- What are the specific jobs, tasks, or projects that must be done in the organization?
- Is it more cost-effective to use volunteers or staff to accomplish activities and objectives? What is the potential to enhance or compromise the quality of programs and services with volunteers versus staff?
- How can jobs best be broken down in terms of responsibilities, time commitment, difficulty, interest, and balance? For example, in trying to attract busy, working people, consider how jobs can be structured to be accomplished and monitored on weeknights or weekends when many people are more likely to be available.
- What are the volunteer benefits associated with each job?
- Are you looking for "members" with long-term needs (social, self-actualizing, learning, contributing) or "joiners" with short-term ones (social contacts, affiliation, status)?

> According to the 2014 State of Volunteering in America study by the Corporation for National and Community Service, the "top volunteer activities included fundraising or selling items to raise money (25.4 percent); collecting, preparing, distributing, or serving food (24.2 percent); providing transportation and general labor support (19.6 percent); tutoring and teaching youth (18 percent); mentoring youth (17.3 percent); and lending professional and management expertise (15 percent)."

JOB DESCRIPTIONS

Drafting job descriptions serves several purposes. From your organization's standpoint, it forces you to summarize the work that needs to be done—assessing how many people are required, estimating work hours, projecting deadlines. It makes actual recruitment simpler and clearer. From the volunteers' viewpoint, it offers a more realistic picture of what they are getting into and what they can expect to gain by being involved in your organization.

The job description most often expresses an ideal. In recruiting it is important to remain appropriately flexible and to balance the pros and cons of what each applicant has to offer. Perhaps two people with complementary skills can do the job better than either one alone. Keep in mind the implications of compromises, however. Two people require twice as much oversight on your part, at least at first.

Allow room to grow. Aim for balance between specifying responsibilities and leaving room for the volunteer's own initiative to shape the job. Example:

Sample Volunteer Job Description

JOB TITLE

Publicity assistant for On the Road Theater

JOB DESCRIPTION

Assist publicity coordinator with the following tasks:

- write press releases;
- write radio advertising copy;
- make and follow through on media contacts (feature writers, television, and radio personnel);
- arrange guest spots on local radio and TV shows;
- update media mailing and email lists; and
- orchestrate mass mailings and e-mailings.

SKILLS AND INTERESTS NECESSARY OR HELPFUL FOR JOB

- Good writing and interpersonal communication skills
- Computer skills helpful, but will train
- Knowledge of and interest in theater preferred

JOB BENEFITS

- Receive intensive one-on-one training in various aspects of publicity
- Gain knowledge of how a touring theater group functions
- Gain free admission to all shows or one complimentary ticket per show

TRAINING PROVIDED

- Copy writing
- Targeting markets
- Writing press releases
- Information/mailing systems management
- Developing media relationships

HOURS PER WEEK RECOMMENDED

Six to ten, depending on flow of local and regional tour schedule

ANTICIPATED LENGTH OF INTERNSHIP

Minimum six months or ongoing

OTHER INFORMATION/COMMENTS

The volunteer will have the chance to work with and learn from a lively and credentialed promotion staff of two! She or he will also have opportunity to get to know the artists in the company during down time through special seminars set up for volunteers.

On the Road Theater can work with college students and appropriate college programs to help students earn college credit for this volunteer opportunity.

Staff Person:_____ Date:_____

WHERE TO FIND VOLUNTEERS

Sources of volunteers are many. It is useful to first profile who your current volunteers are since they reflect likely sources of new recruits. What are their characteristics? What has motivated them to volunteer with you?

To focus your recruitment, determine the type of volunteers you are seeking, considering factors such as:

- special skills or knowledge (bookkeeping, social media expertise, database management, research);
- particular ages and backgrounds (nearby residents, teens, people of color, seniors, low income, young professionals, people with disabilities); and
- numbers (for example, large numbers needed for a short-term opportunity such as a festival or fundraising campaign).

These factors will suggest likely places to look for qualified prospects, as described by the volunteer coordinator for a children's museum:

> It is important for the Children's Museum to recruit young people as volunteers. We wanted the youngest children who come to the museum to have role models from their community, and we needed the perspectives of young people as part of our team. Those who had grown up using the museum were a likely source of youth volunteers. We used our membership lists and also went to local junior and senior high school art classes. The Latino children who live in the community where the museum is located had not visited the museum much. We decided to put together a teen council comprising Latinos to advise us on programming, image, and other things which would help us better serve this community. We identified Latino youth with the help of the nearby church and a Puerto Rican neighborhood center.

Besides identifying skills and characteristics to define sources of volunteers, use your accumulated list of volunteer factors to help you to narrow down the field of prospects. Then conduct targeted recruitment.

RECRUITING AND INVOLVING FOR DIVERSITY

As communities experience increasingly diverse populations, there is value in diversifying your arts organization's volunteer base to reflect and connect with that diverse community. However, methods and approaches for recruiting and providing positive experiences that have worked effectively in more homogenous settings may not be as useful in more diverse environments. Arts organizations need to understand and be sensitive to cultural norms and life circumstances that may affect how various groups will respond to your organization and its volunteer needs. They will need to develop culturally-sensitive ways to reach these diverse groups. In an article for *The Journal of Volunteer Administration*, diversity consultant Santiago Rodriquez explained that in the United States, there are a great number of community-based organizations focusing on volunteer activities. But he explains:

> …this phenomenon may not be representative of many other societies where extended family groupings, religious organizations, and government may play greater roles…. Community-based volunteerism, for example, is relatively rare in the traditional Hispanic and Asian contexts—families and churches may play a greater role…. Activities such as fundraising, how people are managed, and how decisions are made within groups are affected by different cultural norms. Diversity, then, is about learning to include different perspectives and processes so that the work of the organization can be as effective as possible.

If people of color, senior citizens, people with disabilities, teens, people who are economically disadvantaged, or others are not frequenting your programs or using your services, it is almost a sure bet that they are not volunteering in or reflected in the leadership of your organization either. As is true in

Sources of Volunteers

COMMUNITY AND PROFESSIONAL ASSOCIATIONS

- Civic organizations
- Church groups
- Trade associations
- Fraternal associations
- Labor unions often offer union gatherings and newsletters for the purpose of publicizing volunteer opportunities; some labor unions provide expertise of union members.

YOUTH

- Schools
- Arts-related programs (dance schools, drum corps)
- Clubs (scouts, 4-H)
- Church groups
- Vocational schools

BUSINESSES AND CORPORATIONS

- Companies sometimes have an executive loan program which enables employees to provide expertise or consultation to community organizations on company time.
- Business Volunteers for the Arts

PEOPLE OF COLOR

- Urban League
- National Association for the Advancement of Colored People (NAACP)
- Ethnic organizations
- Church groups
- Political, advocacy organizations
- African-American fraternities and sororities
- College departments (African American, Native American, Asian, Latin American studies)
- Neighborhood associations

VOLUNTEER AGENCIES

- City Cares of America
- Business Volunteers for the Arts
- Singles organizations

PEOPLE LOOKING FOR JOB RETRAINING OR CAREER SKILLS

- Unemployment office
- Career counselors

SENIOR CITIZENS

- Councils on Aging
- Senior centers
- RSVP (Retired and Senior Volunteer Program)
- Nursing homes
- Retirement communities

PEOPLE WITH DISABILITIES

- Statewide Very Special Arts (VSA) programs
- Associations for Retarded Citizens
- Schools and clubs for the deaf or blind
- State agencies for deaf and hard of hearing and blind

College Students

- Academic departments
- Internship programs
- Work/study programs
- Sororities and fraternities
- Clubs and service organizations
- Campus arts organizations
- Career services

Specialized Sources of Unpaid Workers

- Prison inmates or individuals with community service sentences
- U.S. Army Corps of Engineers (for traffic control, leveling earth, hauling major equipment, loaning and erecting tents)

any effort to engage and involve diverse populations, you must first look at how you are currently serving the interests of diverse groups through your programs. You may find that there is work to be done that first ensures that your organization is relevant to various segments of the community.

In recruiting volunteers from diverse populations, be clear on why you are interested in including them in your organization. Are you seeking multiple viewpoints, better service to constituencies, or enlightenment on issues or needs? Be sure your reasons are authentic and clear to you before you begin a recruitment plan.

Involve individuals from these groups to identify, recruit, and manage volunteers. If recruitment overtures, for example, are carried out exclusively by white or able-bodied members of your organization, these may be met with skepticism by those you are hoping to involve.

Make use of culturally specific media, organizations, and other resources in recruitment.

INTERNSHIP PROGRAMS

Internships are structured volunteer experiences which offer formal training and are designed as focused learning opportunities. Some arts organizations have developed internship programs, typically attracting college students wanting practical experience, but often times drawing adults who may be in career transition or recently retired and looking for meaningful experiences. Many college programs encourage—and even require—students to do internships as field training. Graduate degree programs in arts administration often require students to do full-semester, full-time internships to fulfill their degree requirements. In these cases, students are usually paid by the arts organization. In the case of internships, expectations on both the volunteer's and the agency's part are high, so special care must be taken in assessing needs, making placements, and providing specific training and formal evaluation.

Recruitment

Recruiting volunteers is not as simple as posting flyers saying that you need help. Effective recruitment first targets the people you believe offer what you're looking for and who might be interested in volunteering with you. Then you find the best way to connect with them. A positive impression will convince discriminating people that you can provide an interesting, well-organized, and personally meaningful experience with your organization.

Recruitment, whatever form it takes, should answer basic questions a volunteer may ask.

- What is the purpose of your organization?
- Why do you need volunteers?
- What will a volunteer get out of working with you?

You should be able to demonstrate to a potential volunteer that:

- your organization is a worthy, credible one;
- you are well-organized, take volunteers seriously, and won't waste the volunteer's time;
- your organization can provide a meaningful, fulfilling, and challenging experience while being flexible given the volunteer's time limitations and need for appropriate training;

- you have specific opportunities in the form of job descriptions; and
- others with similar experiences have been involved in a productive way in the organization.

RECRUITMENT TECHNIQUES

The same range of publicity and promotion opportunities that you use to market programs and services can be employed to announce volunteer opportunities as well. See the Marketing the Arts chapter for additional ideas.

Print and online. Through press releases, announcements on your social media sites, and online volunteer listing services like idealist.org or volunteermatch.org, you can reach broad segments of your community. More specialized media (an African-American newspaper, an online community with a large teen following) are effective in reaching certain segments.

Feature articles and interviews on local television shows. These are great ways to recognize a particular volunteer's efforts or a recent major accomplishment, and to promote the program at the same time.

E-Newsletters. Your organization's e-newsletters can offer an effective way to target those who are familiar with your organization.

Brochures, flyers, mailing inserts. To satisfy ongoing or specific volunteer needs, a promotional brochure or information sheet can provide immediate information and be used to reach targeted groups.

Personal contact. Because volunteering is a people affair, the most effective recruitment techniques are those enabling prospective volunteers to meet face-to-face with people involved in the organization. Presentations by staff and volunteers can be an excellent recruiting tool. Remember that volunteers who have had a good experience with your organization are often the most effective recruiters.

Person-to-person recruitment may take the form of:

- presentations to clubs, corporations, senior groups, schools;
- presentations before or after performances when people are excited about what you do;
- door-to-door, neighborhood meetings;
- open house; or
- word of mouth.

To recruit large numbers of volunteers for one purpose, the pyramid approach can be effective. Each board, staff, and key volunteer is responsible for recruiting a certain number of volunteers (say five), who in turn must each recruit additional volunteers (say two). By beginning with 20 individuals, you can recruit 200.

> The most effective recruitment techniques are those enabling prospective volunteers to meet face-to-face with people involved in the organization.

Volunteer agencies. Explore how national volunteer organizations can promote your arts organization to prospective volunteers:

- **Corporation for National and Community Service** (CNCS) is an independent federal agency and leading funder of volunteer service in the U.S. The CNCS runs several national volunteer programs, including SeniorCorps and AmeriCorps, and provides funding and support through its social innovation fund.
- **Points of Light Foundation** works in partnership with the **HandsOn Network** to help mobilize people and resources to find creative solutions to community problems.
- **Youth Service America** (YSA) is a resource center that partners with thousands of organizations committed to increasing the quality and quantity of volunteer opportunities for young people, ages 5-25, to serve locally, nationally, and globally.
- **VolunteerMatch** offers a variety of online services to support a community of nonprofit, volunteer, and business leaders committed to civic engagement.
- Other resources which may operate volunteer placement services include local volunteer liaisons, chambers of commerce, community development agencies, libraries, councils on aging, and other community-based organizations.

Consider the following to determine which techniques to employ:

- Are your volunteer needs ongoing or sporadic? Recruiting 500 festival volunteers for a three-day event requires different strategies than recruiting five volunteers who will share receptionist duties year-round.
- How much time and resource do you have for the recruitment process itself? What are your capabilities for handling response to the recruitment process?
- What technique(s) will be most effective in eliciting the response you would like?

Above all, when communicating with prospective volunteers, make it easy to say yes. While it is important to have an application process, avoid cumbersome and protracted application procedures. Be honest. Don't minimize challenges, time commitments, or other factors which you fear might discourage a volunteer. Whenever possible, send recruiters whose backgrounds reflect the types you are recruiting (i.e., send teens to recruit teens). Finally, stress the potential benefits to the volunteer and the people you serve rather than how your organization benefits from volunteers.

> When communicating with prospective volunteers, make it easy to say yes.

Selecting and Placing Volunteers

For responsible volunteer positions, especially longer-term or ongoing ones, it's important to choose volunteers who can be the best match for the job. Four steps are helpful in assuring appropriate selections:

1. Involve the person who will work most closely with the volunteer in the selection process.
2. Use a written application, but make it simple and suitable to the responders; use it to gain basic information about the person and his or her interests and qualifications.
3. Interview applicants to get to know each other's aspirations, goals, and interests, and to assess if a mutually beneficial match can be made.
4. Check references for volunteers who will be placed in highly responsible positions. In some states, you are required to conduct a criminal background check for volunteers who will come into con-

tact with children. You may wish to consider background checks as a part of your routine volunteer screening activities.

Ask yourself these questions when making final selections:

- What is the individual seeking from a volunteer experience?
- Can your needs be met given the skills, interests, and capabilities of the applicant?
- What are the applicant's personal qualities and how would she or he fit in the office?
- What is the applicant's availability?

REJECTING AND CONFIRMING VOLUNTEERS

It's not easy to reject an applicant for a volunteer position. The reason may be that you cannot make the right match of skills and job so that both the volunteer and your organization benefit. It's a good idea to state at the outset that sometimes more people are interested than you can accommodate. Even so, honestly assess an individual's skills and suitability. Suggest skill areas to strengthen. And provide alternatives, referring the applicant to local volunteer agencies or other arts groups with whom the applicant may find a more suitable opportunity.

Whether or not you accept an applicant, make decisions expeditiously and notify candidates on the status of their applications. Too much elapsed time leads good people to lose interest and pursue other opportunities.

Getting a Good Start

Once a volunteer is on board, a number of practical steps can be taken to ensure a successful experience for both the volunteer and the organization. Primary among them are a memorandum of agreement, orientation, and training.

MEMO OF AGREEMENT

At the outset clarify expectations about the volunteer's role on a project or in the organization. For a volunteer assigned to your fundraising auction, simply explaining expectations before the volunteer goes on duty, perhaps with a written information sheet for referral during the job, may suffice. If the volunteer position is long-term—for example, a semester-long student internship or a yearlong festival chairmanship, a memo of agreement can formalize the understanding of expectations for both parties. Such an agreement is generally similar to a job description and specifies:

- the volunteer's responsibilities and tasks;
- the volunteer's personal goals for the job; and
- the organization's obligations (travel reimbursement, training opportunities, evaluation procedures, etc.).

A memo of agreement fosters a sense of commitment by both parties to meet their obligations to each other. It may establish a trial period during which both volunteer and organization can assess if things are working out. It is also a reference tool as the volunteer's experience is periodically evaluated. At the same time, a memo of agreement should remain flexible and open to revision as the job needs to change or as a volunteer grows into new responsibilities.

ORIENTATION

Orientation integrates volunteers into your organization's activity. It should address needs on three levels: individual, group, and task.

Individual Needs

Individual needs are most basic and should be addressed first. Take care to make new volunteers feel welcome, comfortable, and a part of your organization. This may be accomplished by developing a buddy system where seasoned volunteers can help new volunteers get started, learning individual interests of volunteers and engaging in non-work conversation, providing the volunteer with a space to work, giving sufficient attention and training in the early stages, and, most importantly, monitoring how the individual's own motivating factors are being met.

Group Needs

Orient new volunteers to your organization. Cover the background, history, achievements, and aspirations of the organization, its programs, procedures, timelines, staff structure, and relevant policies. This may be done by inviting a new volunteer to a staff meeting, holding a special orientation meeting for several new volunteers, or making available annual reports, newsletters, and other written materials that convey a picture of the group. Volunteers should feel like they can get to know staff members even if they may not work directly with all of them.

Make sure that staff and board members introduce themselves and their roles to new volunteers individually or at an orientation meeting or reception so that volunteers connect to the people of your organization. Show how each member works toward and contributes to the larger picture. This team building creates a sense of belonging, of place, and helps to establish work and social relationships.

> Team building creates a sense of belonging, of place, and helps to establish work and social relationships.

Task Needs

Even the most experienced professional or savvy volunteer may benefit from orientation to the steps and mechanics of the tasks at hand. Struggling with the quirks of the office copy machine can be as frustrating to completing a task efficiently as composing a fundraising letter for the first time. For any new undertaking, stop and remember that this may be a new skill for the volunteer—newcomer or veteran volunteer.

Orientation to tasks is most often accomplished one-on-one between a supervisor and a volunteer. Procedures manuals and instruction sheets are useful written tools. More extensive training may be critical for more demanding activities, such as making fundraising calls or coordinating an artist residency program.

Training

Training is an investment in your organization. It helps a volunteer to acquire knowledge and skills beyond specific individual tasks. Through training, volunteers understand their jobs better, take initiative, and therefore contribute in a deeper, more meaningful way. It is also an expression of your belief in volunteers' capabilities and value to the organization.

> Training is an investment in your organization.... It is also an expression of your belief in volunteers' capabilities and value to the organization.

Training may take a variety of forms, depending on the nature of the job and the skills being taught. These might include:

- one-on-one training, provided by a staff or board member, or a senior volunteer;
- in-house workshops, presentations, discussions, practice, or role play; or
- attendance at conferences or workshops, or enrollment in continuing education or college courses.

Volunteer Management

In rewarding relationships, there is a balance reflecting what both parties are getting from the association. If one party stands to gain disproportionately and this is apparent to the other, productivity sometimes diminishes. Everyone deserves to gain the satisfaction they expect.

Volunteer management is simultaneously the management of human relations and the management of work that needs to get done effectively. To be most productive and fulfilled, volunteers need to be supervised and nurtured on an ongoing basis, with special attention given to keeping each person motivated. Central to this process is effective communication. This means setting up regular opportunities to check on one's progress on specific tasks, to work out problems which arise, and to talk about how the volunteer is feeling about her work. It also involves ongoing evaluation and a willingness to make changes as the volunteer adjusts to the position.

> Volunteer management is simultaneously the management of human relations and the management of work that needs to get done effectively.

LEADERSHIP

Effective volunteer managers recognize potential in people and maximize opportunities to develop and utilize talents while keeping their eyes on the goals of the organization or project at hand. To accomplish this, those overseeing volunteers need to recognize that different situations call for different approaches or styles of leadership and problem solving. Good leadership utilizes the potential and resources of the individual or group. When a volunteer is involved in and buys into pertinent decisions, confidence is built and commitment is reinforced.

> Those overseeing volunteers need to recognize that different situations call for different approaches or styles of leadership and problem solving.

The Volunteer Coordinator

Recruiting, training, and managing volunteers requires time, energy, and planning. For an organization intending to work regularly with volunteers, a coordinator to oversee volunteers and to work with staff is essential. The coordinator could be a staff member, a board member, or even a volunteer. In any case, the volunteer coordinator's job includes many responsibilities.

PLANNING

- Guide staff to define volunteer positions.
- Identify volunteer needs for various projects.
- Develop timelines for recruitment and training.
- Research `potential volunteer sources.

RECRUITMENT, PLACEMENT, AND ORIENTATION

- Recruit volunteers.
- Oversee or implement the review and selection process.
- Orient volunteers.
- Train and monitor training by others.
- Lead by outlining organizational goals, modeling professional behavior, and providing direction, guidance, and assistance.

MANAGEMENT

- Organize meetings.
- Monitor morale, work load, quality, and quantity of work, the learning experience, and additional volunteer needs.
- Replace volunteers who leave.
- Keep records on the volunteer program, including volunteer contact information, letters of recommendation, and quantifiable information such as the number of volunteer hours contributed per year and the economic value of program.
- Facilitate information flow among staff and volunteers through meetings, email announcements, etc.
- Provide support and recognition.

EVALUATION

- Provide mechanisms for assessment of volunteer work through meeting and discussion, and for volunteer assessment of the project, organization, and volunteer program.

RECOGNITION

- Monitor staff or others who are overseeing volunteers' work to ensure ongoing recognition.
- Provide meaningful recognition, suitable to the volunteer's job, tenure, and accomplishments.

Effective leaders:

- develop trust among those who work together;
- introduce challenges at appropriate times and accept risk;
- balance learning by mistake with averting mistakes;
- demonstrate confidence in volunteers, once it's earned;
- share individual and collective achievements with the entire group;
- model professional behavior and standards;
- project a positive view of the organization, its work, and people;
- perceive unspoken needs and foster a communicative environment;
- keep focused on the vision and the goals, and keep the work in context of its significance and impact;
- help unravel and break down tasks;
- provide information tools;
- help solve problems effectively; and
- empower volunteers with decision-making opportunities when they are ready.

See the Volunteer Coordinator sidebar for the roles embodied in this position.

RETAINING VOLUNTEERS

Some organizations have taken into account the changing conditions described at the beginning of this chapter and restructured their volunteer programs to accommodate flexible opportunities for people with demanding lives. They have, for example, shifted their expectations from longer- to shorter-term commitments.

Yet organizations still need long-term commitments from board members or other key volunteers where continuity is an advantage. So it is frustrating when a board member resigns prematurely, a key volunteer leaves due to burnout, or a promising volunteer mysteriously quits midstream. Problems of volunteer retention can often be traced to ineffective recruitment, placement, orientation, training, or management. Many of these experiences can be averted by following some of the advice provided throughout this chapter.

Below are common reasons organizations lose volunteers and suggested approaches for prevention.

Burnout
- Recruit enough volunteers.
- Divide labor to reduce the work load.
- Allow longer lead time to accomplish the work.
- Encourage delegation among volunteers.
- Provide leaves of absence.
- Respect people's limits.
- Make time for fun!

Loss of interest
- Make sure the position matches the volunteer's interests and expectations.
- Provide enough to do.

- Offer more challenge.
- Make clear the ways that the position makes a difference—the reasons for routine or clerical tasks—and provide support.
- Recognize accomplishments on a regular basis and when a volunteer's efforts have helped to meet project/organizational goals.
- Offer outside opportunities for new learning or ways to understand the big picture of the organization.
- Rotate responsibilities to offer variety.
- Lighten up and have fun!

Lack of motivation
- Match assignments with interests and motivations.
- Equip the volunteer with the information, tools, and support to tackle the job.
- Steer activity toward clear-cut successes.
- Offer more challenge.
- Provide opportunities for advancement and participation in decision-making or new programs.
- Validate positive effort through recognition and appreciation, both formal (events, certification, awards) and informal.
- Have fun!

Low energy
- Check the work conditions—space, supplies, scheduling, transportation—for possible problems.
- Keep an eye on the work load, providing a balance between work and play. Have fun!
- Be sensitive to personal or other factors competing for a volunteer's attention.

Interpersonal difficulties
- Keep lines of communication open.
- Detect problems before they flare up; anticipate trouble spots.
- Check organizational attitudes toward volunteers.
- Reassign a volunteer to a new staff person.

RECOGNITION AND THANKS

Volunteers need ongoing recognition and thanks for their contributions. Most important, recognize and thank an individual volunteer in a way that is meaningful to him or her. If a volunteer is motivated to learn new skills, then sending him to a weekend workshop may be exactly the recognition needed: It says that you believe in his capabilities enough to invest in his training. A corporate executive who has volunteered time to put your books in order may be best served by a letter of thanks praising her help and sent to her employer as evidence of community service. For another volunteer seeking to make a difference in the lives of disadvantaged children, seeing the play produced in an artist residency may be the greatest possible reward.

Arts organizations have approached this important aspect of volunteerism in a variety of creative ways.

- Training opportunities
- Promotion to increased responsibility
- Involvement in decision-making
- Certificates of appreciation

- Complimentary or reduced price tickets to programs
- Recognition in the media through feature articles, thank you ads, letters to the editor, or newsletter features
- Birthday celebrations
- T-shirts, pins, etc.
- Parties
- Special opportunities, such as meeting guest artists

However you show appreciation, tailor it to the individual as much as possible. Both individual and team recognition can help people feel good about their work and their contributions to the organization.

> Over 500 volunteers support the work of the Springfield Museums in Springfield, Massachusetts, a complex of art, history, and science museums in the center of this mid-sized city. The two art museums have a strong corps of docents (volunteer tour guides) that lead tours for schoolchildren and adults, and assist with many other educational programs offered by the museums. Docents are carefully trained in the art work they are interpreting through a semester-long course in art history, and new docents shadow experienced docents to learn how to give highly interactive tours for schoolchildren. Every docent is carefully interviewed for the volunteer position, and each signs a contract promising to deliver a certain number of tours after they are trained. At the end of each year, their exceptional service is rewarded at an annual awards ceremony. Informal volunteer recognition events are held throughout the year, such as picnics and other gatherings, to help to build camaraderie and good will amongst docents.

EVALUATION

Supervision and evaluation also should be appropriate to the job and the volunteer. A new ticket seller may need to be monitored by a veteran volunteer during her first shift or two. Volunteers involved in more extensive roles benefit from regular feedback on their work. Ongoing monitoring and feedback helps ensure quality and detects problems before they flare up. It is helpful when a new volunteer comes on board to discuss how you plan to monitor and evaluate work and to ask what will be the most helpful way to provide feedback.

Evaluation is a two-way street. It is as important for you to know how the volunteer experience is working for the volunteer as it is for the volunteer to know how he is doing. Evaluation questionnaires are useful for collecting information from volunteers about their own experience and about the volunteer program, both midstream and at the end of a volunteer experience. Organizations should also consider some deliberate way of learning volunteers' opinions about and recommendations for the job they did—an evaluation form, an exit interview, a lunchtime debriefing, or a project staff meeting.

Conclusion

A successful volunteer program meets the needs of both the organization and the volunteer. This shows in the achievement of your organization's goals and in the personal and professional growth of your volunteers. Strive to create an environment in which people are encouraged to give their best and to grow in qualities such as commitment, confidence, productivity, initiative, cooperation, imagination, self-esteem, and pride in work well done.

Financial Management in the Arts

CHRISTINE BURDETT
with contributing editors
SALLY ZINNO, MAREN BROWN, *and* CAROL HARPER

Many volunteers and staff of community arts organizations are intimidated by the prospect of managing the financial aspects of their organizations or programs. Preparing and analyzing budgets is often delegated to an accountant or banker on the board—or assigned to a staff member who lacks training in financial management. In many cases, such people bring their personal financial habits to their work environments. If someone in a financial management position is accustomed to accumulating credit card debt and unsecured personal loans, or failing to balance his or her checking account, the effect can be devastating if these habits are transferred to the financial management of an organization.

By law, financial responsibility rests with every member of the board, who are "fiduciaries," caring for the nonprofit organization as a public trust for the rest of the community. Financial management is such a fundamental aspect of organizational sustainability that every board and staff member should understand the basics. Fortunately, the principles of financial management are easy to understand and well within the grasp of every key member of an organization. Even in organizations with extensive programs and significant budgets, the board and staff can find qualified financial advice to ensure that the financial operations and data are appropriate.

Good financial management provides vital support to arts programs and important evidence of organizational stability to funding sources. Keeping accurate, up-to-date financial records guarantees that you will be ready any time records are requested by the IRS, donors, loan officers, or members. Those records are proof that the organization has upheld its fiscal responsibility. Most important, good financial management helps board members to govern effectively and staff members to operate efficiently, and it assures your constituency that your organization is run responsibly.

This chapter will help you understand the terminology and practices of financial management, so that your organization can prosper in good times and bad. It covers how to:

- designate responsibility for financial planning and evaluation;
- set financial objectives;
- learn an 8-step process for developing and monitoring a budget;
- evaluate options for record keeping;
- apply basic principles of accounting that affect nonprofits;
- prepare and read financial statements;
- analyze an organization's financial health using ratios;
- meet reporting requirements common to most nonprofits; and,
- foresee financial problems and opportunities.

The Management Control Cycle

In essence, financial management consists of three activities, constituting basic management controls:

- **First,** develop an annual budget that reflects your objectives, in measurable terms, for each program (such as art classes) or "business" area (such as a retail shop).
- **Second,** carry out your programs according to that financial plan, and measure financial performance against the objectives using operating statements at regular monthly or quarterly intervals.
- **Last,** compare actual revenues and expenses and cash flow to those predicted in the budget, and if necessary, adjust the projected budget to reflect corrective actions or to enable unanticipated opportunities.

Board Responsibility

When it comes to financial management, the ultimate responsibility lies with the board of directors. Financial management is the board's fiduciary responsibility, both as individuals and as a group. When board members take their financial responsibility seriously, they can feel confident that they are fulfilling their duty to build and retain public trust. Doing so makes it much less likely that they will encounter legal difficulties from mismanagement or debt. See the Board Development chapter for more information about the role of boards of directors.

One of the board's primary responsibilities is to ensure that the organization has the resources available to achieve its mission. That responsibility includes approving the budget and monitoring actual performance, as well as setting and enforcing fiscal policy. Ordinarily the board is advised by the treasurer, the finance committee, and a professional staff member (when there is one). It is each board member's responsibility, however, to understand the financial information they review, in order to make informed decisions.

Board and staff members need adequate time to review financial information before discussing or voting on it. Financial statements, budgets, and written explanations of the impact of the financial status on the organization should be available in advance of meetings to allow for examination and questions.

THE TREASURER'S ROLE

The treasurer is the board's chief financial representative. In smaller organizations with no director or finance staff, the treasurer may be responsible for signing legal financial documents, loan applications, or grant reports. The treasurer is also responsible for other key functions which may include bookkeeping, writing checks, reconciling bank statements, monitoring petty cash, preparing financial statements, and filing state and federal tax forms. When paid or volunteer staff members are assigned any of these tasks, the treasurer oversees their activities so that financial operations are performed in a responsible and ethical manner.

The treasurer is the primary communicator to the board concerning the organization's financial position, and helps the board to understand the organization's finances. Most meeting agendas include a treasurer's report to update the board on financial activity.

THE FINANCE COMMITTEE

The finance committee plays a key role in overseeing the financial operations of the organization and building public confidence in the organization's fiscal management. The committee advises the board on financial matters. Typically, it also:

- recommends an annual operating and capital budget and the multiyear budgets needed for long-term planning;
- monitors income and expenditures against budget and cash flow projections during the year and recommends changes to meet established goals;
- reviews and recommends financial policy and ensures compliance with legal reporting requirements; and
- oversees investments.

The Budget

A budget is a financial plan expressed in quantitative, monetary terms over a specific time period. It is the central instrument of financial planning and control. If a budget is prepared correctly and evaluated throughout the year, an organization can be forewarned of financial difficulty and take measures to prevent or minimize its impact.

Budgets may be presented in various formats, but they always reflect revenues and expenses and the difference between them. In financial management, the term revenues is used interchangeably with the word income, and the word expenses is sometimes substituted by the word costs. The difference between revenues and expenses is termed a surplus when revenues exceed expenses, and a deficit (a negative figure) when expenses exceed revenues.

WHY PREPARE A BUDGET?

A budget is the means by which arts managers allocate resources to fulfill organizational goals and objectives. A budget:

- provides a plan that helps guide management decisions;
- guides subsequent spending decisions and serves as a yardstick to measure actual performance;
- spurs the keeping and maintaining of adequate financial records;
- clarifies the need to expend scarce resources effectively and make appropriate investments;
- supports grant applications and fundraising campaigns; and
- provides an objective standard for evaluation.

WHO DEVELOPS THE BUDGET?

A budget projects anticipated revenues and expenses based on the organization's operational plan for the year. In all but the smallest organizations, the budget should be generated from the bottom up. People who make the day-to-day spending decisions and must live within a budget should have key roles in creating the budget. The program managers are closest to the action and understand best what expenses are incurred and what revenues are likely to be generated. If the board has a committee related to a particular program, the program manager often works with that committee chair or the committee as a whole to review the budget recommendations. The arts education manager, for example, would work with board's education committee on the budget for education programs and services.

THE BUDGET PROCESS

There are four basic types of budgets.

- Organizational budget: a financial plan developed for an overall operation.
- Program budget: a financial plan developed for a single project.
- Cash-flow budget: a projection of available cash over a specified time period.
- Capital budget: a projection of the facility, equipment, or leasehold improvements needed over a period of time that are greater than the organization's annual budget.

An organizational budget is created by combining all of the individual program budgets and adding general administrative revenues and expenses. A capital budget is created by establishing baseline information on existing fixed assets (facility, furniture, equipment, leasehold improvements) and projecting replacement and repair costs associated with those fixed assets over time.

Planning for the Replacement of Fixed Assets

Virtually every cultural nonprofit owns a variety of fixed assets. For some it may be an entire building, for others it may be sound equipment installed in a leased space. Whether it's a large fixed asset such as a building or something smaller, such as computers and printers, it's necessary to plan for its obsolescence, repair, and eventual replacement.

Each year an arts organization uses its assets to help achieve its mission, and each year these assets depreciate. In order for an organization to continue to operate, each year it should not only address preventative maintenance issues and repairs, but should also replace assets that have reached the end of their useful life. For example, based on materials and usage, roofs may need to be replaced every 20-30 years, furnaces every 10-15 years, furniture and fixtures every 5-7 years, ticketing equipment and computers every 3 years, and so on. The useful life of many of these assets can be estimated using IRS depreciation methods or more carefully evaluated by a trusted architect, engineer, or local tradesperson. Planning for the replacement of these items is an integral part of the organization's overall financial planning.

A cultural organization should proactively address its fixed-asset needs by creating a spreadsheet that tracks its fixed assets—estimating when they will need to be replaced and how much it might cost—and including some level of funding for depreciation in a maintenance reserve on its balance sheet. Most arts organizations choose to put this exercise on the back burner because the annual expense numbers can be quite daunting. However, it would be much worse to have the furnace fail during a week-long run of The Nutcracker and pay a premium for emergency repair services.

The process of evaluating an organization's fixed assets should begin with an inventory of what the organization already owns, identifying when each item was purchased and for how much, and if and when the items will need significant repairs. This inventory should include the organization's building(s), furniture, fixtures, and equipment. If the organization has a long-term lease and is responsible for major asset repairs and upgrades, as in a condominium arrangement, it should have some sense of what repairs are being planned by the lessor or management company and what the assessment would be.

Once an inventory has been completed, the organization should work with a knowledgeable board member, architect, engineer, or local tradesperson to evaluate the condition of the assets and project when these assets will need to be replaced. Once an inventory spreadsheet has been created, the organization should project in what year each item might be replaced and how much that item will cost, remembering to account for inflation. An accounting professional should be able to help estimate these future costs.

Most organizations have a significant amount of annual maintenance that is deferred to future years. These projects should be reviewed and completed in a systematic manner, such as one section of the building at a time, or when the facility is not at its peak use. All deferred maintenance issues should be prioritized and reassessed each year by the organization. Health and safety issues should always be at the top of the list. Smoke detectors, elevators, and other life and safety systems may need to be inspected yearly by the local authorities and must therefore always be code compliant. Replacing, repairing or modernizing items like these also involves other system reviews like electrical and water, and can be more complicated than initially planned. Ideas on how to integrate energy-saving measures into these improvements can be found in the chapter on Greening Your Arts Nonprofit.

Always pay attention to changes in the industry as well as in safety and building codes. For example, by 2014 all major feature films were produced digitally, and if cinemas had not upgraded their equipment in time, their ability to show feature films would have ceased. Fires at crowded events often result in public officials changing current health and safety regulations. Although some resources are devoted to updating older facilities, organizations ultimately have to comply with local building codes, as well as ADA regulations, in order to operate. Further discussion of ADA regulations are in the Cultural Access chapter.

Another factor to consider is the related cost of expanding or renovating facilities. Many arts organizations build new additions without factoring in the impact on annual operating costs associated with increased energy usage, maintenance, and other necessities.

One nonprofit organization that may be able to help work through this evaluation with you is the Nonprofit Finance Fund (www.nonprofitfinancefund.org), which has created a Systems Replacement Plan to help organizations review their fixed-asset needs.

Each organization's budget process must be developed to fit its governing procedures and mix of board and staff members. Some boards will expect their treasurer or finance committee to take the lead on budgeting, while others will entrust budget development to professional staff. Boards that meet quarterly should plan their budgets earlier in the fiscal year than boards that meet monthly.

An annual budget is based on the program and operational plan determined by the board and staff as well as the capital investments indicated in the capital plan for the coming year. The board and staff must first agree on the annual program goals and priorities and the administrative and operating objectives required to achieve them. The budget process, then, attaches expenses and revenues to the strategies required to implement the plan.

Eight Steps to Budgeting

Preparing a budget is a dynamic process that follows eight key steps. We will illustrate these steps using a fictional organization, "the City Center for the Arts" (CCA), as a hypothetical case study.

1. *Establish budget guidelines.* The board determines budgetary guidelines, including setting the fiscal year (accounting period covering 12 consecutive months over which an organization determines earnings and profits); anticipated percentage increases in salaries or inflation; the target for the annual bottom-line budget surplus; dates by which budget drafts and the final version must be prepared; and other general guidelines.

   > CCA's budget covers one fiscal year, July 1 to June 30. Its general guidelines are that the total budget must generate a surplus in the range of $8,000–$15,000 and that salaries and general overhead will be presented in separate budget lines, rather than prorated among the various programs).

2. *Develop program budgets.* Program managers, working with committee chairs as appropriate, create a revenue and expense budget for each program area and earned income service, such as a retail store. (See the shaded Artist in Residence column in Figure 1.). Costs must be researched and revenues conservatively estimated for each program. Individual programmatic budgets are considered tentative until the full organizational budget is approved by the board.
   Capital expenditures, if needed, are part of a separate capital budgeting process that plans for asset investments that make the most sense for the organization. Program managers, together with either the chief executive or the facility manager, research costs and prepare a budget and timeline for the work.
3. *Draft the organizational budget.* The chief executive or finance committee adds together the program budgets with overall administrative expenses and needed capital expenditures into a single organizational budget for the year, as illustrated in Figure 1a.
4. *Refine the budget.* The board reviews the total picture to see if it meets budget guidelines and is realistic and achievable. It then negotiates potentially conflicting uses of resources, eliminates excessive costs, and combines resources to prevent deficits. Income projections from grants and contributions are discussed, approved or changed by the fundraising committee and development staff.
5. *Consider and approve the final budget.* Though one cannot underestimate the importance of program-level budgeting, the budget presented to the board should include a "total" column that summarizes all expenses and revenues by line item. This enables the board to more easily focus on the overall mission and operating activities needed to support the organization. See Figure 1 Total Column.

   > If the program summary format is used, the same presentation of income and expenses should be used in a statement of activities report that compares budget to actual performance throughout the year (see the Statement of Activities section below). The figures in the Projected Budget column of the sample Statement of Activities below correspond to the totals from the worksheets completed in steps 2 and 3, above. The board compares these to the previous year's actual figures and budget. Unusual deviations, higher or lower, are explained in accompanying notes.

   The budget for the following fiscal year should be approved before the start of that year.

Figure 1a: City Center for the Arts' Organizational Budget

DESCRIPTION	TOTAL	ADMIN - General Admin.	PROGRAMS - Artists in Residence	PROGRAMS - Jazz Concerts	PROGRAMS - Arts Festival	PROGRAMS - Theatre Performances	FUNDRAISING - Member Ship	FUNDRAISING - Special Events	FUNDRAISING - Other
Program Expenses									
Artists' Fees	**125,000**		72,000	20,000	3,000	30,000			
Materials	**27,500**		17,000	1,000	2,500	7,000			
Production Expense	**26,000**			4,000	2,000	20,000			
Ad/Print/Design Fees	**14,000**		3,500	3,000	3,000	3,500		1,000	
Special Event Expense	**12,500**							12,500	
Subtotal Program Expenses	**205,000**								
% of Total Expenses	40%								
% of Total Revenues	39%								
Occupancy Expenses									
Utilities	**19,000**	7,500	3,000	2,000	1,500	4,000		1,000	
Insurance	**26,000**	21,000	1,000	1,000	1,000	2,000			
Equipment	**0**								
Purchase *	**0**								
Repair	**30,000**	14,000	5,000	2,000	2,000	5,000		2,000	
Rental	**0**								
Interest Expense	**27,100**	27,100							
Depreciation/Amortization	**33,190**	16,615	3,315	3,315	3,315	3,315			3,315
Subtotal Occupancy Expenses	**135,290**								
% of Total Expenses	26%								
% of Total Revenues	26%								
Administrative Expenses									
Salaries	**101,000**	15,000	15,000	10,000	5,000	15,000			41,000
Payroll Taxes	**10,100**	6,000							4,100
Benefits (15%-30% of salary)	**30,300**	18,000							12,300
Supplies/Postage/Other	**5,700**	1,000					2,000	2,000	700
Travel/Training/Entertainment	**3,900**	1,000					900	1,000	1,000
Audit/Legal/Other Fees	**10,000**	10,000							
Computer Fees/Web Licenses	**10,000**	5,000					2,500		2,500
Bank & Other Fees	**5,500**	5,500							
Subtotal Admin Expenses	**176,500**								
% of Total Expenses	34%								
% of Total Revenues	33%								
Total Operating Expenses	516,790	147,715	119,815	46,315	23,315	89,815	5,400	19,500	64,915
Building & Equipment Purchases	**60,807**								
Cash Reserve	10,000								

Note that the Building & Equipment purchases and cash reserve are not operating expenses, but capital expenses and reserve funds that are part of the capital planning and reserves to cover cash flow needs, which is why they are not included in the total expense figure.

Figure 1b: City Center for the Arts' Organizational Budget

DESCRIPTION	TOTAL	ADMIN General Admin.	PROGRAMS Artists in Residence	Jazz Concerts	Arts Festival	Theatre Performances	FUNDRAISING Member Ship	Special Events	Other
Individual Contributions	18,000	18,000							
Membership Drive	45,000						45,000		
Board Contributions	30,000	25,000							5,000
Corporate Grants	55,000	5,000	10,000	10,000	5,000	20,000			5,000
Foundation Grants	50,000	5,000	10,000	5,000	15,000	5,000			10,000
Government Grants	0								
Federal	2,500			2,500					
State	20,000		5,000	7,500	5,000	2,500			
Local	2,000				2,000				
Special Events	28,000							28,000	
Total Contributed Revenue	250,500								
% of Total Revenues	48%								
Ticket Sales	90,000		2,000	35,000	5,000	48,000			
Class & Workshop Tuition	145,000		115,000	10,000		20,000			
Rental Income	23,000	23,000							
Retail Shop Sales	12,000	12,000							
Advertising Sales	6,400			2,400		4,000			
Total Earned Revenue	276,400								
% of Total Revenues	52%								
Investment Income	100	100							
Total Investment Revenue	100								
% of Total Revenues	0.02%								
TOTAL REVENUES	527,000	88,100	142,000	72,400	32,000	99,500	45,000	28,000	20,000

6. *Share the final budget with others in the organization.* The board or chief executive communicates the approved budget back to the committee or staff responsible for each program.
7. *Monitor the budget.* The staff, treasurer, and finance committee monitor revenues and spending throughout the fiscal year, generally at regular intervals, such as quarterly or monthly, using a statement of activities to compare actual revenue and expenses to the equivalent time period in the budget.
8. *Make financial adjustments.* Staff and committee chairs adjust programs and spending decisions throughout the fiscal year to keep the budget on target. If there is a significant difference between projected revenue or expenses, the organization will adjust its financial plan. For instance, the budget might have included anticipated income from a grant that was not received, or ticket sales projections for a performance were overly optimistic. Before taking corrective action, the board will need to assess if these losses can be offset with higher revenues in other areas of the operation or a reduction of future expenses.

Additional Budget Concepts

Zero-based budgeting is a popular approach to developing a budget. Each revenue and expense line item is justified by current programs and conditions without regard to previous years' figures. The budget, in other words, is built from scratch.

Historical-based budgets are developed by reviewing the organization's expense and revenue history over a three-to-five-year period and adjusting the budget by a factor that compensates for new conditions—inflation, economic trends, new programs, etc. In practice, most planners use a combination of the historical and zero-based approaches.

Fixed and variable costs are useful for distinguishing expenses during budgeting. Some costs—like administrative salaries, rent, or insurance—are not affected by the number or kinds of programs that are presented or by audience turnout. These are fixed costs. Variable costs depend upon the kinds and numbers of programs and include artist salaries, printing, advertising, technical staff, concessions, etc.

Relevant costs are those that staff and/or board members consider as they decide whether or not to continue an existing program or develop a new one. Program costs and revenue are among the issues that determine program value. The costs directly related to the program—including, for example, artist fees and marketing expenses—are clearly relevant costs in a decision about whether or not to expand a concert series. The mortgage payments on the theater are not relevant to making such a decision, unless these program costs would drain current earnings being used to pay the mortgage. Usually only the variable and direct costs for that program are relevant to making the decision.

Depreciation expense should be accounted for throughout the budgeting process (see expense worksheet above). Depreciation represents the wear and tear that programs have on the organization's facility and fixed assets (see "Planning for the Replacement of Fixed Assets"). While usually calculated using the generally accepted accounting principles known as GAAP standards,[1] an organization should use its depreciation expense as a barometer for its annual capital investment or reserve. If some portion of depreciation is not "funded" each year (items repaired or replaced or a reserve set aside for more expense items like a new roof or boiler) then an organization's fixed assets would diminish to a zero value over time on its statement of position (balance sheet).

BUILDING THE BUDGET

As illustrated in Figure 1B, building a budget is the most fundamental step in the financial management process. It is based on careful estimates of your anticipated revenues and projected expenses.

Estimating Revenues

Always calculate revenue first. A realistic assessment of the anticipated level of revenue will guide the level of expenses that you can afford. If you calculate expenses of $1,000 first, it is too tempting to predict that you'll sell 100 tickets at $10 each, even if your experience makes this number unrealistic. Protect yourself from optimistically inflating revenues to match the expenses you want to meet by realistically estimating revenues first.

Facility Planning

Most directors, staff, and boards of arts organizations at some point want a new or renovated building to "better" fulfill the organization's mission. However, planning for a new space involves more than simply hiring an architect and an experienced project manager, it involves understanding the true role a facility plays in your organization's overall strategic planning and capitalization. How will the new space affect the organization's mission, programs, organizational capacity, and capital structure?

When considering a facility project of any kind, an arts organization and its board must also consider the impact that the facility will have on its financial stability, organizational capacity, mission, and programs. While the gift of a building can be very seductive, it can also destabilize even the largest arts organization if not holistically planned. The truth is, the majority of arts organizations undertaking facilities projects are small to mid-size organizations that are undercapitalized and financially fragile. Years of operating losses weaken an organization's balance sheet and its ability to have the unrestricted cash necessary to support a facility project.

In pure accounting terms, improvements to facilities consume unrestricted cash (capital campaign funds and/or debt) and increase fixed costs. Organizations are left trying to pursue their programs with less available cash than before and their building or leasehold improvements now dominate the percentage of assets on their balance sheets, while cash has been reduced and potentially debt has increased. Additionally, the new facility project will inevitably lead to an increased earnings gap for the organization driven by the increased fixed assets and/or programming required. (An earnings gap is the difference between earned income and total expenses. It represents the amount of money the organization needs to raise each year just to break even.)

So what should be considered when undertaking a facility project?

First, truly understand why your organization is undertaking this project, within the context of the organization's value to the community it serves. Communicate the need for the facility project to all constituents including staff, board members, funders, community leaders, and program participants.

Second, understand your organization's financial history, and do not assume that, for example, increased seats or classrooms will automatically increase revenues. The facility's fixed costs (insurance, utilities, interest from a loan, etc.) will increase immediately. Programmatic costs may also increase (new employees, supplies), and classes may not immediately fill to capacity. Completing the capital campaign will continue to need employee attention and organizational funds.

Third, make sure, if there are not experts on staff, that experienced individuals are hired and the project manager has direct experience not only with cultural facilities, but with the type of project the organization is undertaking. Free advice may be attractive, but your negotiating leverage is compromised when issues arise. Understand what you don't know and hire the right people to advise you.

Finally, research what it will take to keep the facility operating over the long term. Annual maintenance and replacement of systems should be reviewed in a system replacement plan (SRP) that guides your annual facility investment decisions. After all, if the roof begins to leak or the boiler breaks, programs will cease, revenues will be lost, and audiences and students will seek out alternative programs. "Greening" a facility will also require holistic thinking, so make sure all aspects of your facility are being reviewed as part of such a project. For example, the savings from installing a new energy-efficient HVAC system may not be realized if leaky windows and inadequate insulation are not also considered. (See the chapter on Greening Your Arts Nonprofit for more information.)

Estimate the amount you can conservatively expect to collect from each of the proposed activities. Don't guess. Consider past sales records, the current economic climate, changes in your planned promotions, how competitors are doing, how peer organizations fared with similar programs, and other related factors. Based on this information, develop models that help you to predict results and reduce guesswork.

To estimate revenues from ticket sales, for example, you could multiply the seating capacity for each performance by your usual percentage from previous sales (See Figure 2, Method 1). If you have historical information about ticket sales for each type of performance, it is best to modify this base figure according to the anticipated popularity of each of the proposed performances, also factoring in the attractiveness of the ticket price, and the likely success of your marketing campaign (See Figure 2, Method 2). Variably priced seats must also be accounted for in your estimates. Take the same approach for calculating likely registration fees for a workshop or sales in a gift shop.

> In this example, the City Center for the Arts' program manager first determined the average number of tickets sold per performance in the past. She then reviewed the sales history for past theater events and determined that they had routinely sold out, allowing her to reliably estimate an above-average audience. For the jazz performances, a newer series that had not yet built a large audience, she budgeted for below-average attendance.

Revenue forecasting should be made in conjunction with a marketing plan. A program that has a strong publicity and promotions plan is more likely to realize earned income objectives than one that has minimal promotion. See the chapter on Marketing the Arts for more information on how to develop a marketing plan and employ different pricing strategies. ▌

Figure 2: Estimating Revenue from Ticket Sales

METHOD 1: Average overall ticket sales		
Seating Capacity		800
Usual Paid Attendance	x	70% (.70)
Total Tickets Sold		560
METHOD 2: Modified according to anticipated popularity of program		
Jazz Concert (predicted to draw smaller than average audience)		460
Average Ticket Price	x	$76
Total Anticipated Income		$34,960
Theater Performance (predicted to sell out)		800
Average Ticket Price	x	$60
Total Anticipated Income		$48,000

Although it is tempting to inflate revenue projections, you should always utilize the most conservative figures to protect the organization from deficits. List grant funds as revenue only if you are certain you will receive them. Base estimated fundraising revenue on previous successes and this year's planned campaign. As with the ticket sales examples, use your average membership renewal rate and your own past experience with a membership solicitation campaign to predict revenue. Be wary of dramatically increased fundraising goals, and exercise caution in estimating a big increase in any revenue figure unless there is a specific, achievable plan for realizing the increase, including the expenses needed to carry out the plan.

Estimating Expenses

The sample expense worksheet in Figure 1 lists possible areas in which you may incur expenses. Add to it any categories that apply specifically to your organization. Expenses should relate directly to the programs in which you expect to generate income. You may choose to list general administrative or fixed expenses first and then the variable expenses necessary to create the programs.

Take time to consider what it will actually cost to run each program. Base estimates on your own experience or the related experience of others. Call printers, insurance agents, and suppliers to get cost estimates. Consider the effects of the rate of inflation on last year's expenses and the impact of increased activity in a program or administrative area.

Be conservative. If in doubt about which of several likely values to assign for an expense, select the one with the highest cost: it is better to have a surplus at the end of the year, rather than a deficit. In developing draft budgets you may use ranges of expense and related revenue to determine what you can do with the available funds. You may also wish to add a budget line for contingencies—unexpected or miscellaneous expenses—as the sample expenses worksheet provides in the "cash reserve" line item.

In some organizations, administrative expenses are allocated proportionately for each program. Staff salaries, rent, utility bills, insurance, postage, and other overhead expenses are charged to each program according to the amount of staff time or facility space that each one requires. This method more accurately projects the resources and costs necessary to conduct each program, but is more complicated to calculate. While this may not be the easiest way to allocate expenses, it is beneficial for the leaders of an organization to occasionally step back from a "business-as-usual" mentality and revisit how staff time is truly being spent on programs, administration, fundraising, etc. See expense worksheet for an example of how expenses were allocated across CCA programs.

A budget's expense lines should reflect an organization's priorities. For example, if your organization is committed to an education program but is spending ever-decreasing sums to support it, you should take a closer look at the program and objectively evaluate where staff time and effort is going instead.

CASH-FLOW BUDGET

Cash management is a critical issue for most nonprofits. Cash must be available when the organization needs to pay bills, salaries, and other obligations. However, the annual business cycle for most organizations usually results in an uneven flow of cash through the year. A cash-flow forecast can help predict cash shortfalls and times of surplus. Knowing in advance of an impending cash shortage or surplus allows you to manage cash flow rather than be managed by it. To prevent a cash flow crisis for the organization, it is strongly recommended that you maintain a cash reserve equal to at least 3-6 months' of your operating expenses. These general recommendations should be adjusted according to your organization's unique circumstances. For instance, if you know you have a large expense due early in the year, you will need to plan for this cost by having funds on hand to cover it.

If a shortage is predicted, you can negotiate a short-term bank loan, ask a donor to advance a planned gift, or make spending decisions that minimize or eliminate the temporary shortage. Conversely, the prediction of a temporary cash surplus can allow the financial manager to invest in short-term certificates of deposit to realize a higher interest return.

A cash-flow budget begins by determining the opening cash balance for the period, then adding anticipated revenues received and deducting expenses that will be paid for each month. The ending cash balance for January becomes the opening cash balance for February, and so on. Projections are based on past experience, anticipated activities and events, and anticipated obligations. All staff that has responsibility for program revenue and authorizing expenses should provide ongoing information for the cash-flow budget.

Cash-flow projections are useful only if they are compared to actual performance. At the end of each month, when the actual cash results are known, the future cash-flow projection should be revised. (See Figure 3.)

Tracking and Measuring Performance

The previous section considered budgets. Now we look at some fundamental principles of accounting—what you need to account for with bookkeeping, how to track cash, and then how to summarize the many daily transactions into summary financial statements.

Since nonprofits hold assets in trust for the public good, they must establish and maintain financial operations and controls that ensure that they function in a responsible and ethical manner. In addition, the board and staff need to rely on systems and reports that allow them to monitor results and measure performance against expectations established in the budget. The management control cycle outlined earlier shows how the interdependent elements of financial management intersect: financial projections reflected in budgets; performance measured through record keeping; comparison and monitoring made possible with financial statements.

Nonprofits' financial systems records, like those of all businesses, provide critical data needed by board and key staff and are subject to monitoring by outside authorities. As a result, they should be set up and maintained carefully and reviewed periodically by a person with accounting expertise so that the nonprofit is run according to generally accepted accounting principles (GAAP).

These standards provide the basis for sound accounting policies and procedures. Due to scandals in the corporate community, nonprofits are under increasing scrutiny, which has added to the complexity of doing business. Unfortunately despite formal reviews and accounting policies and procedures, there will always be corporations as well as nonprofits that push the envelope of the law. When this occurs it places increased outside scrutiny on organizations from funders as well as government officials.

Figure 3: City Center for the Arts' Cash Flow Projections

CITY CENTER FOR THE ARTS	July	August	September	October	November	December
CASH FLOW PROJECTIONS						
Beginning Balance	80,703	77,397	44,591	79,835	105,554	112,123
EXPENSE						
Program Expense						
Artists' Fees - non-salaried	2,500	2,500	15,000	15,000	15,000	15,000
Materials	2,000		5,000		5,000	
Production Expense				5,000	5,000	10,000
Advertising/Printing/Design	525	7,000				
Special Event Expense		1,000	1,500	10,000		
Occupancy/Facility Expense						
Utilities	1,500	1,500	1,500	1,500	1,500	1,500
Insurance (non-employee related)	13,000					13,000
Maintenance/Repair	500	15,000	500	500	500	500
Interest Expense (loans)	2,250	2,250	2,250	2,250	2,250	2,250
Administrative Expense						
Salaries - Administrative	8,410	8,410	8,410	8,410	8,410	8,410
Payroll Taxes	841	841	841	841	841	841
Employee Benefits Health Insurance	2,525	2,525	2,525	2,525	2,525	2,525
Supplies/Postage/Other	475	2,000	475	475	475	475
Audit/Legal/Other Fees	2,500	2,500	2,500	500	500	500
Travel/Training/Entertainment		1,000			150	
Bank Fees/Other	450	450	450	450	450	450
Other Fees/Licenses (Web)	830	830	830	830	830	830
Expense Total	*38,306*	*47,806*	*41,781*	*48,281*	*43,431*	*56,281*
Cash Balance Subtotal	*42,397*	*29,591*	*2,810*	*31,554*	*62,123*	*55,842*
REVENUE						
Contributed Revenue/Income						
Individual Contributions			1,000	1,000	5,000	1,500
Membership Drive		5,000	25,000	10,000		
Board Contributions	30,000					
Corporate Grants		5,000		5,000	20,000	
Foundation Grants			25,000			10,000
Government Grants					10,000	
Special Events			10,000	18,000		
Earned Revenue/Income						
Ticket Sales			5,000	15,000	10,000	5,000
Class and Workshop Tuition			10,000	25,000		8,500
Rental Income	5,000					10,000
Shop Sales					5,000	5,000
Advertising Sales		5,000	1,000			
Investment Revenue/Income						
Interest Income			25			25
Revenue Total	*35,000*	*15,000*	*77,025*	*74,000*	*50,000*	*40,025*
Closing Cash Balance	*77,397*	*44,591*	*79,835*	*105,554*	*112,123*	*95,867*

For this reason, financial records should be maintained by a qualified bookkeeper or a person with specific training.

ESTABLISHING YOUR FINANCIAL RECORDS

Reasonably priced and user-friendly accounting software is available to nonprofits and should serve as the cornerstone of your accounting system, comprising the manual and electronic processes you use to record your financial transactions and information. Using financial software facilitates the process of managing financial information and producing financial reports.

Selecting which software to use will be easier if sufficient time is allocated for research, software testing, installation, and practice. Before investing in accounting software (that lives on your computer) or online accounting systems (that live in the "cloud"), evaluate your existing system and determine what features you want in the new system, compare the features of several financial packages, talk to other nonprofits using the software, "test drive" several, and compare prices before making a decision. Key considerations should be ease of use and the availability of training for staff and/or volunteers who will use the system.

Accounting Software

User-friendly and affordable accounting software packages are readily available and greatly ease the work of the bookkeeper and enable managers to get reports more quickly. At the time of this writing, the nonprofit service organization Tech Soup offers discounted accounting software for nonprofits and unbiased reviews of different software packages on their website. Most accounting software includes basic ledgers and the ability to prepare budgets, cash-flow reports, check writing, and payroll. While basic systems will work for many nonprofits, larger or more complex organizations may choose systems designed for nonprofits that provide additional system features, such as links to ticketing and fundraising components.

Spreadsheets

Spreadsheet programs computerize the simplest mathematical functions and provide the ability to prepare specialized reports and graphs. While they are not a replacement for accounting software, they are excellent tools for developing initial budgets and analyzing your financial results. Microsoft Excel, Google Sheets and Numbers (for Apple computers) are among the most common spreadsheet programs as of this writing. Basic software packages that come with most computers include spreadsheet software. Microsoft Office, for example, includes Excel. The accounting software packages provide links to spreadsheets; some versions are able to download data directly from the accounting system into a spreadsheet so a specialized report can be created without re-entering all the data.

ACCOUNTING METHODS

Accounting is the process of financial record keeping. A nonprofit typically chooses one of three methods to record revenues and expenses: cash basis, accrual, and modified cash basis. (Recording a transaction means entering it in your ledger or accounting system.)

Cash basis accounting records when revenues are received and expenses are paid, much like a checkbook. Neither accounts receivable nor payable are recorded in a cash basis system. Accounts receivable are monies owed to you but which you have not yet received, such as grants or donations that have been pledged but not yet received. Accounts payable are expenses you are obligated to pay in the form of a purchase order or a contract to a vendor. While the cash basis method is easy to understand and implement, it often results in misleading financial information because it does not reflect financial obligations that may have been incurred but have not yet been recorded. Similarly, it may understate income that is pledged but not yet received. In addition, cash basis accounting does not comply with GAAP regulations, so an auditor cannot offer an unqualified opinion that the financial statements comply with these regulations (which can be a red flag for funders and donors). For this reason, only nonprofits with no auditing requirements are exempt from accrual accounting (the National Council of Nonprofits offers a breakdown of auditing requirements by state at www.councilofnonprofits.org).

In accrual basis accounting, all committed income and expenses are entered in the books, whether or not they have been actually received or paid. In this system of accounting, all cash basis revenues and expenses are reflected, as well as accounts receivable revenue and accounts payable expenses. For this reason, the accrual method provides a more accurate picture of the organization. While accrual basis accounting requires more familiarization with accounting methods than cash basis, it is recommended that the accrual method be used by your nonprofit because it allows more accurate information.

Modified cash basis accounting is often used by smaller nonprofits. Under this method, some transactions are recorded on an accrual basis, such as unpaid bills and depreciation, while other transactions, such as uncollected income, are recorded on a cash basis only. This approach allows a smaller organization to see the impact of unpaid bills on their accounts, without having to implement a more complicated accrual method accounting system.

ACCOUNTING PROCEDURES

It is usually wise to seek the help of an experienced accountant or bookkeeper when setting up a bookkeeping system. If your organization's financial activities are substantial, the ongoing services of a bookkeeper or accountant are essential. The following briefly explains key terms and procedures involved in bookkeeping and accounting.

Bookkeeping. A well-designed bookkeeping system enables an organization to track income and expenses, produce financial statements, monitor the budget, and provide a "trail" of transactions for future workers to review. As such, it provides the basis from which an audit is completed.

Internal controls. These are procedures and policies that improve security and avoid mismanagement of funds. A primary control measure is separation of duties, which requires that different people be responsible for aspects of the financial process such as check approval, check signing, and bookkeeping. In an all-volunteer organization or when there is only one staff member, the minimum safeguard is to require two signatures on checks. Often board members become involved in check signing and approval, especially for expenses over a specified dollar amount. An experienced bookkeeper or certified public accountant (CPA) should review your internal control practices periodically and make recommendations for improvement. A CPA will also provide you with a management letter that reviews internal controls and, if necessary, makes recommendations for improvements.

Chart of accounts. A chart of accounts assigns a number or code to each type of transaction, using five categories: revenue, expense, assets, liabilities, and net assets. This makes it easier to keep track of transactions and produce reports in a consistent manner.

Several nonprofit support organizations have developed a Unified Chart of Accounts for Nonprofit Organizations (UCOA).[3] The system is designed so that nonprofits can quickly and reliably translate their financial statements into the categories required by IRS Form 990 and other government reporting formats. UCOA is extensive, but any nonprofit can select the categories that apply to their own operations. Examples of some UCOA sample account categories are shown in Figure 4.

Recording cash transactions. Many nonprofits maintain small petty cash accounts for last minute purchases or handle cash from sales at art events that need to be integrated into the organization's financial recordkeeping system. Be sure to document these cash transactions carefully by saving receipts for expenses and providing receipts for income. Create a separate account in your accounting system for petty cash expense and income (see the sample chart of accounts) and properly record these transactions immediately, to prevent fraud.

Reconciliation of accounts. Your monthly bank and credit card statements as well as petty cash should be reconciled in your accounting software each month. The reconciliation is the primary control over cash accounts and should be completed as soon as your statements are received to verify that the recorded information is correct.

Grants and contributions. The Financial Accounting Standards Board (FASB) defines separate standards for recording and reporting grants and contributions. These should be checked to determine if the funds are restricted (for example, to a particular program rather than for general operating expenses). Restricted funds should be coded accordingly, and tax deduction acknowledgement forms may need to be sent to donors to comply with applicable regulations. In-kind contributions and donated services, including volunteer hours, are also recorded in the accounting system.

OTHER FINANCIAL RECORD KEEPING

Your accounting system should establish specific procedures for recording and reporting payroll expenses in accordance with procedures mandated by the federal and state governments. The IRS and designated state government agencies can provide guidance in setting up procedures and preparing reports. Since organizations that fail to comply with the requirements are subject to penalties, the board and staff must ensure that the proper procedures are always followed.

FINANCIAL STATEMENTS

Financial statements provide the information that the board and staff need to measure the financial status of the organization. The three core financial statements are the statement of position (SOP, also known as the balance sheet), the statement of activities (SOA, also known as the income or operating statement), and the cash flow statement. Data for all three reports are compiled from the accounting system.

The GAAP standards set guidelines for financial statements, and those guidelines are always followed when an auditor conducts a financial audit. For internal reporting, a board may modify the formats to provide data they need for decision making.

Statement of Position

The statement of position (SOP), or balance sheet, is a snapshot of an organization's financial position (assets, liabilities, and net assets) as of a specific date, such as the end of a month or fiscal year. It shows what an organization owns and owes, and summarizes the difference between the two. That difference, or total net assets, is similar to the net worth of for-profit organizations, and is an important indicator of organizational health. An SOP has three key sections:

Total assets are what an organization owns and is owed by others (such as in the case of a multi-year pledge receivable). Assets are divided into groups based on liquidity: current assets, or those that are available to generate cash within the year; longer-term assets taking more than a year to generate cash, such as multi-year pledge receivables or prepaid deposits; and fixed assets that usually must be sold to generate cash for the organization.

Total liabilities are what the organization owes. Liabilities are divided into two sections, current liabilities, or those due within the year, and long term liabilities due beyond the year, such as a mortgage.

Total net assets are the value of the assets minus the liabilities. GAAP groups the net assets of a nonprofit into three classifications: unrestricted, temporarily restricted, and permanently restricted. Collectively, the unrestricted, temporarily restricted, and permanently restricted assets comprise your organization's net assets, which are the cumulative amount of your revenues less your expenses from the inception of your nonprofit. A description of each type of net asset is offered below.

- Unrestricted net assets have no donor-imposed restrictions and can be used for any operating and programmatic expenses authorized by the board. Restrictions placed on funds by the board, but not by the donor, are considered unrestricted. Examples of unrestricted funds include revenue from ticket sales, membership, and retail operations, and an annual appeal for general operations. The board may choose to set aside cash reserves for future use such as deferred maintenance or the creation of new programming; however, in accordance with GAAP, these board-directed reserves usually remain unrestricted in audited financial statements, but are worthy of inclusion in the notes to the financial statements.
- Temporarily-restricted net assets have a donor or funder-imposed purpose or time restriction. For example, your organization may receive a grant for a school program from a local community foundation. You are permitted to use these funds to support the program as defined in your contract with the funder (to pay artists, for instance), but not for other general organizational purposes

---

Fixed assets are the property and equipment owned by an organization and valued over a certain amount. Accounting guidelines define how the purchase or donation of fixed assets is recorded. Because equipment and property lose value over time as they are used, their value is reduced over time according to guidelines for "useful life." The process of reducing the value is called depreciation and is recorded in the accounting system.

Figure 4: Chart of Accounts Example.

1 **ASSETS**
- 1000 Cash
- 1040 Petty cash
- 1100 Accounts receivable
- 1200 Contributions receivable—pledges, grants, etc.
- 1210 Pledges and grants receivable
- 1300 Other receivables—notes, loans, etc.
- 1420 Inventory for use
- 1600 Fixed operating assets—land, buildings, fixtures, vehicles, etc.

2 **LIABILITIES**
- 2010 Accounts payable
- 2020 Grants and allocations payable
- 2100 Accrued liabilities—payroll, paid leave, taxes, etc.
- 2500 Short-term notes and loans payable
- 2700 Long-term notes and loans payable

3 **EQUITY—UNRESTRICTED AND TEMPORARILY OR PERMANENTLY RESTRICTED NET ASSETS**

4 **CONTRIBUTIONS/SUPPORT**
- 4000 Direct contributions—individuals, corporate, small business, etc.
- 4010 Individual and small business contributions
- 4100 Donated goods and services
- 4150 Donated art, etc.
- 4200 Nongovernment grants—corporate, foundation, etc.
- 4230 Foundation and trust grants
- 4410 United Way or CFC contributions
- 4500 Government grants—federal, state, local
- 4520 Federal grants
- 4530 State grants

5 **EARNED REVENUES**
- 5000 Contracts/fees—federal, state, local, etc.
- 5100 Program-related Sales—service fees, etc.
- 5210 Dues—individual and organizational members
- 5800 Special Events

6 **OTHER REVENUE—UNREALIZED GAIN (LOSS), NET ASSETS RELEASED FROM RESTRICTION**

7 **EXPENSES (PERSONNEL RELATED)**
- 7000 Grants, contracts, and direct assistance
- 7200 Salaries and related expenses
- 7240 Employee benefits (not pension)
- 7500 Contract services—fundraising, accounting, legal, etc.

8 **EXPENSES (NONPERSONNEL RELATED)**
- 8100 Nonpersonnel—supplies, postage, printing, etc.
- 8200 Facility and equipment
- 8300 Travel and meetings
- 8500 Other—list rental, contingency provision, etc.
- **8600** Business—taxes, bad debt expense, etc.

9 **NON-GAAP EXPENSES—FIXED ASSET PURCHASES, ADDITIONS TO RESERVES, ETC.**

Excerpted from Unified Chart of Accounts, version 3.0

unrelated to the program. Any funds remaining after the grant period has concluded should be discussed with the funder as to their use.
- Permanently-restricted net assets are made up of contributions for which the donors require the funds be used in a specific way indefinitely. A gift to an endowment usually has a permanent restriction. Such restricted funds must be tracked separately from funds donated for use in general operations. Regardless of how funds are designated, management has the obligation to use these various funds for the purposes for which they were intended and not use restricted funds inappropriately.

The total assets presented on an SOP will equal the total liabilities plus the total net assets—hence the term balance sheet. Many organizations compare the statement of position on the same date over several years to examine organizational change over time. An annual audit compares the end of the fiscal year audited to the end of the previous fiscal year. (See Figure 5.)

The SOP is an essential tool for board and staff to monitor on a regular basis in order to determine whether the organization is financially healthy or at risk. Each organization should set a target for the level of assets it needs in order to support its mission for the long term. Board and staff also need to identify key indicators that they will use to monitor change.

Note that organizations embedded in larger institutions (such as art centers in colleges or universities or departments in a municipality) will find an SOP somewhat meaningless for their department, since the actual owner of assets such as an auditorium or gallery is the parent institution. Should such an organization be requested to provide an SOP for a grant application, for instance, it should submit its parent institution's SOP instead.

Statement of Activities

The statement of activities (SOA) summarizes revenues received and expenses incurred throughout an accounting period. The SOA, sometimes called the income or operating statement, uses the same format as the budget, so that the board and staff can compare actual financial performance with that projected in the budget.

Differences between what the budget projects and what actually occurs are noted as variances. Unfavorable income variances mean that revenue is less than expected. Unfavorable expense variances indicate that spending is greater in a category than was forecast. In either case, a variance means that the leaders need to look more closely at that income or expense item to learn what has happened. Lower-than-forecast contributions could suggest that donors are not responding to the annual appeal as usual. Or lower earned-income figures could simply reflect that the annual benefit auction will not take place until the next month. For clarification, the SOA should include a column with the projection for the end of the fiscal year so the annual budget can be compared to the expected results for the year.

The SOA should be prepared monthly, quarterly, and at year's end. The monthly report should be reviewed by the staff and treasurer; the finance committee should review the SOA at least quarterly. Regularly scheduled reviews will enable board and staff to observe discrepancies and take steps to protect the organization from spending more money than it receives. This allows an organization's leaders to manage, not merely report the group's finances.

STATEMENT OF POSITION CITY CENTER FOR THE ARTS	YEAR 1 ACTUAL	YEAR 2 ACTUAL
Assets		
Other		
Cash - Operating	101,697	80,703
Accounts Receivable	12,500	10,000
Prepaid Expenses	1,500	3,500
Inventory	1,200	1,500
Grants Receivable	15,000	10,000
Total Current Assets	**131,897**	**105,703**
Other Assets		
Pledges Receivable	8,000	2,000
Other Assets	6,550	6,550
Total Other Assets	**35,050**	**29,050**
Fixed Assets		
Land & Buildings		
Land	7,000	7,000
Building	500,000	500,000
Building & Improvements	235,000	285,000
Total Land & Buildings	**742,000**	**792,000**
Furniture & Equipment		
Furniture & Equipment	193,140	203,947
Total Furniture & Equipment	193,140	203,947
Accumulated Depreciation	(428,500)	(455,875)
Net Fixed Assets	**506,640**	**540,072**
Total Assets	**673,587**	**674,825**
Liabilities		
Current Liabilities		
Accounts Payable	13,500	15,400
Accrued Liabilities	3,500	3,400
Gift Certificates	1,500	2,500
Deferred Revenue	30,000	35,000
Other Liabilities	562	320
Working Capital Bank Loan		
Current Maturity of Long Term Debt	17,500	17,500
Total Current Liabilities	**66,562**	**74,120**
Long Term Financing		
Loan from Bank for Building	280,000	262,500
Total Liabilities	**346,562**	**336,620**
Net Assets		
Unrestricted Net Assets	300,000	306,525
Net Income Current Year	6,525	11,180
Permanently Restricted Net Assets	20,500	20,500
Total Net Assets	**327,025**	**338,205**
BSheet Check (Assets - (TL+FB))	(0)	(0)

Figure 5. City Center for the Arts Statement of Position

Figure 6: City Center for the Arts Statement of Activities

STATEMENT OF ACTIVITIES CITY CENTER FOR THE ARTS					
	Actual YEAR 1	Actual YEAR 2	% increase/ decrease	YEAR 3 Projected Budget	% Change from Actual YEAR 2
Income/Revenue					
Contributed Revenue/Income					
Individual Contributions	$ 15,000	$ 15,000	0%	$ 18,000	20%
Membership Drive	$ 35,000	$ 40,000	14%	$ 45,000	13%
Board Contributions	$ 20,000	$ 25,000	25%	$ 30,000	20%
Corporate Grants	$ 45,000	$ 50,000	11%	$ 55,000	10%
Foundation Grants	$ 50,000	$ 45,000	(10%)	$ 50,000	11%
Government Grants	$ 33,000	$ 30,000	(9%)	$ 24,500	(18%)
Special Events	$ 25,000	$ 30,000	20%	$ 28,000	(7%)
Total Contributed Revenue	$ 223,000	$ 235,000	5%	$ 250,500	7%
Earned Revenue/Income					
Ticket Sales	$ 80,000	$ 85,000	6%	$ 90,000	6%
Class and Workshop Tuition	$ 120,000	$ 135,000	13%	$ 145,000	7%
Rental Income	$ 11,000	$ 19,500	77%	$ 23,000	18%
Shop Sales	$ 11,000	$ 12,000	9%	$ 12,000	0%
Advertising Sales	$ 6,000	$ 6,300	5%	$ 6,400	2%
Total Earned Revenue	$ 228,000	$ 257,800	13%	$ 276,400	7%
Investment Revenue/Income					
Interest Income	$ 250	$ 100	(60%)	$ 100	0%
Total Investment Revenue	$ 250	$ 100	(60%)	$ 100	0%
Total Revenue/Income	$ 451,250	$ 492,900	9%	$ 527,000	7%
Expense					
Program Expense					
Artists' Fees - non-salaried	$ 100,000	$ 110,000	10%	$ 125,000	14%
Materials	$ 25,000	$ 26,500	6%	$ 27,500	4%
Production Expense	$ 22,000	$ 25,000	14%	$ 26,000	4%
Advertising/Printing/Design	$ 12,000	$ 14,000	17%	$ 14,000	0%
Special Event Expense	$ 15,000	$ 12,000	(20%)	$ 12,500	4%
Total Program Expense	$ 174,000	$ 187,500	8%	$ 205,000	9%
% of Total Revenue	38.6%	38.0%		38.9%	
Occupancy/Facility Expense					
Utilities	$ 19,500	$ 18,600	(5%)	$ 19,000	2%
Insurance (non-employee related)	$ 22,000	$ 24,000	9%	$ 26,000	8%
Maintenance/Repair	$ 35,000	$ 31,970	(9%)	$ 30,000	(6%)
Depreciation	$ 21,500	$ 27,375	27%	$ 33,190	21%
Interest Expense (loans)	$ 30,625	$ 28,875	(6%)	$ 27,100	(6%)
Total Occupancy Expense	$ 128,625	$ 130,820	2%	$ 135,290	3%
% of Total Revenue	28.5%	26.5%		25.7%	
Administrative Expense					
Salaries - Administrative	$ 85,000	$ 92,000	8%	$ 101,000	10%
Payroll Taxes	$ 8,500	$ 9,200	8%	$ 10,100	10%
Employee Benefits Health Insurance	$ 21,000	$ 27,600	31%	$ 30,300	10%
Supplies/Postage/Other	$ 5,000	$ 5,500	10%	$ 5,700	4%
Audit/Legal/Other Fees	$ 9,000	$ 9,800	9%	$ 10,000	2%
Travel/Training/Entertainment	$ 4,000	$ 4,300	8%	$ 3,900	(9%)
Bank Fees/Other	$ 4,000	$ 5,000	25%	$ 5,500	10%
Other Fees/Licenses (Web)	$ 5,600	$ 10,000	79%	$ 10,000	0%
Total Administrative Expense	$ 142,100	$ 163,400	15%	$ 176,500	8%
% Total Revenue	31.5%	33.2%		33.5%	
Total Expense	$ 444,725	$ 481,720	8%	$ 516,790	7%
Total Income/Surplus (Loss/Deficit)	$ 451,250	$ 492,900	9%	$ 527,000	7%
Total Expense	$ 444,725	$ 481,720	8%	$ 516,790	7%
Total Operating Surplus (Loss)	$ 6,525	$ 11,180	71%	$ 10,210	(9%)
Total Surplus/(Loss)	$ 6,525	$ 11,180		$ 10,210	

The SOA also relates directly to the statement of position. The net income—the excess or deficiency of revenues over expenses—is added to the net assets on the SOP. If the net income is positive (surplus), the net asset amount is increased. If the net income is negative (deficit), the net asset amount is decreased. Thus, all revenues and expenses flow to the SOP. For the City Center for the Arts (see Figure 6), the net income/surplus from the SOA in Year 2 amounted to $11,180. This amount was added to the net assets as shown on the SOP.

How to use an SOA. Compare total revenues to total costs to determine if the surplus will be maintained. Compare administrative expenses to program expenses, and direct the majority of your resources to mission-directed activities. Be alert to an increase in the percentage you spend on administration, especially if it is a trend over several years. You may also compare your results with those of similar organizations to determine if your trends are similar. However, such comparisons should be used only to indicate that added research is needed, since each organization's circumstances are different.

Express each program's revenues and expenses as a percentage of total revenues and expenses. Look for programs that consume more than their share of expenses and contribute less than their share of revenues. If such a program is also peripheral to the fulfillment of your mission, it is a likely candidate for cost-saving measures or elimination. Look for significant changes in a revenue or expense category by comparing several years of operating statements. A drop in ticket sales, grants, or fundraising should cue a close examination of the cause. Compare program expenses to attendees, fundraising expenses to contributed revenue, or advertising and marketing as a percent of total program revenue to gauge program effectiveness.

Cash-Flow Statement

The statement of cash flow helps organizations to view how they are managing their cash over time. It consists of three parts: cash from operating activities (contributions and the purchase and sale of good and services), cash from investing activities (the sale and purchase of investments), and cash from financing activities (borrowing and debt repayment). Often unappreciated by arts leaders, the cash flow statement is an important barometer of the ability of an organization to meet its immediate financial obligations. As mentioned above under cash flow budgeting, if the organization does not have sufficient cash on hand, it will face significant operational risks. See Figure 7 for a sample cash flow statement.

FINANCIAL RATIOS

An additional way to test an organization's financial health is to use financial ratio tools, which reformulate financial statements into quick indicators of fiscal stability. Financial ratios should only be used to diagnose potential problems, and not become the sole indicator of fiscal health. Further investigation can help to uncover problem areas. Here are some examples:

- **Months of Operating Cash** shows the organization how long it could operate if no further income were earned. A per-month figure for operating cash is calculated by subtracting total expenses from unrestricted cash plus short-term investments and dividing by 12. It is prudent to have approximately three months of cash on hand, though this may vary, based on the organization's projected income and expenses.

Figure 7: City Center for the Arts Statement of Activities Cash-Flow Statement

STATEMENT OF CASH FLOWS CITY CENTER FOR THE ARTS	
Year End 12/31	YEAR 2
CASH FLOWS FROM OPERATING ACTIVITIES:	
Net Income/Surplus	$ 11,180.00
Adjustments to reconcile changes in net assets to net cash used in operating activities:	
Depreciation	$ 27,375.00
Realized Gains (Losses)	
Unrealized Gains (Losses)	$ -
Over/Under	
Adjusted Net Income	$ 38,555.00
Balance Sheet Changes	
Grants Receivable	$ 5,000.00
Pledges Receivable	$ 6,000.00
Accounts Receivable-Other	$ 2,500.00
Prepaid Expenses	$ (2,000.00)
Inventory	$ (300.00)
Endowment	$ -
Accounts Payable	$ 1,900.00
Accrued Liabilities	$ (100.00)
Gift Certificates	$ 1,000.00
Deferred Revenue	$ 5,000.00
Other Liabilities	$ (242.00)
NET CASH USED BY OPERATING ACTIVITIES	$ 57,313.00
CASH FLOWS FROM INVESTING ACTIVITIES:	
Change in Fixed Assets	
Land	$ -
Building	$ -
Building & Improvements	$ (50,000.00)
Furniture & Equipment	$ (10,807.00)
NET CASH PROVIDED BY INVESTING ACTIVITIES	$ (60,807.00)
CASH FLOWS FROM FINANCING ACTIVITIES:	
Repayment of Bank Debt	$ (17,500.00)
NET CASH PROVIDED BY FINANCING ACTIVITIES	$ (17,500.00)
NET (DECREASE) INCREASE IN CASH AND CASH EQUIVALENTS	$ (20,994.00)
Cash and Cash Equivalents Beginning of Year	$ 101,697.00
Changes	$ (20,994.00)
Cash and Cash Equivalents End of Year	$ 80,703.00
B/S Check Mgmt Statements	
Difference from Actual	$ 80,703.00

- **Working Capital** evaluates the unrestricted resources available to fund an organization's operations and provides it with the financial flexibility necessary to meet obligations as they come due or the ability to manage additional risks. It is conservatively calculated as unrestricted current assets (not including unrestricted endowment investments) minus current liabilities. If working capital is negative due to seasonal programming, an organization may need a working capital loan to sustain its cash flow.
- **Unrestricted Net Assets** (URNA, the net total of property, plant and equipment) should be a positive number. The extent to which this calculation is positive indicates the organization's accumulated net earnings over the years supporting its capital structure and providing a liquidity cushion in the event of losses. It is calculated as URNA minus (net fixed assets minus mortgage debt). If your figure is negative, it is advisable to speak with an accountant about how to plan to replenish the unrestricted net assets of the organization to cushion it from further losses. See the Kresge Foundation website at kresge.org for an excellent discussion of this topic and a worksheet to calculate this ratio.
- **Fixed asset ratio** (Fixed Assets—land, buildings, furniture, fixtures and equipment, leasehold improvements, and accumulated depreciation—divided by total assets) evaluates an organization's financial flexibility/liquidity. If this number is greater than 50 percent, meaning more than half the assets are invested in highly illiquid fixed assets, the organization may not have the financial flexibility to effectively deal with unplanned challenges.
- **Fundraising Efficiency** (fundraising expenses as a percentage of contributed revenue) indicates how much is being spent to raise contributed income. It is calculated by dividing fundraising expenses by contributions (excluding grants). A percentage of 65% or above is recommended. Increasingly, funders are looking at this ratio to see if an organization's fundraising efforts are effective as well as efficient.
- **Earnings Gap** is an indication of an organization's ability to support its operations strictly through its programs. The gap that is shown in this ratio represents the amount of funds necessary to be raised to meet all of its expenses. The greater the gap, the more fundraising is necessary. The earnings gap can be expressed as total earned revenues minus total expenses or as the ratio between total earned revenues and total expenses.

Arts organizations should become familiar with a number of traditional financial ratios, but they also should monitor other financial measurements that are integral to their business, such as total expenses per ticket sale, changes in specific categories of contributed revenue over time, or seasonality of earned income compared to working capital needs. These are all financial measurements that can be used to strategically monitor an organization's financial health and the health of its programs.

AUDITS

An independent accountant can review an organization's various financial statements and operations and produce an opinion as to the organization's financial health, in the form of a full audit or a review, or prepare a compilation of financial records and statements. An auditor tests transactions to evaluate the accuracy of accounting records and the degree of reliance he or she can place on the organization's internal controls.

- **Audit.** An auditor renders an opinion as to whether the financial statements are free of material misstatement, based on an examination in accordance with GAAP standards.
- **Review.** An auditor reviews a limited scope of the organization's financial statements in order to provide limited assurance that the statements conform with GAAP.

- **Compilation.** An auditor compiles financial data for the accounting period and prepares a financial statement without expressing assurances that the statement complies with GAAP.

The compilation and financial review are most common for smaller organizations. Full audits are usually performed only when required by state regulations and funding sources or where dictated by the size and complexity of an organization. While there are no federal audit requirements for submitting a Form 990, in some states nonprofit organizations must submit audited financial statements as part of their registration process.

Audit Opinions

The end result of an audit is the expression of an opinion. The auditor may render one of four basic opinions.

- **Unqualified.** The financial statements are considered to be fairly presented in conformity with GAAP.
- **Qualified.** The auditor takes exception to some specific part of the financial statements as presented or is unable to form an unqualified opinion because of some contingency which might affect the financial statements.
- **Adverse.** In the auditor's opinion, the financial statements do not present fairly the financial position in conformity with GAAP.
- **Disclaimer.** The auditor is unable to form an opinion due to limitations of scope, uncertainties in the future, or poor bookkeeping by the client.

Benefits of an Audit

Credibility of financial statements. The purpose of financial statements is to communicate in a direct manner what has transpired during the fiscal period. An auditor's opinion helps in this communication, since an independent expert has examined and determined that the financial statements are presented fairly. If an organization can tell its financial story accurately and completely, and it is accepted at face value, the potential contributor is more likely to feel that the organization is well managed.

A CPA can provide key assistance in this process. She or he can help an organization prepare meaningful financial statements in a format that will be clear and understandable to outside entities; advise the board on how to strengthen internal controls or simplify bookkeeping procedures; and help submit reports to regulatory agencies or the IRS.

REPORTS TO THE INTERNAL REVENUE SERVICE

Annual tax return. Organizations with 501(c)(3) nonprofit status must file a yearly tax return, IRS Form 990, 990EZ or 990N. As of this writing, if gross receipts are normally not more than $50,000 an organization need only file a 990N (which is described as an electronic post card), but may choose to file a full return. However, changes in IRS guidelines and requirements as well as state tax filing requirements should be reviewed each year. Some states may require a full tax return regardless of the organization's federal exemption. In some states, nonprofit status may be withdrawn (on the state level) if certain forms are not filed, such as a certificate of good standing. Remember that your organization's tax returns are a matter of public record.[4] The nonprofit organization Guidestar routinely indexes the tax forms of nonprofits whose annual revenues are $1million or greater, as do other nonprofit charities such as the Foundation Center.[5] Nonprofits can establish free accounts at Guidestar to upload their tax forms and other information to promote full transparency.

Salaries and wages. Several IRS forms are required when an organization has employees:

- Form W-4, Employee's Withholding Allowance Certificate, enables an employee to define the correct amount of federal income tax to be withheld from pay.
- Form 941, Employer's Quarterly Federal Tax Return, report tax liability to the IRS.
- Form W-2, Wage and Tax Statement, provided by an employer to an employee to summarize gross wages and deductions.
- Form W-3, Transmittal of Income and Tax Statements, the cover sheet accompanying W-2 forms sent to the IRS.

Organizations also must submit forms when employing contractors.

- Form W-9, Request for Taxpayer Identification Number and Certification, given to the employer by the contractor. When the contractor is an individual, this form is used to report his or her social security number.
- Form 1099–Miscellaneous, the contractor's equivalent of a W-2 form.
- Form 1096, the cover sheet accompanying 1099 Miscellaneous forms sent to the IRS.

Additional Resources

Several nonprofit service organizations provide online resources pertaining to financial management.

Guidestar Blog (trust.guidestar.org) is designed to help "nonprofit professionals and their supporters become more efficient and effective." The blog often includes entries on financial management for nonprofits.

National Council of Nonprofits (councilofnonprofits.org) provides a number of helpful tools and resources in the Financial Management section of its website.

Nonprofits Assistance Fund (nonprofitsassistancefund.org) offers an excellent glossary of financial terms for nonprofits in the Resources area of its website.

Nonprofit Finance Fund (nonprofitfinancefund.org) provides a wealth of resources in the Nonprofit Services and Tools and Resources areas of its website.

Endnotes

1. GAAP standards, which are defined by the American Institute of Certified Public Accountants (AICPA) and the Financial Accounting Standards Board (FASB), provide the basis for sound accounting policies and procedures.

2. Available from www.independentsector.org.

3. A copy of the UCOA is available from the National Center for Charitable Statistics at the Urban Institute (nccs.urban.org). Note that most nonprofit accounting software has a chart of accounts built into it that is aligned with both the Unified Chart of Accounts and the accepted categories on IRS Form 990.

4. "An exempt organization must make available for public inspection and copying its annual [tax] return." Public Disclosure and Availability of Exempt Organizations Returns and Applications: Documents Subject to Public Disclosure at www.irs.gov.

5. See, for example, the Foundation Center's 990 Finder at www.foundationcenter.org.

Greening Your Nonprofit Arts Organization: The Role and Practice of Environmental Sustainability in Arts Management

SARAH SUTTON *and* DEE BOYLE-CLAPP

Introduction

ENVIRONMENTAL SUSTAINABILITY — WHAT AND WHY?

The arts and artists have long been on the forefront of change, and as climate change and its effects threatens the planet, it is not surprising that artists and arts organizations are responding by creating and presenting work that addresses these concerns. Arts organizations increasingly recognize that leading by example and greening their own organizations saves money while reducing their carbon and chemical footprint. To many arts managers and others who are considering environmental sustainability for their arts institutions or even a once-a-year outdoor festival, the processes and concepts are outlined here to reduce their complexity. This chapters' goal is therefore to provide a basic greening template that can be extended to multiple decision-making needs, and provide guideposts for navigating the new or unexpected. This chapter also holds that greening is good for people, the planet and institutional pocketbook.

Why should an arts organization concern itself with environmental sustainability? What has it got to do with one's mission? Put simply, arts organizations exist to engage their community in creative, challenging and fulfilling ways that bring beauty, joy, ideas, and additional meaning to life. Many arts organizations are the leaders in their communities. Should they not challenge themselves and address the very issues that challenge their constituents and everyone on the planet? Climate change, financial sustainability, and serving as a community role model are closely linked.

Think holistically for a moment: When attendees visit a sculpture park and walk past a gorgeous garden, there is beauty and joy; but if staff used harmful chemicals to create that beauty, and those chemicals kill bees or enter watersheds where they negatively affect plant and aquatic life, has the sculpture park cared for its full community? If a public arts program commissions the creation of a work of art, but insists that the work be made from plastic and be lit 24 hours a day, the program has allowed the art to become tainted. A responsible and creative arts organization works with the artist to identify the best resources with the least negative impact.

It is not enough to ask staff and audience members to turn out a light, use less water, or recycle when an organization decides to "Go Green;" instead the organization must take measures to make each effortless, teach everyone how or where to participate, and thank them for doing so. The greening organization must replace aging or outmoded systems whenever the opportunity arises; must prevent the consumption and waste of resources through careful purchases; and should track how much it has saved not only in terms of dollars, but water, materials, carbon, and energy. Financial savings found by doing business in a new and effective way allows the organization to spend more on programs and one's good work. Green can be very, very good for an arts organization.

I. Myths, Fears and Inertia

For some – be they funders, board or staff members – taking steps to become green can be accompanied by fear of the unknown or resentment as people resist change or are concerned that they may be blamed, directly or indirectly, for their practices. Delays in addressing issues are opportunities missed. Inertia – or intentionally ignoring the ideas of those most excited to green their arts organizations- creates disillusioned workers; try not to dampen staff enthusiasm. Some board or staff members cite myths to avoid change. Let's examine some of the most common myths and concerns below:

MYTH #1 — GREEN IS DIFFICULT

Learning to make good choices, in any new area of work, requires some degree of research and effort. Greening is a process, and as such some simple decisions, such as replacing incandescent bulbs with now-required compact fluorescent or LEDs, can seem complex (or bothersome) if there is new information for staff to recognize, price or interpret. Because environments are tapestries of interconnected organisms and systems, information-gathering should be viewed as a continuum of learning, interpreting, experimenting, adjusting and observing. To simplify, below are some maxims that may help sort through the array of information and options your organization may encounter as it makes environmentally-sustainable choices.

- No one goes all-green: perhaps someday if one builds a new net zero facility; but certainly not in an existing facility or historic house, (even the two-day Garlic & Arts Fest in Orange, Massachusetts creates (amazingly) two bags of trash.
- No one goes green all at once: large systems may be too complex to change quickly and capital funds are not always available.
- Green is local – very local: what works next door won't necessarily work at another institution; make choices appropriate for individual situations.
- Green is creative and offers unique opportunities for each institution's organization, climate, facility or programs to determine individual needs; a cookie cutter approach is not realistic.
- Consider the quadruple bottom line: to the single bottom line approach of profit, add three more goals for return on investment — people, planet and program.
- Support the program or mission: that's the fourth "p"; how does green support core work and mission?
- Think like an ecosystem: everything is connected, so choices in one area can affect many others.
- Respect the law of unintended consequences: because one's institution is a system, there will be many unexpected results – good and bad; one cannot expect to anticipate them all, but that should not stop an institution from starting.
- Pilot everything: plan to refine small changes or tackle a full-scale project based on discoveries
- Educate everyone; teach both staff and visitors about the choices made so that all learn together and support one another.

> How can you showcase far-reaching savings? The Environmental Protection Agency's website features calculators that can show savings in terms of the number of trees, gallons of water or barrels of oil saved and represent the savings in a tangible manner that people can quickly comprehend.

MYTH #2 — GREENING COSTS MONEY AND IS "MORE" EXPENSIVE

To say green is more expensive is much like saying clothes or cars are more expensive. Than what? Which ones and over what period of time? Yes, there are costs when adding or changing complex systems, buying new materials, or making changes at a time that is not optimal; but greening offers opportunities to create savings. Here are some brief examples.

Green does not have to be bought or fancy. Does it cost more to use less electricity? Training staff to turn out lights as they leave an area may reduce energy costs significantly with little-to-no-expense. However, if the goal is to significantly use less electricity, a large institution may first need to install a building management system and related sensors to cut back on energy use in lighting and the Heating, Ventilation and Air Conditioning (HVAC) system. The initial cost of installing that system is an expense, but over the life of the system if it saves energy so the organization is financially ahead, then green is not more expensive.

Consider office consumables. How can it cost more to use less paper by using scrap paper for drafts? A one-time cost to install water filters on faucets rather than purchasing bottled water has a cost, but if one adds in the cost of inventorying and reordering, trucking, plastic bottle production, disposal costs, and more, then the investment of a filter reveals additional savings. By carefully examining institutional habits to reduce redundancies and waste, it is easy to find that institutions can continually make improvements while buying less and savings can mount!

Timing can shift an equation. It is expensive to put in a green roof (one with living plants) when the roof was just replaced last year. This is because the organization will have to consider the cost of the recent nvestment in the the current new roof plus the green roof; but what if the green roof is installed only when a new roof is needed anyway? Assuming the structure can hold the weight, the green one can save energy and help the roof membrane last much longer. And if there is a need for more programming space or an improved view from other parts of the building, a living roof has even more advantages than the old one. It may turn out to be highly cost-effective over the life of the product especially as a new roof is needed anyway: timing can shift an equation.[1]

MYTH #3 — GREEN IS MORE SHOW THAN SAVINGS

Early in this decades' green movement, people made obvious statements of green practice to make their point and to lead the way. Often a photovoltaic (PV) solar array or a wind turbine or wind spire

> Tip: Cannot afford a green roof? Installing a light colored one saves energy by reflecting light and not collecting heat, thus saving cooling costs. Even small changes can make a big difference!

symbolized the organization's adoption of green practices. Sometimes these choices made less sense for sustainability than for marketing ploy. Though this may have been very valuable to the movement, on an individual basis it suggests it may have been more drama than savings or environmental impact. Because the early solar arrays were expensive and only offset a portion of an institution's energy use, it set a tone that only wealthy institutions could go green. This is rapidly changing. In some states, programs offer deep incentives and some energy service companies (ESCO) will "rent" an institution's roof, offsetting a portion of the organization's electric bill while the ESCO obtains the tax credits. ESCO's pay the upfront material, installation and electric company connection costs, and after a set number of years, [typically 10-20] the panels belong to the institution so it can continue to reap the rewards. Partnering with an ESCO enables an institution to take no financial risk, make their statement, contribute their "real estate" to green energy, and get a break on the electric bill.

Where such opportunities do not exist, the arts organization may create them by developing a partnership with an energy company or a technology training school that can install PV or other systems. The arts organization can seek funds or invest in materials, and the choice results in cleaner energy. It's a balance of the four bottom lines: people, planet, profit, and program. If the project meets needs, creates green energy, is paid for from grants or is supported by the community or outside vendors, or if it provides more than it takes in terms of dollars, then institutions have turned their statement into a profitable "win" for their bottom line.

MYTH #4 — GREENING INVOLVES COMPLEX TECHNOLOGY

Greening is not always a technical solution. More often behavioral change is what's green. Encouraging staff carpooling or biking to work rather than driving alone saves fuel and reduces carbon production. It does not require special technology to dedicate a printer drawer for drafts, to use the blank side of recycled office paper, to encourage staff not to print at all, or to buy used instead of new furniture.

A sculpture park or museum building a rain garden to address a run-off problem is an example of using a low-tech solution to capture and slow rain water runoff, simply with plants and soil processes. The rain garden requires design and engineering – professional planning on a small or large degree depending upon the site and capacity – but once installed, the system works energy-free with low-maintenance for years. Transforming the rain garden INTO art meets a dual purpose. It may help find funders willing to pay for the work and could encourage visitors to stop by an underutilized site, providing additional opportunities for teaching and learning.

Sometimes *simple* technology can provide low-cost solutions to greening problems. Online services that allow people to meet face-to-face instead of driving across town or flying to meetings across the country provides enormous savings, and is no more complex than downloading a program to one's computer.

MYTH #5 — GREENING IS RISKY

Green is perceived as risky because some of the materials, concepts and approaches are new; however as more institutions have gone green there are ample opportunities to see processes at work. Not every stakeholder believes in environmental sustainability and, for some, there may be concern that going green may be alienating; or perceived as off-mission and wasteful. This is an opportunity for information sharing and creating buy-in. Consider taking a board field trip to a successful green organization or inviting a well-informed special guest to present at the next staff meeting. Inviting questions in a safe place can turn the doubtful into green believers.

Good leaders know how to manage risk. They make choices based on supporting the mission, researching and testing the approach, and sharing why a decision was made at a particular time and with specific financial support. This type of risk-management work will stand the organization in good stead and prepare it to take some important strategic steps.

MYTH #6 — ONLY LARGE ORGANIZATIONS SHOULD GO GREEN OR CAN MAKE AN IMPACT

Not true! Smaller organizations may have an easier time instituting changes, and their impacts can be equally dramatic in terms of savings on water, electricity, and leadership for a community. A smaller institution may find that turning on the copier only when the first person actually needs it (not when staff arrive in the morning), or putting the microwave on a switch then turning it on only when needed (so the clock isn't on all the time), reduces hours of energy use each day.

> One small western Massachusetts nonprofit arts organization located in a former mill building cut their power use by 50% by adopting many of the simple changes noted above. They also traded in their electric water cooler with a ceramic water container which used no electricity but kept the water cold. Seasonally, they installed clear, removable window covers that sharply reduced their heating bill.

II. Steps to Greening — How To Start

What are the primary consumers of energy in the arts facility? No doubt it is a combination of electricity, HVAC and program-related equipment such as kilns, stage lighting and projectors. To make the greatest possible impact GET AN ENERGY AUDIT! Often the local utility will provide it free of charge. The audit gives concrete examples of where to make substantive changes to save energy and therefore money. It's the easiest way to start, but there are times when an audit is not forthcoming, or sometimes leadership or landlords are unwilling, or financially unable, to act on information. If an audit is impossible (for the moment), begin greening where it makes the most sense.

If an audit is possible it will inform the organization where the most savings can be found, and it may provide a clear and attainable fundraising opportunity. If the facility is found to be too costly to run, then perhaps the audit could be the deciding factor in whether or not to move, downsize, or push to purchase the space so the organization has full control. An electric company or firm devoted to energy audits should conduct the audit and then make appropriate recommendations. The auditor will describe ways to reduce energy consumption (such as improving insulation, replacing "leaky" windows, and recommending efficient equipment), and (by scheduling lighting and HVAC systems more efficiently, and making better use of daylight options) can set systems that can improve indoor comfort. One recommendation may be to capitalize on a solar electric program, and another may be or to add sensors to vending machines to save energy without compromising food storage conditions. There will be large and small projects to consider.

Since environmental sustainability is all about ecosystems, and ecosystems are interconnected, that means environmental sustainability is a continuous loop – no beginning or end. After the energy au-

> **How to Make Discoveries and Build Staff Buy-in**
>
> One new green team started by conducting a kick-off meeting of all staff, sharing why the team thought going green was a good idea. Leaders asked for input on ways to save energy, water, and more. Ideas came fast and furious, and quickly revealed that the primary concern was temperature. Simultaneously some staff were too hot, while others too cold (some so cold in fact that individuals were running space heaters under their desks in summer!). A map of the space was drawn, inexpensive thermometers were handed out to those in different parts of the building and at set times over two days, staff filled out a form noting temperature and what they felt. The team learned that their facility had zones that the building manager could adjust, and suddenly everyone was more comfortable. The team demonstrated their value and buy-in was immediate, making future changes easier to implement.

dit, the institution can choose what is believed to be the best way for the organization to start, whether it is the path of least resistance, or the path most strategically aligned with mission and goals.

Will this be a piecemeal, low-hanging fruit approach, or more strategic? For very plan-driven organizations, taking out the strategic plan and the multi-year budgets and align planned or desired actions with sustainable methods and solutions may be a welcomed approach. If there are many priorities of similar values, then look for the barriers and opportunities, deficits and excesses to find clearer choices. If one starts as piecemeal, then the planning will likely become more strategic, but starting is important: it allows time to develop expertise that will make the planning stage more effective once it is reached.

Find the entry point by examining excesses or deficits, barriers and opportunities. An excess is too much trash or shipping pallets, or costs that are too high. A deficit may be too few parking spaces or not enough money to purchase gala decorations or hire needed staff. Examples of barriers may be zoning by-law restrictions or not owning one's facility and getting no support to make changes from an unmotivated landlord. An opportunity may be the gift of space for a sculpture garden or the energy company's need to generate renewable energy through solar arrays on local roofs. Each of these situations requires a solution; sustainable solutions often offer a better return on investment making green its own reward. Where there is a problem, call on the creativity and ingenuity of new green solutions!

Early changes are more likely to succeed if they have a champion to lead them, have a clear project scope with a widely-supportable goal, and involve a shared process so more than a few supporters share the effort and glory while also spreading the word and setting a great example.

III. Green Teams

A green team is charged with the research and implementation of greening plans. Institutions generally have two choices in forming a team. They can start working and collecting team members as they go or they can launch a strategic project to identify team members and set up a plan of work. Either works, but starting somewhere begins to develop staff expertise that will make the planning stage more effective.

There is a great deal of green team information available online. Much is dated, simply because the concepts are now well-established. However here are some important issues to consider to suit one's institutional needs and culture:

- A green team will evolve through phases: over the months and years ahead look for ways to adapt its design and work practices to remain relevant to institutional needs and interests.
- Identify a natural green leader or two to be the champion(s). They are already recycling, buying green products, or agitating for purchasing green power.
- Work to attract representatives from across the institution to seed green ideas, bring a wide perspective to tasks and better understand the impact that one decision will make on a variety of departments.
- The team may feel pretty ad hoc at first, but usually a volunteer group is more committed than one made of conscripts. If the green team's activities are not part of a job assignment, they will be put aside for more pressing responsibilities. The ideal is voluntary participation by all with full backing of their supervisors.
- Remember to share the news and celebrate. Good green works encourages more, so reward successes and encourage others to join a joyful team. A green board in the kitchen or break room, or emailing a weekly Green Tip or Green Tip of the Hat to a staff member will keep the excitement alive.

There are three basic types of green teams: institution-wide, departmental, or ad hoc. If a green team is either institution-wide or departmental, it is often a formal organization. If the green team is ad hoc, then it most likely will be pretty informal. It is hard to say if most green teams started as grassroots affairs or were created by leadership. Often an ad hoc green team triggers another, more formal and top-down approach within a year or two - if the group has had some clear successes and leadership recognizes the green value.

By piloting green changes through an ad hoc green team an institution can learn a good deal about what the barriers and opportunities, excesses and deficits are for the organization and for green team work. If the organization moves from informal to formal, recognize the contribution of the first green team members, and ask them to help with the transition and shape the change. The original team may have the most "green expertise" in the institution – don't let that get away.

IV. Assessments

Assessing is the step that helps organizations to know what to change and how to manage efforts going forward. There are many informative assessing opportunities in environmental sustainability: energy

---

Thinking about issuing a mandate to go green?

This is one way to direct the ecosystem of green practices, but a mandate works best in a hierarchical institution. Arts organizations with creativity as a focus are usually fluid, even entrepreneurial in their approaches, not hierarchical, and the staff and volunteers want input and direct participation. For a large, well-established organization with a deep staff and a broad list of departments, a mandate may be the only way to create a cohesive approach that can work effectively. Be sure to leave room for creativity so greening projects will benefit.

and waste audits; supply and chemical inventories; electricity and water metering; and temperature and humidity monitoring. If all the meters and systems were already in place to measure energy and water use, track waste and purchases, and calculate carbon emissions, there would be no need to do an energy audit, create a preferred-purchases list, or track the mercury-containing light bulbs. But, since this is still the beginning of change, some tracking and managing systems may need to be developed.

The energy audit is the simplest assessment – and as noted above — due to the scale of our heating/air conditioning needs, offers the largest cash savings. But what other assessments are helpful?

- Simply asking people not to waste water may be insufficient. In water-sensitive areas, (and increasingly elsewhere) it makes sense to conduct a water-use audit, and adopt every possible water saving device, such as low-flow or multi-option toilets, automatic faucets (set to be frugal), and designing the outdoor space for best utilization of run-off.
- Waste audit: measuring garbage and recycling, both by type and volume, over time can identify where the biggest changes might be made and help determine the costs and advantages of those changes. (One small office replaced the annual waste of 30,000 paper coffee cups by gifting one mug per staff member and making additional mugs available for guests. Staff were encouraged to place one-time use plastic pods from the coffee maker into a container which green team members emptied, composted and spread on outdoor plants.)
- Supply inventory: understand all the things purchased to determine which ones are already green which the organization can boast about, and which can be replaced with greener options. Changes can be made by department or product type. For example, each department can change a few products a year or set a 12-month goal of a 25 percent increase in green product choices, or reduce by cost. An easy starting point is to recommend Energy Star® appliances, and those certified as using renewable sources and sustainable process for paper and wood production. Put these items on a preferred-purchase list and train staff to choose from this list first. Be sure to delete the old products from the purchase list!
- Chemical and finishes inventory: similar to a supply inventory it includes all the cleaning chemicals (any applied to landscapes, walkways and parking areas); adhesives; and all finishes for floors, walls, furniture and carpeting. This is an important area to tackle because it can be so large and hidden, but by specifying low/no-VOC items (Volatile Organic Compounds) – many of which are harmful to humans and pollute the environment – the chemical footprint can begin to be reduced. Build this list simply by noting items used or purchased over a full work week, then adjust seasonally. Ask others to add any missing items. One arts nonprofit realized that applying an insecticide on their lawn had a broader implication: children played on the lawn during breaks, and all were tracking chemicals into the building on their shoes. This exposed everyone, especially the full-time office staff, to the dangers.
- Electrical plug inventory: count and identify the number of items plugged into outlets organization-wide to determine which unnecessary ones can be left unplugged much of the time to save money. Anything plugged in draws some energy; if it has a light indicating it's plugged in, then it is actively drawing energy (phone chargers and printers, for example). Follow up this inventory with a staff awareness session. Encourage plugging multiple items into a single power strip to reduce the draw when the strip is "on", and to allow a single switch to turn items off at the end of the day. Institute an 'off at night and weekend' rule, then make occasional check-in tours to monitor plug habits. Share the changes in the electrical usage to show the collective impact.

> Savings can quickly mount. One university green team calculated that if all staff and students turned off their computers each day by 10 pm (an average to balance those who left at 5 pm for the inevitable late night students), the institution would save over $2 million annually!

- Building retro-commissioning: if one's building were brand-new, this would be called commissioning. Doing this years later is called retro-commissioning: an intense review of the HVAC system and the building's design to make sure the air, energy and water systems are working as intended. Choose an experienced engineering company or energy service company to scour the building. To fund this activity, seek a community foundation interested in capacity building, or a long-time donor interested in a gift that keeps on giving. The recommendations can provide strategic plans for system improvements, replacements or upgrades, while providing good returns on energy efficiency and reduced maintenance concerns.

Each of these inventories and audits provides the information for making decisions. They may be small and immediate, or larger and more strategic. Each provides a recommended path for change to help get started. Be sure to act on what you can as soon as possible so the information does not become so out-of-date it requires a new assessment.

> We use our programmable thermostats faithfully and the local utility company said we had cut the gas and electric use in our building 50 percent from the previous tenant. They called and wanted to know what we were doing that reduced usage so much – we told them we use the programmable thermostats. They said they tell people that and if they will use them they can drastically save on their energy bills.
>
> —Jennifer Case, Managing Director, Case School of Music, Sioux Falls, South Dakota[2]

V. Plan Capital Changes

From this day forward commit to including sustainable solutions as part of all discussions of repair, replacement, expansion or adaptations to the building. This means the capital changes for a new water heater, a gallery renovation, a new catering kitchen, or a new wing.

For new construction, if the work involves an architect, engineer, designer, or plumber, make it clear that sustainability is a value to be included alongside cost, appearance, ease of use, and durability. Ask them to provide the pros and cons of all solutions including the sustainable ones. Consider as well the benefit of meeting any of the sustainability standards such as Living Building, Leadership in Energy and Environmental Design (LEED), Energy Star®, Sustainable SITES (for landscapes), or ExhibitSEED. In addition to "proving" that a standard has been met, the benefits include PR opportunities which can raise the institutional profile for not only programming, but for fundraising and gaining support from those who appreciate and wish to reward institutions that work sustainably. These standards programs are most useful and efficient if they are part of the earliest planning discussions. Regardless of achieving certification, their tenets may prove very valuable in identifying important options in planning.

Again, visit other green buildings – arts organizations and others – to learn from their experiences and to widen exposure to the many available and creative options.

If a project involves a renovation, it is important to consider embodied energy in the calculations. If the boiler, roof, patio, or parking lot has reached the end of its life, then the organization has capitalized on all the embodied energy in it – the energy spent finding and collecting the materials and processing them, manufacturing the final item, and installing it at the site. But if the chiller unit in the HVAC system is new or a motor is only five years old, or the parking lot was just repaved, replacement now wastes the value of the materials and effort spent on producing the not-so-old item unless there is a way to reuse or repurpose it. The ideal approach is to use it up before replacing it. That is where strategic capital planning helps an institution make strategic green choices. Replacing end-of-life items with new, sustainably-sourced and manufactured materials or items is the appropriate next step.

> As the film industry replaced reels with digital projectors, a small nonprofit cinema agreed to serve as a case study organization for students from an Arts Extension Service greening course. The cinema had selected, but not yet purchased, new digital projectors. Students quickly researched equipment options, this time with an eye toward energy use, and found equipment meeting the same specifications, but requiring 50 percent of the energy to operate.

Changes may be made over time or in key areas while an institution waits for adequate financial resources. For example, an organization may need to save for an HVAC system upgrade, and meanwhile add sensors to help improve the functioning of the current system and to save money until it is replaced. Or it may choose to refit old toilets with low-flow ones in the bathrooms with the most visitor and patron use, and delay refitting the others until ample funds are available. There are times to go ahead and get the new system because a donor offers it or because critical functions require it; at this point, it is wise to consider what related changes can be made to capitalize on the opportunity or to minimize its impact. It may be that the new on-demand water heater uses so much less space than a traditional water heater that – finally – it is possible to create storage for tables and chairs and free up classroom space. Efficiencies pop up in unexpected places.

> Sometimes being smart turns out to be green. The New England Youth Theatre in Brattleboro, Vermont, was required by the city's floodplain ordinance to have 20-inch high floodgates at the ready. These simple panels slip into place inside and at the bottom of the main doors. They are fastened to create a seal. In 2011 Hurricane Irene devastated major areas in the Northeast. The theatre staff report that the water came nearly to the top of the panels, but inside there was only minimal carpet damage. Low tech, preventive work saved the organization the cost in cash – and interruptions – of a full scale replacement of carpet and perhaps much more, keeping all that material out of the landfills and not requiring new items to be installed.[3]

VII. Public Program Considerations

These will cluster generally in three areas: choices of activities, materials used, and locations.

The location choice has a great deal to do with energy: lighting, heating and cooling, and travel. Can the program occur in natural daylight? Can the event take place in the space that requires the least energy use for user comfort by starting out in the sunny area in the morning, but retreating to a cooler place in the afternoon in summer, or vice versa in winter? Where can the event be held that requires the fewest fuel miles for presenters and guests? For example, it may be possible to take a busload of people to New York to the Met, or, like the Avalon Theater in Easton, Maryland, is there the option to have it streamed live into one's auditorium. An in-person experience is preferable, but offering options onsite is the greener choice.

Choosing more sustainable materials is an ongoing process, so celebrate the first steps taken and build from there. One's goal is to always consider materials based on the concepts of the chemical impact of the product and/or the process of manufacturing it, renewability of the resources in the product, location of the source materials, ease and longevity of use, and the ease of end-of-use steps (repurpose, reuse, recycle, compost). In the book Upcycle, the authors demonstrate how every product can be designed for its 'next life', for example creating a piece of furniture without the use of glues and toxic finishes so it can be transformed later into something new with minimal impact. By planning beyond a one-time use, items can be repurposed more easily.

Until all products are planned this way there will be trade-offs, so select the materials that make the most sense. For example, art supplies made in another country and shipped here travel too far to be sustainable, but if a program truly requires them, there may be no choice. In that case, see if purchasing in bulk can reduce packaging, and be sure to manage the end-of-use aspects as sustainably as possible. For another activity, supplies found at a yard sale, or recycled yogurt containers for paint pots, may fit the bill perfectly, helping to balance impact.

Regardless of the program, the place to start is with an inventory of what is currently in use. Encourage others to make green choices by providing an easier path to compliance. Look at the labels and invoices to determine content, source, cost and the amounts regularly consumed. Begin to track rate of use and plan for bulk purchases to save packaging and travel. Check the inventory list before a purchase to avoid duplications. Create a preferred purchases list that highlights sustainable choices. Post this publicly and encourage others to add to it. For new products, ask a volunteer or intern to research a green alternative and add it to the list. Gradually this list will grow, and all can celebrate the progress noting for example that the institution is now using 30, 50, or 70 percent or more green products.

Choosing to green activities may appear challenging, but with practice it becomes easy. Once an activity idea comes forward, the first green steps are to consider the location (where) and materials (what) are already on hand. Then consider the how and why parts. Here are some examples of more sustainable approaches that improve efficient use of materials:

- Students could paint individual pictures (yet again) in a class, and they could take them all home (yet again); or they could paint a wall mural at the local nursery school instead. What's the sustainability factor there? The wall already exists, but now students won't consume 15 pieces of paper, cardboard or canvas. Logistically this is more complex, and eventually the region may run out of available walls, but sharing the art makes green sense.

> Tip: Store items in full view. If staff, board and volunteers can see what is on hand, they won't buy more unless it's needed. Keep a clear and obvious system of organization for costumes and costuming supplies, exhibit and stage building materials, special events and office supplies, and any other item that commands a significant amount of the supply budget. Keep the storage area as tidy as possible so people won't avoid using it and will learn to keep it organized as well.

- Perhaps an ensemble class has a participation requirement of two performances per session. Could one of those be at a community Earth Day event instead of an evening auditorium concert?
- Can a "found" art class be scheduled to follow the area nonprofits' combined supply swap event using only items left over after the swap?

With a little practice, this gets easy.

> **Green Revolution**
>
> "Would your organization like to reduce its carbon footprint? Have you thought about ways to incorporate/reuse/recycle materials from old exhibits, activities, or projects? Would renewable energy, organic food, climate change, and other environmental issues strike a chord with your visitors or community?"
>
> This is the promotion for the Smithsonian Institution's Travel Exhibition Service's exhibit "Green Revolution". If an institution is looking for a green project that comes with guidance, the Smithsonian's virtual exhibit guide offers fabrication plans and graphic designs in pdf format which can keep the costs and the environmental impact down while providing some great creative and green education for the audience. This isn't just for museums – any creative group should consider it.

VIII. Changes to Core Practices

Some aspects of an organization's work are neither basic operations nor public activities, but core practices. For a museum this is collections care work and exhibits. For a theater, dance, or opera company this is costuming, lighting design, and stage/scene construction. For an arts school or sculpture studio, core practices may create chemical exposure from printing solutions or concerns from breathing clay or plaster dust. Staff must be the final arbiter of green decision in specialty areas, but there are many approaches for use of art materials, staging and costuming, lighting, and museums exhibits and collections care that can provide opportunities to go green and protect staff and patron health.

A. ARTS MATERIALS

For toxicity of materials, the Art and Creative Materials Institute Inc. (www.ACMInet.org) has a searchable products database that can help with research. ACMI identifies approved products and those with cautionary labeling to help make safer choices about the health and disposal of materials. Always consider fumes, not simply the materials that are handled and disposed of. ACMI can warn about needs for ventilation – natural or artificial. The Occupational Health and Safety Administration's (OSHA) guidelines can also help share information regarding toxicity of chemical use. The Environmental Protection Agency (EPA) has disposal requirements that should also be identified on material labels with hazardous characteristics. See Monona Rossol's The Artists' Complete Health and Safety Guide for ideas on how to mitigate issues.

B. STAGING AND COSTUMING

For organizations with intense costuming needs, sourcing materials and material content will be most important. How natural are the materials? How far away is the manufacturer? What processes provide the material finishes and how are the garments cleaned? To get the glitter or flow or required appearance may be difficult in sustainable materials, so begin by recognizing needs and developing new sources for materials gentler on the environment. Reuse whatever possible to make them and to make them over for reuse. One's local Goodwill, Salvation Army or second-hand stores are a great source of wedding and prom dresses that may offer the desired special fabrics while giving longer life to a single-use dress. Or simply ask patrons to donate their unwanted fancy dress items.

> Tip: To earn money some companies rent out their costumes, enabling others to save money, fulfill need, and keep costumes in use rather than in perpetual storage.

Regularly building new sets, refreshing backdrops, replacing all the orchestra seating, and keeping the showplace of the work presentable is an expense that is likely to have some serious repercussions for environmental sustainability. Fabrics – their cleaning and finishes – are often sources of volatile organic chemicals; furniture construction often includes harmful adhesives and fabrics with toxic finishes; and frequent making and breaking of theater staging involves wood, adhesives, finishes and lots of dumpsters. Consider the material choices discussed in the last section. If one does not exist, now is the time to build a strong relationship with the used furniture providers in the area and with other performance groups so that all can share props and staging. Consider durability as well. Whatever components – modular or otherwise – that could be reused, engineer them to last. When they are no longer needed, consider if they or their components can have another life with other organizations or projects.

At this stage of the sustainability revolution creating a zero-waste staging plan while keeping up with the expectations of patrons or the demands of performances may be difficult, but do begin to mitigate the effects of any consumption using these three approaches – gradually incorporate greener alternatives for the most commonly-consumed items; cultivate a broader and more active reuse and redistribution system for materials and furniture; and examine the performance selection process to consider if the program goals can support, or gradually become supportive, of less-intensive resource use. When making changes in production materials and appearance, it will be very important to educate staff, donors and the audience. It may help them understand the reasoning behind the changes, and it may even attract new supporters. Take note of any alternative materials in use, and invite the supplier to be a sponsor, and then together spread the good green word.

> Tip: Theaters (and museums) near a university, community college or tech school, should schedule with the art department or shop instructors to create opportunities for students to pick up sets as they are broken down. Students will have resources, the dumpster will remain (mostly) empty, and the cross-pollination of departments can build alliances.

> Sometimes environmental sustainability is the creative outlet. Consider the Museo Subaquatico de Arte (MUSA) in Cancun. (Yes, it's underwater.) A sculptor worked with marine biologists to create cement installations designed to become habitat for aquatic life. Over time the sculptures will act much a like a coral reef in attracting organisms. This strategically-placed museum's real goal is to attract divers who are overusing and damaging the natural coral reefs around Cancun. The first installation was a series of human sculptures, and the second was an underwater suburb of cement 'homes'. As the aquatic life – flora and fauna – take over, the art installation evolves – attracting return visitors year after year.[4]

C. LIGHTING

The advances in the lighting industry are making it much easier to use efficient lighting while still achieving desired effects on stage or in museum exhibits. Lighting manufacturers are aggressively pursuing better, more appealing lamps (bulbs) and fixtures making the casual user unable to keep abreast of all options. A lighting designer, or energy provider, and/or lighting materials supplier should help with efficient approaches and share information about state and local efficiency programs that offer rebates and discounts. Include these professionals in discussions about upgrades to help make the greening process more affordable. This is one area where institutions are very likely to find financial support and make a big impact on energy costs and bottom line.

D. MUSEUM EXHIBITS AND COLLECTIONS CARE

In greening exhibitions, museums should consider exhibit construction materials, exhibit lighting, and demands of traveling exhibits for safe and efficient artifact storage.

Considering their collections energy efficiency for providing temperature and humidity for proper, and perpetual, care is paramount. These environmental conditions are required for collections care whether in storage or exhibit areas. According to Brophy and Wylie in *The Green Museum: A Primer on Environmental Practice,* 2nd edition, "New conservation science has shown that most collections are best preserved at cool temperatures combined with moderate relative humidity, or RH. This work was presented at a roundtable at the Museum of Fine Arts, Boston in 2010 where conservators and collection managers from three dozen of the country's top collecting institutions discussed new ways of thinking about environmental conditions in their institutions." There is a growing body of evidence that HVAC system shutdowns and temperature setbacks, temporarily at night and on weekends, may support substantial energy savings without compromising collections care. "The new thinking is a far cry from the traditional 70°F, 50% RH flat-line condition" adopted by the field in the 1970's and followed religiously ever since. Of course there are inappropriate conditions for considering such changes: highly-sensitive collections should not be subject to such practices, and extreme seasonal or weather conditions prevent this practice as does a building with poor insulation and much air infiltration, but under certain conditions this is becoming a powerful, respected approach to sustainable collections care.

Exhibit lighting approaches are changing. Museums are steadily replacing lighting systems for the more advanced, color-appropriate LEDs. The physical materials impact of exhibit design, construction and deconstruction is substantial, just as for performance groups. exhibitSEED's green checklist is a valuable guide for development teams. There are five strategies: reduce new materials; use local resources; reduce waste; reduce energy consumption; and reduce toxic emissions. The checklist provides ideas not just for materials but also for working with stakeholders and advisors collaboratively; sourcing components and encouraging batch processes for building; standardizing components and designing for reuse; maintaining easily accessible storage for odd cuts and leftovers for use on other projects; and focusing on local resources, vendors and advisors. The checklist's sixth section encourages innovation such as re-using or repurposing materials, and identifying new solutions to common problems that will help continuously green exhibit work.

> Recycling is mandatory for bulbs with mercury content (fluorescent tubes, CFLs, black lights and high-intensity discharge lamps among others). Plan to inventory lamps as they are delivered, save their shipping boxes, and put each burnt-out lamp back in its box (covered) to await return to the manufacturer for recycling. Determine who is responsible and who will manage the process, and monitor how diligent they are. Include electronic fixtures and controls in the recycling program. When in doubt, consult the EPA's Energy Star® program to learn where to recycle these products. As the price of LED lights has dropped, using these energy savers makes green sense.

Travel – for exhibits and loaned objects – is a high-consumption component of museum exhibits. Clearly museums will not stop sharing exhibits or objects, but can they make the process more sustainable? Some of the solutions developed are shared below:

- Use nuts and bolts to build travel crates instead of a "glue-and-screw" approach to allow crates to be disassembled, stored and reused.
- Standardize sizes and shapes where possible so travel crates – at least the exteriors – can be used safely for more than one object over time.
- Consider reusing crates as storage where appropriate rather than building storage shelves and crates for many items.
- Use sustainably-sourced materials for making travel crates and continue the practice of choosing no-VOC materials and finishes to protect the objects and the environment.
- Whenever possible, choose the most-fuel efficient transport method.
- Work to develop a travel schedule that limits miles covered by focusing on reasonably adjacent geographic area.

IX. Gift Shop, Supply Shop, Café

As with materials choices, there may be many opportunities for greening the retail part of the institution. Begin with an inventory. Look for items sourced locally, made with sustainable materials (reused, repurposed or rapidly-renewable materials; responsibly cultivated, with low/no chemical impact, and using green energy and/or little water, for example), and responsibly packaged.

- The Buy Local movement may mean that locally crafted materials may sell as well as imported items and provide an opportunity for the institution to become a supporter of local artisans, farmers, bakers and others. Make it a goal to become as locally-sourced as possible, feature items to raise awareness and grow sponsorships.
- Does a best-selling item come individually packaged? Ask the wholesale provider to send them in bulk with less packaging. This reduces materials use for packaging, saves time unpacking the items, and creates less waste to store and pay to haul away.
- If a consumable such as coffee is a popular item, many opportunities exist to sell it with limited negative environmental impact. For coffee this means bird-friendly and shade-grown so the growing lands are not clear-cut for plantations (eradicating all local flora and fauna and exposing the land to erosion), organic if possible, and fair trade so the farmer is fairly compensated and treated.
- Some vendors advertise that their products are made in factories powered with clean energy. If this is verified by a reliable source, it is a good green practice to support.

Whatever green choices are made, be sure to tell the public. Buyers with sustainability inclinations are likely to pay more for a green item than a standard one. Green buyers are also more likely to choose the green item among many, so be sure to give these buyers what they're already looking for.

A green gift shop should consider more than its products, but also lighting and display. Daylight enhances mood and saves energy and money too. Often vendors offer special promotional displays that require energy and may use cases with unsustainable characteristics (plywood that emits – off gas – harmful chemicals such formaldehyde-based glues, or unsustainable wood sources). Resist this and opt for a greener display approach. If the gift shop has a vending machine or cooler for items, make sure it is the most efficient possible by purchasing an Energy Star® appliance or the Energy Miser® add-ons.

Last (perhaps most of all) encourage buyers to bring their own bags. If the shop has an overflow of packing peanuts and cardboard boxes, give what cannot be reused or recycled to UPS or the local pack-it shop. Recycle everything, and insist that the institution recycles all cardboard, paper, bottles and cans.

IX. Financial Considerations and Fundraising

What about covering those initial costs? The good news is that new income options often come with sustainability projects and potentially new donors, but don't count on this being a solution to all problems.

There is an adage "Money must do more than one thing". This maxim is generally an excellent approach to creating fundable projects: if a grant for a project fulfills more than one goal for the arts organization or the funder, then its impact multiplies. This attracts and rewards more funders and encourages renewed support.

This is also why green projects attract funding. The best green projects affect many areas of one's organization positively, therefore making money "do more than one thing". Here are some examples:

- When funding the installation of a green roof, donors' funds support a new roof, energy efficiency, a potential new entertainment or program space, and habitat. A safe green roof outside a rooftop café provides a lovely view in inclement weather, an expanded service area in good weather, a fantastic location for a fundraising event, a great backdrop for magazine photo shoots, a terrific rental space, and a good place for messy art projects.
- If the energy audit recommends purchasing and installing occupancy sensors to manage lighting and to reduce energy costs, a donor can see the value in an immediate cost savings that continues for years.
- Selling new seats in the auditorium to a new and younger group of supporters may be easier if they are attractively made from renewable resources and low-VOC materials.
- Replacing the lawn with xeriscaping makes sense in areas of the country experiencing water shortages as does planting native plants everywhere else.

Each of these situations involves some trade-offs. For example, after 15 to 20 years that solar array will not be as productive as it had when new, but it will still produce free energy. Xeriscaping, while becoming increasingly popular in the Southwest, may require signage to explain why the choice was made to remove the lawn, and should include information about saving water, saving work (no more mowing) and using native plants.

Some supporters will not be interested in multiple benefits. If they have an agenda, they'll be focused on a single interest: energy efficiency, water conservation, or sourcing local foods for the café and receptions. These donors will say what motivates them. They may want to work side by side with staff to develop a good solution and to make the final choices, so be prepared to be a partner in the project, not the leader.

Some single-focus supporters will bring funding with them: the local energy supplier or state energy office; lighting provider; and the solar or wind power company. There may be regulatory or provider groups offering rebates or incentives for program participation because an agency must meet a quota or is interested in building a market sector. This is common in the lighting industry and its extensive rebate programs. It is also common where an energy provider must meet a quota of renewable energy provision but needs the real estate for building arrays; they may be interested in an institutions' roof or parking lot. The DSIRE.org database lists all the state agencies that provide rebates, tax incentives, or grants to support alternative energy use. There are strict criteria and timeframes to follow, so read the fine print, but definitely explore these options when considering funding capital projects.

There are not many private foundations currently touting green projects as their funding focus, but increasingly funders are asking for descriptions of applicant's sustainability practices in proposals. Certainly if a group of proposals has similarly competitive projects, the one with solid thinking in environmental sustainability will have an edge with some funders.

Federal agencies also support some projects through grants. The Environmental Protection Agency has programs to fund energy efficiency and environmental education. Federal funding often seeps into state agencies so the Energy Efficiency Community Block Grants or other grants may be appropriate opportunities. Energy projects are subject to annual changes in focus so beware: this year's interest in all things solar may give way to small-scale wind next year. Tap the board or key staff member's advocacy skills and ask them to stay in touch with the state's energy office interested in these projects. (See the Advocacy Chapter for more information. ▌) They may call with opportunities or may include the institution in an application they submit — remember, agencies need a place to showcase their ideas, too! The more these agencies understand the arts organization's interests, the greater the chances to help fulfill each other's goals.

In addition to the energy providers, some large companies have quiet but important sponsorship programs – usually in their home regions — that promote high-visibility sustainable programs. Boeing and Toyota, for example, have re-granting programs in partnership with nonprofits fostering green community work. Whether this is a promotion approach or a genuine green approach, consider using it to advance the arts organization's green agenda if values match. Observe others' green projects, research their funders, and be sure to apply if the arts organization qualifies.

It will be easy to develop a list of individual donors motivated by green options. Keep that list active and work with individuals to develop and fund green projects. Consider green-themed annual appeals, fundraising events, and materials donations programs. Each will expand efforts forward and increase the institution's profile as a green agency. For those green projects requiring many person-hours, such as building rain gardens or reducing invasive plants on the property, inviting volunteers to help can begin to cultivate engaged, green supporters.

X. Boost Profile and Stand Out

As the financial, environmental, and popular value of a green approach becomes a greater part of mainstream thinking, all organizations will be expected to effectively describe their sustainability work. The time remaining to set the arts organization apart by defining and promoting green efforts is coming to a close. As for-profit organizations have already figured out the value of this approach, the public has become sensitive to green-washing: promoting aspects of a product or practice as environmentally sustainable when they really are not. Be sure that any green attributes promoted on one's website or to audience members are truly green and valuable.

Celebrate Success! The Orange, Massachusetts Garlic and Arts Festival reduced their trash each year by creating systems limiting items entering the grounds to those that could be recycled, and stationing volunteers to help attendees sort their food and other items into compostable, recycling or trash. In a few short years they celebrated just two bags of trash for a two-day, busy festival and aim for no trash at all!

- Early successes will be quickly overshadowed by new projects as the staff gain confidence and momentum, so be sure to keep a running record of the accomplishments.
- Begin to record and report on green work quarterly or annually. Those assessments will help establish baseline numbers for illustrating progress in energy or water saved and waste reduced. Also record actions such as installing new water bottle filling stations, creating a preferred purchases list, or finding a vendor willing to collect compost after special events.
- Set up a green page on the website to post green plans, activities, and successes. Add requests for donations of reused materials or new LED bulbs (be specific about your needs); and offer to make the institution's used items available to other agencies or local schools.
- Test ideas! Brand one summer camp week as a 'green' one, and then do the same for other scheduled programs such as a special performance, or a monthly guest column in the newsletter.
- Develop a version of the organization's logo with a green tinge — literally — or environmental representations so that it can simultaneously promote the organizational brand and highlight green activities.
- Invite the local paper to cover work around the annual Earth Day celebrations in April. They will be hungry for topics and may not have thought of the local arts organization over a scouting group.
- Enter local green competitions or submit achievements for green business awards. The local chamber of commerce or the state economic council might know of appropriate competitions.

Gradually recognize green partners and options to begin and continue to green, and then cultivate a habit of looking for green angles and green promotional outlets. Key staff will know that the institution has made an impression when others begin asking the arts organization to partner.

> The arts have unlimited capacity to raise awareness of climate change. In April 2013 the City of Montreal hosted "Polar Bear on Thin Ice"; a project sponsored by Équiterre, a nonprofit "Inspiring Change on a Daily Basis", the World Wildlife Fund (WWF) and northern Quebec's Inuit communities. Équiterre commissioned a bronze sculpture by artist Mark Coreth. He worked with Quebecois and Inuit artists who created an ice sculpture of a giant polar bear over Coreth's life-size skeleton. It is a fleeting exhibit — less than a month. Ice melts; sometimes while bystanders watch. "This sculpture is interesting from several points of view: in its design, which combines the efforts of artists from diverse backgrounds; in its form, which is an interesting mix of urban and traditional Inuit art; and particularly in its purpose, to raise public awareness on a critical issue… A real encounter between culture and citizen engagement on climate change… ."[5]

Conclusion

It is important that arts organizations lead their community on greening their own institution so they can showcase ideas, opportunities, and share the ease of going green and saving money. By remembering the mantra that no one goes all-green, or green all-at-once; allowing and encouraging staff and volunteers to develop the skills and aptitude for sustainability; that involving, educating and engaging the community in green work builds community support; and that making thoughtful green decisions are leadership choices, arts organizations will go green and prosper.

Endnotes

1. In the summer of 2015 France announced that a new requirement for roofs. They must either be living roofs — covered with plants — or must contain solar panels. What was once considered fringe is quickly becoming the norm.

2. Email from Jennifer Case, Managing Director, Case School of Music, Sioux Falls, South Dakota, March 2013.

3. "Flood proofing: from low-tech to high tech", *GreenSource* Magazine, January-February 2013.

4. www.muacancun.org accessed February, 2013

5. www.equiterre.org/en/communique/polar-bear-on-thin-ice-exhibition-launches-at-the-place-des-festivals, accessed April 2013. (pg 18)

Resources

Brophy, S. & Wiley, E. (2013). *The Green Museum: A Primer on Environmental Practice,* 2nd Edition. Lanham, MD: AltaMira Press

Hitchcock, D., & Willard, M. (2006). *The Business Guide to Sustainability: Practical Strategies and Tools for Organizations.* London, UK: Earthscan.

McDonough, W., & Braungart, M. (2013). *The Upcycle: Beyond Sustainability—Designing for Abundance.* New York, NY: North Point Press.

Rossol, M. (1994) *The Artists' Complete Health and Safety Guide,* New York, NY: Allworth Press.

The Worldwatch Institute, Prugh, T., & Renner, M. (2014). *State of the World 2014: Governing for Sustainability.* Washington, DC: Island Press.

Tumber, C. (2012). *Small, Gritty, and Green: The Promise of America's Smaller Industrial Cities in a Low-Carbon World.* Cambridge, MA: The MIT Press.

Stringer, L. (2009). *The Green Workplace: Sustainable Strategies that Benefit Employees, the Environment, and the Bottom Line.* New York, NY: Palgrave Macmillan.

Sutton, S. (2015). *Environmental Sustainability at Historic Sites and Museums.* Lanham, MD: Rowman & Littlefield

www.ACMInet.org

www.exhibitSEED.org

www.sites.si.edu/greenRevolution/

PART THREE

Programming and Participation

Program Development

PAM KORZA *with contributing editors*
DENISE BOSTON-MOORE *and* MAREN BROWN

> *In today's environment, we are going to have to do more than simply provide the work that will draw adult audiences back to our stages and museums: we are going to have to help them value, connect with, and engage in the arts. In this respect, we need to view our task not as a matter of an educational structure, but as a function of human experience, interaction, growth, and learning.*
>
> —*Nello McDaniel and George Thorn,*
> Learning Audiences: Adult Arts Participation and the Learning Consciousness[1]

Many arts managers would say that programming is the most creative function of arts organizations. Curators, artistic directors, and program coordinators have the core and exciting responsibility to develop creative and meaningful programs that connect art with people. The way that arts organizations conceive and implement their programs has evolved tremendously in the last few decades in response to a variety of factors. Many adults lack grounding in the arts as a result of limited arts education in school. The commercial entertainment industry has influenced consumer habits. Demands of daily life restrict leisure time, and a variety of technologies make it easier to have whatever form of entertainment you want in the comfort of your own home. The demographics of communities are rapidly shifting as newcomers arrive and the baby boomer generation ages.

These trends, however, have flip sides. They present opportunities to use the power of arts and culture to fulfill human needs for connection, have meaningful leisure experiences, and build community. Increasingly, arts organizations of all types and sizes—from local arts agencies to major museums—are seeking inspiration and leadership from artists, audiences, their neighborhoods, and social and civic leaders in redefining programs to be relevant to community needs and interests. They are taking advantage of technology to expand access to the arts and make it available to wider audiences. They are programming less as independent producers of arts and more as collaborators with school systems, tourism and economic development agencies, urban planners, and a host of other community groups and institutions to ensure that arts and culture are integrated elements of broader community ventures. In these ways, arts organizations are encouraging a community-wide recognition and celebration of cultural diversity, social change, youth advocacy, appreciation of aging, and neighborhood vitality.

The arts are but one aspect of cultural life, which encompasses history and heritage, culinary traditions, lifestyles, and religion—all expressions of the creative human spirit. Programs which embrace these various creative expressions may include presenting or producing activities, community-based arts endeavors, residencies, festivals, thematic series, educational programs in the arts, and public art, to name a few.

As you read this chapter, imagine your own arts, culture, and programmatic frames of reference to make it relevant to your own work. The chapter provides a structure for conceiving, planning, and implementing programs that will help meet the needs of artists and the community, fulfill organizational mission, and aim to advance the arts themselves. These key questions are addressed:

- What values and philosophy underlie your program directions and choices?
- What difference do you want to make through your programs?
- Who should be involved in program planning? How might you involve representatives of your target audience(s) and stakeholders?
- What are some key considerations in designing programs to achieve organizational, artist, partner, and audience goals?
- Is your program feasible? Does it have the necessary resources to meet its full potential for success?
- How will you know if your program has succeeded?

Program Philosophy

An arts organization's program philosophy encompasses the values, principles, and creative point of view that guide its decisions and approach to artistic work as well as the way it connects that work to audiences and community. Your program philosophy should take into account the following considerations.

Organization mission. Programs should reflect the organization's purpose and whom it serves. A local arts agency may leave arts programming to the wide range of cultural organizations in the community and focus instead on services, grantmaking, and advocacy in order to build the capacity for local arts organizations to thrive and for citizens to have access to a breadth of cultural programs. However, new opportunities often emerge as contexts change or as an organization strives to serve the needs of particular communities or audiences. Developing a public art program, for example, may be a compelling new direction for a local arts agency when new public buildings are being constructed in a community, and no other agency is poised to lead such a program. Analyzing each new opportunity in relation to how it may support the organization's mission can keep the organization performing in a vital way while ensuring that it stays focused.

Concept of "audience" or "community." Some organizations are expressly committed to serving youth, a specific cultural community, or a community of circumstance (such as inmates in the prison system). Others may serve artists in a particular discipline or the full range of artists in a region. Still others may broadly define the residents of a defined county as its community.

In the 21st century, changing demographics in the United States should prompt an assessment of how current or new programs can effectively serve new members of a community, however it is defined. A community concert association in a rural Midwestern town, for example, used to serve a fairly homogenous white, middle class community. Today its programming considers a growing senior population, a declining population of young adults who don't return to their hometown after college for lack of job opportunity, and an immigrant population, attracted by jobs at local vegetable packing plants.

Commitment to making programs accessible. To what degree can you make programs accessible to audiences and artists with disabilities or special needs? Can you commit the resources necessary to do so? See the chapter on Cultural Access for more on program accessibility.

Sources of program ideas. How are board, staff, volunteers, members, citizens, and stakeholders such as artists or youth or culturally-specific populations involved in defining your programs? How successfully do you balance being responsive with being proactive vis–à–vis artists and the community in developing new program directions?

Relationship to the world of art and ideas. Art is at the core of what we do, whether your organization is a producing organization that creates new work, presents the work of contemporary artists or those of the past, or works collaboratively with schools to develop arts education programs. Are you abreast of what is current in your part of the arts and culture world? Arts organizations, particularly those that preserve art of the past, are increasingly challenged to find creative ways to make their offerings relevant to social or civic concerns, community or economic development priorities, or broader quality of life goals.

Risk-taking threshold. How much does your organization challenge itself and its audiences, versus relying upon certain comfortable and cautious program choices? Reasoned risk that meets audiences at new and appropriate learning points can stretch them toward new interests in their engagement with the arts. Artists continually explore new art forms and are often at the vanguard of excavating the meaning of difficult contemporary issues. To what extent does your organization embrace artistic investigations and programs that may be controversial, and is it prepared to defend such choices if controversy arises?

Definition of success. What difference are you trying to make through your programs? How will you evaluate the impact of your programs and who will do the evaluating? What criteria will you use? A new music series that presents adventurous programming may need to take a long view to build audiences over time. The measures of success may be repeated audience attendance and modest audience growth over a longer time period than an established program, or how the program is serving artists' creative investigations. Notions of success and failure may need to be reconsidered to see the big picture; in other words, some programs may not immediately and fully meet artistic, audience, or community goals, but the cumulative effect over time shows advancement.

If your programming aims to meet educational, community development, or economic development goals, partners and stakeholders may have different definitions of success which must be considered. See the Program Evaluation chapter for additional information.

Program Planning

Arts organizations are continually presented with opportunities to develop new programs. They also face circumstances that suggest modifying, and sometimes terminating, existing programs. Program planning may be prompted by constituent need; artistic initiative; new or reduced funding opportunities; influences of a changing social, political, or cultural environment; or simply someone's great idea!

Examples:

> **Modifying an existing program.**
> An arts council staff member believes that expanding the successful holiday season craft sale to a year-round craft shop with an online sales presence can better serve the region's craftspeople and provide additional revenue.
>
> The arts agency's grantmaking program has withstood two consecutive years of severely diminished funds from state and local government sources. The trend will likely continue. The agency considers making targeted grants for specific programs as an alternative to its operational support grants, to reflect diminished resources and community need.

> **Developing new programs.**
> A social service organization serving several neighborhoods approaches an arts center to help develop afterschool programs which would build respect between teens and elders.

> **Eliminating programs.**
> A performing arts series presented for decades by a campus-based art center has seen a precipitous decline in attendance for each of the past five years. The campus leadership is questioning the benefit of the performing arts series, and suggests that the arts center eliminate the program and use these resources to support their popular residency programs that link more closely to the academic experience and to area schools.

The program planning process helps an organization choose intelligently from various options and test their feasibility. Specifically, the process:

- gauges support for the idea and identifies potential partners;
- assesses and plans for the financial viability of the program, including financial risk;
- avoids overtaxing human and other resources; and
- formulates a workable plan of action.

The planning stage could take weeks, months, or longer depending on the complexity of the program. The program stands the best chance of smooth implementation and success in serving its participants and audience if you invest the time to plan.

SIX STEPS TO DETERMINE PROGRAM FEASIBILITY

This section discusses six steps which will help you gauge the feasibility of a program opportunity and create a program plan.

1. Assess program need.
2. Agree on the program's purpose, goals, and objectives.

3. Define the program specifically—who, what, when, and where.
4. Examine resources you need, have, and can get.
5. Identify and evaluate critical issues, obstacles, and opportunities.
6. Finalize the plan.

Step 1. Test need and interest in a program

Talk with potential program beneficiaries, artists, partners, and organizational partners to determine if there is a need for—and interest in—the program concept. In doing so, the organization begins to clarify:

- perceptions of the needs and interests held by various collaborators and potential participants;
- who can benefit from the program and how;
- what support systems are available; and
- whether your organization is the best one to implement the program.

Example:

> A neighborhood center staff member suggests that a Latin dance project would offer community youth an afterschool activity that's fun and connected to their cultural heritage. She invites a locally-based Latino dance company to become a partner to help design the program and offer dance classes. Possible assumptions are: dance is the most effective art form to achieve the goal; the dance company has experience working with youth; a partnership is needed versus contracting with the dance company to simply offer a class; and such a project is a better use of scarce resources than other options. These assumptions can then be tested with potential program partners and participants, who can help to shape the program ideas.

Step 2. Agree on Program Goals and Objectives

What difference do you want to make with this program? Who do you hope to serve with this program? This step:

- ensures that everyone is working from a common understanding of shared goals as well as any that are distinct to participating artists, partners, and stakeholders;
- guides decisions in program development and implementation and keeps you on course;
- provides a clear and consistent message to your community, members, funding sources, volunteers, and the media about why you are doing what you're doing; and
- forms the basis for evaluating the impact of the program.

To arrive at clear program goals, some level of audience or community assessment—such as public meetings, focus groups, or surveys—may be important. The Marketing the Arts and Strategic Planning chapters ▌ discuss various assessment processes, as well as how to write purpose, goals, and objectives statements for your programs. See the Arts and the Economy and Creative Placemaking chapters for information to address community or economic development goals. ▌

Example:

> The Houston Youth Symphony's (HYS) Coda Music Program, a new afterschool project that offers string ensemble instruction to third through fifth graders, exemplifies a project developed with a clear sense of goals in response to community need. When a nonprofit that was offering afterschool arts instruction at five, low-income elementary schools in Houston withdrew their programs, the HYS Board of Directors and staff worked with school administrators, civic leaders, parents, students, and teaching artists to establish an afterschool orchestra program that could fill the void at two of the schools. Using Venezuela's El Sistema program as a model, HYS offers classical music education through group instruction as a tool to strengthen community ties and improve student outcomes. Not wanting to replace music in the school day, but to enhance the educational experience of students, HYS's goals focus on improvements in student's academic, artistic, and personal success. Already, HYS is seeing reduced behavioral issues and better school attendance rates for participating children. By measuring outcomes against program goals, HYS can determine if the pilot program is a success and can be adopted in additional schools.

Step 3. Define the Program

Visions are amorphous by nature. It is difficult to project a budget, technical needs, or the terms of a partnership based solely on the vision you may have for a program. Eventually a specific program concept (or a few variations on it) needs to be nailed down in order to evaluate its feasibility. To bring your program idea from that initial fluid vision to a clear and more specific concept, determine who, what, when, and where.

Who.

Define who the program will benefit. An organization's programming may be grounded, first and foremost, in a commitment to support artistic investigation and advancement. Other organizations may define community or audience interests as the driving force in their program choices and directions. They may develop programs to attract targeted community populations, broaden audiences, or serve current audiences. Whether you start with art or the desired audience, carefully consider the relationship between the two. One may emerge as primary, and therefore shape the program in a certain way. See the Marketing the Arts chapter ▌ for more information about building audience participation.

Example:

> When the Indianapolis Children's Museum mounted a major exhibition of Alexander Calder's work, the city's cultural organizations saw an opportunity to build local audiences as well as attract regional tourist audiences. With coordination and marketing from the Indianapolis Arts Council, they mounted a city-wide festival celebrating Calder and creativity. The event succeeded in drawing local audiences, but made limited advances with a regional market. Organizers assessed that, if a future event were designed to attract a regional market, it would need to produce one or more major attractions to entice audiences and capture media attention, offer incentives such as family packages, and be more concentrated in time to allow visitors to attend several activities during their visit to Indianapolis.

Estimate the number of people to be served. Clear audience estimates will help you to design programs that best meet the interests of your audiences; attract artists; raise money; secure sponsors; negotiate a facility or setting for the program; determine ticket prices; and develop a marketing strategy. If your program relies on fee-based income from ticket sales or registration fees, making a considered attendance estimate to develop a realistic budget is crucial.

Estimating the number of people may hinge on such factors as:

- capacity limits of the space;
- drawing power of the program or artist;
- availability of the targeted audience or community;
- what it will take to effectively promote to this audience;
- competition for the targeted audience; and
- what is considered reasonable and appropriate for the scale of the activity and its goals.

Clarify who will be involved in program planning and implementation. In what ways are the board, staff, program director, or executive director responsible? It must be clear who advises and who has final authority to make artistic decisions. In all volunteer organizations, board members may serve on various program committees and choose and work directly with artists. Generally, if an organization has paid staff, the board helps to define overall program philosophy and policies but staff implements programs, including the choice of artists. Determine if and how artists should advise or be involved in program design and planning. When community advisory boards or committees are formed to help plan or implement programs, their roles should be clear as well. In public art programs, for example, sometimes community advisory groups help to define the criteria for public art projects in a particular place and may meet and speak with prospective artists, but may or may not be charged with actual artist selection.

Will you work with partner organizations? As arts organizations extend the reach of their programs to various populations and toward civic, social, or economic goals, they find it necessary to work in partnership with other organizations. Partners can help cultural organizations better understand the needs and interests of these participants and frame goals that reflect their concerns. They can provide access and help build trust to navigate systems. Consider what benefits each partner will receive, and how your program can advance the mission of each partnering organization. Clarify expectations about each partner's roles and responsibilities, financial and other contributions, and how you plan to communicate regularly about the project.

See the People Resources under Step 4 for further discussion.

What.
At the planning stage, outline specifics about content, scope, and format or structure of the program to give shape to your vision. For simple programs, it may be easy to define details. For more complex or extended programs, frameworks for key elements may be defined. Many community-based and public art projects define the goals and shape of a project only after a period of activity with community members, making it impossible to map out the entire program at the outset. In any case, enough sense of the program elements and their technical, time, and other requirements is needed in order to create a plan, understand resources needed, etc.

Where.
The real estate industry sums everything up as "location, location, location!" For arts and cultural programs, as well, location is one of several important factors that can make or break a program. The choice of location can emphasize particular goals of the program. For example, alternating a weekday lunchtime concert series between the downtown business district, neighborhood parks, and soup

kitchens helps to meet the goal of providing access to art for all citizens. Undesirable locations are sometimes deliberately targeted for transformation by arts and cultural activity.

Arts organizations with a goal of serving culturally diverse populations need to consider how various segments of the community perceive different settings. The art center or museum may not be perceived as a welcoming space. Practical issues of transportation may make it difficult for some people to get to certain facilities. Present programs in locations where people feel comfortable.

An organization should consider the following in determining where to hold its program:

- **Suitability.** Will the facility do justice to the art form? Does it have suitable technical support?
- **Capacity.** Can it accommodate the expected number of people?
- **Aesthetics.** What can the space or setting lend aesthetically or conceptually to the program?
- **Accessibility.** Is the location physically accessible to people with disabilities? Is the location close to public transportation? What psychological perceptions may exist concerning accessibility to the location?
- **Availability.** Is the space available on the date(s) wanted? Get to know the booking patterns of various facilities so that you can plan well enough in advance.
- **Cost.** Are rental costs or costs of adapting the location feasible and consistent with your budget projections?

When.

Choosing a program date can involve as much strategy as choosing the right location. Factors to consider include:

- availability of time to plan and promote the program;
- ability to meet funding application deadlines;
- compatibility with the target audience's program preferences and schedules;
- opportunity to expand the audience by connecting with complementary programs at the same location;
- possibility to block–book an artist with another organization;
- availability of desired space(s);
- probability that inclement weather will impact outdoor programs;
- and ability to establish an annual date.

Step 4. Examine Resources

Having defined your program concept in greater detail, test its feasibility against the money, time, and people needed to make it a reality. This step requires some objective assessment.

Financial resources. Only by developing a specific, research-based budget can you assess the financial feasibility of your program. Define expense and income limitations and potential, how much money needs to be raised, and what's needed to raise it.

The budgeting process is usually one that requires a give-and-take between the expense and income sides until the bottom line is acceptable. Do not approach this as an exercise in creative arithmetic, however. Each shaving of an expense or increase in an income projection must be honestly and realistically assessed, considering its implications to the program.

See the Financial Management chapter ▌ for more detailed discussion of budget development and the Marketing the Arts chapter ▌ for information about pricing strategies.

Financial objectives. Here are some pointers for developing program budgets.

- Estimate income conservatively.
- Maximize earned income potential.
- Save money wherever possible by getting in-kind donations.
- Don't give away too much. Determine complimentary ticket policies thoughtfully. Should corporate contributors be given a free ad in your program book or should they be asked to pay for advertising beyond their other contribution?
- Don't spend too much money raising money. Carefully evaluate the costs involved in certain fundraising activities. Visit Charity Watch online to learn about recommended amounts you should set aside for fundraising.
- Spend money where it counts. Compensate artists fairly for their efforts. Consider the terms of agreement with significant partners to ensure there is an appropriate balance between investment and return.
- Understand what your cash flow needs are and how you will accommodate them.
- Minimize the chance for surprise expenses. Think specifically about what you will need. Don't base projected costs on ballpark estimates or old information. Research as exhaustively as possible to determine expense lines. If you have no way to determine costs, ask others in similar organizations to share their experiences with you.
- Include a contingency expense figure. Five to ten percent of total direct expenses (other than salaries and overhead) is common.
- Be careful about developing programs in response to a specific grant or funding initiative, without considering grant requirements, such as matching funds, in your overall budget. More than one programmer has received funding for a project and has been heard to groan, "Oh no, now I have to do it!" when they receive a grant.

If expenses are greater than income, evaluate the possible courses of action.

- Can the program be scaled back? Can certain expenses be cut? Consider the implications of these actions in relation to your programmatic goals and maintaining the integrity of the art.
- Can expenses be shared with collaborative partners or other community organizations?
- Can certain expenses be amortized? A festival purchasing tents, a theater company creating portable sets for a tour, an art center purchasing display cases for an exhibition—these costs can be amortized on the organization's balance sheet (see Financial Management chapter ▌) or spread across a certain period beyond the program at hand since they will support other programs in the future.
- Can income be increased? Estimate cautiously.

Play out different budget scenarios. It is useful to develop two or three budget scenarios that anticipate varying degrees of income.

- **The ideal scenario.** Your dream program achieves its income potential.
- **The compromise scenario.** A modified program can be mounted with anticipated lower income. This scenario should reflect acceptable programmatic compromises.
- **The no program or delayed program scenario.** This assumes that adequate income cannot be secured or earned to support program variations which still meet your programmatic goals. This may also suggest that an alternate timeline should be considered which allows for sufficient fundraising or the setting of a deadline by which a decision must be made to go forward or not.

In the fundraising stage, organizations often generate a budget for funders which reflects the ideal program, and a fallback internal budget which reflects the compromise program the organization is willing to present with a defined minimum assured raised or earned income.

The appropriate staff, board, and, perhaps, advisers in the community should review the financial picture drawn in this feasibility stage. At this point the review should test the validity of the figures. Did you project realistically? Are all potential expenses outlined? Have incomes been reasonably projected? Are there any that have not been identified?

People resources. Arts organizations are notorious for greeting every exciting program idea with a resounding, "Yes, let's do it!" Such passion has also launched many an arts organization's staff or board into a state of perpetual overdrive. Whether a single event or an ongoing program, the ebb and flow of work should be carefully considered, as well as the specific skills and expertise required.

- Do the necessary skills, expertise, and connections exist within the organization?
- Is it feasible for staff or board members to devote time and energy to the program? If so, can other regular activities be sustained without compromising quality?
- Will volunteers or new staff be required? Will training be necessary? Do you have the time and money to make this happen?

If you must seek expertise outside the organization, consider a friends group or existing volunteer corps, an ad hoc advisory group, contracted staff or a consultant, or partnerships with other organizations.

Partnerships require:

- trust and an appreciation of each other's expertise and unique identity and contributions;
- familiarity with each other's language, ways of working, and the systems within which each partner works;
- agreement on program goals and a commitment to help achieve them;
- understanding of each partner's particular goals and the development of a program design which aims to satisfy them;
- regular communication;
- delineation of decision making authority, accountability, and each partner's roles and responsibilities;
- identification of a point person to manage project details;
- agreement on financial risk–taking and gain; and
- a written agreement outlining the above.

See the Arts Extension Service's workbooks on arts partnerships at www.artsextensionservice.org for more information about how to start and sustain partnerships in the arts.

The program should be based on a realistic assessment of the time it will take to plan, raise funds, and implement the plan. Identify critical deadlines, including:

- research (program components, community involvement, artists' availability, market potential, costs, funding sources, potential partners, technical concerns);
- fundraising (grant application deadlines and notification dates, and other fundraising efforts);
- staffing (recruitment, hiring, and training of paid or volunteer personnel to staff the program);
- a finalized program when artists, artwork, and program participants are all secured and other components and design are set;
- final dates for bidding out contracts for services (if applicable); and
- key promotional opportunities and marketing deadlines.

Timeline. A suggested timeline format looks like a grid with one axis for the months or weeks leading up to (and throughout) the program and the other axis for specific tracks of activities—such as administration, fundraising, program development and implementation, marketing, and technical support. (See the sidebar with a sample timeline.) These tracks may correspond to specific committees working on the program, and such a master timeline shows the relationship between activities. For example, in order for the publicity committee to initiate on online marketing campaign six weeks before the concert series, the program committee must submit to the publicity committee a final lineup of artists with descriptions and photos four weeks before the marketing campus deadline, allowing time for the publicity committee to develop each component of the plan.

In addition, the timeline helps everyone to visualize the plan's progress, the interdependence of various committees, and periods when staff or board may be in greatest demand. An agency timeline showing all of the organization's programs and services also helps place this program activity in a context of the total demand on the board, staff, and volunteers. For more complex projects, you may wish to use a project management program which helps to deal with multiple interdependent variables.

Should we use project management software to manage our programs?

While a program can be managed with paper forms, software can greatly simplify the process and enhance the accuracy of your program plan. Programs that require you to manage the work of more than one individual and/or the delivery of materials and equipment from vendors are especially suited to software applications. Software specifically designed to manage projects can be time consuming to learn and somewhat expensive, but the benefits are substantial when you are managing the work of multiple individuals. If you have a simple program that involves only one or two people, spreadsheet software like Excel or Google docs will suffice (as will the sample timeline we have provided in this chapter). More sophisticated programs can benefit from project management software, such as Liquid Planner, Microsoft Project, or Mavenlink—to name a few currently available on the market. Sign up for trial versions of the programs that interest you before purchasing them, and determine if the program will meet your needs. Idealware and the Nonprofit Technology Enterprise Network (NTEN) often provide free reviews of project management software programs for nonprofits on their websites, and Techsoup frequently offers discounted and free project management software for nonprofits.

Step 5. Identify and Evaluate Issues, Obstacles, and Opportunities

Defining program and resource needs will undoubtedly identify issues and obstacles, as well as opportunities, which your organization must analyze and evaluate. For example, a consultant conducting a feasibility study for a national festival to take place in a major city discovered that local cultural organizations were fearful that county arts council funds would be significantly diverted to support the new festival, reducing allocations that were an important part of the arts groups' revenue base. The county arts council had to determine how it could support the new event without unfairly stressing its ongoing constituents.

Some useful questions to ask are:

- What do we lose if the program does not meet our criteria for success? What are the implications of losing these things?
- What can we and others—such as artists and audiences—learn by doing this program?
- What relationships might be built?
- Can we sort out certain short-term activities from those that require long-term planning?
- What internal or external conditions must be met before we can proceed?

Step 6. Finalize the Plan

At this point you should have the information you need to decide the likelihood of achieving your goals and objectives. Your options may be:

- Go ahead with the program with a better understanding of what you need to do to make it a success.
- Refine the program concept to bring it in line with resources you can reasonably secure.
- Delay until you are able to secure the resources you need.
- Stop if the program poses too great a financial risk, you don't have the time or personnel to carry it off, you don't have adequate community support, or it's outside your scope.

Program Design

Regardless of the type of program or service you offer, its design should consider policies to guide actions and decisions; finding, selecting, and working effectively with the right artists; ensuring access, and creating a meaningful artistic experience for participants or audience members. This section explores these concerns.

PROGRAM POLICIES

Policies are guidelines that help an organization act consistently and in keeping with its values, principles, and mission.

Examples:

> **An artist market** that values originality and authenticity prohibits exhibitors whose work is made from kits or is not the original design of the exhibiting artist.

Greek Folk Arts Festival Timeline

	October	November	December	January	February
Administration	Corporate and local fundraising completed		Budget meeting: staff and committee chairs	Trip to Greece raffle tickets on sale Admission tickets copy to marketing committee	Raffle drawing at Mayor Petrakis' honorary reception
Performance	Research performers: • Greek cultural center • State arts council • Regional touring program • NEA folk arts • Public radio and TV	→ → → → → → → → →	Prioritize list and invite performers	Performance confirmed: contracts out Create schedule	Collect promo photos for marketing committee Determine all performers' technical requirements
Demonstrations and Exhibition	Research artists: • Church bulletins • Greek cultural center • Hellenic journal • University	→ → → →	Prioritize list and invite artists	Artists confirmed; contracts out Create schedule (work with performance committee)	Collect promo, photos Show local participants their spaces; determine technical needs
Food	Meet with board of health about regulations	Bids out: beer, wine, soda	Bids back and selections made	Confirm food demos and local groups providing food ID gaps in food fare	Publicity out to solicit other food vendors
Publicity	Press release: "Looking for Artists" Introduction letter to arts editor Revise media mailing list	Research radio, talk TV shows	Secure radio station to help make PSAs Press release: "Poster Artist"	Press release: "Raffle" Admission tickets to designer	Select photos: releases and press packets Photo with caption: "Raffle Winner!" Solicit talk shows
Promotion	Research artists for poster		Select poster artist	Brochure, poster distribution plan Deadline for confirmed program from program committee (1/25)	Brochure copy drafted Poster copy to designer
Volunteer			Create volunteer needs assessment forms and distribute to committees	Deadline, volunteer needs assessment, all committees (1/30)	Volunteer recruitment kick off at raffle drawing
Site and logistics	ID exhibit, stage demo spaces with programmers	Major equipment, service needs determined (tents, sound, etc.) Site design, map done in draft	Bids for major needs	Equipment, supply needs from all committees Refinements to site plan	Electricity, plumbing needs from all committees Secure in-kind materials, services

> **A presenter** concerned that programs are accessible to economically disadvantaged community members creates policies which ensure child care and subsidized ticket pricing.

> **A theater company** committed to cultural equity institutes a policy of selecting works that present multiple cultural perspectives, and hiring actors from a variety of cultural backgrounds as performers.

> **An art museum** only offers educational programs that relate to its permanent collections or temporary exhibitions.

> **Board and staff** should create policies with input from the people who are most directly affected by the policies. When policies are grounded in the principles and values of an organization, they generally require minimal revision over time.

QUALITY: A MULTIDIMENSIONAL VIEW

Most arts organizations would agree that they strive to support the highest quality in the art they present, produce, or support. Mediocre or poor artistic content, form, or execution will negatively affect a community's view of the arts and its value, and betrays audience trust.

Absolute standards of excellence are found to be limiting, though, when other social, civic, or educational goals are linked to the creative endeavor. The conventional paradigm that focuses solely on the artistic product is making way for an expanded framework that considers the quality and impact of process and the value or meaning of the artistic experience for participants or audience members, in addition to artistic excellence. Here are some general guidelines about defining and fostering quality.

Consider who defines criteria and standards. Involve people with expertise in the discipline, genre, and language to articulate standards of excellence. Hip-hop artist Rennie Harris observes that critics who write about his work without an historical understanding of hip-hop tend to perceive the pieces only as acrobatic spectacle, and this often reinforces cultural stereotypes about black males.[2] Artists themselves should be involved in articulating criteria and standards as well as knowledgeable critics. Others involved in community-based cultural work advocate that community members affected by the work have valuable contributions to make in defining what is artistically excellent and meaningful.

Articulate criteria specifically. It is important to be as specific as possible when communicating with those who are applying for opportunities or evaluating artistic submissions, such as artist applicants, grant panelists, organizational staff, or judges who are making artistic decisions. Aesthetic criteria might relate to artistic-cultural vision, accepted discipline- or genre-based criteria, craftsmanship and skill in execution, and risk-taking. Criteria sometimes can be effectively expressed in terms of what is not desirable. For example, the town of Amherst, Massachusetts, values its historic architecture and personages, such as poets Emily Dickinson and Robert Frost. As community members discussed aesthetic standards for environmental changes, they advocated for design standards that maintain the integrity of the historic district, but also cautioned against the potential to overdo historic references,

> ### *African in Maine*: What Constitutes "Quality"?
>
> *African in Maine* was a two-year programmatic effort by the former Center for Cultural Exchange (CCE) to respond to the cultural needs of refugee Sudanese, Somalian, and Congolese communities in Portland, Maine. CCE supported these three communities to define and implement cultural programs, drawing upon contemporary and traditional African music and other art forms, to represent themselves to each other and the wider Maine community. Below, former CCE Artistic Director Bau Graves offers his views on the question of what constitutes quality:
>
>> American arts professionals often decry the lack of "professionalism" and "quality" in community-based art. However, communities themselves rarely make such distinctions. *African in Maine* offered moments of extreme artistic virtuosity, such as the performances by Papa Wemba or Kanda Bongo Man. It included events that held special significance for the insider communities, such as the performances by Emanuel Kembe and Shego Band. But it also included many events that were amateur attempts by local community members to represent themselves.
>>
>> From the perspectives of the participants and their communities, this is irrelevant. Indeed, the events that featured community members acting, singing, and dancing onstage had an emotional resonance with their audiences that exceeded the response to the stars. This does not imply that community members lack insight into aesthetic nuance; they know very well what constitutes quality within their own cultural sphere, and they want that, too. It does state that issues of quality are often secondary considerations in the value of cultural events to insiders. Who is onstage can be far more important than what is onstage. The imposition of outsiders' views of what constitutes "quality," puts a frame around ethnic performance that is foreign to the experience of most community members. This particular, often-voiced preoccupation with "quality" within the American public arts community (especially among funders) is a red herring, itself a reflection of the elitism that still prevails in too much public cultural work.
>>
>> —Bau Graves[3]

trivializing Amherst's history. By describing what was not acceptable, townspeople further clarified the originally stated design goal.

Understand and employ culturally-specific criteria when presenting forms of a particular culture. Artwork that is created outside of the dominant culture is often judged according to European or Western standards. As a result, its formal qualities, meaning, and the nuances of aesthetics are misunderstood or misrepresented. People who are of the cultural community being evaluated should be a part of the system assessing quality. See the *African in Maine* sidebar.

Uphold artistic integrity in presenting art. Adapting a traditional ethnic dance form that is rooted in ritual to Western stage presentation, for example, might render it inauthentic. Presenting an artist's laser art event on a foggy night to keep to schedule could so diminish the intended visual effects that the artist's reputation and yours could be hurt. Involve the artists or specialists to determine if and how reasonable adaptations can be made without compromising integrity.

Develop methods of evaluating quality that are fair, accountable, and enable the work to be assessed in its best light. Such methods might include review of work through in-person viewing, various digital media, or other reproductions. Note that some work may only demonstrate its full meaning with the benefit of audience interaction or in the setting for which it is originally intended, for example, sacred spaces, natural environment, or the city street.

Defining Quality of Experience

The most outstanding performance of *La Traviata* may not be rewarding for a viewer who is unfamiliar with opera or who does not understand Italian. Preexisting perceptions of the arts or of your programs must also be addressed. Elements that may contribute to quality of the artistic experience include:

- meaning that audience or participants derive from the work, their participation in its development, or educational or interpretive tools which provide context and new insight (interpretive strategies are further discussed later in this chapter);
- accessibility of language through presentation of the artistic work in the first language of non-English speaking participants or sign interpretation for people who are Deaf or hard of hearing;
- relationship made with artists through informal opportunities to talk with the artist;
- media coverage and criticism which is thoughtfully developed in tandem with the arts organization or relevant partners; and
- overall tone and feeling of the program established by the demeanor, respect, helpfulness, and energy of staff and volunteers.

FINDING AND SELECTING ARTISTS

Many arts organizations develop rosters of artists as a result of their own research, services, and programming. They also contact colleagues and solicit artists to be included in rosters, artist directories, and slide registries. The Internet has opened up vast informational resources as well, with artists' own websites as well as arts service organizations which list or link to member artists or other listings. See the Ways to Identify Artists sidebar for additional ideas.

Generally, there are three ways to select artists for your programs: direct invitation; first come, first served; and application or a call for proposals.

Direct invitation. When you know what you want and which artist can satisfy your goals, make a direct invitation to that artist.

First come, first served. This process obviously requires the least amount of effort but also provides the least opportunity for quality control or programmatic design. You might employ some basic parameters to define who can submit work. A first-come-first-served approach may be quite suitable for a broad-based community event which celebrates everyone's creativity, or where balance or differing levels of quality are not a concern in the work presented.

Application or call for proposals. Applications or proposals are often solicited when the organization does not have a preconceived idea about which artist to choose, wants to give many artists equal opportunity to participate in a project, or simply wants to make choices from a wide range of possibilities. Artists are commonly solicited for festivals, public art projects, or to apply to granting organizations for funding. Applicants are evaluated according to pre-established criteria. An advantage of an application process is that it can uncover new talent. Therefore, it is important to get the word out in as many ways as possible.

Applications or calls for proposals should include:

- a description of the program or project (mission, format, location, anticipated audience, schedule);
- eligibility requirements;
- selection criteria;

Ways to Identify Artists

SCOUT ARTISTS THROUGH DIRECT CONTACT.

- Attend festivals, exhibitions, performances, and other events. Make note of and contact artists of interest.
- Visit artists' studios during open house events or by appointment.

TIE INTO NETWORKS.

- Get recommendations from other programmers.
- Ask artists for recommendations.
- Talk to folklorists in your region or state (ask your state arts or humanities council or historical commission).
- Explore the talents of local college or university faculty or students through art departments, outreach programs, and speaker bureaus.
- Contact your local arts agency, statewide assembly of local arts agencies, or discipline-specific arts service organizations in your region.
- Connect with national service organizations that represent your interests, such as the Association of Performing Arts Presenters, Americans for the Arts, or National Performance Network. Attend booking conferences and showcases that allow you to view artists' work first hand and talk directly with artists and agents.
- Connect with local libraries or other non-arts entities which work with artists.

IDENTIFY SOURCES OF ARTIST LISTS.

- Visit artist websites and online listings.
- Seek out artist agencies and representatives.
- Get recommendations from staff at state arts agencies (applicants and recipients of fellowships, project and artist residency grants, slide registries, artist survey lists, or lists developed to promote artists in the state).
- Talk to staff at regional arts organizations (New England Foundation for the Arts, Southern Arts Federation, Arts Midwest, Mid-America Arts Alliance, Western States Arts Federation) for performing arts touring rosters and touring exhibitions.
- Search online for artist organizations in your region.
- Contact Young Audiences, VSA, and other national organizations with state affiliates whose services include linking artists.

FIND TRADITIONAL OR COMMUNITY-BASED ARTISTS.

- Churches
- Music stores
- Community schools of the arts
- Local newspaper, radio, or television
- Ethnic clubs or associations
- Senior citizen clubs or homes
- Civic organizations

- documentation required to represent the artist's work, such as digital images (and resolution requirements) and other media (with length requirements), etc.;
- description of the review process;
- application deadlines; and
- dates by which artists will be notified of decisions.

Administering a call for proposals or applications and then conducting a review or jurying process to evaluate what has been submitted involves time, staff resources, and expense to promote the opportunity.

Selection by jury. A jury or peer panel involves one or more individuals with relevant expertise who select artists by reviewing examples of work (usually digital images or media) or proposals. While staff or volunteers might serve as jurors, outsiders can lend a fresh perspective and may, if notable, lend credibility and attract artists to participate. Composing a selection jury or committee is an art in itself. Consider these variables for the right balance of expertise and perspective:

- knowledge of the art form(s) being reviewed;
- other important knowledge or expertise, such as an educator would bring to a residence teaching artist selection committee;
- belief in your program goals;
- representation of diverse cultures or, for culturally-specific programs, significant representation by members of that culture;
- gender balance; and
- appropriate geographic representation.

It is important to determine how important reviewers' familiarity with the locale or region might be to achieving decisions that support the program goals. For example, an urban neighborhood arts program whose goal is to stimulate dialogue on issues important to residents warrants strong local representation. In any case, it is important to orient jurors to program goals and policies in order to make decisions that meet your interests.

WORKING WITH ARTISTS

Artists are your most valuable partners, and treating them and their work with respect is important to the end result and to your organization's reputation. Once again, the specifics will vary from program to program, but some common guiding principles can help ensure good artist relations and a quality program.

Include artists as program advisers and in planning. Artists' experience and insights are particularly important when venturing into new or unfamiliar areas of programming, or when program goals warrant that artists become familiar with the context for their work, such as residencies or public art projects. Artists can:

- help frame the goals of a program;
- help design the specific content or format of a program;
- serve on selection committees and juries;
- determine possible educational or interpretive activities;
- advise on technical aspects of presenting their work most effectively; and
- help identify audience segments who might be attracted to their work and suggest promotion strategies.

Pay artists professional fees. Artists are professionals and deserve professional rates of compensation. Cultural groups should not ask for donated services or artwork from artists who are trying to make their living from their work. When estimating artists' fees, consult with artists, colleagues, or agents before you prepare a budget. Research fees for a variety of artists to become aware of the going rate. It is common practice, particularly when dealing with agents, to negotiate fees. You may be able to reduce the cost of a performance by block booking with other presenters in your region. Some artists will reduce their fees if there are other clear advantages which you can offer, such as the sale of artwork or the promise of multiple engagements (performances coupled with master classes, for instance) in a small geographic area. If you ask artists to do something not anticipated in the scope of the original contract, respect that the artist is providing additional service and is due additional compensation. Depending on what is requested, the artist may choose to do it at no cost, but this should never be assumed.

Consider the fairness of artist entry fees and of asking artists to donate work. Entry fees are commonly charged in competition programs, festival markets, and other situations, often to offset costs of processing entries, provide return shipping of entry materials, insure work, etc. There is debate about the fairness of charging artists to "take a chance" since there is usually no guarantee that an artist will be accepted, win a prize, or make money by participating. Many artist organizations have lobbied against such fees. In general, organizations should make every effort to earn revenue from other sources first.

Likewise, artists are often asked to donate a performance or artwork for a fundraising event or auction. Arts organizations should examine the fairness to artists of such requests. If you choose to make a request, ask what is something "concrete and valuable" to offer the artist in exchange for his or her donation.

Develop a contract. Contracts protect the artist's and your rights by spelling out precisely the responsibilities and requirements of each party. Contracts need not be formidable documents but should clearly outline the terms of the relationship. The complexity of the contract depends upon the complexity of the artistic service and on certain institutional requirements. Major artistic productions, public art commissions, or extended residencies may have voluminous contracts. Remember that all contracts are negotiable and, if it is your first time entering into such an agreement, it is wise to seek help from an experienced arts administrator or legal counsel. For help on legal issues, contact your nearest Volunteer Lawyers for the Arts.

Work the system to support artists' interests. Arts organizations which are part of local government or state institutions sometimes face challenges working within bureaucratic systems never designed to accommodate artists' needs and timelines. It often becomes necessary to advocate that the system operate more flexibly to support artists' needs. This is particularly true when hiring international artists, who are under greater scrutiny with the advent of more stringent visa regulations. This can greatly extend the contracting time for artists, especially in governmental agencies, and it is wise to work with officials to ameliorate any potential difficulties before they arise. Examples:

> Contracts may need to be adapted to include a planning as well as implementation phase for projects that cannot be fully defined until planning efforts are completed.

> Provide advance or midpoint payments. Paying artists and reimbursing expenses after "services are rendered," typical in public agencies, can put an undue burden on artists, particularly with projects where there is significant development work or upfront costs. Artists, unlike a commercial construction company, do not usually have the cash reserves to cover up-front costs for a major public art project.

Prepare artists with what they need to know. Artists will do their best job if they are informed in advance about the program goals and theme, the kind and size of audience to expect, the nature and limitations of the space in which their work will be presented, and that you care about their well-being, their work, and their success.

Logistical information such as the following should be summarized in a preprogram letter or in the contract for the artist's reference:

- travel and hotel arrangements made for the artist;
- information, including directions, on where the artist needs to go;
- the time the artist is expected to arrive onsite and the time needed for setup;
- hospitality that will be provided to the artist, whether through individuals to greet and escort the artist or meals offered during the artist's stay;
- assistance that will be provided to the artist to help unload equipment, set up, or support during rehearsals, exhibitions, or workshops; and
- the technical specifications and dimensions of the stage or exhibition space and the audiovisual equipment available (many performing arts spaces offer this in downloadable form on their websites, which can be particularly helpful for traveling shows).

Treat artists as professionals and as people. If artists feel well treated, they will want to work with you again. Consideration, respect, and enthusiasm should extend through staff and volunteers in their interactions with artists, even in the most difficult moments. Ask artists their preferences. While it may be true, for instance, that local hosts could provide home-cooked meals and the comforts of home to artists staying in your community (not to mention saving you hotel and per diem costs), the artist may need and prefer the privacy and down time of a hotel. Recognizing the work of artists after an event or exhibition with a handwritten letter and small personalized gifts can make your organization stand out from other venues when you are seeking to hire the artist in the future.

Strategies to Connect Art and Audiences

Keeping core audiences is essential to survival. However, for many reasons, arts organizations are constantly working to develop new audiences and to stretch current audiences to try new things. Practically speaking, new and more adventurous audiences can mean more revenue. More importantly, though, engaging more and varied segments of the community mutually supports their needs and interests and an organization's mission and goals. In addition, thoughtful efforts to build audiences for art, be it conceptual music or independent film, supports artists' desire to connect their work with open and appreciative audiences.

Here are some strategies that have been used successfully by artists, arts educators, and arts organizations to sustain old audiences as well as engage new people. For more information about audience participation, please see the Marketing the Arts chapter.

SEQUENTIAL PROGRAMMING

Sequential arts programming is based on the same premise as any sequential learning—meeting learners at their current level of skill or familiarity and challenging them to engage on a deeper level of discovery. For years, arts presenters and museum educators, among others, have used these theories to understand how adults learn and what motivates them to do so.

Sequential programming first defines entry points for adults to have a meaningful encounter with art. Either through the choice of art or the interpretive strategies that accompany it, a programmer creates a way for the participant or audience member to find relevant personal or cultural associations between the art's content and his or her own ideas, experience, knowledge, or understanding.[4] Over time, other artwork or experiences are offered that build on this encounter, and the work may become more complex, challenging, or adventurous as participants or audience members gain familiarity, confidence, and deeper appreciation. Example:

> Some orchestras have used a sequential programming strategy to move current audiences from the expected repertoire of works from the classical canon to lesser-known works of the past as well as work by contemporary composers. A "new" work might be presented in each program of the season, with commentary by the conductor and an opportunity for the audience to engage each other in questions that help make personal connections, such as: Did this work make you think of any other music with which you're familiar? or Knowing that this work was influenced by sounds of nature and concerns for environmental preservation, is there anything that you heard within it that suggested such interests? As audiences gain more exposure and understanding, the orchestra may begin to expand the kinds of offerings within a program or create programs focused on new work.

MAKING CONNECTIONS

Making connections between the arts and other subjects or fields with which people are familiar and interested is a prime strategy for making the arts more accessible and meaningful. Programs might explore the physics of dance or the religious purposes of stone carving in history to interest science buffs or faith-based communities, respectively.

> We may talk about audience development or building community, but art is experienced first and foremost on an individual level. A successful experience may be an emotional, visceral, or intellectual connection, but it is always a personal connection.

FREQUENCY

Providing audiences with multiple opportunities to experiment with and get used to unfamiliar forms of art can enhance their interest in and understanding of that art form. Example:

> Hancher Auditorium at the University of Iowa has built an enthusiastic audience for dance over three decades. Through a combination of frequent dance performances in the auditorium, community residencies by visiting dance companies, and a long-term relationship established with the Joffrey Ballet, Hancher has seen some amazing demonstrations of its audience's commitment. For example, 2,000 children attended a matinee performance of one dance performance, despite the fact that it was held on a school holiday.

EXTENDED OR RETURN ENGAGEMENTS

Multiple encounters with the same artists and their work help people to gradually understand and appreciate them on deeper levels than a single encounter might allow. Residencies are a common form of extended engagement. They typically involve some mix of presentation of the artist's work, education or training about the work, and participatory art making. Residencies can last from a couple of days to many months. Many artists whose community-based work addresses social or civic goals work over a period of time with a particular group of community members.

Such extended engagements enable artists to get to know their audience and to develop specific experiences in response to the needs and interests of the audience. Likewise, the audience gets to know the artist as both a professional and as a human being. Example:

> For over a decade, the Asian Arts and Culture Program (AACP) at the University of Massachusetts Amherst has offered artist residency programs in partnership with area schools. AACP Director, Ranjanaa Devi, is committed to the educational mission of her program, and almost always incorporates educational experiences into her artist presentations. AACP has brought hundreds of artists to the schools to share culturally-authentic art forms, ranging from traditional Chinese dance to Japanese flower arranging. Partnering schools eagerly anticipate the offerings, helping to raise funds to support the residency programs, and working with Devi to identify artists that relate to their curricular goals.

INTERPRETATION

Interpretation of artists' work can help audiences to gain deeper understanding and greater appreciation of the work. Some artists conduct audience discussions before or after people experience the work. Program books or exhibition catalogues and labels may include artistic intent statements, contextual information, artist biographies, and insight about the creative process. Interactive computer displays that allow visitors to learn about the history of the art and its historical context, and to experiment with light, sound, and art making that is related to the work have exponentially expanded the way that museum visitors can access information. Providing video and contextual information online provide visitors the opportunity to preview the work and the personality behind it. Demonstrations give perspective on the process of art making, especially for more complex or esoteric art forms.

Some artists resist interpreting their work for their audiences, preferring instead that the work speak for itself. The programmer's role is to balance the artist's wishes with the needs of the audience.

Developing Interpretive Materials

Determine when to introduce information. In viewing exceptionally challenging work, audience members might benefit from information before a presentation. At other times, it might be the artist's or programmer's preference to wait until the presentation concludes in order not to influence the viewer's own interpretation.

Use user-friendly language. Develop information that is engagingly written and free of art jargon or terms. Whenever feasible, offer translations for non–English speaking audiences.

Be creative in providing information. Old conventions of art interpretation take a didactic approach, emphasizing dates and chronologies, movements, and formal analysis. A newer approach instead offers questions for viewers to reflect on, provides opportunities for personal engagement with the art form or ideas, and prompts audiences to establish relevant connections with the work.

Make interpretive information accessible. Use accessible fonts and type sizes, and make information available in a variety of forms for people with different needs. See the Cultural Access chapter for more information. ▌ Example:

> New York's Cooper Hewitt Museum (CHM) went through a significant transformation in creating interactive experiences designed to engage visitors more deeply in the art forms on display. Visitors are now provided with handheld devices that enable them to create a virtual gallery of their favorite works that they can access after their visit to CHM. CHM also incorporated electronic displays that enable visitors to experiment with art concepts, and a gallery was converted to an art making studio for family visitors. Many museums now view their websites as an extension of their collection, allowing audiences to learn more about the history and context of the artwork, even if they are unable to visit. This trend is not isolated to museums: many performing arts and media organizations are also harnessing the power of technology to extend the visitor experience.

Programming Considerations

When offering work that may be provocative, controversial, or outside of what is familiar or accepted, arts organizations need to venture knowledgeably and with forethought regarding how various constituents or audiences may respond. They need to be aware of political, cultural, and economic contexts that can affect how work will be perceived and received. The challenges of such opportunities shouldn't be avoided. They may actually offer a chance for important dialogue to occur and an opportunity for building alliances and bridging ideological differences. Below are some pointers on two programming considerations deserving thoughtful approaches: managing controversy and presenting culturally-specific work.

CONTROVERSIAL WORK

Many factors in contemporary times—competition between the arts and other sectors for decreasing public dollars, ongoing and newly emerging social concerns, vigorously wielded political and religious agendas—have made the environment for the arts more volatile. Sometimes predictably and sometimes not, arts organizations need to act thoughtfully to try to avert controversy, as well as deal constructively with it when it does arise. Here are some measures that might effectively prevent or help deal with controversy.

Be accountable in making program choices. Involve community people on the selection committee, hold community focus groups to discuss new program directions, or involve arts professionals who can substantiate the artistic merit of a project. Working closely with community partner organizations can help you understand how the work may be perceived and received by different community segments. This, in turn, can help frame and present the project with concern for the values and interests of those who might find the work controversial.

Prepare project and organization leaders. Discuss the work within the organization so that board and staff members at all levels understand its intent, how it relates to the organization's mission, and how the organization will publicly support this choice. Clarify in advance of the program with board, staff, and other key partners the process to deal with controversy in the event that it arises. What kinds and degree of negative response warrant action?

Be clear and consistent about your organization's position. It is important for everyone associated with the controversial program to be able to articulate why it was undertaken and to be supportive of it and the artist, even if the work is personally not their cup of tea. Designate one person to speak to the press and concerned parties on behalf of your organization in order to be consistent with statements and responses.

Educate the media in advance. Draw upon positive relationships with feature writers, bloggers, editors, and producers to try to secure advance media coverage that will prepare the community about the project. Offer the press a private preview with the artist present to provide them background information and a clear statement of artistic intent.

Provide interpretive materials. Sometimes people are just confused by the underlying meaning of a work of art or performance. Interpretive materials can help to clear up any misunderstandings and objections by clearly stating the artist's intent behind the work.

Respect differing opinions. Provide opportunity for opinions different from your organization's position to be expressed and dialogue to take place. Allowing for different opinions in your interpretive materials can also help to advance understanding and stave off negative reactions.

Engage supporters. Invite them to write letters to the editor or make calls to city council members or other leaders who should know that community members support your organization's program.

Conflict and challenge are not necessarily bad things. They can uncover issues beyond those at face value that, if addressed, can lead to new understanding—and even to healing within communities. Although easier said than done, arts leaders can transform controversy into constructive results. Find ways to educate and engage before, during, and after a controversial program has happened. Finding ongoing opportunities to engage the community in discussion about your program objectives and highlighting positive attention to your programs from other places and professionals can help create inroads toward constructive exchange.

CULTURALLY SPECIFIC WORK

Culture comprises a set of practices and expressions—language, behavior, ritual, values, food, and art—shared by a group of people. Cultural groups can encompass an ethnic community; youth; gay, lesbian, bisexual, and transgendered people; people who are Deaf or hard of hearing; and newcomers to the United States. Supporting and presenting the creative expressions of specific cultures well requires knowledge and sensitivity about those cultures and their creative forms. Ideally, a culturally-diverse staff and board can lend relevant cultural perspectives, expertise, and oversight to offering and supporting culturally-specific work. Absent that, working closely with partners, artists, advisors, or community members helps ensure that the integrity of the work is upheld. Many cultural organizations form advisory committees to advise on the faithful presentation of culturally-specific work.

Cultural representation is a complex matter that deserves attention beyond what this chapter can address. Concerns regarding self-determination, authenticity, appropriation, or exploitation can arise, even with the best of intentions. In addition, strategies for audience education and cross-cultural audience development are often needed to help understand meaning embedded in the work. Here are some fundamental considerations in developing culturally specific programs.

Aim for authenticity. Authenticity is most commonly thought of in relation to origins or authorship—for example, whether a painting is an authentic Rembrandt. However, authenticity also relates more broadly to whether the art is a true expression of a culture's values and beliefs. When working with traditional or folk art, authenticity is typically defined in terms of continuous tradition, that is, aesthetic forms and practices that are passed down through families or members within a culture. When folklorists or traditional artists look for authenticity, they not only look for continuity in the materials, form or style, function, and craftsmanship, but also in the spiritual, social, or cultural meaning of that work.

Questions that may arise around authenticity of work include: Can an artist of one culture effectively interpret art of another culture? How far can traditional artists exercise personal creative freedom before the work is no longer authentic or true to the tradition?

Consider appropriate presentation modes. Meaning and authenticity can be lost or compromised in presenting work out of its intended social, religious, or environmental context. Arts programmers need to ask such questions as: Can an African ancestor ritual be performed in a concert hall without stripping it of its meaning and authenticity? Or, What essential defining qualities are lost when hip-hop is taken out of the context of urban streets and put on stage? Evaluate these opportunities with the advice of the artists, and provide the artists with additional orientation to the project and its goals, a description of the audience, space, language, format, etc.

Recognize cultural norms. Not everyone who is used to clapping along with the music would know that folk fiddlers find audience clapping disruptive to the rhythm and to the way the music should be heard. Presenting the traditions of a culture unfamiliar to your audience often warrants informing audience members about what to expect and about appropriate behavior.

Discourage the commodification of traditional culture. In the American Southwest, Native American cultures seek to protect the integrity, privacy, and spirituality of religious dances. To safeguard sacred ceremonies from being reduced to the status of tourist attractions, many are not performed publicly. Through your own program choices, as well as advocacy among other local presenters, arts organizations should take care to avoid romanticizing, commercializing, or otherwise commodifying cultural traditions.

Understand the needs of artists of contemporary and traditional art forms. Many artists of a particular culture create work that makes little or no reference to their cultural traditions. Others may combine traditional and contemporary sensibilities. Still others may draw upon cultural references but evolve an altogether new, contemporary style. Do not assume that artists who are of a particular culture are traditional or folk artists.

ACCESSIBILITY

Involving artists with special needs and making programs accessible to people with disabilities are important concerns for programmers. It requires forethought and resources to address how people who are Deaf or hard of hearing might experience a theater production or how people who use wheelchairs can view artwork. See the Cultural Access chapter for a full discussion of this issue.

Logistics

Whether you are producing a weeklong outdoor festival in a city park, running a grant program, or transforming a solid waste management plant into a community environmental educational facility through public art, the vast volume of technical and logistical considerations never ceases to amaze and sometimes poses significant obstacles to arts programmers.

For most programs, there are common areas of concern. These include: site design; regulations, permits, and licenses; signage; equipment, supplies, and services; insurance; and security. Develop an operations manual for repeated programs to help streamline the planning and implementation of future programs.

SITE DESIGN

How you use your space and situate various elements within it affects the quality of the experience that artists, audience, and organizers have. Before making decisions, consult with appropriate individuals—such as the manager of the facility or property, police and fire marshals, and others who have used the space—to learn about any overriding rules and concerns regarding the site. Following are some questions to answer in designing your site.

How can the site design support effective presentation of the art? What relationship to the art and what experience do you want people to have? What characteristics of the location support this? Are there relationships between various program components that need to be reinforced through their proximity to each other?

What will be the flow of people through the space? What are givens and how can you manipulate traffic flow to serve artistic goals as well as to ensure safety, security, etc.? How will such concerns affect the location of program components, such as directional signs? How can you encourage or discourage people in and out of certain areas?

Example:

> An annual outdoor sculpture exhibition on the grounds of an historic estate displays sculpture on the lawn adjacent to the main house and along the walking trails in a more remote wooded area. While the woods offer a beautiful setting for the work, many artists have complained that visitors often overlook those pieces. The organizers improved signs and stationed volunteer tour guides at certain locations to encourage more people to venture beyond the lawn display.

How might weather conditions affect outdoor program sites? Check historical data and consider alternative dates for inclement weather or plan for dealing with weather issues during an event.

REGULATIONS, PERMITS, AND LICENSES

Rules governing required licenses and permits vary from place to place. To learn exactly what you need, check with the license commission, liquor commission, police and fire departments, building and electrical inspectors, and the board of health. This section addresses those areas for which permits or licenses are usually required.

Alcohol. If the facility you are using doesn't already have required licenses, you will need to get a liquor or beer and wine license as well as liquor liability insurance.

Food. Unless you are in a facility which has a food operation and is already approved by the board of health, all food vendors are required to get food permits from the local board of health to ensure sanitary food preparation, proper refrigeration, etc.

Gambling or raffles. Raffles, casino nights, and other pay-for-a-chance kinds of activities require a permit. Find out who authorizes such permits in your town by calling the city clerk's office.

Electrical. For significant modifications made to accommodate your electrical needs, a special electrical permit may be required.

Building permits. Attachments to buildings, such as signs or banners, or construction or erection of permanent or temporary art works or other structures may require permits from your local building commission.

Street closure or assembly permits. In some communities, festivals, parades, and other special events that take place in public settings require permission to close off or assemble in public ways.

Fire code compliance. Local fire marshals will want to evaluate the safety of your site in terms of maximum capacity, ingress and egress (where people enter and exit the location), and to ensure that standard fire lanes are adhered to for access by fire trucks. In addition, certain materials and objects—such as tents, projection screens, or curtains that you might bring to a location—must meet fire retardancy standards. In the latter case, the supplier might have a guarantee in writing from the manufacturer, or the fire marshal may require a sample of the material for testing.

Signage. Signs should help people get to and navigate within the program site. Find out from local officials if permission is needed to post temporary signs and at what point in time they may go up.

EQUIPMENT, SUPPLIES, AND SERVICES

Nothing is too big or too small to be considered in this area of logistics: from masking tape to media players, podiums to portable dance floors, rented tables to tents, track lighting to theatrical lighting, sound systems to assistive listening systems, backhoes to bucket trucks. Here is where your detail-oriented people must think thoroughly about what is needed. The costs of renting or purchasing goods, equipment, or services can easily consume a budget, so it is best to determine early which of these might be donated or borrowed, or what can be secured in-kind or purchased at a reduced price.

Artistic integrity could be easily compromised to save a few dollars. Providing dancers with an inadequate floor on which to perform may not only affect the quality of the performance, it could cause injury. Determine artists' needs very specifically. Talk honestly about shortcomings related to your site or

> **The Devil's in the Details! Visualizing What You Need**
>
> Identifying all of the logistical needs can seem like an overwhelming task. One effective technique for anticipating a program's logistical needs is called visualizing. It involves putting yourself in the shoes of the various key individuals involved in the program—an audience member, artists, VIPs, volunteers, etc.—and imagining yourself moving through the program moment by moment.
>
> Set aside ample quiet time and have what you need to begin to make lists. You might do this alone or with one or two others who are working with you. Picture how the program will look. Be very detailed in this visualization. Imagine yourself attending the event. How you will get to the program? Where will you park? Where are you entering? What signs do you need to find your way? Who is greeting you? Imagine the artist's arrival. What equipment will she or he need to set up? What kind of volunteer or technical staff will be there to help? Imagine the concession stand. How many tables and chairs do you need to display the merchandise and seat the sales staff? What signs are needed to indicate prices? How will purchases be accepted (cash, credit)? Is seating needed for the program? What configuration will work best, and how many chairs will be needed?
>
> The objective is to give yourself the time and space to imagine every detail. Don't censor any part of your visualization; the point is to reveal items or processes that you might not think about without the benefit of time and space. If program planners do this for their area, in addition to requesting logistical needs from artists, community partners, and others involved, they can begin to put together the master list of logistical needs.

technical support before you contract with an artist and review carefully the technical needs outlined in the artist's own contract rider.

> The vocalist and her voice should be the center of attention…not the sound system.

INSURANCE

There are many kinds of insurance that can protect you, artists, artwork, and the public. Consider what your programs might require among these basic insurance types.

Personal liability insurance. Your organization may already be insured for personal injury for your own facility. If you present programs in other locations, understand who is responsible for liability coverage. Some facilities will insure rental users. Others will require you to purchase liability insurance. Ask for proof of liability coverage through a policy currently covering your organization or agree to a hold harmless clause in a contract.

Liquor liability insurance. At many arts festivals, concert intermissions, and fundraising events, alcohol sale is a reliable revenue generator. If you sell alcohol, you must do so responsibly.

1. Evaluate the potential for abuse. Is the audience you expect likely to consume excessively and put themselves and others at risk?
2. Ask the site management if there are any rules or laws prohibiting the sale or serving of alcohol. Some places, for example, have open container laws that prohibit individuals from walking around with alcohol in open containers. This can affect festivals, outdoor concerts, etc.
3. Consult with police or the local liquor board regarding specific rules about who can serve alcohol and what kind of training may be required.

4. Determine the coverage and cost of securing liquor liability insurance. Weigh the enhancements alcohol offers to your program and profit margin against the added cost of insurance. Many arts organizations present alcohol-free programs in order to be socially responsible and because the legal and financial risks are too great.

Inclement weather insurance. Weather insurance protects against loss of profit or extra expenses caused by inclement weather conditions. This may be especially attractive to outdoor festivals or concerts which stand to lose significant admission or concession revenues if crowds are kept away by bad weather. The costs are generally quite high, and you must evaluate the fine print carefully. Cost and coverage of rain insurance are determined by complicated definitions of what constitutes damaging rain or other attendance–prohibiting weather.

Rain insurance premiums are typically calculated by mixing ingredients from the following recipe:

- the probability of rain as determined by the insurance company's weather maps;
- the projected revenue lost by the insured if it does rain; and
- the deductible as expressed by the amount of rain in inches that you can tolerate over a given time period.

So, for example, an event might pay a certain amount for rain insurance only for the most lucrative hours of the festival. Another might purchase rain insurance to cover a defined dollar amount of loss in the instance of "five continuous hours of rain" as specified in the policy.

Insurance for theft, damage, or loss. Valuable artwork, cultural artifacts, artist's equipment, and any other valuable objects should be insured for theft, damage, or loss. Insurance companies require the exact value of each item and specific information about security measures to be taken.

SECURITY, SAFETY, AND EMERGENCIES

Security encompasses the protection of people, art, the facility, equipment, onsite cash, and other valuables. Volunteers may be suitable to perform certain security functions—such as guarding artists' equipment or seeing that the fire lane on your festival grounds is kept free of vehicles. However, official police security may be a necessary precaution for guarding the ticket office where cash is handled, a major celebrity who might pose a crowd control problem, a beer concession, or valuable artwork.

Some emergencies can be averted. A prolonged heat wave, for example, prompted one festival organizer to purchase huge quantities of water to help visitors and participating artists stave off heat prostration. Staff at a partnering juvenile detention center should orient artists-in-residence to potential behavioral problems in advance of their onsite work and may need to attend and oversee residency workshops.

By nature, however, most emergencies are unpredictable. No matter what the program, you should be prepared for medical emergencies. Staff and volunteers should know:

- who has training in CPR;
- if there are onsite medical professionals, where they are located, and how they can be contacted quickly;

- where telephones are for calling 911;
- where first aid for minor accidents can be received; and
- what the plan is for halting or continuing program activities in the event of a disruptive emergency.

Other kinds of emergencies include severe weather for outdoor events, lost children, fire, or crowd control problems. Emergency procedures should be prominently displayed in program materials to inform the public how and where to get help. If you are running programs for young people—such as classes or camps—carefully define what staff can and cannot do in informational materials sent to parents. For instance, many parents may expect staff to administer injections or other medications, yet doing so could open your organization to lawsuits if improperly administered. Similarly, you must be careful about screening artists and staff members who work with young children in unsupervised settings. All of these precautions help to ensure the safety and security of your program participants.

After the Program

Program wrap-up should be done with the same care and attention given to program planning. There is a range of post-program activity.

FOLLOW-THROUGH AND THANKS

Agreements made before the program should be dutifully kept in a timely way. Return borrowed items. Pay bills promptly. Write and send final reports to funding sources and partners.

Everyone affiliated with the program should receive a thanks as personalized as is possible. Involve various volunteers or staff who had contact with participants, volunteers, etc., to take responsibility for drafting letters. To let people know their role has been important, it is a good idea to have letters cosigned not only by those who had most direct contact with them but also by the executive director, president of the board, or the director of the program.

Using Threat Assessment as a Proactive Tool for Planning

Threat assessment (also referred to as business continuity planning, when applied to an entire organization) is an exercise that examines three dimensions of any potential threat to your program: (1) probability: the probability that a threat will occur, (2) impact: the degree of impact this threat would have on your program (if it occurred), and (3) control: how much control you have in preventing the threat from occurring.

To engage in this process, brainstorm a list of potential threats that could impact your program with the core group of staff or volunteer event organizers. Then rate each of these threats on a scale of 1 to 5, with 1 being very unlikely, and 5 being very likely for each of the three areas: probability, impact and control. Tally up the scores, and—as a group—discuss strategies for how to mitigate against those threats that have the highest scores.

When you are done, commit your ideas to writing and communicate the threat mitigation plan with others who are affected by these issues. Take any steps that will help to minimize threats now, before any problems occur.

PROGRAM DOCUMENTATION AND EVALUATION

The Program Evaluation 🔖 chapter provides an in-depth discussion of program evaluation principles and practices, including documentation that supports your evaluation interests. A couple of notes are worth reinforcing.

Program Documentation: Things to Collect

Consider which items on this list will serve your evaluation needs, as well as serving as useful documentation for procedures manuals and planning future programs.

ITEMS TO HELP WITH EVALUATION

- Program purpose, goals, objectives
- Projected and actual budgets
- Projected and actual timeline
- Attendance figures
- Copies of media coverage and online publicity
- Program brochures and other printed pieces (retain a certain number of copies for posterity, future funding proposals, etc.)
- Evaluations from artists, audience, and other participants and summaries written
- Final evaluation report, when completed
- Video documentation
- Photo documentation
- Copies of website and social media pages

ITEMS TO HELP WITH FUTURE PROGRAM PLANNING AND IMPLEMENTATION

- Copies of essential and standard correspondence
- Contracts
- Background information about artists and other participants
- Copies of marketing materials, including social media postings, press releases, and other promotional tools
- List of key contacts: address, phone, email, why contacted, results of contact, recommendations for working with each person
- Mailing lists
- Site and sign requirements list
- Procedures unique to the program (such as how to obtain insurance for gallery exhibitions)
- Volunteer needs and lists of volunteers with contact information

Plan for documentation and evaluation from the beginning. Be sure staff and volunteer organizers know what information and documents they should be collecting and organizing as the program is developed and implemented as well as after the fact.

Encourage an expeditious closure to the program. Hold wrap-up and evaluation meetings very soon after the program has concluded while ideas and impressions are fresh, and before people begin to move on to other things. Set a deadline by which final summary reports should be completed.

The types of information that should be documented or compiled are listed in the sidebar, Program Documentation: Things to Collect.

Conclusion

Many arts programmers say that developing arts programs draws equally upon the left and right sides of the brain. From the right side, they exercise vision, knowledge, and creativity to conceive and design exciting arts and cultural activity and to support and champion artists and their aesthetic investigations. They develop educational, interpretive, and participatory ways to link art with people and communities which leave a lasting impression and a desire for more. The left side of the brain figures out how to make it real—how to organize and execute the myriad of details in order to support the art and people's experience of it. This chapter has introduced how to muster the whole brain to develop meaningful and successful arts programs from the mundane elements to the sublime!

As do other *Fundamentals* chapters, this chapter underscores the increasingly integrated ways in which arts organizations are working in their communities. Innovative program collaborations have enabled cultural organizations to connect with community members in new and meaningful ways. The program development process has become as much about the process, exchange, and learning that results from making programs together as it is about the envisioned outcome.

Endnotes

1. McDaniel, N. & Thorn, G. (1997). *Learning Audiences: Adult Arts Participation and the Learning Consciousness.* Washington, DC: The John F. Kennedy Center for the Performing Arts and the Association of Performing Arts Presenters.

2. Kuftinec, S. (2002). *Critical Relations in Community-Based Performance: The Artist and Writer in Conversation.* Retrieved at http://www.americansforthearts.org/AnimatingDemocracy.

3. Graves, B. & Juan Lado, M. (2005). Áfrican in Maine. Cultural Perspectives in Civic Dialogue: Case Studies from Animating Democracy. Washington, DC: Americans for the Arts, 55-56.

4. Ibid, 41.

15

Marketing the Arts

MAREN BROWN *with contributing editors*
BARBARA SCHAFER BACON, DOROTHY CHEN-COURTIN,
and SHIRLEY SNEVE

With arts organizations facing tremendous competition for the attention and support of their constituencies, and with audiences that are increasingly discerning in their need to engage authentically with arts and cultural groups, the imperative for arts marketers to build a clear message that engages participation from their communities is more urgent than ever. When done well, arts marketing embodies these interrelated goals--strengthening dialogue with constituents and increasing audience participation in programming.

Marketing is a means of clarifying and communicating what the organization is, what it does, and how the public can be involved. Whether the reader represents a cultural group or a local arts agency, successful marketing strategies can accomplish key tasks to strengthen the organization. These include:

- promoting events, artists, and cultural resources;

- developing audiences and increasing ticket sales;

- attracting donors, volunteers, and members; and

- advocating for policies that support arts and cultural development.

Evolution in the meaning of arts participation, continuous developments in technology and communications, and shifts in demographics and economics have all seismically impacted what it means to market the arts. With change as a constant in the field, this chapter focuses on the *foundational principles* that undergird a successful approach to arts marketing and introduces *core marketing concepts* that are relevant to the many challenges faced by cultural organizations and local arts agencies.

> The American Marketing Association (ama.org) offers this definition of marketing:
> "Marketing is the activity, set of institutions, and processes for creating, communicating, delivering, and exchanging offerings that have value for customers, clients, partners, and society at large."

Building on the "Four P's"

In his landmark 1960 book, *Basic Marketing: A Managerial Approach*, E. Jerome McCarthy attempted to isolate those factors that are not within the control of marketers, versus those that marketers can control. While audience turnout at cultural events can be impacted by a variety of factors that are outside of the arts marketer's control, such as weather, local economics, and personal obligations, McCarthy described four marketing elements that *can* be controlled. He called them "The Four P's": product, price, place, and promotion.

According to McCarthy, the "Four Ps," are necessary and mutually dependent ingredients in the marketing mix, and they should be considered when looking to meet the needs of a particular audience.

- **Product** is the mix of programs and services an organization provides.
- **Place** is the location (both physical and virtual) in which these programs are offered.
- **Price** is the price at which programs and services are offered for sale.
- **Promotion** is the specific promotional strategies used to promote the programs and services to target audiences.

The marketing cycle (Figure 1) incorporates all the elements of McCarthy's Four P's, while adding two components considered critical to a successful marketing approach:

- **Understanding audience** as an ongoing process that is central to an organization's marketing strategy; and
- **Incorporating evaluation** to better understand the impact of these marketing efforts and to refine the approach in a responsive manner.

Figure 1: The Marketing Cycle

STEP 1: UNDERSTANDING YOUR PROGRAMS/SERVICES
- What programs or services are provided?
- Where are they offered, and through what distribution methods?
- What is unique about these programs?
- What price should be charged?

STEP 4: EVALUATING YOUR EFFORTS
- What marketing efforts were effective, and which weren't?
- What can be done to improve marketing efforts in the future?

STEP 2: UNDERSTANDING YOUR AUDIENCE/CONSTITUENTS
- Who are the current and intended audiences/constituents?
- What are they willing to pay to participate in programs?
- What do they value about the programs and services?

STEP 3: SELECTING THE BEST MARKETING CHANNELS
- What are the best marketing channels to use, given the audience, budget, and capacity?

©2015, Maren Brown, used with permission

Marketing is *cyclical* in cultural organizations, requiring a continuous process of investigation and renewal to be truly effective. The *marketing cycle* illustrated below is a four-step process for organizing your marketing efforts.

Step 1: Understanding Your Products and Services

Programs and services are the mix of events, products, and services an organization offers to the public, such as concerts, exhibitions, residencies, education workshops, and publications, or, for a local arts agency, grants. The variety of programs offered by cultural organizations is truly endless and varies greatly by the type of organization. The most creative programmers or curators integrate the assets of the organization and its community in the design of programs and services.

Here are the key questions to ask when evaluating your products and services: What programs or services are provided? Where are they offered? What distribution methods are employed? What is unique about these programs? What price should be charged?

WHAT PROGRAMS AND SERVICES ARE PROVIDED?

Programs and services should be selected with target audiences in mind, and marketing strategies should be central to the design of these offerings. In many cultural organizations, there is a lack of consideration of audience preferences in the design of programs, often due to a concern that "populist" programs will lack artistic merit. The most successful organizations balance audience needs with artistic excellence. Direct communication between those responsible for programming and those responsible for marketing is essential to ensure an organization's responsiveness to its intended audience and for the implementation of effective marketing.

Many staff and volunteers at cultural organizations are unfamiliar with the full range of programs and services they offer. For example, it is not uncommon for cultural organizations to fail to create a comprehensive list of programs and services offered *across* the organization, such as internship programs, detailed educational offerings for schools, community outreach programs in off-site locations, curatorial advising on private collections, etc. Arts organizations need to inventory their programming every year and work with the arts marketer to promote the full range of programs and services offered by the organization. The arts marketer, in turn, should categorize these programs into logical groupings, such as exhibitions or performances, school programs, courses or workshops, internships, community outreach events, etc. This will help in the design of marketing strategies for specific audiences. How to link these offerings to target audiences is discussed later in this chapter.

WHERE ARE THE PROGRAMS AND SERVICES OFFERED?

The convenience, aesthetics, and accessibility of a location can affect the marketability of a program. Considerations for choosing a particular location are many: Does a regional touring format make sense for a theater program, or would a central downtown location be more appropriate? Should the programming be offered in an arts center, a business lobby, a youth center, or an urban park, or should multiple locations be considered? Does the venue have convenient parking, accessibility features, and public restrooms? Amenities such as parking, opportunities for socializing and dining, and activities for children may all contribute considerably to the quality of the consumer's experience. Therefore, such amenities should be designed and promoted with the program and considered as part of the programs and services offered to participants.

There are many competing priorities for a consumer's leisure time that need to be considered when devising marketing strategies. For example, when considering whether or not to attend a cultural event in the evening, many consumers compare the ease of staying at home to the potential obstacles of attending an art event, such as difficulty parking or driving distance. These issues of "place" can have a tremendous impact on audience participation. Potential audiences do not necessarily prioritize artistic considerations when making decisions about arts participation. For this reason, it is important to understand what obstacles prevent participation by these audiences and to overcome them through the marketing message. How to surface these issues for specific audiences, and address them in marketing materials is discussed later in the chapter. Example:

> As cities and towns recognize the value of the arts and culture to attract tourists and revitalize the economy of a region, they are also grappling with the issue of place. Because art venues are often situated in historic districts or within multiuse structures, they are frequently difficult to find. Recognizing a need to make the arts more accessible, the city of Worcester, Massachusetts devised new wayfinding systems, including dynamic signage and informational kiosks, to enable arts patrons to more easily locate the cultural attractions in the city.

WHAT DISTRIBUTION METHODS ARE EMPLOYED?

Consider the means by which programs and services are made available and accessible to buyers. Are tickets available online, through the mail, or only at the box office? How easy is it to get information about the program or event? Honestly assess any barriers that prevent visitors from patronizing programs and events, and devise ways to overcome these obstacles.

Many cultural organizations utilize sophisticated software, called customer or constituent relationship management systems (CRMs), for tracking communications with customers and ticket sales. Depending on the capacity of the organization, CRMs are an excellent way for an arts marketer to provide customers with the convenience of purchasing tickets online, while also enabling more refined insight into the success of organizational marketing efforts (see evaluation section at the end of this chapter). At the time of this writing, many cultural organizations utilize ticketing programs such as Tessitura, The Patron Edge, Vendini, and others to sell admission to their programs and events. The nonprofit technology research organizations Idealware, Techsoup, and Nonprofit Technology Network often provide free research and reviews of online ticketing and CRM systems that are worth investigating.

WHAT IS UNIQUE ABOUT YOUR PROGRAMS?

The question of uniqueness is, by far, the most difficult question for nonprofit arts marketers to answer. It requires a deep understanding of the distinctive assets of the organization, as well as a comprehensive assessment of similar programs and services offered by other nonprofits in one's service area. What is meant by "distinctive assets"? Simply put, the arts marketer needs to probe what their organization does better than anyone else in their service area. This perspective is informed by audience research, as well as through internal reflection by staff and volunteers.

The most distinctive assets are often overlooked. For example, a performing arts center might not consider the uniqueness of their decades-long contemporary dance series, and how this has both spawned an entire generation of local dancers and provided audiences with an unmatched, artistically rich experience. Museum collections provide yet another example. For instance, museums often have dominant collections that are considered so familiar to staff and volunteers that they fail to notice their uniqueness in the context of the region.

In addition to content, arts marketers should consider other qualities that make their offerings unique to their service area: Are the programs less expensive, more in-depth, serving a particular community, more centrally located, offering much-needed family programming? It is up to the arts marketer to unearth these distinctive capabilities and find ways to highlight them for the audiences the organization wishes to serve.

WHAT PRICE SHOULD BE CHARGED?

Price is the monetary value placed on the programs and services an organization offers to the many publics it serves. A delicate balance must be struck when determining price: not be so high as to prohibit participation and not so low as to shortchange income potential. In developing a pricing strategy, "what the market will bear" is an often-repeated recommendation that suggests a single formula. In truth, the process of determining pricing involves many possible strategies. As the following sections demonstrate, determining the needs of the various constituencies––the many "markets" of the organization—assessing the larger matrix of cultural offerings in the arts organization's community, and considering the uniqueness of each of the programs and services, are all necessary steps for arriving at the appropriate price point.

When considering pricing, it is important to first examine the types of programs and services that generate earned income in cultural organizations. Most commonly, earned revenues come from admission or workshop fees, gift shop sales, book, publication, or ticket sales, refreshment sales at events, subscriptions, and advertisements in program books. Less common sources may include licensing of images in a permanent collection for reproduction (for which the organization owns the copyright), travel programs, and the live broadcasting of performances or events. This is certainly not a comprehensive list, but gives one a feeling for the range of possibilities.

Free and reduced pricing

Many cultural organizations offer their programs and services free of charge, or at a substantially discounted price, in fulfillment of their nonprofit mission to reach underserved audiences and in an effort to provide public value to the community. These programs are subsidized with grants, donor and endowment income, or surplus earned revenues. When setting prices, consider who is excluded at what price levels and how to keep programs open to those less able to pay. Some approaches to keeping price affordable are:

- free or low-cost admission or registration (scholarships, free community performances, off-peak matinees, or abbreviated events);
- exchanges for volunteer labor (ushers at performing arts events or festival support in exchange for free attendance);

- complimentary tickets (unsold seats offered free of charge to social service organizations); and
- sliding scale (a price range, with people asked to pay according to ability).

Example:

> Many orchestras trying to turn around an elitist image have begun offering Casual Concerts, an alternative to traditional classical music concerts. A shortened, hour-long version of an evening concert is performed, with friendly and informative discussion from the director, and the musicians and audience members dress casually. A reduced admission price reflects the shortened program.

While it is important for arts organizations to provide free or subsidized services in fulfillment of their mission, it is also critical to identify ways to raise earned revenues to sustain the organization. In fact, many programs that begin as free events often transition to paid admission in order to continue operating, resulting in some degree of consumer dissatisfaction. An educational process can help audiences appreciate the cost of presenting the arts, as well as their role in supporting their community's cultural assets. Some cultural organizations have launched entire marketing campaigns aimed at educating the public about the real cost of their events, such as using the graphic image of a dollar, with the percentage of real costs contrasted with the percentage covered through ticket sales. Example:

> An arts council produced a popular folk festival. Initially offered free, the event attracted thousands of people. The arts council anticipated the financial reality that it would have to begin charging admission, so in order to retain its audience, paid admission was phased in gradually. First they set up unattended donation boxes; the next year people were personally invited by volunteers to make a donation at an attended donation box; then they suggested a specified donation amount; finally, they charged a ticket price equal to that amount. The council was able to sustain attendance throughout the transition.

Eight Pricing Strategies

Most arts marketers find it extremely difficult to establish prices for their earned revenue programs and services, often defaulting to "gut feel" when setting prices. Effective pricing strategies can play a significant role in the success or failure of a program or service, and—if properly applied—can help to sustain a program or organization for many years. Arts marketers should consider the following eight strategies when establishing program and service fees.

1. **Cost-based pricing:** This method considers the costs incurred for producing or presenting programs and services. A thoughtful budget analysis of the organization's programs and services (including allocated staff and overhead costs) can help to establish a realistic picture of the true cost of a program. Cost-based pricing includes the examination of such factors as the cost of staffing, overhead and materials used in the presentation of the program, the constraints imposed by the capacity of the venues where a performance is to be held or a workshop offered (for instance, how many seats does the theater have? how much display space exists?), and the number of seats or admissions that can realistically be sold.
2. **Competitive pricing**: This form of pricing takes into consideration what others in your service area—your "competitors"--are charging for similar products and services, such as cultural events, classes and workshops, or admission fees. To use this method, it is best for arts marketers to get a comprehensive sample of competitor prices for similar programs in the service area, to compare

them "apples to apples," and determine if there are any differentiating factors that could affect pricing. In this research, it is important to evaluate competitor prices on many levels. For example, if the organization is offering art classes to a specific community, it is wise to research other classes within a 30-minute driving radius and examine their pricing for similar classes (studio art vs. art appreciation, children's vs. adult offerings, for instance), materials provided (what is included in the course fee), duration of the course (the number of contact hours students have with an instructor, the number of weeks a class is offered, etc.), timing of the class (time of year, day of week, time of day), and uniqueness of the offering (the most common courses offered and those that are offered less frequently). This concept can be applied to any form of program or service, though the questions would vary, depending upon the type of program or service offered.

3. **Customer-segment pricing:** This pricing concept offers different levels of pricing for various types of audiences or constituents. For example, an arts organization may offer reduced admission to school groups at performances, or may offer special discounts for members in the gift shop. Customer segment pricing can also be used in collaboration with other businesses, such as hotels and restaurants that offer discounts to the organization's patrons.

4. **Differential pricing:** This model establishes pricing levels based on other differentiating factors beyond customer segments, such as the distribution method, the timing of a promotion, the quantities sold, the combination of similar products and services (bundling), and other features. The most common form of differential pricing is subscription tickets that offer patrons a discount for purchasing admission to several performing arts events in advance of or early in the season. Differential pricing can also be used in gift shops, where patrons can purchase multiple items for a discount.

5. **Versioning:** In this pricing structure, programs and services are organized according to a value scale. For instance, prices may vary for different program lengths (one hour vs. all day) or different levels of travel programs (domestic vs. international trips).

6. **Product-form pricing:** In this model, products and services within the same art form have different pricing based on the reputation of the artist. Tickets for a well-known dance company are likely to be more expensive than those for an emerging troupe. Similarly, it is not unreasonable to charge more for a full symphonic concert than for a quartet.

7. **Variable pricing:** This method calls for charging different prices based on the timing of an event, such as higher prices on the day of a performance, to discourage late purchases, or less for a matinee versus an evening performance. As ticketing programs become more sophisticated, more cul-

---

Three Forms of Value-Based Pricing

In chapter 3 of his book *The Art of Pricing: How to Find the Hidden Profits to Grow Your Business* (2005), Rafi Mohammed discusses three forms of value-based pricing. While his emphasis is on for-profit businesses, many of these lessons can be adapted to nonprofit arts organizations:

1. **Enhanced service:** What kind of service do you offer your customers? Do you remember their preferences? Do you make it easy for patrons to purchase your tickets?

2. **Insurance:** How do you ensure the satisfaction of your customers? Many cultural organizations offer lost ticket "insurance," as well as full refunds for unsatisfactory programs and services.

3. **Financing:** Do you allow your patrons to pay in installments for larger purchases, such as travel programs or visits by large school groups? Can you offer other payment plans that would help them to more easily afford an expensive item?

tural organizations are using complicated formulas to predict times of high demand, and charge more at different times for tickets, much as the airline industry has done for years.

8. **Value-based pricing:** In this version, prices are based on the value the program or service offers to customers, not on the cost to produce or deliver the service. Many pricing theorists now argue for the importance of this approach. In order to price effectively, they say, marketers need to understand what their customers value most: Do they value convenient parking or a pre-event reception? Do they value programs that target their age group? Determine what patrons value most and then develop pricing structures to capture that value. See the sidebar, *Three Forms of Value-Based Pricing*.

By carefully considering these eight strategies in establishing pricing for programs and services—and integrating at least three or more of them—arts marketers are almost certain to increase the income generated from earned revenue programs and services, which can support both the programs and the organization.

An example using three pricing strategies

A community arts center is planning to offer a musical concert at its main performance venue, which seats 200. Ticket sales are the organization's sole source of revenue, so they need to price the performance to maximize revenue. They have chosen to examine three pricing strategies in establishing a price for the event.

COST-BASED PRICING

The cost to produce the event (artist fees, sound equipment, space rental, marketing, staffing, and other costs) is $3,000. The organization usually gives away ten complimentary tickets at each performance to VIPs and friends of the artist, so the highest number of tickets it could sell at each event would be 190, based on the seating capacity of 200. Looking at its average ticket sales for previous concerts, the arts center anticipates that it will sell 80 percent of the total available seats, or 160 tickets. Using a cost-based pricing scheme alone, the ticket range would be $15.78/ticket ($3,000 divided by 190 tickets) to $18.75/ticket ($3,000 divided by 160 tickets).

COMPETITIVE-BASED PRICING

Extensive research into similar performances in the region has determined that ticket prices range from $20–$30 per ticket.

PRODUCT-FORM PRICING

The organization anticipates that its own audience will pay $20–$25 per ticket, based on the artist's reputation and what patrons who responded to a pricing survey indicated they would pay to see the artist.

Now let's look at the numbers. The chart below summarizes the potential income from pricing the concert at $20 per ticket or $25 per ticket. In either scenario, the organization will come out ahead, based on costs of $3,000 and its attendance history. In general, it is best to set prices at the highest levels the organization believes their audience can afford. Remember that any surplus income can be used to support other programs that may be more experimental in nature or help to subsidize seats for those who are not able to pay the full price, such as students and seniors.

Ticket Price	Minimum # Seats Needed to Cover Costs of $3,000		Average # Seats		Maximum # Seats	
	# Seats	Gross Revenues	# Seats	Revenues	# Seats	Revenues
$20	150	$3,000	160	$3,200	190	$3,800
$25	120	$3,000	160	$4,000	190	$4,750

Step 2: Understanding Your Audiences

Audiences (also known as constituents and patrons) are the lifeblood of cultural organizations. Without them, arts marketers cannot realize their organizational missions, nor can they survive financially. While arts marketers express interest in knowing their audiences, far too few take the time to really understand who their audiences are and how these audiences interact with the organization. Arts marketers who adopt this attitude of ignorance often rely on impressions culled from vocal participants in programs, allowing these few individuals to define the arts marketer's conception of the audiences the organization serves.

Marketing involves identifying, selecting, and cultivating targeted audiences. It is not an attempt to entice the general public. In market *segmentation*, specific groups are identified and research conducted to understand their attitudes about the arts and gain insight into their lifestyles. Marketing campaigns are then directly targeted to capture their attention and elicit a response.

Target marketing is effective for drawing more of the kinds of audiences already supporting the organization and for developing new audience segments. And, it can be key in discovering how to overcome barriers to participation for previously excluded populations. Example:

> A music presenter in a suburban area learns from national research that young singles and couples are good audience prospects for jazz performances. The program committee wants to offer a short series of Saturday night concerts that will appeal to a younger audience. Before investing in this new venture, however, the organization conducts two focus groups and gets some surprising feedback about the attitudes, beliefs, leisure activity patterns, and media habits of the target population:
>
> - Many affluent singles and young couples frequently go away on weekends.
> - Weeknight performances are more likely to draw singles and young couples because they have no family obligations or childcare needs.
> - Many singles are as interested in the social aspect of cultural events as in the artistic content.
> - People think of jazz as "serious."
> - Everyone goes to the Wednesday night two-for-one deal at the local cinema.
> - A widespread perception exists that "there is nothing to do on weeknights."
>
> This information is shared with the program committee, which uses it to design a Thursday night series featuring cabaret-style performers, sale of refreshments, and plenty of intermissions during which audience members can socialize. These events are promoted as a relaxed "jazz coffeehouse" evening and developed as a joint promotion with the local cinema. By the third month, these performances are considered the thing to do for this market segment.

To better understand the audiences for an organization's programs and services, arts marketers need to look for clues to answer three central questions:

- Who are the current and intended audiences/constituents?
- What do they value about the existing programs and services?
- What are they willing to pay to participate in current and future programs?

Carefully conducted audience research can help an arts marketer to answer all of these questions.

Figure 2: Understanding audiences.

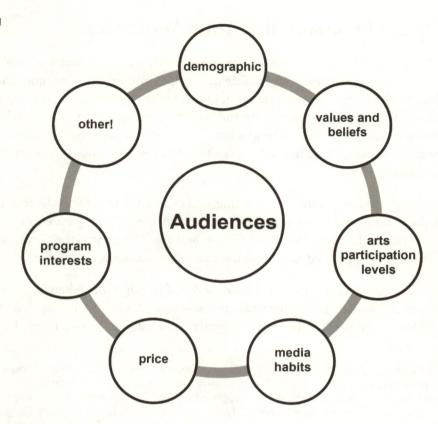

AUDIENCE RESEARCH

Audience research is the process of investigating information about existing or prospective audiences to inform one's programming and marketing decisions, and help minimize the risk of offering programs and services that do not meet needs in the community. Its goal is to gain insight into the interests and behavioral patterns of these target groups.

Audience research methods might be employed to:

- test interest in a new program direction;
- understand why membership is dwindling;
- learn about the interests of potential new audiences;
- identify a disinclined group's barriers to participation;
- gather market profile information needed to identify and secure media or corporate sponsors; or
- determine the best placement for publicity, promotion, and advertising.

As Figure 2 illustrates, audiences can be understood on a number of different levels. It is important to gather information about the demographic characteristics of an audience, such as their age, ethnicity, geographic location, gender, and income levels, as well as other characteristics. With this information, arts marketers can begin to develop a more accurate picture of their audiences, which can help them to better meet their needs and communicate with them about the programs and services offered by the organization.

Examples of information that can be gathered through audience research

VALUES AND BELIEFS

- Impressions of cultural life in the community
- Beliefs about the importance of the arts
- Feelings about the arts and culture that are currently available
- Perceptions of cultural activities lacking in the community

ARTS PARTICIPATION

- Attendance at cultural events or institutions—including kinds of events and frequency
- Obstacles to attending cultural events
- Impressions of particular events, organizations, or institutions

LEISURE ACTIVITY

- Available leisure time
- Current ways of spending leisure time
- Most preferred leisure pursuits
- Feelings about the amount and kinds of activities available for adults and children

MEDIA HABITS

- Sources used to obtain information about cultural and leisure activities
- Typical advance planning time to participate in cultural activities

DEMOGRAPHIC PROFILE

- Age, gender, and income level of participants
- Number of children, if any, in the family

FEEDBACK ON COMPLETED PROGRAMS AND EVENTS

- Inclination to attend (support) the program again
- Suggested improvements to make the program better serve interests or needs
- Other programs that would be of interest to patrons

PRICE

- Opinion about fair price for the program
- Feeling about investment of time required to participate in the program

PROMOTION

- Response to the marketing campaign message and image
- Recommendation about different or additional information for marketing materials

PLACE

- Opinion about convenience and desirability of the location
- Opinion about the date and time of the program
- Ease of registration or ticket purchase
- Opinion about accessibility for people with disabilities
- Recommendations for improvement

FEEDBACK ON ONGOING ACTIVITIES (FOR EXAMPLE, MEMBERSHIP)

- How members first became aware of the organization
- Benefits that convinced members to join
- Most positive experience(s) since joining
- Negative experience(s) with this organization
- Most important benefits of belonging
- Suggested other offerings
- Reasons for renewing or not renewing membership

Audience Research Methods — Existing Sources

Information about audiences can be gathered in a variety of ways, beginning with the examination of existing sources that are augmented with new information that focuses more specifically on the unique characteristics of one's audiences.

Here is a sampling of the methods researchers use to learn more about nonprofit cultural organization audiences. *Note that due to space limitations, the resources are entirely U.S.-based.*

- **Internal customer records:** Cultural organizations frequently look at the information contained in their mailing lists, ticket sales lists, and other databases to gain insights into the demographic composition of their audiences and the buying habits of these groups.
- **Marketing analytics programs:** Another excellent method for gathering information about audiences is to examine analytics programs that run on the back end of websites, social media sites, and email service providers. At the time of this writing, Google Analytics is widely used by arts organizations on their websites, as are analytics programs on Facebook and YouTube.
- **Federal data:** For an overview of U.S. arts audiences, the first stop should be the National Endowment for the Arts publications and research division (www.arts.gov/artistic-fields/research-analysis). There are a number of important studies about arts audiences on this website. The U.S. Census website (www.census.gov), while somewhat difficult to navigate thanks to the volume of information on the site, is a treasure trove of information about the demographics of individuals and businesses within a focused geographic region in the United States. FedStats (fedstats.sites.usa.gov) is a central aggregator of data gathered by 100 federal agencies. Depending on one's marketing goals, there may be some important information available in this centralized resource.
- **State and regional data:** Regional, state, and local arts agencies are an important resource for data about the organization's region. A list of regional and state arts agencies is available at the National Assembly of State Arts Agencies. Americans for the Arts may provide a listing of local arts agencies in a particular region. Other valuable sources of information about regional, state, and local audiences include economic development agencies, area colleges, and state department of education websites.
- **Arts service organizations:** Most arts service organizations (such as Americans for the Arts, National Assembly of State Arts Agencies, National Guild for Community Arts Education, American Alliance of Museums, Association of Performing Arts Presenters, and others) maintain a vast repository of information about arts audiences on their websites. If an organization is presenting a particular art form, it is wise to examine these sites for best practices and marketing strategies that work. The National Arts Marketing Project is a great general resource for arts marketers.
- **Foundations:** Foundations can be an excellent source of audience research and marketing information. Visit the Foundation Center website to learn about which foundations support the arts in any region of the country, and examine their websites to learn more. Grantmakers in the Arts' website features research into arts audiences and other topics of relevance to arts marketers. The Pew Research Center website offers topical research about marketing trends that can be very useful.
- **Market research firms:** Many commercial market research companies offer information about audiences and marketing preferences for free on their websites. While these research reports are generally focused on for-profit companies, they can provide valuable clues about marketing strategies that are effective with specific audience demographics. Visit the American Marketing Association website for a list of members and resources.

Gathering New Information:

After existing sources are fully investigated, gathering new information can offer insight into the organization's specific audience composition and preferences. Many of these methods benefit from the impartial perspective of skilled professionals who are experienced in this form of research. See the Program Evaluation chapter for more information about the methods below ▌.

- **Observation**: Observing the audiences that attend events is one of the easiest and most frequently employed audience research methods used by arts marketers. Most people count participants, and make rudimentary judgments about the types of people in attendance (such as age, gender, income level, etc.).
- **Surveys:** Surveys are a common method for gathering audience information. These can be administered online, in paper form, and through an audience intercept process (where visitors are stopped and asked a short list of questions by trained researchers or volunteers). Surveys are useful for gathering basic details about patrons, such as their marketing and programming preferences, and allow an efficient gathering of information from large groups of people.
- **Interviews:** Informal and formal interviews are another method that arts marketers use to better understand their audiences. Most often, these take the form of informal interactions with patrons, and yield valuable insights.
- **Focus groups:** Focus groups offer arts marketers the opportunity to gather more in-depth information about audiences from a small sampling of the audience they wish to study (usually 6-10 people who share common characteristics). Focus groups are best conducted by a trained professional and are often an excellent way to explore strategies to reach new audiences.
- **Competitive research:** Another important strand of research is to assess similar programs and services in the arts organization's service region. It is helpful to identify 5-10 organizations serving a similar target market (regardless of the art form they present), and to assess the program and service offerings, pricing, facilities, marketing strategies, and other aspects of the organization that can provide insight into the marketing messages currently used.

Audience Participation Strategies

An important goal of audience research is to increase participation levels in programs and services. For more than a decade, researchers have focused on audience participation trends in arts organizations. A landmark study for the Rand Corporation by Kevin F. McCarthy and Kimberly Jinnett, *A New Framework for Building Participation in the Arts* (2001), dramatically changed the way cultural organizations think about their audiences. The study states that a central strategic issue involves deciding what an institution means when it says it wants to increase participation. According to this research, an institution can increase participation in three basic ways:

1. **Broaden it** by capturing a larger share of the existing market by attracting individuals who constitute a natural audience for the arts but are not currently participants.
2. **Deepen it** through intensifying its current participants' level of involvement.
3. **Diversify** it by attracting new markets composed of individuals who typically would not entertain the idea of participating in the arts.

4. An organization that decides to pursue all three approaches at once faces a difficult challenge, because each of these methods requires a different engagement strategy.

This framework helps us to understand that audience development goes beyond simply increasing attendance. It occurs when new groups of people are attracted to a program or organization and develop an interest, connection, or commitment. By combining program development and promotional strategies, arts marketers can provide bridges to connect new audiences with opportunities for expression and enrichment.

Cultural organizations must determine how participation-building efforts fit with their overall purpose and mission, available resources, and the community environment in which they operate. In other words, arts organization must take an integrative approach to building participation, one that:

- links the organization's participation-building activities to its core values, purpose, and goals;
- identifies clear target groups and bases its tactics on good information about those groups;
- clearly understands both internal and external resources that can be committed to building participation; and
- establishes a process for feedback and self-evaluation.

How much time and money should be allocated to marketing?

While there are many possibilities for marketing arts programs, not all are effective choices. What's more, the availability of money, time, and labor forces organizations to choose methods within their means that will bring them closest to their objectives. While some organizations allocate 10 percent of their programming budget for marketing expenses, there are no rules of thumb. Organizational resources differ, and diligent use of in-kind services, volume or nonprofit discounts, and partnerships can all affect the amount of cash needed.

Often the toughest marketing decisions concern whether or not to spend money on high-cost marketing strategies. If these avenues hold real promise for reaching one or more target markets, it is important to evaluate the potential reach (how many people will see the promotion) and effectiveness (how many people may respond) in relation to the cash cost. For example, to promote an annual folk festival, a multicolor, artist-designed poster, despite its expense, may work more effectively than an inexpensive flyer. The poster not only calls the community's attention to the upcoming event but also may have a lasting impact if the image is popular and posters are sold at and beyond the event. At other times, less costly promotions, such as email, may be more than adequate. One cannot apply the same marketing formula to every activity and event.

Many organizations solicit partners or underwriters to support special, more costly promotional strategies that advance the marketing objectives in significant ways. Media and business sponsorships and donations of goods and services can extend the impact of limited marketing dollars.

Marketing campaigns also require skills, information, and equipment. Staff time is a real cost—one that is often overlooked in the marketing budget!—and it is important to carefully weigh the investment of labor for each promotional method to assess its effectiveness. Marketing campaigns may also require specialized skills in writing, editing, or graphic design, as well as access to specialized equipment (such as videography equipment) that needs to be included in the budget.

All of these costs should be enumerated in a marketing plan. See the APPENDIX to this chapter for an outline of an organizational marketing plan.

With significant funding from the Wallace Foundation, the principles posited in the 2001 study were tested throughout the nation. In 2014, the foundation supported an in-depth review of these efforts in an effort to extract best practices and lessons learned. The study, *The Road to Results: Effective Practices for Building Arts Audiences,* by Bob Harlow, isolates nine practices that characterize successful audience participation efforts:

1. **Recognize when change is needed.** Organizations that developed awareness of "a pattern of audience behavior that presented an opportunity or a challenge for their financial viability, artistic viability, or both" were more likely to succeed in their audience participation efforts. This awareness was often signaled by a drop in attendance or reduction in ticket sales, creating a sense of urgency that supported change efforts.
2. **Identify the target audience that fits.** Organizations that succeeded were more likely to recognize a need to identify audiences with whom they had a reasonable chance of success in growing participation, as well as those audiences that were consistent with their mission to serve.
3. **Determine what barriers need to be removed.** After identifying the barriers to participation, successful organizations were able to develop strategies that helped overcome obstacles to participation.
4. **Utilize audience research.** Successful efforts were more likely to employ data to support their understanding of audiences, such as the target group's level of arts involvement, interests, and opinions of the institution. This aided the development of strategies that were better aligned with the target audiences.
5. **Define what success looks like.** It is important for arts organizations to "spell out a vision of the relationship" they want to have with the audiences they are targeting. This encompasses anything from how the organization interacts with audiences to the mix of programs and services that are offered to these targeted groups.
6. **Provide multiple points of entry.** Staff provided target audiences with many different opportunities to connect with their organization.
7. **Align the organization around the strategy.** Internal buy-in was an essential component of success, including the definition of audience participation objectives, staff roles and responsibilities, and other factors.
8. **Build in learning.** Successful organizations were more likely to engage in ongoing assessment of their efforts, in order to understand what works and what doesn't.
9. **Prepare for success.** While success is certainly a desirable outcome, it can also strain staff with increased workloads, a need to develop new competencies, and other unanticipated pressures. This last point asks arts marketers to contemplate what happens when an audience participation effort is so successful that they can't accommodate everyone who arrives, or how the organization will deal with frustrated staff members who are overburdened with throngs of people arriving to an event where there is limited capacity.

Step 3: Selecting The Best Marketing Channels

TYPES OF MARKETING CHANNELS

After audience research has been concluded, an arts marketer should have a clear sense of the programs and services that would interest their target audiences, as well as the pricing and location that would best serve them. Research should also point to the best marketing channels to use in communicating with these audiences.

Generally, marketing channels fall into four categories:

- **Online:** Defined here as online delivery methods such as websites, social media, online advertising, email promotions, mobile applications, online coupon promotions, blogs, texting, and other tools.
- **Print media:** While many consider print media "dead," in fact, many community- and campus-based arts organizations use print strategies to great effect. These include posters, brochures, tourism rack cards, advertisement in print media, billboards, table tents, flyers, and other physical marketing
materials.
- **Newspapers, magazines, and broadcast media**: Arts marketers are often adept at garnering coverage from local media sources, even in markets where there is an oversaturation of art events. They also regularly advertise their programs and events on television, radio, newspapers, and magazines.
- **Other**: Additional methods used by arts marketers to promote programs and services offered by their organizations include presentations at clubs and community gatherings, offering "schwag"—free promotional items with the logo or name of the organization on them, and previews of programs or events.

Once the media preferences of one's target audiences are understood, the arts marketer can make informed choices about the best marketing channels to reach them.

THE SIX STEPS TO IDENTIFYING THE BEST MARKETING CHANNELS

1. Inventory existing marketing efforts

Unless their organization is new, without any prior history of marketing, most arts marketers are well advised to conduct a thorough inventory of all the marketing channels the organization currently utilizes to understand those that are successful, as well as those that are not as effective. To do this, the following process is recommended:

- **Interview current and former staff and volunteers** who were involved in marketing the programs and services of the organization to unearth current and former marketing efforts. Learn what marketing channels are currently in use, and why these strategies were selected. Inquire about strategies that were once utilized but have since been abandoned, and why these fell out of favor.
- **Conduct a simple web search** to fill in any information gaps. It is not uncommon for organizations to have "abandoned properties" on social media sites or websites that people have long since forgotten. Conducting a web search with the organization's name in quotes can help to unearth any forgotten sites and provide an opportunity to update or remove outdated information.

- **Gather together any data** that quantifies the success of current and previous efforts. Collect available data from the organization's ticket sales database, website, email communications, social media sites, and other information sources to determine which marketing channels have the highest levels of traffic, audience engagement, and/or conversion rates.
- **Pull together audience research** that identifies the marketing channel preferences of the organization's target audiences. Review the results of audience research to determine which marketing channels are preferred by the organization's target markets.
- **Note the marketing channels** where there is a high correlation between target audience preferences, high levels of marketing success (as determined by high traffic, engagement or conversion rates), and existing marketing efforts. When there is a high correlation, this is a strong indicator that investment in these efforts is likely to yield positive outcomes.

2. Define marketing success

Determine how marketing will support key organizational objectives. Here are some examples of typical organizational objectives that are supported by arts marketers:

- A 10 percent increase in attendance at the jazz series this year vs. last year.
- A 20 percent increase in participation by youth between the ages of 10–14 in this year's summer arts camp vs. last year's.
- An increase of 20 percent in revenues from school performances this year over last year.
- Selling out an average of 50 percent of seats two weeks prior to shows vs. the average rate of 30% for the last two years.
- A 10 percent increase in positive perception of the organization compared to an audience survey conducted last year.

Notice the specificity in these statements. It is important to articulate success measures that are *specific, measurable,* and *time bound.* If these terms sound familiar, they are: the terminology we are using in this chapter corresponds to the *objectives* discussed in the Strategic Planning chapter. Marketing is one function within the larger organizational enterprise (alongside finance, programming, fundraising, and other functions in the organization). Because of this, the marketing effort must always relate to the larger goals and objectives of the organization as a whole.

Remember that marketing is just one part of the larger whole in supporting these organizational objectives. It is not uncommon for lack of communication across departmental lines to result in fractured organizational goals. For instance, in most arts organizations, the artistic director or curator is assigned responsibility for selecting and presenting programs, often without relevant input from the arts marketer. Given that the quality and potential popularity of these programs or exhibits can greatly impact attendance levels, organizations that design *an overall strategy in collaboration with others across the organization* are more likely to achieve their broader organizational objectives. While this book presents the functional areas of arts organizations as separate chapters, the truth is that the most successful organizations work in cross-functional teams.

3. Build an online anchor

After inventorying the organization's existing efforts, and analyzing the relationship between these efforts and the preferences of the target audiences, the next step is to create a solid online "anchor" that offers detailed information about the organization. This should include a listing of board and staff, the programs and services offered, contact information and directions, as well as other relevant details that help audiences and constituents to easily find what they need to engage with the organization. Typically this anchor site is a website, though cultural organizations are increasingly abandoning websites in favor of a strong presence on a social media site or blog. At the time of this writing, the strongest recommendation is to maintain a website, since it allows for greater organizational control and is still widely expected by consumers.

Invest time and thought in developing an anchor site that is visually appealing, easy to navigate, informative, consistent with the look of other organizational marketing materials, and that incorporates links to the other online marketing channels the organization maintains. Arts marketers must maintain an anchor site that continually incorporates new technologies and appeals to contemporary sensibilities. To stay current with ever-changing technologies, a good rule of thumb is to plan on significantly redesigning the organization's anchor site every two to three years to take advantage of developments in new technologies and evolving consumer preferences, with revisions to back-end functionality every year.

Once an anchor site is created, arts marketers can reference it in other marketing channels as a source for more detailed information about the organization and its programs and services.

4. Concentrate on selected marketing channels

One of the most common dilemmas arts marketers face is how to make the best use of their limited time and budget in promoting their organization's programs and services. Remember that more is *not* better when marketing arts programs. Instead, it is best to review the audience research conducted in step 2 and carefully analyze what channels the organization's target markets are most likely to use when seeking out information. *Focus* is the key here. Once a discrete set of marketing channels are identified that are both *utilized by the organization's audiences* and are *capable of being* fully harnessed, the arts marketer can concentrate efforts accordingly.

Social media simultaneously presents one of the greatest opportunities and one of the most formidable challenges for arts marketers. On the one hand, social media is free, offers the potential to reach millions of people, and provides significant "behind the scenes" data about users. On the other hand, social media challenges organizations to distinguish themselves from others, requires that arts marketers develop familiarity with the technology that drives the sites, and demands a significant amount of time to maintain an active and lively presence. Because social media is a two-way channel (as opposed to the one-way communication of print media and many websites), it is essential that organizations maintain a frequent, engaging presence. There are no prescriptions for how frequently one needs to post, since conventions vary for each site. So it is up to the arts marketer to understand the standards for each social media channel, and maintain a site that is consistent with the norms in each social media community. Consult sites like the National Arts Marketing Project to learn more about the conventions for each marketing channel, and look at the blogs or books of nonprofit marketing experts like Beth Kanter and Heather Mansfield.

It is not uncommon to find established arts organizations with multiple abandoned efforts on social media sites that were initiated by well-meaning volunteers or staff, but have subsequently been allowed to languish with dated and irrelevant content. If it is determined that the organization's target audiences, or other visitors, do not use these sites, it is time to shut them down. Example:

> The local arts agency of a small city completed an analysis of its marketing presence, and after conducting detailed audience research, decided to inventory their marketing channels. Staff learned that the organization's presence on the photo-sharing site Flickr had not been used in three years. Audience research showed that none of their target markets used this site for information, and Flickr site data showed little recent use by visitors. When discussing options, several staff members noted that the Flickr site showcased rental facilities that the organization wanted to highlight. Since rentals were an important earned revenue source, they wondered how "it could hurt" to retain the site. However, after reviewing the responsibilities of the arts marketer and her capacity to promote the organization effectively across all its marketing channels, it was decided to shut down the Flickr site and redesign the organization's website with a new section devoted to rental facilities that would make use of the best photos from the Flickr site. Staff also decided to move images to their existing account on Instagram (another photo-sharing site) that was identified as a preference by their target audiences.

Another challenge for arts marketers is the transition from consumer preferences for print media vs. online marketing channels. Some audiences still prefer print materials, yet the cost to produce these can be exorbitant. Their design, printing, and mailing costs, as well as the staff time required to produce them, can easily consume one's marketing budget. What to do? To cut costs and integrate some audience preferences for print media, many organizations are using postcards to promote a new season and directing patrons to websites and social media sites for more information. Other organizations have moved in the opposite direction, again noting target audience preferences. For these organizations, using print media helps them distinguish themselves from others, and is more effective than many online strategies in driving attendance at events. Here again, it is essential to look carefully at target audience preferences to discover what works best for the constituency the arts marketer is trying to reach.

The decline of traditional arts journalism is another frequently cited concern of arts marketers. In the past, performing and visual arts critics were a mainstay of newspaper and broadcast media. These positions are quickly vanishing from the landscape. Instead of appealing to a limited set of experts to provide in-depth coverage of their programs and services, arts marketers must now be aware of which online media sources (both formal news media sites and influential individuals who have set up blogs and online publications) to direct their messages. Here, audience research can provide helpful insights into where coverage of programs and services influences arts participation.

5. Create a consistent brand across all marketing channels

After completing the steps above, it is now time to consider the element of *branding*.

A brand is the symbolic expression of the cultural organization, as expressed in the images and messages utilized. Increasingly, arts professionals appreciate the value of branding as a critical component of their overall marketing strategy. The power of branding is that these messages and images combine to elicit an emotional response on the part of audiences, such as excitement, trust, fun, and other desirable emotions. Practically speaking, the brand is expressed in the logo, the colors and images used in marketing materials, the website's look and feel, email communications, social media sites, and even the name badges and clothing that staff members wear. The more consistent the "look" associated with the organization, the stronger the brand. Before embarking on a branding campaign, think strategically about what key idea or ideas the organization wishes to be fixed in the minds of audience members: Should it be seen as a cutting edge museum? Is it to be known as an elegant "night out" performing arts center? Is it a place for family-friendly art experiences? All of these ideas suggest different strategies, and require thinking about how best to express the core mission in marketing materials. Audience research can help to test the success of these ideas before "going live" with a consistent brand.

It is important that the arts marketer pay attention to *consistency* in branding across all the organization's marketing channels, including social media. Many organizations have beautiful websites, but fail to pay attention to the design of their social media sites (or vice versa!). This confuses audiences and contributes to a lack of trust when they click on links to social media sites that look nothing like other organizational marketing materials. See the Online Fundraising Chapter for more on this. ▌.

6. Carefully time the release of each marketing strategy

The timing and interrelationship of different marketing components is a key part of a campaign strategy. The most critical deadline is when the organization wants people to act, but it is also important to consider when particular markets are *likely* to act. For example, by what date must the total number of advance ticket sales to a key fundraising event be known in order to give caterers a head count? If the local audience makes decisions to attend an outdoor festival within three to five days of the event, then advertising and feature stories in the local paper should be planned to culminate during that period. A social media campaign might be planned to reach potential participants three weeks before the event to provide target markets with the information they need to attend. By determining these key audience action points, arts marketers can then project backwards to give audiences enough time to get information and the arts organization time to implement marketing activities.

Other timing factors to consider include:
- demands on staff or volunteer time to coordinate various marketing efforts;
- deadlines for program details to be set in order to include them in materials;
- service timelines, such as for graphic designers; and
- media deadlines.

Step 4: Evaluate the Effectiveness of Your Marketing Strategies

The final step in the four-part marketing cycle is the evaluation of the marketing efforts. In earlier steps, the organization's program and service offerings were defined, target audiences were researched and identified, and appropriate marketing channels were selected that most closely aligned with the preferences of these target audiences.

Evaluation helps arts marketers to see whether they are reaching these target audiences, how well they are engaging these audiences, and whether their marketing is succeeding in drawing audiences to the organization's programs and services. Most of all, evaluation helps arts marketers answer crucial questions about their marketing efforts:

- How well is the marketing supporting overall organizational objectives?
- What marketing efforts were effective, and which weren't?
- Was the staff and volunteer time and money invested on these efforts the best use of these limited resources?
- What can be done to improve future marketing efforts?

INVENTORY MARKETING DATA

One of the first steps that arts marketers should take in setting up an evaluation system is to inventory what data is currently being captured through the organization's existing marketing channels. Marketing data being gathered by arts organizations commonly includes the following:

Marketing budget and staffing data

It is crucial that the organization have a clear understanding of the staff and/or volunteer time available for marketing the organization, and the financial resources that can support the effort. Key metrics that draw from this information include:

- number of hours spent to market specific events, broken down by each marketing channel;
- dollars spent on marketing specific events, broken down by channel.

Ticketing system metrics

An organization's customer relationship management (CRM) or ticketing system is one of the most important sources of marketing information. Depending on the type of system the organization has at its disposal, data can include:

- number of names in the database, and ability to track if the number grows over time;
- number of tickets sold, broken down by multiple segments, such as: day of week sold, individual performance or event, type of event, etc.;
- ticket buyer's location;
- frequency of attendance (first time buyer, repeat visitor, etc.).

Website analytics

These programs run quietly in the background of many websites and capture a wide array of information about visitors to the site, including:

- number of unique visitors;
- average time spent on site;
- geographic region of visitors;
- number of repeat visitors;
- page referrals (where visitors came from).

The most common web analytics program used by arts organizations is Google Analytics (because it is free at the time of this writing). There are many other competing web analytics programs that provide similar information.

Social media metrics

Most social media sites have analytics programs, which vary in detail. Facebook Insights is very detailed, others are not. Many marketing companies specialize in monitoring social media sentiment, and this can be very useful for larger organizations with a robust social media presence. Typical social metrics include visitor demographics (age, gender, etc.), as well as the number of:

- likes, followers, etc.;
- comments or likes on a post;

- views of online videos or photos;
- times a post is forwarded to others.

Email metrics

Email service providers like Constant Contact, Mail Chimp, and others offer organizations the ability to send out mass emails to a list of subscribers. They have the added feature of offering a data "dashboard" that tracks information about how users interface with the emails, including:
- number of emails sent for each campaign;
- open rates (number of people who open the email);
- click through rates (number of people who have clicked on links in the email);
- unsubscribe rates (number of people who have unsubscribed);
- subscriber retention rates.

Advertising data

Many arts marketers employ online advertising to promote their organization and its programs. Advertising can be purchased on most social media sites and through most online search engines, as well as in print newspapers and magazines. Online advertisers offer added tracking features that are not as accessible in local print media, though this is changing quite rapidly. Common tracking features include:
- number of "impressions" (either physical copies of ads printed or times it is served up to viewers);
- click-through rate (in an online ad, the number of times people click on the ad).

Other data examples

Arts organizations also often capture the number of:
- presentations given in the community;
- articles in local media about an event;
- schwag items distributed;
- survey respondents who answered a question affirmatively.

While this is not a comprehensive list, it should stimulate thinking about what measures might be available to your organization. The arts marketer won't use all of these measures but will select those that are aligned with key organizational objectives.

DETERMINE HOW TO EVALUATE MARKETING RESULTS

There is no single or ideal solution for an effective arts marketing campaign. When confronted with the same organizational objectives, two arts marketers will often arrive at different marketing strategies to support these objectives. Here's where the importance of audience research is crucial, because marketing strategies should be informed by target audience research. In considering the results of this research, each organization's marketing strategy necessarily will be unique. So how can the arts marketer evaluate these efforts if they are all so different?

The marketing strategies to use are typically based on the following criteria:

1. relevance to the organizational objectives to be addressed through the marketing campaign;
2. historical success with previous marketing approaches. and
3. best practices in the field, whether comparable or aspirational.

So how to apply these concepts?

Relevance to organizational objectives

In step 3, several sample organizational objectives were outlined that might inform a typical marketing campaign, such as increasing ticket sales for a jazz series by 10 percent. Evaluation systems should be designed to help to measure whether marketing is advancing these organizational objectives. In that example, ticket sales for that series before and after a marketing campaign would be compared to see if there has been an increase of 10 percent or more. Usually, organizational objectives can be measured by internal data, such as financial information or ticket sales. But in some instances, organizations are looking at "softer" measures, such as increases in audience awareness, and these require more sophisticated approaches. See the Program Evaluation chapter for more information.

Historical success with previous marketing approaches

Examining previous successful marketing efforts for the same target audiences can provide baseline data for measuring improvements in the organization's marketing efforts. Begin by holding a one-hour debrief session with those who planned and executed similar marketing campaigns for comparable programs in the past. Ask everyone to reflect on the following questions:

- What organizational objectives were addressed through this marketing campaign?
- What made this marketing campaign successful, if anything?
- What evidence, if any, do we have that demonstrates this success? (Look at the list of marketing data above to stimulate ideas.)
- What could be improved in this marketing campaign?

Once this information has been gathered, the arts marketer can design evaluation systems to measure any changes (both increases and decreases) between current and past efforts, and refine marketing strategies based on the results. For example, this research may reveal that the timing of an email campaign for a particular event series is strongly correlated with increases in ticket sales. The arts marketer will then want to track two metrics very carefully to determine the optimal timing of emails: (1) when the emails were sent, and (2) the number and timing of tickets sold for the event. The arts marketer can then test whether there is an optimal time to promote the event through email, and even whether email is an effective marketing strategy for the organization.

Best practices in the field

Especially for new organizations and programs with a limited track record, researching the marketing strategies of comparable organizations that are seeking to reach similar audiences (such as K-12 teachers or family audiences) can provide a reasonable starting point for developing the marketing approach. Evaluation systems can then assess which strategies are most effective at fulfilling organizational and programmatic objectives. See the following examples from real arts organizations (whose names have been changed) that have designed evaluation systems to measure the success of their marketing efforts.

> **Example 1: A multi-layered approach**
>
> The Mesa Performing Arts Center was interested in increasing attendance and ticket sales revenue at its performing arts series for school-age children. Audience research revealed that area teachers were most likely to be the decision-maker for school field trips, and that they preferred Mesa over other field trip options. One of the biggest barriers to participation by the schools was lack of information about the series. Teachers indicated that they were most receptive to print mailings and email notices about the programs, and that they liked to visit Mesa's website for more detailed information after receiving the initial mailing. Research showed that teachers were often not receiving their mailings, and Mesa's staff attributed this primarily to outdated contact information on their database. In addition, the website did not have the most current information, and email notices (when received) were not timed to key periods when teachers made decisions about field trips. As a result of these insights, Mesa's staff installed a multi-pronged effort to address deficiencies and track results. A staff person was assigned to update the mailing list every year, a new schedule for website updates was implemented, and the timing of emails was altered to coincide with key decision periods for field trips. To assess the effectiveness of these changes, they monitored several metrics, which were compared to baseline data gathered before changes were made:
>
> - the number of brochure returns from wrong addresses;
> - the number of instances teachers reported hearing about the program through each marketing channel (a phone log was kept to track word of mouth, brochure, website, email, etc.);
> - the number of people who clicked links on the emails promoting the program;
> - the number of people in attendance at the performances; and
> - the amount of revenues from ticket sales.
>
> Through these small changes, they saw a sharp increase in the number of tickets sold and income generated from these sales, meeting their original criteria for success. An additional benefit was that they noticed performances selling out much more quickly than in previous years!

> **Example 2: A focused approach**
>
> An opera company trying to build its audiences for a new Wednesday evening performance series launched a social media campaign in which discount coupons were offered to these events on selected social media sites. Using ticketing software, arts marketers were able to track the number of patrons who redeemed the coupons to determine which site was most effective at attracting patrons. They repeated this promotion four times over the course of the year, and saw a strong correlation between coupon redemptions and one particular social media site. This led them to develop a stronger presence in that site for the Wednesday evening series, and expand their marketing strategies on the site. This example shows us that evaluation can both measure the fulfillment of organizational objectives (in this case, to increase participation in the performance series), and help the arts marketer to more precisely target his or her efforts (in this case, to concentrate more effort on a particular social media channel).

As these examples illustrate, evaluation can benefit the arts marketer by helping to gauge success in reaching one's objectives and whether the investment of resources was commensurate with the result. Please see the Program Evaluation chapter for more information.

Conclusion

Far too often, the approach to arts marketing is focused on promotional tools and ignores the essential component of audience research. Quick, symptomatic fixes are often used while underlying strategic causes are ignored. Since nonprofits are increasingly required to be accountable for both the short and the long term, a well-thought-out marketing plan is an important step in that direction.

The Appendix for this chapter outlines an approach to developing a marketing plan that is equally relevant for an organization or for an individual program. In brief, a successful marketing plan will be developed with as much whole-organization participation as possible and will provide action items and responsibilities for different programs and functions. The plan will become a common road map for the fiscal year, serving to unite the shared vision of the organization as it moves toward a common goal.

Resources

American Marketing Association Definition of Marketing. Accessed 9/23/15 at https://www.ama.org/AboutAMA/Pages/Definition-of-Marketing.aspx.

Harlow, Bob. (2014) *The Road to Results: Effective Practices for Building Arts Audiences*. New York: Bob Harlow Research and Consulting, LLC and the Wallace Foundation.

McCarthy, K. F., & Jinnett, K. (2001). *A New Framework for Building Participation in the Arts*. Rand Corporation.

Mohammed, Rafi. (2005). *The Art of Pricing: How to Find the Hidden Profits to Grow Your Business.* New York, NY: Crown Publishing. Pages 60-78 cover value based pricing.

McCarthy, E. J. (1960). *Basic marketing: A managerial approach*. Homewood, Ill: R.D. Irwin.

Appendix

THE MARKETING PLAN

Use this outline of an organizational marketing plan to help you structure your own plan for your organization or for individual programs.

1. Executive Summary

2. Statement of general organizational mission and goals, and specific marketing objectives

3. Market Situation Analysis

    a. Market threats and opportunities

    b. Audience analysis

  c. Competitor analysis

  d. Positioning statement

 4. Marketing Strategy

  a. Product

  b. Price

  c. Place

  d. Promotion

  e. People

  f. Process

 5. Action Steps with Timeline

 6. Marketing Budget

 7. Monitoring and Contingency Planning

1. Executive Summary

Ideally one page, it captures the salient points of the analysis, summarizes the plan's objectives, and presents the action plans. It should be written *after* the marketing plan is completed.

2. Mission, Goals, and Marketing Objectives

The marketing plan furthers the organization's mission and long-range goals, as described in the strategic or long-range plan. If the marketing plan is embedded within the organization's strategic plan, the mission and goals will have been stated. If the marketing plan is a separate document, the mission and goals should be restated with emphasis on marketing objectives.

- **Mission.** In a very general way, the mission statement answers the questions What is our business? What should our business be? Why do we exist?
- **Goals.** Develop general marketing goals with related, specific objectives and tactics within a separate strategic marketing plan.
- **Objectives.** Objectives describe specific results, often in quantifiable terms with a timetable. For instance, if a goal is to attract more families, an objective may be to improve hands-on educational programs for children to involve more parents.

Example:

> To increase family patronage by 10 percent at year's end with an investment of $3,000 to support program upgrades and additional marketing communications to reach the target audience of families.

3. Market Situation Analysis

- **Internal and external forces.** Analyze external opportunities and threats and internal strengths and weaknesses as they relate to marketing. What internal strengths (skills, successful programs, good will) can you draw upon? What internal weaknesses (financial, personnel, facility, past mistakes) must you overcome? What potentially negative external threats (competition, economic stress, trends in philanthropy) must you accommodate? What positive external opportunities (partners, public opinion, growth, demographic changes) can you use to good advantage in marketing planning?
- **Audience analysis.** Summarize who are your markets, what are their defining characteristics (age, gender, ethnicity, etc.), and what are their interests and needs. Depending on strategic plan goals, you may need to analyze specific audience segments.
- **Competitive analysis.** Understand who are your direct (arts) and indirect (sports, Internet, films, etc.) competitors. It is critical to understand the alternative ways your audiences meet their needs.
- **Positioning statement.** Describe how your organization or program relates both to your target audience and to the competition. Do not name your competition in this statement, but distinguish how your program uniquely meets your audience's needs.

Consider developing your positioning statement as a longer narrative or list of key words and phrases that helps you articulate the various elements of product, competition, and customer needs. Then distill this into a compact and memorable statement that can be used as a tag line in marketing materials.

4. Marketing Strategy

A marketing strategy outlines how the *Product*, its *Price*, the *Place* it occurs, the means of *Promotion*, and the *People* it seeks to engage, and the *Process* of executing and evaluating the strategy will combine to connect products with intended audiences.

At this planning stage, evaluate the need for additional market research. You may find areas for which there is insufficient information to make decisions. For instance, in the example above, you may not know how many families live within 15 miles of the organization, how to reach them, and what these parents' top concerns are for their children. This is essential information when making product content, pricing, distribution, promotion, and investment decisions.

Review alternatives based on the assumptions that guide your plan. Determine the best option(s), then determine the marketing strategy. Some of your marketing strategy can be expressed as a narrative with bulleted highlights. The rest can be portrayed with a timeline and budget.

5. Action Steps with Timeline

A marketing plan indicates who must do what by when. Start by identifying necessary tasks.

Group related activities together, then create a process for each group and express it in a graphic timeline. A timeline ensures that you see all the tasks, plan adequate time to implement them and to meet deadlines, identify bottlenecks ahead of time, and facilitate cooperation within your organization. See the Program Development chapter ▌ for a graphic format that can be adapted for a marketing timeline.

6. Marketing Budget

The marketing budget reflects the costs associated with the different marketing strategies, such as product development, targeted marketing, or email campaigns.

Ordinarily it is integrated into and allocated a percentage of the organization's overall annual budget (10 to 20 percent is not unusual). For program or series-specific expenses, budget for each program or series and then present the budget on a program-by-program basis, broken down by category into projected expenses and expected revenues. This way, you can more easily track the financial costs and income associated with each program or series. Revenues and expenses that benefit all programs—such as corporate sponsorships, telephone and Internet access, or organizational brochures—should be presented as separate organization-wide expenses in the marketing budget. If your marketing plan includes new programs, first determine revenue and expense categories, and then estimate the amounts. At the minimum, determine the expense categories related to your marketing plan and estimate the cost for each.

Marketing Costs Categories
- Marketing-staff salaries and benefits
- Marketing-related printing
- Design
- Postage and mailing supplies
- Email service provider fees
- Domain name registration fees
- Advertising
- Purchased mailing lists
- Marketing photography
- Marketing share of general administration (may not be in separate marketing budget)

7. Monitoring and Contingency Planning

Periodically monitor the effects of marketing activities, particularly in the context of the strategic plan, to allow adjustments to be made to the marketing plan. Also develop a contingency plan that considers questions such as: What if no corporate sponsorship is available? What if we find that our planned product offering has little appeal to the targeted audience? What if, by mid-year, we have reason to believe that we will not be able to increase family patronage by 10 percent at the end of the year?

Cultural Access: Extend the Complete Invitation

GAY HANNA *with* LISA KAMMEL

Shifting demographics are affecting communities and institutions. These changes are reflected in the composition of our public and private organizations—schools, healthcare and social service agencies, businesses, cultural organizations, etc.—and underscore concerns for inclusion and equal access. According to Elaine Ostroff, founder of Adaptive Environments,[1] "our expectations have changed: we expect to have choices about what we do and where we go without regard to age or ability."

However, ancient taboos still exist regarding disabilities, perpetuating forms of discrimination. Some cultural organizations simply ignore access issues due to other priorities. The results can be thoughtless acts of exclusion in the planning, implementation, and evaluation of cultural facilities and programs.

There are many opportunities for growth by reaching out and opening up programs to older Americans and people with disabilities. For-profit businesses across the country recognize this and attend to the concerns and needs of these burgeoning populations through advertising and realistic, positive images of the targeted populations. Cultural organizations stand to gain a new and larger audience from those who want to become involved in making and appreciating the arts.

Accessibility is a work in progress because there are always new technologies and developments that advance inclusive programming. It is essential to review and evaluate—on a regular basis—policies and procedures, facilities and programs, print materials and websites, and to include an accessibility component in all board, staff, volunteer, and constituent training.

Cultural organizations that are not actively concerned with accessibility and inclusion for staff, board, volunteers, and constituents not only risk the loss of funds and invite lawsuits, but are missing the opportunity to grow and learn about 19% of this country's population or 56.7 million citizens with disabilities who represent potential patrons, artists, teachers, students, administrators, and audiences.

The Ordinariness of Difference in Ability

Some US Census statistics highlight this ordinariness: 30.6 million Americans report some difficulty with walking or climbing stairs.[2]

- One in five Americans (20 percent), 45 years of age or older, reports some form of vision impairment. Of these 8.1 million people, 2 million are reportedly considered blind.
- 7.6 million Americans have some level of hearing impairment

AGING IN AMERICA

- There are 76.4 million baby boomers in America (those born 1946 - 1964).

- The Arthritis Foundation estimates that 50 million Americans have arthritis.

- According to the Administration on Aging, Americans 65 years or older represent 14.1 percent of the US population and are expected to grow to represent 21.7 percent of the population by 2040.

Inclusion is a key issue to create cultural accessibility. All organizations need to extend a complete invitation to people regardless of their age, race, religion, and/or disability. Cultural organizations should do more than just invite people that have been excluded in the past to attend their programs. They must also work with their communities to remove the physical and attitudinal barriers that prevent a diverse population from participating in their organizations.

> 'Nothing about us, without us' was the theme that emerged from the 1970s disability rights movement and continues to be echoed today by individuals with disabilities and even by older adults. Inclusion is the essential word in making the arts fully accessible. Make sure that you involve these targeted populations not only in planning for inclusive programming, but as staff, board members, panelists, creators, volunteers, and as audiences.
>
> —Paula Terry, former director, AccessAbility Office, National Endowment for the Arts

This chapter discusses accessibility through an introduction to basic philosophy, terms, best practices and model programs, tools, and resources. In learning ways to adapt existing facilities and programs readers will bring the community into the organization and the organization into the community. This, in turn, can create exciting institutional changes.

Extending a full invitation to participate in your organization requires more common sense than funding. Attitude is of greater importance than the latest adaptive technology. Connections are made person to person with dignity and respect.

Cultural Access Is Social Justice

> The most important thing to remember when interacting with people with disabilities is exactly that—they're people.
>
> —Rose Marie McCaffrey, former program director, The Associated Blind, Inc

The basic premise of cultural access is one of social justice. It is an ongoing process that assumes diversity of users and that a broad spectrum of abilities is ordinary, not special. Sharon Sutton, Ph.D., professor of architecture, urban design, and planning, University of Washington, refers to a community as "the great public theatre where all can perform their part." In order to attain inclusion and the gradual democratization of society, cultural accessibility seeks to give a voice to disempowered persons in shaping their social and physical environments.

Though the disability rights movement grew up along side other identity-based movements in the 1960s and 70s, the particular discrimination disabled people have suffered—attitudinal, employment, and architectural barriers; educational and social segregation; institutionalization; even forced sterilization—kept many isolated from one another. This made the formation of the disability subculture difficult, if not impossible. Only after several decades of disability activism—which has brought about landmark civil rights legislation, independent living centers, and the formation of a distinct community—has the disabled American voice begun to reach a wider audience, both on and off stage. A growing number of playwrights and performance artists have given artistic expression to the experience and culture of disability from an insider's perspective.

—Carrie Sandahl[3]

DESIGNING THE GREAT PUBLIC THEATER: ACCESS FOR ALL AGES

Cultural access, the process of creating "the great public theatre," links physical and attitudinal changes with individual and community empowerment. All players want to participate in society and find their way independently. Based on professional literature and practical examples from Access for All Ages[4], the following points describe a philosophy of cultural access:

- **People are the measure of all things.** The user should not have to adapt to the environment and service: the environment or service should adapt to the user.
- **The average person does not exist.** The fact that everyone is different does not mean that separate accommodations should be made for each person in each group. People's varying and differing needs should be translated into provisions usable by everyone.
- **Realize the relation between age and accessibility.** To serve children and older adults, accommodations should be designed to support their differences in size, physical endurance, and perceptual changes. Issues regarding safety and independence should be addressed as well.
- **Design for all.** The maximum number of people must be physically and mentally able to have access to the services they want to use.
- **Start with services that are frequently used.** Achieving cultural access for all requires great effort with scarce resources. First, analyze the services most frequently used.
- **Connect form and content.** Accessibility means more than a good building: more important is the organization's welcome attitude at all levels and phases of service.
- **Communication is key to cultural access.** The realization of cultural accessibility is good communication with the user, both during the design phase of a certain service or accommodation and its use.
- **There is no end point, but a continuous process.** Because each situation is different, new questions are constantly raised. Cultural access as a stream of experiences with challenges and opportunities has no end point, but is a continuous process of attention and communications.

From public parks to the private rooms of hospice patients, cultural programs are providing new avenues for community service. Case studies and best practices are available in each arts discipline—music, dance, drama, visual arts, and literature—as well as a listing of artists and arts organizations which are considered leaders in the field of cultural access. For more information on cultural access, see the National Endowment for the Arts (NEA) Office for AccessAbility on their website, www.arts.gov.

Knowing the Language of Cultural Access: Terms and Types

Accessibility means different things to different people. Barriers to access can be based upon economic disadvantages, cultural or ethnic bias, ageism, and physical or mental disability. This section outlines the public mandate for access in the United States and provides a vocabulary to stimulate individual conversations and community partnerships to establish a space that is accessible to everyone.

ACCESSIBILITY

According to *Everyone's Welcome: The Americans with Disabilities Act and Museums*[5], accessibility means making the site's exhibits and programs available to all visitors. The goal is to eliminate physical, communication, and attitudinal barriers.

- **Physical** access means removing barriers to allow all people to move independently throughout a facility.
- **Communication** access means providing graphic information along with alternative formats such as assistive listening devices and visual aids, such as a raised line map of the space, to help all people receive and communicate information effectively.
- **Attitudinal** access means being sensitive to human diversity, so that all people feel respected and included.

Providing access not only helps people with disabilities but also make life easier and more convenient for everyone involved. It also is not just a choice; it is a law. The Americans with Disabilities Act (ADA) was passed in 1990 as a comprehensive civil rights act enforced by the U.S. Department of Justice.

AMERICANS WITH DISABILITIES ACT

The ADA is a federal civil rights law created to ensure equal access for people with disabilities to employment, government programs and services, and privately owned places with public accommodations, transportation, and communications. It is modeled after earlier civil rights laws that protect individuals from discrimination based on race, color, sex, national origin, age, and religion. Unlike other civil rights legislation, non-discrimination laws for people with disabilities have specific design and technical provisions and requirements in order to provide equal opportunities for participation.

> Accessibility begins as a mandate to serve people who have been discriminated against for centuries; it prevails as a tool that serves diverse audiences for a lifetime.
>
> —Janice Majewski, former accessibility program coordinator, Smithsonian Institution

According to the ADA, an individual is considered to have a disability if he or she:

- has a physical or mental impairment that substantially limits one or more major life activities (such as people with paralysis, hearing or visual impairments, seizure disorders, HIV infections or AIDS, mental retardation, or specific learning disabilities);
- has a record of such an impairment (such as cancer survivors or people who have recovered from a mental illness); or
- is regarded as having such an impairment (such as people who have severe facial or other disfigurements that are substantially limiting only because of the attitudes of others).

The ADA also covers a person on the basis of a known association or relationship with a person with a disability, such as a family member, friend, or acquaintance.

The ADA has five sections that address a specific category of coverage:

- **Title I.** Employment
- **Title II.** Programs, services, and activities of state and local governments, including public transportation
- **Title III.** For-profit and nonprofit organizations that operate places of public accommodation or commercial facilities, or which offer certain types of examinations and courses
- **Title IV.** Telecommunications access
- **Title V.** Miscellaneous provisions which are applicable to all other titles.

The ADA and other laws like it must have a system of implementing regulations that establish enforceable requirements. For example, the ADA requires the Department of Justice to establish regulations for Titles II and III, including cultural organizations such as museums and performing arts centers. The Department of Transportation also issues implementing regulations for Titles II and III. Title I has implementing regulations issued by the Equal Employment Opportunity Commission. Most cultural organizations, whether public or private, must adhere to the employment provisions of Title I.

Further, temporary events, rented facilities, and contracted program services must be accessible and in compliance with the ADA.

TECHNICAL LOCAL AND STATE ACCESSIBILITY ASSISTANCE REQUIREMENTS

Many state and local governments have more stringent accessibility requirements than the ADA. For further assistance on local accessibility requirements, contact your state and local governments or refer to the Disability and Business Technical Assistance Center (DBTAC) or www.disability.gov online. Information below is excerpted from *Everyone's Welcome: The Americans with Disabilities Act and Museums.*

Which Title Should I Follow, Title II or Title III?

If your cultural organization is owned and operated by a state or local government, you must follow Title II. If your cultural organization is privately owned and operated or a nonprofit, you must follow Title III. If you are privately owned but receive funds from a state or local government, then you will follow Title III. However, the government funding source may, as a means of meeting its Title II obligations, require you to comply with certain Title II provisions.

Title II. Local and State Government Cultural Organizations

Cultural organizations...

- must ensure that individuals with disabilities are not excluded from services, programs, and activities because buildings are inaccessible or because of policies or practices, unless to do so would result in a fundamental alteration;
- are not required to take any action that would result in a fundamental alteration in the nature of the service, program, or activity, or in undue financial and administrative burdens;
- must ensure equally effective communication with individuals with disabilities; and
- must maintain accessible features of facilities and equipment.

Existing Facilities

- State and local government cultural organizations must conduct a self-evaluation of all programs and activities to identify any physical or policy barriers that may limit or exclude participation by people with disabilities.
- Cultural organizations must choose to modify the facility, relocate the program or activity, or provide the activity, service, or benefit in another manner that meets other ADA requirements.
- If modifications are done, physical changes must comply with the ADA Standards for Accessible Design (ADA Standards) or the Uniform Accessibility Standards (UFAS).

Alterations. Any alteration that affects the usability of the facility must comply with the requirements of the ADA Standards (without the elevator exemption) or the UFAS to the greatest extent feasible.

New Construction. New construction must comply with relevant requirements of the ADA Standards (without the elevator exemption) or the UFAS.

Administrative Requirements. In addition to self-evaluation, entities with 50 or more employees must:
- develop a grievance procedure;
- designate an individual to oversee ADA compliance;
- develop a transition plan that catalogs the physical changes that will be made to achieve program accessibility; and
- retain the self-evaluation for three years.

Title III. For-profit and Nonprofit Cultural Organizations

Cultural organizations...
- must provide goods and services in an integrated setting, unless separate or different measures are necessary to ensure equal opportunity;
- must eliminate unnecessary eligibility standards or rules that deny individuals with disabilities an equal opportunity to enjoy the goods and services provided;
- must make reasonable modifications in policies, practices, and procedures that deny equal access to individuals with disabilities, unless a fundamental alteration would result; and
- must maintain accessible features of facilities and equipment.

Existing Facilities Open to the Public

- Cultural organizations must remove architectural and structural communication barriers in existing facilities where it is readily achievable to do so.
- Cultural organizations must provide readily achievable alternative measures when removal of barriers is not readily achievable.

Alterations. Any alteration that affects the usability of the facility must comply with the requirements of the ADA Standards to the greatest extent feasible.

New Construction. Cultural organizations must design and construct new facilities to comply with the ADA Standards.

What Are the Meanings of Readily Achievable and Undue Burden?

Readily achievable indicates whether an action is easily accomplished and able to be carried out without much difficulty or expense. An undue burden is a significant difficulty or expense. Cultural organizations should consider the following factors when considering whether an action, such as barrier removal, is readily achievable or poses an undue burden:

1. nature and cost of removal;
2. the cultural organization's overall financial resources, number of employees, effect the action will have on expenses and resources, legitimate safety requirements necessary for safe operation (including crime prevention measures and necessary steps for protecting the integrity of art work), artifacts and historical structures on display, or any other impact on the organization's operation;
3. the geographic separateness and administrative or fiscal relationship of the cultural organization to any other associated cultural organizations or parent entities;
4. if applicable, the overall financial resources and size with respect to the number of employees of any associated cultural organizations or parent entities, as well the number, type, and location of their facilities; and
5. if applicable, the type of operation or operations of any associated cultural organizations or parent entities, including the composition, structure, and functions of their work forces.

Making All Guests Feel Welcome

The following steps, used to make visitors with disabilities feel welcome and comfortable, may be included as part of an organization's plan for providing effective communication:

- provide orientation brochures and guide maps (including raised line maps) which identify accessible features with disability symbols of accessibility;
- provide orientation and information brochures in large type so that all users can use the same brochure;
- provide an advertised incoming TTY (text telephone) line so visitors with hearing or speech impairments may contact the organization or a video phone (VP) where Deaf consumers can sign to Deaf staff;
- offer sign language interpreted tours for visitors with hearing disabilities; and
- provide captioned and audio-described orientation videos.

—*Everyone's Welcome: The Americans with Disabilities Act and Museums*

A greater level of effort is required to meet the undue burden standard than the readily *achievable* standard for removing barriers in existing Title III cultural organizations.

Meeting Ongoing Obligations of the ADA

Monitoring ADA obligations is an ongoing process. Title II cultural organizations must continually provide accessible programs and communications. Title III cultural organizations must, when readily achievable, remove barriers. Alterations, reconstructions, additions, or new construction for all cultural organizations must meet ADA requirements.

Cultural organizations should also understand how their local, state, and federal laws affect each other. All cultural organizations must comply with the ADA Standards; however, additional steps may need to be taken to comply with state or local laws.

ADA Resources

Information about specific ADA requirements for Title II or Title III cultural organizations is available online at www.usdoj.gov, www.ada.gov/regs2010/titleII_2010/titleII_2010_regulations.htm, www.ada.gov/t3hilght.htm, or through the ADA Information Line at 800-514-0301 (voice) or 800-514-0383 (TTY).

> The disability community is coming of age with the advent of technology, changing social/political attitudes and a growing understanding of abilities over disabilities. Like in the case of other minority groups, arts are an area that can give this previously stifled community a stage on which to present its issues, aspirations and triumphs.
>
> —Douglas Towne, founder and CEO, Disability Relations Group

Notify visitors regarding access services. Every event, activity, and program should be accessible to people with disabilities. If the event is publicized, cultural organizations should provide people with disabilities the opportunity to request accommodations. To find out if accommodations are needed, list the following statement on all notices about the program, e.g., website, newspaper ads, and flyers.

> For individuals with disabilities requiring access accommodations, please contact [insert name of contact] within a minimum of [insert number] hours prior to the program so that proper consideration may be given to the request.

The recommended notice is a minimum of 72 hours. In most cases this provides the required time to make the necessary arrangements. A more advance notice can be requested.

Building Inclusive Communities

This section describes universal design, a planning strategy that goes beyond minimum access standards. Universal design and targeted program development serve as the building blocks for an inclusive community.

Cultural organizations that go beyond the minimum standards to design programs and places for all ages and populations create bridges from access to unlimited opportunities. *People First* language is an excellent first step in building inclusive arts environments. It costs nothing yet changes attitudes while opening the door to broadening opportunities for everyone.

THE PRINCIPLES OF UNIVERSAL DESIGN

Universal design is the design of products and environments to be usable by all people, with disabilities and without, to the greatest extent possible, without adaptation or specialized design. According to Adaptive Environments, the seven principles listed below may be applied to evaluate existing designs, guide the design process, and educate both designers and consumers about the characteristics of more usable products and environments.

- **Equitable use.** The design is usable and marketable to people with diverse abilities. For example, provide stair and smooth surface options for people.
- **Flexibility in use.** The design accommodates a wide range of individual preferences and abilities. For example, provide different forms of vertical access such as stairs and an elevator.
- **Simple and intuitive use.** Use of the design is easy to understand, regardless of the user's experience, knowledge, language skills, or current concentration level. For example, use clear parking zone signage that includes way-finding arrows.
- **Perceptible information.** The design communicates necessary information effectively to the user, regardless of ambient conditions or the user's sensory abilities. For example, provide maps for orientation in different sensory forms such as tactile and visual models.
- **Tolerance for error.** The design minimizes hazards and the adverse consequences of accidental or unintended actions. For example, provide lighted shapes that begin at the front door and continue to the reception desk so the path of entry is clear to all.

People First Terminology

Place the person before the disability. For example, say "person with a disability" rather than "disabled person."

Avoid referring to people by their disability, for example, "an epileptic," "blind people," or "a deaf person." A person is not a condition. Instead, refer to people with disabilities as "a person with epilepsy," "people who are blind," or "a person with a hearing loss."

People are not "bound" or "confined" to wheelchairs. They use them to increase their mobility and enhance their freedom. It is more accurate to refer to a person in a wheelchair as a "wheelchair user" or "a person who uses a wheelchair."

—*Adaptive Environments*

- **Low physical effort.** The design can be used efficiently and comfortably and with a minimum of fatigue. For example, provide a door that requires a low physical effort to open, such as a sliding door with an automatic eye.
- **Size and space for approach and use.** Appropriate size and space is provided for approach, reach, manipulation, and use regardless of user's body size, posture, or mobility. For example, provide water fountains that are the appropriate size and space for the approach and use by all.

TIPS FOR PROGRAM DEVELOPMENT FOR FIVE TARGET POPULATIONS

Requests for on- and off-site arts programs and services provide opportunities for new partnerships that serve target populations with unique individual needs. Universal design can be partnered with adaptive or assistive technology to meet unique individual needs and be the foundation upon which broad-based community cultural access is built.

An organization's first priority should be basic facility and program accessibility. However, it is important to explore potential relationships with community partners to develop outreach programs that meet specific individual and group needs. There are basic protocols and best practices to follow for outreach programs to serve target populations with a high level of staff and environmental support.

Below are descriptions of program considerations for five major target areas of arts outreach: arts education that includes students with disabilities; health care; juvenile justice and corrections; lifelong learning in the arts and aging, which includes intergenerational activities; and art centers for adults with disabilities.

Arts Education for Students with Disabilities

The inclusion of students with disabilities in school and community arts education programs is a reality that often catches educators unprepared. The prospect of adjusting teaching styles, instructional strategies, and classroom management is a daunting task. The dynamics of arts education welcome such innovations. In *Strategies for Inclusive Classroom Environments*[6], VSA arts emphasizes the compatibility between the arts and a diverse student population.

> The arts appeal to diverse learning styles, creating greater opportunities for students and teachers to connect in productive ways.
>
> The arts make learning more interesting by correlating learning experiences to life experiences.
>
> The arts provide a forum for creating innovative teaching strategies.
>
> Multicultural aspects of the arts foster appreciation and acceptance of diversity.

The arts educator should keep the following list of tips and strategies in mind while creating an inclusive classroom environment.

- Capitalize on students' individual interests and suggestions for both content and strategy.
- Utilize content to reach or interdisciplinary lesson plans to stimulate interest and dialogue.

- Tap the network (exceptional student or special educator specialists, parents, and other support staff) for moral, instructional, and financial support.
- Discuss appropriate roles for teaching assistants or student aides beforehand in order to prevent potentially uncomfortable or goal-defeating situations.
- Understand the Individual Educational Plan (IEP) process and incorporate arts education as a means to accomplish important goals.
- Modify the classroom environment to promote inclusive principles.
- Welcome ongoing evaluations, modification, and reinforcement.

All arts education programs, including artist residencies and performances, must provide accommodations for students with disabilities. Including all students in arts education is not only the right thing to do, but is also a powerful way to effect positive change in the academic and social life of students with disabilities.

For further information regarding best practices, model programs, and technical assistance for developing inclusive arts programs explore the resources available through Very Special Arts, www.vsarts.org.

> I'm not someone who just sits in a wheelchair all day. Singing has changed the way people perceive me.
>
> —Jenna Feci, VSA youth performer

Arts in Health Care

> Throughout the ages the arts have been used to uplift the human spirit, provide expression for feelings, and create a sense of community. Increasingly, these strengths of the arts are becoming ever more valued for their contributions to the health and welfare of our communities and to individuals. As a consequence, the arts are flourishing in hospitals, hospice, clinics, and nursing homes for their ability to reduce stress, enhance the healing environment, improve doctor-patient relations, communicate information, and provide patients with dignity, self expression, and release from pain.
>
> —Naj Wikoff, former director, Healing and the Arts, C. Everett Koop Institute, and president, Society of the Arts in Healthcare

John Graham-Pole, MD., founder of Arts and Medicine at Shands Hospital at the University of Florida in Gainesville, acknowledges the coming of a second renaissance—one that celebrates the marriage of art and science in medicine. No longer confined to the orchestra pit and the gallery wall, the arts are infiltrating the hallowed halls of hospitals nationwide. Modern scientific evidence supports this direction. The list below provides examples of controlled studies on the effect of art in health care in diverse settings.

- Aesthetic environments shorten postoperative recovery and hospital stay.
- Artmaking reduces anxiety in patients with cancer and blood diseases.
- Artmaking raises circulating endorphin and natural killer cell levels.
- Cooperative play-acting and theater games raise pain thresholds and mood.
- Creative writing lessens the physical symptoms of asthma and arthritis.
- Creative writing reduces anxiety, depression, and doctor visits.
- Dancing improves circulation, coordination, and alertness in elders.
- Music enhances sleep patterns, alertness, and growth of newborns.
- Music lowers state and trait anxiety in patients after myocardial infarctions.
- Music raises pain thresholds and reduces postoperative pain medications.
- Sharing stories regularly lengthens lifespan of advanced cancer patients.
- Sustained laughter lowers blood pressure and stress hormone levels.

> Arts programs for healthcare environments are no longer optional amenities; they are an important characteristic that distinguishes facilities in their communities and attracts patients, staff, and donors.
>
> —Annette Ridenour, president, Aesthetics, Inc.

World-class art collections and performances inhabit the public spaces of major health care centers from Seattle, Washington and Iowa City, Iowa to Gainesville, Florida. Artist residencies bring the arts to bedsides while impromptu dance and play-back theater groups can engage patients, families, and their caregivers outside of hospital rooms. The opportunities for community cultural organizations to enrich the lives of their constituents in hospitals, hospices, and long-term care facilities are expansive.

Arts for Juvenile Offenders in Retention and Corrections

States pass bond issues to build more prisons and begin to imprison youths as adults at younger and younger ages. The cost of lost youth and the societal burden of fully maintaining incarcerated youth are staggering. Grady Hillman, an award winning poet and technical assistance director for the arts partnership program sponsored by the NEA and the U.S. Department of Justice's Office of Juvenile Justice and Delinquency Prevention, writes that evidence from adult and juvenile correctional arts programs have clearly determined that reduced recidivism rates occur among participants. Some states like California, with its Brewster Report, have quantified institutional benefits into cost savings for taxpayers.

Correctional arts programs take place in three unique settings, according to Hillman: school alternative learning centers, community probation programs, and detention facilities (county jails, prisons, or juvenile detention). Each has its own set of specific considerations for artists and arts administrations similar to other partnership programs. It is important to note that 50 percent to 75 percent of the youth involved in juvenile crime have an identified disability, such as a learning disability, severe emotional disturbance, or a form of mental retardation compounded by cycles of poverty, neglect, and abuse.

Many at-risk youth need accommodations of special education with supporting therapy. The arts offer youth involved in juvenile offenses a positive alternative to finding self-expression, increased self-esteem, and windows of opportunity to achieve academic success. Artists become important role models as well. Hillman offers the following advice regarding artists working in juvenile and corrections environments.

> Artists need to be prepared for restrictions on art supplies and space.
>
> Artists should not try to "rescue" students.
>
> Artists should ensure that students' artwork is protected between sessions.
>
> Artists should never make promises they cannot keep.

Experience is critical to longevity and to gaining acceptance within the correctional system. Accountability is key, as well as clear and ongoing communications within the arts and juvenile justice partnerships. According to the Office of Juvenile Justice and Delinquency Prevention and the NEA, the results of arts programs in the lives of youth involved in juvenile crime are shown in reduced disciplinary infractions in alternative education and correctional facilities, improved attendance in alternative education settings, and reduced recidivism upon release from correctional facilities. The arts offer at-risk youth ways to re-enter community life and contribute successfully to it.

For further information, contact the U.S. Department of Justice, Office of Justice Programs, www.ojp.usdoj.gov.

> The arts programs helped to set our girls free from the constraints placed on them by the lives they have led, the crimes they committed and the consequences they are now dealing with. They learned to think and express themselves by setting words and dance to the music within themselves.
>
> —Jacque Coyne, executive director, Florida Institute for Girls

Arts and Older Americans

Betty Friedan suggested that age allows us to pioneer and explore new horizons for society and our communities. In regard to the current "age wave," creativity is becoming an emerging metaphor with new possibilities for aging with integrity. It is an unprecedented time for America with:

- More than 70 million baby boomers aging;
- Americans living longer, with life-expectancies rising from 45 to 75 years of age; and
- A declining birthrate juxtaposed against an aging culture.

To Andrea Sherman, Ph.D., an intergenerational specialist at the Mill Street Loft, this population revolution presents an extraordinary opportunity and challenge for arts organizations, artists, and aging communities. In the *Americans for the Arts Monograph,* "The Arts and Older Americans," Sherman identifies specific ways in which the arts can be involved in this age shift.[7]

1. The arts can be used as a vehicle to help us understand and define aging, through conversations created through writing workshops, forums, theatre, and dance.
2. The arts offer the opportunity for self-expression amidst loss, for achievement, and in reengagement amidst voids and uncertainty. Many older adults face frequent loss in their lives—jobs, spouses, health, friends, or income.
3. The arts can provide ample opportunities for lifelong learning and service to others.
4. Arts organizations can expect older adults to participate and need arts programming.
5. The arts can benefit from people's contributions and resources. Older adults can be creators, mentors, teachers, tutors, and advisors, sharing the wisdom they have gained through a lifetime of experience.

Arts programs unite generations to develop mutual understanding—young and old celebrating culture and rebuilding communities together. Opportunities to enter this new paradigm of program service and resource development have the potential to reinvigorate cultural activities community wide. However, cultural organizations must remember to address the "age wave" as it relates to the ADA accommodations in order to provide accessible and inclusive programs and services. For further information regarding best practices and model programs for services for older Americans, explore The National Center for Creative Aging, www.creativeaging.org.

> We are on the threshold of a powerful and challenging time—an 'age wave'—where new paradigms for creative aging continue to be developed.
>
> —Susan Perlstein, Founder Emeritus, The National Center for Creative Aging

Arts Centers and Community Day Programs for Adults with Disabilities

Many arts centers offer programs developed primarily to meet the needs of adults with disabilities through creative expression in the arts. These centers, now established nationwide, also provide pre-vocational and vocational training in the arts and arts-related fields, thanks to the leadership of Florence Ludins-Katz, MA, and Dr. Elias Katz, Ph.D. at the National Institute of Art and Disabilities. In the 1980s, due to the large-scale transfer of people with profound mental and physical disabilities out of large dismal state institutions to community residential facilities, the number of day programs for adults greatly increased. According to Ludins-Katz and Katz in *Art and Disabilities: Establishing the Creative Art Center for People with Disabilities*[8]:

In contrast to earlier beliefs, there is widespread agreement that disabled people not only belong in the community but should be active members of the community.

The Process for Cultural Accessibility

Strategies to create cultural access should begin with making the difficult easier. For example, ask the questions: What change can be made to enhance communications for all users? and Who should be involved? The Global Universal Design Educator's Network then recommends drafting strategies to make it happen.

The American Association of Museums, in *Everyone's Welcome: The Americans with Disabilities Act and Museums*[9], presents a process that cultural organizations, particularly museums, can use to plan, implement, evaluate, and advertise accessibility at their sites. The short-term goal is compliance with the ADA minimum requirements. The universal design long-term goal is to achieve totally accessible programs and facilities at every level.

COMPREHENSIVE ACCESSIBILITY PLAN

The American Association of Museums suggests nine building blocks to achieve accessibility. Some of the steps provided below are required by the ADA, while others provide guidance in improving accessibility of programs, goods, services, and facilities. Section 504/ADA coordinators are designated within each state arts agency to monitor and assist cultural organizations with accessibility compliance and planning.[10]

> The Ohio Arts Council has a long standing commitment to ensure that everyone has access to the arts including involving people with disabilities on our grant panels. In 2015 we celebrated our 50th anniversary and the 25th anniversary of the Americans with Disabilities Act (ADA). These milestones remind us of where we've been and the work we have yet to do.
>
> —Kim Turner, Accessibility Coordinator, Ohio Arts Council

Nine Building Blocks to Accessibility

Include a statement of commitment. A commitment to accessibility should be included in the institution's general policy or mission statement. The statement should affirm that the institution welcomes people with disabilities and strives to provide access for all to the institution's programs, goods, services, and facilities. This is similar to the ADA Title II requirement for providing notice to the public. Embracing the concept of accessibility is essential and should have full support of the director, board, and all staff.

Designate an accessibility coordinator. The overall responsibility of the accessibility coordinator is to oversee the implementation of the institution's accessibility plan. This plan should be institution-wide from facilities, programs, and public relations to financial, volunteer, and staff development. The accessibility coordinator could be a single individual or a group of employees. Facilitating access within the institution could be the individual's sole responsibility or, in smaller organizations, it could be one of several duties the individual carries out. Training should be provided to individuals who do not have knowledge and experience with disability and accessibility issues. Local centers for independent living are excellent resources for training and ongoing technical assistance support. If a group of employees serves as the accessibility coordinator, then each employee should serve as a resident expert for a particular accessibility goal, and one person should be responsible for the overall coordination.

Obtain input from people with disabilities. An effective way to achieve this is to organize an accessibility advisory council, which typically consists of staff members, at least one board member, people with disabilities, and those who represent people with disabilities. Individuals should be chosen to participate because of their experience, knowledge, or interest in issues affecting how people with disabilities use cultural institutions, and they should reflect varied points of view on disabilities other than their own. The institution should have clear procedures for reviewing and implementing recommendations of the council.

Train staff on accessibility. All personnel—staff, volunteers, board members, and outside consultants—should become familiar with accessibility issues, including the ADA and relevant state laws. In order to achieve this, institutions should train staff on a regular basis. Training should include an initial orientation to educate existing staff about disability issues, and assistance with the evaluation process and ongoing support. Accessibility training should include, but not be limited to meeting and hearing from individuals with disabilities as a first step in providing specific and accurate information on the needs of people with disabilities; the institution's legal responsibility concerning non-discrimination of people with disabilities and compliance with accessibility laws; and development of staff expertise on various-accessibility related solutions. Local training can be conducted by your local Center for Independent Living Center. Nationally, the Very Special Arts of Massachusetts' Cultural Access Institute provides annual national training.

Review facilities and programs. Cultural institutions should examine all of their activities, programs, communications, services, policies, and facilities to identify existing barriers and discriminatory policies or practices. This is considered self-evaluation and is required by the ADA Title II. An accessibility study should review: language of the institution's policies and practices; accessibility of programs, activities, events, website, and publications from a communications standpoint; accessibility of buildings where programs, activities, and events take place or where goods or services are provided; and adequacy of staff training for visitor and volunteer access. The review process should incorporate discussions by staff, volunteers, board members, the accessibility advisory council, and specialists or consultants.

Implement short and long term accessibility efforts. After an institution has conducted an accessibility self-evaluation, it should begin planning for needed accessibility modifications in areas including programming, barrier removal, effective communications, and new construction or alterations. Short-term modifications should be determined and handled immediately. Long-term modifications should be identified, and a transition plan should be developed to help institutions implement the transformation to accessible programs and facilities in a realistic and cost-effective way.

Promote and advertise accessibility. All promotional ads, institutional literature, postings, and announcements should be accompanied by accessibility symbols where appropriate. Accessibility symbols include the following types of access: wheelchair accessibility, sign language interpreted programs and text telephone (TTY) availability or VP phones (video phones). Institutions should also use other means of standard communications such as targeting specific media and contacting disability related organizations, services and social groups. Visit the Graphic Artists Guild Foundation web site for downloadable accessibility symbols at www.gag.org.

> **Process Checkpoint List**
>
> Use the following list of checkpoints to help you achieve universal accessibility.
>
> ☐ Form an advisory committee on accessibility.
>
> ☐ Make an institutional commitment to universal accessibility.
>
> ☐ Do an accessibility survey.
>
> ☐ Develop a long-range plan with input from board, staff, and the advisory committee.
>
> ☐ Develop a fundraising plan with input from board, staff, and the advisory committee.
>
> ☐ Develop a marketing plan that includes outreach to new audiences.
>
> ☐ Make sure your goals are clear to everyone and that staff and volunteers are aware of how they are expected to participate in achieving them.
>
> ☐ Employ architects and other professionals to work with your staff, board, and advisory committee to achieve facility accessibility.
>
> ☐ Review programming choices.
>
> ☐ Review the way-finding plan.
>
> ☐ Review marketing and advertising promotions.
>
> ☐ Reevaluate on a regular basis.
>
> —*Beyond Access to Opportunity: A Guide to Planning a Universal Environment for the Arts*

Establish a grievance process. The ADA Title II law requires that entities with 50 or more employees have a grievance procedure. As the ADA does not establish a specific process, many institutions use the same procedures as with other civil rights complaints. Under the ADA, visitors and volunteers have the legal right to file complaints and lawsuits against cultural institutions that do not provide accessible programs and facilities. Institutions may be able to resolve potential disputes before formal complaints are filed by providing a grievance policy. By working with a complainant to identify and correct access problems, experience has shown that institutions can resolve most informal and verbal complaints.

Conduct an ongoing review of accessibility efforts. The ADA requires cultural institutions to continually evaluate remaining barriers to determine whether or not their removal has become readily achievable. Institutions should develop long-term policies and systems to incorporate accessibility into all new projects, programs, and activities. Because accessibility is a work-in-progress, institutions should also periodically reevaluate themselves to make sure they are meeting the needs of staff and visitors in the most cost-effective ways possible.

DISABILITY ISSUES

Organizations should consider people with disabilities as persons with *varying* abilities as this is how many people with disabilities see themselves within communities. Nine Building Blocks to Accessibility[11] addresses the issues of sensitivity training and developing an ongoing community advisory group to guide the creation of a universal environment for the arts. In the following section, Douglas Towne, from the Disability Relations Group, describes three key issues that determine the level of participation from people with disabilities—economy, transportation, and cultural identity.

> **What is a Universal Environment for the Arts?**
>
> A universal or inclusive environment for the arts is one that is usable by everyone, people with and without disabilities and people of all ages. It is an environment with a physical plant (buildings and grounds) and communication systems that go beyond minimum access standards to serve the broadest public. It is an environment where the choice of programs and exhibits reflects a commitment to being part of an inclusive community.
>
> In response to the passage of federal legislation requiring public institutions to make it possible for people with disabilities to use their programs and services, we saw the development of what are now commonplace architectural design features, curb cuts and ramps being the most familiar. Interestingly, the design elements originally developed for people with disabilities were adopted by people without disabilities. For instance, ramps are used by people pushing strollers, people making deliveries, and many others without disabilities.
>
> The way people choose to use so-called accessibility adaptations makes an important point: places and products can be designed that work better for everyone. We shouldn't be asking ourselves how to construct a ramp for one group of people and a staircase for another. We should ask ourselves how to create an entrance that everyone can use. The same is true of non-space issues. A tactile model can enhance everyone's enjoyment of a work of art. A readable print presentation is just that: more easily readable for all.
>
> Using the model of universal planning moves the discussion beyond separate accommodations for people with and without disabilities to a discussion of how to create an environment that works for and is respectful of the independence and culture of everyone. Universal planning makes choices that recognize that we are all different, that we have different ways of doing things, and that we have different preferences about how we access information and how we communicate. Universal planning makes choices that create flexibility so that, as the designer Satoshi Kose suggests, "we modify the environment, instead of modifying people to adapt to the environment."
>
> —*A Universal Environment: Beyond Access to Opportunity,* New York State Council on the Arts

Economy. Although there are increasing numbers of highly successful professionals with disabilities in every area of employment, among the disabled population in America, there is a 59 percent average unemployment rate. Many survive on the limited Social Security income or Supplemental Security income payments they receive from the government. In 2015, this average monthly Social Security benefit ranges from between $1000-$1200 per month. Cultural organizations should consider these factors when involving people with varying abilities as volunteers or participants. The cost of cab fare alone could keep them from participating in your organization. A ticket price of $20 could quite literally be two percent of their monthly income.

Transportation. Transportation is one of the most difficult barriers that block people with varying abilities from full community inclusion. You will find that transportation systems vary depending on your community. If you have a local transportation authority that provides mass transit, under the ADA they are required to provide access to their system for people with disabilities. This includes paratransit services for those who cannot use the fixed route system. Check with your state and local government to determine what other resources may be available. It may be necessary to partner with other community nonprofits that have the ability to offer accessible transportation. It is important to remember that accessible transit is costly. A partnership with your local Center for Independent Living is recommended so that you avoid any misstep and get the necessary support from the disability community. It also can tell you the state of accessible transportation in your community, so that you can include people with varying abilities from the onset of your program.

Cultural identity. When identifying different disability cultures, the Deaf and blind communities often times may be best accessed through other local organizations such as the Deaf Service Bureaus or the local chapters of the American Council of the Blind and the National Federation of the Blind. These groups, in some cases, consider themselves separate cultures but still can be contacted through your local Center for Independent Living. Should you have any difficulty in accessing assistance locally, you can also connect with the Disability Relations Group, www.drgglobal.com.

Tools for Creating a Universal Environment for the Arts

UNIVERSAL ENVIRONMENT=USABILITY=OPPORTUNITY

Recently, studies have shown that architectural and other accessible adaptations that have been developed to serve people with disabilities are being used by people without disabilities as much if not more than people with disabilities. *Everyone's Welcome: The Americans with Disabilities Act and Museums* presents the following example for a universally designed museum exhibit:

> Suppose [a museum exhibit] was designed for use by a visitor in a wheelchair, labeled with large-print text, offered with tactile alternatives, and included an audio-description tour. This case now offers greater access and convenience to families with babies in strollers, visitors at the back of a large group, and small children not yet able to read.[12]

It is evident that people with disabilities, as well as the general public, are being served better by organizations that offer an environment that is usable by all. It is in an organization's best interest not only to address the ADA standards, but to reach out to all audiences with an environment that can be utilized by everyone. There are many important factors to consider when creating such an environment.

Developing an Accessible Facility: Enhancing Mobility, Vision, and Hearing

Staff, volunteers, and visitors should first and foremost be able to safely and successfully find, enter, and move through a public facility and its designated visitor areas.

Provide a safe and independent route of travel for the site and its buildings that is accessible by all people, especially those who use wheelchairs, walking aids, walk with difficulty, or have a visual impairment. Everyone, including people with disabilities, must be able to move about the site with safety and ease.

- A single, continuous, accessible pedestrian path should be provided that is at least 36 inches wide, firm, stable, and slip resistant without low or overhanging hazards or obstructions, and not require the use of stairs.
- All circulation paths provided must be free of protruding objects.
- The accessible route should provide a direct path from parking, bus stops, drop-off areas, and sidewalks into a primary building entrance that links or joins all designated visitor areas, such as exhibits, program spaces, gift shops, drinking fountains, and restrooms.

Provide an accessible route to the entrance of the facility.
- The route provided should be free of steps or have a ramp, elevator, or a gently sloped walkway to change levels.

- Another entrance can be provided or converted into an accessible entrance if the existing main entrance is inaccessible, difficult to modify, or modification would destroy historic significance.
- Signage should be installed at the accessible entrance if multiple entrances are available.
- If all entrances are not wheelchair accessible, signage should be installed at the inaccessible entrances directing people to the accessible entrance(s).

Provide an accessible ticket booth or information front desk, center, or area.
- The ticket booth or main information desk, center, or area should be on the accessible route that connects the parking and the accessible entrance.
- If there is an information desk or ticket booth, there should be sufficient space that allows a person using a wheelchair to approach and maneuver into a position to receive information or pay for a ticket.
- To be wheelchair accessible, a section of the desk or counter must be no higher than 34 inches.
- The information desk should provide a brochure that explains the facility's overall layout. The ADA requires directional information found in brochures to be available in alternative formats such as tactile or audible.
- A raised line-map or tactile model of the floor plan, with raised lines and Braille labeling, is helpful to all visitors.

Provide an accessible circulation route throughout the facility.
- The circulation route should be well lighted, clearly defined, and have a simple geometric layout that is easy to follow.
- The accessible route should be smooth, level, slip-resistant, and not have stairs or steps.
- Avoid highly glazed ceramic tile because its surface is slippery and makes it difficult for a person in a wheelchair to get sufficient traction.
- Sufficient room should be provided so a person in a wheelchair can maneuver throughout the space.

Eliminate protruding objects.
- Protruding objects must not infringe on any interior or exterior pathway.
- Building elements such as fire extinguishers, signs, drinking fountains, or plants may not protrude from walls or hang down from the ceiling in any way that a person with a visual impairment could run into the element and be injured.

Provide adequate signage, lighting, and other way-finding cues.
- Signage should be located in standard, logical, and predictable places that are perpendicular to the visitor pathway.
- Signage required to be accessible by the ADA Standards is divided into two categories: signage that identifies permanent rooms and spaces must be tactile and visually accessible; and signage that provides information about or directions to functional spaces must only meet the visual criteria.
- Directional signage must be high contrast and have a nonglare finish.
- Lighting of at least five to ten foot-candles should be provided along the accessible route.
- Changes in illumination can be provided to indicate changes in direction.
- Pathways or accessible routes can be indicated by different surface texture.
- Signage should refer to the direction or accommodation and not to the users, i.e. "ramped entrance" or "accessible parking."

Use a consistent system of control barriers throughout the facility.
- Barriers, so as not to be a hazard themselves, should be cane detectable. A barrier's leading edge or

detectable element must be no higher than 27 inches above the floor to be cane detectable.
- Barriers should not prevent a visitor from seeing, hearing, or interacting with a program, performance, or exhibit.

Provide an accessible emergency system.
- Provide as many accessible emergency exits as the number of fire exits required by the National Fire Protection Association's Life Safety Code (NFPA 101).
- Provide emergency exits that lead to the main accessible entry route or another accessible route.
- Provide notification about accessible emergency exits at key points in the facility.
- Provide both visual and audible fire alarm systems.

Developing Accessible Communications in Public Programs

It is equally important to ensure that people are provided with accessible information and services while visiting a cultural organization.

Readable print. Provide legible printed materials—such as publications, brochures, programs, and signage—that address the needs of people with disabilities, older adults, those learning English as a second language, those trying to read materials in low lighting, and those in groups reading to children.
- Use a simple serif or sans serif font for printed material and labeling. Helvetica, New Century Schoolbook, Arial, and Times Roman are among the most legible fonts.
- All publications should use a minimum 12-point type size.
- Use upper and lower case type. Type set in all caps is difficult to read and should be limited to titles and headlines.
- Avoid very condensed, extended, extremely bold or light typefaces, and underlined text.
- Type should exhibit a high degree of contrast from its background. Text and visuals should be at least 70 percent darker or lighter than their background.
- Illustrations and text should not be printed over each other.
- Make margins justified on the left and ragged on the right. A matte or non-shiny paper or background that will not produce a glare is recommended for printing.
- The size and shape of a publication should be manageable by someone with a hand or motor disability.
- Spiral binding is recommended for large publications so the piece will lie flat if someone is using a reading machine.
- Assure that electronic text is compatible with screen reader software.

Exhibition Labels
- Avoid the use of complex English, jargon, and technical language in text panels unless such language is explained within the text or in supplementary handouts.
- Use the active voice in text panels; limit sentence length.
- Use a maximum of 55 characters per line in exhibit text because text containing too many characters on a line is difficult to read.
- Provide a short overview paragraph set in clear, large print at the beginning of introductory and thematic label panels which allows visitors to gather key information without having to read all of the text.
- Carefully link sentences and paragraphs and try to limit a sentence or paragraph to one idea.
- Provide line drawings, silhouettes, and photographs that complement label text to aid comprehension for those with reading difficulties.

- Main exhibition label information must be available within the galleries in alternative formats—such as Braille or audio—for people who cannot read print.
- Do not set text in all caps and avoid the use of script and italic type for essential information. Alternatives to italic type—such as underlining, boldface, quotation marks, or another color—should be used for book citations, artwork titles, foreign words, and quotations whenever possible.
- If an exhibition title is presented in an ornate or decorative type, it should be repeated in a clearer type at an accessible location near the exhibition entrance.
- Select type size appropriate to the viewing distance. Keep in mind the effects of crowds on actual viewing distance when calculating distance. At any distance, people who have low vision will need larger type than other visitors.
- Print only on a solid background. Print on imaged backgrounds, textured surfaces, or backgrounds with differing colors and tones are unreadable for people with low vision and perceptual difficulties.
- Mount labels so visitors can get very close to read them. People with low vision often must be within 75 mm (three inches) of a label to read it. Label and location should be situated so that the reader does not block his own light and should be out of the way of barriers, protruding objects, stairs, or the swing of a door.
- Keep in mind the natural line of sight when mounting labels. Labels mounted at 45 degree angles to the front of an exhibition case or vitrine are more accessible to people who have low vision than those that are mounted flat on the floor of the case.
- Mount wall labels at a height comfortable for both those seated and standing. Wall labels mounted with a centerline at 1370 mm (54 inches) above the floor are at an optimum height for everyone.
- Locate labels in consistent locations throughout an exhibition.
- Provide sufficient light to read labels. For text to be readable by people with low vision, lighting on the label must be between 0 to 30 foot-candles.
- Offer audio versions of text labels for individuals with visual loss.

Audio description. Audio description, a narration service that allows people to hear what cannot be seen, allows people with vision loss to experience theater performances, film presentations, and museum exhibitions. Audio describers capture the essence of a scene and provide detailed information in clear, concise statements; see all of the visual elements of an image or an event; determine and convey the images most necessary to an understanding and appreciation of the event or program being viewed in as few words and in as little time as possible; and complement the program or exhibition with descriptions and do not interfere with it.

Samples of audio description from Audio Description Associates can be found online at www.audiodescribe.com.

Conveying audible information. Provide appropriate services to convey audible information effectively. Methods offered that allow people with hearing loss to experience programs will vary depending on the complexity of the program, the information being conveyed, and an institution's budget.

Captioning. Captioning translates the spoken word into simultaneously displayed text in programs such as films and video productions. There are several different captioning methods that may be used.
- **Open captioning** is a useful method for displaying spoken portions of video programs because the captions always appear on the screen. It is important to consider the placement of the captions so they do not obstruct the screen and viewing of the program. Open captioning is preferred by many and is an excellent example of universal design as it improves reading skills, allows the audio volume to be turned down, and is used by many to learn English as a second language.

- **Closed captioning** is similar to open captioning except it allows captioning to be turned on or off. All televisions now include the decoder chip needed to display the captions and control buttons for video displays.
- **Rear Window Captioning System®** displays captions in reverse on a light-emitting diode (LED) text display mounted in the rear of a theater. People who wish to view the captions have a transparent acrylic panel attached to their seats to reflect the captions so they are superimposed on the movie screen.

Assistive listening devices and other assists for people with hearing loss
- **Assistive listening devices (ALD)** increase the volume of sound. They can be used in live performances, films, lectures, and guided tours. The three types of ALDs are: (1) inductive loop, which transmits sound using an electromagnetic field; (2) infrared systems, which transmit sound via light waves; and (3) FM systems, which transmit sound via radio waves. The equipment needed for ALDs depends on how they will be used; however, a transmitter and several receivers will be needed. Provide ALDs that increase the volume of desired sound without increasing the loudness of background noises.
- **Signaling systems** such as flashing lights or vibrating receivers alert visitors with hearing loss that a program or performance is beginning, going into intermission, or ending.
- **Sign language interpretation** by certified interpreters should be available by request for meetings, special events, and programs. The most common from of sign language interpretation is American Sign Language (ASL), though Signed English is another form of interpretation that is used. Note in all publications, advertisements, registration forms, and at information desks who visitors should contact and by what deadline to arrange for an interpreter. Scheduling interpreter services is an accommodation request that commonly requires two weeks to arrange. Be sure to include this early deadline in publications.

TIPS FOR DEVELOPING DISABILITY AWARENESS

These tips are to be used as a starting point to develop a better understanding of disability issues and the disability community as a whole.

General Suggestions to Improve Access and Positive Interactions
- Offer assistance, but do not insist. Always ask before you assist someone and do not help without permission. If you do not know what to do then ask the person what would be helpful.
- Focus on what the person is able to do, rather than on their disability. Be aware that alternative ways of doing things can be equally effective.
- Be aware of limitations specific to a disability, but do not be overprotective. Do not exclude someone from an activity because you think his or her disability would be a problem. People with disabilities need to be able to take risks and make their own decisions.

Suggestions to Improve Access and Positive Interactions for Major Disabilities

Blindness and visual impairments
- When guiding a person who is blind, let him or her take your arm. If you encounter any obstacles, such as steps or curbs, pause briefly and identify them.
- Speak directly to the person in a normal tone and speed.

- Do not pet or play with a working service animal.
- Inform him or her that you are entering or leaving a room.
- When a person with vision loss is meeting many people, introduce them one at a time.

Deafness and Hearing Loss
- It is important to remember that the major issues for people who are Deaf are the challenges they experience in trying to communicate with people, not their inability to hear, and gaining information from the hearing society.
- When talking to people with hearing loss, use a normal tone and speak clearly and distinctly.
- Use facial expressions, body language, and written communication.
- If there is a sign language interpreter, speak directly to the person who is Deaf, not the interpreter.
- If you do not understand a person with hearing loss, ask them to repeat themselves.

Learning Disabilities
- It is important to remember that learning disabilities do not mean inferior intelligence.
- Be aware that periodic inattentiveness, distraction, or loss of eye contact by a person with a learning disability is not unusual.
- Discuss openly with a person with a learning disability the preferred way to communicate.
- Be aware and sensitive that some information-processing problems may affect the social skills of someone with a learning disability.

Mental Illness
- It is important to remember that people with mental illness do not have lower intelligence.
- Be aware that people with more serious forms of mental illness may have difficulty processing or expressing emotions.
- Be aware and sensitive to the fact that a person with a mental illness may react strongly to emotionally charged topics or discussions.
- It is helpful to learn more about the nature of a person's diagnosed mental illness.

Developmental Disabilities (which can include autism, cerebral palsy, brain injuries, and other neurological impairments)
- Interact with a person with a developmental disability as a person first.
- Avoid talking around or about a person with a developmental disability when they are present. Speak to the person directly.
- Provide clear and consistent information in multiple modes—orally and in print.
- If necessary, involve an advocate when communicating with a person with a developmental disability. Be sure this is an option for informed communication and never as a means of talking around the individual.

Mobility Impairments
- Do not be afraid to shake hands with someone who has very little grasping ability.
- Do not hold onto a person's wheelchair because it is seen as part of the person's body space. Holding on to, touching, or leaning on a person's wheelchair is both inappropriate and can be dangerous.
- Talk directly to a person in a wheelchair, not someone who is attending to them.
- Consider sitting down when talking to a person in a wheelchair to share eye level.
- Use people-first terminology such as "person with a physical disability." Avoid using inappropriate terms such as "cripple," deformed," or "wheelchair bound."

Tactile presentations

Provide tactile opportunities whenever possible. Touch allows people with vision loss to experience programs such as visual art exhibitions.
- Use original art and artifacts whenever possible for tactile exploration. Since most original art cannot be touched, casts and reproductions should be added, ideally for everyone to touch.
- Provide clear and concise verbal descriptions of works of art being touched to enhance the experience.
- Provide tactile pictures and hands-on art activities to supplement information about the artwork.
- For very large sculpture, small replicas may be mounted adjacent to the original at an appropriate height that allows people seated in a chair or children to explore it through touch.

Developing Accessible Communications in Promotions

People generally find out about cultural programs and events from newspapers, radio, mailings, posters, newsletters, television, and websites. In order to effectively inform people with disabilities about accessible programs and events, alternative approaches to providing public information should be practiced.

Simple statements. Provide simple, low-key statements regarding accessibility in all publicity—for instance, "This facility is accessible to all people." Do not use the word "handicapped" or the phrase "accessible to the handicapped."

Disability access symbols. Use disability access symbols in publicity and promotional materials to indicate what type of accessibility the facility offers. The most recognized symbol is a stylized wheelchair, the International Symbol of Accessibility. Other common ones denote availability of TTY, sign language, Video Phone, live audio description, large print, and access for people who are blind or have low vision such as guided tour or tactile description. Disability access symbols can be downloaded free of charge from The Graphic Artists Guild at www.gag.org.

Broadcast media. Use broadcast media when possible, particularly to reach people with visual and cognitive disabilities. Television can potentially be the ideal way to communicate to people with disabilities because it provides audio and visual elements as well as many programs that are audio described or captioned.

Accessible website. Specific steps must be taken to ensure that your website is usable by everyone, including people with sensory loss. Use navigation that is simple, intuitive, and easy to follow. Make the text scalable to allow visitors to view the text at whatever size is comfortable for them to read. Use text-based browsers as well as conventional graphical browsers, and add audio to visual information and screen readable print descriptions to graphics and visual aids that the viewer with limited sight cannot perceive whenever possible. Some specific features to make websites accessible are:
- **alt-text tag** (audio descriptions of the content of an image which interface with voice activated computers);
- **D-link** (provides a longer, more complete description of what an image looks like);
- **captions** (multimedia captions can be used to make video or audio clips in websites accessible); and
- **descriptions** (descriptions of static images or more in-depth narration of a video clip to describe what is taking place).

Telecommunications. Publicity and promotional materials should provide and promote accessible telecommunication devices, such as TTY and video phone as well as relay service numbers.

Local disability organizations. Notify local disability organizations and groups about accessible activities, programs, or services. They can usually be found in the resource pages of the telephone book. Additional information can be found through centers for independent living, school systems, health care organizations, and local government.

Funding Accessibility

Usually, one of the first concerns of accessible adaptations is the cost. Since the development of universal design, however, designs and renovations are no longer considered as costly, disruptive, or unsightly as they were before the ADA. It is estimated that for a new building, universal design elements amount to less than one percent of total construction costs. Universal design was developed to eliminate the need for costly special features that benefit only a small group, and instead creates structures that are more easily adapted to the changing needs of all building occupants and visitors.

Examples of Funding Sources for Disability-related Programs and Services
- **Department of Housing and Urban Development** offers Community Development Block Grants which provide funds each year to state, county, and city governments for projects that remove barriers in both public and private cultural facilities and programs.
- **NEC Foundation of America** provides grants that focus on science and technology education and the application of assistive technology for people with disabilities.
- **Mitsubishi Electric America Foundation** funds projects and organizations that advance the independence, productivity, and community inclusion of young people with disabilities through technology.
- **MetLife Foundation** supports various educational, health and welfare, and civic and cultural organizations. MetLife's initiative, Access to the Arts, funds innovative programs that encourage organizations to make the arts more inclusive and accessible for the special-needs community.
- **The Foundation Center** provides resources by geographic region and subject area to private and corporate foundations.

When applying for funding and writing grants, the Association of Science and Technology Centers (ASTC) recommends the following:
- **Include target audience** statistics when describing the need for an accessibility project. For example, about 20 percent of the U.S. population is classified as having a disability, with nearly half considered to have a severe disability.
- **Use demographics** of the cultural organization's surrounding community. Visit the Census Bureau website (www.census.gov) for population data in your particular area. Local government and organizations that serve people with disabilities also maintain current statistics.
- *Use input* from focus groups, visitor surveys, or advisory committees in writing grant proposals to make sure the project responds to its target audience.
- **Include costs of program accommodations**—sign language interpretation, audio description, or large print programs—in your project budget when applying to a federal agency, such as the National Endowment for the Arts.

Conclusion

The "design for all" principle is an advantage for all ages. A complete invitation can and should be extended for the great public theater where everyone is a player.

To paraphrase *Access for All Ages*, providing cultural access to all creates these advantages.
- The arts become accessible to more people.
- The arts remain accessible in each phase of people's lives, especially for children and older adults.
- Everyone profits from an accessible society because sooner or later everyone will belong to a special category.
- Fewer additions and provisions will be needed for targeted populations, which will make arts facilities and program operations more durable and, in the end, cheaper,
- An accessible arts environment contributes to the realizations of other policy objectives related to social justice, safety, and quality of life, such as independent living for all including young people with disabilities as well as older adults.
- Arts programs and productions will profit from a larger circle of employees, volunteers, and patrons.
- Accessible programming is sustainable while accommodations for every event are often not sustainable in the long term.

Creating cultural accessibility through a universal environment where all can participate may require systemic change within the organization, but the rewards will launch your programs and make your facility a vibrant part of community life.

Endnotes

1. Adaptive Environments is an educational nonprofit committed to advancing the role of design and enhancing experience for people of all ages and abilities. Its work balances expertise in legally required accessibility with promotion of best practices in human centered or universal design.

2. *Nearly 1 in 5 People Have a Disability in the U.S.*, Census Bureau Reports, https://www.census.gov/newsroom/releases/archives/miscellaneous/cb12-134.html

3. Sandahl, C. (2001, April). "Access, Activism & Art," American Theatre, 18(4),

4. *Access for All Ages.*

5. Salmen, J. P. S. (1998). *Everyone's Welcome: The Americans with Disabilities Act and Museums.* Washington, DC: American Association of Museums.

6. VSA Arts. (1998). *Strategies for Inclusive Classroom Environments.* Washington, DC: Author.

7. Sherman, A. P, (1996, November). The Arts and Older Americans. *Americans for the Arts Monographs,* 5 (8). Retrieved at http://pubs.artsusa.org.

8. Ludins-Katz, F. & Katz, E. (1990). *Art and Disabilities: Establishing the Creative Art Center for People with Disabilities.* Cambridge, MA: Brookline Books.

9. Salmen.

10. The Americans with Disabilities Act (ADA), passed in 1990, builds upon Section 504 of the Rehabilitation Act of 1973. Whereas Section 504 prohibits recipients of federal funds from discriminating on the basis of disability, the ADA expands this into a prohibition of discrimination on the basis of disability. For more information, visit www.usdoj.gov/crt/ada/cguide.htm.

11. Salmen.

12. Ibid.

17

Arts Education: Policy and Practice

MARETE WESTER *and* JUDITH ANN SARRIS CONK

Arts Education: Promise and Challenge

The work of artists, arts organizations, state and local arts agencies, and education agencies intersects productively in numbers of ways to advance quality arts education, for many students, in many schools across America. Still, evidence has shown that access to arts education for Blacks and Hispanics remains persistently and significantly lower than for their White peers, and has indeed has been steadily declining for three decades.[1] Achieving equity in arts education, for all students in all schools across the country, remains an elusive goal.

A surge in efforts over the past decade to provide exemplars and "models" of good practice has yielded valuable knowledge. Yet there remains no one plan, formula, or "magic bullet" that will guarantee the success of arts education programs in all environments.

To the schools, whose primary concern is to engage students in learning, the arts are concrete manifestations of one of the higher orders of human achievement impacting student cognitive, personal, social, and civic development. To the nonprofit arts agency, whose primary concern is for artists or the perpetuation of an art form, education is the infrastructure within which students' artistic talent is discovered, nurtured, and developed——either as creators or audience members. No art can thrive without education; no education can be complete without the arts.[2]

> In the 21st century humanity faces some of its most daunting challenges. Our best resource is to cultivate our singular abilities of imagination, creativity and innovation. Our greatest peril would be to face the future without investing fully in those abilities.
>
> — Ken Robinson, *Out of Our Minds: Learning to be Creative*

The arts are among the most powerful means we have to address issues that concern a broad and diverse set of public interests. Through well-publicized research efforts, the arts have made the case for their role in the revitalization of neighborhoods and communities, as well as for their economic impact. The United States relies heavily on the creative energy of its citizens to drive its economy, heal a wounded spirit, and bring communities together; consequently, the arts occupy a fundamental role in the lifeblood of democracy.

The inclusion of the arts in federal and state policy in the late 1990s, including educational goals and standards, opened the doors for encouraging more schools to incorporate the arts as a sequential component of a quality K–12 education and challenged schools to find the resources to do so after decades of neglect. Yet despite significant advances in policy and strong advocacy initiatives at national, state, and local levels, arts education as part of a student's core education is still unevenly delivered, often providing the least to the most vulnerable student populations. Findings by UCLA researcher James Catterall provide evidence that low-socioeconomic-status students who are engaged in arts learning demonstrate increases in critical areas, including high school academic performance, college entrance rates and grades, and holding jobs with a future—yet the decline of arts education is most pronounced in these underserved populations.[3]

In local communities, arts organizations serve to educate the public in, through, and about the arts. Adults across multiple generations are able to participate in learning that allows them creative freedom, self-expression, and refinement of skills. The trend towards more experiential, participatory, and interactive experiences impacts both school-age and adult classrooms, as well as programs offered by performing arts groups, museums, and cultural centers.

These trends help fuel a greater interest from all sectors in the critical role the arts are playing in our society. The link between arts education and the development of 21st-century workplace skills has recently become more widely embraced by employers and educators alike. Among these skills, those most closely aligned with skills developed through the arts are: communication; critical thinking and problem solving; and creativity.

> The College Board believes that the arts expand student potential by encouraging creativity, innovation, collaboration, and critical thinking. A comprehensive arts education is an effective tool for developing the whole child, keeping students in school and promoting high achievement. It is an essential element for the emotional and intellectual maturity of young people, encouraging them to open their minds to other disciplines and broadening their cultural diversity.
>
> The College Board's Arts at the Core Advocacy and Education Initiative, 2011

Business leaders understand that the cultivation of employees' minds is more important than ever in our global economy. The IBM 2010 Global CEO Study surveyed 1,500 chief executive officers from 33 industries in 60 countries. Among the key findings were that CEOs believe that creativity helps employees capitalize on complexity, and that creativity is the most important leadership quality.

In the realm of education reform, arts education is a subject that inspires passionate debate, as it impacts both the development of the brain and the whole human condition. Those working in arts education—whether in schools, community agencies, or cultural institutions—must be prepared to be advocates, to understand the breadth and scope of a field in constant dynamic change, and to continually work towards achieving a common agenda that will help create a supportive environment.

This is an enormous task. Only by working together can we, as educators, artists, administrators, and supporters, continue to make the cultural shift from "making the case" for arts education to "making it happen." As the demands on our already scarce resources continue to grow, we must explore and invent better ways to collaborate and deliver high-quality arts education experiences.

This chapter attempts to provide some navigational tools to help individuals and organizations engage in arts education in multiple ways—from advancing and advocating for stronger policies at the national, state, and/or local levels, to building sustainable community partnerships, to creating and implementing successful programs. Each approach requires understanding the existing environmental conditions, and what tools and strategies are required to achieve impact.

Arts Education Policy and Advocacy: Evolving from Frill to Focus

THE ARTS IN THE SCHOOLS: A BRIEF HISTORY

The evolving role of the arts in public education and their educational role in the community has held a place in the former since the 1800s, and the latter since this country's inception. All artistic disciplines, most frequently music and visual arts but also dance and theater, have been present in elementary and secondary curriculums to a greater or lesser extent throughout the history of public education. External partners have historically stepped up to mitigate the inevitable loss of in-school arts programs due to local funding crises or downturns in economic cycles.

Here is an outline of important milestones in this century.

Federal Efforts

Arts education was embedded in the founding of the National Endowment for the Arts (NEA) in 1965. Initially, the NEA focused more of its energies on supporting the work of artists and arts institutions in the broader education realm, and less on efforts directed toward improving the arts in K–12 education.

The U.S. Department of Education and the John F. Kennedy Center for the Performing Arts, seeking to strengthen state policy for arts education, created a network of state alliances for arts education in the 1970s, which became the Kennedy Center Alliance for Arts Education Network. This program established a foundation for state planning efforts for arts education and helped to lay the groundwork for the education reform movements of the 1980s and 1990s.

In the mid-1980s, Congress expanded the role of both the NEA and the National Endowment for the Humanities (NEH) in arts and humanities education in the schools. The NEA moved toward a greater funding focus on curriculum-based arts instruction, instituting the Arts in Schools Basic Education Grants (AISBEG) Program, which created statewide arts education programs and joint state agency planning processes in nearly two-thirds of the states.[5]

Despite a more than a 50 percent reduction in its federal budget during the mid-1990s, the NEA continued to support arts education, not only through its grant programs to state arts agencies and nonprofit arts organizations, but increasingly through its leadership initiatives, resulting in a strengthened national support network for arts education. This work was substantially bolstered by the pivotal passage of the Goals 2000 Educate America Act in 1994, which included the arts in the National Goals for Education. A major achievement for arts education, it set the stage for the arts to be included in education appropriations as well as legislative authorization language.

The Private and Nonprofit Sectors

Private foundations in the 1970s and 1980s were also developing and promoting strategies and initiatives aimed at improving public school arts instruction, most notably the Getty Center for Education in the Arts and the JDR 3rd (John D. Rockefeller III) Fund.

During this same period, complementary local and community efforts to bring learning in the arts to children and citizens were underway, their roots in the country's rich folk arts traditions, the community guild schools for the arts movement, and the emergence of children's theaters, as well as other arts- and arts education-based nonprofit organizations.

The emergence of the local arts agency (LAA) movement as a force in community cultural development impacted arts education as well. LAAs from rural to urban areas began taking on new roles, depending on the needs of their particular communities—from strengthening local policies and interest in arts education and reform, rallying community support, and advocating for new resources for the arts, to conducting and/or funding artist residencies and other arts education in community- or school-based programs. These efforts transcend fluctuations in national and state policies, since program implementation and resource allocation decisions—from curriculum to staffing to facilities—are almost always made locally.

MAKING THE ARTS BASIC: STANDARDS-BASED EDUCATION REFORM

National Standards

Perhaps no other single policy initiative in arts education has been as pivotal in uniting the arts community around a central vision for arts education—and encouraging collaborative action over the years—more than the development of the National Standards for Arts Education in 1994. The development of the National Standards for Arts Education was groundbreaking for several reasons:

- **Impact on policy.** The inclusion of the arts in the national standards movement firmly embedded the arts in national education policy, setting in motion changes in state education policy and, subsequently, local education policy.
- **Stimulus for systemic change.** The inclusion of the arts as a core subject area in the National Education Goals triggered other major policy shifts, including the opportunity to access funding opportunities through the Elementary and Secondary Education Act (ESEA). Since 1994, ESEA funding supported the development of state and local arts standards; assessments, research, and professional development programs for teachers; it also opened up competitive state and local grant initiatives to include arts education. These funds provided incentives for states to develop state standards and assessments in arts education, and to include the arts in a state's overall plan for standards-based education reform.
- **Catalyst for collective action.** In the 30-plus years of the modern arts education movement, progress has tended to be impeded by the competing voices holding differing views of arts education. The National Standards provided a unique opportunity to bring together arts specialists, artists, and nonprofit arts leaders in the disciplines of dance, music, theater, and visual arts to achieve

some consensus through a broad-based process on what a quality education in the arts is, can, and should be.
- **Common ground.** By articulating a clear set of principles of what children should know and be able to do in all artistic disciplines, the National Standards have provided a valuable resource both to educators and to the arts community. The concept of standards is a principle that is readily accepted by educators, business leaders, parents, and politicians. These standards, and their more recent incarnation, the National Core Arts Standards, have become the banner under which arts education can collectively move forward, and the means by which the previously ephemeral has become concrete.

21ST-CENTURY EDUCATION REFORM

No Child Left Behind

The 21st century has seen education reform grow more volatile with the advent of each new presidential administration and the changes in congressional leadership. This was no more evident than with the 2002 authorization of the Elementary and Secondary Education Act (ESEA), under the new reform banner of "No Child Left Behind" (NCLB).

From 2002 to 2015, NCLB policies resulted in many unintended consequences to schools, teachers, and students across the country. NCLB ushered in an unprecedented national emphasis on math and reading through the establishment of "adequate yearly progress" (AYP) requirements. The hyper-focus on testing in a few subjects is widely blamed for the erosion of arts instruction over the life of NCLB, as increased pressure to perform on key tests has led to the stifling of other curricula, leaving other core academic subjects—like the arts—to be reduced, or in some places, eliminated.

Common Core State Standards Initiative

The emergence of the Common Core State Standards Initiative in 2009 contributed to that general erosion. Sponsored by the influential National Governors Association and the Council of Chief State School Officers, the initiative seeks to establish consistent educational standards for what K–12 students should know in English language arts and mathematics across the states, as well as to ensure that students graduating from high school are prepared to enter credit-bearing courses in two- or four-year college programs or to enter the workforce. The application of the nationwide tests, which over time have been adopted and put into process by more than 40 states, have proved to be controversial among teachers, administrators, and parents. 2015 saw several states requesting waivers from the U.S. Department of Education, or putting the tests on hold. At this writing, it remains to be seen how much of a continued impact this initiative will have on schools over the long run, yet its influence as a driver of school change has been substantial and will have lingering effects.

National Coalition for Core Arts Standards

Despite the significant challenges throughout this period, the arts education community maintained its commitment to advocacy and collective action. In response to Common Core, the initial partnership that created the original national arts standards expanded to include additional national arts and education associations to help lead the new National Coalition for Core Arts Standards[6] effort in 2013. This coalition continued to advocate for the inclusion of all the disciplines of the arts (dance, media arts, music, theater, and visual arts as defined by the National Core Arts Standards), and sought to ensure that the arts are eligible under the definition of "core academic subjects" contained in any proposed federal education legislation.

Every Student Succeeds Act

The coalition of arts education advocates legitimately claimed victory on a number of fronts the Every Student Succeeds Act (ESSA) was signed into law on December 10, 2015. This coalition has included the discipline-specific groups representing dance, media arts, music, theater, and visual arts education, as well as groups representing community-based and out-of-school time programs.

ESSA, the first significant piece of education legislation in more than 14 years, includes these key arts education priorities:

- inclusion of the arts in the "well-rounded education" definition with over a dozen references in the bill ensuring, among other things, that the arts continue to be eligible for Title I funds—the largest federal funding source to local educational agencies and schools;
- dedicated funding for arts education through the "Assistance for Arts Education" grant program; and
- integration of the arts in STEM (science, technology, engineering, math) programs—recognized in the field as "STEM to STEAM"

ESSA reinforces the trend towards more local control and state level accountability in education. This law means that states must invest in new arts education learning standards and resourcing of arts education to encourage creativity in our nation's classrooms. ESSA also places emphasis on providing all students with an education that is shared and coordinated between classroom teachers, arts specialists, and community partners.

The following section provides a more detailed account of some of the major areas of the law and its impact on arts education.

1. ESSA defines support for a "well-rounded education" which includes the arts. Instead of defined core academic subjects, the bill is clear in its support for well-rounded education (Sec. 8002, "Definitions"). In the bill, the term "well-rounded education" means "courses, activities, and programming in subjects such as English, reading or language arts, writing, science, technology, engineering, mathematics, foreign languages, civics and government, economics, arts, history, geography, computer science, music, career and technical education, health, physical education, and any other subject, as determined by the State or local education agency, with the purpose of providing all students access to an enriched curriculum and educational experience." (emphasis added)

This key language appears in Title I, the largest portion of funds, and is also carried through in over a dozen additional locations of the bill, including within targeted and school-wide grants.

2. ESSA provides funding specifically for arts education. The bill (in Sec. 4642) includes key, dedicated, and distinct authorization to promote arts education under a new program, Assistance for Arts Education. Similar to the current Arts in Education program, the program will promote arts education for disadvantaged students through activities including professional development for arts teachers, development and dissemination of arts-based educational programming in multiple arts disciplines, and national outreach activities that strengthen partnerships among local education agencies, communities, and national centers for the arts—all helping ensure that all students have access to a well-rounded education that includes the arts. Significantly, under the program, those receiving grants are also encouraged to coordinate with public or private cultural agencies, institutions, and organizations, including "museums, arts education associations, libraries, and theaters."

3. ESSA gives the arts equal footing with other academic subjects in other grant programs. In the bill, dozens of federal grant programs were consolidated in a new Student Support and Academic Enrichment grant program (Sec.4104). At least 20 percent of the funds are directed to well-rounded education, which includes "activities in music and the arts." This funding is distributed according to a formula (totaling $1.65 billion for FY17 and $1.6 billion for FY18–20), reaching states and school districts. Two additional programs of note in the new bill include:

- Preschool grant program. The bill authorizes a preschool grant program (Sec. 9212) that was funded by Congress in 2014 and, for the first time, included the arts within the "Essential Domains of School Readiness" definition as an approach to learning. In addition, the program allows local preschool programs to coordinate with local arts organizations. This authorization helps solidify the program going forward.
- Promise Neighborhoods. The bill authorizes grants for this program (Sec. 4624), which is designed to help improve educational outcomes and transform communities. These plans include eligibility for extended learning time and partnerships between schools and community resources. By extension, these community resources may include local arts organizations.

4. ESSA requires each local education agency to describe how they will monitor students' progress in meeting state standards. Acute disparities in access to arts education for students are pervasive throughout the country, despite the impressive and well-documented benefits of arts education.[7] A remedy for this situation has been hampered by the lack of transparency and reporting in how much (or how little) arts education is being offered to our nation's students. ESSA now includes some plan provisions designed "to ensure that all children receive a high-quality education, and to close the achievement gap between children meeting the challenging State academic standards and those who are not." Under the bill, each local educational agency plan is required to describe how they will monitor students' progress in meeting state standards, and how they will implement "a well-rounded program of instruction to meet the academic needs of all students." Outlining these steps and requiring the reporting will better help ensure that plans are met.

5. ESSA changes STEM to STEAM. Thanks to the efforts of Rep. Suzanne Bonamici (D-OR) during the conference committee's amendment process, the bill now includes the arts as part of the support given to schools that provide a well-rounded education through programs that integrate academic subjects into STEM (science, technology, engineering, mathematics) courses. With the signing of ESSA into law, "STEM to STEAM," long a rallying cry among arts advocates, is now a reality.

6. ESSA continues authorization for 21st Century Community Learning Centers. The 21st Century Community Learning Centers program supports afterschool, out-of-school, and expanded learning time in schools. A critical source of funding for many afterschool arts programs, especially in lower-performing school districts and higher-poverty areas, the program in 2015 served over 1.6 million children with a budget of just over $1 billion annually. Continued authorization was successfully added (with bipartisan backing) to the Senate version of the bill during earlier committee consideration through a restoration amendment. It continues in the final ESSA bill, although at slightly lower authorized funding levels.

7. ESSA improves accountability for lower-performing schools. Another positive and significant development took place in the reauthorization bill around the School Improvement Grant (SIG) program. SIG was a source of funding for Turnaround Arts, serving the lowest-performing 5 percent of elementary and middle schools. In the bill, states are still required to improve student learning within the lowest-performing 5 percent of their schools. While the new bill eliminates the current School Improvement Grants as a separate program, the previous 4 percent set-aside by states from their Title I allocation for school improvement is now increased to a minimum of 7 percent, to help target additional funds to these schools. Arts-based solutions like Turnaround Arts have demonstrated improved academic achievement, reduced disciplinary referrals, and increased classroom attendance.

8. ESSA improves testing and standards. Under the bill, the "adequate yearly progress" (AYP) requirement is replaced with multiple measures—an innovation of the states—including student engagement and post-secondary readiness. The arts are a proven way to increase engagement, student attendance, and academic achievement.[8]

Each state will have full control of the "challenging academic standards" within their state. Fortunately, the new arts standards—which serve as a model to be used for state-level adaption and adoption– were conceived and developed by leaders from all arts disciplines across all 50 states. Throughout the new legislation, states have gained more responsibility for their education reform efforts and will be the major drivers in the foreseeable future.

9. Teachers. Under ESSA, arts educators are eligible for professional development support (under Title II) since the bill provides some resources to states and school districts to implement various activities to support teachers, principals, and "other educators." The bill also adjusts the allocation of Title II formula funds so that states with higher numbers of students in poverty receive a higher proportion of funding.

10. Grants directed to Alaska Native organizations. The arts are once again listed in this grant program as an activity that increases graduation rates and assists students in meeting challenging state academic standards.

The Growth of Research in Arts Education

The efforts in the 1990s to make the case for arts education also drew attention to the fact that the arts were among the least researched areas of the curriculum, placing arts advocates at a distinct disadvantage when confronted with school administrators or politicians asking for proof that it works.

The NEA was an early leader in efforts to stimulate longitudinal research that attempted to provide evidence of the impact of the arts in the curriculum, releasing Schools, Communities, and the Arts: A Research Compendium in 1995. Shortly thereafter, the President's Committee on the Arts and Humanities and the National Assembly of State Arts Agencies released Eloquent Evidence: Arts at the Core of Learning, which summarized the key research findings.

Champions of change. In the late 1990s, James Catterall and colleagues analyzed data from the National Educational Longitudinal Survey, a study of 25,000 secondary school students over four years. They found significant connections between high involvement in arts learning and general academic success, including lower dropout rates. These findings were published in a major research compendium, Champions of Change.[9] Other studies found further positive benefits of arts education that can help explain the lower dropout rate:

- The arts reach students who might otherwise slip through the cracks.
- The arts reach students with different learning styles.
- The arts create a feeling of connection and cooperation between students.
- The arts create schools that are exciting places for learning and discovery.
- Arts education may also help students stay excited about school right through graduation.

In 2012, Catterall and two colleagues compared three additional data sets with the findings from the 1999 study.[10] These results corroborated the link between high arts involvement and academic success.

Critical links. In 1999, the NEA and the U.S. Department of Education provided grant support to the Arts Education Partnership to commission and manage the development of a second compendium, Critical Links.[11] Released in 2002, the collection explores the arts as forms of cognition—ways of acquiring and expressing knowledge—which help every child reach the levels of achievement needed for academic and social success. Profiling 62 studies of learning in dance, drama, music, visual arts, and multi-arts, Critical Links focuses on the cognitive capacities used and developed in learning and practicing the arts, and the relationship of these capacities to students' academic performance and social interactions and development.

COMMUNITY INVOLVEMENT

Communities' involvement in arts education ranges from program delivery to increasing levels of influence in local decision- and policy-making. The 1988 Arts and Education Handbook: A Guide to Productive Collaborations outlined the kinds of programs and services LAAs and nonprofit arts groups have typically engaged in developing and/or supporting:[12]

- **Resources for education,** such as curriculum development, artist residencies (in schools and nontraditional settings), arts classes or workshops outside of schools, and providing help in organizing advocacy efforts on behalf of mandated K–12 arts curriculum in schools.
- **Information and technical assistance,** including curriculum consulting, developing in-service workshops for teachers and other teacher-training models, and connecting the schools to cultural resources in the community.
- **Events,** such as festivals for children and adults, performances, tours, exhibitions, workshops, and projects.
- **Artist listings,** including directories of local artists with their contact information and artistic disciplines.
- **Artist rosters,** comprising those local artists who do residencies and those who are part of official state, regional, or national residency programs that take place locally.
- **Preassembled exhibits,** offering collections of a single artist's work, a regional show, or a thematic collection, with information materials and presentations often connecting across regions with public, university, and private collections and educational programs.

- **Touring services,** helping to link schools with regional touring agencies or artist representatives, keeping costs down by "block booking" a touring artist in a number of schools or communities, or even creating touring educational programs.
- **Facilities, equipment, and space access,** helping to support schools without proper equipment or studio, rehearsal, or performing space, and/or expanding students' experience beyond the school setting.
- **Field trips,** creating access to a cultural facility or to an arts or cultural theme in local, regional, or even international settings.
- **Advocacy assistance,** training parents, teachers, and the arts community to be effective advocates, and helping them to lobby for changes in local school curriculum or policy toward the arts.
- **Fundraising experience and activities,** supporting additional activities in the schools, cosponsoring activities with other organizations, identifying an underwriter, or making key contacts with the private sector.

Additional growing areas of community support include:

- Partnership building to enhance relationships with other cultural, civic, social, or governmental agencies that share similar goals.
- Community cultural planning, which helps to identify the community's desire for increased opportunities for youth and adults to engage in the arts, and leads to creative strategies and new local partnerships with government and education agencies.

ADVOCACY FOR ARTS EDUCATION: WHOSE JOB IS IT?

The steady progression of the arts embedded in education reform, despite its ups and downs, is testimony to the power of collective action in support of a common goal. The initial omission of the arts in the first incarnation of National Goals for Education recommended by the nation's governors in the early 1990s galvanized the arts education community to take action. Since then, coalitions have engaged in sustained advocacy efforts that have alternately made significant advances for the arts and beaten back challenges. These efforts provide evidence that even the most diverse groups, with at times conflicting agendas and priorities, can succeed when enough voices make themselves heard, if they are willing to work together.

Educating decision-makers as to the value of the arts in education begins with every election cycle and new policy reform effort—no matter whether it is taking place at the national, state, or local level. The results of every new debate that alters or changes federal legislation will inevitably be felt in policies and actions at the state level and in local districts and schools.

Arts advocates themselves are constantly challenged to remain educated on the issues affecting education as a whole, since often one new policy development can have major impacts on another. Standardized testing, driven by national policy directives, has become the major focus of most schools and districts—and the arts have once again frequently found themselves on the "chopping block," despite their previous gains. Facing pressures from education reform movements, school administrators claim that with the increased emphasis on improving reading, writing, and math test scores, they have no time and few resources for the arts. Advocates must help school officials better understand the role that the arts can play to enhance the performance of students.

Whose problem, then, is the lack of widespread and equitable distribution of quality arts education programs in schools? The answer is plain and simple: ours. If we, as a community concerned about the arts as a whole, do not fight for it, it will not be there.

Advocacy for arts education is not easy—yet it has been proven both necessary and effective. Voicing support for arts education needs to be a part of the mission of every nonprofit arts organization, local arts agency, and cultural institution—even if they are not directly involved in providing or supporting arts education programs.

Effective advocacy efforts bring all interested voices to the table. Engaging in local school politics can be messy, but it is essential to effect changes in policy. Arts advocates can play a vital role by being active in school groups, such as parent committees or planning efforts, and, perhaps more important, by working to make sure supportive arts voices are elected to local school boards. With the passage of federal education legislation in December 2015 that grants greater authority and oversight to states to guide their education policy, advocates gained a new opportunity to focus their attention on how their state is rising to this challenge.

As we have seen, history has proven that reaching a common vision for arts education, and making significant policy strides, is achievable. But without vigilance, that success can be fleeting. It is clearly in the best interests of children and the public good that the arts grow and flourish in lifelong learning opportunities in school and beyond. This requires a concerted effort by all who share in this vision. See the Arts Advocacy chapter for more information about processes and strategies.

First Things First: Preparing to Take the Plunge

IS ARTS EDUCATION THE RIGHT THING FOR YOUR ORGANIZATION?

> To do well in the arts-in-education business, you must ground your organization's efforts in a clear understanding of education and of what you hope to accomplish. You must be able to articulate an education mission, strategy, and program to avoid criticism that your education program is just a marketing scheme to put bottoms in seats. To compete for funds to support education programs, you must excel in education, not just the arts.
>
> — David O'Fallon[13]

Embarking on a program in arts education requires thoughtful planning. In order to be effective, the program must be integral to the mission of your organization, affirmed by stakeholders, and well within your organization's capacity to sustain it. Funders increasingly demand greater accountability for programs, both to advance educational outcomes and to demonstrate long-term impact. The costs to the organization—both human and financial—are substantial, and are only sustainable if the program is built on a sound mission-based philosophy and purpose, and not merely to satisfy a funding requirement.

The impact of limited resources and competing pressures. Occasionally, the lure of potential funding informs the decision whether or not to work in arts education—which often leads to unsustainable programming if the goal of the education activity is not clearly articulated and understood. Public funders, foundations, and corporations often provide funding specifically for arts education; however, engaging in fundraising to support arts education and/or artistic programming should be balanced and relevant to your organization's mission.

Conducting a self-audit. With the myriad opportunities available for arts education to address the needs of pre-K children through senior citizens, it is essential for an organization to first assess its own values and mission in relation to that work. Without a clear sense of direction, it is easy to become overwhelmed by the multitude of directions to pursue. A self-audit is a valuable tool for understanding if the driving imperative for developing an arts education program is mission-based and serving a critical audience or constituent need.

The Self-Audit Worksheet in Figure 1 can be helpful in determining to what extent arts education should be part of your planning and programs. The Strategic Planning chapter ▌ also explains many techniques and strategies applicable to a community cultural planning process.

WHAT ARE THE NEEDS IN YOUR COMMUNITY?

As more local arts agencies (LAAs) have become involved in conducting community cultural planning, many also choose to engage in additional planning efforts that focus specifically on the needs of education in the arts, for children as well as adults.

Conducting a community assessment. The Kennedy Center Alliance for Arts Education Network has developed a useful planning tool to guide efforts in community assessment of arts education called A Community Audit for Arts Education: Better Schools, Better Skills, Better Communities It is designed to help local education, community, and cultural leaders assess the status of school district arts programs through the lens of 13 critical factors essential to implementing and sustaining comprehensive arts education programs. These factors are organized under three larger categories: Community Connections, Informed Leadership, and Educational Content.

Working with schools on community planning. Schools present a special challenge for those seeking to integrate education into community planning efforts. Often the local education system, representing the largest local government expenditure, wields significant political clout. The emphasis on testing and accountability places pressure on already scarce arts program resources. Yet, the local school system is an important potential ally in a community's overall cultural plan, and key to any effort to improve K–12 sequential education in the arts.

Spheres of influence: understanding the players and their needs. More often than not, successful arts education programs operate within complex systems. It helps to develop a working knowledge of the significant players who influence or are impacted by education, along with an understanding of what their beliefs and motivations are, in order to identify potential allies and helpers, as well as obstacles to be overcome.

The Arts Education Field Guide, published by Americans for the Arts in 2012, helps arts education advocates understand and find the connections and partnerships that will strengthen arts education in

Figure 1: Self-Audit Worksheet: Deciding whether arts education is for you.

Reflection Exercises for Boards and Program Planners

Adapted from O'Fallon, D. (1996). The Arts Organization and Public Education: A Guide to Conducting a Self-Audit. In J. Remer (Ed.), *Beyond Enrichment: Building Effective Arts Partnerships with Schools and Your Community.* Washington, DC: Americans for the Arts.

FOCUS QUESTION 1
What is our philosophy of education?

- What does "education" mean to our organization?
- What does "education" mean to the people we serve?
- Where are the arts in this philosophy? What is the role of the arts in the national education reform agenda? How is it playing out in our state? In our community?

PURPOSE OF EXERCISE: Developing a solid philosophy of education helps establish a strong sense of purpose and create an identity for the organization's role in arts education. It also lends credibility to the organization seeking to develop sustained relationships with educational institutions—especially in the public school system. The self-knowledge gained helps the organization clarify intent, and avoid being drawn into practices and activities that fall outside the agency's mission and strain the organization's capacity. The program will suffer if the educational goals become fragmented or are not clear from the start.

FOCUS QUESTION 2
How are our core values related to education and our education programs?

- Is building knowledge or awareness *about* an art form or artist our primary educational goal?
- Is building personal skills or creative abilities *in or through* the arts the primary goal?
- Is it a combination of the two?
- What role can we do best?
- What role is in the best interests of the organization?

PURPOSE OF EXERCISE: The core values as defined by the organizational mission should form the foundation of the education program. For example, an organization founded with the mission of advancing American jazz as an art form would be ill-advised to decide to develop its education program around the American musical theater because that's what the middle school wants. While this seems self-explanatory, many organizations can get pulled in the wrong direction by trying to adapt themselves to fit a school's or funder's agenda that extends beyond the scope of their mission. By acting on its strengths, the organization will be better able to define the goals, purpose, and resources available to launch the program effectively, as well as develop the will and capacity to sustain it.

444 | FUNDAMENTALS OF ARTS MANAGEMENT

Figure 2: Who Calls the Shots at a School?

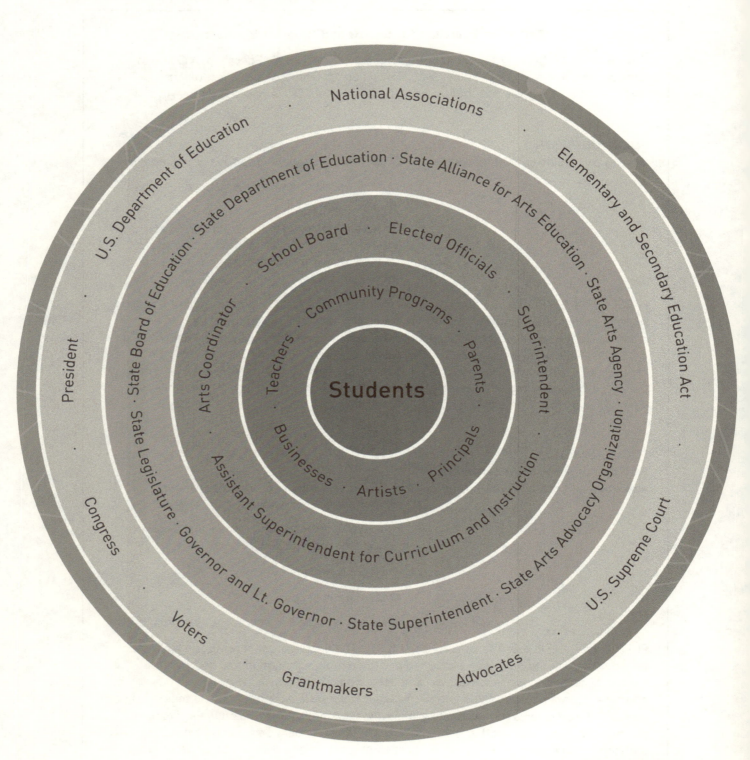

From Arts Education Field Guide, courtesy of Americans for the Arts.

their communities. The summary, in brochure format, identifies key players and decision-makers. The full guide provides detailed information about each stakeholder: their motivations and connections in arts education, in order to help advocates build more effective relationships. See the Tiers of Influence in the Appendix.

At the local and state level, the major participants who impact arts education include the students, teachers, administrators, arts specialists, parents and parent advisory groups in Pre-K through 12 public school systems; deans of arts and education departments, art galleries and performing arts centers, and student arts groups in universities and colleges; nonprofit arts organizations, individual artists, and community art institutes; public and private funders; municipal governments and chambers of commerce; and state arts agencies and departments of education.

Who is really calling the shots? Determining the process behind a school's decision-making often requires some careful detective work. According to the school's organizational chart, the chain of command may seem obvious. However, the power structure active in local schools is very much an individual phenomenon, based on how much school policy is being driven by state mandate, local initiative, or a mix of the two. Figure 2 is a visual representation of this complexity. Understanding how decisions are made at the school with regard to programs, and who the decision-maker or decision-makers are (for example, administrators, teachers, and parents, as well as students) is important to developing productive partnerships.

Building a network of critical friends. It is almost impossible for one person to know everyone and all the dynamics at play in schools. Developing a network of "critical friends" who can advise you is essential. Ideally, this network will include those who are outside of your program. Key decision-makers and leaders central to early planning efforts can remain involved as informal advisors. Their expertise can help you avoid making mistakes, determine whether this is an environment that is conducive to ensuring a successful program, and, most important, decide if it is ultimately worth the investment of precious time, energy, and resources in the first place. Maintaining open, ongoing, and positive relationships with the people involved in your planning strengthens the foundation for successful implementation later on.

Programs that suit the community's needs. Arts education programs taking place in the community tend to fall into two general categories: those that take place in the K–12 setting or are integrally connected to the school curriculum; and those that take place beyond the school setting in the community at large.

The after-school/out-of-school movement. The late 1990s saw an increase in national attention and the direction of federal resources to after-school programs. In 1998, the federal Twenty-First Century Community Learning Centers Program sent hundreds of millions of dollars to schools, in collaboration with nonprofit and public agencies, community-based and social service organizations, and businesses, to support the development of quality after-school programs in rural and inner-city neighborhoods.

In 2000, leaders from the Kennedy Center Alliance for Arts Education Network and the Kennedy Center's Partners in Education program created a protocol for the development of quality after-school arts education programs, in order to help groups understand what constitutes excellence in after-school arts programs and how they can be designed to complement in-school programs. Their report, "The Arts Beyond the School Day," identifies nine essential elements of arts-based, student-centered after-school programs that, when taken together, forge the framework for ensuring the development of a quality arts-based after-school program. These programs:

1. are focused on student needs.
2. offer unique opportunities for imaginative learning and creative expression.
3. employ and support quality personnel.
4. are structured to maximize student learning.
5. engage families with their children.
6. are actively supported by school leadership.
7. invite collaborations with community partners.
8. are committed to ongoing planning and evaluation; and
9. leverage a wide variety of resources.[14]

The preschool movement. The National Goals for Education catalyzed an interest in improving the quality of early childhood education by establishing as the first goal that all students will start school ready to learn. In 1998, the Arts Education Partnership established the Task Force on Children's Learning and the Arts: Birth to Age Eight, charging it with developing a framework and resources to help guide arts organizations in creating arts-based, developmentally appropriate early childhood programs, and in linking the arts to the literacy of young children.

The task force's report, "Young Children and the Arts: Making Creative Connections," defined three guiding principles to be thoroughly integrated into the development of arts-based programs and resources for young children.

- **The child.** Children should be encouraged to learn in, though, and about the arts by actively engaging in the processes of creating, participating in, performing, and responding to quality arts experiences, adapted to their developmental levels and reflecting their own culture.
- **The arts experience.** Arts activities and experiences, while maintaining the integrity of the artistic disciplines, should be meaningful to children, follow a scope and sequence, and connect to early childhood curriculum and appropriate practices. They also may contribute to literacy development.
- **Learning environment and adult interactions.** The development of early-childhood arts programs (including resources and materials) should be shared among arts education specialists, practicing artists, early childhood educators, parents, and caregivers, and the process should connect with community resources.

Planning and Implementing the Program

Arts education programs target different audiences and may take place in many different settings. The chapters on Strategic Planning, Program Development, and Program Evaluation ▌ contain information and examples that will help you structure program development in community settings. This section focuses on planning for arts education programs that either take place in schools or are designed to help support school learning and curricular goals.

There are four critical phases to an effective arts education program: exploring its feasibility; designing the program; developing the curriculum; and, once the program is completed, reflecting on its outcomes.

EXPLORING THE PROGRAM'S FEASIBILITY

The first step in developing an effective arts education program involves asking these critical questions:

- Who initiated the idea? If it was the arts organization or cultural institution, planners should have the capacity to follow through and retain the notion of "under-promising and over-delivering." If the school or district initiated the idea, planners must be clear with their partners on whether the idea fits within the respective missions of both organizations.
- What are the school's educational priorities? Ask for the school's mission statement in order to assess whether the program goals are aligned with the school's goals.
- What are the current national or state standards that impact the school? Become familiar with the prevailing national and state standards, which can be found on the state education agency's website. While the English Language Arts are easy to link with, don't ignore subjects like mathematics and science. Grounding some work in these standards will help teachers and leaders see the arts as a creative way of approaching standards rather than something to do after the "real" work is done.

DESIGNING THE PROGRAM

Plan with the End in Mind

The most critical part of the design process is establishing the outcomes for the program. This involves projecting "backwards" from the anticipated results to the specifics of how to achieve them. Regardless of the duration or configuration of engagement, the questions "What will success look like?" and "How will we know we are successful?' must be answered first.

Developing the outcomes for the program can be a challenging design task. The hardest is creating outcomes that are measurable or observable and are realistic for the program at hand. A tool that is helpful in writing outcomes is a framework called SMART goals.[15] The outcomes you design for your program should be:

- **S**pecific: what? why? how?
- **M**easurable: with clear criteria for measuring program results.
- **A**chievable: able to be attained in the time allotted.
- **R**elevant: to connect with the students.
- **T**ime bound: designed within a clear time frame.

The quality of the goals that are set will drive the success of any program, so the organizations involved should be in agreement on these from the beginning.

Collect the Necessary Data

The second step, and a critical consideration in program design, is deciding how you will collect the data necessary to assess the success of the program. Funders and partners will want to know how you know a program is successful at the end of the designated time period. The goal must be somehow measurable—for example, through observations, surveys, student work, or participation. This design for the summative assessment occurs early in the process, even before you begin to design the specific curriculum and consider logistical implications. The assessment must be designed to evaluate each of the designated SMART goals. This should be documentable and allow the groups involved in the program to "tell the story" about it. See the chapter on Program Evaluation for further details.

> Educative assessment requires a known set of measurable goals, standards, and criteria that make the goals real and specific (via models and specifications), descriptive feedback against t hose standards, honest yet tactful evaluation, and useful guidance.
>
> —Grant Wiggins and Jay McTighe, *Understanding by Design*

When we begin a conversation regarding the assessment of student learning in the arts, too often the automatic reaction is that we are reducing an arts experience into a "true or false" standardized test. Such assessments do, indeed, divert students' attention from understanding large ideas and processes to mastering facts. In Taking Full Measure: Rethinking Assessment through the Arts, Dennie Palmer Wolf and Nancy Pistone argue for the use of assessment as an "episode of learning." They lay out a framework of three "essential lessons" about monitoring or measuring student learning:[16]

1. The contents of assessment should address the full range of what is involved in making a work of art—a process of complex problem solving that is deliberately multidimensional. Within this framework, the contents of assessment are expanded beyond the quality of the final piece or performance to include early and ongoing processes, such as investigations into ideas, reflections, actions based on critique, and responses.
2. The conduct of assessment suggests that assessment—as opposed to testing—is a process of ongoing monitoring of progress and quality, where students are active participants. Assessment is more than an occasion to assign grade or rank: it becomes an ongoing "episode of learning."
3. The tools of assessment support assessment as an ongoing component of learning. Since learning is measured over a longitudinal time frame, tests that measure knowledge or recall at a particular moment—that is, multiple-choice or end-of-year exams—give way to "process portfolios," which are "longitudinal histories of themselves as people learning an art form." Journals, self-critiques, and portfolios by their very nature are designed to provide evidence of knowledge of the processes and values, as well as sustained work and reflection.

Logistics

The final part of "backwards design" involves actually planning the activities of the program. This involves two types of consideration: curriculum and logistics. Both are important to the success of the program.

Logistical decisions should be made early. These include:

- Who the participants will be. The more defined the constituent population for the program can be, the greater the ability to develop targeted and focused activities that can successfully meet program objectives.
- The number of participants. Depending on the environment in which the program is taking place, there may be competing views of what is possible versus what is preferable. A teaching artist who is brilliant with small groups of children may feel overwhelmed if the school insists on an assembly program for the whole fifth grade. Conversely, a fully staged production of Macbeth performed

for a single seventh-grade English class would be an opportunity lost if not presented to the whole middle school. The key decision here becomes the needs of the learner.
- The school's experience and support. What is the school's previous experience with an artist in residence, if any? Is someone from the school designated to serve as a liaison with the arts organization and the artist(s) "on the ground"?
- The venue. Where will the work be conducted? Besides cost implications, the available space will dictate what the possibilities are for the program activities and curriculum.

These issues remain constant beyond the school environment and are appropriate, with some adaptations, for other settings such as social service agencies, hospitals, and community centers.

DEVELOPING A STUDENT-CENTERED CURRICULUM

A student-centered curriculum is based on the assumption that the learner, and not the event or artwork itself, is the primary focus within the learning experience and environment. To distinguish between the two focuses, consider the difference between the educational goals in these two learning tasks:

> **To help students know more about the choreography of Martha Graham.** To support this goal, students may read a biography of Graham, view videotapes or films, or see a dance performance of Graham's work in a school assembly or at a performing arts center. At the end of the lesson, students should be able to answer basic questions about Martha Graham's life, her work, and various aspects of dance as it pertains to her artistic vision.

> **To help students make a personal statement by creating a dance in the style of Martha Graham.** Obviously, many of the activities outlined above would still be appropriate—but to learn about Graham's work, students will also study how her concepts developed, what techniques she used, and what influenced her work. They would then apply this knowledge by creating a personal artistic statement through dance. In this example, the student is actively engaged in understanding a process—an understanding that extends beyond a single artist, performance, or event.

While the first goal emphasizes facts about a specific artist, the second puts the focus on the students' understanding through application and using the knowledge in a new and different situation.

Understanding developmentally appropriate curriculum. The stages of artistic development in children are based in part on their overall cognitive and motor abilities and also on how much and what kinds of arts experiences have been available to them in their homes, school, or community.

Very young children are naturally drawn to the arts. Children who have not yet fully developed verbal skills will still move their bodies to sounds, respond to singing, and try to imitate their parents' facial expressions. With appropriate adult facilitation, these basic forms of play can evolve into the acquisition of skills and frames of mind that we recognize as rudiments of the artistic process. In arts education:

- Children learn to observe, organize, and interpret information they receive from their environment. As they grow, these observations gain greater depth, more intricate patterns emerge, and interpretations grow more insightful.
- Children learn to make decisions, even at the most basic level. By engaging in the arts, children must take action and can see the results of their decisions in the product or event they create.
- Children learn that they can communicate in many ways—with adults and with each other, through words, sounds, movements, and pictures.

Arts education program planners should have a general understanding of the stages of learning development and how they work in the learning environment. An art experience given to an eight-year-old with absolutely no background or frame of reference for the art form presented could prove overwhelming: the child is likely to become frustrated and shut off from the learning experience. The same experience given to an eight-year-old with an extensive background and grounding in the fundamentals of the art form might view it as remedial: this child is likely to be bored and disinterested. In both cases, the child will have a negative view of the arts experience. The program you design, therefore, should be adaptable, so that if the population encountered is either less prepared for the program than anticipated or more advanced in knowledge and abilities, it can easily be adjusted. The more careful the preplanning, the less likely the artist or arts group is to step into a situation for which he or she is not prepared.

There are many resources to assist program planners in an examination of age-appropriate activities, including the Kennedy Center's ArtsEdge and the Getty Center for Arts Education, which have curricular models and ideas based on actual field practice. ArtsEdge, for instance, is a robust multimedia platform with many features, including a Lesson Finder, where educators and programmers can access free arts-based lesson plans and projects for classrooms and after-school programs. Lesson Finder is searchable by Keyword, Grade Band (K-4, 5-8, 9-12), Arts Subject (Dance, Literary Arts, Media Arts, Music, Theater, Visual Arts), and Other Subject (such as English, Math, Science, Technology and World Languages).

Arts learning standards. The National Core Arts Standards (along with most state standards in the arts) define both content—what students should know and be able to do in the arts disciplines—and performance levels: those specific competencies within each of the disciplines, according to grade clusters, that together demonstrate whether the student is proficient in the content. These voluntary national standards were developed to guide arts curriculum, instruction, and assessment in America's schools. They emphasize the process-oriented nature of the arts and arts learning, and are being delivered to the field through a web-based platform designed to meet individual teacher and local district needs. Thus standards represent a good starting point for program planners. (More information about the National Core Arts Standards may be found at www.nationalartsstandards.org.)

The very best strategy an artist or arts group can follow when developing curriculum for a particular age group is to involve their own local experts. Education professionals—including arts specialists, classroom educators, educators who work with special populations, early-childhood educators, curriculum developers, and administrators—undergo extensive training to understand how and when children develop different cognitive and motor skills. They can provide useful feedback as to whether a program is appropriately targeted.

What essential questions will the program answer? The essential questions framework is a useful planning and organizational tool which helps establish content themes; organize outcomes and activities around big ideas for artists, teachers, organizers, and students; and stimulate inquiry-based learning. It also engages the students in the process of learning and making connections to previous and ongoing learning in other disciplines.

Artists and arts groups can work with teachers and students to develop essential questions for the educational program. Essential questions can be derived from a number of sources: from an exploration of a particular standard area (how dances are made); a specific part of the arts group's artistic season (the upcoming retrospective festival of the work of August Wilson); a critical issue for the students (bullying); or the identification of a specific theme (the year-long celebration of the town's centennial).

REFLECTING ON THE RESULTS

The final stage of the process is the final reflection, sometimes referred to as a "debrief" or "post-mortem." Unfortunately, this stage is often not given the importance that it needs, due to lack of time or moving on to other programs, yet the reflection by all parties, students, teaching artists, the arts organization, and even partners, is a critical tool for learning and growing.

A key tool for reflective practice is creating documentation along the way. This documentation can include written observations, video records, etc., as well as the products created as part of the final assessment. Ask everyone, including the participants, the teaching artists, and the institutional partners, "What have we learned as a result of this program?" Taking the time needed for this reflection will close the feedback loop. Reflective practice allows participants to synthesize the most important learnings. It allows teaching artists to repeat those activities and strategies that were successful and to reconsider those that were less so. And it provides the arts organization or cultural institution the opportunity to learn from the experience.

See the Program Evaluation chapter for a detailed discussion of post-project reflection and assessment.

WHO SHOULD TEACH THE ARTS?

> The sustainability and success of arts education programming is due in large part to a commitment across communities for both shared delivery of arts instruction by arts specialists, teaching artists, and general classroom teachers and shared leadership for arts education among arts agencies, education agencies, parents, and businesses.
>
> —Arts Education Navigator, Americans for the Arts

One of the most enduring, needlessly polarizing, yet fundamental questions in arts education is: Who should teach the arts to students? The answer is complex, for in reality; many people are responsible for—and can play a role in—teaching the arts to students, whether at home, at school, or in the community. Figure 3 illustrates this concept of shared endeavor.

If a focused arts education program is to succeed, attention must also be paid to the excellence of the experience as both a learning opportunity and an artistic event. This requires valuing the skills of both the trained arts specialist and the professional teaching artist for the strengths each brings to the learning process. In order to identify and engage the most qualified specialist to deliver the program, it

Figure 3: Arts Education for America's Students: A Shared Endeavor

Certified Arts Educators
A career commitment to and accountability for the delivery of sequential, standards-based arts curriculum

Community Arts Providers
A career commitment to deep expertise in an arts specialty, connecting real-world practice to arts standards and the classroom

Certified Non-arts Educators
A career commitment to and accountability for the delivery of sequential, standards-based non-arts content areas

The definitions here are minimal statements of quality.
What additional strengths do your partners bring in support of quality arts education in your community?

Common Qualities of Effective Teaching Artists

- *Artistic quality and professional integrity.* The teaching artist will possess exceptional skills in his or her discipline, present a body of professional work, and be able to demonstrate professional success in the art world.

- *Ability to communicate.* An effective teaching artist will not only be able to verbalize ideas and concepts about the art form in an interesting way, but will use multiple means of demonstrating, illustrating, and otherwise imparting understanding about the art form. Good communicators tailor their presentations to the age group and make an effort to understand special needs or challenges.

- *Ability to engage the learner.* One of the most valued aspects of an artist residency is hands-on activity. These activities should encourage the learner to unlock the creative skills within and not merely provide a carbon copy of the teaching artist's work. Effective teaching artists help the learners establish their own creative identity.

- *Flexible working style.* The school environment is different from the studio: artists must be prepared to take the good with the bad. A willingness to understand and work within the confines of the school structure is essential to fostering a strong working relationship.

- *Respect for educators.* An effective teaching artist makes the classroom teacher a partner in the residency. Teachers have expectations for what a residency can accomplish, and what experiences and activities could enhance educational objectives. By working together, the artist and the teacher can maximize their strengths for the benefit of the students.

- *Motivation for teaching.* Above all, effective teaching artists want to teach—and love doing it. Teaching is an important part of who they are.

is incumbent upon the program planner to determine what skills are needed to effectively deliver the objectives of the program.

Ensuring quality program delivery likewise requires an understanding of the roles general classroom teachers and nonprofit arts and arts education providers can play. Americans for the Arts has useful online resources to help advocates and planners better understand the interplay and shared roles among all these groups in both delivery of effective programs and leadership in sustainable community partnerships.[17]

What is a "teaching artist"? There is no universally accepted definition of teaching artistry. Eric Booth, who has spent a great deal of his career working with and developing teaching artists, says, "A teaching artist is an active artist who chooses to also develop the skills of teaching in order to activate a variety of learning experiences that that are catalyzed by artistic engagement."[18]

One of the most important roles an arts organization or local arts agency can play is to help artists become partners in education programs. Consequently, an essential component of a successful program is the selection of artists who excel not only in their art form but also in their ability to impart their knowledge and skills effectively through engagement with the students. Not all great artists are effective teachers; therefore, the arts organization must match the skills of the teaching artist with the needs of the learners.

Partnerships

Partnerships in arts education often involve multiple sectors, including nonprofit, for-profit, and public arts and education agencies; schools; private funders; and parents, volunteers, and community groups. The general enthusiasm for starting a partnership can sometimes be eclipsed by the challenges of sustaining one. Therefore, it is important for an organization to consider whether a partnership or collaboration is really the best strategy for meeting a need.

Conclusion

Making the decision as an organization to engage in arts education should not be done lightly. In the preceding discussion, both the opportunities and challenges have been outlined. No matter what process is being used, the focus should always be on the students: What do they need to engage in highly developed, age-appropriate arts learning, and how can the arts organization or cultural institution provide this within their mission and capacity?

In the end, successful program development in arts education—whether for school students or the community at large—depends on identifying needs, building quality relationships, developing mutually supportive goals, and establishing a firm commitment to work toward achieving a greater good. It involves clearly articulated plans, strong partnerships, and artists who are committed to teaching, in the best sense of the word.

Practically speaking, this takes time and a willingness to plan for the journey, in order to successfully reach your destination. This means investing time, effort, and resources in the practices that will lead to success. As with most worthwhile endeavors, it is important to bear in mind that in the long run, there is much wisdom to be gained from the journey itself, rather than rushing without intention or reflection to reach the final destination.

Endnotes

1. Americans for the Arts, "Arts Facts ... Access to Arts Education is Not Equitable," 2014, www.americansforthearts.org

2. See Charles Fowler, *Arts Education Handbook: A Guide to Productive Collaborations* (National Assembly of State Arts Agencies, 1998).

3. Cited by Nick Rabkin and E. C. Hedberg in *Arts Education in America: What the Declines Mean for Arts Participation* (NEA Office of Research & Analysis, 2011).

4. "Capitalizing on Complexity: Insights from the IBM 2010 Global CEO Study," IBM Corporation, 2010, www.ibm.com.

5. Nancy Welch, Andrea Greene, et al., *Schools, Communities, and the Arts: A Research Compendium* (NEA, 1995).

6. www.nationalartsstandards.org.

7. "Arts Education Navigator: Facts and Figures," Americans for the Arts, 2014, www.americansforthearts.org/sites/default/files/pdf/2014/by_program/networks_and_councils/arts_ed_network/navigator_series/AFTA_Navigator_Facts-and-Figures.pdf

8. Ibid.

9. Edward B. Fiske, ed., "Champions of Change: The Impact of the Arts on Learning," *Arts Education Partnership and President's Committee on the Arts and the Humanities,* 1999, www.aep-arts.org.

10. James Catterall et al., *The Arts and Achievement in At-Risk Youth* (NEA, 2012).

11. Richard J. Deasy, ed., *Critical Links: Learning in the Arts and Student Academic and Social Development* (Arts Education Partnership, 2002).

12. Jonathan Katz, ed., *Arts and Education Handbook: A Guide to Productive Collaborations* (National Assembly of State Arts Agencies, 1988).

13. David O'Fallon, "The Arts Organization and Public Education: A Guide to Conducting a Self-Audit," In J. Remer, ed., *Beyond Enrichment: Building Effective Arts Partnerships with Schools and Your Community* (Americans for the Arts, 1996).

14. Judy Conk, "The Arts Beyond the School Day: Extending the Power—A Report of the After-School Protocol Task Force" (Kennedy Center Alliance for Arts Education and Kennedy Center Partners in Education, John F. Kennedy Center for the Performing Arts, 2000).

15. George T. Doran, "There's a S.M.A.R.T. Way to Write Management's Goals and Objectives." Management Review 70 no. 11 (Nov. 1981): 35–36.

16. Dennie Palmer Wolf and Nancy Pistone, *Taking Full Measure: Rethinking Assessment through the Arts,* 2nd ed. (College Entrance Examination Board, 1995)

17. See "Arts Education for America's Students: A Shared Endeavor" and the Arts Education Navigator, www.americansforthearts.org.

18. Eric Booth, "The Universal Elements of Teaching Artistry," *Teaching Artist Journal* (Nov. 6, 2012).

Appendix

Tiers of Influence

The structure of our education system is often seen as a linear hierarchy, but each partner below has a different role and a different amount of influence. Your strongest ally is not always just one step above, below, or beside you. How can we build more relationships within and between tiers in order to help arts education thrive within this ecosystem?

Federal
- White House • Congress • U.S. Department of Education • National School Board Association • National PTA • National Association of State Boards of Education • Arts Education Partnership • Americans for the Arts • National Associations for the Various Arts Disciplines • State Agencies of Education Directors of Arts Education • Kennedy Center Alliance for Arts Education Network • American Association of School Administrators • National Endowment for the Arts • National Education Association

State
- State Legislatures • State Department of Education • State Board of Education • State Superintendent • State Department of Education's Director of Arts Education • State Arts Agency • State Arts Advocacy Organization • State Alliance for Arts Education • Governor and Lt. Governor • Teachers Unions State Affiliates

Local
- School Board • Superintendent • Assistant Superintendent for Curriculum and Instruction • Arts Coordinator • Principal • Teachers Unions Local Affiliates • Arts Specialists • General Teachers • Teaching Artists • Parents / PTA • Mayors • City Elected Officials • Local Arts Agencies • Arts & Culture Organizations • Community Leaders • Community Programs • Grantmakers • Colleges • Businesses • Voters

Students

www.AmericansForTheArts.org/go/FieldGuide

© Americans for the Arts 2012

Fundamentals of Program Evaluation: Looking for Results

CRAIG DREESZEN

Program evaluation has become a fundamental skill for arts managers who must manage programs that work well and raise the funds to do so. Many managers, who first evaluated programs at the insistence of funders, have continued evaluating because it works. A focus on results helps us insure that programs are making a difference for people, helps us improve our programs, builds support, and helps managers make critical management decisions.

Understanding the Principles of Program Evaluation

FOCUS ON RESULTS

Effective nonprofit leaders have learned to shift from primarily managing activities to managing for results. No, arts leaders haven't stopped paying attention to getting tasks done, but competent leaders are no longer content to simply cross tasks off to-do lists or report that programs have been completed as planned. They also ask, "Did we achieve the results we intended?" This may seem a subtle shift of emphasis, but the implications are profound.

If results define success, leaders value productivity, not busyness. They sustain programs that work and change or discontinue those that do not. They decide what works with evidence from evaluation. Organizations that have incorporated evaluation into their practice are skilled at defining what they plan to accomplish and then tracking their progress. It has been truly said that "the odds of hitting your target go up dramatically when you aim at it."

> From this chapter, you will gain the confidence, skills, and commitment to consistently look for evidence that your programs are making the positive difference you intend for the people and communities you serve.

Most program evaluations measure change. The gold standard is a comparison of the situation before and after a program or intervention, for example: "Three-quarters of artists receiving fellowships report more visibility and two-thirds report increased sales or commissions after their recognition." This requires baseline data, pre- and post-tests, or questioning participants about the change in their circumstances attributable to your program. Other evaluations compare program participants with a similar group that did not benefit from the program.

> **Good Evaluation Questions**
>
> Evaluation asks these kinds of related questions:
>
> - What did you intend to achieve with your program?
> - Were program activities consistent with your intentions?
> - If so, did you observe the intended outcomes?
> - How do you account for the variations between observed outcomes and intended objectives?
> - How likely is it that observed outcomes were caused by your program activities?
> - What were the program's unintended outcomes? You may achieve some positive results or negative consequences that were not part of your plan.
> - What did you learn from your evaluation that will improve your program or plan new ones?
> - Did this program serve the public interest?
> - Was this a good use of your funding?

Evaluation is closely related to strategic planning. In planning, organization leaders determine the results they wish to achieve (intended outcomes) and in evaluation they measure actual outcomes achieved.

A New Era of Accountability

The funding paradigm has shifted. This is an era of accountability. It is no longer sufficient to promise in a grant application that you will change people's lives with your arts programs but then note in your final report that lots of people attended and seemed to have a good time. The audience size does not measure whether lives were changed. Knowing that you must measure the changes that you promise will help you aim at a target you can reach.

FUNDAMENTALS OF ARTS MANAGEMENT'S APPROACH TO EVALUATION

While it is possible to apply evaluation more broadly to whole organizations, this chapter focuses on the evaluation of specific programs. Programs may be evaluated at any point in their cycle. Assessments during the planning stage help determine needs and feasibility of a new program. Program monitoring during activities determines whether tasks are being completed as planned. Formative evaluations while the program is still underway measure initial progress on outcomes to see if adjustments should be made. Summative evaluations at the conclusion of a program evaluate outcomes or results.

Evaluation begins with a clear idea of what you want to achieve. You envision a certain change that you hope will happen. This change, or result, is called the outcome. You do the program, which includes certain activities or products. These elements are called outputs. Then you measure whether the anticipated change has occurred and note unanticipated results.

Evaluation doesn't need to be shrouded in mystery or jargon. It doesn't need to be complicated to be effective. This chapter explains the concepts and language of evaluation, suggests a simple, six-step process to define your anticipated results, and explains how to look for evidence that results were achieved, or not. This text prepares you to plan and implement an evaluation of a program. See the Appendix for additional instruction and worksheets.

THE LANGUAGE OF EVALUATION

Much of the mystery surrounding evaluation relates to its terminology. Common words have specific meanings in evaluation and many similar terms have subtly distinct differences. To complicate matters, evaluators sometimes disagree on what the words mean. If you consult another reference on evaluation, you may find different usage and definitions. But if you keep firmly in mind the flow from envisioning a certain change for people, through doing the program that you believe will create the change, to measuring whether the change has happened, you can cut through the thicket of vocabulary words.

Here are some key vocabulary words:

Outcomes are the specific results that can be attributed to your program. Most evaluators insist that an outcome must describe specific positive benefits to program participants. The United Way says that "outcomes are benefits for participants during or after their involvement with a program. Outcomes may relate to knowledge, skills, attitude, values, behavior, condition or status." When assessing educational programs, educators often describe the new skills or knowledge they intend their students to learn as learning outcomes.

- *Short-term outcomes* are the immediate effects of your program. For example, "Nearly all participants said they learned more than they had expected."
- *Intermediate outcomes* are effects that linger over time. "Six months after the program the majority of participants were using what they learned in their work."
- *Long-term outcomes* are lasting impacts of your program. "Participants have incorporated what they learned and improved performance is the result."

Objectives is a term used in planning to describe intended outcomes. An outcome is an achieved objective. Some planners and evaluators use outcomes and objectives interchangeably, although objectives generally refer to future, intended results and outcomes to results actually achieved. (Note that objectives are distinct from goals, which generally refer to very long-term results. However, some organizations do use the term goal to mean nearly any result, short- or long-term.)

Activities are the things you do to produce and implement your programs—raise funds, produce concerts, market events—and what program participants do to achieve your outcomes.

Outputs are the immediate products of your program activities—a concert, book, or curriculum. Outputs are not measures of changed behaviors or environments (those would be outcomes). This chapter is an output of a publications program; your learning about program evaluation is the intended outcome. (Note: Some use the term process outcomes instead of outputs to mean the immediate results of activities. To minimize confusion from equivalent terms, we use the term outputs in this text.)

> *Note*: While it may be more difficult to measure outcomes than outputs, participant benefits (i.e., outcomes) are what you ultimately aim to achieve, so that's what should be observed and reported. While it is good to know that 600 people attended the event, it is even better to know that 80 percent of a representative sample reported they valued the experience.

Indicators, sometimes called performance measures or metrics, are evidence that show the extent to which an intended outcome has been achieved. Indicators may be quantifiable (e.g., test scores, graduation rates, participation numbers, etc.), so that the evaluation results can be measured as the number or percentage of program participants who achieved the intended outcome, or performance target. Some qualitative outcomes, like audience satisfaction, may not be directly observable and may only be measurable by asking participants' opinions. Indicators can be proxies for what you cannot measure directly, providing indirect, or approximate, evidence.

> *Example*: Our intended learning outcome is that children participating in the artists' residency program will improve their self-esteem. As self-esteem cannot be observed directly, one indicator will be higher scores on the Coopersmith self-esteem test after the program compared with scores before our program. A second indicator will be new behaviors consistent with improved self-esteem, as observed by teachers over the course of the program.

Note that the first indicator in this example is readily quantifiable (test scores), and the second (changed behavior) is less so. Of course, with enough time you could ask the teacher to reflect on the behavior of each child and then quantify how many children demonstrated behaviors consistent with higher self-esteem.

As you look for indicators, ask yourself, "What does the outcome look like when it occurs? How do you know it has happened? What do you see?"

> If you think of an outcome as the answer to the question, "What change will this program make in the world?" you can think of indicators as "what would you accept as evidence?"
>
> —Lynn Griesemer, Donahue Institute

Mark Friedman, developer of Results-Based Accountability, is among those who call indicators "performance measures" and recommends that you focus on the best, most persuasive performance measures and collect data on no more than five. Picture yourself defending the performance of your program in public, perhaps before a skeptical funder or an anti-arts-funding journalist. What evidence of your program's results would be most powerful? This becomes the most important indicator for which you will collect data.

The United Way's training kit for measuring program outcomes has some additional useful definitions:

> **Outcome targets** (also called performance targets) are numerical outcomes for a program's level of achievement of its outcomes. For example, "We expect 60 percent of artist-in-business students to report improved sales after working with their mentors."
>
> **Benchmarks** are performance data that are used for comparative purposes. For example, you may compare your results to a similar program or this year's results to last year's. "We compared our staffing model with six arts producing organizations in our region with similar budgets and found our personnel costs are 4 percent lower, indicating we're well within the norm."

Milestones are significant steps or interim achievements that mark progress toward the achievement of outcomes. "We have raised 60 percent of our capital improvement target halfway through our campaign."

TWO EVALUATION MODELS

Many funders ask applicants to communicate evaluation plans according to a standard model. Two of the most common are the "logic model" and "outcome-based" evaluation.

Logic Model

There are many styles of logic models. There is no one right way. Richard Penna describes the basic logic approach this way: "If the program is what we do, and the output is the product of what we do, the outcome is what happens because of that product.... The outcome is the link between our action or activity and our mission; it is the tangible evidence that our activity is leading to our vision."

Figure 1 is a simple graphic that illustrates the logic of your program design and intended results.

To use the simple logic model in Figure 1, work backward from the intended end result. Start at the right of the model with the outcomes you wish to achieve, then determine what activities will produce those outcomes or results and then what funding and other resources are required to implement the activities. Your plan, in other words, should be logical. If you do planned activities, is it logical to expect your anticipated outcomes? Have you allowed for adequate resources to produce those activities?

Suppose that the intended result (the outcome) you want to achieve is that children learn how to analyze paintings. You believe that a new arts-integrated curriculum that includes team teaching by three teachers including the art teacher will achieve this result. To build this approach, you get the school board's and principal's blessings, and secure a grant. The funding and the go-ahead are the inputs. The curriculum and the classroom activities are the outputs. The ability of the students to analyze paintings is the outcome. Some evaluators call this your "theory of change"—your explanation of the logical connection between what you put into a program and the benefits you expect to see achieved.

The United Way and Kellogg Foundation add layers to the simple logic model shown in Figure 1. Figure 2 distinguishes between kinds of outputs and the continuity or changes in outcomes over time.

Figure 1: Simple Logic Model

Figure 2. Logic Model

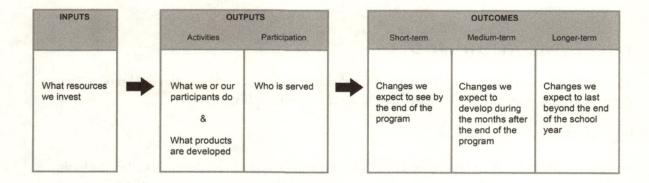

Outcome-Based Evaluation

The outcome-based approach to program evaluation compares intended short-term results (objectives) to actual results (outcomes). Outcomes should be consistent with, and advance, organizational goals. Since goals generally envision very long-term results, these are not usually evaluated.

Evaluation starts at the shorter-term level of objectives. The best evaluations define elements at the outset that will later be observed or measured for evidence that the intended outcomes were met, or not. (Evaluation can also discover unforeseen outcomes in programs.)

In Figure 3 you can clearly see the relation between planning—setting long-term goals and short-term objectives—and evaluation.

Figure 3: Outcome-Based Evaluation Framework

DEFINITION	EXAMPLE
Goal Long-term result (not subject to evaluation)	Students will get a well-rounded education with arts integrated into the curriculum.
Objective Intended results (tangible or not) projected in planning to help fulfill a long-term goal	White and Latino eighth graders in JFK School will learn mutual respect through theater project.
Indicators Predicted evidence that, if observed, will show the extent to which objectives are achieved	1. Fewer stereotypes will be mentioned in interviews. 2. Teachers observe improvement in respectful behavior. 3. Fewer disciplinary reports will be filed. 4. Play will demonstrate excellent artistic standards, appropriate to eighth graders.
Program activities Actions that implement planned arts education program	Playwright works with kids who produce their own play illustrating respect for other cultures.
Outputs Immediate products of a program	The script of the students' play, casting, and performance are immediate products, or outputs of the program.
Evaluation questions Questions about activities or outcomes to be answered in evaluation	1. Do kids describe each other with more respect? 2. Do kids demonstrate more respect? 3. Did the play demonstrate artistic merit?
Evaluation measures Observation of indicators to document outcomes	1. Pre and post-event student interviews 2. Teacher observations and reports 3. Vice Principal report 4. Critic reviews 5. Visiting artist observations and reports
Outcomes Actual results that include achieved objectives and unanticipated consequences	1. 60% of students report fewer stereotyped remarks after production. 2. Teachers report less harassment. 3. Race-based disciplinary actions down 30%. 4. Play demonstrated artistic excellence.

> ### Apples and oranges: outputs and outcomes in basic art and applied art
>
> We might debate endlessly the distinction between art for art's sake and art used to achieve some specific benefit. It is not productive here to compare which of these is more valuable. It does, however, make a difference in how we evaluate.
>
> When we present performances and exhibitions that are intended to delight or inspire the audience, we are challenged to measure intrinsic outcomes. Outcome evaluation, as described in the United Way Logic Model, specifies initial, intermediate, and long-term outcomes. Changes such as increasing understanding or ennobling the spirit are not often affected by a single exposure to art and even if they were, they would be difficult to measure. So we measure how many people we serve and how well they think we serve them. We count heads and ask opinions. Although these short-term measures may be less satisfying than understanding long-term outcomes, they may be good enough to plan and improve our art programs.
>
> In contrast, in the realms of education, social service, juvenile justice, and economic development, arts programs may be intended to influence readily observable behaviors like learning to read, staying drug-free, or getting and keeping a job. In such cases, evaluations should align more closely with the norms of outcome evaluation. If you say that your poet in the school program will help kids learn to write, or that your AIDS education theater will raise AIDS awareness, then you must demonstrate results. Schools and health educators have embraced the need to be accountable for outcomes. In arts education or community action programs managers must follow the stricter standards of accountability. In these cases it is not sufficient to measure outputs. Funders and our partners want to know how many kids improved their reading (outcome) not how many kids studied with our poet (output).

Other Evaluation Systems

If your primary funder has adopted a specific approach to evaluation, it would be prudent to learn and apply their system. In Connecticut, for example, the legislature has mandated that nonprofit organizations seeking direct state funding and final reports use the Results-Based Accountability (RBA) planning and evaluation system in their applications and final reports.

Richard Penna's *Nonprofit Outcomes Toolbox* summarizes several evaluation systems, including two with particular relevance for nonprofit arts organizations.[1]

Results-Based Accountability (RBA) uses a five-step process with specific questions arrayed in a four-square grid to guide managers through planning and evaluating programs. The questions ask, "How much did we do?" to track participants, kinds of activities, and outputs; "How well did we do it?" to monitor constituent satisfaction and activities accomplished; and "Is anyone better off?" to evaluate outcomes.

The Common Outcome Framework to measure nonprofit performance defines 14 kinds of nonprofit programs and suggests outcomes and indicators appropriate for each sector.

Preparing for the Evaluation

Before you start to evaluate a program, you should ask yourself a series of questions—the Why, What, When and Who of evaluation—and be clear about your responses.

WHY EVALUATE?

Why do you need to evaluate? There are essentially two motivations.

Evaluate to improve programs, that is, to:

- design a better program that achieves intended benefits;
- better manage the program;
- collect information to plan the next program;
- provide feedback to program participants (for instance, artists, teachers, administrators, or students).

Evaluate to be accountable, that is, to:
- report results to your director or board;
- report to program funders;
- advocate for support of your program.

Note that the need to present outcome evidence of results and the need to demonstrate persuasive evidence to support advocacy and funding may sometimes be in conflict with each other. You also have to be open to the possibility that you may not have achieved your outcomes. Funders should not expect that every funded program will work. Innovation entails risks, and stakeholders should value candid reports of what did and did not work. Learning what did not work through program evaluation is one of the benefits.

IS IT FEASIBLE?

Evaluator David Karraker starts with an "evaluability assessment"—what's involved in doing the evaluation. "As you size up the evaluation task," he advises, "consider what is involved in doing it. You don't want to evaluate a program if it's harder or more expensive to evaluate than to do the program itself! Be clear about the purpose of the evaluation. Ask where information already exists. Consider how easy it is to get and use the information. Do you have to reorganize the data? Is there some information that we can get at easily enough, well enough to make competent decisions about the program?"[2]

WHAT CAN FEASIBLY BE EVALUATED?

Which of your intended results can be observed? An observed result can be evaluated. Evaluate outcomes, not long-range goals.

You can plan to achieve profound or simple results. Many program outcomes can be readily evaluated and some cannot. In general, the more tangible the intended result, the more readily it can be observed and therefore evaluated. Intangible results, such as changed human attitudes, may also be assessed in evaluations. In this case, evidence, such as perceptions, may be sought through interviews; such indicators may suggest whether intended results have been achieved.

The United Way offers three tests to determine if you have described outcomes that can be evaluated:[3]

1. Is it reasonable to believe the program can influence the outcome in a non-trivial way, even though it can't control it?

> **Intangible Outcomes**
>
> Assume that you are doing an exhibition of contemporary Navajo rug weaving. You hope people will attend and enjoy the show and learn to better appreciate Navajo culture. You have two anticipated outcomes:
>
> ENJOYMENT
>
> Gallery visitors enjoying the show is a worthy outcome, but difficult to measure. The best way is to ask them. A volunteer could ask visitor to write comments in a guest book, hand exiting visitors a short feedback form, or ask a few questions orally. To avoid bias, volunteers should be given a protocol to ask every nth visitor—every tenth, for example. (Note that in social service programs, user satisfaction is not usually considered an outcome.)
>
> APPRECIATION
>
> For this outcome, it's easy to think of indicators. The question is whether it is feasible to collect the data. One good indicator would be that people score better on a test about the Navajo culture after seeing the exhibition than before. This is pre- and post-testing. It can be quite reliable, but may take more time, money, and visitor patience than you can muster. An alternative indicator would be that people say they learned to appreciate the Navajo culture when asked as they exit the exhibition.

2. Would measurement of the outcome help identify program successes and help pinpoint and address problems or shortcomings?
3. Will the program's various "publics"—staff, volunteers, participants, collaborating organizations, funders, and the general community—accept this as a valid outcome of the program?

WHEN WILL YOU EVALUATE?

Evaluations are done while programs are in progress (formative) in order to make adjustments while there is still an opportunity to affect the outcomes, and at the conclusion (summative) to observe what outcomes were accomplished.

- **Formative evaluation.** You should evaluate while the program is in progress, while it is still forming. Formative evaluations are often informal and are done primarily to improve programs. The program staff or volunteers typically do formative evaluations.
- **Summative evaluation.** You may need to evaluate at the conclusion of the program. Summative or final evaluations tend to be more formal and rigorous and are often done to demonstrate results in the service of accountability for funders or governing boards. They can also improve programs. They may be conducted by professional evaluators.

HOW OFTEN DO YOU NEED TO EVALUATE A PROGRAM?

You don't have to measure everything all the time. Once evaluated, a program doesn't necessarily need continuous scrutiny until something significant changes in the program, its environment, or its constituents. If conditions do not change, you can use your evaluation over time to seek funding and plan subsequent programs. You will know when things have changed enough that a re-evaluation is in order. Some program managers conduct regular participant evaluations and then less frequently do more rigorous external evaluation.

> ### A Note about Proving Impact
>
> We must recognize that our programs are just part of the many forces that act upon our constituents and communities. It is difficult to prove that a program causes a specific result. If low-income kids in your arts-education program do better in school, was it your program that made the difference or was it a parallel supplemental reading program? Even when we can't cite proof that program A caused outcome B, we can say that there is a positive correlation between our program and an observed result. In other words, we ran our arts infusion program for disadvantaged youth and we saw their grades, school attendance, and interest in learning go up. We should explore alternative explanations for the results we observe, but if we see the outcome we intended, we can cite it even if we can't conclusively prove a cause-and-effect relationship. We don't have to prove that there was no other cause of the improvement.
>
> Our observations are even more valid if we can compare this outcome with another time or place. What were these kids like before our program and after? How did our group of participating kids compare with a similar group without our arts experience? The former can be thought of as pre- and post-intervention testing. The latter proof is what evaluation researchers call control group experimenting.
>
> We know art does save lives, but can we prove it? You don't have to abandon your higher aspirations, nor must you measure every hoped-for outcome. But don't hold yourself accountable to measure your progress against these higher goals. You can aim high for your goals and evaluate more modest outcomes: Did the kids enjoy the program and would they come again?

TO WHOM WILL YOU ADDRESS EVALUATION RESULTS?

An evaluation may be serving funders, stakeholders, and partners in addition to your own interests. Different audiences may want to learn different things from evaluation and value different kinds of evidence. A parents' group may be moved by a compelling anecdote and a foundation may require experimental test results. Sometimes the same data can be reorganized to respond to the interests of different constituents. Consider who are the primary "audiences" for your evaluation: your board of directors, program participants (especially those who helped with the evaluation), funders, public officials, and news media.

WHO CONDUCTS THE EVALUATION?

Often program managers undertake evaluations of their own programs. Internal evaluations have the advantages of economy, first-hand knowledge, and expedience. In addition, evaluation skills are cultivated within the organization and lessons learned can be implemented immediately. A disadvantage is that self-evaluation presents the risk of bias. An evaluation consultant may be perceived by funders and other stakeholders as more reliable and unbiased. This is more costly, but may yield more credible results. Whether or not you employ an outside evaluator, you must be clear about your program's intended outcomes for your evaluation to be meaningful.

WHAT IS THE EVALUATION BUDGET?

It is best to budget for evaluations by estimating each expense. See the Financial Management chapter for advice on budgeting. ▌ Rules of thumb and agency policies allow from 1 to 20 percent of a program's budget for evaluation, depending upon the scope and rigor of the evaluation plan. If you use

> **More Difficult Outcomes to Measure**[4]
>
> *If your contact with an audience or constituent is short-term, you won't be able to determine changes over time.* We don't have the advantage of a social service provider who sees a client over time or a school that can track individual students over years. If your outcome will take a long time to achieve, you will most feasibly look for short- or intermediate-term outcomes that suggest progress on your longer-term results. If your outcomes are intangible you will use qualitative measures. See Rubrics, page x.
>
> *If your outcomes require someone else to act (advocacy, technical assistance, community organizing, grant making) you are not directly responsible for the intended outcomes.* Service organizations and funders are challenged by the fact that their interventions are indirect. You award a grant to achieve a program outcome, but it is up to the grant recipient to implement the funded projects. In these cases you may measure outputs (e.g., we awarded $150,000 in grants to 20 agencies) and note progress toward achieving your outcomes.
>
> *If your programs are intended to improve a community, region, or state it may be difficult to demonstrate that a single program influences a wide geographic area.* Your cultural tourism website may intend to increase visitors to the region, but it would be very expensive to ask visitors why they chose to visit unless you build this question into research undertaken by a state tourism agency. You may need to be content to count numbers of visits to your website as an indication of interest.
>
> *If your programs aim to prevent a problem, it is difficult to measure events that did not occur.* If your youth writing program intends to keep kids safe from drug abuse or violence, how can you tell if the kids avoided these risks? Control-group experiments with a similar group of kids would work, but if your budget is modest, you may have to rely on testimony from the kids about their attitudes or observations from their teachers about apparent behaviors.
>
> *If your program intends multiple outcomes*—for example, a single program might generate a series of benefits for kids, for their parents, and their community—then you might choose one or two of these outcomes as the focus for your evaluation.

an outside evaluator, this cost may be the single largest expense. If you integrate evaluation into the program design, a do-it-yourself evaluation need not be expensive. While funders value evaluations of results, many are wary of high overhead expenses.

PROGRAM MONITORING

Program monitoring or documentation is the reporting of activities and outputs—what managers and participants did in a program. When funders request evaluations, they sometimes get descriptions of tasks and activities instead. These are valuable functions that can inform evaluations, but they do not measure results, as outcome-based program evaluations do.

Undertaking the Evaluation

Having made the decisions outlined in the previous section, it's time to begin the evaluation process. That process can be divided into four steps:

1. Design the evaluation plan
2. Collect the data
3. Analyze the data
4. Report the results

Figure 4. Evaluation tasks plan[5]

Goal. Integrate the arts into JFK Middle School curricula.

Intended outcomes	Indicators	Data sources	Data collection methods
1. Teachers will learn to develop arts-infused lesson plans	Plans will have more arts sections than before	Teacher lesson plans	Meet with teachers and review lesson plans
2. Two artists in residence will help students learn their local history unit through story telling.	Higher scores on standard tests for participating students compared to similar classes	Scores of tests designed to measure student learning for this curriculum standard	Gather scores from participating classes and from comparable group without residency
3. Arts curriculum specialist will be hired by August	Employment will occur, line item in budget for position	Principal and school budget	Call principal

STEP ONE: DESIGN THE EVALUATION PLAN

The tasks to planning for evaluation are:

- Re-state your long-range goal to provide context
- Write your intended outcomes or objectives (tangible and intangible)
- Determine indicators (evidence)
- Identify the source of evaluation data
- Describe the methods to collect evaluation data
- Assign evaluation tasks

You may summarize your evaluation tasks with a sheet like the one in Figure 4 for each of your program's intended outcomes. These tasks are described in greater detail (complete with worksheets and guidelines) in the Evaluation Planning Workbook, found in the Appendix.

STEP TWO: COLLECT THE DATA

You should aim first to use readily available information and then plan to collect new data.

By first identifying existing sources of information, such as those described below, you can make evaluation easier—and save both time and money. This baseline data can be used to compare your results with the situation before your program existed, or to compare your program constituents to a more general population and look for improvements. Program partners, such as schools and social service or health agencies, may also provide a ready source of data on their constituents.

There are many places you can seek existing data:

- Your own records: attendance, sales, annual reports, community assessments done for strategic planning, previous evaluation reports.

- Your grant records: proposals, interim and final reports, grant-review panel scores and comments.

- Partner records: for instance, if your partner is a school, it will have data such as attendance records, scores for standardized tests, grades, disciplinary actions, reports of assessments, studies, evaluations, or plans.

Even if you use existing information, it is likely that you will need additional material that relates to your specific outcomes. You have at least three options. You can design experiments, plan to observe directly, and ask questions of participants.

Experimental Designs

The use of control groups, longitudinal studies, and other scientific methods that carefully examine cause-and-effect relationships are more common in scientific and medical research than in arts-program evaluations, primarily due to higher personnel costs relative to other forms of evaluation. However, experiments do have the potential to be more rigorous and persuasive, so they are worth considering, but they must be built in during the early planning stages of the program. The challenge is to design an experiment that controls the many variables of cause and effect—for instance, how can you be sure that improved racial tolerance is the result of your theater program and not another factor like parental influence?

Here are four experimental designs you might consider using:

- **Pre- and post-tests** evaluate changes within a group over the course of your program. You administer a test that measures attitudes, knowledge, or skills related to your intended outcomes before the program begins, and again at its conclusion. If your tests are accurate, then measured improvements represent positive evidence that you are achieving your outcomes. Because of its relative simplicity, this is probably the most common experimental design for program evaluation.
- **Portfolio examination** is a fairly common evaluation method for visual arts and writing programs. Examinations are conducted by qualified persons who review and note changes in student visual artwork or writing over the course of the program, or note differences in the work produced by students participating in the program and those not participating. Using rubrics (see below), this method can also be readily applied to programs that produce presentations, recitals, performances, or other products that can be observed.
- **Control group studies** compare some aspect (indicator) of the program in an experimental group with the same aspect in a closely comparable group that does not participate in the program being evaluated. So if you were developing health-awareness theater programs for a group of at-risk teens, you would identify another group of teens outside the program. Control group evaluations are simpler to design if you have access to existing information that may serve as an indicator of outcome achievement. For example, it is relatively easy to determine if your arts program improves standard test scores or school attendance in your experimental school compared to a similar school without your program. Look for indicator data that your partners routinely track.

- **Longitudinal studies** track an experimental group of participants over time. Because some arts program outcomes may only be realized over several years, a longitudinal study might provide the most effective evaluation. For this kind of experiment, you would follow a specific group of individuals and measure one or more indicators at specific intervals over time. For arts program evaluations, this may be most feasible with contained populations such as a class of school children or residents of a retirement home or correctional facility. Longitudinal studies are relatively rare in the arts because they involve so much time and expense, but using existing data collected by your partner institution makes this evaluation design more feasible than if you observe or interview your sample over many years.

Observation

This method may be overlooked since it's so obvious, but it is quite common to employ observation in program evaluation. Most arts managers routinely use observation to monitor whether their programs are working or not. The risk, of course, is that evaluations based on simple observations may not be valid if care isn't taken to maintain rigor and avoid bias. Observations may be conducted by participants or an outside evaluator, or you may observe indirectly by asking questions of participants.

Participant observer. Any knowledgeable participant in a program can be recruited to help evaluate as a participant observer. Teachers, artists, or program coordinators may be oriented to the task of systematically recording observations about the effects of the program.

An external funder may be skeptical of an evaluation based on observations by participants who have a stake in finding positive outcomes. To counter this risk and to be effective, you should develop a rubric or other measurement checklist, along with a research protocol that prescribes when and how observations are to be recorded.

Outside observer. You may employ a professional evaluator who observes the program and documents results, which may be more credible than a participant observer, but also will likely increase your expenses.

Indirect observation. You may choose to observe indirectly to save costs, to protect privacy of participants, or to avoid any effects on the program caused by the presence of observers during the program. A portfolio review is a kind of indirect observation. Other indirect observation tools include:

- Photo, video, or audio documentation of process and/or results. These can be also advocacy and fundraising tools, if the program is successful.
- Journal writing: students or other program participants record their thoughts and observations in personal journals, which are reviewed by knowledgeable persons to answer one or more evaluation questions.

Rubrics. Observation becomes a more reliable method to evaluate programs if you use rubrics to rank what you see against a scale of pre-determined indicators. Teachers frequently use rubrics to evaluate student learning and a quick Internet search will yield examples for most disciplines. A rubric is a simple chart that compares level of performance against standards, which may be expressed as dimensions or criteria. If you've ever taken a child in pain to a clinic, you may have seen a pain rating scale, which is a kind of rubric (see Figure 5). Even children who cannot yet speak can point to the face that represents their level of pain, allowing a nurse to report a quantitative rating to an intangible feeling.

Figure 5: Example of a Visual Rubric

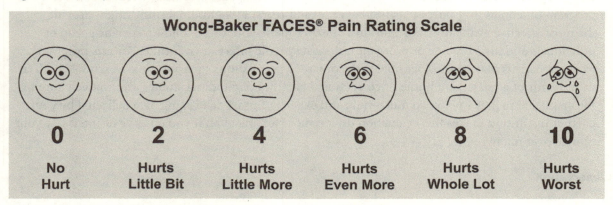

To create a rubric, design a grid in a table on your computer or a spreadsheet with columns to indicate a three- or four-point performance scale, then rows that indicate the dimensions (or criteria or standards) by which you will evaluate performance. The National Education Association describes four parts to a rubric: "1) the task description, 2) the levels of performance, 3) the dimensions (criteria), and 4) the description of the dimensions."[7]

To use the rubric, the observer watches the student performance and/or audience reaction and circles or notes the score of the description of the criteria that best matches each observed behavior in the rubric. An event can be evaluated with a score for each performance dimension and a single, total score. This is how judges convert their observations of a dance competition or an athletic competition into a single score. An artist in residence can do the same thing with her students' learning of acting skills.

Figure 6: Rubric Template

Task description					
	Levels of performance (scale)				
CRITERIA		4. Exceeds evaluation criteria	3. Fully meets criteria	2. Somewhat meets criteria	1. Fails to meet criteria
		Describe criterion	Describe criterion		
	Criterion 1				
	Criterion 2				
	Criterion 3				

> ### Sampling
>
> We must digress a bit into statistical science. When you talk to just a few people in the program you're evaluating, there is a risk that your evaluation may be biased if those people differ in some significant way from others in your program whom you didn't talk with. You should therefore understand the distinction between a population and a sample.
>
> If you observe all events or interview everyone who participated in your program, evaluation is easier because you are contacting the whole population for your program. This makes for a thorough evaluation with no risk for statistical error. But this can be too time consuming, expensive, or unfeasible for large populations.
>
> Most evaluation observes some of the programs and/or asks questions of some of the participants. The evaluators sample the population of activities and participants. If the sample is representative of the whole population, conclusions drawn from the small, observed group will be true of the larger group. The evaluation will be free from sampling errors. Errors occur when the observed group differs in some significant way from the larger population. For example, if you only interview people who volunteered to help with evaluation, you risk a sampling error by missing people who are less prone to participate. You minimize the risk of sampling bias by being deliberate about the people you question.
>
> #### SAMPLING METHODS
>
> - Random sample: Pull names from a hat, or number each participant; obtain a list of random numbers from a statistics book or computer program and sample the corresponding numbers from your population.
> - Systematic sample: Select every tenth (or third or whatever) name or event.
> - Segmented or stratified sample: Group your population into similar clusters (i.e., by age, artists and teachers, etc.) and then select a random or regular-interval sample from each cluster.
> - Deliberate sample: Intentionally select individuals from the population to make the mix of your sample representative of the whole population.

Figure 6 is a template that you can use; Figure 7 is an example of how a teacher might grade a class using this template.

Ask questions

Asking questions of participants and recording their answers is another kind of indirect observation. Questioning is perhaps the single most common way to collect new information to evaluate a program. You have lots of choices, from oral interviews and group meetings to written evaluation forms and surveys. These can be as simple as a phone conversation with a member of your audience or as sophisticated as a stratified sample survey. (See the Strategic Planning chapter ▮ for more information on asking questions. As you will note, many planning methods are useful in program evaluation as well.)

See Conducting Interviews in the Appendix for more information on interviewing.

Moderated group discussions (focus groups of participants and expert panels of observers). Group discussions are more efficient than one-on-one interviews because one conversation taps the opinions of as many as ten or so people. Group interactions may also lead to richer information than single interviews through productive interactions among participants where one person's comments stimulate others to contribute related ideas. In some settings, however—particularly when people of differing

Figure 7. Simple Grading Rubric for Online Course[8]

	Performance Indicators				
Objective/Criteria	Exceeds minimum expectations (Letter grade = A)	Exceeds minimum expectations (Letter grade = B)	Needs improvement (Letter grade = C)	Does not meet minimum expectations (Letter grade = D)	No participation (Letter grade = F)
Written Assignments and Exams	○ (4 points) EXCELLENT level of analysis that applies course concepts to case study organization. Paper demonstrates the student has learned the assigned principle or task. Student's original work responds fully to the assignment. Papers are presented professionally, clearly and on time.	○ (3 points) THOROUGH level of analysis. Would be A level work except lacks either supporting evidence from course lectures and readings, professional presentation, and/or original thinking. Student responds fully to assignment. Paper is posted on time.	○ (2 points) BASIC level of analysis or did not fully respond to assignment. Paper may be poorly organized or containt significant grammar or spelling errors.	○ (1 points) SUPERFICIAL level of analysis, minimal effort, or paper is late and downgraded accordingly. Student does not respond fully to the assignment or provides incomplete or missing answers.	○ (0 points) No posting, posted late*, failed to revise returned work, work is plagiarized. (*See syllabus for policy).

rank or social status within a hierarchical organization are meeting together—some people may be more cautious and less candid in group discussions and may be inhibited to share critical information.

- Select a representative sample.
- Set a date and place and allow from 60 to 90 minutes.
- Invite enough people to have about eight to ten in the discussion.
- Offer an incentive to participate (food is good).
- Develop a short list of questions—could be the same as your interview guide.
- Choose someone to moderate the discussion—preferably not the note-taker.
- Take notes and/or record the discussion.
- Summarize results.

Public meetings (facilitated meetings of parents, neighbors, or other constituents the program intended to impact). Public agencies may be obliged by law to evaluate their programs or overall efforts using open public forums.

Evaluation forms and surveys. Written questions and answers to evaluation forms or survey questionnaires may be the most efficient way to sample opinions from large numbers of constituents. Think of these as written interviews. Unlike interviews, however, you cannot clarify answers that don't make sense or probe for deeper answers. Evaluation forms are often collected on-site at the time of a program and may be shorter than surveys, which may be conducted online, mailed, or conducted by phone interviews after a program.

Evaluation forms. The evaluation form must be short and simple and the questions clear. You can ask two kinds of questions: open-ended questions that request a narrative answer, and fixed-response questions for which the respondent checks a box or circles their choice among a number of prepared answers. A good evaluation form includes both kinds of questions to combine the flexibility of narrative answers and the expedience and economy of fixed responses. (See the Strategic Planning chapter for examples of open-ended and fixed-response questions.) ▌

Evaluation forms are often handed out to participants at the conclusion of a program. Instructions can be repeated orally and the evaluator can answer questions about the evaluation form. Because they are often administered within the program itself, evaluation forms must be very concise, as time will be limited.

Your evaluation questions should ask if your outcomes have been realized. One way to do this is to paraphrase the outcomes you seek to measure and ask to what extent these have been realized. For example, "How confident are you, after our workshop, that you could evaluate your arts program? This approach is quite clear and direct and works with both open-ended and fixed-response questions, but does risk that people will say what they think you want to hear. You may also miss results that you did not anticipate in your fixed-response questions. A less directed approach is to ask people to simply describe what resulted from their experience with your program and compare their answers with the outcomes you intended. This has less risk of bias, but requires open-ended questions and may generate lots of information unrelated to your intentions.

Surveys. Written surveys are a simple way to distribute evaluation forms to small or large groups of people and collect their responses. Online surveys seem largely to have replaced mailed questionnaires, as the latter require a cover letter, a paper survey, envelopes, and postage, followed by data entry of responses. Web-based surveys allow for many kinds of questions. The best of the commercial and free versions are simple to set up and use, and lead you through a process to design fixed-response, scaled answers, fill-in-the blank, and open-ended questions.[9] Then you can send an announcement to your email list, social media friends and followers, and post on your website. Recipients of your email message are linked to a website where they can view the survey and submit their answers online.

With an online survey, you don't need to do any data entry. These e-survey applications also summarize responses and allow you to import raw data into a spreadsheet, word processor or statistical program to do further analysis. However, surveys are complicated enough that you may wish to seek professional help. While many online surveys look easy and you may be tempted to do it completely yourself, ambiguous or incorrectly asked questions can skew or invalidate your findings. Evaluation consultants, marketing or social science faculty, graduate students or planners could help with your survey.

See the Appendix for a checklist on designing and implementing a printed survey.

Sample Program Evaluation Form

1. What was the best part of the program?

2. What could have been improved?

3. Did you learn what you had hoped?
   - ☐ Yes, very much, ☐ Yes, somewhat,
   - ☐ No, not very much, ☐ No, not at all

Please rate with a check mark your ranking of each of the program components.

Insert intended program and learning outcomes	Extremely well	Well	Fairly well	Poorly	Comments
How well did the program [insert an intended outcome]….					
How well did you learn [another outcome]…					

Additional comments:

ALTERNATIVE FORMAT FOR QUESTIONS

Did you _____? [insert learning outcome(s) from evaluation plan]
☐ Yes, very much, ☐ Yes, somewhat, ☐ No, not very much, ☐ No, not at all

Did the program meet _____? [insert program outcome(s)]
☐ Yes, very much, ☐ Yes, somewhat, ☐ No, not very much, ☐ No, not at all

STEP THREE: ANALYZE THE DATA

Evaluation data comes to you mostly in numbers, words, and sometimes images. If your data is primarily numeric, you are doing quantitative research. This has historically been considered the most credible form and is the domain of statistics. If your evaluation data consists of anything other than numbers—words, portfolios, etc.— you can call your evaluation qualitative research. As you will see, these labels are overlapping insofar as you can also quantify common elements within qualitative data.

You can do some simple analysis without statistical training. Alternatively, the following brief summary should prepare you to seek statistical analysis from your evaluation consultant or friendly college faculty member.

Quantitative analysis

The overall process in quantitative analysis is to reduce the bulk of data, to display it, to analyze the results, and to decide what it means.

Reduce the data. To analyze numeric data, you first have to reduce the information into summary form. If you collected data with an online survey, much of this is done automatically. If you have 150 paper surveys, evaluation forms, or test scores, you must summarize this information. The low-tech way is to manually count the number of responses in each fixed-response category and record the results. Tick marks on a blank evaluation form are a low-tech way to keep track until you type up the summary.

Setting up a spreadsheet and entering the data from each completed form simplifies the process. Typically, spreadsheet programs allow for summing, averages, and simple statistical analysis. For more sophisticated analysis, you may export the finished spreadsheet into a statistical analysis program. Some analyses, such as cross tabulations (see below), are much simpler with statistical programs.

Display the data. Now, present the key trends or results, using graphs or charts as appropriate.

Analyze the results. Trends or results may be revealed by doing mathematical and statistical calculations for quantitative data. These include:

- Counting responses: For example, "12 artists completed evaluation forms." "240 kids participated in the program."
- Calculating mean or average: "The artists had, on average, 15 years' experience." "The average residency was 10 days long."
- Calculating the median: "While the average was 15 years' experience, the median experience of participating artists was 10 years." When there are a few very large or very small numbers in a group, sometimes the median number (the midpoint of a set of numbers, half of them above and half below) represents that group better than the mean.
- Looking for patterns: "There were two groups of artists, those with significant teaching experience and those without."
- Noting most frequent responses: "Most often artists reported they learned more than they had expected."
- Doing cross tabulations: "All of the six artists who had not previously taught in classrooms said they would readily do so again." Select responses from one variable (new teaching artists) and compare to another variable (willingness to teach again). This can be done slowly by manual sorting, but is simple with an online survey or statistical program. Performing statistical significance tests: "While

students preferred painting to sculpting by a slight margin, the difference was not statistically significant." If you are asking questions of a sample rather than the whole population, be aware that some differences may be so small that they could be the result of chance. Pollsters describe such differences as being within the margin of error. You may want to search for an online margin of error calculator.

Informal evaluations probably don't need statistical significance testing. But if you skip this step, be wary of making too much of small differences in your findings, especially if your sample is small. So if 20 percent of your sample said they learned a lot and 24 percent said they learned a little, you may not be able to say with confidence that more learned than didn't. You don't have to worry if you have asked questions of the whole population of program participants. Significance testing only applies to samples within larger populations.

Decide what the numbers mean. Now you can determine what all of this is telling you, and what should be done with the program in light of these results.

Qualitative analysis

Analyzing content is similar to analyzing numbers. You reduce textual data to summary form, analyze the contents of the texts, and report the results.

Much of arts program evaluation information is gathered from interviews, focus groups, and written answers to open-ended questions. The results are expressed in words. Pages of notes may be intimidating, but it is possible to boil these down into a credible summary with content analysis. This analysis will still be subjective, but it is possible to rigorously analyze written data. Just as in numerical analysis, the bulk of text must be reduced, analyzed, and reported to be useful for evaluation. Researchers who do a lot of content analysis may use text analysis software. There are simple online word and phrase counters and more sophisticated academic and commercial text analysis programs. If you are associated with a school or university, check to see what site licenses are available.

The Appendix has instructions for manual content analysis.

STEP FOUR: REPORT AND USE RESULTS

Evaluation results must be communicated if they are to do any good. Formal evaluations should be reported in writing. Be clear about your intended audience. Potential readers of the evaluation report may include your own director or governing board, key partners, funders, your program staff and volunteers, constituents, program participants, or outside decision-makers like school board or city council members. Select typical quotes or anecdotes to make your results more meaningful.

> A study of Massachusetts state legislators who authorized funding for arts programs found that most legislators wanted evidence of results with both anecdotes and quantitative data.[10]

Tailor the message and format to your intended audience, possibly creating different versions. You will not distort results, but you may stress different findings for different readers. Your board of directors or funders may want to see that you achieved your outcomes. A school board member may want to see findings about student learning. Your partners may want to see, in addition to this information, if and how the program may need to change.

Evaluation becomes most useful when it is used. Evaluation results can be used to:

- improve programs;
- plan future programs;
- make decisions to cut or add programs;
- allocate resources among competing programs;
- be accountable;
- provide solid information for advocacy and fundraising; and
- improve program or organizational marketing.

Conclusion

This chapter opened by acknowledging that evaluation has become a common expectation. You may have read this chapter because someone has required you to evaluate your program. Whether or not it is a requirement, evaluation has real power to help you run better programs that make a positive difference for your constituents and community.

If your programs are working well, evaluation gives you credible evidence. You can use this evidence to win support for your programs and to educate funders and others about your program achievements. If evaluation shows that your programs are not having the impact you intended, the evidence gives information to help fix what is not working. You may either improve the programs or design new ones.

Evaluator David Karraker has said, "Evaluation can make you feel better about your work, in that you can be grounded and clear in what you intend to do and actually do. Even when things don't work as you hoped, you know where you stand. Better find that out before you spend more time and energy doing more of what doesn't work. Then you can develop some strategies to improve it. Clarity is better than ambiguity."

Outline of an Evaluation Report

Cover page

Acknowledgements: funders, partners, program participants, evaluators

Table of contents

Executive summary

Evaluation methods

Evaluation findings (results of statistical and/or content analysis)

Recommendations

Appendix

    Evaluation questions

    Interview and survey forms

    Copies of program descriptions and materials

Appendix

Evaluation Planning Workbook

CONDUCTING INTERVIEWS

Most people have experience with interviews, so this is the easiest way to ask questions. Yet, for credible evaluation results, you must approach interviews with care. First, determine your sample. Ask yourself whom you will interview. If you are doing interviews and focus groups, consider who might best be heard individually or in a group. You may want to interview leaders or other designated spokespeople for groups (for instance, the president of the neighborhood association) or you may interview a representative sample of the group itself (for instance, a random group of neighbors).

Next, determine the questions you will ask. Ordinarily you will ask simple, conversational questions at the outset and work toward more challenging questions. It is good to start with some factual questions, like "Would you please tell me what the program looks like?" to get the conversation going. Then ask tougher questions, like "What worked well?" and "What could have been improved?"

Prepare an interview form that lists your questions, for consistency among different interviews. Your form may provide a space to summarize answers or just prompt you as you take notes. If you take extensive notes you will want to summarize key points on the interview form. This is particularly important if more than one person will be doing the interviewing. You might add prompting questions that you can use if your interviewee is reticent. For example for the question "What could be improved?" some interviewees will go on at length about problems with the program. Others may need prompting questions such as "Knowing what you know now, what might you have done differently?" or "Where were the problems?"

For the most accuracy, you may audio- or video-record the interview, transcribe it, and then summarize. You may find that this is more time-consuming and expensive than just taking notes during the interview, but it is more accurate. Research has documented that interviewers tend to hear what they expect and disregard contrary information. An alternative to recording is to have two note-takers who then compare their notes to reach a common understanding.

Conducting an interview

1. Determine sample of participants to interview
2. Schedule interviews
3. Develop an interview guide of evaluation questions
4. Ask your questions:
5. Explain why you are asking questions and what will be done with the information
6. Promise anonymity (and keep that trust!)
7. Ask for permission to take notes or record the conversation
8. Ask and/or observe and record demographic questions (age, gender, race, etc.)
9. Ask your program-evaluation questions, starting with simple descriptive inquiries ("What did you do?") and move toward more subtle questions ("How did you feel?")

10. Listen well
11. Probe as needed to clarify answers or elicit more details
12. Take notes
13. Thank the interviewee

Summarize the interview on a form such as this:

Interview Guide

Program _____

Interviewee _____

Interviewer _____

Date of interview _____

Hi, I'm _____ from _____. I understand you took part in the _____ program.

I'm asking a few students some questions to help us learn how well the program worked and how we can make it better. Would you have a few minutes to talk? Thanks (If not, schedule a later time).

I'll report what you say but won't report who said it. OK?

Question 1.

Question 2.

Question 3.

Printed and Mailed Evaluation Survey Checklist

1. Select a sample that represents the population (random, systematic, or deliberate)
2. Design the questionnaire
3. Keep survey to one page
4. Test the questionnaire on a small sample and correct any ambiguous questions
5. Print and distribute
6. Send with brief cover memo that explains why and requests response
7. Enclose self-addressed return envelope—a stamp improves response
8. Follow up with reminders (if you want a good return)
9. Collect surveys
10. Code open-ended questions
11. Enter survey responses into a computer spreadsheet or statistical analysis program (or summarize responses by counting various responses with tick marks on a blank survey form)

12. Make sense of the results (statistical analysis of numbers and content analysis of texts)
13. Summarize and write report of findings

How to Do a Manual Content Analysis of Texts

1. Gather the summarized interview or focus group notes or the evaluation forms with narrative answers. (If each interview or focus group meeting is not summarized into a page or two, you should do this first.)
2. Read over the answers to one particular question in all of the evaluation forms or summary notes.
3. As you read, look for patterns and make notes of recurring answers or themes.
4. You can copy and paste a section of text into an online word or phrase counter to help identify key words. Just note that these words are not put in context, so "good program" and "bad program" will count as two references to the word "program" but with opposite meanings.
5. Make a short list of words or phrases that capture the sense of each recurring answer. Label each of these items with a word, number, or letter to create a code sheet. If several interviewees cited artistic quality as a problem, then "quality" becomes a category and perhaps you will choose "Q" to be your code.
6. Read back through the answers again and code similar statements (for instance, code every mention of a concern for artistic quality as "Q"). Some people use numbers, so that "quality" concerns would be coded 1, "funding" problems coded 2, etc.
7. Count coded items and note your results.
8. Select typical quotes to make your results more meaningful.
9. Write up your findings, citing numbers and using representative quotes. "Sixteen survey respondents, or 20 percent, noted artistic quality was a big concern. One teacher expressed a typical sentiment: 'Even as we strive to improve standard test scores, we can't ignore the quality of the artistic experience. It is the high quality of the arts process that gives this program the power to help kids learn.'"

Resources

The American Evaluation Association's website has a resource section with links to online evaluation how-to manuals. http://www.eval.org/

Animating Democracy Toolkit. Tucson Pima Arts Council and Americans for the Arts, 2011. http://www.tucson-pimaartscouncil.org/

Animating Democracy. *Resources for Evaluating the Social Impact of the Arts.* http://animatingdemocracy.org

Anita M. Baker, Evaluation Services website. http://www.evaluationservices.com

Anita Baker and Beth Bruner. *Integrating Evaluative Capacity into Organizational Practice: A Guide for Nonprofit and Philanthropic Organizations and Their Stakeholders,* The Bruner Foundation, 2012. http://www.evaluativethinking.org/docs/Integ_Eval_Capacity_Final.pdf

Kelly Barsdate, *A State Arts Agency Performance Measurement Toolkit.* National Assembly of State Arts Agencies, 1996.

Deborah Bedwell, "Measuring Joy: Evaluation at Baltimore Clayworks," in Outcome-Based Evaluation: A Working Model for Arts Projects, National Endowment for the Arts, FY 2004 NEA Grants for Arts Projects: Outcome-Based Evaluation. http://isites.harvard.edu/

Richard A. Berk and Peter H. Rossi. *Thinking about Program Evaluation 2.* Sage Publications, 1999.

Bond, Sally, Sally Boyd, and Kathleen Rapp. *Taking Stock: A Practical Guide to Evaluating Your Own Programs.* Chapel Hill, NC: Horizon Research, 1997.

John Boulmetis and Phyllis Dutwin. *ABC's of Evaluation: Timeless Techniques for Program and Project Managers.* San Francisco, Jossey-Bass, 2000.

Bruner Foundation. Effectiveness Initiatives, evaluation web portal. http://www.evaluativethinking.org/

Boston Youth Arts Evaluation Project Workbook, 1st edition. Boston Youth Arts Evaluation Project and Raw Art Works, Massachusetts Cultural Council. http://www.massculturalcouncil.org/services/BYAEP_Workbook.pdf

Suzanne Callahan, *Singing our Praises: Case Studies in the Art of Evaluation.* Washington, DC: Association of Performing Arts Presenters, 2005.

Mary Campbell-Zopf, *Strategic Evaluation. Focusing the Light: The Art and Practice of Planning,* vol. 4. Ohio Arts Council, 2008.

Institute of Museum and Library Services. Outcome Based Evaluation Basics. http://www.imls.gov/applicants/outcome_based_evaluations.aspx Accessed 2/10/2015

National Endowment for the Arts. Program Evaluation Resources. http://arts.gov/grants-organizations/art-works/program-evaluation-resources

Shaping Outcomes. Online course in outcomes-based planning and evaluation. http://www.shapingoutcomes.org/

Brian M.Stecher, and W. Alan Davis. *How to Focus an Evaluation.* Newbury Park: Sage Publications, 1987.

W.K. Kellogg Foundation, Evaluation Handbook, 1998. Free at http://www.wkkf.org/

W.K. Kellogg Foundation Logic Model Development Guide, 2006. Free at http://www.wkkf.org/

Endnotes

1. Cited by Robert M. Penna in *The Nonprofit Outcomes Toolbox: A Complete Guide to Program Effectiveness, Performance, Measurement, and Results,* (2011), p. 69.

2. United Way of America, *Measuring Program Outcomes: A Practical Approach,* 1996, p. 62.

3. United Way of America, *Measuring Program Outcomes, Training Kit,* 1996.

4. Ibid., p. 19.

5. Penna, op. cit. For more information about RBA evaluations, see resultsaccountability.com. For more information on the Common Outcome Framework, see the Urban Institute, www.urban.org or the Center for What Works, www.whatworks.org.

6. David Karraker, personal contribution to this chapter.

7. United Way, *Measuring Program Outcomes, Training Kit.*

8. Adapted from United Way, *Measuring Program Outcomes: A Practical Approach,* pp. 76-78.

9. Adapted from a framework developed for the Arts Extension Service by David Karraker and Dyan Wiley. http://www.umass.edu/aes/learningpartners/index.htm

10. Donna L. Wong, Marylyn Hockenberry-Eaton, et al., *Wong's Essentials of Pediatric Nursing,* 6th ed. (2001).

11. The Do It Yourself Rubric, http://www.nea.org/home/34451.htm

12. For simplicity, this grading rubric illustrates just one criterion. In practice, other criteria such as class discussion and final presentations are included in the rubric.

13. See, for example, surveymonkey.com. Simple surveys can be conducted free, while more complex surveys require a subscription. Some customer-relations management systems like SalesForce.com or Constant Contact also have survey capabilities.

14. Massachusetts Cultural Council, *Creative Economy Program Plan Recommendations & Analysis* (Arts Extension Service, 2008).

15. Personal communication to the author.

Contributors

TOM BORRUP has been a leader and innovator in nonprofit cultural and community development work for over 25 years. Based in Minneapolis, Tom consults with foundations, nonprofits, and public agencies across the United States. He has written many articles for publications in the arts, city planning, and philanthropy. His book, *The Creative Community Builders' Handbook,* was published in 2006 by Fieldstone Alliance. It tracks communities that have transformed themselves through the arts, and includes a how-to guide. In 2002, Tom was a Fellow in the Knight Program in Community Building at the University Of Miami School Of Architecture. As executive director of Intermedia Arts in Minneapolis from 1980 until 2002, he developed a nationally recognized cross-disciplinary, crosscultural organization in a diverse urban community. Tom has served on many boards—including the Jerome Foundation, the National Alliance for Media Arts and Culture, and Appalshop— as well as funding and policy panels, for numerous funding institutions. He teaches for the Graduate Program in Arts Administration at Saint Mary's University of Minnesota, and for the Institute for Arts Management at the University of Massachusetts. He received his B.A. in Liberal Arts and M.A. in Communications and Public Policy from Goddard College and his Ph.D. in Leadership and Change at Antioch University in 2015.

DENISE BOSTON-MOORE, PH.D., is an educator, consultant, and expressive arts specialist. She earned her Ph.D. in counseling psychology from Walden University, M.A. in psychology from Goddard College, and a B.F.A. in theater at the North Carolina School of the Arts. Boston-Moore specializes in play therapy, expressive movement, and mixed media. She has conducted numerous workshops and training programs for parents and professionals, as well as rites of passage adolescent training programs for urban youth.

DEE BOYLE-CLAPP is the Director of the Arts Extension Service (AES) and teaches in AES's online and on-campus arts management degree and certificate programs, leads training programs in artist in business, entrepreneurship and public art, and is a consultant for artists and nonprofit arts programs. Dee is a sculptor, installation artist and has over 25 years of experience in the arts, teaching studio, art history and arts management courses at UMass, museum schools, and community colleges. She teaches Introduction to Arts Management, Arts Entrepreneurship, Fundraising and Greening Your Nonprofit Arts Organization, a course she created, and is the co-editor of the 6th edition of the Fundamentals of Arts Management. Dee is the co-founder of the Arts Entrepreneurship Initiative and oversees the National Arts Policy Archive and Library, a collection of 50+ years of arts policy materials from the NEA, AFTA, TAAC, NASAA and independent arts policy advocates. She has a long history in community arts and was a founding member and the first director of the Art Bank community arts center, and was program coordinator for the Fostering the Arts and Culture Partnership Creative Economy project, and co-owned the Artemis Gallery. Dee holds bachelor's degrees in art and art history from the University of Wisconsin at Madison, an MFA in Sculpture from UMass Amherst, and a Master's in Nonprofit Management from Regis University in Denver. She is a member of the Leadership Council for MASS Creative and is on the board of the Pioneer Valley Creative Economy Network.

MAREN BROWN is the Principal of the arts management consulting firm, Maren Brown Associates, which consults on arts planning and evaluation with a wide range of clients nationwide, including state, regional, and national arts agencies, as well as performing arts organizations embedded in colleges and universities. She is the co-founder of the University of Massachusetts' arts management degree program with the University Without Walls, and has developed and taught a variety of subjects in the program. Brown is the co-editor of the 5th and 6th editions of Fundamentals of Arts Management. She is a national expert on arts partnership development and has co-authored two workbooks on the topic, and delivered training and consulting to thousands of arts practitioners and civic leaders on this subject around the U.S. She is also the co-founder of the National Arts Policy Library at the University of Massachusetts, with collections from the National Endowment for the Arts and Americans for the Arts, among others. Prior to her work as an arts management consultant, Brown worked for over two decades as an arts management practitioner. Brown holds an MBA from the University of Massachusetts and is a nationally-certified human subjects researcher.

CHRISTINE D. BURDETT is an administrator, consultant, and educator in the nonprofit sector. She is development director at the Center for Children and Families in Norman, Oklahoma. Tina is also an instructor in the Master of Arts in Arts Administration program at Goucher College in Baltimore where she teaches the distance learning course Financial Management of the Arts. Tina's background in the arts includes community arts development with local arts agencies, statewide assemblies, and national service organizations.

DOROTHY CHEN-COURTIN, PH.D., is an independent marketing and management consultant for nonprofit organizations. With a background in both the for-profit and nonprofit sectors, she adapts best practices from the forprofit sector in her work with nonprofits. Her clients include national and regional foundations, state art commissions and art councils, as well as performing and visual arts organizations and museums. A frequent speaker on management and marketing issues nationwide, Dorothy is also a regular contributor of articles on the subject. She developed the arts marketing module for the distance learning course on arts management for the Arts Extension Service. She is a board member of the Arts Extension Institute, The Bostonian Society, Fruitlands Museums, and the Herald Tribune World Youth Forum Association. A Barnard College graduate, Dorothy earned a Ph.D. in oriental art history from Columbia and an M.B.A. from Northeastern.

JUDITH CONK is an educator who has taught and administered at all levels of education from preschool to graduate school for more than forty years, working in urban and suburban school systems as a Principal, Assistant Superintendent and Superintendent, where she won recognition for outstanding educational programs that recognized the individual in each student. Judy retired from administration to devote more time to supporting creative teaching and learning. She is principal of *Consulting for Results,* and works with national and international clients spanning Pre-K to University level and concentrates on leadership, teaching and learning, and the arts. Judy is a speaker, author and educator trainer, and works on topics such as infusing the arts into the content classroom, school change, leadership development, assessment, staff development, instructional strategies, and multiple intelligences in the classroom. She has worked extensively with schools in the area of curriculum development to meet the needs of students and has served on a variety of state and national panels in aligning standards with classroom practice. Judy received a Governor's Award in Arts Education as Outstanding Superintendent of 2001 and has served as Chair of the Kennedy Center Alliance for Arts Education Network, and President of the Alliance for Arts Education/NJ. She continues to serve on the Board of Directors of various arts organizations. In May of 1996, she was awarded the prestigious Distinguished Service Award for Educational Leadership from the New Jersey Association of School Administrators, recognizing her work as an advocate for a high quality education for every child.

CRAIG DREESZEN, PH.D., directs Dreeszen & Associates, a consulting firm in Northampton, Massachusetts. Craig provides planning, evaluation, teaching, facilitation, and research for nonprofits, foundations, and public agencies. He is an educator, consultant, and writer who works nationally with arts and other community organizations on organizational development and strategic planning, collaborative planning, program evaluation, and community cultural planning. Craig earned his Ph.D. in planning and his M.ED. in organizational development at the University of Massachusetts Amherst. He is author of books, articles, and courses on planning, board development, arts education collaborations, and program evaluation. Craig directed the Arts Extension Service for 12 years.

MARYO GARD of Gunnison, Colorado, provides an array of services to the nonprofit world in general, and the community arts world in particular, through keynote speaking, writing, consulting, training, and teaching. Her specialty is community development and the arts—the linking of the arts to the furthering of broader community ends. She is especially interested in the history of community arts development, and increasingly her work focuses on this history and its implications for community arts workers today. Maryo began her 40-year community arts career working in The Arts and the Small Community project in rural Wisconsin—the first rural arts award ever made by the National Endowment for the Arts. She has worked for community arts councils in Connecticut, and for state arts agencies in Illinois and Colorado. She currently serves on her local arts center and community foundation boards, among others. Recent honors include the 2004 Arts Advocate of the Year award from the Gunnison Arts Center; the 2003 Arts Are the Heart award for service to the arts in Colorado; and, in 2001, an honorary doctor of humane letters degree from Goucher College. Maryo received the Selina Roberts Ottum Award from Americans for the Arts—its highest award for community arts development—in 1995.

GAY POWELL HANNA, PH.D., is the executive director of the National Center for Creative Aging, and was the former executive director of the Society for the Arts in Healthcare (SAH), an interdisciplinary membership organization dedicated to the integration of the arts into healthcare. Through faculty positions at Florida State University and University of South

Florida from 1987 to 2002, Gay directed VSA arts of Florida, providing arts education programs for people with disabilities, including people with chronic illness. In 2001, she established the Florida Center for Creative Aging at the Florida Policy Exchange Center on Aging at the University of South Florida. A contributing author to numerous articles and books, Gay is noted for her expertise in accessibility and universal design. In addition, she is a practicing artist who maintains an active studio with work in private and corporate collections through the Southeastern United States. Gay holds a Ph. D. in arts education with a specialization in arts administration from Florida State University; a M.F.A. in sculpture from the University of Georgia; and a B.A. in studio art from Old Dominion University.

CAROL HARPER is a consultant with more than 30 years' experience in management, finance, and economic development in the arts and cultural nonprofit, for-profit, and public sectors. She has served as financial consultant to EmcArts, grants advisor to the Massachusetts Cultural Council, director of the NonProfit Finance Fund Massachusetts office, and program director for the Massachusetts Department of Housing and Community Development as well as Director of Planning and Community Development for the Town of Franklin, Massachusetts. She began her career as a commercial lender with Bank of Boston, spending more than a decade managing a multimillion dollar loan portfolio and mergers and acquisitions in both national and international markets. Carol has an MBA from Boston College's Carroll School of Management and a BA from Mount Holyoke College.

DAN HUNTER is the former executive director of the Massachusetts Advocates for the Arts, Sciences, and Humanities, a statewide advocacy and education group. An award-winning playwright, songwriter, and humorist, Dan also has more than 20 years of experience in politics and arts advocacy, serving as director of the Iowa Department of Cultural Affairs (a cabinet appointment requiring Senate confirmation) and running a successful advertising and political consultancy firm in Des Moines, Iowa. Dan is the author of two books, *Let's Keep Des Moines a Private Joke* and *The Search for Iowa (& We Don't Grow Potatoes)*. He has written several plays, including *Un Tango en La Noche,* winner of a Kennedy Center Short Play Award, and *The Monkey King,* a finalist for the 2004 Heideman Award from the Actors Theatre of Louisville. He has performed a one-man show of topical humor in original song and has made numerous radio and television appearances (ABC's *Good Morning America,* National Public Radio, BBC, and CNN *Nightly News*). Dan earned his B.A. from Hampshire College, his M.A. in creative writing from Boston University, and an honorary doctor of humane letters from Goucher College.

LISA KAMMEL is an arts consultant with an M.A. in arts administration from Florida State University. After completing her graduate degree, she spent four years working in North Carolina at the United Arts Council of Raleigh and Wake County and the Southeastern Center for Contemporary Art in Winston-Salem. Lisa returned to Florida where she worked with Arts for a Complete Education, with the VSA arts of Florida as a fundraising consultant and program coordinator for Putting Creativity to Work, and as a program specialist in the School Choice Office at the Florida Department of Education on research and public outreach with charter schools.

NORTON J. KIRITZ was the founder and president of the Grantsmanship Center. In 1971, he left his position as director of planning for Los Angeles County's anti-poverty agency to establish the Grantsmanship Center. His goal was to help community groups, nonprofit organizations, and public agencies that hoped to start programs or keep them alive, but lacked the know-how to make the potential benefits clear to donors. In the next three decades, Norton built the Center into the world's best-known training center for fund development and nonprofit program planning. In 2000, the California Community Foundation described his text, *Program Planning and Proposal Writing,* as "the proposal writer's bible." As president of the Grantsmanship Center and publisher of the organization's quarterly magazine— which has a circulation of more than 200,000 nonprofit and government agencies worldwide—Norton influenced the careers of nonprofit executives and the field at large. Norton passed away in 2006.

PAM KORZA co-directs Animating Democracy, a program of Americans for the Arts that inspires, informs, promotes, and connects arts and culture as potent contributors to community, civic, and social change. She co-wrote *Civic Dialogue, Arts & Culture,* and the *Arts & Civic Engagement Tool Kit*. She co-edited *Critical Perspectives: Writings on Art & Civic Dialogue,* as well as the five-book *Case Studies from Animating Democracy*. She has consulted and offered workshops and presentations on arts and civic engagement for artists, cultural organizations, funders, and at cross-sector gatherings across the country and in China and South Korea. Pam is co-chair of the Assessing Practices in Public Scholarship research group for Imagining America (IA), a consortium of colleges and universities that advances public scholarship in the humanities, arts, and design and was a two-term member of IA's National Advisory Board. As a consultant, Pam has partnered with Barbara Schaffer Bacon in organizational planning, program design and evaluation for cultural organizations, state arts agencies, and private foundations. As an independent consultant, her activities have included organizational assessment for a children's initiative by internationally renowned book artist Eric Carle, evaluation of a citywide arts festival and published report commissioned by the Indianapolis Arts Council and the Lilly Endowment Inc., planning with the Maine Arts Commission for expanded artist services, and consultation with individual artists. She began her career with the Arts Extension Service where she coordinated the National Public Art Policy Project and co-wrote and edited *Going Public: A field guide to developments in art in public places*. She also directed the New England Film & Video Festival.

ROBERT L. LYNCH is president and CEO of Americans for the Arts, which is dedicated to advancing arts and arts education in every American community. With over 40 years of experience in the arts industry, he has guided the services and membership of Americans for the Arts to grow to more than 50 times their original size. Nationally, Mr. Lynch serves on the Independent Sector Board of Directors and has served two terms on the U.S. Travel and Tourism Advisory Board, a position appointed by the U.S. Secretary of Commerce. For three consecutive years, the *NonProfit Times* selected him as one of the most influential executives in the sector. Mr. Lynch earned a bachelor's degree in English from the University of Massachusetts-Amherst, and plays the piano, mandolin, and guitar. He lives in Washington, DC.

HALSEY M. NORTH and **ALICE H. NORTH** jointly head The North Group Inc. Since 1987, they have been assisting nonprofit arts agencies, theaters, performing arts centers, and arts service organizations with fundraising feasibility studies, capital and endowment campaigns, annual operating campaigns, solicitor training, strategic planning, board development and retreats, cultural planning, organizational assessments, business plans, and workshops on fundraising, board development, and planning. Halsey is the former executive director of the North Carolina Arts Council, the Charlotte Arts & Science Council, and New York City's Cultural Council Foundation. He has also been vice president of C.W. Shaver & Company and corporate contributions manager of Philip Morris Companies.

Alice is a former investment banker. Halsey and Alice are both M.B.A.s and, between them, have received the Distinguished Service Award from the North Carolina Association of Arts Councils, the Chairman's Award from the National Assembly of Local Arts Agencies (now Americans for the Arts), and the Fan Taylor Award from the Association of Performing Arts Presenters.

STAN ROSENBERG is a 1977 graduate of the University of Massachusetts, Amherst, where he majored in arts management and community development. As a student, he founded the Arts Extension Service, an arts service organization dedicated to encouraging the use of the arts as a tool for social change and leadership development among artists and arts organizations. Stan has served in the Massachusetts legislature since 1987, first as a state representative and, since 1991, as a state senator. Among the Senate positions he has held are member, Committee on Education, Arts and Humanities, and leadership posts including assistant majority leader and president pro tempore of the State Senate. Stan became Senate President in 2015. He has been the author and chief legislative strategist for a number of pieces of arts legislation, including an endowment incentive program, annual appropriations battles, and the recently approved cultural facilities program, a $500 million public private partnership to improve cultural facilities throughout the Commonwealth of Massachusetts. Stan has continued to serve as an arts consultant specializing in board retreats, strategic planning, and arts advocacy.

BARBARA SCHAFFER BACON co-directs Animating Democracy at Americans for the Arts. Co-author of *Civic Dialogue, Arts & Culture: Findings from Animating Democracy,* Barbara has written, edited, and contributed to several publications, including *The Cultural Planning Work Kit* and *Fundamentals of Local Arts Management*. She served for 13 years as executive director of the Arts Extension Service at the University of Massachusetts at Amherst. Consulting work includes program design and evaluation and arts management education for state and local arts agencies and private foundations nationally. Projects include a five-year plan for the New York State Council on the Arts, a twenty-year review of the North Carolina Arts Council's Grassroots Arts Program, and cultural plans for Northampton, Massachusetts and Rapid City, South Dakota. A University of Massachusetts graduate, Barbara is a board member of the Fund for Women Artists and currently serves as a member of the Massachusetts Cultural Council. She is president of the Arts Extension Institute, Inc..

SHIRLEY SNEVE is director of radio and television at Vision Maker Media (formerly Native American Public Telecommunications), where she directs the television production fund and the AIROS Radio Network. NAPT supports the creation, promotion, and distribution of Native public media. She moved to Nebraska from Amherst, Massachusetts, where she was director of the Arts Extension Service from 2001 to 2004. A member of the Rosebud Sioux Tribe in South Dakota, Shirley was a founder of Northern Plains Tribal Arts Juried Show and Market, the Oyate Trail cultural tourism byway, and the Alliance of Tribal Tourism Advocates. She has been the director of the Washington Pavilion of Arts and Science Visual Arts Center in Sioux Falls, assistant director of the South Dakota Arts Council, and minority affairs producer for South Dakota Public Broadcasting. Shirley has been adjunct professor in Native American Studies at Augustana College and the University of Sioux Falls, and a community cultural planning consultant. She is a graduate of South Dakota State University. Graduate work at the Universities of South Dakota and Massachusetts focused on management, community building, and the arts. Shirley serves on the boards of the Arts Extension Institute and The Association of American Cultures (TAAC).

SARAH SUTTON leads Sustainable Museums, a consultancy helping the staff and leadership of cultural and natural resource organizations plan for a more sustainable future. She and her team work with zoos, gardens, museums, aquariums and historic sites to identify and fund greener approaches in programs, operations, and building and site management. She has worked with the Minnesota Historical Society, Peoria Riverfront Museum, Strawbery Banke Museum, Detroit Zoological Society, and the United Keetoowah Band's John Hair Cultural Center. She has been in the museum field for over thirty years as a grant writer, and has consulted on sustainability for the last decade. She is leading the movement to establish environmental sustainability as a Characteristic of Excellence in museum practice. Sarah is the author of Is Your Museum Grant-Ready? Assessing Your Organizations' Potential for Funding, Environmental Sustainability at Historic Sites and Museums, and The Green Nonprofit: The First 52 Weeks of Your Green Journey. She is co-author, as Sarah Brophy, of both editions of The Green Museum: A Primer on Environmental Sustainability.

MARETE WESTER, M.S., is director of arts policy information at Americans for the Arts. Previously, she was an arts management writer and consultant, and served as executive director of Dance New Jersey. While at Dance New Jersey, she instituted the first strategic planning and fundraising efforts aimed at building organizational capacity for web-based marketing and technical assistance services. She tripled the organization's membership by positioning Dance New Jersey as the state affiliate of the National Dance Education Organization, uniting dance educators with professional companies and artists under one umbrella. She serves as adjunct professor for arts administration in Seton Hall University's Graduate Department of Public and Healthcare Administration, and as an online instructor for the Arts Extension Service. In addition to authoring the chapter on arts education in *Fundamentals of Arts Management*, she has written several monographs published by Americans for the Arts. Marete has been executive director of the Alliance for Arts Education/New Jersey, acting program specialist for presenting organizations at the National Endowment for the Arts, and associate director of program operations at the Staten Island Council on the Arts. She holds a B.A. of music performance degree from Wilkes University, Pennsylvania, and an M.A. in arts administration from Drexel University.

SALLY ZINNO was a consultant who worked with leaders of arts and cultural organizations and their funders to strengthen governance, management effectiveness, and financial results. She was a senior associate with National Arts Strategies (formerly National Arts Stabilization), where she directed the Columbus, Ohio, stabilization project. Before starting her consulting practice, she directed the administrative and financial operations at the Delaware Art Museum and the Harvard University Art Museums, and was the chief administrative officer at the Boston Museum of Science. She taught graduate courses in nonprofit administration and finance at Harvard, George Washington, and Tufts Universities. Sally passed away in 2005.

About the Arts Extension Service

The Arts Extension Service (AES) develops the arts in communities and community through the arts with professional development and education for arts managers, artists, and civic leaders.

AES achieves its mission through the following programs and services

The Arts Extension Service's award-winning classes, workshops, and training programs are designed to meet the needs of artists, arts managers, board members, local arts agency staff and others interested in working to develop the arts in their community. A pioneer in online education, AES translated its *Fundamentals of Arts Management* text into a comprehensive series of Web-based courses that can be taken towards a Certificate in Arts Management, and in 2007, created the nation's first (and only) online Bachelor's Degree in Arts Management through the University Without Walls. AES offers one- or multi-day workshops and intensive trainings for artists anywhere in the country interested in learning artist-in-business skills or how to run a public art project.

COURSES, DEGREES AND CERTIFICATES

For local, national and international online students, AES offers the nation's only online Bachelor's Degree in Arts Management, several non-credit certificates in arts management, and an à la carte menu of single offerings to expand one's skills and knowledge base or to earn CEU's.

For the UMass campus community AES offers an exciting array of arts management and arts entrepreneurship courses, an Undergraduate Certificate in Arts Management and arts entrepreneurship and art-skills programming, as well as an internship program that bridges the community's artists and arts nonprofits with arts students.

ARTS ENTREPRENEURSHIP INITIATIVE

The Arts Entrepreneurship Initiative works to advance our region's culture, community and creative economy by supporting artists and their businesses through an escalating offering of services and trainings that build skills, cultivate relationships and strengthen ties between students, artists, community leaders and the University.

Artists in the Pioneer Valley of Western Massachusetts are not only professionals, often holding multiple degrees and having decades of experience in the creation of their work, but they are potent economic drivers in their communities. The Arts Entrepreneurship Initiative helps artists and arts-based businesses benefit from their participation in the creative economy by providing the skills to help them thrive. These programs include: courses, workshops and professional development trainings, internships, and consulting.

CONSULTING

Launched with the Arts Entrepreneurship Initiative, the Arts Extension Service's artist-staff members serve as consultants for artists seeking to launch or expand their businesses. Through a network of independent consultants, the Arts Extension Service offers an array of services for the field, including its Peer Advising Network Training Program. The program, offered throughout the United States in response to the increasing need for management assistance services of those with limited financial resources, trains members of the community arts field to provide management, program consulting, and training to their peers in community arts organizations.

PUBLICATIONS

AES publications provide practical information and tools for arts management and community cultural enhancement. AES has developed a variety of publications of value to arts administrators, educators, students, economic development specialists, artists, municipal officers, cultural advocates, regional and urban planners, civic leaders, tourism officials, and human service organizations. These highly practical books are written by working practitioners in the field who have a wealth of experience to share and include Partners in Creative Economy, Arts Festival Work kit, and Going Public: A Field Guide to Developments in Art in Public Places.

SPECIAL PROJECTS

The field of community arts is in a state of constant flux and change, and the Arts Extension Service is continually developing new courses and training programs that respond to the most urgent developments in the field.

Index

Note: Page numbers in *italics* indicate figures.

A

accepting volunteers, 281
accessibility
   comprehensive plan for, 417–419
   definition of, 406
   of programs, 341, 363
   See also accessibility and inclusion; cultural access
accessibility and inclusion
   building inclusive communities, 411–416
   difference in ability, 403–404
   funding issues, 428
   overview of, 429
   universal environment, 421–428
accessibility coordinators, 417
accessibility symbols, 418, 427
accountability
   of board, 166
   era of, 458
   objectives and, 131–132
   program evaluation and, 465
   of schools, and ESSA, 438
accounting methods, 304
accounting procedures, 304–305
accounting software, 303
accrual basis accounting, 304
actions
   of board, monitoring and following through on, 177
   definition of, 133
activities, definition of, 459
ADA. *See* Americans with Disabilities Act
Adams, John, 73, 76
adaptive challenges, 119–121, *120,* 153
Addams, Jane, 7, 9
ad hoc green teams, 323
ad hoc task forces, 189
administrative consolidations, 186
adults with disabilities, community day programs for, 416
advertising
   data from, 394
   as marketing expense, 224
advisory group of persons with disabilities, 418
advocacy
   for arts education, 440–441
   by board members, 211
   to businesses, 76–77
   campaign strategy and timeline example, 92–93
   continuum of activities, 90–91
   creating messages, 82–83
   definition of, 72
   designing campaigns, 83–84
   to foundations, 76
   goals for, 79–80, 82
   IRS limits on, 72–73, 88–90
   knowing elected officials, 84–85
   making specific requests, 81–82, 85–86
   to media, 77
   meeting elected officials, 85–86
   networks for, 78–79
   one-to-one, 77
   as part of daily mission, 87–88
   setting agendas, 80–81
AES planning process. *See* Arts Extension Service (AES) planning process
after-school/out-of-school movement, 445–446
age-appropriate activities, 449–450
agenda
   for advocacy campaign, 80–81
   for board, *174,* 174–175
aging population, 404, 415–416
Albrechts, Louis, 60
alcohol, permits for, 365
Allison, Michael, 115, 148
all-or-nothing concept of crowdfunding sites, 264–265
all-volunteer organizations
   governing responsibilities in, 171
   organizational structures for, 188
Alternate ROOTS, 189
American Association of Museums, 417
Americans for the Arts
   Animating Democracy program, 4, 11
   Arts Education Field Guide, 442, 445, 455
   Arts Education Navigator, 451
   National Arts Index, 127
   Policy Wheel, 108, *108*
   Prosperity Index, 79
   2012 Arts and Economic Prosperity Study, 102
Americans with Disabilities Act (ADA)
   ongoing obligations of, 410
   overview of, 406–407
   readily achievable and undue burden terminology in, 409–410
   resources on, 410
   technical local and state accessibility assistance requirements, 407
   Title II, 408, 419
   Title III, 408–409
   welcoming visitors, 409
annual report and fundraising, 204
annual work or operating plans, 122, *123*
Appendix section of grants, 250–251
application programming interface (API), 249
applications for artists, 354
appreciated securities, gifts of, 221
Appreciative Inquiry, 119
approve and commit stage of planning, *136,* 152
Art and Creative Materials Institute Inc., 328
Art Garden, Shelburne Falls, 260
artistic boards, 189
artistic dividend, 18
artistic policies, 179
artist live/work projects, 26–27
artists
   culturally-specific work of, 363
   definitions of quality and, 352–353
   extended or return engagements for, 359–360
   finding and selecting, 354–356
   interpreting work of, 360–361, 362
   program design and planning and, 345, 356
   "teaching artists," 453
   working with, 356–358
ArtPlace America
   origins of, 21
   Vibrancy Indicators, 63
arts
   benefits of, 18–19, 73–74
   connecting audience and, 358–361
   cultural life and, 339
   engaged, 11–12
   fundraising for, 200–201
   isolation of, 9–10
   philosophy of program and, 340
   in schools, history of, 433–439
   universal environment for, 421–425
   See also arts education; arts policy
Arts Culture Trade (ACT) Roxbury, 56
arts education
   advocacy for, 440–441
   after-school/out-of-school movement and, 445–446
   community involvement in, 439–440
   community needs for, 442, 445–446
   designing program for, 447–449
   ESSA and, 436–438

evaluation of organization and, 441–442
exploring feasibility of program for, 447
overview of, 431–433, 453–454
as policy issue, 103
preschool movement and, 446
in public schools in Massachusetts, 74
reflecting on results of planning for, 451
research in, 438–439
student-centered curriculum for, 449–451
for students with disabilities, 412–413
teachers for, 451, *452,* 453
Arts Education Partnership, 439, 446
arts excellence and community-building work, 4
Arts Extension Service (AES), 489–490
Arts Extension Service (AES) planning process
approve and commit stage, 152
assess stage, 140–144
decision making stage, 144–150
envision stage, 137–139
evaluate and adapt stage, 154
implement stage, 153–154
organize stage, 135–137
overview of, 134–135, *136*
write plan stage, 150–152
arts materials, greening, 328
arts policy
federal, 105–106
influence of, on social policy, 104
overview of, 95–97, 110
of U.S., 102–105
See also cultural policy
arts service organizations, as sources of data, 384. *See also* local arts agencies; state arts agencies
Arvold, Alfred, 7, 9, 10
Asian Arts and Culture Program, University of Massachusetts Amherst, 360
asking questions for program evaluation, 473–476, 480–482
assessment
of community needs for arts education, 442
definition of, 133
of energy use, 321
of fixed assets, 293
of need for volunteers, 274
of online fundraising personnel, 254–258
of opportunities for environmental sustainability, 323–325
of place of culture in ecology, 41–42
of readiness for creative placemaking, 66–67
as stage of planning, *136,* 140–144
of threat, 368
of websites, 255–257
See also critical issues from assessment; evaluation
asset-based approach
to community building, 18, 35–40
to creative placemaking, 57–58
to planning, 118–119
Asset-Based Community Development, 57–58
assistive listening devices, 425
Association of Science and Technology Centers, 428
associations, presentations to, 107
assumptions, 130

attitudinal access, 406
audience
connecting art and, 358–361
marketing and, 381–387, *382*
philosophy of program and, 340
for program evaluation reports, 478
for programs, 344–345
research on, 382–387
audience development, 3, 385–387
audio description/narration service, 424
audits, 313–314
authenticity of culturally-specific work, 362–363
Authorize.net, 259

B

Baeker, Greg, 59–60
Bedoya, Roberto, 53
beliefs, terms describing, 130
benchmarking, 141
benchmarks, definition of, 460–461
benefits (events) for fundraising, 208
bequests, 222
blindness, improving access for, 425–426
blogs, 108
board development
building sense of team, 173–174
changing governing structure, 184–190
clarifying governance responsibilities, 169, 169–171, *170*
conflict management, 177–178
flexible approach to, 163–164
helping members understand roles, 171–173
improving effectiveness of current team, 168–184
keys to, 190
meeting management, 174–177
orientation, 182–183
policy development, 178–179
president, role of, 179–180
recruiting members, 180–184
resources on, 190
retaining members, 183–184
strategies for, 168
Board Development Profile Grid, 180, *195*
board manuals, 182–183
boards of directors
accountability of, 166
approval of budget by, 296
approve and commit stage of planning and, 152
characteristics of, 187
chief executives and, 192
expectations of, 167–168
as fiduciaries, 289
financial management and, 166–167, 290–291
fundraising and, 201–202, 210–211, 218
leadership of, 167
profiling personnel needs, 193–194
responsibilities of, 135, 164–167, 172, 192–193
role of, 163
Self-Audit Worksheet, 442, *443*
See also board development
BoardSource, 165, 174, 186, 187
Bonamici, Suzanne, 437
bookkeeping, 304
Booth, Eric, 453
Bowling Alone (Putnam), 17–18, 29, 54–55

Boyne City, Michigan, 31
Bradford, Neil, 54
Brain, David, 19
brainstorming, 142
branding, 391–392
Braslow, Laura, 29, 64–65
Bridges, William, *Managing Transitions,* 173
Brophy, S., 330
Brownell, Baker, 8, 10
budget
boards and, 166
cash-flow, 292, 301, *302*
development of, 292
expenses, estimating, 300–301
facility planning, 298
linking plans to, 150
marketing, 386, 393, 400
of NEA, 97, 104
organizational, 292, 294, *295–296*
overview of, 291
for planning, 137
preparing, 294, 296–297
for program development, 346–349
program evaluation, 468–469
purpose of, 291
replacement of fixed assets, 292–294
revenues, estimating, *299,* 299–300
as type of plan, *123,* 124
types of, 292
Budget section of grants
nonpersonnel, 248–250
personnel, 246–248
building permits, 365
building retro-commissioning, 325
burnout of volunteers, 285
businesses
advocacy to, 76–77
contributions from, 208, 224–225
business plans, *123,* 124
Buy Local campaigns, 30, 331

C

calls for proposals, 354
candidate forums, 107
capital budgets, 292
capital changes, planning to go green, 325–326
captioning, 424–425
Carver, John, 98, 99, 109, 170, 191n6
Case, Jennifer, 325
case for giving, 204, 217
cash basis accounting, 304
cash-flow budgets, 292, 301, *302*
cash-flow statements, 311, *312*
cash gifts, 221
cash transactions, recording, 305
Catterall, James, 432, 439
CDCs (community development corporations), 20–21
census data, evaluating, 36
Center for Cultural Exchange, *African in Maine* program, 353
Chait, Richard, 164, 180
change
community organizing and, 4
in core practices for greening organizations, 328–331
in governing structure, 190
program evaluations as measuring, 457
See also transition

channels, marketing
  identifying best, 388–392
  types of, 388
charitable contributions to nonprofit arts organizations, 72, 75
charitable foundations, 76
charitable gift annuities, 222
charitable lead trusts, 222
charitable remainder trusts, 222
chart of accounts, 305, *307*
Chautauquas, 6, 9, 10
chemical and finishes inventories, 324
chief executives
  boards and, 192
  role of, 167, 170, 172, 185, 188
City Beautiful movement, 5, 10
civic aesthetics movement, 5–6
Civil Rights movement, 10
closed captioning, 425
coalitions of arts organizations, 189
collaboration
  in community building, 43–44
  institutional, 185
collaborative plans, *123,* 126, 128–129, 156
collections care, greening, 330–331
collective efficacy, 30
College Board, Arts at the Core Advocacy and Education Initiative, 432
Comer, Virginia Lee, 6–7
commodification of traditional culture, 363
Common Core State Standards Initiative, 435
Common Outcome Framework, 464
communicating with elected officials, 85–87
communication access, 406, 423–425, 427–428
community
  arts education and, 439–440
  arts education needs of, 442, 445–446
  boards as representing, 167
  definitions of, 3, 16–17
  elements in health and sustainability of, 18
  identity of, 24, 38
  inclusive, building, 411–416
  philosophy of program and, 340
  program choices and, 361
  See also community-building work; community organizing
community and economic development, resources on, 32–33. *See also* economic development
Community Asset Inventory, 38, 45
community-building work
  arts excellence and, 4
  assessing place of culture in ecology, 41–42
  asset-based approach to, 18, 35–40
  collaborating across sectors, 43–44
  overview of, 48
  partnerships for, 44–45
  paying for, 45–46
  principle of, 54
  readiness checklist, 47
  role of "intermediary," 42
community capacity building strategy, 29–30
community centers, 7
community concerts, 6
community cultural plans, *123,* 126–127

community day programs for adults with disabilities, 416
community development
  creative placemaking and, 55–57
  culture in, 20–21
community development corporations (CDCs), 20–21, 55–57
community interviews, 143
community organizing
  definition of, 3–4
  examples of, 11–12
  headwaters goals for, 10–11
  history of, 5–9
  ways for arts organizations to lead, 12–13
CompassPoint Dual-Bottom Line Matrix, 148, *149*
competitive pricing, 378–379, 380
competitive research, 385
conflict management, 177–178
conflict over planning, 129
consent agenda, 175
consolidations, 186
consultants
  choosing, 157
  deciding to use, 156–157
  in grant proposals, 248
content analysis of texts, 482
contingency plans, *123,* 124
contracts with artists, 357
contributions
  from artists, 357
  from national corporations, 209, 224–225
  to nonprofit arts organizations, 72, 75
  recording and reporting, 305
  tax deductions for, 220–221, 262
  See also funding
control group study, 470
controversial work, 97, 361–362
Cooper Hewitt Museum, New York, 361
Cooperrider, David L., 119
Coreth, Mark, 334
Corporation for National and Community Service, 280
corporations. *See* community development corporations; national corporations; nonprofit corporations
correctional arts programs, 414–415
cost-based pricing, 378, 380
cost of going green, 319
costuming, greening, 328–329
cover letters, 239
Covey, Stephen, 153
Coyne, Jacque, 415
Creative CityMaking Program, Minneapolis, 60
creative class, 17, 18, 62
Creative Community Builder's Handbook (Borrup), 22, 36
creative economic plans, *123,* 127
creative economy
  background on, 17–21
  definition of, 15–16
  sustainable, 61–62
creative industries, 61–62
creative placemakers, characteristics of, 57
creative placemaking
  assessing readiness and getting started, 66–67
  as emerging field, 55
  inclusive approach to, 65–66

  listening to and gathering stories, 58–59
  making or producing space, 52–55
  outcomes and measures, 63
  overview of, 51–52
  preparation and ongoing practice, 67
  principles and outcomes of, 52
  processes and practices of, 61–62
  sustainability, unintended consequences, and, 64–66
  sustainable creative economies, 61–62
  tools of, 55
  traditional community planning and development and, 55–57
creativity and leadership, 432
"critical friends," network of, 445
critical issues from assessment
  identifying, 144
  resolving, 147
Critical Links, 439
critical questions, defining, 146–147
CRM (Customer Relationship Management) system, 258–259, 376
crowdfunding, 264–266
cultural access
  ADA and, 406–410
  inclusion and, 404
  philosophy of, 405–406
  process for, 416–421
  as social justice, 404
  terminology for, 406–410
cultural advocacy. *See* advocacy
cultural democracy, 8–9
cultural heritage tourism, 25–26
cultural identity, 421
culturally-specific criteria for quality, 352–353
culturally-specific work, 362–363
cultural policy
  of agencies and organizations, 100–101
  characteristics of, 98–99
  culture in, 97
  in law, 99–100
  overview of, 95–97, 110
  in plans, 100
  stated and actual, 101
  See also arts policy
culture
  assessing place of in ecology, 41–42
  community development and, 20–21
  creating healthy places and, 19
  in cultural policy, 97
  definition of, 17, 58, 97
  economic development and, 22–32
  as public benefit, 73–74
  See also cultural access; cultural policy
curriculum for arts education, 449–451
Customer Relationship Management (CRM) system, 258–259, 376
customer-segment pricing, 379
cycle of planning, 125. *See also* marketing cycle

D

Dang, Steven, 56, 58, 60
dashboard reports, 175, *176*
data analysis for program evaluation, 477–478
data collection
  for marketing evaluation, 393–394
  for program design, 447–448

for program evaluation, 468–475, *472*, *473*–*476*, *474*
date for programs, choosing, 346
Davis-Dubois, Rachel, 8–9, 10
deafness, improving access for, 426
decision making in board meetings, 175–176
decision making stage of planning, *136*, 144–150
de facto U.S. arts policy, 102–105, 110
deferred maintenance issues, 293
de Gaulle, Charles, 71
departmental green teams, 323
depreciation, 293, 297
designing programs
    arts education, 447–449
    finding and selecting artists, 354–356
    policies, 350, 352
    quality criteria, 352–354
    working with artists, 356–358
designing websites for online fundraising, 258–259
developmental disabilities, improving access for, 426
Devi, Ranjanaa, 360
differential pricing, 379
difficulty of going green, myth of, 318
disability
    definition of, 407
    participation from persons with, 419–421
    See also accessibility
disability access symbols, 418, 427
Disability and Business Technical Assistance Center, 407
disability awareness, 425–428
distinctive assets, 376–377
distribution methods for products and services, 376
diversity, recruiting and involving volunteers for, 276–278
documenting
    board decisions, 176
    interviews, 481
    priorities and decisions when planning, 149
    programs, 369–370
    reflective practice and, 451
donations. *See* contributions; fundraising
donors
    acknowledging, 219
    developing, 206
    files on, 218, 258–259
    green options for, 332–333
    identifying, 199
    lists of prospective, 215
    methods of individual giving, 221–223
    needs of, speaking to, 198–199
    online, 266–267
    reasons for giving of, 200–201
    researching prospective, 215–216, *236*, 263
    rewards for, 265
    thanking, 212, 237
    top, appeals to, 262
    written acknowledgment of contributions from, 220–221
Donor Tools, 249
Drummond, Alexander, 7, 9, 10
DSIRE.org database, 333
Duany, Andres, 19
Duncan, Arne, 103

duty of care, 165, 166
duty of loyalty, 165
duty of obedience, 165

E

earnings gap, 313
economic development
    based on cultural assets, 32
    creative placemaking and, 61–62
    culturally driven strategies for, 22–31
    culture and, 22
    researching local and regional economies, 37–40
economic diversification strategy, 27–28
economic impact studies, 79
economy, culture, and communities, 17–18
education system, tiers of influence on, *455*
effective interdependency, 3
Eisenhower, Dwight D., 125
elected officials
    knowledge of, 84–85
    support from, 208–209
electrical permits, 365
electrical plug inventories, 324
email
    CRM system for, 259
    metrics, 394
    testing subject lines, 261
email lists for fundraising campaigns, 259–260
Emanuel, Rahm, 116
emergencies
    accessibility and, 423
    during programs, 367–368
emergent planning, 126, 127
employee matching gifts, 224
end-of-year giving, 262
energy audits, 321
Energy Efficiency Community Block Grants, 333
energy service companies (ESCO), 320, 332–333
engaged arts, 11–12
entry fees for artists, 357
Environmental Protection Agency, 328, 333
environmental sustainability
    assessing opportunities for, 323–325
    choosing materials for, 327
    overview, 317–318
    standards for, 325
    See also "greening" organizations
envision stage of planning, *136*, 137–139
equipment costs in grant proposals, 248–249
ESCO (energy service companies), 320, 332–333
ESSA (Every Student Succeeds Act), 436–438
evaluate and adapt stage of planning, *136*, 154
evaluation
    of accessibility efforts, 418, 419
    of arts education feasibility, 447
    of arts education in organization, 441–442
    designing into arts education program, 447–448
    of fundraising capacity, 207–210
    of marketing strategies, 392–397
    of products and services, 375–377

    of quality, 352–354
    of volunteers, 287
    See also assessment; program evaluation
evaluation forms, 475, 476
Evaluation section of grants, 244–245
Evans, Graeme, 28
Every Student Succeeds Act (ESSA), 436–438
exercises to clarify board responsibilities, 172
exhibition labels, accessibility of, 423–424
expenses, estimating, 300–301
experience, quality of, 353–354
experimental design, 470–471
extended engagements of artists, 359–360
external assessments, 140, 143

F

face-to-face recruitment of volunteers, 279
face-to-face visits for fundraising, 201
facility projects, planning for, 298
Feci, Jenna, 413
federal government
    data from, 36, 384
    funding from, 75, *76*, 228
fees for artists, 356–357
fiduciary mode of governance, 164–167
finance committees, 291
financial management
    audits, 313–314
    boards and, 166–167, 289, 290–291
    budgets, 291–294, *295*–*296*, 296–297, *299*, 299–301, *302*
    control cycle of, 290, 301, 303
    facility projects, planning for, 298
    financial statements, 306, 308, *309, 310*, 311, *312*
    overview of, 289
    replacement of fixed assets, 292–294
    reports to Internal Revenue Service, 314–315
    resources on, 315
    tracking and measuring performance, 301, 303–306, 308
financial ratios, 311, 313
financial records, 303–304, 305–306
financial resources for program development, 346–348
financial statements
    financial management and, 306, 308, *309, 310*, 311, *312*
    grant proposals and, 250
    internal assessments and, 140–141
fire code compliance, 365
501(c)3 organizations
    definition of, 72
    funding for, 75
    limits on advocacy of, 72–73, 88–90
    tax deductions for contributions to, 207
fixed asset ratio, 313
fixed assets, 292–294, 306
fixed costs, 297
Florida, Richard, *The Rise of the Creative Class,* 17, 18, 62
focus groups
    for external assessment, 143
    for marketing, 385
    for program evaluation, 473–474
    for strategic planning, 157–158
"folk plays," 7
food permits, 365

Ford Foundation, 11, 21, 95
formative evaluations, 466
for-profit cultural organizations and ADA, 408–409
Foundation Center, 226, 428
foundations
  advocacy to, 76
  contributions from, 208, 209, 225–226
  grant proposal packages to, 239
  as sources of data, 384
free events, 377–378
French, Samuel, 7
frequency
  of program evaluation, 466
  of programming, 359
Friedan, Betty, 415
Friedman, Mark, 460
"Friends of..." or membership programs, 219–220
fringe benefits in grant proposals, 247–248
Fukuyama, Francis, 29
functional agenda, 175
funding
  for arts education, 436–437
  for community-building work, 45–46
  for disability-related programs and services, 428
  era of accountability and, 458
  from federal government, 75, 76, 228
  grant proposals and, 245–246
  from NEA, 75, 104
  for nonprofit organizations, 102, *102*
  policies related to, 101, 106
  See also fundraising
fundraising
  annual reports and, 204
  boards and, 166, 167–168, 187, 210–211
  capacity for, 207–210
  capital and endowment campaign example, *230–231*
  case for giving, 204
  developing donors, 206
  elements of successful, 199–200
  evaluating internal resources, *232–233*
  face-to-face visits for, 201
  financial information and, 203
  from foundations, 225–226
  goals for, 210
  from governments, 226–229
  for green projects, 332–333
  identifying donors, 199
  from inside, 201–202
  leadership and, 205–206
  legal readiness and, 207
  linking to strategic plan, 154, 201, 203
  mission and, 203
  from national corporations, 224–225
  organizational attitude and, 204–205
  overview of, 197
  partnerships and, 228–229
  planning, 209–211, 215–218, *234–235*
  reasons donors give, 200–201
  as relationship building, 198–199, 229
  "rights" of, 213
  sources for, 197–198, 207–209
  special events for, 223–224
  staff and office resources for, 206, 212–214
  from top down, 202
  See also individuals, contributions from; online fundraising
fundraising efficiency ratio, 313

Future and Other Necessary Funding section of grants, 245–246

G

GAAP (generally accepted accounting principles), 303, 306
Gadwa, Anne, 31, 51, 64
gambling, 365
Gard, Robert, 8, 10
Gard Ewell, Maryo, 124
Garlic and Arts Festival, 333–334
Geithner, Tim, 117
generally accepted accounting principles (GAAP), 303, 306
generative mode of governance, 164–165
gentrification, 28, 62, 64
gift shops, greening, 331–332
"Giving Tuesday," 262
goals
  for community building, 41–42
  for fundraising, 210, 219
  long-range, 131, 144–145
  for programs, 343–344
  for student-centered curriculum, 449–451
  worksheet for, 159
Goals 2000 Educate America Act, 434
Goals and Objectives section of grants, 243–244
governance modes of boards, 164–165, 169–171
governing boards. *See* boards of directors
governing structure
  changing, 190
  examples of, 188–190
  overview of, 184–185
  restructuring options, 186
  rethinking assumptions, 185–187
government, levels of, 74–76
governments, raising money from
  federal, 228
  grant proposal packages to, 239–240
  local, 227
  overview of, 75–76, *76*, 208–209
  state, 227–228
grading rubric, *474*
Graf, Helmuth Karl Bernhard, 125
Graham-Pole, John, 413
Grams, Diane, 20
grant proposals
  Appendix section, 250–251
  Budget section, 246–250
  Evaluation section, 244–245
  Future and Other Necessary Funding section, 245–246
  Goals and Objectives section, 243–244
  Introduction section, 240–241
  Methods section, 244
  packages to foundations or corporations, 239
  Problem Statement or Needs Assessment section, 241–242
  sections of, 240
  Summary section, 240
grants
  recording and reporting, 305
  writing, 198, 428
  See also grant proposals
The Grantsmanship Center, 251
grants policy, 98
grassroots advocacy campaigns, 83

Gratz, Roberta Brandes, 27
Graves, Bau, 353
greening organizations
  assessments before, 323–325
  boosting profile and standing out, 333–334
  capital changes, planning, 325–326
  core practices, changing, 328–331
  environmental sustainability and, 317–318
  financial issues and fundraising, 332–333
  gift shop, supply shop and cafe, 331–332
  holistic thinking for, 298
  mandate for, 323
  myths, fears and inertia, 318–321
  overview of, 335
  public program considerations, 326–328
  resources on, 335
  starting, 321–322
Greenpoint Manufacturing and Design Center, 24
green teams, 322–323
Griesemer, Lynn, 460
grievance process, 419
group process, 173

H

Hancher Auditorium, University of Iowa, 359
Harlow, Bob, 387
Harris, Rennie, 352
Hartford Foundation for Public Giving, 97
Havel, Václav, 71
headwaters goals for community organizing, 10–11
Healey, Patsy, 59–60
healing function of arts, 12–13
health care, arts in, 413–414
hearing loss
  enhancements for, 421–423
  improving access for, 426
Heifetz, Ronald, 119, 120, 121
Hillman, Grady, 414
historical-based budgeting, 297
history
  of arts in schools, 433–439
  of community, mapping, 35–38
  of community organizing, 5–9
  creative placemaking and, 53–55
  of marketing strategies, 395–396
  of placemaking, 53–55
Holbrook, Josiah, 6, 10
Hotchkiss, Dan, 170, 171
Housing and Urban Development Department, Community Development Block Grants, 428
Houston Youth Symphony Coda Music Program, 344
Hughes, Sandra, 163, 175
Hurford, Diane, 60

I

identity
  community, 24–25, 38
  cultural, 421
impact, proving, 467
implement stage of planning, *136*, 153–154
inclement weather insurance, 367
inclusion. *See* accessibility and inclusion

Indianapolis Children's Museum, 344
indicators, definition of, 460
indirect costs in grant proposals, 249–250
indirect observation, 471
individuals, contributions from
    "Friends of…" programs, 219–220
    fundraising calls, *237*
    methods of giving, 221–223
    overview of, 208, 214
    researching, planning, and cultivating, 215–218, *236*
    soliciting, 218–219
    tax-deductibility of, 220–221
in-kind contributions, 225
Insightly, 259
institutional collaborations and mergers, 185
institution-wide green teams, 323
instrumental benefits of arts, 18–19
insurance
    gifts of, 222–223
    for programs, 366–367
Intermedia Arts, 60
"intermediary," role of, 42
intermediate outcomes, 459, 468
internal assessments, 140–142
internal control procedures, 305
internal customer records, 384
Internal Revenue Service. *See* IRS
internship programs, 278
interpretation of work of artists, 360–361, 362
interviews
    of audiences, 385
    for external assessment, 143
    for internal assessment, 141
    for program evaluation, 480–481
Introduction section of grants, 240–241
Inuit, 259
inventories
    Community Asset Inventory, 38, 45
    of existing marketing efforts, 388–389
    of fixed assets, 293
    of marketing data, 393–395
    of opportunities for environmental sustainability, 324
investment attraction strategy, 26–27
IRS (Internal Revenue Service)
    determination letters, 220
    form 990, 178
    Publication 1771, Charitable Contributions--Substantiation and Disclosure Requirements, 220
    reports to, 314–315
    See also 501(c)3 organizations
isolation of arts, 9–10
Ivey, Bill, 53–54

J

Jacobs, Jane, 24
Jacobs Center for Neighborhood Innovation, San Diego, 65–66
Jinnett, Kimberly, 385
job creation strategy, 23–24
job descriptions for volunteers, 274–275
Johnson, Amanda, 61
Johnson, Barry, 121
joint programming, 186
joint venture corporations, 186
journalism, traditional arts, 391
Junior League of America, 6–7

jury selection of artists, 355–356
Justice Department, Office of Justice Programs, 415
juvenile offenders, arts for, 414–415

K

Karraker, David, 465, 479
Katz, Elias, 416
Kaye, Jude, 115, 148
Kearns, Kevin, 147
Kennedy Center Alliance for Arts Education Network, 433, 442, 445
Kennedy Center ArtsEdge, 450
King, David, 18, 62
Koch, Frederick, 7, 9, 10
Kretzmann, John, 18, 57–58

L

LAAs. *See* local arts agencies
Land Bridge Project, 11
Landry, Charles, 54, 64
Lanesboro, Minnesota, 26
language
    of planning, 129–133
    of program evaluation, 459–461
    See also terminology
La Piana, David, 116, 125, 133
Lasswell, Harold, 71
law, policies established in, 99–100
leadership
    adaptive, 119–120
    board meetings and, 174
    boards and, 167
    creativity and, 432
    fundraising and, 200, 205–206
    planning and, 135
    vision and, 138
    volunteer management and, 283, 285
learning disabilities, improving access for, 426
learning organizations, 154–155
Lefebvre, Henri, 52, 58
legislative hearings, 107
legislators
    getting to know and meeting with, 84–86
    support from, 208–209
letters
    to editors, 108
    IRS determination, 250
    of support or endorsement in grant proposals, 251
    of transmittal, 239
life insurance, gifts of, 222–223
life insurance proceeds, gifts of, 222
lighting
    for accessibility, 422
    greening, 329–330, 331
Liquid Planner, 349
liquor liability insurance, 366–367
livability indicators, 63
lobbying and advocacy, 72, 107–108, 109
lobbyists, 82
local arts agencies (LAAs)
    ADA and, 408
    as coalitions, 189
    emergence of, 434
    funding from, 104
    history of, 6–7
    policies of, 101, 106

    as public commissions, 189
    strategic plans of, 107
local disability organizations, 428
local governments, funding from, 75–76, *76*, 227
location
    for programs, choosing, 345–346
    of programs and services, 375–376
logic model, 461, *461, 462,* 464
longitudinal studies, 470–471
long-term outcomes, 459, 468
Ludins-Katz, Florence, 416
Lyceum movement, 6, 9, 10
Lynch, Robert, 108

M

MacKaye, Percy, 9, 11
Madison Park Development Corporation, 56
Majewski, Janice, 407
major gifts, soliciting, 218
management
    governance compared to, 165, *169,* 169–171, *170*
    of volunteers, 283–287
management policies, 179
mapping history of community, 35–38
Mapplethorpe, Robert, 97
Market Creek Plaza, San Diego, 65–66
marketing, 373–374, 386. *See also* marketing cycle; marketing plans
marketing analytics programs, 384
marketing cycle
    evaluating effectiveness of strategies, 392–397
    overview of, 374, *374,* 397
    selecting best marketing channels, 388–392
    understanding audiences, 381–387, *382*
    understanding products and services, 375–380
marketing plans
    outline for, 398–401
    revenue forecasting and, 300
market research firms, 384
market segmentation, 381
Markusen, Ann, 18, 26, 31, 51, 62, 63, 64
Massachusetts Museum of Contemporary Arts, 28, 39
matching gifts, 221
matching support in grant proposals, 247
materials for fund drives, 217
Mavenlink, 349
McCaffrey, Rose Marie, 404
McCarthy, E. Jerome, 373–374
McCarthy, Kevin F., 385
McDaniel, Nello, 339
McKnight, John, 18, 57–58
McLuhan, Marshall, 59
McTighe, Jay, 448
measuring performance. *See* performance, tracking and measuring
media
    advocacy to, 77
    controversial work and, 362
    interviews, 107
    print, marketing in, 388, 390–391
    See also social media
meeting management, 174–177
member boards, 189
membership programs, 219–220

memos of agreement with volunteers, 281
mental illness, improving access for, 426
mergers, 185, 186
messages for advocacy campaign, creating, 82–83
methods, terms describing, 133
Methods section of grants, 244
MetLife Foundation, 428
Microsoft CRM, 259
Microsoft Project, 349
Midtown Global Market, Minneapolis, 30
milestones, definition of, 461
minorities, access to arts education for, 431
Mintzberg, Henry, 115
mission
 definition of, 130–131
 fundraising and, 203
 governing structure and, 184
 philosophy of program and, 340
 vision compared to, 139
 writing or revisiting, 144
Mitsubishi Electric America Foundation, 428
mobile-ready websites, 255, 256, 257–258
mobility impairments, 421–423, 426
moderated group discussions, 473–474
modified cash basis accounting, 304
Mohammed, Rafi, 379
months of operating cash, 313
Morgan, Arthur, 62
motivations of volunteers, 271, 285–286
Mulcahy, Kevin, 95
Mumford, Lewis, 51, 58
Murphy, Tom, 15
Museo Subaquatico de Arte, Cancun, 329
museum exhibits, greening, 330–331
The Music Man (movie), 5

N

National Center for Creative Aging, 416
National Coalition for Core Arts Standards, 435–436
National Core Arts Standards, 450
national corporations
 contributions from, 209, 224–225
 grant proposal packages to, 239
National Council of Nonprofits, 304
National Endowment for the Arts (NEA)
 arts education and, 433
 budget of, 97, 104
 establishment of, 74, 80, 95
 funding through, 75, 228
 livability indicators, 63
 Office for AccessAbility, 406
 online grant applications, 268
 policy initiatives of, 105–106
 reauthorization of, 104
National Endowment for the Arts and Humanities Act of 1965, 103
National Endowment for the Humanities, 74
National Goals for Education, 434, 440, 446
National Standards for Arts Education, 434–435
NEA. *See* National Endowment for the Arts
NEC Foundation of America, 428
Needs Assessment section of grants, 241–242
needs of donors, speaking to, 198–199

nested policies, 98–99
networks for advocacy, 78–79
New England Foundation for the Arts, 79, 127
New England Youth Theatre, Brattleboro, 326
news media. *See* media
No Child Left Behind Act, 435
nominal governing boards, 188–189
nominal group process, 142
non-partisan election activity, 72
nonprofit corporations
 accountability practices of, 178
 ADA and, 408–409
 definition of, 72
 funding for, 75–76, *76*
 funding sources for, *102*
 limits on advocacy of, 72–73, 88–90
 profit-making subsidiaries of, 189–190
 tax deductions for contributions to, 220–221
 See also boards of directors
Nonprofit Finance Fund, 293
Nonprofit Outcomes Toolbox, 464
Northeast (Minneapolis) Arts District, 29

O

objectives, definition of, 459
objectives and outcomes
 accountability and, 131–132
 for arts education, 447–449
 defining, 149–150
 focusing on, 153
 for marketing, 389–390
 relevance of marketing strategies to, 395
 worksheet for, 159
observation
 of audiences, 385
 as method for program evaluation, 471–472
Occupational Health and Safety Administration, 328
O'Fallon, David, 441
Ohio Arts Council, 417
Olmsted, Frederick Law, 5–6
one-to-one advocacy, 77
online anchors, 390
online fundraising
 assess stage, 254–258
 benefits of, 254, 266
 campaigns, 260–261
 crowdfunding, 264–266
 drawbacks to, 266–267
 email list for, 259–260
 end-of-year giving, 262
 overview of, 253
 peer-to-peer, 265–266
 people to people concept and, 263–264
 resources on, 268
 social media and, 260
 software and systems stage, 258–259
 special giving days, 262–263
online marketing, 388
open captioning, 424
operating meetings, 175
options, comparing against criteria, 147–148, *148*
Oracle CRM, 259
Organizational and Partner Assessment Form, 41, 46
organizational budgets, 292, 294, *295–296*

organize stage of planning, 135–137, *136*
orientation
 of board members, 182–183
 of volunteers, 282–283
Osborne, Alex, 142
Ostroff, Elaine, 403
outcome-based evaluation, 462, *463*
outcomes
 in basic and applied art, 464
 creative placemaking and, 63
 definition of, 459
 intangible, 466
 measurement of, 468
 See also objectives and outcomes
outcome targets, definition of, 460
outputs
 in basic and applied art, 464
 definition of, 459–460
outside observers, 471

P

Paducah Artist Relocation Program/Paducah Renaissance Alliance, 27
parent-subsidiary organizations, 186
parliamentary procedures, 175–176
participant observers, 471
participation, building or increasing, 385–387
partisan election activity, 72
partnerships
 for arts education, 453
 for community building, 41, 44–45
 with energy service companies, 320
 for fundraising, 228–229
 for program development, 345, 348–349
Pathway to Peace Neighborhood Gateway, 11
The Patron Edge, 376
PayPal, 259
Peck, Jamie, 28, 61, 64, 65
peer-to-peer fundraising, 265–266
Penna, Richard, 461, 464
Pennekamp, Peter, 2
People First terminology, 411
performance, tracking and measuring
 accounting methods, 304
 accounting procedures, 304–305, *307*
 audits, 313–314
 financial ratios, 311, 313
 financial records, 303–304, 305–306
 financial statements, 306, 308, *309, 310*, 311, *312*
 overview of, 301, 303
performance measures, 460
Perlstein, Susan, 416
permanently-restricted net assets, 308
personal liability insurance, 366
personal property, gifts of, 221–222
personnel. *See* staff
personnel costs in grant proposals, 246–248
personnel policies, 179
person-to-person recruitment of volunteers, 279
Peters, Thomas, 154
petitions, 86
philanthropic gifts, 224
philosophy of program, 340
physical access, 406, 421–423
place, definition of, 19

placemaking, 19, 53–55. *See also* creative placemaking
planning meetings, 175
planning paradox, 118
planning process for community building, 36–39
planning programs
  arts education, 446–451
  budget and resources, 346–349
  defining program, 344–346
  finalizing plan, 350
  goals and objectives, 343–344
  issues, obstacles, and opportunities, 350
  overview of, 341–342
  software for, 349
  testing need and interest, 343
  threat assessment and, 368
  See also Arts Extension Service (AES) planning process
planning retreats, 137, 156–157
plans
  annual work or operating, 122, *123*
  collaborative, *123,* 126, 128–129, 156
  cultural policies in, 100
  fundraising, 209–211, 215–218, *234–235*
  marketing, 398–401
  program, *123,* 124–125
  program evaluation, 469, *469*
  See also planning programs; principles of planning; strategic planning
Points of Light Foundation, 280
"Polar Bear on Thin Ice" project, Montreal, 334
Polarity Management, *121,* 121–122
policy
  boards and, 178–179
  cycle of, *108,* 109
  defined, 96
  development of, 106
  influencing, 107–110
  of nonprofit boards, 187
  program design and, 350, 352
  setting, 105–106
  for volunteers, 273
  writing, 109–110
  See also advocacy; arts policy; cultural policy
Policy Governance prescriptive board system, 191n6
politics
  campaign intervention, 72, 85
  cultural, 97
  definition of, 71
  See also advocacy
Ponzini, Davide, 66
portfolio examination, 470
position papers, 108
pre- and post-test design, 470
preschool grant program, 437
preschool movement, 446
presidents of boards, role of, 172, 179–180
press releases and conferences, 107
pricing strategies, 377–380
principles, definition of, 130
principles of planning
  adaptive challenges, 119–121, *120*
  alternatives to planning, 127–128
  approaches, 128–129
  building on assets, 118–119
  cycle of planning, 125
  keeping planning simple, 117–118, 153
  language of planning, 129–133

managing polarities, *121,* 121–122
planning paradox, 118
purpose and benefits of planning, 117
types of plans, 122, *123,* 124, 125–127
printed materials, accessibility of, 423, 427
print media, marketing in, 388, 390–391
priorities
  documenting, 149
  scheduling, 153
  setting, 146
problem-centered planning, 118–119
Problem Statement section of grants, 241–242
procedure manuals, elements in, 156
procedures, policies compared to, 96–97
product-form pricing, 379, 380
production of space, 52–53, 58
products and services, evaluating, 375–377
professional policies, 179
profiling board personnel needs, 180, 193–194
profit-making subsidiaries of nonprofit organizations, 189–190
program budgets, 292, 294
program development
  accessibility issues, 363
  for adults with disabilities, 416
  arts education, 447–451
  connecting art and audiences, 358–361
  controversial works, 361–362
  culturally-specific work, 362–363
  design, 350, 352–358
  documenting and evaluating, 369–370
  equipment, supplies, and services, 365–366
  follow-through and thanks, 368
  in health care, 413–414
  insurance needs, 366–367
  for juvenile offenders, 414–415
  logistics, 364–368
  for older persons, 415–416
  overview of, 339–340, 370
  philosophy and values, 340–341
  planning, steps in, 342–350
  regulations, permits, and licenses, 365
  security, safety, and emergencies, 367–368
  site design, 364
  for students with disabilities, 412–413
  universal design and, 412–416
program evaluation
  audience for results of, 467
  budget for, 468–469
  data analysis for, 477–478
  data collection for, 468–475, *472, 473–476, 474*
  designing plan for, 469, *469*
  feasibility of, 465
  focusing on results in, 457–458
  frequency of, 466
  language of, 459–461
  logic model, 461, *461, 462,* 464
  of objectives and outcomes, 132
  outcome-based, 462, *463*
  overview of, 369–370, 458–459, 479
  purpose of, 465
  reports of, 478–479
  resources for, 482–483
  staff for, 467
  timing of, 466
program monitoring, 468
program plans, *123,* 124–125

program policies, 179
programs and activities, greening, 326–328
project management software, 349
Promise Neighborhoods, 437
proposals, writing, 229
pros and cons, listing, 147
prospects. *See* donors
public benefit, arts and culture as, 73–74
public commissions, 189, 197
public forums, 143
public meetings for program evaluation, 474
public spaces, active, 19
Putnam, Robert, *Bowling Alone,* 17–18, 29, 54–55

Q

qualitative analysis, 478
quality of programs, defining and fostering, 352–354
quantitative analysis, 477–478
questions
  critical, defining, 146–147
  for program evaluation, 458, 473–476, 480–482

R

raffles, 365
rain gardens, 320
Rapson, Rip, 52, 56, 60
real estate, gifts of, 223
real time strategic planning, 116, 125
Rear Window Captioning System, 425
recognition for volunteers, 286–287
reconciliation of accounts, 305
recruiting
  board members, 168–169, 180–184
  volunteers, 216–217, 275–280
recycling light bulbs, 330
Redpath, James, 6
reduced pricing, 377–378
reference checks on volunteers, 280–281
reflection on planning process, 451
regeneration, culture-led. *See* creative placemaking
regulations, permits, and licenses, 365
rejecting volunteers, 281
relationship-building, fundraising as, 198–199, 229
relevant costs, 297
renting costumes, 329
replacement of fixed assets, planning for, 292–294
reports
  annual, and fundraising, 204
  dashboard, 175, *176*
  to Internal Revenue Service, 314–315
  of program evaluation, 467, 478–479
requests for advocacy campaign, making, 81–82, 85–86
research
  in arts education, 438–439
  on audiences, 382–387
  on donors, 215–216, *236,* 263
  on foundations, 225–226
  public policy and, 108
resources
  age-appropriate activities, 450
  Americans with Disabilities Act, 410
  board development, 190

community and economic development, 32–33
financial management, 315
greening organizations, 335
online fundraising, 268
program evaluation, 482–483
strategic planning, 155
responsive design, 255
restructuring options, 186
results, terms describing, 130–132. *See also* objectives and outcomes
Results-Based Accountability, 464
retail operations, greening, 331–332
retention
  of board members, 183–184
  of volunteers, 285–286
retro-commissioning building, 325
return engagements of artists, 359–360
revenues, estimating, *299*, 299–300
reviewing and revising draft plans, 151–152
rewards for donors, 265
Ridenour, Annette, 414
The Rise of the Creative Class (Florida), 17, 18, 62
risk of going green, myth of, 320–321
risk-taking thresholds of organizations, 341
Roadside Theater, 5, 12
Robinson, Ken, 431
Rockefeller Foundation, 95
Rodriquez, Santiago, 276
roofs, green, 319
Rosenfeld, Stuart, 23
Rossi, Ugo, 66
Roxbury Center for the Arts, 56
rubrics, 471–472, *472, 474*
Ryan, William, 164

S

SAAs. *See* state arts agencies
safety policies, 179
salaries in grant proposals, 246–247
Salesforce, 259
sampling, 473
Sandahl, Carrie, 405
Sandercock, Leonie, 60
SAP CRM, 259
Sarkissian, Wendy, 60
scenario planning, 125–156
scheduling board meetings, 174
Schneekloth, Lynda, 53, 54, 58, 59, 60
schools
  decision making in, *444*, 445
  history of arts in, 433–439
  working on community planning with, 442
  See also arts education
Schuster, J. Mark, 98
Schwartz, Peter, 125–126
science, technology, engineering, arts, mathematics (STEAM), 437
security, safety, and emergencies, 367–368
Seifert, Susan, 20
self-assessment questionnaires, 141
Self-Audit Worksheet, 442, *443*
Senge, Peter, 116, 119, 126, 154
sequential programming, 358–359
Serrano, Andres, 97
Settlement House movement, 7, 10
Sherman, Andrea, 415–416

Shibley, Robert, 53, 54, 58, 59, 60
short-term outcomes, 459, 468
show, going green as, 319–320
signage, 365, 422
signaling systems, 425
sign language interpretation, 425
Simon, Ed, 115
simultaneous loose/tight principle, 154
site design, 364
size of organization and going green, 321
slogans, 131
small organizations, governing responsibilities in, 171
SMART mnemonic, 132, 447
Smithsonian Institution Travel Exhibition Service, "Green Revolution" exhibit, 328
SOA (statement of activities), 308, *310,* 311
social capital, 17
social capital building strategy, 29–30
social justice, cultural access as, 404
social media
  analytics programs, 394
  as marketing channel, 390–391
  as online anchor, 390
  postings on, 108
  tying to online fundraising, 260
software
  accounting, 303
  online fundraising, 258–259
  project management, 349
  spreadsheet programs, 303–304, 477
solicitation phase of fundraising, 218–219
SOP (statement of position), 306, 308, *309*
sources
  for artists, 355
  of audience data, 384–385
  for fundraising, 197–198, 207–209
  of program ideas, 341
  for volunteers, 277, 279–280
space/facilities costs in grant proposals, 248
special events for fundraising, 223–224
special giving days, 262–263
spending, linking to strategic plans, 154
sponsorships, 224
spreadsheet programs, 303–304, 477
Springfield Museums, 287
staff
  fundraising and, 212–214, 215
  green teams, 322–323
  online fundraising and, 254–255
  planning and, 135, 137
  program development and, 348–349
  responsibilities of, *169,* 169–170, *170*
  training on accessibility, 418
staffed organizations, governing structures for, 188–189
staging, greening, 328–329
stakeholders, identifying, 180–181, *181*
state and regional data, 384
state arts agencies (SAAs)
  ADA and, 408
  as allies for advocacy, 79
  NEA and, 105
  policy of, 106
  strategic plans of, 107
  support from, 208
state governments, funding from, 75, *76,* 227–228
statement of activities (SOA), 308, *310,* 311
statement of position (SOP), 306, 308, *309*

STEAM (science, technology, engineering, arts, mathematics), 437
Stern, Mark J., 20
stories of place, 58–59
storing donor data, 258–259
strategic mode of governance, 164–165, 171
strategic planning
  consultant for, 156–157
  format options for plans, 151
  learning organization and, 154–155
  linking fundraising to, 154, 201, 203
  overview of, 115–116, 122, *123*
  process of, 125
  resources on, 155
  responsibility for, 135
  sequence of steps in, 135
  structure of plans, 133–134
  See also Arts Extension Service (AES) planning process; principles of planning
strategic restructuring, 186
strategy, definition of, 115, 133
street closure or assembly permits, 365
Strengths, Weaknesses, Opportunities, and Threats (SWOT) analysis, 141–142, 147
success, definition of
  audience development, 389
  marketing, 389–390
  program development, 341
Summary section of grants, 240
summary version of plan for public, 152
summative evaluations, 466
supply costs in grant proposals, 249
supply inventories, 324
surveys
  of audiences, 385
  for external assessment, 143
  for program evaluation, 475, 481–482
  for strategic planning, 158–159
Sutton, Sharon, 404
SWOT (Strengths, Weaknesses, Opportunities, and Threats) analysis, 141–142, 147
symbolic capital, 29
system replacement plans, 298

T

tabular agenda, 175
tactile presentations, 427
tag lines, 131
Taleb, Nassim Nicholas, 116
talent attraction strategy, 18, 62
talking through planning questions, 146–147
target marketing, 381
tasks
  of boards, monitoring and following through on, 177
  definition of, 133
  of volunteers, 282
tax deductions for contributions, 220–221, 262
taxes for arts investment, 105
tax returns, 314–315
Taylor, Barbara, 164
teachers for arts education, 451, *452,* 453
team building on boards, 173–174
technical problems compared to adaptive challenges, *120,* 120–121
technology for going green, 320

Temali, Mike, 38
template for rubric, *472*
temporarily-restricted net assets, 308
terminology
    in ADA, 409–410
    for beliefs, 130
    for cultural access, 406–410
    for methods, 133
    People First, 411
    for results, 130–132
    See also language
Terry, Paula, 404
Tessitura system, 259, 376
texts, manual content analysis of, 482
thanking
    donors, 212, 219, 237
    foundations, 226
    program participants, 368
    volunteers, 286–287
theft, damage, or loss insurance, 367
thermostats, programmable, 325
Thomas, Lewis, 3
Thompson, Joe, 28, 39
Thorn, George, 339
threat assessment, 368
ticket sales
    data from, 393
    estimating revenue from, *299*, 299–300
time commitment
    for marketing, 386
    for planning, 135–136
timed agenda, 175
timeline for program development, 349, *351*
timing of marketing components, 392
Tocqueville, Alexis de, 74
total assets, 306, 308
total liabilities, 306
total net assets, 306, 308
tourism, cultural heritage, 25–26
Towne, Douglas, 410, 419
tracking performance. *See* performance, tracking and measuring
trade stimulation strategy, 25–26
traditional board meetings, 175
training
    on accessibility, 418
    for volunteers, 282–283
    See also orientation
transition
    board role in, 172–173
    plan for, *123*
    teams for, 107
transportation issues, 420
travel costs in grant proposals, 249
travel for exhibits and loaned objects, greening, 331
treasurers of boards of directors, 290–291
trust and fundraising, 212
trust building strategy, 29–30
Tuan, Yi-Fu, 24
Tuckman, Bruce, 173
Turner, Kim, 417
21st Century Community Learning Centers, 437–438, 445

U

Unified Chart of Accounts for Nonprofit Organizations, 305, *307*
uniqueness of programs, 376–377
United Way Logic Model, 464
universal design, 411–416
universal environment for arts, 420, 421–428
university extension services, 7, 9, 10
unrestricted net assets, 306, 308, 313

V

Valentine, Mark, 11–12
value-based pricing, 379, 380
value enhancement strategy, 28–29
values, 130
variable costs, 297
variable pricing, 379–380
Vawter, Keith, 6
Vazquez, Leonardo, 52, 56, 59, 61, 64
Vendini, 376
Venturelli, Shalini, 16
versioning, 379
Very Special Arts, 413
Vibrancy Indicators, 63
videos for crowdfunding, 265
Village Improvement movement, 5, 10
Villani, John, 26
Vincent, John, 14
virtual board meetings, 177
vision
    definition of, 130
    importance of, 138–139
    translating into strategies, 115
visual impairments, 421–423, 425–426
visualizing programs, 366
visual rubric, *472*
voice activated technology, 257–258
volunteer coordinators, 284
volunteer management, 283–287
Volunteer Match, 280
volunteers
    assessment of need for, 274
    attracting, 272
    components of programs for, 273
    demographics of, 272
    designing programs for, 272–273
    evaluating, 287
    fundraising and, 212–213
    internship programs for, 278
    job descriptions for, 274–275
    leadership of, and fundraising, 205–206
    memos of agreement with, 281
    motivations of, 271, 285–286
    orientation for, 282–283
    recognizing and thanking, 286–287
    recruiting, 216–217, 275–280
    retaining, 285–286
    role of, 271, 274
    selecting and placing, 280–281
    soliciting for fund drives, 218
    at Springfield Museums, 287
    training, 282–283
    See also all-volunteer organizations

W

Walker, Chris, 25
Wallace Foundation, 387
Warr, Michael, 20
waste audits, 324
Waterman, Robert, 154, 155
water-use audits, 324
wealth retention strategy, 30–31
Webb, Debra, 52, 55
Website Comparison Worksheets, 256, *257*
websites
    accessibility of, 427
    analytics programs, 394
    assessing for online fundraising, 255–257
    mobile-ready, 255, 256, 257–258
    as online anchor, 390
"well-rounded education," 436
Western States Arts Foundation (WESTAF) Vitality Index, 79, 127
Whitney, Diana, 119
Whyte, William, 19
Wiggins, Grant, 448
Wikoff, Naj, 413
Wisconsin Idea, 8
Wong-Baker FACES Pain Rating Scale, *472*
Worcester, Massachusetts, 376
working boards, 171
working capital, 313
work plans, 122, *123*
Works Progress Administration (WPA), 17, 74, 97
Wright, Frank Lloyd, 6, 10
writing
    to elected officials, 86–87
    policy, 109–110
    proposals, 229, 239–251
    strategic plans, *136*, 150–152
Wylie, E., 330

Y

Yellow Springs, Ohio, 62
Youth Service America, 280

Z

zero-based budgeting, 297
Zukin, Sharon, 29, 64–65